T0316975

Thorstein Veblen

The Anthem Other Canon Series

Anthem Press and The Other Canon Foundation are pleased
to present **The Anthem Other Canon Series**. The Other Canon – also
described as 'reality economics' – studies the economy as a real object rather than as
the behaviour of a model economy based on core axioms, assumptions and techniques.
The series includes both classical and contemporary works in this tradition, spanning
evolutionary, institutional and Post-Keynesian economics, the history of economic
thought and economic policy, economic sociology and technology governance,
and works on the theory of uneven development and in the tradition of
the German historical school.

Other Titles in the Series

Thorstein Veblen

Economics for an Age of Crises

Edited by
Erik S. Reinert and
Francesca Lidia Viano

ANTHEM PRESS
LONDON · NEW YORK · DELHI

Anthem Press
An imprint of Wimbledon Publishing Company
www.anthempress.com

This edition first published in UK and USA 2012
by ANTHEM PRESS
75-76 Blackfriars Road, London SE1 8HA, UK
or PO Box 9779, London SW19 7ZG, UK
and
244 Madison Ave. #116, New York, NY 10016, USA

Non-exclusive distribution in Norway by Res Publica, Oslo.

British Library Cataloguing-in-Publication Data
A catalogue record for this book is available from the British Library.

Library of Congress Cataloging-in-Publication Data
Thorstein Veblen : economics for an age of crises / edited by Erik S. Reinert
and Francesca Lidia Viano.
p. cm. – (The Anthem other canon series)
Includes bibliographical references and index.
ISBN 978-1-84331-858-3 (hbk. : alk. paper)
1. Veblen, Thorstein, 1857–1929. 2. Economists–United States–Biography. 3. Economics–
United States–History. I. Reinert, Erik S., 1949- II. Viano, Francesca Lidia, 1973-
HB119.V4T495 2012
330.092–dc23
2012036082

ISBN-13: 978 1 84331 858 3 (Hbk)
ISBN-10: 1 84331 858 X (Hbk)

This title is also available as an eBook.

Dedicated to the memory of
Knut Odner and Marjorie Gluck Plotkin

Unveiling the Veblen monument at Høre school, Valdres, Norway, on the farmland from which Thorstein Veblen's parents left for the United States in 1847. Thorstein Veblen left no direct descendants, but members of the family attended.

From left to right: Doris Langseth, whose grandmother was Thorstein's cousin; Knut Wollebæk, Norway's ambassador to the United States; Kari Veblen, Veblen's great-niece (her grandmother was Thorstein's elder sister Emily Veblen Olsen); Knut Haalien, mayor of the municipality of Vang, Valdres.

Photo credit: Geoffrey Hodgson.

CONTENTS

ACKNOWLEDGEMENTS

Thorstein Bunde Veblen was born on 30 July 1857 and passed away on 3 August 1929, exactly one month before the US stock market peaked and less than three months before Black Thursday saw the US economy collapse into the Great Depression. Veblen's warnings against the negative aspects of a market economy – of 'the price system' – that favoured finance at the neglect of production very soon proved to be more than justified.

This book is the result of a conference marking the 150th anniversary of Veblen's birth, held in Valdres, Norway, from where his parents migrated ten years before Thorstein was born. The conference was held at Radisson SAS Resort Beitostølen, where it is possible to see all the way to the summer pastures of the Veblen farms. The organising committee consisted of Knut Odner, Ingeborg Kongslien, Terje Hasle Joranger – all from the University of Oslo – and Erik Reinert of The Other Canon Foundation. Kongslien and Joranger both hail from Valdres.

Following the international conference, a very well attended public meeting was held at Høre School, located on the former property of the Veblen farm. The unveiling of the Veblen memorial stone, shown as the frontispiece of this volume, formed part of this meeting with the people of Valdres. Another meeting, in Norwegian, marking the Veblen anniversary was held at Stalheim Hotel, Voss, organised by Trygve Refsdal and the group behind the well-known *Skjervheim Seminar.*

The Veblen anniversary in Norway was also marked with a book exhibition at the main university library in Oslo, organised by librarian Pål Lykkja, also from Valdres. The speech made by Head Librarian Bredo Berntsen on the opening of the exhibition was – appropriately for the Norwegian setting – entitled 'Thorstein Veblen – The forgotten social scientist'. This book exhibition later moved to Vang Municipal Library in Valdres.

The Valdres conference was made possible by grants from Vang Kommune (Municipality of Vang), Vang Sparebank (Vang Savings Bank), Mr William C. Melton – who also financed the restoration of Veblen's childhood home in Nerstrand, Minnesota – and from Stiftelsen Fritt Ord (Freedom of Expression Foundation), Oslo. The organising committee and the editors are grateful for all the support given to the Veblen commemorations in Norway by the people and institutions mentioned above, to the authors who contributed to this volume, and to numerous others who helped revive the memory of Veblen and his work. A special thank you goes to Fernanda Reinert whose invaluable assistance extended from the preparations for the conference to the last galley proofs, and to the publishing staff supporting the Anthem Other Canon book series. The editors are also grateful to Leif Høeghs Stiftelse (Leif Høegh's Foundation), Oslo, for its generous support. Professor Reinert's research for this volume was partially funded by grant No. 8097 by the Estonian Science Foundation.

It so happened that the 150th anniversary of Thorstein Veblen's birth took place just a few months before the start of a new financial crisis which once again made important, but almost forgotten, aspects of his work extremely relevant.

LIST OF CONTRIBUTORS

Russell H. Bartley is professor emeritus of history at the University of Wisconsin-Milwaukee, with a special interest in cultural history and the history of ideas. He has published, with Sylvia Erickson Bartley, 'In the Company of T. B. Veblen: A Narrative of Biographical Recovery' in the *International Journal of Politics, Culture and Society* 13, no. 2 (1999).

Sylvia Erickson Bartley is a public historian, archivist and photographer, with a special interest in visual history and the history of alternative social movements. She has published, with Russell H. Bartley, 'Stigmatizing Thorstein Veblen: A Study in the Confection of Academic Reputations' in the *International Journal of Politics, Culture and Society* 14, no. 2 (2000).

Paul Burkander wrote 'Veblen's Words Weighed', for which he received the Gockerman Award for outstanding paper, while earning his BSc in economics at Eastern Michigan University. In 2009, he began his doctoral studies in economics at Michigan State University, which he plans to complete in 2014.

Charles Camic is John Evans Professor of Sociology at Northwestern University and editor (with Geoffrey Hodgson) of *Essential Writings of Thorstein Veblen* (2011).

Stephen Edgell is professor of sociology at the University of Salford, UK. He is the author of *Veblen in Perspective: His Life and Thought* (2001).

Robert H. Frank is H. J. Louis Professor of Management and professor of economics, at the Johnson Graduate School of Management, Cornell University. He is the author of numerous books including *The Darwin Economy: Liberty, Competition, and the Common Good* (2011).

James K. Galbraith is Lloyd M. Bentsen, Jr Chair in Government/Business Relations and professor of government at the Lyndon B. Johnson School of Public Affairs, University of Texas in Austin, and is president of the Association for Evolutionary Economics for 2012. His latest book is *Inequality and Instability: A Study of the World Economy Just Before the Great Crisis* (Oxford, 2012).

Geoffrey M. Hodgson is research professor in business studies at the University of Hertfordshire, UK, and author of numerous works on institutional and evolutionary economics. He is the editor (with Charles Camic) of *Essential Writings of Thorstein Veblen* (2011).

Terje Mikael Hasle Joranger received his PhD in history from the University of Oslo and is affiliated with its Department of Literature, Area Studies and European Languages. He was born and currently resides in Valdres, Central Norway, from where Veblen's parents migrated.

Kåre Lunden is professor emeritus of history at the University of Oslo. Also an agricultural economist, Lunden specialises in Norwegian history in the period 850 to 1850, and is author of numerous books including *Frå Svartedauden til 17. mai. 1350–1814* (2002).

Knut Odner (1924–2008) was a Norwegian archeologist and anthropologist who taught at the universities of Bergen and Oslo. His many publications include *Thorstein Veblen: Forstyrreren av den Intellektuelle Fred* (2005). This volume is the result of his initiative.

Eyüp Özveren is professor of economics specialising in institutional political economy at the Middle East Technical University in Ankara, Turkey. He is co-editor of *Transnational Social Spaces: Agents, Networks and Institutions* (2004).

Sidney Plotkin is professor of political science at Vassar College. He is the author (with Rick Tilman) of *The Political Ideas of Thorstein Veblen* (2011). Since 2004, he has served as president of the International Thorstein Veblen Association.

Erik S. Reinert is chairman of The Other Canon Foundation in Norway and professor of technology governance and development strategies at Tallinn University of Technology, Estonia. He is the author of *How Rich Countries Got Rich…and Why Poor Countries Stay Poor* (2007).

Sophus A. Reinert is assistant professor in the Business, Government and International Economy Unit at Harvard Business School. He is the author of *Translating Empire: Emulation and the Origins of Political Economy* (2011).

Francesca Lidia Viano is a graduate research associate at the Centre for History and Economics at Harvard University and is currently working on her second PhD in history at King's College, Cambridge University. She is the author of *Thorstein Veblen: Fra mito e disincanto* (2002) and *La statua della libertà: Una storia globale* (2010).

L. Randall Wray is professor of economics at the University of Missouri-Kansas City and senior scholar at the Levy Economics Institute, Bard College, Annandale-on-Hudson, NY. His most recent book is *Modern Money Theory: A Primer on Macroeconomics for Sovereign Monetary Systems* (2012).

Chapter 1

INTRODUCTION

Erik S. Reinert and Francesca Lidia Viano

Thorstein Bunde Veblen (1857–1929) may no longer feature on the curricula of most economics students, but in terms of editions of his books published and doctoral work dedicated to his work and legacy he remains America's most famous economist. Veblen is the intellectual father of the two most influential economic schools to offer an alternative to today's mainstream economics: evolutionary economics and institutional economics.[1] He vivisected modern capitalism and redrew the very framework of social science, and his renown goes well beyond the Ivory Tower. His name, alongside his signature concepts such as 'conspicuous consumption' and 'vested interests', appears in scholarly studies as well as novels and popular media, from the works of novelist John Dos Passos to *Fortune Magazine*. Other great economists may be cited in academic articles, but theatrical plays are rarely dedicated to their persons and their names are seldom invoked in comedy films as is Veblen's.[2] His international reach extended far beyond the Atlantic communities: six of Veblen's books have been translated into Japanese,[3] and at least two into Chinese.[4] But who was he?

In a 1924 letter – written on the stationary of the New School for Social Research where he was employed at the time – Veblen describes himself to a certain 'Mr. Pritchard' as 'an average person with few and slight ties of family or country, being born of Norwegian parents in America and educated at various American schools, and having never been hard at work or very busy'.[5] The present volume, the proceedings of an international conference held in Valdres, Norway, to commemorate the 150th anniversary of his birth, can fruitfully be seen as a meditation upon these words. It is obvious from the response that Mr Pritchard had wished to learn who Veblen was, where he came from and what had made him such a penetrating observer of the modern world; he had wished, in short, to get under Veblen's skin. Veblen disappointed his hopes, but we hope that this volume will go some way towards satisfying the curiosity of a Pritchard, shedding light on Veblen's simultaneously evasive and revealing reply.

Veblen's reply to Mr Pritchard gives some indication of the tenor of this volume. While far from average and often (if quietly) overworked, Veblen was indeed born to Norwegian parents and educated at various American universities, and a cipher for deciphering his enigma lies precisely in the interplay of these distinctive elements of his personal history, ever obscured by his penchant for irony and understatement, or even by his playfulness.[6] Tellingly enough, his two stepdaughters gave him the nickname *toyse*, rendered as *toyse*,[7] which means 'kidding' or 'playing games' in Norwegian.[8]

Partially because Veblen himself, however indirectly and ambiguously, had suggested the relevance of his personal experiences for his intellectual development, scholars have often given biographical emphases to the study of his ideas. This book shares this emphasis, but is based on a broader conception of Veblen's 'persona', comprehensive of his family background as well as academic experiences and the institutions that shaped both, and aims at opening up new avenues for interpreting the relation between Veblen's person and his ideas. It is divided into four main sections, containing essays on different aspects of Veblen's personal and intellectual story: his cultural origins and personal life; his education and intellectual formation; his politics; and his economics. Some of the contributions focus on Veblen's writings, and others purely on his biography, but our hope is that the sum of this commemoration, like a literary diorama, will end up giving a holistic view of Veblen's intellectual background and development, from the moment his family left Norway to sail to the United States, to Veblen's Cassandra-like premonitions of the Wall Street Crash of 1929.

Part of Veblen's enduring appeal lies in his evocative analysis of the 'modern' condition, which he depicted as characterised by two major sacrifices: the sacrifice of technological concerns to the worlds of speculation, advertising and sabotage of technological change, and that of savings and investments to financial capitalism and a widespread frenzy of conspicuous consumption. Even if posterity has not appreciated Veblen's prophetic vocation with the same enthusiasm it has those of Alexis de Tocqueville and Max Weber, the contemporary resonance of Veblen's ideas has increasingly been recognised, much like the similarities between our era and the 'Gilded Age' that inspired his criticisms. 'History does not repeat itself', Mark Twain is supposed to have said, 'it rhymes'. The precise context and epic crises faced by Veblen are crises of the past; yet their consonance with our present predicaments is food for thought. Though the present endeavour seeks to contextualise Veblen's life and writings to a greater extent than has been done before, it also includes contributions that draw explicitly on his insights and develop them in light of current concerns. After all, as was remarked at the 100th anniversary of his birth, Veblen formulated 'a theory of becoming, not a theory of being', a theory meant to dialogue with future interlocutors.[9] In the same spirit, this collection of essays represents a waypoint, at which one can pause to contemplate the varied terrain that has been covered and chart future courses for scholarship on this remarkable man and his remarkable ideas.[10]

Erik Reinert's preliminary essay, following this introduction, argues for the interdependence of the different sections of the book as seen from a variety of Veblenian contexts: Valdres, the original home of the Veblens; Veblen's work in relation to contemporary Norwegian culture and its idealistic zeitgeist; his type of economics in the setting of a contextual – rather than whiggish – understanding of the history of economic thought; and Veblen in relation to industrial sabotage and financial crises as they recur again today.

Norwegian Origins and Personal Life

The question of Veblen's heritage, and how this influenced his personality and his work, has always played a curious role in Veblen scholarship. It is true that, in the wake of the Great Depression, he was allowed into the hallowed club of dead white prophets of social science, but his role in the canon was never free from ambiguity.[11] From the 1950s onwards, economics and sociology underwent an epistemological revolution favouring specialisation over the interdisciplinarity so characteristic of Veblen's work. At the same time, mathematics became the dominant language of economics and brought the discipline away from Veblen's evolutionary approach. Finally, growing opposition to communism made Veblen's critiques of 'vested interests' and 'absentee ownership' politically suspect. In hindsight, it is indeed striking that the same period which witnessed the nadir of Veblen's fame as an individual, when David Riesman drew on second-hand sources to describe him as 'put off and alienated from his parents' parochial culture but without the ability fully to assimilate and accept the available forms of Americanism', coincided with that in which his ideas, though often divorced from his name, enjoyed the greatest currency.[12] In fact, Veblen's supposedly 'outsider' criticisms of advertising, the hegemony of the leisure class, conspicuous consumption and big business ethics, like his analysis of the relation between management and ownership, gave birth to a central current of quintessentially *American* criticism, which included such luminaries as David Chandler, Charles Wright Mills and John Kenneth Galbraith, who often developed largely independently of Veblen's name.[13] Galbraith himself hinted at this when, in private correspondence, he admitted that 'while I am a great admirer of Veblen, I am not that much of a scholar of his works'.[14]

This curious divorce between Veblen – the 'misfit' or the assumed crypto-Marxist – and his ideas produced paradoxical results: Veblen's marginality in many ways supplanted his ideas as the primary object of scholarly attention. Curiously enough, Veblen himself was responsible for this development. In a once famous article on the 'Intellectual Pre-eminence of Jews in Modern Europe', Veblen offered an image of himself in the guise of a sceptical Humean and wandering Jew, 'a disturber of the intellectual peace', a 'wanderer in the intellectual no-man's-land, seeking another place to rest, farther along the road, somewhere over the horizon'.[15] This poetic self-portrait, which almost sounds like an epitaph, profoundly influenced the earliest accounts of Veblen's work and life, beginning with Joseph Dorfman's epic 1934 biography. Not only, however, did Dorfman fail to appreciate the idealism of Veblen's self-representation, he did not distinguish carefully enough between Veblen's pride in intellectual marginality and his supposed *social* alienation. This is why he traced both back to Veblen's solitary youth in a transplanted Norwegian environment – a sort of "Scandinavian ghetto" in Manitowoc County, Wisconsin – where ostensibly not a word of English was spoken.[16] Since then, with a few exceptions (such as C. Wright Mills's attempt to Americanise Veblen by presenting him as 'the best critic of America that America ever produced'), scholarship revelled in Veblen's supposed social dysfunctionality, his lecherousness and his complete contextual alienation until Sylvia Yoneda, Russell Bartley and Rick Tilman inaugurated a new, revisionist trend in Vebleniana in the 1980s.[17] Yoneda and other revisionist scholars have highlighted Veblen's sociability and re-evaluated the importance of the Manitowoc neighbourhood as a multilingual community of immigrants, in which Veblen familiarised himself with English, learned German and assimilated to the American way of life. Most importantly, they have demonstrated that Dorfman greatly exaggerated the Veblens' poverty, instead unveiling an enterprising family of above average means who were willing and able to send their children to a progressive co-educational institution like Carleton College.

Indeed, Veblen's self-assimilation to the Judaic diaspora disclosed aspects of his intellectual and 'spiritual' life, not of his social uneasiness. It is a fact that Veblen presented as a universal prerequisite of intellectual perspicacity the scepticism induced by the wandering along and across 'frontiers', a fruitful but exhausting process that caused the Jew to lose 'his secure place in the scheme of conventions into which he has been born' while 'finding no similarly secure place in that scheme of gentile conventions into which he is thrown'.[18] But intellectual alienation did not correspond, in Veblen's eyes, to spiritual alienation. Like the idealised Jew, who refused both his old and new cultures, yet was homesick and *spiritually* attached to his ancestry, Veblen saw himself as an intellectual wanderer who, spiritually, remained a Norwegian 'chauvinist', as his former student Isador Lubin once defined him.[19] For 'the heart-strings of affection and consuetude', Veblen noted, 'are tied early, and they are not readily retied in after life'.[20]

The first section of this book traces Veblen's travels across and along American and Norwegian frontiers. It shows the complex process he underwent of intellectual estrangement from, and attachment to, Norwegian and American cultures, and explores his hidden spiritual links with his parents' homeland. There can be no doubt, as many of the contributors to this volume emphasise, that an important key to understanding Veblen lies in a better understanding of his Norwegian-American background, seen not as a vague catch-all category for immigrant alienation and the odd Ibsen reference but as a conflux of specific cultural, institutional and intellectual traditions and conditions which influenced his formation. As Odd S. Lovoll has demonstrated, 'Norwegian-American culture' was uniquely resilient, characterised by 'interaction rather than assimilation with American society'.[21] As the founder of the influential nationwide association of *bygdelag* – organisations comprised of the descendants of emigrants from rural Norway to North America – Thorstein's elder brother Andrew Veblen was one of many Norwegian-Americans to nurture his multi-ethnic background carefully. That Andrew Veblen became a professor of science and physics at Johns Hopkins University, but retired to own and operate a farm in Minnesota, indicates the ease with which the family conciliated rural and academic life.[22] Although Thorstein was less vocal than his brother Andrew in nurturing his multi-ethnic background, one of the strengths of this volume is to bring his cultural mediation to light without falling back on Dorfman's tired account of estrangement.[23]

In his contribution to this volume, Kåre Lunden, one of Norway's leading economic historians, begins to chart this terrain by providing us with a synthetic account of Norwegian cultural and economic history over the past millennium. Against this background, he places particular emphasis on the unique role played, and status enjoyed, by peasants and freeholders such as Veblen's family in the country's *longue durée*. Norway, like Switzerland, was one of very few areas of Europe to escape the yoke of feudalism, a salient characteristic which would influence institutional structures and popular culture there for centuries. In a comparative European perspective, Lunden concludes, Norwegian peasant society was characterised by a penchant for insubordination and industriousness, traces of which Lunden detects at the core of Veblen's life and thought.

There are many different ways to explain the origins of Veblen's ideas, and the ambition of this book is to gather and compare a variety of them. Although free from feudal hierarchies, Norway knew other forms of discrimination at the time, particularly from a non-democratic regime vesting disproportionate power in civil servants appointed by the King (*embetsmannsveldet*). It was because of a strict observance of the rights of primogeniture (*odel*), as Terje Mikael Hasle Joranger argues, probably united with some form of religious dissent, as Knut Odner suggests in a path-breaking essay, that Veblen's parents were deprived of their land and forced to emigrate to the United States. In this context, Joranger and Odner offer new, more concrete sociological accounts of the *neighbourhood community* at Høre, in Valdres, where Veblen's parents grew up and from where they emigrated ten years before Thorstein was born.

In Valdres, a silent and scantly habited place, where each farmstead was surrounded by large tracts of green land, Veblen's parents experienced two personal tragedies: they were not only deprived of their land, but lost their first child just before embarking on the voyage to America, and they were being deprived of their land due to a strict observance of the rights of primogeniture (*odel*). Joranger places their migration from Norway in the wider context of Norwegian–American immigration and reconstructs the networks of friendship and kinship which helped them cross the Atlantic and resettle on the shores of Lake Michigan, first in Sheboygan and then in Manitowoc County in Wisconsin, where Thorstein Veblen was born. Scandinavians, Odner explains in his chapter, had the tendency to socialise among themselves while abroad, and Veblen was no exception. By drawing on new archival evidence, Odner differentiates between Norway's official and dissenting currents of thought, and reconstructs some of the American links through which the latter might have reached Veblen and his family. According to Odner, Veblen was not only influenced by Marcus Thrane's socialist movement, but he developed this and other Norwegian traditions of progressive politics within the liberal framework of a Quaker education. The latter hypothesis could help explain a wide range of surprising choices made by the Veblen family, like that of educating women – quite radical in light of paternalist traditions of the time – and of assisting Indians in the Midwest, a group habitually looked down upon by settlers. Although Odner doubts that Veblen endorsed Quakerism as a faith, he further suggests that its ethics might have nurtured his hostility to conspicuous consumption.

Veblen's student Isador Lubin once said that 'when it came to Norway, Veblen was as great a chauvinist as anybody I ever knew'.[24] It is undeniable that Veblen had Norway and Scandinavia in mind when translating the *Laxdæla Saga* in 1889, when he smuggled Vikings into his lectures and dug into comparative archaeology with a project of comparative research on Scandinavian and Aegean antiquities during the Late Bronze Age.[25] What this volume aims to demonstrate, however, is that Veblen's Norwegian inheritance was not a monolithic block of fixed and consolidated traditions. As Veblen suggests in his article on Jewish intellectuals, such cultural inheritances rather took the form of intellectual legacies, ever intermixed with those of one's new land, as well as sentimental solidarities and attachments. Filtered and inflected by American institutions, 'Norwegianness' shaped Veblen's appreciation of social and economic mechanisms in numerous ways: through family memories, dissenting criticisms, literary solidarities, and even, as Bartley and Bartley demonstrate in the last article of this section, private spaces. Pioneers of Veblenian revisionism, their article depicts a further and less appreciated manifestation of Veblen's relation to Norway and his lifelong romance with Scandinavian nature and literature (from Henrik Ibsen to Peter Christen Asbjørnsen, the collector of Norwegian fairy-tales, to Icelandic sagas) through the spaces he traversed and inhabited.

American Education

As Veblen wrote to Pritchard, however, he was not simply the product of Norwegian parents in America; he was also the product of some of America's premier educational institutions. Even if a Norwegian heritage helped steer Veblen's attention towards Baltic, Scandinavian and Icelandic history and institutions, an independent academic path armed him with the instruments necessary to interpret these subjects and to incorporate them into the wider theoretical schemes for which he was celebrated. Veblen's intellectual breakthrough has habitually been relegated to his years at the University of Chicago in the 1890s, where he supposedly first encountered Darwinian influences on social science. Veblen, however, entered Chicago as an associate professor at the age of 36, after a circuitous academic career, and scholars have recently begun to seriously explore the intellectual contexts in which he moved during his university education. After graduating from Carleton College in 1880, Veblen moved to Johns Hopkins to study philosophy and, after only a year of study, embarked on a three-year PhD in philosophy at Yale. Notwithstanding his astonishing results and laudatory letters of recommendations, Veblen was unable to find an academic position, and was forced to 'lie low', as he put it, at his family farm and that of his wife's family for a period of seven years. These years were 'spent to no purpose', he reminisced, and in 'parts' were 'some of the most enjoyable times I have had'.[26]

Veblen's hiatus ended in the spring of 1890 when he entered Cornell for a second PhD, now in history and political science. Francesca Viano's chapter re-evaluates his formation by analysing previously undiscovered archival materials concerning Veblen's studies at Cornell up to 1892.[27] Building on more than a decade of published research, she argues that Veblen's Cornell years played a unique role in his graduate formation, introducing him to contemporary currents of 'institutional history' inspired by explicitly Darwinian critiques of teleology, to a form of Darwinism weighted down with less theological baggage than the one spread by neo-Darwinians like C. Lloyd Morgan or George Romanes, one more applicable to the explanation of institutional delays, inefficiencies and useless survivals. *The Theory of the Leisure Class* can then be seen as a continuation of Darwin's meditations on sexual competition and social aggregation in the light of data on institutional growth accumulated and only partially understood by nineteenth-century historians.

In his chapter, Charles Camic draws on analogies from the field of evolutionary biology to present a synthetic account of Veblen's educational history. By applying the 'logic of comparative genomics' to the sequence of Veblen's university experiences, Camic argues that the clue to understanding Veblen's heterodoxy lies in the 'order' of his 'segments of schooling': the economics of John Bates Clark at Carleton; the history of H. B. Adams and the economics of Richard T. Ely at Johns Hopkins; the sociological anthropology of Charles Sumner and the philosophy of Noah Porter at Yale; and his encounter with Laurence Laughlin's institutional neoclassicism and Darwinian historiography at Cornell. The sequence of Veblen's educational experiences, in short, was far from immaterial for the development of his ideas.

What emerges from these new, detailed studies of Veblen's educational history is that his heterodoxy consisted not so much in his allegiance to radical currents of thought as in his ability and inclination to 'short circuit' the orthodox relations between disciplines (history and sociology, biology and economics, anthropology and history) and to simultaneously draw on different national and linguistic traditions. This is why, even if, as H. G. Brown wrote in 1925, few economists had 'such radical proclivities as Veblen', he found sympathetic supporters and like-minded academics along every step of the way.[28] Veblen was not Minerva, leaping fully formed from the head of Zeus, but an extraordinary product of his time, galvanising pre-existing evolutionary tendencies and institutional forces in American academia with impressive results.

Veblen's Politics

In a letter of recommendation written on Veblen's behalf (without his knowledge, it seems) to Stanford president David Starr Jordan, Cornell professor Charles Hull noted: 'he writes in a brilliant but somewhat paradoxical manner and has, it seems to me, rather a stronger bent towards social diagnosis than social therapeutics.'[29] Carlton Qualey similarly portrayed Veblen as a 'sardonic observer' and a 'diagnostician', and John Diggins followed suit, arguing, 'Veblen, who seemed to be able to analyse and explain everything, could affirm nothing.'[30] Although Veblen, in his mature years, took over the editorship of the left-leaning New York magazine *The Dial*, he was neither a policy maker nor a reformer in the classical sense. It has become something of an academic hobby to find hidden references to Tocqueville and Weber in Veblen's writings. But Veblen hardly ever mentioned the word 'power', and sidestepped the problems with which the political scientists and sociologists of his day usually grappled, whether the institution of representation, oligarchic and elitist tendencies in politics, or party structures. Veblen indeed shared Tocqueville's and Weber's concerns with the degeneration of modern societies, but framed his theories independently of their influence and with an autonomous vocabulary.

Quite curiously, given his neglect for mainstream political language, Veblen harboured a secret passion for political reform. When his affectionate student Isador Lubin brought him to Washington to work for the Food Administration during World War I, Veblen famously failed to ingratiate himself by suggesting they should remedy the cultivators' shortage in the north-west by stipulating a contract with the radical International Workers of the World (IWW) and excluding individual cultivators in the area. Similarly, he proposed to replace the retail system with a centralised mail delivery system and employing the workers made thusly available in more useful, 'productive' occupations.[31] As Veblen's forays into the realms of economic policy and reform testify, he cared little for the fundamental mechanisms of real politics, such as the reliance of Congressmen on the vote of cultivators and retail shoppers. He did politics neither theoretically, nor, seemingly, practically.

As Sidney Plotkin notes in his chapter, the fact that Veblen did not use the traditional reference system of contemporary political theorists and reformers does not make his ideas any less political. Plotkin cuts the Gordian knot of Veblen's alleged political aloofness by dwelling on the subtle divide between Veblen's realism, as it emerges from his predatorial vision of business life, and his omnipresent idealism regarding man's natural sociability and inborn tendency to work. The solution, according to Plotkin, resides in the fact that Veblen rejects the definition of power 'as a natural phenomenon', but interpreted its evolution in naturalistic terms. In Plotkin's view, Veblen saw power as emerging from the process of 'self-delusion' implicit in the basic processes of mental perception and elaboration of the outer world. Since the earliest stages of his development, man has shown a tendency to project his own structures onto the outside world, to 'humanise' it, and then subject it to his own goals. Power, according to Veblen, resulted from this intellectual struggle and consisted in the 'gratification' that came 'with breaching barriers and overcoming resistance'. Plotkin further explores the way in which Veblen applies his definition of power to formal political notions by analysing his theories of the state, international relations and class conflict.

Veblen's theory of knowledge is viewed from a complementary angle by Eyüp Özveren in his study of Veblen's analysis of the American system of higher education, *Higher Learning in America*.[32] Through *business schools* and *economics departments*, universities served the interest of managers and businessmen, who instilled in students a passion for exploitation and a disinterest in questions of common concern. Veblen believed universities fostered the old hierarchic and exploitative version of science inherited from barbaric times. Furthermore, the shaping of universities along business lines prompted competition between different institutions offering the same kind of knowledge, resulting in waste and the useless duplication of posts and professorships. Veblen's proposed solution drew on his theory of human instincts. Men were naturally inclined to work and take care of their offspring, family and also the community at large by virtue of their innate 'instinct of workmanship' and 'parental bent'; but they were occasionally driven to wasteful emulation by predatorial institutional structures. Men were also endowed with what Veblen called 'idle curiosity', an instinct which regulated knowledge and discovery by stimulating human proclivities for play and the disinterested association of ideas. Özveren brings forth the complicated relation between idleness and instrumentality at the base of Veblen's account of academic institutions, and discusses it against a wider background of theories on similar topics, from those of Karl Polanyi to those of Max Weber and Joseph Schumpeter. Finally, in re-discovering the importance of 'useless' instincts such as 'idle curiosity' in Veblen's analysis of higher learning, Özveren joins Plotkin in re-directing the discussion on Veblen's evolutionism towards his largely neglected treatment of hermeneutic processes.

Equally interested in the often neglected aspects of Veblen's writings, Stephen Edgell, one of the pioneers of Veblen revisionism and one of the earliest scholars to highlight the European origins of Veblen's sources in Anglophone debates,[33] shifts the attention from knowledge and hermeneutics to war and peace, production and predation. He explores

Veblen's development of Immanuel Kant's famous *Plan for a Perpetual Peace* and the relationship between Veblen's ideas on war and peace and his personal commitments during the Great War.[34] Edgell's chapter, vast in scope, revisits Veblen's political economy in its entirety, concluding with a personal application of these ideas to the problems of war and economics today.

Veblen's Economics

Although Veblen's impact in the social sciences was tremendous, he principally considered himself an economist, and it was in that field he advanced some of the most pertinent currents of academic inquiry of his day. In particular, he helped progress the application of evolutionary schemes from biological sciences to economic phenomena; the role of institutions in economic life; the nature of economic crises; and the relationship between consumption, productivity and happiness. As he writes in a now famous letter to Sarah Hardy of 23 January 1896,

> Economics is to be brought into line with modern evolutionary science, which it has not been hitherto. The point of departure for this rehabilitation, or rather the basis of it, will be the modern anthropological and psychological sciences [...] the science, taken generally, is to shape itself into a science of the evolution of economic institutions.

This, he admits, might 'strike' one as 'pretty fantastic'. In fact, he asks Hardy not to be 'disturbed' by any 'apprehension that I am about to write a compendium of this rehabilitated science. It will take a lustier pen than mine to write out even a working scheme, if it is ever done.'[35] The result was his extraordinary 1898 methodological manifesto, 'Why is Economics not an Evolutionary Science?'.[36]

Since the late 1980s, Geoffrey Hodgson, one of the contemporary academics most responsible for the current renaissance of interest in Veblen's evolutionary political economy, has taken up where Veblen's manifesto left off. Not only spearheading the project of revisiting Veblen's debt to Darwinism and the close relationship he inaugurated between institutional and evolutionary currents in economics, Hodgson has done more than anyone to chart what modern evolutionary, institutional economics might look like, the 'working scheme' imagined by Veblen. In a series of seminal books and essays, he has shown how Veblen drew on the evolutionary theories elaborated by his colleagues at the University of Chicago, where he began teaching in 1893, to escape the sterile teleology of neoclassical economics, Marxism and the German Historical School, and drawn on his insights to produce original work. Hodgson's contribution to this volume is both his most sophisticated take on this problem and an assessment of the nature of evolutionary and institutional economics as such.

Macmillan nearly rejected *The Theory of the Leisure Class* by virtue of its obtuse language – a shortcoming Veblen was 'quite sensible of' – and even favourable readers like John A. Hobson lamented its style.[37] In a short essay, Paul Burkander deciphers one of Veblen's most famous and most convoluted passages in his 'Why is Economics not an Evolutionary Science?' as a means of approaching Veblen's essential critique of contemporary economics.[38] In doing so, he suggests that although the passage – which draws heavily on the lexicon of biology – is in line with Veblen's main purpose with the article: to re-shape the economic discourse in biological terms, it can also shed light on why Veblen's central ideas often were ignored by economists: they simply didn't get what he wrote, something which Frank Hahn, for one, has readily admitted.[39]

In his chapter L. Randall Wray – who has emerged as a main expert on today's financial crisis – discusses Veblen as a theorist of crises. Wray suggests that the 2007 crash resulted from processes that replicated the problems analysed by Veblen – in his *Theory of Business Enterprise* – and that even if Keynes may have provided the best framework of analysis, Veblen provides a more critical analysis of the actual processes of the crisis than Keynes does. Wray also compares Veblen crisis theories with those of Hyman Minsky. In spite of Minsky's acknowledged debt to Keynes, Wray argues that, coming from the tradition of the University of Chicago, Minsky had an institutional and specific approach that in many ways was more similar to Veblen than to Keynes.

Sophus A. Reinert and Francesca Viano examine a different aspect of Veblen's political economy, this time in relation to contemporary debates about how economic expectations contributed to financial crises. They complicate the vision of Veblen's total alienation from the economics profession by highlighting his clear indebtedness to a certain tradition of utilitarian thought, one stretching from eighteenth-century sensualism to John Stuart Mill's *Principles of Political Economy*. In their essay Reinert and Viano first discuss the neo-Kantian influences under which Veblen revised the sensualist and utilitarian traditions, and then show the effects of this epistemological turn on the entire range of Veblen's theories, from those concerned with production and consumption to those dealing with financial crises.

At a previous Veblen anniversary, it was decreed that Veblen was 'America's greatest social critic of the first half of the twentieth century', and that it was 'perhaps too much to ask that the second half of the century produce another such brilliant diagnostician'.[40] As history would have it, America produced Robert H. Frank and James Galbraith, the modern economists who have done the most to advance Veblen's analytical agenda. James Galbraith, heir to an eminently Veblenian legacy, draws on Veblen's theories to analyse the role of predation in modern economies and to formulate a plea for an economic science open to predatory politics and the regulations necessary to counteract them. Galbraith, in fact, maintains that predatory systems such as those described by Veblen – systems adopting a 'strategy for competitive self-enrichment' – are fostered by deregulation and smothered by regulation. This he describes as a contrivance for 'redistributing economic power', correcting the inefficiencies inevitably attached to what in conventional economics is called 'asymmetry of information' and guaranteeing the authenticity and quality of products. In doing so, Galbraith begins to trace the contours of a truly Veblenian economic policy.

Robert Frank has analysed the relationship between consumption and happiness on the one hand and the biological forces influencing economic behaviour on the other. Through a number of important studies, he has confirmed Veblen's major premises that consumption is context dependent, and that we 'come into the world equipped with a nervous system that worries about rank', which is solicited more in urban and anonymous contexts than in 'stable environments with long-standing social networks', a context in which ever-intensifying conspicuous consumption is the logical, though not necessarily optimal outcome of the interplay between biology and the economy.[11] This need to contextualise the choices of economic actors, suggested by Veblen and proven by Frank, poses a threat to orthodox economics because it negates economic life in the simplicity of absolute standards, not to mention the illusion that the interplay of individual choices optimally distributes resources by default. Frank's contribution to this book, in fact, dwells at length on 'arms races' in economics, those of consumption being the most visible, which create conditions of Veblenian systemic waste.

Commemorations

'It is also my wish', Veblen wrote in a note shortly before passing away, destitute and largely ignored, on 3 August 1929, 'that no obituary, memorial, portrait or biography of me, nor any letters written to or by me be printed or published, or in any way reproduced, copied or circulated'.[12] To some, this may sound rather like an encouragement, for how many unemployed academics had portraits painted of them at the time, as Veblen had? For others it testified that 'Veblen justifiably had confidence that the power of his writings would outlast any marble memorials erected in a misguided effort to perpetuate his essence'.[13] Fact remains that, of all the items on Veblen's list of things we should not do in his memory, the only one still undone at the 150th anniversary of his birth was a proper memorial. It is, in a sense, to live up to his iconoclasm that we have resorted to iconolatry, raising a traditional memorial – similar to a traditional runic *bauta* – made from local stone, outside the Høre elementary school in the Valdres valley, located on the land from which Veblen's parents emigrated, as a means of marking this event and its transatlantic connotations. The frontispiece of this book shows the unveiling of the Veblen *bauta*, fashioned in the tradition of the eleventh-century *Vangsteinen* (the Vang Stone) which adorns the entry to the main church in Veblen's municipality, Vang in Valdres.

The 100th anniversary of Veblen's birth was celebrated with a conference at Cornell University in 1957, at a time when Veblen's fame was ebbing. Nobody knew at the time what Veblen had accomplished at Cornell, and not a word of regret was spent for having let Laughlin escape to Chicago in 1893 to lay the basis of what would become a famous economics department. The collection of essays which came out of the conference dealt above all with economic aspects of Veblen's thought, from his evolutionism to his theory of business cycles and his ideas about engineers and technical progress. Veblen was still largely the tragic forecaster of the Great Depression, the evolutionist and the crypto-Marxist.[14] When, in 1966, Carleton College celebrated its 100th anniversary, the event was marked by celebrating its 'perhaps most significant alumnus' Thorstein Veblen, the celebration was much more enthusiastic and celebratory in spirit than the one at Cornell nine years earlier. It also divided its contributions between the biographical and the analytical, both in terms of his oeuvre and of the future of capitalism, and underlined the fact that Veblen's theories now enjoyed a 'relevance' greater 'than anyone had anticipated', as well as their prophetic virtues: Veblen, it was said, 'was one who could lift himself above the turmoil of his time and take the long view'.[15] By the centenary of his 1899 *The Theory of the Leisure*

Class, contemporary questions of consumption, gender and inequality ranked higher on the agenda of the publication to mark the occasion, entirely overshadowing the work's context and broader analysis, but emphasis was still on the prophetic nature of Veblen's work. In effect, its contributors were asked to 'reread *Leisure Class* and think about it with respect to its meaning for the twenty-first century', its editor asking 'to what extent can we find ideas in it that will help us solve our social and economic problems?'[46] Veblen's ideas were largely looked to for their capacity to explain *our* present and to sketch out the future of capitalism. Sound forecasting has always been a valued intellectual dowry, but appreciations of Veblen's prophecies have often been dissociated from any interest in the genesis of his thought.

The present volume, commemorating the 150th anniversary of Veblen's birth, brings together all these disparate strands of Vebleniana, the biographical, the analytical and the actualising: where some of the chapters engage with Veblen's life and intellectual development, others purposefully draw on aspects of his thought to explore its resonance in the present and make active proposals for policy.

Instead of being detrimental to the economy of the book, the mixture of different styles and methods is faithful to Veblen's own approach, combining historical analysis with political criticism and drawing on different disciplines and methodologies. What has emerged from these essays is that there is a sore need for a new, complete and up-to-date intellectual biography of Veblen. The shortcomings of Joseph Dorfman's 1934 epic are many, but it is still the master narrative on which Vebleniana rests; we criticise Dorfman, but rely upon his specific arguments when it is convenient for us to do so. This is a state of affairs which cannot last, and hopefully the essays collected in this volume go some distance towards foreshadowing what such a new biography might look like, with a more balanced assessment of Veblen's cultural origins, a more nuanced exploration of his personal and intellectual formation, and including a more rigorous analysis of his ideas in appropriate historical contexts of the past and of the present.

For in addition to the themes more frequently associated with Veblen's name, from psychology to consumption and business enterprise, the contributors to this volume have also explored new or relatively neglected topics of Veblen scholarship, whether his Norwegian origins, political realism, thoughts on war and peace, hermeneutics, or his more general reflections on the evolutionary and economic concept of utility. Veblen is seldom thought of as a practical thinker. The image resulting from this collection, we hope, is thus an unconventional one, in which we can begin to rediscover some neglected aspects of Veblen's background and education, both in Norway and in Norwegian-American circles in the New World, but also to appreciate Veblen better as a political being. We think that Veblen's transatlantic 'education' and political interests are both indispensible to fully understand his interpretation of the mechanisms of political and economic crises, but also to fully appreciate his continuing relevance.

Notes and References

1   Alternatively referred to as 'neoclassical economics' or 'standard textbook economics'.

2   See for example John dos Passos, *U.S.A.* (London: Penguin, 2001), 554–5, 806–15; Leonard Solomon Silk, *Veblen: A Play in Three Acts* (New York: Augustus M. Kelley, 1966); Whit Stillman, *Metropolitan* (Allagash Films and Westerley Film, 1990), in which Veblen's name is mentioned

several times. For a Veblenian take on Hollywood, see Stella Bruzzi, *Undressing Cinema: Clothing and Identity in the Movies* (London: Routledge, 1997), 84.

3   *The Theory of the Leisure Class* (1924, 1956, 1998), *Vested Interests and the Common Man* (1925), *The Theory of Business Enterprise* (1931, 1965), *Absentee Ownership* (1940), *The Engineers and the Price System* (1962). *The Instinct of Workmanship* was published in Japanese for the first time as late as 1997.

4   *Theory of Business Enterprise* (1959), *Theory of the Leisure Class* (1969).

5   Thorstein Veblen to 'Mr. Pritchard', 28 October 1924, in the Reinert Collection.

6   See for example Charles Hull to David Starr Jordan, 27 April 1905, in Francesca Lidia Viano, 'Ithaca Transfer', in this volume; P. L. van Elderen, *Der Triomf der Ironie: Thorstein Veblen (1857–1929) als Radicaal-Burgerlijk Criticus van de Moderne Cultuur* (Tilburg: Tilburg University Press, 1991); Clare Virginia Eby, *Dreiser and Veblen: Saboteurs of the Status Quo* (Columbia: University of Missouri Press, 1998).

7   See Bartley and Bartley, 'Physical World', in this volume.

8   Once asked by a young girl living on the same farm as Veblen in Cedro, CA, what his initials T. B. (Thorstein Bunde) stood for, Veblen replied 'Teddy Bear', upon which the girl always called him that. Knut Odner, *Thorstein Veblen. Forstyrreren av den intellektuelle fred* (Oslo: Abstrakt Forlag, 2005), 168.

9   Myron W. Watkins, 'Veblen's View of Cultural Evolution', in *Thorstein Veblen: A Critical Reappraisal. Lectures and Essays Commemorating the Hundredth Anniversary of Veblen's Birth*, ed. by Douglas F. Dowd (Ithaca, NY: Cornell University Press, 1958), 249–64, esp. 250.

10 A full bibliography of Veblen's writings is found in *Essential Writings of Thorstein Veblen*, ed. by Charles Camic and Geoffrey M. Hodgson (Abingdon: Routledge, 2011), 577–84.

11 On Veblen's historiography, see, among others, Rick Tilman, *Thorstein Veblen and his Critics 1891–1963* (Princeton: Princeton University Press, 1992); Rick Tilman, *The Intellectual Legacy of Thorstein Veblen: Unresolved Issues* (Westport: Greenwood Press, 1996); John Patrick Diggins, *Thorstein Veblen: Theorist of the Leisure Class* (Princeton: Princeton University Press, 1999), 208–24. Sidney Plotkin and R. Tilman, *The Political Ideas of Thorstein Veblen* (New Haven: Yale University Press, 2011).

12 David Riesman, *Thorstein Veblen: A Critical Interpretation* (New York: Seabury, 1960), 206.

13 A similar argument is discussed in Joseph Dorfman, 'New Light on Veblen', in *Thorstein Veblen, Essays, Reviews and Reports: Previously Uncollected Writings*, ed. by Joseph Dorfman (Clifton, NJ: Kelley, 1973), 326n.

14 John Kenneth Galbraith to William Targ, 30 March 1964, in the Reinert collection.

15 Thorstein Veblen, 'The Intellectual Pre-eminence of Jews in Modern Europe', *Political Science Quarterly* 34.1 (1919): 33–42, esp. 39.

16 Joseph Dorfman, *Thorstein Veblen and His America* (New York: Viking, 1934), 7.

17 Charles Wright Mills, 'Introduction to Thorstein Veblen', *The Theory of the Leisure Class* (New York: New American Library, Mentor Books, 1953), vi. For important contributions to this debate, see Tilman, *Thorstein Veblen*; Russell H. Bartley and Sylvia E. Yoneda, 'Thorstein Veblen on Washington Island: Traces of a Life', *International Journal of Politics, Culture and Society* 7.4 (1994): 589–613; Stephen Edgell, 'Rescuing Veblen from Valhalla: Deconstruction and Reconstruction of a Sociological Legend', *British Journal of Sociology* 47.4 (1996): 627–42; Elisabeth Watkins Jorgensen and Henry Irvin Jorgensen, *Thorstein Veblen, Victorian Firebrand* (Armonk: M. E. Sharpe, 1999).

18 Veblen, 'Intellectual Pre-eminence', 33, 39.

19 Isador Lubin, 'Recollections of Veblen', in *Thorstein Veblen. The Carlton College Veblen Seminar Essays*, ed. by Carlton C. Qualey (New York: Columbia University Press, 1968), 131–48, esp. 135

20 Veblen, 'Intellectual Pre-eminence', 41.

21 Odd S. Lovoll, *Norwegian Newspapers in America: Connecting Norway and the New Land* (St. Paul: Minnesota Historical Society Press, 2010), 5.

22 In 1904, Andrew Veblen wrote the following about the *Valdris* (modern Norwegian: *Valdres*) *Samband* (a *bygdelag*): 'One of the chief aims is to gather, preserve and impart knowledge of Valdris and people of Valdris origin; to serve as a bond between them and to keep alive their common traditions, to foster knowledge of their ancestry and cherish a filial interest in the beautiful ancestral home of the race. By the operation of natural causes the language of our fathers will be forgotten among our descendants a very few generations hence. But the sentiment and interest that called the Samband into being need not die with the language. They should endure as long as there is Valdris blood to transmit; and to keep them alive and perpetuate them is a special function of the Valdris Samband.' Online: http://www.valdressamband.org/about/veblen.htm (accessed 9 April 2012).

23 Lovoll, *Norwegian Newspapers*, 5, 224; see also Norlie, *History of the Norwegian People in America*, 436–37. For an example of the Valdres dialect spoken in the Veblen household, see the appendix to Chapter 2. Norwegian and English, but also the vernacular dialects, were languages employed in the total of some 280 secular Norwegian periodicals in North America. Thorstein's brother Andrew was one of the Norwegian-Americans who also published in the vernacular Valdres dialect in America.

24 Lubin, 'Recollections', 131–48, esp. 135.

25 A similar argument is discussed in Joseph Dorfman, 'New Light on Veblen', in *Thorstein Veblen, Essays, Reviews and Reports: Previously Uncollected Writings*, ed. by Joseph Dorfman (Clifton, NJ: Kelley, 1973), 326n.

26 Thorstein Veblen to Sarah Hardy, 28 October 1895, in Jorgensen and Jorgensen, *Thorstein Veblen*, 188.

27 An earlier exploration of this theme is her 'Passaggio a Cornell: Veblen e gli esordi della storiografia Americana' (Passage to Cornell: Veblen and the Beginnings of American Historiography), in *Annali della Fondazione Einaudi* 39 (2005): 91–123

28 H. G. Brown to J. M. Clark, 24 September 1925, in Dorfman, 'New Light on Veblen', 272.

29 Charles Hull to David Starr Jordan, 27 April 1905, in Francesca Viano, 'Ithaca Transfer', in this volume.

30 Carlton C. Qualey (ed.), 'Introduction', in *Thorstein Veblen: The Carleton College Veblen Seminar Essays* (New York: Columbia University Press, 1968), 10, 15; Diggins, *Thorstein Veblen*, 212.

31 Thorstein Veblen, 'Interim Report on the I. W. W. and the Food Supply', in *Essays, Reviews and Reports: Previously Uncollected Writings*, ed. by Joseph Dorfman (Clifton: Augustus M. Kelley, 1973), 583–86; Lubin, 'Recollections', 137–42.

32 Thorstein Veblen, *The Higher Learning in America: A Memorandum on the Conduct of Universities by Business Men* (New York: B. W. Huebsch, 1918).

33 Stephen Edgell, *Veblen in Perspective: His Life and Thought* (Armonk: M. E. Sharpe, 2001).

34 Immanuel Kant, 'Perpetual Peace: A Philosophical Sketch', in *Kant: Political Writings*, trans. by H. B. Nisbet, ed. by Hans Reiss, 2nd edn (Cambridge: Cambridge University Press, 1991), 93–130; Thorstein Veblen, *An Inquiry into the Nature of Peace and the Terms of its Perpetuation* (New York: Macmillan, 1917).

35 Thorstein Veblen to Sarah Hardy, 23 January 1896, in Jorgensen and Jorgensen, *Thorstein Veblen*, 194.

36 Thorstein Veblen, 'Why is Economics not an Evolutionary Science', *Quarterly Journal of Economics* 12.4 (1898): 373–97.

37 In Dorfman, 'New Light on Veblen', 9, 22–23, alongside numerous other sources on Veblen's linguistic limitations in written English, an argument often demonised in recent historiography.

38 A sentence discussed, among others, by Diggins, *Thorstein Veblen*, 49–50.

39 Frank Hahn, 'Is Economics an Evolutionary Science?', in *Is Economics an Evolutionary Science? The Legacy of Thorstein Veblen*, ed. by Francisco Louçã and Mark Perlman (Cheltenham: Edward Elgar, 2000), 114–24.

40 Qualey (ed.), 'Introduction', in *Thorstein Veblen*, 15.

41 Robert H. Frank, *Passions within Reason: The Strategic Role of the Emotions* (New York: Norton, 1988).

42 Dorfman, *Thorstein Veblen*, 504.

43 Jorgensen and Jorgensen, *Thorstein Veblen*, 182.

44 Contributions collected in Douglas F. Dowd (ed.), *Thorstein Veblen: A Critical Reappraisal. Lectures and Essays Commemorating the Hundredth Anniversary of Veblen's Birth* (Ithaca, NY: Cornell University Press, 1958).

45 Contributions collected in Carlton C. Qualey (ed.), *Thorstein Veblen: The Carleton College Veblen Seminar Essays* (New York: Columbia University Press, 1968), see Qualey's, 'Preface' and 'Introduction', vii–viii, 14.

46 Doug Brown (ed.), 'Introduction', in *Thorstein Veblen in the Twenty-First Century: A Commemoration of the Theory of the Leisure Class (1899–1999)* (Cheltenham: Edward Elgar, 1998), xii.

Chapter 2

VEBLEN'S CONTEXTS: VALDRES, NORWAY AND EUROPE; FILIATIONS OF ECONOMICS; AND ECONOMICS FOR AN AGE OF CRISES[1]

Erik S. Reinert

After Ireland, Norway is the country that lost the largest part of its population through migration to America, and one of the Norwegian areas that lost the most was Veblen's Valdres. Most Norwegians have some family or relation who left for America, and I am no exception. I grew up with stories about the United States and what to me seemed like an exotic tribe: the Norwegian-Americans (*norskamerikanerne*).

I later found it fascinating that one of these Norwegian-Americans was an important economist, but I found reading Veblen challenging. Eventually, however, I was able to make the words of a 1920 reviewer of Veblen my own:

> Reading him tightens the muscles and stiffens the intellectual spine. One comes away from him a bit bruised and panting but with a sense of power exerted and power achieved. It has been suggested that someone ought to rewrite Mr. Veblen, to put him into such flowing measures as would delight the readers of the *Saturday Evening Post*. But then there would be no Mr. Veblen.[2]

Reading Veblen in the 1970s, the capitalism he described was as unfamiliar as Marx's 'army of the unemployed'. Veblen's idea that business could represent some modern version of piracy sounded just as strange as when he proposed that one of the tools of business was sabotage. But in today's context, when money is made in a financial casino which feeds on shrinking national economies, as Greece presently experiences, when Enron had its regulated electricity prices increased in California after having created an artificial blackout, and when close to half of Spanish youth is unemployed, these concepts again make eminent sense. Veblen's is a type of economics which comes alive in times of crisis. Contexts are therefore indispensable in order to understand him and his work.

Context 1: Valdres, Norway and European Idealism at the time of Veblen

'Veblen the Norwegian' is well covered in the next three chapters of the book.[3] This section provides some additional comments relating specifically to Veblen's Valdres and to his ideals from a Norwegian and European perspective.

Valdres, from which Veblen's parents migrated, is both central and peripheral in Norway. Central because it is geographically in the middle of the country where it is at its widest. Therefore, in spite of its remoteness, the postal route between Oslo and Bergen once led through the valley. But the mountain area of Valdres is inaccessible and, as we shall see below, an important Norwegian author once noted it was a white spot on Norwegian maps, like certain areas of Africa, at the time Veblen's parents left the valley. Henrik Ibsen situates the play *Peer Gynt* – his attempt to portray a Norwegian 'national character' – in the mountain areas just north of the homes of the Bunde and Veblen families. The area is probably – together with the inner parts of Finnmark in the north – the least affected by Norway's period under Denmark, the period Ibsen refers to in *Peer Gynt* as the '400 years' night'. Nature in the Valdres area – valleys, mountains, lakes – is stunningly beautiful.[4]

A key feature of Norwegian economic geography, compared to the rest of Europe, is the absence of villages, a product of its non-feudal past as Lunden emphasises (see Chapter 3). Instead of the normal European pattern of villages surrounded by tilled land, the Norwegian pattern is one of individual farms surrounded by their tilled land. Instead of being clustered, houses are on separate 'islands'. The area from where Veblen's parents migrated, Høre in Valdres, displays this same pattern today. A student of Freud travelling in Norway remarked:

> In Norway I was intrigued by the reserved, even secretive character of the people. I understood it better when I saw the vast distances between settlements and also between individual isolated farms. Even a brief tourist's glance at this landscape makes Norwegian literature much more comprehensive.[5]

Today Høre has something timeless about it. The local church, built in 1180, lies across from the farms from where the Bundes and Veblens came. The ornaments and decorations within the church evoke images of the Viking god Thor as much as those of Christendom. This is the church – then already almost 700 years old – where Thomas Veblen, Thorstein's father, was sexton assisting the priest; the pews with the names of Bunde and Veflen (Veblen) painted on them still stand one behind the other. It is easy to imagine Veblen's parents, Thomas and Kari (née Bunde), sitting there during service. Still today, the collective mailbox stand nearby carries only two family names: *Bunde* and *Veflen* (the name is also spelt *Vøvle* or *Veblen*). Appropriately, the memorial stone in Veblen's honour is situated at the nearby elementary school, built on Veblen family land.

Veblen's rebellious idealism and his instinct of insubordination are generally seen as key elements in his personality. If one looks for them, traces of this independence can be found in historical descriptions of the Valdres character. In his book on Norwegian peasant rebellions, historian Halvdan Koht – who as Rector of the University of Oslo signed the letter inviting Veblen to become a professor there – classified the people from Valdres as the most rebellious of all.[6]

Veblen may also be seen in the broader context of Norwegian literature of his time, and Veblen's insubordination may be seen as a unifying theme. Ibsen's Peer Gynt was strong, independent, flamboyant and adventurous, but weak when confronted with important personal moral decisions. Veblen was also strong with a strong independent will, but – on a professional level – also he avoided direct confrontation. Except for having his portrait painted when he was a young man, there is little flamboyance about Veblen. He dressed shabbily and it is told that once, when travelling in Norway on a first-class railway ticket given him by the government, the conductor wanted to throw him out of the compartment. Men so shabbily dressed did not travel first-class. Compared to the outgoing personality of his elder brother Andrew Veblen, Thorstein was shy and avoided conflict.[7] Veblen obviously had a strong personality, but his passions were not immediately visible. His lecturing style was mumbling, and upon being given a microphone he reportedly put it in the lecture room wastepaper basket.[8] Taking a parallel from mountain lakes, a Norwegian saying postulates that 'the quietest of waters are the most profound'[9] – 'still waters run deep' – the quietest people are the ones who often know the most. Here Peer Gynt is the noisy one and Veblen represents the quietest and, therefore, the more profound waters. But both Peer Gynt and Thorstein Veblen had an ability to charm women, sometimes also those of other men.

The central authors of Norwegian literature (called 'The Grand Four', *de fire store*) are Henrik Ibsen (1828–1906), Bjørnstjerne Bjørnson (1832–1910), Alexander Kielland (1849–1906) and Jonas Lie (1833–1904). In earlier days Kristofer Janson (1841–1917), who wrote from the Norwegian-American milieu, could have been counted as a member of the group, but he was later marginalised in the Norwegian literary canon. Janson is, however, the author most enlightening to us as regards Veblen.

These authors were all in a sense staunch republicans and 'humanist rebels' in a way similar to that of Veblen. Living in a country struggling for political independence (as Norway was from Sweden), they all became voices of a republican, emancipatory sentiment (anti-clerical and positive to labour and rural political movements); and they were read all across Europe. They were all precursors of a later famous Norwegian saying by Arnulf Øverland (1889–1968), 'You must not endure with the greatest of ease the injustice that does not threaten your peace'.[10] A corresponding expression in English would be 'you do not have to be hanged to be against death penalty'.

We know that while at Yale Veblen referred to Ibsen;[11] and as Odner indicates (see Chapter 5), many of Ibsen's characters have a strong Veblenian instinct of what I call idealistic insubordination. The best known in this respect is Dr Stockmann, in the play *An Enemy of the People* – in fact the saviour of the people – who famously declares that 'the minority is always right' and that 'the strongest man in the world is he who stands alone'. At one level, then, it is possible to see Ibsen as an elitist. But there are other aspects of Ibsen which do not fit this impression. He was, for example, of the opinion that the aristocracy of the future – aristocracy meant in a positive sense – would emanate from the women's and workers' movements. In the same positive sense, Veblen was of the opinion that the engineers were the best fitted to be leading the United States. To both Ibsen and Veblen, leaders were needed but the present ones were not those best fit.

Kristofer Janson shares his notes from conversations with Ibsen, who said: 'Majority, what is majority, the ignorant masses. The intelligence is always in the minority.' To which Janson says: 'I admitted that every new idea started as a minority, proposed by a poet, a prophet, or a visionary statesman, and that this often was ridiculed because he was ahead of his time. But this minority should work to become a majority, for only then could it aspire to have its ideas realised.'[12]

Bjørnstjerne Bjørnson is famous for his accounts of Norwegian rural life, but is also famous in the Czech Republic and Slovakia for his fight for the rights of the Slovak minority. Bjørnson's international activism also extended to the French Dreyfus Affair in 1898. He wrote to Émile Zola, 'how much I envy you, how I would have wished to be in your position, how I would have wished to be able to give such service to fatherland and humanity as you now have.'[13] As a true internationalist Bjørnson conveyed this message both in French and German. There is indeed a link between old European political values and Veblenian civic values and virtues, which both oppose a society almost exclusively based on commercial values. Herein also lay, at the time, the difference between the evolutionary philosophy of English philosopher Herbert Spencer and that of Thorstein Veblen.

A common idealism among Norwegian intellectuals at the time did not mean that they agreed on the political issues of the day. In the language dispute that has divided Norway since the time of Veblen, Bjørnson – in spite of his romantic views of rural society – founded the society for the preservation of the Danish-influenced written language of the Norwegian cities (*Riksmålsforbundet*), while urbanite Kristofer Janson patriotically adopted the newly created common denominator of Norwegian dialects, *nynorsk*.[14] Likewise the language spoken in household where Thorstein Veblen grew up has been a matter of strife, in this case among Veblen scholars. An appendix to this chapter, courtesy of Ingeborg Kongslien of Valdres and the University of Oslo, throws light on this issue through samples of the language spoken by Veblen's father Thomas in 1895. It shows the local Valdres dialect interspersed with a contextual American term – the Great Lakes – conjugated in the unique Valdres dialect, plural form, into *leihjidn* (the common pronunciation among Norwegian-Americans is *leikene*). In a letter to Rector Halvdan Koht of the University of Oslo, Veblen himself writes, 'The only Norwegian which I speak at all fluently is a dialect of the Valdres *Bygdemål* [i.e. rural dialect].'[15]

The national language conflict represents what is perhaps a less constructive aspect of the Norwegian instinct for 'anti-feudal' insubordination: such an attitude may lead to uncompromising prolonged trench wars. Acknowledging the risk of moving down the slippery slope of national stereotypes, it is tempting to remark that other nations seem to have mechanisms that better solve such conflicts. The Japanese have an ability to talk themselves to consensus; the Germans seem to resort to authority; the French add humour to authority when conflicts loom; the Italians add to authority an appeal to a special national conflict-solving phrase *lasciamo perdere*: let's drop this argument, with an undertone that 'it is really not worth arguing about'.

Alexander Kielland, an urbanite from a wealthy family in the pious south-western city of Stavanger, is the one who appears to have the least common elements with Veblen. But he, like Veblen, used biting satire in order to fight social injustice, and in him we also recognise Veblen's scepticism toward religion, as we do in Bjørnson and polar explorer and humanist Fridtjof Nansen (1861–1930).

The Veblens were not the only successful émigrés from Valdres. In the 1920s Jens Hansen, as Veblen both a *Valdris*[16] and a Cornellian, librarian at the University of Chicago, was sent by the Carnegie Foundation to introduce the Library of Congress system in the Vatican Library at the time of Pius XI, himself a librarian. While Hansen was in Rome, a delegation preparing the International Bibliographic Congress to be held in 1929 in Rome convened there. To his great surprise, Hansen found that among the eleven delegates there were also two other Norwegians, also they from Valdres, making it three delegates from Valdres versus eight from the rest of the world in this international library meeting in Rome![17] The people from Valdres were sometimes justifiably proud of their achievements.

In his short stories from Norwegian-America Kristofer Janson shows us that Norwegian immigrants were not always looked upon with respect. His stories often contrast sharply both with the combination of idyllic farming and sharp intellectualism of the Veblen family and with the proud *Valdris* librarians referred to above. As the latest arrivals in the ethnic pecking order, the *Norskies,* together with the Irish, were looked down upon. In Janson's novel about Vildrose (Wild Rose), a girl of Norwegian parents whose mother dies early and who grows up with her father close to the Indians, a woman exclaims: 'Norwegian? Indian? They are more or less of the same kind. They are both outside human civilisation.'[18]

Anyone seeking the roots of Veblen's scepticism towards religion will find the explanation in Kristofer Janson's novels.[19] Characterised by an anti-Spencerian desire for ethnic fairness, which is shared by Bjørnson, in this novel one of the characters explains,

> [Y]ou may rest assured that when you have these Indian rebellions, the Indians are in their full right. They can be patient and accept injustice, treachery, and insults for perhaps too long, probably because they see the vainness in fighting against so superior forces. But when the oppression and exploitation go so far that their own children succumb to hunger and thirst due to broken promises, then their rage bursts through all the dams of reason. And then, woe to the guilty or innocent who come in their way. With the unbridled cruelty and blood-thirst of the wild man, they attack everything, crush, murder destroy, nor giving up until they themselves lie crushed on the battlefield.[20]

In this perspective, the desire for fairness to your own kind is reflected in a wish for fairness also towards other ethnic groups.

Janson also wrote a brilliant essay on the famous 15th Wisconsin Regiment during the Civil War, under the legendary Colonel Heg (1829–1863),[21] which consisted exclusively of first generation Norwegian immigrants. Two insights relevant to Veblen emerge from this essay. The first relates to why Scandinavians settled so well in America:

Scandinavians are among the immigrants with least problems feeling at home in America, they love the republican institutions with life and soul. The freer of the political discussions from home, the old spirit of independence which inhabits the [home] nation as a heritage from the past, and the necessity in America to depend on yourself, your own work, and your own wisdom, all contribute to this […]. The Swede has no landlord for whom to crawl, the Dane no *Junker*, and the Norwegian no tax collector or magistrate.[22]

It was exactly against these tax collectors and magistrates Veblen's forefathers in Valdres had rebelled.[23] Are we to seek the reason for Veblen's dislike of Germany – which to myself was long a puzzle because his economic methodology is so similar to German economics at the time[21] – the reason lies in the same *Junkers*, the landed oligarchy (often noble) that dominated Prussia and prevented the kind of personal freedom so cherished in the nobility-free Norwegian tradition.[25]

Janson, himself a Unitarian clergyman, describes the Norwegian church in America:

The Norwegian *Synode* must count among the most narrow-minded and inane churches in the world, taking every word in the bible literally. Dusting off the Old Testament, they had discovered that the bible not only did not forbid slavery, but in certain cases actually demanded it. Owning black slaves was simply in keeping with God's word.[26]

That their own Norwegian religious authorities in the US were in favour of slavery,[27] becomes an explanation for Janson as to why so many young Norwegian immigrants enlisted against the beliefs of their clergy: with the North in the US Civil War.

In all likelihood Veblen would have shared Janson's general view on Norwegian religion in America. It must have appeared as irrational, fundamentalist and in the end anti-humanistic as the Physiocratic *ordre naturel* which Veblen almost makes fun of in his essay 'The Place of Science'. Part of the story of Norwegian religion in the United States is that a less fundamentalist group, the Norwegian-Danish Lutheran Conference, broke out from the *synod* (*konferensen* as opposed to *Synoden*). Janson describes how these two sects sometimes built churches right next to each other, competing for 'customers'. Religious fights are common, but this fight – *Synodestriden* – represents an unusually bitter war of irreconcilable positions within the small Norwegian-American community, thus recalling the language dispute back in Norway.

In the same vein, Ibsen complained about the inability of Norwegians to agree on anything big. Janson notes that Henrik Ibsen criticises Norwegians' inability to accept the full consequences of their thoughts.[28] A few years later Ibsen put this idea into verse:

They go about their tasks, the Norwegian men – weak-willed, wavering, they don't know where they are going. Their hearts shrink, their minds steal away, weak, like waving willows before the wind, they can agree on only one thing in the world, namely, that every greatness shall be toppled and stoned.[29]

The conversations between Janson and Ibsen took place in Rome rather than in Oslo. Although Ibsen was inspired both by Norway and by Italy, where he did much of his writing, he interestingly settled in the area of Europe which seen from the north is called *Südtirol* (South Tyrol); from the south *Alto Adige* (Upper Adige Valley). Here Ibsen would find the best of Europe, just the blend of the Myth of the North – Veblen's Myth – and The Myth of the South which sometimes meet in German culture.

Jonas Lie's novel *Familien på Gilje*[30] ('The Family at Gilje') is of particular interest to Veblenians, because it is set in Veblen's Valdres in the 1840s, at the time when Veblen's parents left the valley. Lie makes the point of how isolated the valley of the Veblens was, in a discussion between a military captain and a student walking in the area:

'I have wondered about that part of the country from the time I was a schoolboy. We had to draw Lake Bygdin into the geography book by hand. It was discovered only a few years ago, in the middle of the broad mountain plateau which only some reindeer hunters knew anything about.'
'Not laid down on any map, no – as blank as in the interior of Africa, marked as unexplored. The locals move between the districts and of course the mountains have their names from ancient times among the common people.'
'True enough, the natives also knew the interior of Africa, but on that account it is not called "discovered" by the civilized world', said the other smiling.'

Even if Jonas Lie has exaggerated, the people of Valdres had reason to keep up their spirit of insubordination against the neglect and positive mischief of the central authorities of Christiania (Oslo). In an infamous incident taking place a few years before the Veblens left, the twelfth-century main church of Vang, deemed too small, was sold against the will of the locals. All valuable woodwork in the church was auctioned off to King Friedrich Wilhelm of Prussia,[31] and sent on a tortuous trip by horse, steamer and river boat to be reconstructed in the village of Bruckenberg in Silesia. The king himself was present when the church was inaugurated in 1844. The old Vang church is still there, but now in Polish territory.

Knud Nordsveen, one of the parishioners, wanted to move the old church across the lake to serve as the local church where the distance to the main church was the furthest, and offered a plot of free land from his own farm for the purpose. His attempts were frustrated, and Nordsveen himself retired from the parish council, sold his farm and left with his whole family and staff for America. Almost 100 years later, the righteous people of Valdres raised a memorial stone – a *bauta* – in his honour on the site to which the church should have been moved. Its inscription reads: 'For this his judiciousness and foresight the congregation of Heensaasen give him thanks and honour by erecting this memorial stone, 22-6-1929.' This took place less than two months before Veblen passed away.

Another Norwegian traveller to the United States was the young Knut Hamsun – born in Lom not too far away from Valdres – who would receive the Nobel Prize in Literature in 1920. In his first book, *Fra det moderne Amerikas Aandsliv* (*The Cultural Life of Modern America*),[32] Hamsun, like Veblen, sees America as a rather uncivilised place and the book title refers more to the absence of cultural life in the over-commercialised nation than to its presence.[33]

Polar explorer Fridtjof Nansen also belongs to this idealist tradition. He later became Norway's ambassador to the League of Nations in Geneva, and is famous in Russia for having contributed to saving millions of people from starvation there, and for saving more than 1 million Armenians during the conflict with Turkey. The efforts in Russia won Nansen the Nobel Peace Prize in 1922, and the League of Nations honoured him by creating the Nansen International Office for Refugees in Geneva, which, in turn, was awarded the 1938 Nobel Peace Prize.

During the run-up towards the independence of Norway from Sweden in 1905, and directly afterwards, a special kind of idealism prevailed which was rooted in the Enlightenment values of the 1700s. This idealism also strongly identified itself with other subdued nations and ethnic groups. This positive kind of national idealism released constructive and inclusive energy rather than xenophobia, and is found also in other 'late-coming' nations that fought for independence or unity in the nineteenth century: in the Italy of Giuseppe Mazzini and Giuseppe Garibaldi and in the Germany of Friedrich List. *Italianità*, *Deutschtum* and *norskhet* (Norwegianness) produced surplus energy to fight for other nationalities as well. Garibaldi physically fought for independence in Latin America; List and Bjørnson fought with their pen for other nations as well as for their own. Both List and Garibaldi were early proponents of a united Europe; their idealistic nationalism also included the rights of other nations to be nationalist.

Veblen uses satire and mockery as a weapon against both social injustice *and* against bad science. In Norwegian literature, we have to go all the way back to Ludvig Holberg (1667–1745) to find Veblen's combination of fighting social injustice and mockery of science. Holberg was part of an Enlightenment tradition that seems to have been particularly vocal in the economically marginalised European periphery. From Ireland, Jonathan Swift (1684–1754) launched his 'Modest Proposal for Preventing the Children of Poor People From Being a Burden on Their Parents or Country, and for Making Them Beneficial to the Publick'. Here Swift takes irony to the extreme by suggesting that the problem of poor children in Ireland could be solved by selling them as food to the English upper classes, providing both recipes and economic calculations. In his *Travels into Several Remote Nations of the World*, the same Swift mocks the scientific establishment in England. This is particularly evident in Gulliver's visit to the land of the giants. Veblen similarly mocks standard economics:

> A gang of Aleutian Islanders slashing about in the wrack and surf with rakes and magical incantations for the capture of shell-fish are held, in point of taxonomic reality, to be engaged in a feat of hedonistic equilibration in rent, wages, and interest.[34]

In his play *Erasmus Montanus*, Holberg delivers a parody of the decayed logic of scholastics, when a learned man makes the following proof to a poor woman: 'A stone cannot fly. Mother Nille cannot fly. Therefore Mother Nille is a stone'.[35] This phrase is famous in Norway and Denmark. Holberg also mocks the Danish feudal upper classes much as Veblen mocked a nascent US 'industry-based feudalism' more than 150 years later.

In France came another voice from the relative periphery of Naples. Ferdinando Galiani (1728–1787), the brilliant secretary of the Neapolitan Embassy in Paris, produced a masterpiece of economic theory mocking the Physiocrats[36] much as Veblen later would mock Ricardian economics. These values were the same as those which Voltaire (1694–1778) and Rousseau (1712–1778) exposed from another anti-feudal bastion, from Geneva in Switzerland. And, it may be argued, there is more than a touch of Rousseau in Veblen. In Italy itself, Venetian playwright Carlo Goldoni (1707–1793) stood for the very same values and method: achieving honesty and a decent humanist society through the mockery of an arrogant nobility and clerics, and their values.[37] But mockery of philosophy and science itself – the method of Voltaire, Galiani, Swift, Holberg and Veblen – is less frequent.

In addition to his Norwegianness, as Stephen Edgell and Francesca Viano have both previously pointed out, there are important European elements in Veblen.[38] He can probably be best understood as a continuation of a European Enlightenment humanist anti-nobility and anti-clerical tradition, and – above all – as someone writing in the Enlightenment methodology of satire and mockery. The conditions giving rise to Veblen's mockery, a new upper class with feudalistic consumption patterns and values, were new to the United States at the time. Satire as a literary strategy for social change was not new in the US, however. Mark Twain (1835–1910) had already used satire against slavery.

Immigrants had left Europe for America by the millions in order to escape societies marred by social stratification, unfair privilege and vested interests. We should therefore not be surprised that someone protested when they saw American society acquiring the very same characteristics that marred the Europe they left behind. That someone was Thorstein Veblen, and in *The Theory of The Leisure Class* he used the same method European authors, from Galiani to Swift and Holberg, had used before him: satire and mockery, holding a mirror up to society to show why they should not like what they saw. Veblen was so original in America essentially because the conditions against which he protested were new at the time. Seen from the perspective of the European Enlightenment tradition, Veblen's values and attitudes were of a quintessentially mainstream kind. By focusing on Veblen as either an American, which he also was, or as a marginalised peasant from the outskirts of civilisation, this important European aspect has not received sufficient attention. The fact that these European values were also those anti-feudal Enlightenment values upon which the United States itself was built – down to the specifics of Thomas Jefferson's scepticism towards the financial sector – makes it relatively unproblematic to reconcile Veblen the European and Veblen the American.

The non-feudal history of Norway – so importantly emphasised in Kåre Lunden's chapter in this book – simply reinforces the point made above; the values Veblen brought with him from Valdres were fully compatible with 'Veblen the European Enlightenment scholar' and 'Veblen the American'. All these three versions of Veblen produce the kind of idealism and spirit of insubordination which is recognisable in Veblen's personality. Veblen 'had an emotional quality, a drive of indignation, a hatred of buncombe and pretence'.[39]

Reflecting on the difference between Norwegian and European idealism at the time of Veblen and now, one observation might be that such idealism has now moved from attacking root causes of unfairness and poverty towards an institutionalised 'regime of goodness' which concentrates on alleviating the symptoms of, rather than curing the causes of, poverty. I refer to this idealism as causing 'welfare colonialism'.[40] Anticipating the analysis that will follow in the next section, I personally see this as a Western retrogression away from a Veblenian anti-Physiocratic *activistic-idealistic* frame of mind in the eighteenth to early twentieth centuries, towards the present day neoclassical (Physiocratic) and *passivistic-materialistic* outlook, where the *ordre naturel* – free trade, etc. – is not questioned, but its symptoms and negative effects are instead treated palliatively.[41]

In 1920, at a time when Veblen had no university position in the United States, he was offered a professorship in *statsøkonomi* ('state economics', i.e. economics) at the University of Oslo. The very friendly invitation letter was signed by university Rector Halvdan Koht.[42] The position required parliamentary approval, and Koht had already secured approval from the head of the Committee on Education, Carl Joachim Hambro (1885–1964). It is noteworthy that Hambro, later head of the Conservative Party, had no objections to such 'radical' thoughts as those Veblen would have brought to Norway. Just as it was still possible for Veblen's student's student Arthur F. Burns, later head of the Federal Reserve (see the last section of this chapter), to refer approvingly to Marx's analysis, intellectual efforts were not yet as politicised along a partisan right–left axis as they later would be. It was then possible to appreciate Marx's analysis of the dynamics of capitalism without being a Marxist. Key to understanding Veblen is also understanding how this all changed after the 1970s, as professional analysis was, as I see it, poisoned by simplistic ideologies guised in equilibrium mathematics. A paraphrase of the Veblenian term 'contamination of instincts' is appropriate here: neoclassical economics 'contaminated' the common sense instincts of economics.

It is worth mentioning that Thorstein Veblen some years later, in 1925, was also offered the prestigious chairmanship of the American Economic Association. An (undated) copy of Veblen's letter to Edwin Seligman rejecting the offer, primarily for health reasons, was found by Knut Odner in the archives of Carleton College.

Context 2: Filiations of Economic Thought and the Revolts of 1848 and the 1890s

Veblen's student Wesley Clair Mitchell (1874–1948) wrote the two-volume *Types of Economic Theory*.[43] The UK translation of Othmar Spann's history of economic thought also carries the title *Types of Economic Theory*.[44] This idea that economics came in different types, with different *filiations,* to use Schumpeter's term, hails back to 1782 when a book grouped the economics profession into either Physiocrats or anti-Physiocrats.[45] In my view, this distinction is still extremely useful in order to come to grips with the history of economic thought and with the crisis of today. A main problem here is that today's textbooks in the history of economic thought virtually unanimously trace the lineage of the profession back to the Physiocrats; while as matter of historical record, the Physiocrats lost all major historical battles except the one in today's economics textbooks.

Veblen stands firmly in the anti-Physiocratic, non-mechanistic tradition, which I refer to as the Other Canon of economics.[46] This Other Canon was virtually doomed to disappear when mathematics, rather than English or other languages, was chosen as the dominating means of communication between economists. I shall argue that this Other Canon type of theory – the anti-Physiocratic one ruled by Man's wit and will rather than by Nature's *ordre naturel* and invisible forces – needs to be brought back in order to solve the present crisis.

In his 1899 article, 'The Preconceptions of Economic Science', Veblen himself uses physiocracy as 'the point of departure in an attempt to trace that shifting of aims and norms of procedure that comes into view in the work of later economists when compared with earlier writers'.[47] Veblen describes physiocracy as being animistic and hedonistic, dominated by a belief in *ordre naturel*, and contrasts it with his own evolutionary approach. While our 1782 taxonomist of economists placed Adam Smith among the anti-Physiocrats, to Veblen '[i]n Adam Smith the two (types of economics) are happily combined, not to say blended; but the animistic habit still holds the primacy'.[48] A prime example of the animistic side of Adam Smith that Veblen refers to is, of course, a belief in an 'invisible hand' that will order economic life harmoniously if only mankind would entrust its fate to it. But this term was only mentioned once in Smith's *Wealth of Nations*, and then only coming into force after a massive dose of policy intervention, i.e. the Navigation Acts, of which Adam Smith greatly approved, had led the English to prefer English goods to foreign imports. So Adam Smith is indeed a blend of the two types, as Veblen says.

Veblen's 1895 translation of Gustav Cohn's *Finanzwissenschaft* provides a world view much broader than finance alone, that of an activistic-idealistic approach to economics. Camic convincingly argues that Veblen's translation of this book, and its version of the German Historical School of Economics, was important in shaping his economic world view.[49] Cohn develops a theory of stages of development of the state. In his work, human welfare is clearly a product of conscious human will, not of any invisible hand of Providence as in physiocracy. Cohn, in Veblen's own translation, quotes Johann Gottfried Hoffman in his *Theory of Taxation*:

> The delusion that security of life and property, the productivity of labour, and the consequent possibility of acquisition and enjoyment, and even the elevation of the spiritual and the ennobling of the moral nature – that these goods came to Man in the gift of gratuities, is itself a proof of the advanced stage of culture which the greater part of Europe at present occupies. As the grown man has long since forgotten the pains it cost him to learn to speak, so have the peoples, in the days of their mature growth of the State, forgotten what was required in order to free them from their primitive brutal savagery.[50]

Gustav Cohn, who was born in the year Hoffman's *Theory* appeared, picks up the argument and continues:

> In point of fact, how significant was the involuntary testimony which the eighteenth Century, with its repudiation of the historic State its yearning after the primordial state of nature, bore to the blessings of the inherited culture which it ungratefully enjoyed.[51]

This description – written well over 100 years ago – also fits the zeitgeist that came to dominate the world after the 1989 fall of the Berlin Wall. The West ungratefully enjoys the result of centuries of wise economic policies, and now, in the spirit of the *ordre naturel* of markets, does its best to undo much of it, including the welfare. Again today, a 'repudiation of the State' and 'the end of the nation-state' – based on English classical and neoclassical economics – is mixed with a 'yearning after the primordial state of nature'. 'If we just managed to get rid of the state [...]' appears to be a Tea Party credo.

As opposed to the Physiocratic *ordre naturel* proposed by feudal landowners, Veblen had his own *ordre naturel:* that of the Baltic Stone Age.[52]

> A small scale system of tillage and presently of mixed farming [...] The scheme of institutions, economic, civil domestic and religious, that would fit these circumstances would be of a relatively slight fixity, flexible, loose-knit and naïve, in the sense that they would be kept in hand under discretionary control of neighborly common sense [...] It is a civilisation of workmanship and fecundity, rather than of dynastic power, statecraft, priestcraft or artistic achievement.[53]

Here, in Veblen's own utopia, we find the issue of small scale and relative self-sufficiency (i.e. a lack of division of labour), which Lunden tells us was a key feature of Valdres society (see Chapter 3). Veblen's love of small scale is in a sense the antithesis of Alfred Chandler's emphasis of *Scale and Scope* as crucial to the development of capitalism, just as Veblen's *out of the North* is an antithesis of Ferdinand Braudel's *Out of Italy*.[54] In German culture, we find these alternative myths – that of the European North and the European South – competing and merging.[55]

Werner Sombart, the important economist of the German Historical School, describes this fault line between the two types of economics in different terms, as static *passivistic-materialistic* (physiocracy) versus dynamic *activistic-idealistic* economics (anti-physiocracy).[56] Originating with the *ordre naturel* of the Physiocrats the former – today founding economics on the metaphor of equilibrium – is individualistic, focuses on trade rather than on production, and dismisses institutions and social synergies such as in the concept of 'society'. The latter focuses on production of knowledge, goods and services, on production rather than trade, and anchors its analysis of economic development in institutions and social synergies, sometimes using the human body as the basic metaphor for society. One fundamental problem of today's economic debate is that the vast majority of participants come from the passivistic-materialistic tradition which – since Adam Smith – has largely exogenised production and unlearned Werner Sombart's definition of capitalism as consisting of 1) the entrepreneur, 2) the modern state and 3) the industrial system, a scheme that would fit Veblen's thoughts. The practical consequences of the disappearance of this Other Canon of economics – of the whole tradition in which Veblen stands – are, I would argue, highly dramatic, both in the Third World and for the crisis the West now faces.

Because Thorstein Veblen's economics belongs to the dynamic *activistic-idealistic* tradition, his approach stands out as being very different from today's mainstream.

However, looking at the context of the 1890s, when Veblen's career as an economist took off, an evolutionary approach to social sciences was, at the time, more 'mainstream' than one would normally assume today. In addition to the discussion found in Hodgson (see Chapter 12), an outline of the broader context will be useful in order to understand Veblen the economist in his historical context.

Ben B. Seligman's *Main Currents in Modern Economics* is an unusual text in the history of economic thought insofar as it is not organised around the history of mainstream economics – normally a requirement for books that aim at high sales – but rather traces the history and fate of the dissenters, among them those found within the American tradition.[57] This may be the reason why John Kenneth Galbraith recognises in his foreword to the second edition of Seligman's book that, in spite of its 'enormous scholarship, wholly acceptable to the diligent layman', it is 'the most overlooked book in the last ten or twenty or fifty years'.[58]

Seligman's history of economics begins in the 1870s with the revolt of the German and English historical schools against the rigidities of the classical school, which peaks in the late 1890s (*The Revolt Against Formalism*, vol. 1), a movement which is countered by *The Reaffirmation of Tradition* (vol. 2) through marginalism – which ends up reinforcing the classical school – and further developed into *The Trust Toward Technique* (vol. 3). In volume 2, the first section starts with a chapter entitled 'From Marginalism to Libertarianism'. Seligman here shows his ability to recognise the long lines of history, where the qualitative understanding in the Austrian economics of Carl Menger degenerated into Mises's 'libertarianism in extremis'.[59]

Seligman's account of Veblen and his theories is perhaps the best synthesis ever produced on this complex topic.[60] On Seligman's huge intellectual canvas, Veblen rather than a loner becomes a participant in a fundamental intellectual revolt against the formalism and sterility of the classical school of economics and its Physiocratic roots. Smith and Ricardo's individualistic teachings, focusing on markets and human bartering, yield to new approaches emphasising human creativity and production where the individual is imbedded in a society. Just as for the members of the German historical school, Veblen's economic theory was anthropocentric in that it placed mankind, *both* as individuals and as society, at centre stage of economics. As Seligman puts it in his analysis of Veblen,

> [t]he plasticity of the human personality was acknowledged, and man became the creative factor in both the physical and social environments. A relationship of complete interpenetration between man, society and the environment was seen as the basis for change and growth.[61]

In this sense, Veblen's economic dynamics is, at its very core, closely related to that of Joseph Schumpeter, 26 years his junior.[62]

As Seligman readily recognises, there were rebels before the 1870s as well. Considering this in a larger context, it seems reasonable to trace the movement for change in economics back to the events that followed the massive financial crisis of 1847 and to 1848, when revolutions erupted in all large European countries with the exceptions of England and Russia. This marked the end of a period of growing influence of David Ricardo's

1817 *Principles of Economics and Taxation*. With hindsight it can be argued that Ricardo's initial influence peaked with the 1846 Repeal of the Corn Laws. John Stuart Mill's 1848 *Principles of Economics* – the canonical textbook which took over after Ricardo's *Principles* – opens for a much broader and more philosophical base of economics than what Ricardo had allowed.[63] Mill's recantation on free trade as a universal principle, opening up for 'infant industry protection', and his call for virtually confiscatory inheritance taxes are but two sometimes ignored aspects of the economics of the great liberal Mill.

In addition to Mill's canonical *Principles of Political Economy* in England, the revolutionary year 1848 also gave birth to two trend-breaking books in continental Europe, and with them came two schools of economic thought. Bruno Hildebrand (1812–1878) published *Die Nationalökonomie der Gegenwart und Zukunft*[64] (*Economics of the Present and the Future*), which came to be the founding work of the German Historical School of Economics;[65] and Karl Marx and Friedrich Engels published *The Communist Manifesto*, the founding work of Marxism. To illustrate the diversity of the persons involved in this theoretical revolt, Hildebrand was so conservative that he had to flee Germany for Switzerland, while Marx was so radical that he had to flee to England. As indicated by Randall Wray (see Chapter 14), the distinction between 'natural economy', 'money economy' and 'credit economy' as used by Veblen is found in Hildebrand.

During the nineteenth century, German and US economics were in close affinity in their opposition of English economic theory, forming an important root of the old American Institutional School. Two influential pairs of American-German thinkers were Friedrich List (1789–1846) and his less well-known but almost equally important US American inspirer Daniel Raymond (1786–1849),[66] and Henry Carey (1793–1879) and Eugen Dühring (1833–1921) who vocally supported each other's work. In his 1924 letter to Mr Pritchard, referred to in the introduction to this volume, replying to a question regarding literature in any language 'bearing on current economic facts' Veblen states that 'the Americans and the Germans have the field pretty much to themselves'.[67]

The *Verein für Sozialpolitik*, active from 1872 to 1932, produced a total of 188 volumes of transactions, and was a focal point of the theoretical revolt. The association included both politically conservative and radical economists working together towards a united goal of 'civilising capitalism'. The 1890s saw what might be considered the three peak performances of revolt against economic formalism, one each in Germany, England and the United States. First came the *Verein*'s founder Gustav Schmoller's in his 1897 inaugural speech as Rector of the University of Berlin, which laments that 'the human idealism of Adam Smith' had degenerated into 'the hard mammonism of the Manchester School'[68] and decries the naiveté of both laissez-faire and communism as 'twins of an ahistorical rationalism'.[69]

The second work of revolt is Cambridge economist Herbert Foxwell's 110-page introduction to a book by Anton Menger,[70] which also distances itself from both political utopias and holds David Ricardo's work responsible for the political ills to both the political right and the political left. His criticism of abstract Ricardian theory has the punch of a Veblen, but takes a different form:

> Ricardo, and still more those who popularised him, may stand as an example for all time of the extreme danger which may arise from the unscientific use of hypothesis

and social speculations, from the failure to appreciate the limited application to actual affairs of highly artificial and arbitrary analysis.[71]

When Veblen mocks Ricardian context-free economics with his reference to the Aleutian islanders, he is essentially making the same point as Foxwell, but in a very different style. In addition to Schmoller and Foxwell, two authors favourably referred to by Veblen,[72] Veblen's own *The Theory of the Leisure Class* can be seen as the third element in this theoretical revolt of the late 1890s.

Other less rebellious economists were also clearly influenced by the changing paradigm of the 1890s, towards a less abstract and more dynamic type of economics. The next canonical textbook in economics after Mill's is Alfred Marshall's *Principles of Economics*, first published in 1890. There is no mention of Smith and Ricardo, nor of Mill, when Marshall – the founder of neoclassical economics – lists his main influences. The two kinds of influences that have affected the book 'more than any other', says Marshall in his introduction to his *magnum opus*, are those of biology, as represented by the writings of Herbert Spencer, and 'of history and philosophy, as represented by Hegel's *Philosophy of History*'.[73] In the same year, Marshall's Cambridge colleague John Neville Keynes – father of John Maynard Keynes – published his *Scope and Method of Political Economy*, a book also very much influenced by continental European and evolutionary thinking.[74] Under the heading 'The conception of political economy as an ethical, realistic, and inductive science', Keynes's father comments that while this school originated in Germany, 'a rising school of economists in the United States, who expressly repudiate the assertion that the new movement is exclusively a German movement', was emerging, and that this type of theory also finds its 'very forcible expression'.[75]

It is difficult to appreciate the enormous influence the evolutionary thinking of English philosopher Herbert Spencer (1820–1903) had both in England and in the United States during his lifetime. Viano details Veblen's meeting with Spencerian philosophy in Chapter 7. Writing on the subject of evolution before Charles Darwin, but later also influenced by him, Spencer saw the evolutionary process as a universal law, applying as much to the stars and the galaxies as to biological organisms and to human society as much as to the human mind.[76] Spencer is now most famously associated with the term 'the survival of the fittest'. However, it is important to note that it was entirely possible to agree with his evolutionary views without subscribing to 'the survival of the fittest'. Andrew Carnegie was a great admirer of Spencer, but gave away fortunes to constructing public libraries across the United States in an effort to counteract this tendency. Veblen was, of course, in the same camp: a tendency towards survival of the fittest needs to be met by policy. Also in the United States – as strongly emphasised in a book by Malcolm Rutherford[77] – Veblen was much more mainstream than scholars hitherto have assumed. Before Marshall, Herbert Spencer's evolutionary thoughts had already found their way into economics by way of Henry Sidgwick – a co-founder, with Marshall, of the Cambridge school of economics – in his 1883 *The Principles of Political Economy*.[78] It should be noted, however, that as with Mill, and in contrast with today's mainstream economics, Spencer's evolutionary utilitarianism was a moral, if dismal, science.[79] Spencer's biology was strongly adaptationist, making use of both inheritance and acquired characteristics, along the lines of Jean-Baptiste Lamarck. In this, but not in his social Darwinism, Spencer's influence lingers on in today's evolutionary economics.

Thus, when in 1898 Thorstein Veblen published his article 'Why is economics not an evolutionary science' his was not a lonely cry in the wilderness, although his focus on the plasticity of human nature – on instincts and proclivities – underlying the evolution was not necessarily mainstream. Both as an economic theorist, as a Norwegian and as a European idealist, Thorstein Bunde Veblen was not quite the loner he is often pictured as being. But he delved deeper into the mechanisms of causality, he was less mechanistic than most of his contemporaries.

Context 3: Technological Change and Financial Crisis, Then and Now

The title of this volume – *Economics for an Age of Crisis* – reflects the belief of the editors that the present multitude of crises and challenges facing us need solutions that are inspired by Veblen's brand of economics rather than by present mainstream theories. It is our conviction that a set of theories based on the notion of equilibrium is totally unfit for today's challenges, and that ideas based on the alternative metaphor of evolution, as Veblen suggested, is needed with considerable urgency.

It is not surprising, therefore, that the greatest interest in Veblen in the United States coincided with the deepest point of the Great Depression, in 1934. When Veblen's *Essays in our Changing Order: Thorstein Veblen's Social Vision*[80] was published that year, the subtitle in *New York Times Book Review*, 30 September 1934, hailed 'a collection …clear and penetrating in their ideas, which proves him to have been at times prophetic'. This was also the year Joseph Dorfman's massive biography of Veblen was published by Viking Press. The newspapers at the time lavished attention and praise on Veblen, who had passed away five years earlier. On 2 December, under the headline 'Analyst of Modern Society', *New York Times Book Review* presented 'the life of a thinker who has had great influence'. The heading of Lewis Mumford's extended book review, 'A stick of dynamite wrapped like candy', was on the front page of *Saturday Review of Literature* on 12 January 1935; while *New York Herald Tribune Books*' 9 December 1934 'Veblen – Freud and Darwin of Economics' was a simultaneous review of Veblen's essays and Dorfman's biography.

The most insightful book review ever published on Veblen's works, also in 1934, gives a very perceptive description of his personality. Well-known *New York Times* critic and author Robert L. Duffus, was uniquely qualified to write it: as a 19-year-old he had spent one year, from 1907 to 1908, in Veblen's household with his brother. Ten years later – in 1944 Duffus went on to publish a memoir of Veblen.[81]

> Veblen was too interesting, too engagingly contradictory and mysterious, too moving in the combination of clarity and bafflement with which he faced life, ever to be ignored. […] Finally he had an exquisite sense of humour which some of his critics seem never to have discerned.[82]

Indeed, Americans could never be sure whether Veblen – *Tøyse* to his stepdaughters – was serious or if he made fun of them.

Figure 1. The Business Climates in Veblen's Life

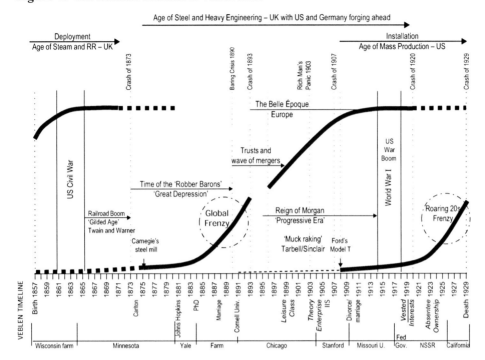

Veblen's life was characterised by disruptive innovations and rapid technological change. Carlota Perez has documented the relationship between such disruptive technical change and financial crises.[83] Perez, who was present at the Veblen conference in Valdres, has kindly matched Veblen's life with the business cycles of the period (see Fig. 1).

As we can see, economic turbulence was extreme during Veblen's lifetime and it clearly influenced his world view. This period bears no comparison to the relative stability which reigned from 1945 to 2007, a result of a wisely regulated capitalism when production rather than finance was at the core of the capitalist system.

Veblen's own understanding of the relationship between finance and production in the creation of business cycles was probably influenced by Gustav Cohn's *System der Finanzwissenschaft*, which he translated in 1895.[84] Veblen's perspective was carried forward by his student Wesley Clair Mitchell in a huge tome, *Business Cycles*, in which Veblen is quoted ten times.[85] Mitchell's volume is in a sense a similar effort to Schumpeter's two-volume work of the same name published 26 years later, in 1939.

Thorstein Veblen's theoretical contributions were – as those of Joseph Schumpeter – fairly unique in linking the understanding of technological change with that of financial crises. As Mark Blaug says about Veblen's most important books:

> No matter which of these books we open, we find the idea that life in a modern industrial community is the result of a polar conflict between 'pecuniary employments' and 'industrial employments', between 'business enterprise' and

'the machine process', between 'vendibility' and 'serviceability' – in short, between making money and making goods. There is a class struggle under capitalism, not between the bourgeoisie and the proletariat, but between businessmen and engineers. Pecuniary habits of thought unite bankers, brokers, lawyers and managers in a defence of private acquisition; in contrast, the discipline of the machine unites workers in industry and more especially the technicians and engineers who supervise them.[86]

The West today sees these same forces – production capitalism versus financial capitalism – again pitted against each other. This is why Veblen's theories are again so relevant. But today's crisis is in many ways more complex than that of 1929. In addition to the financial crisis that started in 2007, the world is facing an energy crisis and a growing environmental crisis involving pollution and climate change,[87] while the West is facing a long-term crisis caused by the growing economic and political power of Asia. At one level, the response to all these crises may be grouped into two schools of thought as introduced above: the Physiocratic and the anti-Physiocratic. Today, the Physiocratic and neoclassical response is focused on the *ordre naturel* of efficient markets, which indirectly creates speculation.[88] This is a focus on Veblen's 'vendibility', i.e. the need for more globalisation; on solving the energy crises through buying and selling of quotas, rather than through new technology, and on purchasing the rainforests in faraway countries in order to preserve them (as is Norwegian official policy), rather than on creating new technologies and alternative employment.

The alternative response – the one we are sorely missing today – is rooted in Renaissance,[89] in anti-Physiocratic, Enlightenment and Veblenian values: scientific curiosity leading to workmanship and production, new knowledge and innovations and a lack of speculation. Asia has now taken over the anti-Physiocratic and Veblenian values, seemingly leaving the West in an animistic belief in Physiocratic natural order, and this is at the root of the crises now facing the West, on both sides of the Atlantic. The West clings to the theories that are useful for countries that have the upper hand in technology and economic power, but which are extremely dangerous to hold on to when technological and economic power is being eroded, as it now is in the West.[90] What we need at this time is to revert to the values of emulation Europe used when it built up world dominance.[91]

Technologically we are in a similar situation to the 1880s and 1890s, when the potential of the steam technology had been exhausted. At a time when the carcasses of dead horses were already a threat to public health, authors predicted that if the volume of traffic in New York and London continued to increase these cities would drown in horse manure. Three options were possible: 1) move back into the countryside, 2) put diapers on the horses, or 3) invent a new means of transportation by employing new technology, i.e. the automobile. But it was not clear what kind of automobile should be invented. In the 1890s, there were prototypes of steam cars and electric cars; electric trams were already working. The solution came from an outsider, from Karl Friedrich Benz and his gasoline-powered automobile.

Technological change: Engineers versus businessmen and finance in the energy sector, then and now

In his 1921 book *The Engineers and the Price System*,[92] Veblen identifies a main conflict in capitalism between the interests of the engineers – we could also call them innovators – and the businessmen who run huge corporations, Veblen's 'captains of industry'. One could argue that profit maximisation in production may be attained in three different basic ways: 1) through reduction of output (which pushes prices higher), b) through process innovations (lowering production costs of existing products), or c) through product innovations (creating new products). Option 1) – increasing profits by reducing output – Veblen calls 'sabotage',[93] or a 'conscientious withdrawal of efficiency'. The way Enron achieved approval of higher electricity prices in California in 2001, by creating artificial blackouts, is an obvious example of increasing profits through sabotage.

It is, however, exceedingly important to notice that Veblen hastens to say that sabotage is not to be condemned as such, sometimes it is both necessary and legitimate to keep profits and employment up by withdrawing capacity. From today's perspective it can be pointed out that the main purpose of the European Coal and Steel Community (ECSC) – the very foundation of the European Union – was to reduce European overproduction of coal and steel in order to achieve profitability: in other words a key objective was a conscientious withdrawal of efficiency. Veblen clearly sees that a 'just degree' of imperfect competition is needed in order to keep profits and employment up, excessive competition may be ruinous. This is why Central European capitalism historically has tended to control industry through cartelisation, limiting output and thus maintaining employment and profits during downturns. But sabotage can also work against the invention and adoption of useful technological change. That Veblen sees both these reasons for controlling output – one legitimate and one illegitimate – shows a much more sophisticated understanding of core issues facing the market economy (i.e. Veblen's 'price system') than that of today's mainstream.

In *The Engineers and The Price System*, Veblen defined the industrial system as 'a system of interlocking mechanical processes', 'on whose due working depends the material welfare of all the civilized people'. This welfare-producing machinery has one enemy, however: 'the captains of finance are working […] to divert whatever they can to the special gain of one vested interest […] at any cost to the rest'.[94] In 2012, the financial crisis of the West – on both sides of the Atlantic – can be seen as these 'captains of finance' making money at the cost of the productive sector. Veblen's analysis is again spot on.

The interest of 'engineers' lies in making profit through innovations, while the interests of mature businesses may lie in the exact opposite: in continuing to make money from already established technologies. No one exemplifies the transition from 'engineer' to 'businessman' and 'captain of industry and finance' better than Thomas Edison.

The 1940 movie *Edison, the Man* – starring Spencer Tracy – gives us the story of how Thomas Edison's light bulb was sabotaged by the operators of gas lights for street lightening. Later Edison himself stood in the way of technological progress, in this way representing, in sequence, both 'engineer' and 'businessman'. Having invested heavily in direct current (DC) Edison fought the technology of alternating current (AC) pioneered by his former employee Nikola Tesla. AC is what we now use, partly because of its high voltage and ability to be transported long distances.

Thorstein Veblen's term 'vested interests' describes a financial stake in a particular outcome. The young inventor Edison fought for his light-bulb against the vested interests of the businessmen who owned the gas light operations. Later, when Edison himself had become a businessman, he fought even more vigorously than the gas light people had against a new and better technology: the alternating current of Nikola Tesla.[95] In other words, engineers have vested interests – promoting innovations – which differ from those of businessmen – the protection of their vested interests. Veblen generalised this conflict between businessmen and engineers by stating that human society would always involve conflict between existing norms with vested interests and that new norms developed out of an innate human tendency to discover and invent based on improving our understanding of the physical world in which we exist. 'Idle curiosity' and 'the instinct of workmanship' were positive proclivities of man that continuously would be fighting the pecuniary interests of those with a vested interest in status quo.

During his lifetime Thomas Edison, then, played both sides in two different Veblenian technology moments; when new technology combats the vested interest of the old. First, Edison the Engineer fought to overcome the vested interest of the gas light industry, and later Edison the Businessman fought vigorously to protect his financial stakes in direct current (DC) against Nikola Tesla's AC. The young and old Edison represent the two different forces – the hero and the villain respectively – in the Veblenian history of electric energy.

Edison tried to protect his vested interests in DC by showing how lethal (high voltage) AC was. During the so-called War of the Currents' his aggressive campaign to discredit the new current took the macabre form of a series of animal electrocutions using AC. Tesla's partner was George Westinghouse, and Edison snidely referred to the killing process as getting 'Westinghoused'. Stray dogs and cats were most easily obtained for these demonstrations, but Edison got his big chance when a local zoo decided that the life of a cranky female elephant – Topsy – had to be terminated.

Just to be on the safe side Topsy was fed carrots laced with 460 grams of cyanide, but with the deadly current from a 6,600-volt AC source that killed her Edison had demonstrated how 'unsafe' Nikola Tesla's alternating current design was. The event was witnessed by an estimated 1,500 people and Edison's film of the event was seen by audiences throughout the United States.

Thomas Edison's sabotage managed to keep an obviously inferior energy technology alive for a long time because he wanted to protect his vested interest. This practice of sabotage is not at all uncommon, but in strategic general-purpose technologies, like energy, its negative effects to society may be very serious.

The energy sector has its Veblenian moments today also. In the past they may have delayed the adoption of superior technologies; in our case today, we continue to pollute the planet longer than necessary. The present version of the Veblenian War of the Currents involves the engineers attempting to produce new and clean energy versus the businessmen with vested interests in the continued use of coal and other fossil energies.

In the name of 'free markets' and against 'government intervention', libertarian think-tanks now play the part Edison himself once played against new technology.

Part of today's rhetoric of sabotage is an indirect use of the equilibrium metaphor – the idea that markets can adjust to any shock – in order to prevent change. In a 2011 interview on Fox News, Anthony Randazzo, Director of Economic Research at the Reason Foundation, argued in favour of closing down five government departments (Energy, Education, Housing and Urban Development, Commerce and Interior). He claimed that 'it is not radical to want to get rid of these departments', because with time the market would adjust to the new situation. The argument skilfully employs what in effect is a parody of neo-classical equilibrium logic where key elements, like knowledge and technology, are absent. The Stone Age was also in equilibrium, as are churchyards. From a Veblenian standpoint, it is fundamentally wrong and counterproductive to employ metaphors from dead matter – as equilibrium from the realm of physics – in order to explain dynamic human societies. Equilibrium, the core metaphor of neoclassical economics, becomes an argument for maintaining status quo.

Based on this equilibrium logic, Reason Foundation's Randazzo then gave his reason why the US Department of Energy should be closed down: 'The Department of Energy destroys jobs because it tries to create these green energy projects that destroy coal-mining jobs.'[96] Again we find the sabotage Veblen referred to: vested interests in previous technologies – as with Edison – mobilise to block new technology. The Bronze Age must be stopped because people in the stone quarries will lose their jobs.

In the US of 2012 the so-called Solyndra Scandal is a replay of the War of the Currents. Solyndra was a California-based company, founded in 2005, producing solar panels. The company received a Federal loan of US$535 million. This money was lost and interests close to coal mining contributed a US$6 million ad campaign to blow the matter out of proportion.[97]

The 2011 annual US defence budget was around US$700,000,000,000 dollars, amounting to US$1,918,000,000 per day. The government money lost in the Solyndra 'scandal' was a mere US$535,000,000 dollars, corresponding to 6.7 hours or 0.28 days of US warfare, in 2011. Hypothetically, if the US government had stopped its wars for 6 hours and 42 minutes during that calendar year, an amount the size of the Solyndra loss would have been saved, making it possible for a new and important technology to pass the hurdle of initial unprofitability that characterises all new technologies.

That the US Department of Energy estimates that China's state support to the solar energy sector amounted to US$30 billion in 2010 – 56 times the Solyndra loss, adds to the drama of lost technological leadership which is presently unfolding.[98] Presently US democracy appears to a large extent to have been hijacked by interests vested in a) old technology and b) financial speculations and manipulations, while the technological leadership '[t]hat used to be US' slowly moves to Asia.[99] Veblen's clear warnings about these mechanisms – which would be perfectly understandable to most businessmen, but lie outside the realm of neoclassical economics – appear to be largely absent from the collective US radar screen.

French Economist Frédéric Bastiat (1801–1850) famously ridiculed vested interests by writing a mock petition from the candle-makers' guild to the French government, asking the government to block out the sun to prevent its unfair competition with their own products. Today the Reason Foundation and the coal mining interests supporting them are fighting the same 'unfair' power of the sun – solar energy – to protect their own vested interests in polluting sources of energy, just as the candle makers did in Bastiat's mock petition. At the same time, none but the very same Reason Foundation sponsors an annual Bastiat Prize and Bastiat Dinner.[100] No doubt the reason for their celebration of Bastiat is his religious belief in free trade. But a master of irony himself, Thorstein Veblen would no doubt have appreciated the irony that the present vested interests fighting the 'unfair' competition of solar energy for light and heat at the same time honour Bastiat – the economist who ridiculed their vested interest.

The world faces similar circumstances of technological uncertainty today as it did during the time of Edison and Tesla, compounded by a much more serious environmental crisis and the additional problem of an energy and climate crisis, regardless of its origins. But, as we shall see, these problems are not being confronted in a sufficiently Veblenian-Schumpeterian fashion, by throwing money at scientific research and new technologies. Instead, on both sides of the Atlantic, more idle money is being created. This money, however, tends to stay in the financial sector and as cash balances in the corporate sector (which may be seen as a prolonged arm of the financial sector). It does not flow out to the real economy mainly because the real economy is being consciously shrunk in the name of austerity, thus also shrinking demand for new investments. This policy will not solve the crisis, but will instead increase the mountain of debt that sooner or later must be repaid or defaulted upon. In the process a new kind of debt peonage is created, one which Enlightenment economists as well as Veblen would probably have seen as a new kind of feudalism, this time based on financial ownership rather than on land ownership.

Financial crisis: Idle financial capital destroying real capital

Financial crises occur when the relationship between the real economy (the total production of goods and services) and the financial economy (money in the widest sense) comes out of balance in such a way that the financial economy no longer primarily supports the real economy, but takes on an independent life of its own in such a way as to damage the real economy. Today's mainstream economics tends to perceive the financial sector only as a mirror image of the real economy: the non-evolutionary – and according to Veblen, animistic and hedonistic – tradition of *ordre naturel* promoted by François Quesnay and David Ricardo does not see financial crises because, in their tradition, there is no monetary or financial sector. This theory fails to perceive financial crises because one of the two parties involved – the financial sector – is non-existent. Financial crises – as well as crises of unemployment and of landless farmers – can only occur when the *ordre naturel* is brought to an end with the introduction of Karl Polanyi's fictitious commodities *money*, *labour* and (private ownership of) *land*. Today's mainstream theory allows for the extremely dangerous perspective of viewing the financial sector as any other sector of the economy, pretending that explosive growth of the financial sector is in some way equivalent to explosive growth in the steel, automotive or IT sectors. This view will deepen the crisis, as we are presently seeing.

Financial crises represent imbalances which – in contrast to inflation and deflation – are not immediately visible in the consumer price index as rising or falling prices, but rather in the form of asset inflation and debt deflation, which in sum have very important impacts on income distribution. The assets, in which massive incomes from the financial sector are invested, will experience an asset inflation. On the other hand, the huge injections of newly created money coupled with falling levels of prices and wages that result from the crises will result in debt deflation, a continually rising amount of outstanding debt.

At the root of financial crises is a Veblenian mechanism of 'vested interest', the desire of the financial sector to get something from nothing (i.e. from speculative activities, not by contributing to the real economy). Capitalism functions well when the interest of the capitalist class is in line with the interests of society at large. When capitalists make money on new technology and production (based on Veblen's *instinct of workmanship*), they automatically contribute to the common weal (i.e. they will display Veblen's *parental bent*). A major achievement of Enlightenment economics was to separate the economic activities where the vested interests contributed to the common good – where wealth-production was a by-product of greed – and where greed produced no such beneficial effects. The concise formula for solving this problem and consolidating the theory of the market economy was expressed by Milanese economist Pietro Verri (1728–1797): 'the private interest of each individual, *when it coincides with the public interests*, is always the safest guarantor of public happiness.'[101] At the time, it was obvious that these interests were not *always* in perfect harmony in a market economy. The role of the legislator was seen as creating the policies that made sure individual interests coincided with the public ones. The role of the 1933 Glass-Steagall Act had precisely been to enforce this Enlightenment vision of the economy, to make sure that the interests which the financial sector could legally pursue stayed in line with the interests of society at large. As it now is, after the Glass-Steagall Act was abolished, enormous amounts of money can be made by destroying economies – as we see in Greece – rather than by building them.

It is normal that capital floods to the newest and most profitable industries that display the highest rate of technical change and growth, be it Carnegie's steel mills, Ford's assembly lines or Bill Gates and his Microsoft. Capitalism collapses, on the other hand, when money flows to the financial sector per se, as if finance were an industry on par with steel, cars or software. Thus, the fundamental flaw behind today's global situation is the failure to distinguish sufficiently between the real economy and the financial economy (see Fig. 2 below). This clear distinction was once understood, not only in Islamic economics as today, but all along the political axis from Marx and Lenin on the left, to social democrat Rudolf Hilferding, a Jew who was killed by the Gestapo, to the conservatives Schumpeter and Keynes, all the way to Hitler's economists on the far right.[102] Unfortunately, the West, and Europe in particular, has not faced the task of a necessary clean-up of its own chamber of horrors of the 1930s.[103] This is one reason why financial crises, once understood along the whole political spectrum, are so poorly understood today.

A necessary ingredient in this economic drama is that the way in which economics was mathematised has contributed to the total dominance of Wall Street over the productive sectors. A failure to distinguish the financial economy other than as a mirror image of the real economy has made it impossible to formalise key basic insights about the role of

Figure 2. The Real Economy vs. the Financial Economy

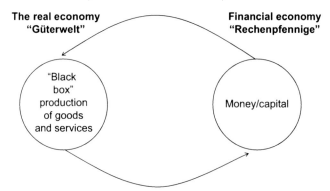

the financial sector. Such insights only come with any analysis made from a book-keeping point of view, where it becomes obvious that the growth of assets in the financial sector will tend to accumulate as liabilities in the balance sheet of the real economy. The real economy enters into a situation of debt peonage to the financial sector.

The transfer of income and assets from the real economy to the financial economy is the most important long-term effect of a financial crisis. If these imbalances are not addressed by making big investments in the real economy, any recovery, however weak, will be driven by demand from the financial sector and the losses in the real economy may be permanent. This is now what is happening in the US and in Europe. The EU's 'internal devaluations' in the Baltic have dramatically reduced real wages, while at the same time unemployment is alarmingly high. Financial crises are the results of a mismatch between the real sector of the economy and the financial sector, illustrated above.

Understanding financial crises requires a terminology that distinguishes the financial economy from the real economy. The financial economy consists of what Schumpeter called *Rechenpfennige*, or *accounting units*. In Veblen's terminology, this is the sector that bases its activities on *pecuniary gain*. The real economy consists of the production of goods and services, Schumpeter's *Güterwelt*, populated by people who in Veblen's terminology are engaged in *material production* based on *the instinct of workmanship* and a *parental bend* (an understanding of being part of society), including, of course, the engineers.

In times when capitalism functions well, the financial sector and the real economy live in a kind of symbiosis; they support each other. The financial sector functions as scaffolding to the real economy or, as Keynes put it, as a 'bridge in time'. In times of crisis the financial sector takes on a speculative life of its own and becomes a parasite weakening the real economy. As the speculative bubble grows, what was once rational (investing in new technology) gradually becomes irrational (investing in pyramid games). The right hand circle in Fig. 2 grows as a malignant tumour and feeds on the real economy in a parasitic way, decreasing wages and shrinking whole economies, as Greece experiences at the moment.

As does Wray in this volume, Giles Dostaler – in his book *Keynes and His Battles*[104] – discusses Veblen's influence on Keynes.[105] Issues that were raised by Veblen and the American institutionalists, and picked up by Keynes, include the link between money, the State and power, as well as the separation between control, i.e. management and ownership of capital. Says Dostaler: 'Economists associated with the institutionalist movement in the Unites States, beginning at the turn of the century with its founder Thorstein Veblen, developed analyses similar to Keynes, who was probably inspired by them.'[106]

Conclusion: Why We Need to Resurrect Veblenian Economics to Solve the Crisis

According to Hyman Minsky, the oil crisis of the 1970s was a financial crisis under a different name; in fact, in the theoretical scheme of Carlota Perez, the background of the crisis was the exhaustion of the technological possibilities of the Fordist mass-production paradigm.[107] Whatever the mechanisms behind it, the 1970s crisis – with Arthur F. Burns (1904–1987) as chairman of the Federal Reserve from 1970 to 1978 – was solved in a way that is virtually diametrically opposed to how the current crisis is being handled. Burns was a student of Veblen's student Wesley Clair Mitchell. Today the Federal Reserve, under Alan Greenspan and Ben Bernanke, and the European Central Bank, under Mario Draghi, have attempted to solve the crisis through *quantitative easing*, i.e. by creating even more money. As indicated above, as long as this policy is combined with *austerity*, the conscious shrinking of purchasing power in the real economy, this will only increase the imbalances and mismatches between the financial economy and the real economy, thereby increasing the amount of debt which sooner or later will have to be paid from the real economy to the financial sector (or defaulted).

The crisis of the 1970s, with Arthur F. Burns heading the Federal Reserve, was solved by the opposite method: demand was kept up creating a demand-pull inflation which reduced the value of the excess liquidity and – due to the considerable negative real interest rates – forced financial capital back into the real economy.[108] This was made possible by the existence of strong labour unions which kept wages, and therefore demand, up. Burns thus rebalanced the relationship between financial capital and the real economy (see Fig. 1). What is today seen as Greek irresponsibility, using more money than the country can afford in order to collect votes had been a common occurrence in Latin America at least since the early 1970s. One may indeed argue that this was a sign of elected democracies: Chile and Costa Rica were both early democracies and both early victims of financial crises. Latin American dictatorships like Stroessner's Paraguay or Duvalier's Haiti did not experience such problems. The Latin American financial crises since the 1970s have always been solved in the same way: by high inflation and defaults. This is how the Argentine crisis (1999–2002) was solved. What is new in today's European crisis is the impossibility of devaluations and the negation of default: a refusal to solve the crisis which can only prolong it and make it worse.

With John Kenneth Galbraith (1908–2006), Arthur F. Burns was probably the last classical institutional economist to have major political influence in the United States. In his own writings, Burns synthesises the explanation of why Veblen and his tradition – not present-day equilibrium economics – is the kind of economics we need during a time of crisis:

> The warnings of a Marx, a Veblen, or a Mitchell that economists were neglecting changes in the world gathering around them, that preoccupations with states of equilibrium led to tragic neglect of principles of cumulative change, went unheeded.[109]

Today's explosive growth of the financial sector while the real economy is allowed to shrink is an example of these cumulative changes that go unheeded.

Here is a core point: in the absence of regulation, the *ordre naturel* in any society employing money and compound interest will be that the real economy will become strangled by debt to the financial sector. This was understood under the rule of Hammurabi in Mesopotamia in the year 1750 BC and was remedied by periodical debt relief ('jubilee years').[110] Now the same tradition of *ordre naturel*, in the guise of neoclassical equilibrium-based economics is creating wide-spread debt peonage in Greece : the very type of crisis that Hammurabi and his advisors managed to prevent in Mesopotamia. Professionally blind to all kinds of cumulative causations, in the conceptual absence of a financial sector and with a propensity to think in terms of equilibrium, the economics profession unknowingly converted itself into claques of an increasingly parasitic financial sector.

On the real side of the economy, a lack of understanding of technology – i.e. of the cumulative effects of Veblenian idle curiosity and material (and service) production – makes the profession impervious to the fact that Asia at the moment is beating the West in its own game. Victims of its own propaganda economics for colonial purposes – Ricardo's idea of comparative advantage is the ideal policy regardless of technology level – the West is declining precisely because the 1954 warnings of Arthur F. Burns went unheeded. Parallel cumulative change – a financial policy which lets speculators enrich themselves at the cost of production, employment and real wages coupled with an extremely superficial understanding of the growth of knowledge and innovations – is causing unnecessary decline in the West.

The last period of big shifts in the economic ranking between European states was the 1700s, when small city states were forced to yield economic power to strong nation-states. Venice and Amsterdam declined, while England and France rose. Faced with a growing real economy in Asia and a vicious circle of financial-sector growth and productive-sector decline at home, the West now faces two possible scenarios: declining like Amsterdam, i.e. relatively, but keeping a healthy productive sector, or like Venice, i.e. declining absolutely, first losing the productive sector and then the financial sector, in the end becoming a big museum. The former will require the resurrection of policy instruments which went out of fashion in the 1970s and started the trend of falling real wages, first in the Third World, then in the Second World and now in the First World: the West. Declining like Amsterdam will require re-establishing a type of economics based on the tradition from anti-physiocracy to Veblen and on evolutionary Schumpeterian economics. A continuation in the tradition of physiocracy and equilibrium economics will lead us down the path of a Venice type decline. What the West needs is what Asia has now learned: the activistic-idealistic economic tradition to which Thorstein Bunde Veblen was a very important contributor.

Neo-liberalism has had a numbing effect on Western society, largely closing the Western economic mind to intellectual discourse, in the same way one of Ibsen's characters claimed liberalism[111] had done in 1882: 'the liberals are the most treacherous enemies of free men. The party programmes wring the necks of all young and viable truths. Considerations of expediency turn morality and justice upside-down, so in the end living here becomes intolerable.'[112] This is the same kind of 'drive of indignation' which the 19-year-old Robert Duffus had observed in Veblen spending a year in his household.[113]

Appendix: Father Thomas Veblen's Accounts, Committed to Paper by Thorstein's Elder Brother Andrew in 1895

A brief sketch of family history

Andris Haldorson [Veblen], han far, va saan has Haldor Haldorson i Oygare o Marit Tørhjelsdøtte, arø hjeringe has. Han Andris jifte se fyst mæ Jartru Tømmøsdotte Tørsta. Ungadn deiris vøro: […] Thomas (Tømmøs) [= forteljaren]
[…]
Ho mor va taa dei storø Tørsta slekten. […] Jartru, ho mor, so va den yngstø taa syshjinno.
[…]
Øystein Bunde, gofa aat mor dikka, hjøftø se in paa Nørre Bunde; […] Han va jiftø mæ ei so eittø Kari, gomo aat mor di. […] Ungadn has Øystein o'n Kari va desse: […] Tøstein […], den trea.
Tøstein vart jift mæ'n Berit Olsdøtte Ejji. Deiris unga vøro: […]
Kari, mor dikka. [f. 1825]
[…]
So fløttø'n far o o mor taa Øvre Helle te Neerhelle […] Der vart eg fød. [1818] Der ifraa fløtte dei norte Vøvle […]

Translation:

Andris Haldorson [Veblen], my father, was son of Haldor Haldorson in Oygare [Øygarden] and Marit Tørhjelsdaughter, his second wife. Andris first married Jartru [Gjertrud] Tømmøsdaughter Tørsta. Their children were […] Thomas [Tømmøs] [the speaker]
[…]
My mother was from the great Tørsta family. […] Jartru, mother, was the youngest of the siblings.
[…]
Øystein Bunde, grandfather of your mother, bought into Nørre Bunde [North Bunde]. He was married to one called Kari, your mother's grandmother. […] Their children were […] Tøstein [Thorstein] […], the third.

Tøstein married Berit Olsdaughter Ejji. Their children were: […]
Kari, your mother [b. 1825]
[…]
Then father and mother moved from Øvre Helle (Upper Helle) to Neerhelle [Lower Helle]. There I was born [1818]. From there they moved north to Vøvle [Veblen] […]

Thomas Veblen's account of the travel from Valdres, Norway, to America in 1847

Mø reistø ut ifraa Drammen. Mø reistø ifraa Vøvle den and'n Mai; laag paa Branæs ei veko, va paa væge te Hamburg ei veko. Mø va i land ei tvo tre gønge imyljo Drammen o Hamburg, taa di dæ va stilt en motvind – stansa i Tønsberg o ve Saltværke. I Hamburg va mø ein maana. Sjepø ifraa Drammen va '*Den Gode Mening*', ein tvomaster; Kaptein Hanevig.

Ifraa Hamburg reistø mø paa '*Haabet*', Kaptein Sven Foyn. Mø landa i Kvebek, Umtrent ellevø veko ifraa Hamburg. Reistø upover Leihjidn, o kom te Milwakee den sextandø September [1847]. E va paa skuldø vørte at i Kvebek paa eit sjukøhus, før feber. Kaftein o ein Hallinggut jøltø me te so e slap førbi døktørn daa fuljiø skuldø te reisø vestover. Hallingen ga me lite brænnevin so e knuddø inni anlætø mit, o'n Sven Foyn haddø me te reinskø væl tunga, føren e skuldø gaa førbi døktørn; o soleise slap e førbi'n o vart mæ fuljie lell.

Translation:

We sailed from Drammen. We left Vøvle [Veblen] on the 2nd of May, waited for a week at Branes [Bragernes, Drammen], spent a week on the way to Hamburg. We went ashore two or three times between Drammen and Hamburg, because of headwinds, stopped in Tønsberg and at the salt works [presumably Vallø near Tønsberg]. In Hamburg we stayed for a month. The Drammen ship was '*Den Gode Mening*' [*The Good Intention*], two masts, captain Hanevig.

From Hamburg we travelled on the '*Haabet*' [*The Hope*], captain Sven Foyn.[114] We landed in Kvebek [Quebec], about eleven weeks from Hamburg. Sailed up the Lakes and came to Milwaukee on the 16th of September [1847]. I almost had to stay behind in Quebec in a hospital because of a fever. The captain and a boy from Hallingdal helped me get past the doctor when the group was going on westwards. The Halling gave me a little alcohol to rub into my face and Sven Foyn had me clean my tongue well before passing the doctor, and so I was allowed to pass and could stay with the group after all.

Notes and References

1   The author is grateful to Håvard Friis Nilsen and Bernt Hagtvet for their comments on an earlier draft, and to Håvard Friis Nilsen also for the translation of the Øverland quote and for supplying the quote from Freud's student.

2   Review of Thorstein Veblen's *The Place of Science in Modern Civilization*: H. A. Overstreet, 'The Place of Science', *The Nation* (New York) 111, no. 2878 (28 August 1920): 250.

3   Previous literature on Veblen in Norwegian, before Odner's 2005 volume (see footnote below), is essentially limited to two articles by Arvid Brodersen (1904–1996), who like Veblen was a

professor at the New School for Social Research: 'Thorstein Veblen som sociolog', *Statsøkonomisk Tidsskrift* 51 (1937): 30–69, and 'Thorstein Veblen, Norsk-Amerikaneren som vart vegbrøytar i moderne samfunns-gransking', *Syn og Segn* 46 (1940): 251–60; and a small book by Bjarne Svare, *Thorstein B. Veblen. En norsk-amerikansk pioneer i moderne samfunnsvitenskap* (Oslo: Samlaget, 1970).

4 There are almost 6,000 photographs from Valdres at http://valdresibilder.no/.

5 Helene Deutsch, *Confrontations with Myself* (New York: Norton, 1973), 97.

6 Halfdan Koht, *Norsk Bondereising* (Oslo: Pax, 1975). 'The people of Valdres were the most stubborn and disobedient when they were under command', 143.

7 'Andrew Veblen was somewhat aggressive and determined to show that he was as good American as any, but Thorstein was highly sensitive. He even preferred to seem to be unable to answer questions in class rather than betray the fact that he did not have sufficient command of the adopted language to express himself well.' Joseph Dorfman, *Thorstein Veblen and his America* (New York: Viking, 1934), 17. Dorfman's point on the shyness seems valid, even if the reason why has not been established. Why should the younger brother of the family have less command of the language when they were both obviously very intelligent?

8 Veblen himself refers to this in his letter to Rector Halvdan Koht of the University of Oslo, dated 1 July 1920: 'You will let me add a word as to my own limitations as a teacher. I am not a successful public speaker, nor have I done well with large classes – say, classes of as many as 50 members. The work in which I may claim to have met with success has been in the way of quite informal lectures, before relatively small classes, and combining more or less open discussion in the classroom', quoted in Olav Bjerkholt, 'Økonomi og økonomer i UiOs historie: Fra Knut Wicksells dissens i 1910 til framstøtet mot Thorstein Veblen i 1920', *Memorandum* 18/2012, Department of Economics, University of Oslo, 26.

9 '*Stillest vann har dypest grunn*' ('The same wind that creates ripples in shallow waters, often fails to move the surface of deeper lakes').

10 I am not at all suggesting that this is a particularly Norwegian value. A Veblenian analysis would, I think, see it as a normal human instinct which is suppressed under certain conditions, such as in feudal Europe, while it flourishes at certain times, as in the European Enlightenment, and under certain conditions, as when nations fight for their freedom. A moving example of a child's instinct against social injustice is found in Peruvian author Alfredo Bryce Echenique's novel *Un mundo para Julius* (Barcelona: Seix-Barral, 1970). The father of the little upper-class boy in Lima dies and his body is carried out by the front door. When, later, his beloved nanny dies, the little boy all by himself arms a small rebellion against social injustice when the adults attempt to carry her body out by the back door.

11 Dorfman, *Thorstein Veblen*, 43. 'He read Ibsen and spread knowledge about him on the Yale campus.'

12 This particular conversation took place in Rome on New Year's Eve 1880. See Kristofer Janson, *Hvad jeg har oplevet* (Kristiania (Oslo): Gyldendal, 1913).

13 Bernt Hagtvet, *Hvor gjerne vilde jeg have været i Deres sted…! Bjørnstjerne Bjørnson, de intellektuelle og Dreyfus-saken* (Oslo: Aschehoug, 1998).

14 For an explanation of the complexities of Norwegian language policy, see Einar Haugen, *Language Conflict and Language Planning. The Case of Modern Norwegian* (Cambridge, MA: Harvard University Press, 1966).

15 Letter dated 1 July 1920, quoted in Olav Bjerkholt, 'Økonomi og økonomer i UiOs historie', 26.

16 A *Valdris* is a person from Valdres.

17 Referred to in Erling Ylvisaker, *Eminent Pioneers. Norwegian-American Pioneer Sketches* (Minneapolis: Augsburg Publishing House, 1934), 161.

18 Kristofer Janson, *Normænd i Amerika* (Copenhagen: Gyldendal, n.d.), 54.

19 On Janson, see Nina Draxten, *Kristofer Janson in America* (Boston: Twayne, for the Norwegian-American Historical Association, 1976).

20 Janson, *Normænd*, 84.

21 At the age of 33 Colonel Heg was the 'father of the regiment'. He died in battle that same year. His statue can be seen in the square in front of the Capitol in Madison, WI.

22 Janson, *Nordmænd*, 131–2.

23 See Koht, *Norsk Bondereising*, and Odner, in this volume (Chapter 5).

24 The German Historical School of Economics and its policy arm the *Verein für Sozialpolitik*, Association for Social Policy (1872–1932).

25 Under the Danes, a few noble families were established in Norway, but this institution never had much practical importance to most people. Nobility was abolished in 1821.

26 Janson, *Nordmænd*, 132.

27 Under the leadership of my great-great grandfather Adolf Carl Preus (1814–1878), who headed the *Synode* at the time.

28 Kristofer Janson, *Hvad jeg har opplevet*, 79.

29 '*Går til sin gjerning de norske menn, viljeløst vimrende, vet ei hvor hen – skrukker seg hjertene, smyger seg sinnene, veke som vaggende vidjer for vindene – kan kun om én ting de enes, den at hver storhet skal styrtes og stenes.*'

30 Jonas Lie, *Familien paa Gilje. Interiør fra Firtiaarene* (Copenhagen: Gyldendal, 1903); English translation: *The Family at Gilje. A Domestic Story of the Forties*, trans. Samuel Coffin Eastman (New York: The American-Scandinavian Foundation, 1920).

31 This purchase by the King of Prussia can of course be seen as an expression of the cult of the Myth from the North. Also Kaiser Wilhelm showed great interest in Norway and frequently went on holiday there.

32 Knut Hamsun, *The Cultural Life of Modern America* (Cambridge, MA: Harvard University Press, 1969), published originally as: *Fra det moderne Amerikas Aandsliv* (Copenhagen: Philipsen, 1889). On Hamsun in the USA, see Richard Nelson Current (ed.), *Knut Hamsun Remembers America* (Columbia: University of Missouri Press, 2003).

33 At the Veblen conference in Valdres, Prof. Sarah Lund of the University of Oslo gave a fascinating paper comparing Veblen and Hamsun.

34 Thorstein Veblen, *The Place of Science in Modern Civilization* (New York: Huebsch, 1919), 193.

35 I discuss mockery of bad science as a literary and scientific tradition starting with Francis Bacon in my article 'Full Circle: Economics from Scholasticism through Innovation and back into Mathematical Scholasticism. Reflections around a 1769 prize essay: "Why Is it that Economics so far Has Gained so few Advantages from Physics and Mathematics?"', *Journal of Economic Studies* 27.4/5 (2000).

36 Ferdinando Galiani, *Dialogues sur le commerce des bles* (London [Paris: Merlin], 1770); see also Steven L. Kaplan (ed.), *La Bagarre: Galiani's 'Lost' Parody* (The Hague: Martinus Nijhoff, 1979).

37 It is of course possible to trace this tradition back to other authors in France.

38 Stephen Edgell, *Veblen in Perspective: His Life and Thought* (Armonk: M. E. Sharpe, 2001); Francesca Viano, *Thorstein Veblen. Fra mito e disincanto* (Aosta: Stylos, 2002).

39 *New York Times Book Review*, 30 September 1934, 4.

40 For a general discussion of this problem, see my 'Development and Social Goals: Balancing Aid and Development to Prevent "Welfare Colonialism"', United Nations Department of Social Affairs, DESA Working Paper no. 14, 2006, online: http://www.un.org/esa/desa/papers/; and in Jose Antonio Ocampo, Jomo K. S. and Khan Sarbuland (eds), *Policy Matters: Economic and Social Policies to Sustain Equitable Development* (London: Zed Books, 2007), 192–221.

41 For more on these concepts, see Werner Sombart *Die Drei Nationalökonomien* (Munich: Duncker & Humblot, 1930) and the discussion referred to below.

42 The full text of the letter is reproduced in Knut Odner, *Thorstein Veblen. Forstyrreren av den Intellektuelle Fred* (Oslo: Abstrakt Forlag, 2005), 257–8. Koht had met Veblen at Stanford eleven years earlier.

43 Wesley C. Mitchell, *Types of Economic Theory from Mercantilism to Institutionalism*, ed. by Joseph Dorfman (New York: Augustus M. Kelly, 1967). Originally published as *Lecture Notes on Types of Economic Theory: As Delivered by Professor Wesley C. Mitchell* (New York: Turtle Bay Bookshop, 1949).

44 Othmar Spann, *Types of Economic Theory* (London: Eden Paul and Cedar, 1929).

45 Georg Andreas Will, *Versuch über die Physiocratie, deren Geschichte, Literatur, Inhalt und Werth* (Nürnberg: G. N. Raspe, 1782). Interestingly, the international comparative table on 71–2 lists both Adam Smith and Arthur Young as anti-Physiocrats.

46 For a discussion of the fundamentally different attitudes and methodology underlying these two different approaches to economics, see Wolfgang Drechsler, 'Natural versus Social Sciences: On Understanding in Economics', in *Globalization, Economic Development and Inequality. An Alternative Perspective*, ed. by Erik S. Reinert (Cheltenham: Edward Elgar, 2004), 71–87. See also www.othercanon.org.

47 Veblen, *Place of Science*, 87.

48 Ibid., 98.

49 Charles Camic, 'Veblen's Apprenticeship: On the Translation of Gustav Cohn's *System der Finanzwissenschaft*', *History of Political Economy* 42 (Winter 2010): 679–721.

50 Gustav Cohn, *The Science of Finance*, trans. by Thorstein Veblen, Economic Studies of the University of Chicago, no. 1 (Chicago: University of Chicago Press, 1895), 60.

51 Ibid., 60–61.

52 In her chapter, Francesca Viano shows how Veblen received inspiration for this at Cornell, from the English history tradition at the time.

53 Veblen quoted in Helge Peukert, 'On the Origins of Modern Evolutionary Economics: The Veblen Legend after 100 Years', *Journal of Economic Issues* 35.3 (2001): 543–55.

54 Alfred Chandler, *Scale and Scope: The Dynamics of Industrial Capitalism* (Cambridge, MA: Harvard University Press, 1990); Ferdinand Braudel, *Out of Italy. 1450–1650* (Paris: Flammarion, 1991).

55 I owe this insight to Professor Helge Høibraaten of the Norwegian Technical University when, during his visiting professorship at Humboldt University, he guided me around the museums of Berlin.

56 Sombart, *Nationalökonomien*. The issue raised here is thoroughly discussed in Erik S. Reinert and Arno Daastøl, 'The Other Canon: The History of Renaissance Economics', in *Globalization, Economic Development and Inequality. An Alternative Perspective*, ed. by Erik S. Reinert (Cheltenham: Edward Elgar, 2004), 21–70.

57 Ben B. Seligman, *Main Currents in Modern Economics*, 3 vols (Chicago: Quadrangle Books, 1971).

58 Seligman, *Currents*, 1:vii.

59 Seligman, *Currents*, 2:328–42. On the 'decay' of Austrian economics, see Erik S. Reinert, 'Austrian Economics and "The Other Canon"', in *Modern Applications of Austrian Thought*, ed. by Jürgen Backhaus (Milton Park: Routledge, 2005), 253–98.

60 Seligman, *Currents*, 129–58.

61 Ibid., 137.

62 Veblen's insistence on 'idle curiosity' and 'spirit of workmanship' reflects Schumpeter's insistence on 'innovations', in both cases as the fundamental moving forces of capitalist societies. In his monumental *History of Economic Analysis* (New York: Oxford University Press, 1954), Schumpeter quotes Veblen four times, all approvingly, but says 'an appreciation, or even characterization, is impossible in the space at our command', 795.

63 John Stuart Mill, *Principles of Economics* (London: C. C. Little & J. Brown, 1848).

64 Bruno Hildebrand, *Die Nationalökonomie der Gegenwart und Zukunft* (Frankfurt: Literarische Anstalt, 1848).

65 It is reasonable to classify Friedrich List as representing a proto-historical school of economics.

66 Francesca Viano (ed.), *Daniel Raymond's Thoughts on Political Economy (1820): A Theory of Productive Power* (London: Anthem, forthcoming).

67 Assuming that Mr Pritchard knows American literature well, Veblen lists the following authors: 'the late W. Rathenau (collected works), Werner Sombart (*Moderne Kapitalismus*, revised edition), R. Ehrenberg (*Zeitalter der Fugger*), Karl Bücher (*Entstehung der Volkswirtschaft*, revised edition, enlarged).'

68 On the Manchester School, see William D. Grampp, *The Manchester School of Economics* (Stanford: Stanford University Press, 1960).

69 Gustav Schmoller, *Wechselnde Theorien und feststehende Wahrheiten im Gebiete der Staats- und Socialwissenschaften und die heutige deutsche Volkswirtschaftslehre* (Berlin: W. Büxenstein, 1897). Online: www.othercanon.org

70 Anton Menger, *The Right to the Whole Produce of Labour* (London: Macmillan, 1899). Online: www.othercanon.org/uploads/MENGER_The_right_1899.pdf

71 Herbert Foxwell, 'Introduction' in ibid., xli.

72 Thorstein Veblen, 'Review: Gustav Schmoller, *Über einige Grundfragen der Socialpolitik und der Volkswirtschaftslehre*', *Journal of Political Economy* 6.3. (June 1898): 416–19. Foxwell's introduction to Menger is referred to by Veblen as 'Foxwell's admirable introduction' in *Essential Writings of Thorstein Veblen*, ed. by Charles Camic and Geoffrey M. Hodgson (London: Routledge, 2011), 375.

73 Alfred Marshall, *Principles of Economics* (London: Macmillan, 1890).

74 John Neville Keynes, *The Scope and Method of Political Economy* (London: Macmillan, 1890). Colleagues, Marshall's and Keynes's acknowledgements to each other in the two books suggest a close professional relationship.

75 J. N. Keynes, page 21.

76 For a study of Spencer's influence on the social sciences in the United States, see Daniel Breslau, 'The American Spencerians: Theorizing a New Science', in *Sociology in America. A History*, ed. by Craig Calhoun (Chicago: University of Chicago Press, 2007).

77 Malcolm Rutherford, *The Institutionalist Movement in American Economics, 1918–1947. Science and Social Control* (Cambridge: Cambridge University Press, 2011).

78 Henry Sidgwick, *The Principles of Political Economy* (London: Macmillan, 1883). Sidgwick acknowledges the assistance of both Marshall and John Neville Keynes.

79 For a classical evaluation of Spencer's contribution to the American character, see Richard Hofstadter, *Social Darwinism in American Thought* (Boston: Beacon Press, 1959).

80 Thorstein Veblen, *Essays in our Changing Order*, ed. by Leon Ardzrooni (New York: Viking Press, 1934).

81 Robert Duffus, *The Innocents at Cedro, A Memoir of Thorstein Veblen and Some Others* (New York: Macmillan, 1944).

82 Robert Duffus, *New York Times Book Review*, 30 September (1934): 4.

83 Carlota Perez, *Technological Revolutions and Financial Capital. The Dynamics of Bubbles and Golden Ages* (Cheltenham: Edward Elgar, 2002).

84 Cohn, *The Science of Finance*, trans. by Thorstein Veblen.

85 Wesley Clair Mitchell, *Business Cycles* (Berkeley: University of California Press, 1913).

86 Mark Blaug, *Great Economists before Keynes. An Introduction to the Lives & Works of One Hundred Great Economists of the Past* (Brighton: Wheatsheaf, 1986), 256–7.

87 Veblen's interest in natural conservation is one aspect we have not managed to cover in this volume.

88 By not distinguishing between the spheres of finance and the real economy, as the anti-Physiocratic and Veblenian tradition does.

89 On Renaissance economics, see Erik S. Reinert and Arno Daastøl, 'The Other Canon: The History of Renaissance Economics. Its Role as an Immaterial and Production-based Canon in the History of Economic Thought and in the History of Economic Policy' (with Arno Daastøl), in *Globalization, Economic Development and Inequality: An Alternative Perspective*, ed. by Erik Reinert (Cheltenham: Edward Elgar, 2004), 21–70.

90 In the words of Kishore Mahbubani, dean of Lee Kuan Yew School of Public Policy at the National University of Singapore: 'The world is entering a new era, an era marked by

two major changes. The first is the beginning of the end of Western domination – not the end of the West, though. The second is the Asian "renaissance", because the 21st century will be the century of Chinese and Indian economies. This is a Western financial crisis, because the problems are the results of Western leaders' failure to understand that they faced a new competition. Western minds couldn't think that other societies were becoming more successful than them. People in the US and the EU live beyond their means. Does "Western wisdom" say keep borrowing despite mounting budget deficits? The West has to "relearn" Western wisdom from the East. Asian societies are doing well [today] because they understood and absorbed the main pillars of Western wisdom, including the market, science, education and rule of law. But Western societies are gradually walking away from these pillars.' See Kishore Mahbubani, 'Move over West, Asia is here', *China Daily*, 23 December (2010): 9.

91 For an account of these strategies, see Sophus A. Reinert, *Emulating Empire* (Cambridge, MA: Harvard University Press, 2011).

92 Thorstein Veblen, *The Engineers and the Price System* (New York: Huebsch, 1921).

93 Sabotage is also treated in the chapters by Plotkin and Edgell in this volume.

94 Veblen, *Engineers and the Price System*, 54.

95 This story is told in Jill Jonnes, *Empires of Light. Edison, Tesla, Westinghouse, and the Race to Electrify the World* (New York: Random House, 2003).

96 Online: www.reason.org (accessed 1 November 2011).

97 Online: http://www.foxnews.com/politics/2012/01/18/obama-campaign-team-buys-ad-time-in-swing-states/ (accessed 15 June 2012).

98 Online: http://www.businessweek.com/printer/articles/13410-firing-up-chinas-solar-market (accessed 15 June 2012).

99 Thomas L. Friedman and Michael Mandelbaum, *'That used to be US'. What Went Wrong with American – And How It Can Come Back* (London: Little, Brown, 2011).

100 Online: http://reason.org/events/show/33.html (accessed 15 June 2012).

101 Pietro Verri, *Meditazioni sulla economia politica* (Genova: Ivone Gravier, 1771), 42; emphasis added.

102 Unfortunately, the fundamentally Veblenian distinction between *schaffendes Kapital* (capital which creates wealth) and *raffendes Kapital* (capital which just grabs wealth without creating) is of fascist origin.

103 As regards the horrors of the 1930s, it is important to note that Veblen's last paper was aimed against the eugenics movement, which was becoming fashionable at the time and which would lead to the Holocaust. See Sophus A. Reinert, 'Iconoclastic Eugenics: Thorstein Veblen on Racial Diversity and Cultural Nomadism', *Revue Internationale de Sociologie/International Review of Sociology* 14.3 (2004): 513–34.

104 Giles Dostaler, *Keynes and his Battles* (Cheltenham: Edward Elgar, 2007).

105 Veblen's contribution is not frequently recognised in today's literature on financial crises, exceptions are J. Patrick Raines and Charles G. Leathers, *Debt, Innovations, and Deflations. The Theories of Veblen, Fisher, Schumpeter, and Minsky* (Cheltenham: Edward Elgar, 2008) and Helge Peukert, *Die grosse Finanzmarkt- und Staatsschuldenkrise. Eine kritisch-heterodoxe Untersuchung*, 3rd edn (Marburg: Metropolis, 2011).

106 Dostaler, *Keynes*, 256.

107 Carlota Perez, *Technological Revolutions and Financial Capital*.

108 It is true that the 1970s crisis was less severe than the present one, but this does not invalidate the arguments as to methods for solving crises.

109 Arthur F. Burns, *The Frontiers of Economic Knowledge* (Princeton: Princeton University Press, 1954), 46. Published for the National Bureau of Economic Research.

110 See Erik Reinert, 'Mechanisms of Financial Crises in Growth and Collapse: Hammurabi, Schumpeter, Perez, and Minsky', *The Other Canon Foundation and Tallinn University of Technology*

Working Papers in Technology Governance and Economic Dynamics, no. 39 (2012). Online: http://tg.deca.ee/files/main//2012040412332727.pdf.

111 Liberalism in the European sense; an ideology favouring a minimum of government and regulations.

112 Henrik Ibsen, *En Folkefiende* (Oslo: Gyldendal, 1992), 113.

113 Robert Duffus, *Book Review*, 4.

114 Sven Foyn later became famous as the founder of the modern whaling industry.

Part One

NORWEGIAN ORIGINS
AND PERSONAL LIFE

Chapter 3

EXPLAINING VEBLEN BY HIS NORWEGIAN BACKGROUND: A SKETCH

Kåre Lunden

Explaining Veblen?

Thorstein Veblen is 'the most creative mind American social thought has produced'.[1] His originality is probably most centrally expressed in his concept and discipline of 'evolutionary economics', intended as a substitute for neoclassical economics. The enduring, penetrating force of Veblen's thinking on these matters has been demonstrated from two angles in these past few years. I think, of course, of the shortcomings of neoclassical economics, revealed by the financial crisis of 2008, and of the renewed relevance of evolutionary theory, even of a biological origin, in social science and history.

It would probably lack credibility to imply that a chief – or nearly sufficient – explanation of Veblen's astonishing originality is to be found in his national or ethnic background. After all there is only one Thorstein Veblen to be found in the rather numerous crowd roughly sharing the same background, e.g. his seven siblings. At the level of methodology it has been said recently that 'Veblen's originality derived from his exploitation of an old historiographical pattern, still submitted to social analysis and practically indistinguishable from it'.[2] Accepting this, it might seem that there is no need to seek an explanation of Veblen outside his quite exceptionally broad erudition in the disciplines of history, biology and political economy, not to mention numerous others, added to a peculiar, personal resourcefulness in combining the very different elements of this erudition.[3]

Nevertheless, I perceive no logical reason why his special background might not be one of the necessary conditions that together explain the very unique scientist/scholar Thorstein Veblen. And the foreignness of Veblen's origin, together with more specific qualities of his background, has rather often been invoked to explain aspects of his writings, such as his denunciation of the American system.[4]

My own hypothesis is that the following qualities in Veblen, all prerequisites of his originality, can plausibly be put in a causal relationship with his family's Norwegian peasant origin:

- A most notable independence of mind, or self-reliance, not in spite of this origin – as one might perhaps more ordinarily expect, but because of it.
- A general scepticism, expressed by him in these words: 'The first requisite for constructive work in modern science, and indeed for any work of inquiry that shall bring enduring results, is a sceptic frame of mind.'[5]
- An oppositionality 'with a knack of standing the accepted doctrines on their head'.[6]
- A more specific insurgency, a quality as a rebel, turning his ire against vested interests of every kind, as represented by 'the predatory capitalist class', or by the established academic life of his America.[7] In this respect, as in Veblen's belief in a golden age in the past, and in 'the Peaceful Savage', one may find in him a way of thinking related to that generally found in peasant rebels.
- A belief in the practical man, represented in modern times by the engineer, and more generally expressed in his concept, 'the instinct of workmanship'.

As for the general credibility of explaining the character of a great intellectual like Veblen by his Norwegian peasant origin, I turn to Max Lerner: Veblen continually reverted to stock figures, such as the Peaceful Savage, the Predatory Barbarian, the Captain of Finance, and so on. Lerner notes that

> the symbol upon which Veblen lavishes his most affectionate adjectives is the Heroic Freeholder of the primitive Icelandic community – the peaceful, sturdy farmer-craftsman-citizen whose passing Veblen laments in his [...] introduction to his translation of the *Laxdæla Saga* [...] It is this genial primitive who seems to have been the touchstone of Veblen's cultural and moral values, and who keeps cropping up in new transformations in the peaceful savage, the scientist, the common man, the engineer.[8]

Veblen surely knew that his paragon Icelandic freeholder emigrated from Norway during the Viking period.

As for Veblen's Norwegian background, I shall not go into the local character of the parish Høre in the district of Valdres, from which his father Thomas, a peasant who was also 'a master carpenter and builder', emigrated in 1847.[9] I defer in that respect to the works of T. M. H. Joranger and K. Odner in this volume, and their references. Instead, I stick to 'the Norwegian' in the more general sense, produced by national history. I present matters which are especially relevant for the history of the peasants, and for the qualities in Veblen I have specified. I include opinions about 'the Norwegian', especially the character of Norwegian peasants, widely spread in Norway in the late eighteenth and the nineteenth century – opinions that some would partly call myths. And I consider how far these opinions after all may have corresponded to important social realities.

I cannot go but superficially into just how I think a form of 'Norwegianism' was transferred to Veblen, born and raised in the USA. But I will presume the most important way to be his internalisation of Norwegian values and culture as he grew up on the farms of his father in Manitowoc County, Wisconsin, and from 1865 in Rice County, Minnesota. In both communities, the Veblen family lived in close proximity to numerous relatives and other immigrants from Valdres and other Norwegian districts.[10] It may be an overstatement to say this upbringing made the boy Thorstein simply a Norwegian in language and culture.[11] It seems more correct to think with Joranger that it made him a specimen of 'complementary identities', where the cultural sphere was, however, largely based on Norwegian traditions.[12] This made Thorstein Veblen to a great extent a Norwegian and a peasant/farmer in culture, irrespective of what he heard told about Norway in his childhood, and irrespective of what he learned later.

Veblen called his father 'the finest mind I ever knew'.[13] Thomas Veblen and his wife, Kari, were among the wealthiest families, both in Manitowoc and Rice Counties.[14] Both descended from Valdres families renowned for their cultural interests. Thomas was a literate and knowledgeable man who even wrote autobiographical notes on the 1847 migration to Wisconsin. He sent all his eight children, including the daughters, to college. Several of them completed BA degrees, and two completed graduate work.[15] We know that he freely conversed about his Norwegian experiences in the family circle, and it is unthinkable that a person with his background would not know the images of Norwegian peasants outlined by the authors I shall be citing.[16] It is very likely that he communicated that picture.

Later on, Veblen's readings, visits to Norway in 1899 and 1914 and contacts with intellectuals of Norwegian stock, such as his friend professor Rasmus Anderson at the University of Wisconsin and, likely, the socialist leader Marcus Thrane, allowed Veblen to 'discuss Norwegian literature, language and politics' fluently with recent arrivals from Norway.[17]

Norwegian Peasants – Opinions, Myths and Other Realities

From 1536 to 1814, the old Kingdom of Norway was a subordinate part of the composite Oldenburg dynastic state, which had ruled Denmark since 1448, with its capital in Copenhagen.[18] 'The first national breakthrough' of Norway occurred in the latter half of the eighteenth century.[19] Among the proponents of this breakthrough were historians, poets and other writers, the likes of Gerhard Schøning, Even Hammer, Christen Pram, Johan Herman Wessel, Johan Nordahl Brun, Claus Friman, Edvard Storm and others. The upshot of their writings was a celebration of the Norwegian peasantry of the past, as well as of their own time as an exceptional phenomenon. The Norwegian people, i.e. the peasants, were found to be uncommonly hardy, courageous and faithful to king and fatherland. Above all, they possessed an exceptional military prowess, so they would never put up with injustice or suppression. This idolisation of Norwegian peasants must partly be seen in connection with typical European ideas of the period, Rousseau's 'back to nature' and physiocracy. But there is no doubt that the idolisation of the peasants in Norway had a quite exceptional intensity.[20]

Similar ideas about the purportedly outstanding qualities in Norwegian peasants were to some extent also expressed by earlier authors, Danes and other foreigners like the poet Thomas Kingo, the statesman Ulrik Fredrik Gyldenløve in 1693, the bishops Bartolomæus Deichmann in 1724 and Erik Pontoppidan in 1747, the dramatist and scholar Ludvig Holberg and others.[21] Even during the union with Sweden from 1814 until 1905, the peasants occupied the foreground of cultural and public life in Norway to a degree that had hardly any parallel in other countries at the time.[22] The general Romantic movement in Norway was a 'peasant romanticism' (*bonderomantikk*). The manifestations of peasant culture were studied, published and celebrated in the form of folk songs (Jørgen Moe), folktales (Peter Christen Asbjørnsen and Jørgen Moe) and folk music (Ludvig Mathias Lindeman). In 1848–50, Ivar Aasen, the son of a peasant, even created a new literary language, based on peasant dialects, intended to replace the traditional and universally used written language, which was Danish. Aasen's Landsmål was eventually placed on a par with the traditional Danish. Instrumental in spreading favourable ideas about the Norwegian peasantry were the clergy, as was well known at the time of the 'revolution' of 1814.

Even if we consider these ideas about Norwegian peasants to be purely ideological, romantic and nationalist conceptions, or myths, they nonetheless constituted a most important part of contemporary, cultural reality; and they surely were more or less internalised by an enlightened peasant such as Thomas Veblen, and to some degree transferred to his children. The abovementioned writers belonged, with the exception of the peasant Aasen, to the upper classes, the royal officials and the merchants' bourgeoisie, generally educated at the University of Copenhagen. The inevitable question that must be asked (which has of course been asked before) is to what degree their ideas about the peasantry corresponded to social and political realities.[23] If there was such a correspondence Thomas Veblen and his son Thorstein presumably shared more or less the qualities ascribed to this peasantry, irrespective of their knowledge of the literary 'myths'. Here are two subordinate questions. To what degree the Norwegian ruling classes – producing the patriotic writers – needed the political and military support of the peasantry, and how did such a need affect their views of the peasants? The other question concerns the conditions that had to be fulfilled for the peasants to be able to provide an effective military and political support. I will sketch some answers.

From about 1730, the Danish Oldenburg state pursued a consistent mercantilist economic policy, concentrating resources and power in the capital Copenhagen.[24] About 67 per cent of the accounted state incomes of the kingdom of Norway went to Copenhagen. The Oldenburg state's privileged manufactures and overseas merchant companies, such as the Asiatic Commercial Company from 1732, the West Indian and Guinean Company from 1733 and the Icelandic Commercial Company, were also concentrated in the city and its hinterland. From 1726, Copenhagen enjoyed a general import monopoly for the entire Oldenburg state, on salt, wine, spirits and tobacco. Danish exporters enjoyed a monopoly on export of grain to the greater part of southern Norway from 1735. Danish manufactures were developed by means of a protective tariff on imports from Great Britain, the dominating market for Norwegian lumber, and the chief source of income for the Norwegian bourgeoisie. The British answer to the protective tariff on manufactured goods was a tariff on the lumber import, detrimental to Norwegian interests. Norway was denied a bank and a university, in spite of continual demands going back to 1660.

By the end of the eighteenth century, the elite of Norwegian merchants and civil servants, though mostly Danish in culture and very often in origin, had come to realise the fundamental clash between Danish and Norwegian interests within the Oldenburg state, caused by, to a great extent, structural economic differences. As a result influential men in the Norwegian elite oriented themselves towards a self-governing Norway within a new union with Sweden.[25] The culmination of this development came with the Oldenburg alliance with Napoleon against Great Britain in 1807 which provoked a British blockade, ruining the Norwegian, lumber-exporting elite and starving the Norwegian masses who were dependent on grain imports.

In spite of this, Norway fought a war against Sweden in 1814. That was because the Oldenburg king in the Treaty of Kiel in 1814 ceded his absolute sovereignty over Norway to the king of Sweden. To secure national independence and the popular sovereignty won by their new constitution of 1814, Norway revolted against the Treaty of Kiel and fought the war against Sweden. The peace of 1815 gave the kingdoms of Norway and Sweden the same legal status in a union under one king.

It is easy to see that the clash of interests between Norway and Denmark within the Oldenburg state in the eighteenth century gave rise to a sharp patriotism and protonationalism in the Norwegian elite. In the usual patriotic way, this meant enhancing everything Norwegian. What is less usual is that the role played by 'the Norwegian' in Norway – where the elite was mainly Danish in language and culture, often in origin – could be played by no other group than the peasants. Celebrating 'the Norwegian' and celebrating the peasants became one and the same thing. For this reason alone it is reasonable enough that the Norwegian peasantry was more idolised than the peasantry in other countries, where the elite itself was more national in language and origin.

It is evident that the Norwegian elite in the conflicts of the eighteenth century and 1814 sorely needed military and political support from somewhere. What is unusual and characteristically Norwegian is that such a support could only come from the peasants. Even more unusual at the time was the peasants' ability to provide such support. The direct cause of this ability was the Norwegian military system. The defence of the kingdom was, from the Viking Age, almost exclusively based on a form of navy service (*leidangr*) levied on all peasants.[26] This popular levy was never – in mediaeval times or later – to any significant degree replaced or supplemented by mercenary forces or by retainers of the nobility, the nobility being very few and weak.

Following a decay of the *leidangr* in the previous mediaeval centuries, a military system based on conscripted peasants was renewed from 1611.[27] The strength of the Norwegian army was 12,000 men in 1650, 30,200 men in 1807. In addition were conscriptions to the navy. Out of 12,900 men in the Oldenburg navy in 1705, 8,300 were Norwegians, mainly peasants. The added strength of army and navy was considerable compared to the military forces of other countries, considering that the total population of Norway was only about 450,000 in 1650, 900,000 in 1807. These conscriptions are demonstrated to have had significant demographic consequences.[28] The army and navy were frequently used in wars, mainly against Sweden, from the sixteenth through the early nineteenth centuries: in 1559, 1563–70, 1611–13, 1624–29, 1643–45, 1657–60, 1675–79, 1709–20, 1762, and 1807–14.

In addition, Norwegian peasants, to some extent, served as voluntary mercenaries in foreign countries in the eighteenth century. Norwegian peasant soldiers were held to have something of a military elite character, as observed by foreign experts like Prussian King Friedrich II (1740–86).[29] The Norwegian peasants then, of course, were never disarmed; on the contrary, they were fined by the king if they did not keep their weapons in shape. This made a radical difference from the regular military European system, based on mercenaries and noble retainers, where the peasants were disarmed.

It is hard to see that the differences in military system alone could anything but give some reality to the 'myths' surrounding the unusual military prowess of the Norwegian peasants celebrated by the patriotic writers of the eighteenth century. The same system must to some extent have widened the mental horizon of the peasants. This gave one of the prerequisites for a national patriotism, even in the peasantry. As to the historical continuity of this system, there are numerous indications of chauvinism to be found, already in the sagas of the Norwegian kings of the thirteenth century.[30] The chauvinism of that time has been connected to the numerous wars and military expeditions then lead by the national king (not by local noblemen). Such expeditions, involving in most cases the popular *leidangr* against Denmark, were led by leaders such as Håkon V, as king or duke, in the years 1284, 1285, 1287, 1289, 1290, 1292–95, 1300, 1305, 1306, 1308, 1310 and 1318. (This king died in 1319, and his reign is usually counted among the more 'peaceful' ones.) The peasants serving on these rather numerous occasions had small choice to be other than 'warlike', and they were extremely slow if they did not understand their importance for the kingdom's military and political system.

Thus, at the time of independence from Denmark in 1814 – when an independent state was renewed – the Norwegian elite had at their disposal an army of conscripted peasants. This peasant army could pursue a policy in harmony with the interests of the elite, and of the people, towards Great Britain and otherwise. But there was also a question of the loyalty of the peasantry. It has been established beyond reasonable doubt – even if some historians still only grudgingly believe it – that the Norwegian peasants of 1814 were rather more patriotic and bent on war than the elite itself.[31] The troops were mutinous because they thought their officers conducted the war too slackly; and there were civilian demonstrations to the same effect. Partly, this patriotism expressed hatred of Sweden, easily explainable by the numerous preceding wars against that country. But the peasants to some extent talked rational, national politics in 1814. One reason for this may be that quite a few of them were owners of forests, and for this reason their interests coincided with those of the elite in important matters like timber export and in national tariff politics.

Whatever the reason, the elite carefully heeded the opinions of the peasants in their revolt against the Treaty of Kiel in 1814. The members of the constitutional assembly at Eidsvoll that year were chosen by parish congregations. Out of 112 members of the assembly 37 were peasants. The constitution they created gave the vote at parliamentary elections (*Stortingsvalg*) not only to the freeholders, but to all tenant farmers with a rental contract of at least five years. This made the Norwegian constitution then the most democratic in existence; and more specifically, it gave the peasants a political prominence unparalleled in other nations. A parallel is, however, to be found in the celebration of the peasants in poetry and ideology.

This situation continued relatively unchanged into the nineteenth century. 45 peasants, as compared to 35 civil servants from the Norwegian upper classes, were elected to Parliament in the elections of 1832 and 1836. The peasants/farmers continued to develop their position as a main force of the political left, with high-water marks at the introduction of parliamentarism in 1884 and the dissolution of the union with Sweden in 1905.

I have stressed the importance of the military system as a cause for an unusual political and cultural prominence for Norwegian peasants, and in the development of a 'national' horizon in the peasantry. The military system is, however, no more than a major part of a larger system, whose other subsystems include judicial and fiscal institutions, the system of land tenure and the legal status of the peasantry. We may add to them the system of rural settlement, and the propensity and direction of peasant revolts.

Since the rise of the national kingdom in the twelfth and thirteenth centuries, Norwegian peasants were under the jurisdiction of the king, in this sense: sentences were passed by officials of the king, or by popular assemblies, administered by such officials, or at least sentences and penalties were appealable to royal courts of law.[32] The main point was that there was no jurisdiction by private, feudal lords, as in feudalised Europe. According to the criterion of Marc Bloch, this distinction constitutes the dividing line between the free man and the serf, or even between the nobleman (*liber homo*) and the common man.[33] By having no other lord than the king, and by the corresponding right and duty to carry arms, the Norwegian peasantry, legally speaking, constituted a kind of gentry in the European sense. There was simply no servile stratum in the Norwegian society after the *trælar* (slaves) disappeared in the twelfth century.

Secular taxes were in Norway paid to the king. The size of the taxes in the Middle Ages, and in principle until Oldenburg absolutism was introduced in 1660, was decided by agreements between the king and popular assemblies. There was never any arbitrary taxation by private lords, as serfs were taxed in feudal Europe. Economically speaking the Norwegian peasants, or the overwhelming majority of them, could in no way be called gentry. They were never uniformly freeholders (*odelsbønder*) in the sense of owning their farms. In 1350, the peasants owned 40 per cent of the agricultural land; by 1660 they owned 19 per cent.[34] As the *odelsrett* (family right to redeem a sold farm) only applied to economic freeholders, the importance of the *odelsrett* for the character of Norwegian peasants was overstated by the patriotic writers of the eighteenth century.[35] But it is implicit in what I have already said about the judicial system that the relation between the proprietor and the tenant was an economic one. The tenants regularly paid only a land rent in kind or money, or very rarely by work. From the seventeenth century onwards, the land rent was regulated by the king. From the 1660s, there was a rapid development, so in 1835 70 per cent of the land was owned by peasants/farmers.

So far we have spoken of the peasants as an estate (*stand*) with a uniform relation to the king and the other estates, irrespective of their wealth, e.g. by the size of their farms.

Beginning in the seventeenth century, economic differences increased both within the peasantry and between the main parts of the country. Already in the sixteenth century, however, and in a certain connection with the timber export-industry, a considerable number of 'big farmers' (*storbønder*) appeared on the scene, especially in the plains of Østlandet (the eastern part of Norway). These big farmers regularly employed some crofters (*husmenn*) and servants. The crofter as well as his employer, the farmer (*bonde*), belonged to the peasantry. The difference was that the *bonde* possessed (owned or rented) a holding (*gard, bruk*), which was a separate unit in the public land register (*matrikkel*). The holding of the crofter (*husmannsplass*) was no such separate unit in the register, only a physical part of a *bondegard* (farm), which the crofter rented from the *bonde*. The rent usually included work for the *bonde*. In 1723 there were in the whole country 12,000 crofters and 68,000 farmers (*bønder*), in 1801 the numbers had risen to 39,000 crofters to 72,000 farmers; in 1855 the numbers were 65,000 to 115,000.[36]

Even the crofters were legally free men insofar as they were under the jurisdiction of the king, not of their employers or any other kind of lords. The *storbønder*, employing several crofters, often enjoyed a gentleman-like way of life. But the overwhelming majority of Norwegian farmers were the smallholders of the coastal districts and valleys (and often of the plains), like in the Valdres of the Veblens. In most cases, such smallholders wintered six to twelve heads of cattle, about the same or at little higher number of sheep and goats, and a horse. They harvested about 12–30 *tønner* (or 139 litres) of grain.[37] The family members of such a farm regularly carried out almost all the work of the farm themselves. The production was mainly for self-subsistence, until a process of change started in the 1850s.

A distinctive feature in Norwegian peasants, still generally found in most of the nineteenth century, was noted by the Dane Arent Berntsen in 1656:

> Among the peasants are quite usually to be found able house builders, ship- and boat-builders, sail makers, gunsmiths, locksmiths, blacksmiths, carpenters, lathe operators, wood carvers, shoemakers and other artisans; so they not only make their own houses, utensils or whatever they need, but even build most of the houses of the town.[38]

Even if some were more able than others, every peasant mostly did his own handicraft. For example, there was regularly a smithy to be found on each farm. In 1780, the royal district judge Hans Arentz in Sunnfjord expressed the hope that professional artisans never would come to be found in the rural districts; that would mean the end of the thrift that the peasants needed.[39] In this respect, the farmer and artisan Thomas Veblen was no more than an outstanding representative of the typically Norwegian peasant of his time.

The unusual propensity to riot

Modern historians have called Norwegian peasants 'the unruly heads of Scandinavia'.[40] Past authorities concur. In writings from the sixteenth and seventeenth centuries it was rather commonplace to call Norway 'a nest of robbers', 'a home for wild undisciplined persons (*villstyringar*)', 'a meeting place for scoundrels', 'a hard, reluctant, disobedient, headstrong, immoderate, unruly, rebellious and bloodthirsty people'.[11] Such words were aimed at the Norwegian people in general, but the peasantry made out 80–90 per cent of the population. These authors are to a great extent corroborated by statistics on the matter. There were 33 major peasant rebellions in the sixteenth century, seven in the period 1600–1660.[12] The second half of the eighteenth century, and the first years of the nineteenth, saw three particularly wide-ranging waves of peasant rebellions, *Strilekrigen* (the War of the *Strilar*, from the coastal area near Bergen) 1762–72, and the ones lead by the peasants Kristian Lofthus (1786–87) and Hans Nielsen Hauge in 1796 and the following years.[13] The mutinous movement of 1849–51, led by the socialist and declassed journalist Marcus Thrane, was also mainly a peasant rebellion; the great majority of the participants were crofters, smallholders and agricultural workers.[14] This last movement may have comprised 30,000 people, and is said to be the biggest of its kind in Europe up to that time in relation to the size of the total population. The particular propensity to rebellion was what the patriotic writers of the eighteenth century chiefly had in mind, when they found that Norwegian peasants would never suffer injustice. Together with their stereotypical warlike quality this characteristic constituted the essence of 'the Norwegian'.

The rebellions up to the *Strilekrig* riot of 1762–72 were rather of the 'classical' type of pre-industrial peasant riots. They were mainly directed against tax demands, in connection with what the peasants considered unlawfulness. New taxes were unlawful if they were not agreed to by the people. The rebellions of Lofthus and Hauge were of a new kind. The former was mainly directed against the mercantilist privileges bestowed on towns and bourgeoisie by the Oldenburg government. The gist of the Hauge movement was a potentially revolutionary challenge not only to the politico-religious hegemony of the State and the upper classes, exerted through the Church, but even to the sovereignty of the State. Hauge and his followers demanded free right for laymen to preach the Scripture, and they did not acknowledge the validity of royal laws, if they were not concordant with the word of God, as interpreted by themselves. The Thrane movement around 1850 partly reflected the growing cleavage within the peasantry, between farmers (*bønder*) and crofters (*husmenn*). A main demand of the rebellious was economic and political improvements for the crofters, including franchise at parliamentary and municipal elections.

The Norwegian peasant revolts partly reflected, partly contributed to, the somewhat unique 'national horizon' of this peasantry. The peasants paid taxes to, were judged by and served as soldiers for the king. So they revolted against the king, or rather against his officials, not against feudal lords. Already in the fifteenth century the peasants expressed a certain 'nationalism' in demanding Norwegian, not Danish, royal officials.[15] The crux is why Norwegian peasants revolted even more than most others – in spite of the fact that their standing – legally and militarily – was close to what could have been considered 'gentry'. They hardly paid heavier taxes than most other peasants, in most periods. They were better trained, militarily. But why were they so aggressive? What reasons did they have to be discontented?

In this context, it is useful to invoke Norwegian sociologist Johan Galtung's 'structural Theory of Aggression'[46]. What Galtung calls 'rank-disequilibrium' is a general explanation of aggression. We have such disequilibrium when actors are highly ranked on some criteria, lowly on others. Norwegian peasants fit the model. They were 'free men' (*liber homines*), carrying arms like nobles, and were made out as a kind of special heroes by the elite ideologists. But they had to work like other peasants, were not better off economically and were often met with demands for taxes to which they had not consented. So had they no reason for aggression?

Diagnosing Veblen as a Case of Norwegianism

> How comes it that men's most important claims to humanity are cast in the accents of group pride?[47]
>
> Clifford Geertz

We have delineated some dimensions of Norwegian culture, especially those related to the peasantry. Some of these dimensions are cultural in the restricted sense; they concern literature, ideology, religion, 'mentality'. Others are usually called economic, political, military or 'social'. But the two main features added together make out Norwegian culture in the broad sense defined by Clifford Geertz. The purpose of my historical sketch, going back to the Viking period, is not primarily to show how this culture came to be, but to demonstrate the deeply ingrained reality of it that continued to exist in the nineteenth century. Explaining Veblen by his Norwegian culture might seem to demand a corresponding inventory of the aspects thus explained, and a somewhat rigorous demonstration of the causal connections between *explanandum* and *explanans*. Something in the latter direction was discussed in section 1 above. But, even if a much longer such procedure were considered necessary, it could not be taken very far in a chapter of this length. And, as I am chiefly concerned with Veblen's background, I take it to be permissible to assume that Veblen's main qualities are fairly well known to the reader, so that the main question is how a thinker like Veblen could come into being.[48]

In my concluding attempt at explanation I now take what Geertz calls the clinical, diagnostical approach of cultural theory. The purpose is not to subsume the observations 'under general laws', but 'to place them within an intelligible frame'.[49] This is his 'method of thick description'. This means to demonstrate how the comprehensive pattern of Veblen's culture, and its 'symptoms', fit the comprehensive pattern of Norwegian (peasant) culture in such a way as to warrant a diagnosis: his is a case of Norwegianism.[50] Even if the aim of the diagnosis is not the prediction of a Veblen, it will be successful to the degree that the reader feels that Veblen is the kind of social scientist you would get if you equipped a Norwegian peasant with Veblen's personal resources and erudition.

By way of specification we point out: Veblen's most general symptom of Norwegianism of the peasant kind is probably a duality in his self-consciousness. On the one hand, he bears a certain social insecurity, revealed in taciturnity and crabbiness, which in a rather usual way would follow from his identification with a peasant stock.[51] On the other hand, we observe what is much more unusual, his pride in this same peasant background, including the continuity between the peasant society of the nineteenth century and the Icelandic-Norwegian, Viking saga-society.[52] We must emphasise this: Veblen is well known as a non-nationalist and as an adversary of brawls.[53] His pride in the bellicosity of his Viking ancestors and of the peasants of later centuries, as well as in the 'national' horizon of these peasants, must therefore be based on their general capacity for self-assertion, and on their relatively high level of politico-social consciousness.

Veblen's other, more specific 'symptoms' of Norwegianism are probably derived from the principal one mentioned above, which partly includes an uncommon self-confidence as a scientist. Veblen's scepticism, oppositionality, pugnacity and rebelliousness can all be explained by the same general theory of aggression, based on the 'rank-disequilibrium' invoked to explain the unusual rebelliousness of his peasant ancestors. The direction of Veblen's aggression against vested interests of all kinds is in keeping with his ancestors' rebellions against the officials of the king, and especially with the rebellions of the crofters and small peasants, ca. 1850, partly directed against the 'big farmers'. His adversity to waste and identification with thrift is to be seen in this same connection.[54]

Veblen's probably most important contribution to science is his rejection of neoclassical economics based on the profit motive as the final measure of all values, and his alternative economics, about the substantive productivity of work. This approach is – at the level of Veblen's motivation – readily explainable through his identification with his father and ancestors, who themselves performed almost all the tasks needed in their society, the production of food as well as of buildings and all utensils. His important concept, 'the instinct of workmanship',[55] must of course be understood in this light.

My conclusive diagnosis is: Veblen's was a case of Norwegianism. But as every patient has other qualities, as well as his suffering from e.g. measles, Veblen surely had other important dimensions beyond his Norwegianism.

Conclusion

My notions of the somewhat special character of Norwegian peasants – in social reality, not only in nationalist ideology – have been exposed at book length.[56] Even if these notions on most points correspond to what other historians have found, they have also been refuted as follows: 'The prenational identity Lunden asserts is interesting, exactly because it is not, like he believes, something uniquely Norwegian'.[57] And, surely, at a high enough level of abstraction all countries are alike – at the same level as all scientists, and indeed all men, are alike. But at another level of abstraction all countries, scientists and men are unique. Only we ourselves choose the level; it is not given by facts. History is an individualising science. And even at a medium level of abstraction we find Norway and Veblen to be unique. They are unique in a way that makes one a case of the other.

Demographically, Norway and Iceland are insignificant countries, bearing together less than 1 *promille* of the world's population. From this perspective it seems it would make little difference if these two countries vanished from the face of the earth. But unlike Norway and Iceland, Thorstein Veblen was undoubtedly a phenomenon of global importance, a quintessential paragon of the scientist, combining devastating criticism with a like measure of creative imagination and erudition. For this reason, the importance of Veblen merits a thorough study of even Norwegian and Icelandic history.

Perhaps it would emerge from such a study that Veblen was not all that original after all. Perhaps his only really distinguishing quality from a global point of view was that he looked upon the world from the point of view of the smallholder. But this was the Norwegian and Icelandic mainstream. This was also the distinguishing quality of the most important Scandinavian contributions to world culture, the Icelandic mediaeval sagas. They are about 'brawling Icelandic peasants'. It was also the chief characteristic of the Nobel Laureate novelists of modern Iceland and Norway, Halldor Laxness, Bjørnstjerne Bjørnson, Sigrid Undset and, to a certain extent, Knut Hamsun. Together with other writers of perhaps an equal professional rank, such as Olav Duun, Arne Garborg, and Tarjei Vesaas, they make peasants/farmers their protagonists, taking them in dead earnest, not only as a class but as individuals. This is quite unlike the literature of feudalised Europe, such as that of William Shakespeare. There, the heroes are, as we know, noblemen and the peasants generally play the parts of clowns and ridiculous fools.

If there are any geniuses to be found in Norwegian historiography, they are probably Johan Ernst Sars and Halvdan Koht. They have in common with Veblen and the Nobel novelists a perception that the outstanding theme of Norwegian history is the unusual role played by the peasantry – which can from one angle be called an aspect of relative poverty and backwardness. This crucial role has nonetheless had a decisive influence on modern Norwegian culture at home, and, through the great nineteenth-century migrations, to some degree in the New World. This was a culture upon which Thorstein Veblen drew and of which, in important ways, he was himself a part. So Veblen was simply like other outstanding Norwegians – or he was rather like the majority of the Norwegian people. As weaknesses of the edifice of the European Union are now becoming apparent – particularly in the EU periphery – it can safely be assumed that Thorstein Veblen would have been proud to belong to the stock of the only European people that voted down their government's decision to join the European Union not once but twice, in 1972 and 1994.

So Veblen was surely a Norwegian.

Notes and References

1 M. Lerner, 'Editor's Introduction', in *The Portable Veblen*, ed. by Max Lerner (Harmondsworth: Penguin, 1977), 2.
2 Francesca Lidia Viano, 'Veblen and the Historical Profession', *History of European Ideas* 35 (2008): 28–61, esp. 7.
3 Ibid., 2.
4 Ibid., 1, 1n.
5 Veblen, in Lerner, 'Editor's Introduction', 474.
6 Ibid., 8.
7 Veblen, *Portable Veblen*, 507–38.
8 Lerner, 'Editor's Introduction', 47.
9 Ibid., 2.

10 Terje Mikael Hasle Joranger, 'Valdres to the Upper Midwest', in this volume.
11 Lerner, 'Editor's Introduction', 2.
12 Ibid., 2.
13 Joranger, 'Valdres to the upper Midwest'.
14 Ibid.
15 Ibid.
16 Knut Odner, 'New Perspectives', in this volume.
17 Ibid.
18 The period of Scandinavian unions started in 1319, but legally the kingdom of Norway was on a par with its union partners. In 1536, Norway lost its separate state council (*Riksråd*), and there was no longer a Norwegian church province.
19 A. H. Winsnes, *Det Norske Selskab 1772–1812* (Kristiania: Aschehoug & Co., 1914).
20 Ibid.; Kåre Lunden, *Norsk grålysing. Norsk nasjonalisme 1770–1814 på allmenn bakgrunn* (Oslo: Det Norske Samlaget, 1992), 75–101.
21 Ibid., 75–101.
22 Arne Bergsgaard, *Frå 17 mai til 9 april. Norsk historie 1814–1940* (Oslo: Det Norske Samlaget, 1958), 125–30.
23 Lunden, *Norsk grålysing*, 102–15.
24 Ibid., 116–49.
25 Ibid., 128–49.
26 Rikke Malmros, 'Leidangr' in *Medieval Scandinavia. An Encyclopedia*, ed. by Phillip Pulsiano (New York and London: Garland Publishing, 1993), 389f.
27 Kåre Lunden, 'Frå svartedauden til 17. mai', in *Norges Landbrukshistorie II* (Oslo: Det Norske Samlaget, 2002), 288. For a shorter version of this book in English, see Kåre Lunden, 'Recession and new expansion 1350–1814', in *Norwegian Agricultural History*, ed. by Reidar Almås (Trondheim: Tapir Academic Press, 2004).
28 Egil Øvrebø, *I kongens teneste. Militær utskriving frå Bergens stift under Store nordiske krig 1709–1719* (Bergen: Riksarkivaren, 1996); Lunden, *Norsk grålysing*, 105.
29 Gerhard Brammer, *Livgarden 1658–1908* (København: Vilhelm Trydes Forlag, 1908), 123; Lunden, *Norsk grålysing*, 107f.
30 Kåre Lunden, 'Was there a Norwegian National Identity in the Middle Ages?', *Scandinavian Journal of History* 20.1 (1995): 20–33.
31 Arne Bergsgaard, 'Folket og krigen i 1814', in *Syn og Segn* nos. 3 and 4: Oslo (1941).
32 Ecclesiastical jurisdiction was also important in the Catholic period until 1536. But in the last resort the Church depended on the royal sword.
33 Marc Bloch, *Feudal Society* (London: Routledge and Kegan Paul, 1961).
34 Lunden, 'Frå svartedauden', 96.
35 Lunden, *Norsk grålysing*, 206 and passim.
36 Lunden, 'Frå svartedauden', 138; Ståle Dyrvik et al., *Norsk økonomisk Historie Band 1 1500–1850* (Oslo: Det Norske Samlaget, 1979), 135.
37 Lunden, 'Frå svartedauden', 214, 223, 228.
38 Ibid., 392.
39 Ibid., 392.
40 Øystein Rian, Bondemotstand i Norge – linjer og utviklingstrekk', in *Kristian Lofthus og hans tid*, ed. by Berit Eide Johnsen et al. (Kristiansand: Høgskolen i Agder, 1998), 46f.; Lunden, 'Frå svartedauden', 339–55.
41 Lunden, 'Frå svartedauden', 353.
42 Steinar Imsen, 'Bondemotstand og statsutvikling i Norge ca. 1300–1700', *Heimen* 27 (1990): 79–95.
43 Andreas Aarflot, *Hans Nielsen Hauge. Liv og budskap* (Oslo: Universitetsforlaget, 1971).
44 Tore Pryser, *Norsk historie 1814–1860* (Oslo: Det Norske Samlaget, 1999), 266–76.

45 Steinar Imsen, 'Unionsregimente og bondemotstand under Erik av Pommeren', in *Konge, adel og opprør: Kalmarunionen 600 år*, ed. by Knut Arstad (Oslo: Forsvarsmuseet, 1998); Lunden, 'Frå svartedauden', 115.
46 Johan Galtung, 'A Structural Theory of Aggression', *Journal of Peace Research* 1 (1964): 95–119.
47 Clifford Geertz, *The Interpretation of Cultures. Selected Essays* (New York: Basic Books, 1973), 30.
48 Ibid., 26.
49 Ibid., 26.
50 Ibid., 26.
51 Knut Odner, *Thorstein Veblen. Forstyrreren av den intellektuelle fred* (Oslo: Abstrakt Forlag, 2005), 21; Francesca Lidia Viano, 'Ithaca Transfer', in this volume.
52 Odner, *Thorstein Veblen*, 53.
53 Ibid., 53.
54 Thorstein Veblen, 'The Theory of the Leisure Class', in Lerner, *Portable Veblen*, 3–214.
55 Veblen, *Portable Veblen*, 7, 21, 306–23.
56 Lunden, *Norsk grålysing*; Lunden, 'Frå svartedauden'.
57 Harald Gustafsson, 'Review of Lunden, *Norsk grålysing*', *Historisk Tidskrift* 1 (1994): 171; Lunden, 'Norge i 1814', ibid., 1 (1995): 75–77.

Chapter 4

VALDRES TO THE UPPER MIDWEST: THE NORWEGIAN BACKGROUND OF THE VEBLEN FAMILY AND THEIR MIGRATION TO THE UNITED STATES

Terje Mikael Hasle Joranger

On 27 April 1847 a young couple from the rural community of Høre in the administrative township of Vang in the Valdres region of Norway visited Pastor Carl Andreas Hansen at the Vang parsonage.[1] They were Thomas Andersen Veblen, aged 29, and his seven-years-younger wife, Kari Torsteinsdatter Bunde. In refined handwriting, the pastor registered the two in the ministerial records as emigrants to America.[2] Five days later, they left Høre to embark on their overseas journey to the land of promise.[3]

This chapter aims to present the Norwegian background of Thorstein Bunde Veblen's parents, Thomas and Kari Veblen, with an emphasis on the period from the beginning of the nineteenth century until their exodus, and analyse their migration and settlement process in the upper Midwest. I do not make any particular mention of Thorstein Veblen, but I do assert that his parents' experiences on both sides of the Atlantic may help us better to appreciate the origins of his ideas. The historical backdrop for this is illustrated by Thorstein's older brother Andrew A. Veblen in his notes *The Veblen Family: Immigrant Pioneers from Valdris*, and by the recollections of their father, Thomas Veblen, particularly with regards to his family background and his journey to America.[4]

The Valdres Region

Kari and Thomas Veblen were born and raised in the Valdres region, a rural highland area in south central Norway consisting of a large inland valley and its smaller side valleys; its main river, the Begna, cuts through the valley from the mountainous areas to the north-west to the forested lowlands to the south-east.[5] The Valdres region has a surface area of 5,409 square kilometres, and, according to the 1907 agricultural census, arable land made up between 0.7 and 4.0 per cent of the acreage in its different rural municipalities.[6] Valdres could be described as a mountain district, since most of its surface has an elevation of 200–500 metres. Yet the region enjoys large topographical variations. On the one hand, 88per cent of the municipality of Vang rises more than 900 metres

Map of the Valdres Region by Administrative Townships and Valley Parishes

Source: Terje Mikael Hasle Joranger, 'Emigration from Reinli, Valdres to the upper Midwest: A Comparative Study', in *Norwegian-American Studies*, ed. by Odd S. Lovoll (Northfield, MN: The Norwegian-American Historical Association, 2000), 156.

above sea level whereas, on the other hand, the southern part of the region consists of hills and forested areas similar to the lowland regions of eastern Norway.[7]

The main road through the region has for centuries formed a central means of communication between eastern and western Norway, and the boundaries between Valdres and the neighbouring regions have remained virtually unchanged since prehistoric times.[8] The northernmost of the six administrative townships in Valdres is named Vang, and its boundaries have also largely remained stable through the centuries. The rural community of Høre makes up the southern portion of Vang.[9] In addition to forming a separate regional unit in civil terms, Vang has, since the Reformation, constituted one of three main parishes in the Valdres region.[10] The settlements in the community of Høre include clusters of farmsteads, single dwelling and isolated farms of which the majority are located in a belt of farmsteads that is three miles long and around half a mile wide.

In this high-lying community all farm clusters, except one, are located at an altitude of 1,500 to 2,300 feet above sea level. Centrally located along this belt of farmsteads was located a cluster of farms named 'Veflen', which in earlier times was spelled 'Veblen'. One of the Veblen farms was the home of Thorstein Veblen's ancestors during the first half of the nineteenth century, when they presumably took 'Veblen' as their family name.[11]

The Peasant Society

The Valdres region in many respects remained a traditional society well into the nineteenth century. For example, extensive farm operating methods rested on a traditional use of labour on infields and outfields during most of the nineteenth century, requiring the participation of a relatively large number of labourers.[12] Furthermore, the region was made up of small communities, each consisting of a circle of neighbouring farms (the so-called *neighbourhood community*), that had many common functions and filled various common needs as if they constituted a single economic agent, superior to the individuals working in it.[13]

As in most parts of Valdres, in Høre the household formed the basis of production. Farming operations were largely based on diversified animal husbandry and grain production, and an extensive use of infields, outfields and mountain resources according to traditional methods.[14] Household economies in the Valdres region were, until the middle of the nineteenth century, to a certain extent characterised by self-subsistence and barter. However, local differences in terms of resources and climate resulted both economically and socially. That said, those segments of the population tied to trade of surplus products from cattle sometimes engaged in monetised exchanges, while peasants in the southern lowlands of Valdres, where forestry dominated, had made the transition to a money economy already in the early eighteenth century.[15] Religious worship also varied across the Valdres region; whereas its southern townships experienced a strong revivalist movement based on the teachings of lay pastor Hans Nielsen Hauge in the early nineteenth century, its northern portions were left practically untouched by this movement.[16] The fact that social and cultural traits differed between regions, but that such traits also could vary within a single region was also noticed by Norwegian folklorist Eilert Sundt on his travels through Norway. During his 1865 tour of Valdres, Sundt noticed local differences in the use of luxury apparel between the outer and upper parts of the region: 'In the upper parts or in Vang one can still content oneself with home-made clothes,' he observes:

> there one can for instance see men with suede trousers made from goat or reindeer, with shoes made from hide like the *komager* of the Finns and other almost old-fashioned dressing customs; but in Aurdal it has come to the point that women both purchase their dress fabric and let city-educated seamstresses sew it beside smartening themselves up with crinolines and the like.[17]

Formally, Valdres society was characterised by a paternalistic and a parental culture, which is especially visible at the family level, where the father enjoyed a position of superiority over his wife and daughters, among other things in choosing his daughter's future spouse. Sons, on the other hand, were favoured in terms of inheritance, receiving double the shares of their sisters, and were the most likely to inherit real property in land, the symbol of economic and social wealth in society, from their parents.[18] Furthermore, the linkage between the independent farm unit in the Valdres region and the family that operated it is consistent with agrarian historian Andreas Holmsen's definition of a 'family society' as a social unit composed by husband, wife and parents.[19] Finally, land was regarded as the symbol of economic and social wealth in rural Valdres, since it gave status and a sense of pride to people on farm units in the region and obliged them to ensure continuity through intergenerational property transfers.[20]

Due to the strong linkage between land and family, the transfer of landed property from one generation to the next included the use of three old institutions, namely the *odelsrett*, the *åsetesrett*, and the support agreement named *føderåd* or *kår*. In this traditional peasant society, the old tie between family and land was found in the *odelsrett*.[21] The right, which already existed in Norwegian provincial law codes from the early thirteenth century, is defined as a person's special right to own agricultural land because the person or his or her ancestors have owned it for a certain period of time. Consequently, the main purpose of the *odelsrett* has been to preserve landed properties within the families originally attached to them. In effect, it implied the right of family lines to redeem lands from more recent owners, as well as the special right to pre-empt said lands in cases where they had been sold out of the family. From the early seventeenth century until the early nineteenth century, the time of redemption and the time of prescription were reduced several times.[22] In addition to the transition to freeholding, the decrease of the time of redemption and prescription contributed to a dramatic increase in the number of peasants endowed with that right as well as the number of farms subject to the *odelsrett*. According to the period of prescription listed in the *odel* law of 1821, farm owners could acquire the *odelsrett* within ten years.[23]

The *åsetesrett* refers to a right of primogeniture by which the elder of two or more heirs has the right to claim the *åsete*, i.e. the main holding, provided that the other inheritors are compensated with other lands or movable property.[24] In 1814, when Norway received its own constitution, both the *åsetesrett* and the *odelsrett* were given constitutional protection, and both institutions were included in a separate law of 1821.[25] With its deep roots in Norwegian history, the longevity of the institution of the *odelsrett* had reflected both a symbolic and a practical significance in Norwegian rural society from its origins until that point.[26] The position of the farm heir was also hedged with traditional regulations, including the duty to support his parents after they had relinquished their rights to the farm. A third institution connected to farm property transfer in Norwegian peasant society is the system tied to the so-called 'support agreement', an arrangement under which owners could transfer their farms to a buyer, often a son, in return for a promise to support them for the rest of their lives.[27]

The Valdres region had a long freeholding tradition as compared to regions in western and northern Norway where a higher percentage of land was in the possession of noble families, officials and the crown.[28] In 1723, for example, around 70 per cent of all farms in the community of Høre were freeholds as compared to 46.8 per cent in the entire

Valdres region and the average 32.5 per cent in Norway. By 1802, freeholders in Vang held 88 per cent of all assessed farm units in which they possessed a share, and by 1850 practically all assessed farms in the region were freeholds.[29]

The use of the *odelsrett* and the *åsetesrett* were only applicable to freeholds where the peasant was a part-owner or full owner of the farm that he operated.[30] Although Kari and Thomas Veblen originated from freeholding families, both their close kin among the Bunde and Veblen family experienced the loss of ownership due to various reasons. This is clarified in an interview with Thomas Veblen made by his son Andrew. Here, the former related that his father, Andris (Anders), was born on a farm in the neighbouring parish but in several instances lost the farm in relation to farm purchases when a relative of the seller used his right of redemption to purchase the farm back. For many years, Andris Veblen rented the upper Veflen farm, a clerical property, and as a tenant farmer he had the right of first purchase when the farm was to be sold in 1854, but the sheriff in Vang convinced him not to bid because he wanted the farm for his son. Andris later moved to a farm in the neighbouring parish where he became a landowner.[31] On Kari's side of the family, her paternal grandfather Øystein had married a widow on the north Bunde farm but risked losing his farm when a relative of the former owner made use of his *odelsrett*. Thanks to a loan from a merchant in Lærdal, Øystein regained possession of the farm and transferred it to Kari's father Torstein. But, since Øystein was not able to meet the terms of the loan and had to sell the farm around 1830, Torstein Bunde and his family migrated to the lowland area of Biri, where Torstein worked at a glass factory and passed away a few years later. Following his premature death, his widow and children returned to Høre where she was given a support agreement on the Bunde farm. She later remarried and resided with her new family on the Bunde farm until they emigrated to America in 1849.[32] The families of Kari and Thomas thus experienced a social degradation due to the abovementioned circumstances, which were specific of an area dominated by a strong tradition of freeholding. As we will soon see, the Veblen couple would become landed, but only following emigration.

The intergenerational transfer of the farm was strictly regulated according to the laws of primogeniture, which in turn were strengthened by strict codes for naming children. The naming pattern in the Valdres region was no exception. Children were usually given one first name. According to custom, the eldest son usually received a name that was linked to the farm, and in most cases he was named after his paternal grandfather, while the second boy was named after his maternal grandfather. As for the girls, the first who was born to a married couple usually was named after her paternal grandmother and the second girl after her maternal grandmother. If the farm had been inherited through the wife, the order was reversed. When the grandparents had been named, younger children were named after great grandparents in the same order. In addition, names of children that died in infancy or of close relatives that died young were usually repeated with the next child of the same gender.[33] The Bunde and Veblen families formed no exception to this rule. As the eldest daughter, Kari Bunde was named after her paternal grandmother Kari Olsdotter Bunde, whereas Thomas Veblen, being the second son in the family, was named after his maternal grandfather Thomas Olson Tørstad.[34]

The peasant society in the Valdres region was egalitarian, especially in areas where freehold dominated and where the number of cotters was relatively low. This is compatible with the case of the community of Høre, where it was the size of the farm and its resources rather than the distinction between freeholder and tenant farmer that dictated a peasant's standing and how he was judged socially. Also, the difference between smaller freeholds and cotter's farms in some areas could be rather vague.[35] In addition to the peasant population, and socially dissociated from it, was a small rural elite consisting of the official class and the church clergy, referred to as 'the upper class' or *de kondisjonerte*, but in no administrative township did they make up more than 0.3–0.5 per cent of the total population.[36]

Factors behind Emigration

According to official statistics available, about 12,000 people emigrated from the Valdres region in the period 1866–1914.[37] Different estimates have also been given by local historians both in America and in Norway, ranging from 17,000 to 21,500 between 1825 and 1920, but neither of these are reliable, being based on educated guesswork, nor comparable, since they refer to different time periods.[38] In the ten-year period 1856–65, for example, 43.6 per cent of all emigrants in Kristians Amt came from the Valdres region which was second only to the region of Sogn in having the highest emigration rates of all regions in Norway both in absolute and relative terms. The overseas migration from the Valdres region ranked among the largest in the entire country in relation to the size of its population. In the period 1846–90, the regional administrative unit of Kristians Amt, of which the Valdres region constituted the western portion, had the highest number of emigrants of any county in Norway.[39]

Regular migration from the Valdres region took place more than twenty years after the first emigrant party left the Stavanger harbour aboard the *Restauration* in 1825. The emigration movement from Norway may be attributed to the interplay between demographic, social, cultural, economic and religious factors both in the sending and in the receiving countries.[40] For example, population growth has been mentioned as a contributing factor to overseas emigration from Norway and also referred to for partly explaining the transformation of the population's social makeup. Demographic growth reached significant proportions in Høre – from where the Veblen family emigrated – where the population increased from 470 according to the 1801 census to 700 in 1855, an increase of around 33 per cent.[41] Due to the strong tradition of primogeniture and the limited access to arable land, farm subdivisions took place in order to keep the pace of population growth. This in turn created opportunities for more families to become landed, but as such divisions reached the point where subdivided units had difficulties in supporting a large family, younger sons were given the opportunity of clearing a croft in the outskirts of the infield. Thus, with increasing rates of population growth, more and more of children on freeholds were channelled into the landless class of crofters, labourers and tenants. The number of landless heads of households and their families in Høre, for example, increased from 26.7 per cent in 1782 to 38.3 per cent in 1855.[42] Couples marrying in the mid-nineteenth century had uncertain prospects of a landed future. Thus, when Thomas Veblen and Kari Bunde were married in 1846, population growth limited their chances of becoming farmers, and their situation was made even bleaker by the absence of alternative opportunities for profitable employment. Consequently, they settled as crofters on the Veblen farm, but decided to emigrate already the following year.[43]

Inheritance was a crucial factor behind emigration. Several transatlantic emigration studies have shown that emigration became a viable option in areas where impartible inheritance was practiced as a means of securing a landed future not only for the landless class, but also for children from landed families who were denied the prospects of inheriting land.[44] In the Valdres region, one heir, usually the eldest son or occasionally the daughter in cases where all children were girls, inherited the family farm, leaving younger siblings to an uncertain future in the home community. In his 1913 description of land tenure in the regional administrative township of Kristians Amt (equivalent to the size of a county), topographer Amund Helland states that the eldest son usually took over the farm on reasonable conditions whereas the other children, who usually could not afford to buy a farm, chose to emigrate instead of becoming crofters or servants.[45]

Many scholars accept the notion that population growth and differences in standards of living in both the countries of origin and destination are the main factors explaining emigration.[46] Helland asserts that emigration was especially heavy in mountain regions in Kristians Amt, where (mostly due to the difficulty in finding work in the winter season, especially in years when spring came late) animal husbandry and agriculture played an important role and where industry and forestry provided limited opportunities.[47] His assertions were later echoed by the leading Norwegian emigrant historian Ingrid Semmingsen who noted that rural communities where emigration to America became a viable option usually were characterised by self-subsistence and little specialisation and division of labour.[48]

Steffen Olsen Helle

By 1847, when the Veblens sailed to the United States, emigration from the Valdres region to America was still very limited, and Kari and Thomas Veblen were one of the first three married couples to emigrate from their parish.[49] The transatlantic migration movement, however, was well known in the rural community of Høre, since families or individuals from this community already had moved in stages to regions that had been hit early by 'America Fever'.[50] We also know that personal connections played a significant role in influencing Thomas and Kari to emigrate. In his autobiographical notes, Andrew Veblen states that his father, Thomas Veblen, followed the example of fellow villager and partner in carpentry and cabinet-making in different regions, Steffen Olsen Kubakke[51]-Helle, among others in the adjoining region of Sogn, where emigration had started in 1839. Andrew Veblen could not recall his father telling how early his parents began to plan to emigrate, but it became a matter of consideration between his father and Steffen Olsen while they were working together.[52]

A man of strong character and ambition, Steffen Olsen Helle deserves further mention. Originating from the same rural community as Thomas and Kari Veblen, he was trained in the military and had received an extraordinary education for his time. In 1846, following the fulfilment of his military duty, Steffen and his brother Ole sailed to America, where Steffen bought lands in both Manitowoc County and Sheboygan County on the shore of Lake Michigan, in north-eastern Wisconsin (which, at the time, was still a territory).[53] The decision of Steffen – or Stephen Olson as he was to be later called – to sail to Wisconsin seems to have been well thought through, as he scouted to find an area for future settlement and purchased several tracts of land west of the present city of Manitowoc. Determined to bring more *Valdris* settlers to his new home in Wisconsin, Steffen returned to Norway in 1847 to lead a large company of emigrants from the administrative township of Vang and adjoining districts back to America in 1848 (including Thomas Veblen's brother Haldor and Kari Veblen's siblings Ole and Ingrid Bunde). According to Andrew Veblen, Stephen Olson also induced peasants in southern Valdres to leave Norway for America that year, and in so doing he initiated a regular migration from the region. The pioneers from this wide geographic area were in turn to influence family members and neighbours in their respective home communities, thus laying the foundation for a self-supporting migration movement once the transatlantic path had been opened.[54] According to Norwegian-American chronicler Hjalmar Rued Holand, Stephen Olson did more to accelerate emigration from the Valdres region than anyone else, a statement that is echoed by Andrew Veblen in his notes on the Veblen family.[55]

The First Settlement Area: North-Eastern Wisconsin

According to English historian Frank Thistlethwaite, it is fruitful to consider conditions both in the country of origin and in the destination in order to understand the entire migration experience. Consequently, instead of regarding emigration and immigration as separate processes, the entire migratory movement should be regarded holistically.[56]

Norwegian emigrants habitually settled in upstate New York in the ten-year period following the initial overseas emigration from Norway in 1825. However, following the opening of the Erie Canal in 1825 and the efforts of Norwegian pathfinder Cleng Peerson, the increasing stream of Norwegian emigrants from the mid-1830s was directed to the upper Midwest. From the 1840s onward, Wisconsin became the main destination of Norwegian emigrants.[57] The migration experience of Kari and Thomas Veblen illustrates the importance of ties in the country of origin for settlement strategies in the receiving country. The personal contact between Stephen Olson and Thomas Veblen in Norway was significant in that the former found work for Kari and Thomas Veblen in Ozaukee County (in north-eastern Wisconsin) following their strenuous voyage to America in September of 1847. Due to their weakened condition following the long trip, Kari and Thomas were compelled to quit their newfound job.[58] Stephen Olson therefore arranged with the Veblen couple to move onto 40 acres of land that he had purchased in adjoining Sheboygan County under the right of pre-emption, but the Veblen family soon moved off the land following trouble with Stephen's brother Ole and instead traded their right to pre-emption to the 40 acres for a tract of 160 acres.[59] In order to have better access to remunerative work, Thomas Veblen erected a dwelling house in the village of Port Ulao, south of Port Washington, which they occupied for a year and where Kari gave birth to their son Andris (or Andrew as he was called in America). According to

Andrew Veblen's notes, the objective of Thomas Veblen all this time was to develop the quarter section that Thomas had traded the previous year into a farm of their own. In the meantime, his brother Haldor had arrived, and he moved in with Thomas and his family. Haldor was single and Thomas thought that it was more convenient to occupy the land by pre-emption, and consequently in February of 1849, the latter filed for the 160 acres. In the spring or summer of that year the entire family moved to the claim.[60] The two brothers divided the land between them and worked together in a sensible arrangement which economised on housing as well as housekeeping.[61]

Upon the payment of their loan, the brothers owned their land free of encumbrances, and for the first time since the arrival of Kari and Thomas Veblen to Wisconsin they now had become landed. As a consequence, Thomas Veblen never again was to do carpentry work for hire except trading his skilled for his neighbours' unskilled labour. The brothers obtained cash by selling cordwood and axe handles which were made from timber cleared from the farmland. Kari and Thomas Veblen had two more children during the period they stayed on the farm, namely their oldest daughter Betsy Jane and their son Østen, later called Orson.[62] Only five years later, in 1854, the brothers sold their shares in the farm in Sheboygan County and moved to the Town of Cato in adjoining Manitowoc County, 33 miles further north. There they purchased eighty acres of wild timber land and later acquired two additional parcels of land including a 40-acre tract of 'swampland' and 80 acres of unimproved land.[63]

What made the Veblen family relocate to a new environment relatively soon following their purchase of the land in Sheboygan County? According to Andrew Veblen, the move was due less to difficulties tied to the strenuous efforts of clearing the dense forest on their farmland than to dissatisfaction with the development of their environment:

> The country all about the Veblens became settled by immigrants from Holland [...] among them the Veblens found themselves strangers, who could have no intercourse with their neighbors, except in their own very limited English, of which the neighbors knew even less than they. [...] We were an isolated family, we could have no social intercourse without making a long journey to find people of our own kind; or we might await the rare occasions when some friend came from far away. There were no opportunities for satisfying religious and spiritual needs [...] There was no organization of coreligionists among the few far scattered compatriots along the Lake before one got days' journey south or north.[64]

Andrew Veblen also adds that the racial isolation experienced by the Veblen family could be not only 'unpleasant and annoying; but it could be a source of great danger'.[65] Haldor had wrongly been accused of stealing a cow by a German who actually had stolen the cow himself; due to his poor English, Haldor was arrested and taken to the county seat at Sheboygan. He was released following bail and was finally acquitted, but the case had caused the family both much trouble and considerable expenses.[66]

From their ethnic isolation in Sheboygan County, the Veblens had now relocated to an environment to a large extent settled by immigrants not only from their own ethnic background but also from their home region in Norway. Owing largely to the efforts of Stephen Olson, the emigrant party of north Valdres immigrants of 1848 and other Norwegians had formed the nucleus in Manitowoc County, Wisconsin. A continuous influx of immigrants from the Valdres region, especially from its northern part, reinforced the settlement's regional flavour.[67]

Chain Migration

The metaphor of *chain migration* is a useful concept for understanding the choice of the Veblen family in leaving their isolation and joining people of the same cultural and regional background. German sociologist Friedrich Heckmann defines chain migration as 'a form of migration where migrants utilize social acquaintances with former emigrants for their migratory process based upon the context of their common origin'.[68] Furthermore, this type of migration is a linkage that develops and connects the point of origin and the destination of migrants, especially those rooted in family ties or in neighbourly relations.[69] In turn, chain migration tends to concentrate an immigrant population of homogeneous origins in a certain locality, often determined by the pioneers' original settlement choices.[70]

    The process of chain migration repeated itself with the westward migratory movement across the American continent. In his essay 'Immigration and Expansion', Marcus Lee Hansen shows how colonial overpopulation resulted in the creation of one or several 'satellite colonies', which in turn attracted newcomers. When the larger settlement in turn became crowded, colonies organised as joint enterprises were sent out to more distant regions, and, as time passed, the process repeated itself.[71] According to historians Jon Gjerde and Walter Kamphoefner, the linkages between immigrants of similar cultural background seem to have persisted within the chain of settlements in spite of the mobility that prevailed in American society in the nineteenth and early twentieth centuries.[72]

    I assert that the relative isolation of the Veblen family was due to two crucial factors, namely the timing of settlement and the availability of land. The couple were early immigrant pioneers who through their acquaintance with Stephen Olson had arrived in an area where Norwegian settlements had not yet been established. As a consequence, they purchased available land close to their initial settlement area. Yet, Andrew Veblen relates that they were in contact with other immigrants from the administrative unit of Vang both during their residence in Port Ulao and on their farm in Sheboygan County. Their spiritual contact during their first seven years, for example, was with Rev. Paul Anderson Norland who emigrated from Vang in 1843 and later become pastor of the first Norwegian Lutheran Church in Chicago in 1848. He later kept in touch with the few *Valdris* immigrants northwards along the coast of Lake Michigan, among others administering the baptismal rites for two of the Veblen children.[73]

The Second Settlement Area: South-Eastern Minnesota

After the Veblens moved to Manitowoc County in 1854, thus entering the confines of a large settlement of *Valdris* immigrants, they observed that several families sold their land and moved westwards where inexpensive government land was available. In 1865, the Veblen family again pulled up their stakes and moved to south-eastern Minnesota where they established their third farm of uncultivated land. They had visited Kari's relatives in Minnesota two years earlier and the sight of the vast Minnesota prairies and the recognition of their economic potential had made a deep impression on Thomas. He sold his 160-acre farm in Wisconsin and instead purchased 290 acres of land in Wheeling Township approximately two miles east of the village of Nerstrand in Rice County.[74]

In Minnesota, Kari and Thomas Veblen and their family (including Haldor) settled in close proximity to Kari's relatives, thus enjoying the closeness of kinship and former acquaintances providing help and support. Kari's brother Ole T. Bunde, her mother, Berit, her new husband, Einar Halvorson, and their family (who formerly lived with them in Sheboygan County,) had preceded them to the area and lived nearby, as did several immigrant families from Vang parish. Furthermore, the area was located in close proximity to a larger Vang settlement further east, which had been established ten years earlier by immigrants from Vang and adjoining communities in northern Valdres. Thus, the Veblen family's migration followed a chain of settlements based on common regional and cultural ties where they again could live next to acquaintances from their home area. In addition to the eight children born in Wisconsin, their three youngest children were born on their farm in Rice County.[75]

The prospect of becoming landed cannot be underestimated as a crucial factor behind emigration. We may assume that this was the case with pioneer farmers, Kari and Thomas Veblen, following the mainstream of Norwegian immigrants in forming the most rural ethnic group among all old immigrant groups, i.e. immigrants mainly from Europe before the Civil War. According to the 1900 federal US census, Norwegians were the most rural of any nineteenth-century group with only a little more than a quarter of all Norwegian-born in the United States residing in towns with more than 25,000 inhabitants. It was the lowest percentage for any European immigrant group. Not only did the first-generation Norwegians have a high percentage of farmers: 54.3 per cent of second-generation Norwegians carried on the tradition, more than any other ethnic group.[76]

Cultural Adaptation to a New Environment

Old world traditions were continued in the Veblen family, but their use was altered by their encounter with a new environment. They relaxed the strict naming patterns inherited from Norway, according to which children should be named after their grandparents and their parents in a certain succession, and gave a single name to the majority of their children, especially the eldest ones. Like many pioneer emigrants, they named their children with Norwegian names, although in some cases they ended up Americanising those names. For example, they followed the Norwegian rule in naming their eldest son Anders both after his elder brother Anders, who died in infancy, and indirectly after his paternal grandfather. But they broke the traditional naming custom with the birth of their next child, who was given two Americanised Norwegian names. As the eldest girl, she was to be named Gjertrud after her paternal grandmother in accordance with Norwegian custom, but she was baptised Betsy Jane, an Americanised form suggested by phonetic resemblance or by the initial letter or sound. The next children born to the couple also broke the naming custom; instead of naming the second boy Torsten after his maternal grandfather, the Veblens named him Østen in remembrance of Kari's oldest brother Østen, who had passed away some time before. And the established succession of names was only re-established when the next child was named Tosten.[77] According to Andrew Veblen, the new naming patterns, especially for the girls, were employed for practical reasons, since they were evidence of successful Americanisation. In the case of the Veblen family, Kari consented to the proposal of her Americanised friends of naming the child with American translations of her grandmothers' names Berit and Gjertrud due to the fact that Americanised equivalents of first names had grown to be accepted among Norwegian immigrants.[78]

Building techniques also helped the Veblens navigate between Norwegian traditions and American customs. Thomas Veblen, who was an able carpenter, started to build his three-story dwelling house in Minnesota in a mixture of techniques in 1866. Its style is clearly American on the outside, while its interior room arrangements have Norwegian traits. He also built a flight of outside stairs from the ground up to the second story, which was not uncommon in the Valdres region at the time.[79] Thomas Veblen also introduced novelties on the farm, among others that of a well inside the house to facilitate access to drinking water. Outbuildings, on the other hand, including a combined hay barn and a cow barn and a smaller barn, were built in the American style.[80]

The thrift of Kari and Thomas Veblen placed them among the wealthiest families in their area both in Manitowoc County, Wisconsin and in Rice County, Minnesota. According to the 1870 population census, for example, taken five years after they moved to Minnesota, they owned $8,000 in combined real estate and personal property. This was the second-highest figure in the township and more than twice the average of households listed as owning property. Ten years later, their real estate alone matched an equal sum.[81] Their economic prominence also gave them opportunities that they were deprived of in their home community. Their large farm house displayed their wealth, but their economic resources and their interest in education may explain why they sent their children, including their daughters, to Carleton College. Three of their children, including Emily, Andrew and Thorstein, completed BA degrees at Carleton College and the two latter also completed graduate work. Emily was the first daughter of Norwegian immigrants ever to complete a BA degree in America.[82]

Whereas the Veblens' thrift and hard work resulted in prosperity in the economic sphere, they continued to adhere to Norwegian cultural customs. Kari and Thomas Veblen were members of the Valley Grove Lutheran Church, a Norwegian Lutheran congregation that mainly consisted of immigrants from Vang and the neighbouring regions of Hallingdal and Sogn. Seven of their eight children that married found Norwegian spouses, and all spoke Norwegian in their homes.[83] The Norwegian institutions relating to the intergenerational transfer of land including the *odelsrett*, the *åsetesrett*, and the support agreement with the older generation did not exist in American law. Yet there is reason to believe that the mentalities tied to these traditions were transplanted to American soil and became altered in the process. Norwegian immigrants may have kept the memory of the institution of the *odelsrett*, for example, in order to retain the farm within the family. This may in part explain the longevity of family-run farms among Norwegian immigrants and their offspring as compared to other ethnic groups.[84]

According to the *åsetesrett* or right of primogeniture, sons were usually the favoured heir in Norway, but none of Kari and Thomas's sons ever took over the family farm in Rice County. This is probably due to the fact that they were either pursuing academic careers or had found work elsewhere, a consequence of the rich opportunities found in American society. However, Thomas Veblen kept some of his land in the family as he transferred the western 90 acres of his farm to his third daughter, Mary, and her husband, Ole T. Hougen, who established their home there.[85] When they retired from farming, the strategy of the Veblens again resulted in a compromise between Norwegian and American cultural patterns. In Norway, the retired farm couple usually cohabited with the next generation in the same dwelling house on the farm, even if there were cases in which (when the farm was larger) they lived in a separate house. This institution, transplanted to American soil also by other ethnic groups (not only Norwegians), would gradually disappear under the influence of old-stock Americans, used to moving away from their farm into nearby towns where they could pursue an education for their children or invest their money.[86] Following the sale of their farms, Thomas, Kari and Haldor followed the American pattern of moving to the village of Blooming Prairie about 35 miles south of Nerstrand. Here, Kari and Thomas's son Orson had established a store, lumberyard and residence and was later followed by his brother Edward; consequently, they could live near their offspring in a new location. In accordance with the traits observed among old-stock Americans, they also invested in the village; Thomas purchased six lots in addition to the one on which he had built his house.[87]

Their son Ed moved to Minneapolis with his family in 1902 and Haldor passed away three years later; as a result, Blooming Prairie became less attractive to Kari and Thomas. According to William C. Melton, the irremediable loneliness caused by these incidents and the prospect that no other family members lived close by, made Kari and Thomas move back to Nerstrand in the spring of 1906 where they had built a home for themselves adjacent to their daughter Mary and her family. Thus, the support agreement from Blooming Prairie was replicated, but they now also practiced a transplantation of the Norwegian support agreement which included the residence of several generations on the same farm. Here, Thomas died in August of 1906 and Kari in February of 1907.[88]

The migration and adaptation process in the case of the Veblens may fit Jon Gjerde's assertion that a rural-to-rural migration is both conservative and innovative, wherein original beliefs and traditions are re-elaborated in the process of being transplanted. According to Gjerde, the significance of chain migration has to be considered critically, as we must be aware of the degree to which studies of chain migrations overemphasise the phenomenon of cultural retention. Besides, he asserts, chain migration may occur more frequently in populations with specific traits; for example, among those with ample economic resources and the correlated ability to acquire information.[89]

Ethnicity has become a fundamental concept in recent studies of American immigration. It has been argued that immigrants move from their former immigrant status to become a kind of ethnic Americans and that, in the process of acquiring an 'ethnicity', they reconstruct their identities by incorporating, adapting and amplifying pre-existing cultural traits and memories grounded in the context of real life and social experience. This process of 'ethnicisation' is shaped within a sphere of collective and interactive behaviour in which negotiations take place between immigrants and the dominant ethnoculture.[90] Gjerde argues ethnic groups were central actors in creating complementary identities, especially a national and an ethnic identity which fused multi-level identities in relation to one another. As a result, ethnic groups could retain their loyalty to American society without losing their ethno-cultural traits.[91]

As their way of life was compatible both with an American and a Norwegian regional culture, Kari and Thomas Veblen represented this complementary identity in their life in America; in the economic sphere they were regarded as successful farmers who adapted well to their American environment, but their social and cultural sphere was largely based on Norwegian traditions and the cultivation of kinship networks. We can learn more about the settlement and adaptation process to American society as experienced by the Veblen family by taking into account conditions both in country of origin and settlement. However, Norwegian-American immigration and adaptation to American society must be regarded as a separate process and must therefore be understood on its own terms; the experience of the Veblen family therefore can neither be characterised as Norwegian, nor as American, but as Norwegian-American.

Notes and References

1 Høre (originally Hurum) forms one of three small valley parishes within Vang main parish. See Anders Frøholm, 'Gardar og slekter i Vang. Høre sokn', in 8 vols, ed. by Ivar Aars (Gjøvik: Valdres Bygdeboks forlag, 1991), 1 (part C): 9–16.

2 A decree passed in 1812 instructed pastors to register all individuals who moved in and out of the parish they served, including age, where they came from and their destinations. Beginning in 1820, the pastor was also asked to note the purpose of migration and to mark whether the individual brought along a certificate or not. (Vang Church ministerial records, 1846–1864, the regional historical State Archive at Hamar, Norway). See Terje Mikael Hasle Joranger, 'På flyttefot fra Valdres', *Årbok for Valdres* 76 (1999): 126–31.

3 The couple's infant son died as they were completing their preparations for the journey, postponing their migration until 2 May 1847. According to Vang's ministerial records, Thomas and Kari Veblen's son Anders passed away on 23 April 1847 at the age of one year, and was buried on 26 April (Vang Church ministerial records, 1846–1864).

4 Andrew A. Veblen's notes are based both on his parents' recollections from Norway and from their initial time in America, and remembrances from his own childhood in Wisconsin until the family moved to Minnesota in 1865. Andrew A. Veblen, *The Veblen Family: Immigrant Pioneers from Valdris*, unpublished manuscript, Andrew A. Veblen Papers, Minnesota Historical Society (undated but probably c.1930).

5 The difference in altitude varies from the Otrøvatn located 970 metres, or approximately 2,960 feet, above sea level to the north to Strømmen in Begnadalen located approximately 150 metres, or approximately 460 feet, above sea level. I have employed two sheets from the cartographical series of the Norwegian Mapping Authority, *Topographical map of Hedalen*, M-711 series in M-1:50,000 (1975) sheet 1716 II, and *Topographical map of Vang*, M-711 series in M-1:50,000 (1989), consisting of sheets 1517 Tyin, 1517 II Øye, 1617 I Sikkilsdalen, 1617 II Slidre, 1617 III Vangsmjøsi, and 1617 Gjende. The latter, which offers a survey of the municipality of Vang, is an enclosure that formed part of A. Frøholm, 'Gardar og slekter i Vang', in id. *Valdres Bygdebok*, vol. 1 (part C). See also Amund Helland, 'Topografisk-statistisk Beskrivelse over Kristians Amt', in *Norges Land og Folk*, 20 vols (Kristiania: Aschehoug, 1913), 5 (part 1): 291–2.

6 I have based the number on the Norwegian Mapping Authority's statement (2003) that the six municipalities in Valdres cover a surface area of 5,409 square kilometres. The total surface area is stated differently in various sources. According to the 1891 census, the Valdres region had a total surface area of 5,438.7 square kilometres, whereas the *Norsk Allkunnebok* states the surface area as 5431.2 square kilometres. The difference between the various sources may be attributed to a lower degree of accuracy on the old topographical maps and the method used to measure the surface area in the region. According to the 1907 agricultural census, around 20 per cent of the area was forested, the rest consisting of outfields, marshes, mountains and lakes. Helland, 'Topografisk-statistisk Beskrivelse', 469, 476; *Norges Offisielle Statistikk*, no. 202 (1894): 22–3. See also *Norsk Allkunnebok* 4 (1952): 76–7, 8 (1957): 999–1001; *Norsk Allkunnebok* 10 (1966): 508–9, 960, 1061, 1314–15.

7 The elevation is equivalent to around 600 to 1,500 feet above sea level. I use the term municipality to describe the present-day local administrative unit in the region, in Norwegian named *kommune*. However, in this chapter, which relates to Valdres until 1900, I use the term 'administrative township' to describe the basic civil administrative unit. In most cases, this unit coincided with the ecclesiastical parish unit, which in its turn was subdivided into smaller parts (valley parishes). For a similar use of the term valley parish, see Orm Øverland, 'Letters as Links in the Chain of Migration from Hedalen, Norway to Dane County, WI, 1857–1890', in *Interpreting the Promise of America. Essays in Honor of Odd Sverre Lovoll*, ed. by Todd W. Nichol (Northfield: The Norwegian-American Historical Association, 2002), 79–103. See also Eirik Fossbråten, 'Jordbruk, jordbruksreiskap og hagebruk', in id. *Valdres Bygdebok*, 5 (part 2): 246–304, esp. 247; Jens Kraft, *Historisk-topographisk Haandbog over Kongeriget Norge* (Kristiania: Dybwad, 1845–48), 197–199; Nils Ödegaard, *Kristians Amt 1814–1914: en kort oversigt* (Kristiania: Grøndahl & Søn, 1918), 19–31.

8 Anders Frøholm, 'Valdres politiske, kyrkjelege, sosiale og økonomiske soge', in *Valdres Bygdebok*, ed. by P. Lillebrænd (1972), 3 (part 1): 17–21.

9 Around 1800, the region was divided in three *tinglag*, which were separate geographical areas with territorial jurisdiction where local affairs were settled and that were identical to the local sheriff districts. Through the passing of the local government acts in 1837, the parishes were given more autonomy in civil-administrative affairs. In 1863, the boundaries were identical to the newly created administrative unit *herred*, from 1918 using the name *kommune*. Since 1894, the Valdres region has consisted of six *kommuner*. See Harald Hvattum, 'Framgang, oppbrot og motstraumar. Valdresbygdene si historie 1800–1914', in id. *Valdres Bygdebok*, 3 (part 2): 349–50, 383; *Aschehoug og Gyldendals Store Norske Leksikon*, 5 vols (Oslo: Kunnskapsforlaget, 1979), 653.

10 Population growth in the first half of the nineteenth century led to the division of Aurdal parish in 1805 to form the parishes of Nord-Aurdal and Sør-Aurdal, while Slidre in 1848 was divided into Øystre Slidre and Vestre Slidre. See Hvattum, 'Valdresbygdene si historie 1800–1914', 343–5.

11 The farm's name in Høre is spelled Veflen, but it is pronounced Vøvle in the Valdres dialect. It has had different spellings since its first mention in the fifteenth century, including 'i Viflini' about 1400, 'Weffle' in 1578, Wefflen in 1664, 1677, 1723, 1761, and 1782, Væblen in 1780, and Veflen since the mid-nineteenth century. 'Veblen' was therefore the official name recognised by administrators from the early nineteenth century to around the middle of the century. And this is the reason why the Veblens (Thorstein's parents) spelled their name with a 'b' instead of an 'f'. The Veflen farm ranks among the oldest farms in Høre, and it has existed as a separate farm since well before the Viking Period (c. 800–1050 AD). According to the linguist Olaf Rygh the meaning of the farm name is a compound of an insect, '*vifill*', a word no longer found in Old Norse, except in the compound '*tordyfill*', a scarab (beetle), and '*vin*' which means a meadow or pasture. The name '*vin*' is used in Norwegian farm names that originate in the sixth or seventh centuries AD, whereas '*vifill*' is found in other Germanic languages including Swedish and Anglo-Saxon. According to Andrew A. Veblen, the first derivation of the name

Veflen came from the Old Norse or Icelandic, 'vifl', which is a beating cudgel used in beating clothes when washing them. It was fancied that the shape of the land had some resemblance to a '*vifl*' in outline or contour, but this explanation does not find support among scholars. In spite of several explanations, it remains unclear if there is a link between these characteristics and the farm's name. See Frøholm, 'Gardar og slekter i Vang. Høre sokn', 10, 199; Andrew Veblen, *The Name Veblen*, undated manuscript in the collection of Andrew A. Veblen's papers at the Minnesota Historical Society, St. Paul, MN.

12 For a useful introduction to pre-industrial farming practices in traditional Norwegian peasant society, see for example Kristoffer Visted and Hilmar Stigum, *Vår gamle bondekultur* (Oslo: Cappelen, 1975); Helland, 'Topografisk-statistisk Beskrivelse', 496; Jens Kraft, *Topographisk-statistisk Beskrivelse over Kongeriget Norge: Christians-, Buskeruds-, Jarlsberg og Laurvigs Amt, Det søndenfjeldske Norge / Topographisk-Statistisk Beskrivelse over Kongeriget Norge/* 4 vols (Kristiania, 1840), 69.

13 Rigmor Frimannslund, 'Farm Community and Neighborhood Community', *Scandinavian Economic History Review* 4.1 (1956): 62–81, esp. 64, 70–73; Andreas Holmsen, 'Det gamle gards-og grannesamfunnet i Norge', in *Gard, Bygd, Rike. Festskrift i anledning Andreas Holmsens 60 års dag 5 juni 1966*, ed. by Bjørkvik et al. (Oslo: Universitetsforlaget, 1966), 104–5; Knut Hermundstad, *Samversskikkar i Valdres* (Oslo: A. S. Norbok, 1975), 9–11.

14 Kraft, *Det søndenfjeldske Norge*, 69. This is in line with Kåre Lunden's thesis, according to which Norwegian peasant society was based not upon the neighbourhood, but upon an even smaller unit, the farm. See Kåre Lunden, *Norges landbrukshistorie 1350–1814: Frå svartedauden til 17. Mai*, in *Norges landbrukshistorie*, 4 vols (Oslo: Det norske Samlaget, 2002), 2:366.

15 Although inferior to the rolling lowlands further east, the soil in Valdres is relatively fertile and gives good crops depending upon the conditions of the subsoil. The slopes facing west and south were the most settled. A monetarised economy also existed among those engaged in cattle trades, those who paid taxes and other charges, and in relation to the distribution of a deceased person's estate to his or her heirs. Helland, 'Topografisk-statistisk Beskrivelse', 434; N. Ödegaard, *Kristians Amt*, 19–31, 263–4; P. Lillebrænd, 'Valdres frå geologisk synsstad', in id. *Valdres Bygdebok*, 2:53–104, esp. 61–86; Knut Ødegård, 'Skogen og skogbruket i Valdres', in id. *Valdres Bygdebok*, 5 (part 2): 308–78; Geir Beitrusten, 'Mot ei ny tid', *Tidsskrift for Valdres Historielag* 56 (1979): 5–21.

16 According to Ola Knutson Ødegaard, a small community of Quaker sympathisers was said to live in Vang in the mid-1840s. See Ødegaard, *Gamalt fraa Valdres*, 3 vols (Fagernes: Valdres Historielag, 1997), 1:104–117; Ole Larsen Kirkeberg, *Minder fra Valdres* [1919] (Bagn: Østfold Trykkeri AS, 1993), 141–57; Knut Odner, *Thorstein Veblen: Forstyrreren av den intellektuelle fred* (Oslo: Abstrakt Forlag, 2005), 95–7.

17 Class distinction was at its highest in Nord-Aurdal, an administrative centre and residence of several upper class families. Cotton was regarded as luxury when woollen clothing became common in Aurdal around 1822. Eilert Sundt, *Husfliden i Norge*, 79–86. Online: http://www.rhd. uit.no/sundt/bind8/eilert_sundt_bd8.html (accessed 2 December 2009); Torstein Høverstad, 'Folket i Valdres', in id. *Valdres Bygdebok*, 2:368–396, esp. 390; Helland, 'Topografisk-statistisk Beskrivelse', 204–6, 353, 359.

18 Until the passing of the law of inheritance of 1854, which put daughters on equal terms with their brothers, a woman was only entitled to her parents' lands as part of an eventual dowry when she was to be married. See Rigmor Frimannslund, 'Søstre fra Middelalderen og ny tid', *Tradisjon* 14 (1984): 74–8; Steinar Imsen and Harald Winge, *Norsk Historisk Leksikon: Kultur og Samfunn ca. 1500–ca. 1800* (Oslo: Cappelen Akademisk Forlag, 1999), 26–7, 490.

19 Holmsen, 'Det gamle gards-og grannesamfunnet', 98–9.

20 Gunnlaug Daugstad, 'Slektskap og jord på gårdsbruk i ei vestnorsk bygd', in *Blod – tykkere enn vann? Betydninger av slektskap i Norge*, ed. by Signe Howell and Marit Melhuus (Bergen: Fagbokforlaget, 2001), 143–63, esp. 159–61.

21 Holmsen, 'Det gamle gards-og grannesamfunnet', 98–9.

22 The time of redemption is defined as the period within which an heir was entitled to repurchase family property that had been sold to non-kin. The time of prescription is defined as the time needed for the buyer of a property subject to the *odelsrett* and his direct heirs to establish the *odelsrett*. Jon Skeie, *Odelsretten og åsetesretten* (Oslo: Gyldendal, 1950), 7–17; *Norsk Historisk Leksikon*, 300; Per H. Norseng, 'Odelsrett – the Norwegian retrait lignager' in *Land, Lords and Peasants, Peasants' Rights to Control Land in the Middle Ages and the Early Modern Period – Norway, Scandinavia and the Alpine Region*, ed. by Tore Iversen and John Ragnar Myking (Trondheim: Department of History and Classical Studies, Norwegian University of Science and Technology, 2005), 201–27, esp. 202–5.

23 Norseng, 'Odelsrett – the Norwegian retrait lignager', 218–19.

24 More precisely, the *åsetesrett* is the right of a living heir to assume the undivided ownership of landed property in cases where a deceased leaves agricultural property, and can only be claimed at the distribution of the deceased person's estate. The general principle introduced in King Magnus the Lawmaker's national code was equal distribution between the children of the deceased, although daughters received only half the share of their brothers. The placing of male heirs before female heirs was characteristic of the western Nordic law of inheritance. See *Norsk Historisk Leksikon*, 26–7, 490.

25 The Norwegian Constitution of 17 May 1814 § 107, Act of 26 June 1821.

26 Norseng, 'Odelsrett – the Norwegian retrait lignager', 202.

27 Ideal supporting institutions are always tied to an agricultural unit and thus were not only applicable for freeholds, but also had validity for tenant farms and crofts as well. Kjeld Helland-Hansen, 'Føderådsordningens historie i Norge', in *Riksarkivarens skriftserie*, 31 vols, CD-ROM edition (Oslo: Riksarkivet, 1997), 3:3–4; Frimannslund, 'Farm Community and Neighborhood Community', 67; Holmsen, 'Det gamle gards-og grannesamfunnet', 98–9.

28 *Norsk Historisk Leksikon*, 179.

29 In the eighteenth and the nineteenth centuries a large portion of crown lands and land owned by the clergy were put on the market, further speeding along the transition to freeholding in the Valdres region, especially in Sør-Aurdal and Vang, where there were relatively many such estates. The change was especially spurred on by the passing of a law legitimising the sale of clerical estates in 1821. Clerical farm properties included both parsonages and residences for pastors' widows in every parish. The upper Veflen farm, for example, where Thomas Veblen was raised, had been set aside as a residence for pastors' widows, but was rented out to tenant farmers until it was sold in 1854. See Frøholm, 'Valdres politiske, kyrkjelege, sosiale og økonomiske soge', 159–87; Frøholm, 'Gardar og slekter i Vang. Høre sokn', 222–6; Hvattum, 'Valdresbygdene si historie 1800–1914', 238–42; *Norsk Historisk Leksikon*, 13–15, 149, 52, 256, 322.

30 We must remember that freehold land did not necessarily mean that entire farm units were owned by the person who farmed the land. In most cases, assessed farms had more than one owner and were divided into portions accordingly; the king; a local church; a central church; private proprietors, such as noblemen, officials, merchants, or wealthy freeholders; or the local pastoral office owned parts of farms in the Valdres region. See Ståle Dyrvik, 'Jordbruk og Folketal 1500–1720', in *Norsk Økonomisk Historie 1500–1970*, ed. by Ståle Dyrvik et al. (Bergen: Universitetsforlaget, 1979), 16–33, esp. 32.

31 Andris Veblen purchased the Jome farm in Vestre Slidre. Notes written down from dictation by Andrew A. Veblen in connection with an interview with his father Thomas A. Veblen in Iowa City, Iowa, summer of 1895, manuscript in the collection of Andrew A. Veblen's papers at the Minnesota Historical Society, St. Paul, MN, 4–6; Frøholm, 'Gardar og slekter i Vang. Høre sokn', 226.

32 When the family moved to Biri, Torstein's daughter Kari Bunde remained in Høre. Notes from Andrew A. Veblen interview with Thomas A. Veblen, 9–10; Frøholm, 'Gardar og slekter i Vang. Høre sokn', 181–2.

33 Outcasts among ancestors usually were not named. See Eli Fure, 'Oppkalling og familiementalitet', *Historisk Tidsskrift* 69.2 (1990): 146–62, esp. 148–9, 155; Frøholm, 'Valdres politiske, kyrkjelege, sosiale og økonomiske soge', 359; Knut Hermundstad, *Ættarminne: Gamal Valdres-kultur part V*, in *Norsk Folkeminnelag*, 162 vols (Oslo: Norsk Folkeminnelag, 1952), 70:22.

34 Frøholm, 'Gardar og slekter i Vang. Høre sokn': 181–2, 226, 325.

35 Frøholm, 'Valdres politiske': 326; Hvattum, 'Valdresbygdene si historie 1800–1914', 250–51, 270.

36 The class of officials around 1800 consisted of people tied to the families of the notary public, pastors and military chiefs. Their numbers totalled 36, or 0.2 per cent of the total Valdres population, both according to the 1801 and the 1900 census. Civil officials, the local district court judge, or the *sorenskriver*, and also the bailiff and the leaders of the military company all had their designated farms, most of which were located in the Aurdal parish in Nord-Aurdal. See Hvattum 'Valdresbygdene si historie 1800–1914', 226–31; Frøholm, 'Gardar og slekter', 222–6.

37 The period 1903–7 is missing in the statistical material. Hvattum, 'Valdresbygdene si historie 1800–1914', 313.

38 In 1922 church historian O. M. Norlie estimated that a total of 21,445 people emigrated between 1820 and 1920, making up three percent of the total number of Norwegians in America by 1920. Andrew A. Veblen, the founder of the *bygdelag* movement in America, suggested that 17,000 people left the Valdres region for America, 11,874 of whom emigrated in the forty-year period 1865–1905. A third estimate was given by teacher and local historian Olaus Islandsmoen in Valdres, who calculated that 15,018 emigrants left the region in the same time period. See Anders M. Sundheim, *Valdreser i Amerika, Aarbok 1922* (Minneapolis: Augsburg Publishing House, 1922), 23–9; Carl and Amy Narvestad, V*aldres Samband 1899–1974: A History of the Oldest Norwegian Bygdelag in America* (Granite Falls: Valdres Samband, 1974), 35–6.

39 Heavy emigration has been explained as the main factor behind the fact that the Valdres population only grew by three percent during the period 1845–55 and even decreased during the following ten-year period. Norges Offisielle Statistikk, *Utvandringsstatistikk* no. 7: 25 (Kristiania: H. Aschehoug & Co., 1921), 28–32; Amund Helland, 'Topografisk-statistisk Beskrivelse over Kristians Amt', in id. *Norges Land og Folk*, 5 (part 4): 308.

40 Historians have traditionally made recourse to 'push' and 'pull' factors to explain the dynamics of migration. However, since the two terms may be criticised for being too impersonal, rigid, and simplistic to explain the complexity of migratory phenomena. I propose to focus on the individual *perception* of the process of migration, and employ the terms 'basic' and 'psychological' to explore the emigrant's subjective experience.

41 Frøholm, 'Gardar og slekter i Vang. Høre sokn', 17, Table 1.

42 Crofters made up 17.5 per cent of the population in the community in 1801, but the number increased to 27.9 per cent in 1855. The joint number of subdivided farm units and crofts between 1801 and 1865 increased from 67 to 100, showing an increase of 33 per cent which almost matched the population increase, but the number of units remained stable following the decrease of the population after 1865. Frøholm, 'Gardar og slekter i Vang. Høre sokn', 17–18, Tables 2, 4.

43 Frøholm, 'Gardar og slekter i Vang. Høre sokn', 232.

44 In Vik parish in the region of Sogn, the class of freeholders made up the majority of all emigrants between 1839 and 1964. If we recalculate the numbers taking into account the gradual reduction of the crofter class, freeholders still made up a majority of all emigrants in the period 1839–1909, both in relative and absolute numbers, except the decade 1860–69, when the crofter class was the most numerous. Among emigrants from Tinn parish between 1837 and 1907, more than 40 per cent belonged to the freeholding class, mostly consisting of sons and daughters of freeholders. The same results can be found among emigrants from the rural community of Ullensaker. See Jon Gjerde, *From Peasants to Farmers: The Migration from Balestrand*

to the Upper Middle West (Cambridge: Cambridge University Press, 1989), 8, 121–4; Arnfinn Engen and Elisabeth Koren, 'Masseutvandringa frå Austlandet etter 1865', in *Utvandringa – det store oppbrotet*, ed. by Arnfinn Engen (Oslo: Det norske samlaget, 1978), 86–107, esp. 104–5; Rasmus Sunde, *Vikjer ved fjorden-vikjer på prærien, Ein demografisk komparativ studie med utgangspunkt i Vik i Sogn* (PhD dissertation, University of Bergen, 2000), 76–81; Andres A. Svalestuen, *Tinns emigrasjonshistorie 1837–1907* (Oslo: Universitetsforlaget, 1972), 125–8.

45 Helland, 'Topografisk-statistisk Beskrivelse', 310.

46 Ingrid Semmingsen, 'Amerikaferd', in *Utvandringa*, 11–19, esp. 12; Robert C. Ostergren, *A Community Transplanted. The Trans-Atlantic Experience of a Swedish Immigrant Settlement in the Upper Middle West, 1835–1915* (Madison: University of Wisconsin Press, 1988), 124.

47 Helland, 'Topografisk-statistisk Beskrivelse', 305.

48 Semmingsen, 'Amerikaferd', 16.

49 According to local ministerial records in the Valdres region only 14 people had been officially registered as emigrants by 1845, but the listings are inaccurate and the exact number of emigrants is therefore not known. Twelve individuals are said to have emigrated from Nord-Aurdal as early as in 1837, but for whatever reason several of the emigrants never got any further than Lærdal in Sogn on their way to Bergen. The only person that supposedly has emigrated, Anders ved Leira, probably lived in Cincinnati, Ohio in the 1830s. See Gerhard B. Naeseth, *Norwegian immigrants to the United States: A Biographical Directory, 1825–1850* (Madison, WI, 1993), 47; A. Veblen, *Veblen Family*, 1; Terje Mikael Hasle Joranger, 'Valdrisbygder i vesterled. Utvandringen fra Valdres til Amerika', *Årbok for Valdres* 76 (1999): 15–37, esp. 21–2.

50 Terje Mikael Hasle Joranger, 'Emigration from Reinli, Valdres to the upper Midwest: A Comparative Study', *Norwegian-American Studies* 35 (2000): 153–96, esp. 168–70.

51 'Kubakke' (Cow Hill) is a nickname that refers to his farm unit, which forms part of the larger Helle farm.

52 A. Veblen, *Veblen Family*, 2; Hjalmar Rued Holand, *De Norske Settlementers Historie* (Ephraim, WI, 1908), 177–8.

53 A. Veblen, *Veblen Family*: 6; Holand, *Historie*, 215.

54 Steffen Olsen Helle also returned to Norway in 1851 and re-emigrated the following year with 134 people from the Valdres region. However, the members of this emigrant party were to experience one of the most tragic incidents in the history of Norwegian emigration history when the ship that transported them on Lake Erie, the steamer *Atlantic*, sank following a collision with the steamer *Ogdenburg* of the rival line; 68 of Stephen's company lost their lives, whereas 66 were saved. A. Veblen, *Veblen Family*, 38–9; Holand, *Historie*, 215–16.

55 Holand states that Stephen Olson's return to his home community was met with respect and curiosity due to his accomplishment crossing the dangers of the Atlantic Ocean twice. Holand, *Historie*, 215–16; A. Veblen, *Veblen Family*, 6, 38.

56 Frank Thistlethwaite, 'Migration from Europe Overseas in the Nineteenth and Twentieth Centuries', in *XIe Congrès International des Sciences Historiques* [1960], in *A Century of European Migrations*, ed. by Rudolph J. Vecoli and Suzanne M. Sinke (Urbana: University of Illinois Press, 1991): 17–33.

57 In Illinois Norwegians established their first settlement at Fox River in LaSalle County west of Chicago in 1834. See Odd S. Lovoll, *Det løfterike landet. En norskamerikansk historie* (Oslo: Universitetsforlaget, 1997), 42–50.

58 A. Veblen, *Veblen Family*, 4.

59 According to the principles of the pre-emption act of 1841, they could hold it for Stephen, who held title to the land. Kari and Thomas Veblen made their home there while Stephen made a trip back to Valdres in 1847–1848. As a compensation for their help to Stephen, they were to receive thirty dollars. The Veblens moved off the land when Stephen's brother Ole Helle refused to pay the compensation Thomas was to receive. See also A. Veblen, *Veblen Family*, 5–6.

60 A. Veblen, *Veblen Family*, 8–13.

61 William C. Melton, 'Ideal Immigrants: Thomas, Kari, and Haldor Veblen', paper presented at 'Vandringer: Norwegians in the American Mosaic 1825–2000', at the Minnesota History Center, St. Paul, MN, 6–8 April 2000, 1–38, esp. 15.

62 A. Veblen, *Veblen Family*, 16,

63 Ibid., 23–5, 33–4, 36, Melton, 'Ideal Immigrants', 18.

64 A. Veblen, *Veblen Family*, 21.

65 Ibid., 22.

66 Ibid., 22.

67 The regional background of these groups in Norway was transplanted to the American scene through the naming of the 'Valders' and 'Gjerpen' settlement areas and the first country congregations in Manitowoc County; A. Veblen, *Veblen Family*, 23, 39; Robert A. Bjerke, *Manitowoc-skogen: A Biographical and Genealogical Directory of the Residents of Norwegian Birth and Descent in Manitowoc and Kewaunee Counties in Wisconsin from the First Settlement to 1900* (Manitowoc: Dobbs, 1994), v; Holand, *Historie*, 215–28.

68 Friedrich Heckmann, *Etnische Minderheiten, Volk und Nation. Soziologie inter-ethnischer Beziehungen* (Stuttgart: Ferdinand Enke, 1992), 99; my translation.

69 Jon Gjerde, 'Following the Chain: New Insights into Migration', *Immigration and Ethnic History Newsletter* 33.1 (2001): 1–8, esp. 1.

70 Walter D. Kamphoefner, *The Westfalians: From Germany to Missouri* (Princeton: Princeton University Press, 1987), 71.

71 Marcus Lee Hansen, *The Immigrant in American History* (Cambridge, MA: Harvard University Press, 1940), 68–73. An early documentation of the process of chain migration is also documented in William I. Thomas and Florian Znaniecki, *The Polish Peasant in Europe and America* (New York: Dover Publications, 1958).

72 Those who displayed a stable residential pattern within the confines of a moving community could reach economic and social advantages. I have found some examples of theological inclinations affecting the choice of settlement in America, but not to such a significant degree as in Gjerde's and Kamphoefner's studies. See Gjerde, *From Peasants to Farmers* and Kamphoefner, *The Westfalians*.

73 A. Veblen, *Veblen Family*, 7, 21.

74 The 200 acres consisted of uncultivated land, but the additional 90 acres consisted of a farm of which half the acreage was made up of woodland that served as a source for building purposes, and it also had several acres under cultivation. They also had shelter during their initial stay on the farm as a log cabin and a stable were located on the 90-acre farm. See Melton, 'Ideal Immigrants', 24–5.

75 Carl and Amy Narvestad, *Valdres Samband 1899–1974: A History of the Oldest Norwegian Bygdelag in America* (Granite Falls: Valdres Samband, 1974), 123–8, Old Valley Grove ministerial church records, 1867–92, in archives of the Norwegian-American Historical Association, Northfield, MN.

76 The percentages are 44 per cent for the second-generation Danes, 32.6 per cent for the Swedes and only 28 per cent for German children of immigrants. Ten years later, in 1910, still only 42 per cent of first- and second-generation Norwegians were urbanised, which means that they lived in towns with 2,500 or more inhabitants. See Odd S. Lovoll, *Innfridde løfter: et norskamerikansk samtidsbilde* (Nesbru: Vett & Viten, 1999), 14.

77 A. Veblen, *Veblen Family*, 50.

78 Ibid., 49–50.

79 Terje Mikael Hasle Joranger, 'Veblen-familien og Amerika', *Valdres*, 10 November 1995.

80 Terje Mikael Hasle Joranger, interview with John Poling, Nerstrand, October 1995. See also William C. Melton, 'Thorstein Veblen and the Veblens', *Norwegian-American Studies* 34 (1995): 23–56.

81 Melton, 'Ideal Immigrants', 20, 29.

82 Ibid., 29–30.

83 Orson Veblen's second wife, Florence Andrus Noble, probably was not Norwegian, and this was also the case with both of Thorstein Bunde Veblen's wives. See *Genealogy of the Veblen and Bonde families*, unprinted genealogical material concerning the Veblen and Bonde families gathered by Helen Bonde Lodmill of Seattle, Washington, a great-niece of Thorstein Veblen.

84 Terje Mikael Hasle Joranger: *The Migration of Tradition? A Study on the Transfer of Traditions Tied to Intergenerational Land Transfers among Emigrants from the Valdres Region, Norway to the Upper Midwest and their Descendants for Three Generations, 1850–1980* (PhD dissertation, University of Oslo, 2008).

85 The 90 acres were sold in two transactions; one on 12 December 1887 and the second on 29 May 1893. The remaining 200 acres were sold to George H. Rauk, to whom they were related by marriage. Melton, 'Ideal Immigrants', 31.

86 Jon Gjerde, *The Minds of the West, Ethnocultural Evolution in the Rural Middle West, 1830–1917* (Chapel Hill: University of North Carolina Press, 1997), 199–200; John C. Hudson, 'The Creation of Towns in Wisconsin', in *Wisconsin Land and Life*, ed. by Robert C. Ostergren and Robert Vale (Madison: University of Wisconsin Press, 1997), 202–18. For example, both Belgian and Bohemian immigrants in the lakeshore counties of Door, Kewaunee and Manitowoc counties cared for the aged in their own homes instead of moving to town; there it was common that parents spent their old age in helping with chores and working the garden. See Fred L. Holmes, *Old World Wisconsin: Around Europe in the Badger State* (Madison: Wisconsin House, Ltd. Book Publishers, 1974), 167–70; Joranger, *The Migration of Tradition?*, 275–89.

87 Melton, 'Ideal Immigrants', 31–2.

88 Melton, Ibid., 32.

89 Gjerde, 'Following the Chain', 8.

90 Kathleen Neils Conzen, David A. Gerber, Ewa Morawska, George E. Pozzetta and Rudolph J. Vecoli, 'The Invention of Ethnicity: A Perspective from the U.S.A.', *Journal of American Ethnic History* 12.1 (1992): 3–41, esp. 4–5, 31–32; Lovoll, *Innfridde løfter*, 35–6.

91 Complementary identity, as defined by Gjerde, is a 'merged allegiance both to national and ethnic group in a self-enforcing dynamic that embedded pluralism into the national fabric as immigrants'. See Conzen et al., 'The Invention of Ethnicity', 4–5, 31–2; Gjerde, 'Boundaries and linkages: Norwegian Immigrants, the United States, and Norway', in *Interpreting the Promise of America. Essays in Honor of Odd Sverre Lovoll*, ed. by Todd W. Nichol (Northfield: The Norwegian-American Historical Association, 2002), 13–29, esp. 18.

Chapter 5

NEW PERSPECTIVES ON THORSTEIN VEBLEN, THE NORWEGIAN

Knut Odner

Although Thorstein Veblen has been recognised by former president Bill Clinton in a presidential address to King Harald of Norway as a great American thinker of Norwegian descent, it is nevertheless a sad fact that he is poorly known in Norway.[1] Most Norwegian scholars ignore Veblen, while Veblen scholars around the world often attribute to Veblen a Norwegian identity he really did not have. Like the Roman scholars who used to attribute certain virtues to almost unknown Germanic tribes in order to contrast them with the debased behaviour of their fellow Romans, Veblen scholars have showed a tendency to insist on certain virtues of the Norwegian peasants in order to stress the corruption of their own society.[2] Some examples will suffice to show that Norwegian peasants did not always live up to such expectations. Folklorist O. K. Ødegaard recalls that Tørkjel Tøpp, Veblen's paternal granduncle, had no mind for working, but he was tremendously talented playing the 'Jew's harp' and at skiing.[3] Accordingly, Tørkjel in the summertime charmed the milk maids on the out farms by playing Jew's harp and received dairy products in return; in wintertime he would ski around to his more provident fellow parishioners to beg for food in order to feed his rapidly growing family. Out of necessity most Norwegian peasants worked hard, but their famous fiddle playing, which great composers like Ole Bull and Edvard Grieg so much admired, shows that they also had time for leisure activities. In this chapter, I seek to navigate the different paths of Vebleniana in order to demonstrate that Norwegian social and historical experiences mattered for Veblen, but only insofar as they allowed him to better understand the great mechanisms of the world institutional history. In other words, as much as he was conditioned by Norwegian values, Veblen would never renounce his 'marginal' identity, of which he was proud.

Veblen's Contact with Norway

Apart from two short visits in 1899 and 1914, Veblen had no direct contact with Norway. Still, nearly all his biographers emphasise his 'Norwegianness',[4] and none of them investigate Veblen's Norwegian identity and reconstruct how it was formed. With the proviso that Veblen learned his Norwegian (which he could speak and write fluently) from conversing with his parents and reading Norwegian-language novels and newspapers published in America, his knowledge seems mainly to have been derived from encounters with Norwegians in America. Drawing on my own experience as a labourer in Canada in my youth, I know that Norwegians abroad often seek each other's company, and in so doing they develop forms of knowledge different from those of the encompassing society. Thus, I suggest that throughout his life Veblen familiarised himself with Norwegian culture through such encounters with fellow Norwegians. With his academic education and his quizzical mentality and radical leanings he is bound to have been eclectic, singling out specific Norwegian personalities or environments as his target. Here I trace his encounters with those Norwegians who I think had the greatest influence on his intellectual development.

As we know, Veblen's parents were of Norwegian extraction and he grew up in a Norwegian environment. It is usually assumed that notions of hard work and frugality that are significant in Veblen's evolutionary theory have their origins in his parents' *oikos*. This is probably true, but there are reasons to suspect that the Veblens remained attached to habits of thought and traditional behaviours originating in their country. We know for certain that the Veblen family kept its links with Norway after moving to America. Veblen's father spoke freely of his Norwegian experiences in the family circle, and these experiences were not limited to his home community of Valdres. As a peddler and labourer in his twenties, he travelled widely both in the western and eastern part of Southern Norway. Being a keen observer, we may assume that he shared with his family the comparisons among the habits then prevalent in different Norwegian districts. And certainly these comparisons left their marks in some of Veblen's writings. Neither must we underestimate the impact of Thorstein's extended family relations on his writings. As a child, Kari, Thorstein's mother, had stayed for a while in the fertile districts west of Lake Mjøsa before sailing to America, from where she must have brought some recollections. Her memories and those of her husband were furthermore kept alive after their arrival in America, by their habit of hosting Norwegian immigrants, often for long periods, on their farm.[5] Most of their guests probably came from their home community in northern Valdres, but there were also representatives from west, east and south Valdres, occasionally also from other parts of the country. Together with their guests, the Veblens would gather around the fireplace in the evenings and listen to the news from home, compare the respective recollections and also tell stories gathered while travelling in Norway and Sweden. These fireside chats would have provided the background of Veblen's first encounter with Norway, which he must have seen through the lens of his parents and their fellow Norwegians.

Veblen's second, more articulated encounter with Norway took place later, in 1880, when he taught mathematics at the Monona Academy in Madison, Wisconsin. There he came in contact with Rasmus Anderson, the son of an early Norwegian immigrant who taught Norwegian studies at the University of Wisconsin and was known for cultivating a selected circle of Norwegian friendships. He was the impresario of the writer Bjørnstjerne Bjørnson on his stormy lecture tour through the Midwest in 1880, and two years later he persuaded a brilliant young author who happened to live in Wisconsin to change his name from Knud Pedersen to Knut Hamsun. He corresponded at length with these authors, as well as with the author Jonas Lie, influential Danish literary critic Georg

Brandes and even female vaudevillian singer Botten Soot, the idol of the Christiania 'merry society' around 1900.

When Anderson met Henrik Ibsen in Copenhagen, Ibsen embraced him and lavished upon him cigars and wine.[6] We do not know how Veblen first reacted to the encounter with Anderson, but they soon became great friends, and it was Anderson who persuaded Veblen to translate Icelandic sagas into English. It is likely no coincidence that some years after his stay at Madison, Veblen was able to discuss Norwegian literature, language and politics with a recent arrival from Norway.[7] In 1890, he addressed Anderson as 'his dear friend', and in 1898 sent him a copy of his first book, *The Theory of the Leisure Class*.[8]

It is impossible to trace all of Veblen's links with the Norwegian community of America. We know that in 1919 he was in contact with the former Norwegian socialist politician Charles E. Stangeland, who at that time worked for the radical National Nonpartisan League in St. Paul, Minnesota.[9] And he might as well have met Marcus Thrane, a Norwegian who lived in America for nearly 30 years, and was the legendary leader of the largest socialist movement in mid-nineteenth century in Europe in relation to the country's population size.

Tracing Veblen's Scandinavian Concerns in his Intellectual Biography

In his 1990 article, Jonathan Schwartz claims that the source of Veblen's 'instinct of workmanship' was his imagination of an innately peaceful Nordic value system, since the instinct was already present in the Baltic early Neolithic culture ('kitchen middens'). In Schwartz's view, Veblen was a romantic immigrant who breathed into the flintstones a spirit of his own homesickness.[10] That the source of Veblen's idyllic value system was his own yearning for a primordial identity is difficult to reconcile with Veblen's own ideal of the researcher as an emancipated Jew, who has abandoned the 'clay vessels' of his own culture without adopting the 'iron pots' of the new one. As it is likely that Veblen transplanted his own marginal identity onto that of the Jew, it is unlikely that he longed for a Norwegian identity. Moreover in Veblen's evolutionary scheme, any 'savage' society, not only a Scandinavian one, was peaceful irrespective of whether they were 'digger Indians' in California, Aleutians in Alaska or shell gatherers on the Baltic shores around 5000 BC. In the introduction to his translation of *Laxdæla Saga*, Veblen himself traces back to the Vikings' raids the origins of the contemporary 'enterprise in getting something for nothing by force and fraud at the cost of the party of the second part.'[11]

All through his academic career Veblen was interested in Scandinavian history, and tried to cover its entirety. He frequented the Scandinavian national museums, and at one stage in his life he wanted to do archaeological comparative research on Scandinavian and Aegean antiquities during the Late Bronze Age (1000–500 BC).[12] His main interest was, however, the Viking period (800–1000 AD) and the Early Middle Ages (1000–1300 AD), particularly as he visualises these periods through Icelandic family sagas. His conviction was that, in addition to their literary peculiarities, the sagas could be understood as sociological documents that shed light on the Lower Barbaric Stage and, more in general, on the development of the Norse nearly egalitarian society of the early Viking Period to the oppressive feudal system 300–400 years later. The sagas are therefore intellectual instruments through which to prove the blind evolution of institutions which, in Veblen's view, characterises the whole history of humanity, and not (as suggested by Schwartz) the literary *locus* of Veblen's nostalgias.

The Nature of Veblen's Norwegian Influences

Norwegian culture may have influenced Veblen in at least two ways: through impulses that create certain basic human values and through concrete historical examples that may have inspired his theoretical categories. According to Douglas Dowd, a good society was, for Veblen, democratic, peaceable, efficient, just and scientific; a bad society, on the contrary, was dominated by tyranny, conformity, patriotism, supernaturalism, privilege, force and fraud.[13] As I will show later, part of this dichotomised framework was inspired by certain political and religious dissent movements that troubled Norwegian society during the nineteenth century. As for the second category, we already know that Veblen had the habit of drawing on his personal experiences to illustrate his theoretical arguments. In *The Theory of the Leisure Class*, for example, he refers to what were probably the printer journeymen's habits of dram-drinking and liberal expenditure as an example of pecuniary achievement; he had experience of this world from the days in which he was a temporary worker in a printing house. We may assume that other examples have Norwegian affinities. For instance, it is tempting to assume that, when he writes about sheltered communities wherein a social transformation had been inhibited, he might have had his parents' Norwegian community in mind, which had existed for centuries at the margin of Danish/Norwegian civilisation, and retained many archaic features.[14] But what kind of features were they?

Even if Veblen's notorious reluctance to reveal his literary sources makes it difficult for historians today to ascertain his dependence on Norwegian history or literature, there are instances where his dependency on Norwegian literature is relatively clear. Both Adorno and Edgell have emphasised Veblen's indebtedness to Henrik Ibsen,[15] and it is difficult to deny that the afterlives of 'dead ideas' in Ibsen's play *Ghosts* influenced Veblen when he formulated his ideas about obsolete institutions. These literary parallels, however, do not exhaust the wide range of Veblen's borrowings from Norwegian culture. Norway, in fact, influenced him above all through political and religious movements of dissent, which took shape in very different sectors and strata of the country.

Norway around the middle of the nineteenth century was in many respects a complex society. There were huge cultural gaps between districts and even between neighbouring communities in terms of social 'progress' and economic arrangements. Apart from some small ethnic minorities (e.g. Lapps, Finlanders, Travellers), all people spoke Norwegian, but the dialects were so different that even persons who lived relatively close to one another encountered difficulties of communication. In 1814, Norway separated from Denmark and became a free nation with the Swedish king as a constitutional monarch. The comparatively rigorous mercantilist system that had been practiced by the Danish authorities was loosened by then: towns and corporations lost their privileges, freedom of movement and religion were gradually introduced. As for religious life, Norway had nominally converted to Protestantism in 1534 (together with Denmark), but dissenting movements had been threatening Lutheran hegemony since early in the nineteenth century. Haugianers, Quakers and other non-Lutheran groups were not tolerated in Norway and, beginning in 1825, they escaped the persecutions by migrating to the United States.[16]

Religious emigration often works as a sort of safety valve, and in Norway in particular it contributed to keep the level of population within acceptable limits. This explains why, when the majority of confessional restrictions were removed in 1845, the total population increased from around 700,000 in 1814 to about one and a half million 30 years later. The most striking consequence was that the living conditions of ordinary people deteriorated to the point where widespread social dissatisfaction culminated in a socialist revolt, organised by the Thrane movement in 1850. And yet Thrane's rebellion was a reaction not only against the worsening of life conditions induced by the increase in population, but also against social inequalities which had increasingly emerged in Norwegian society between 1814 and 1850. It is normally said that, during that period, Norwegian society became highly hierarchical.[17] At the top was a thin crust of officials and wealthy businessmen; the middle layer consisted of shop-owners, artisans and functionaries; and the bottom layer was a heterogeneous group of producers of goods and services (sailors, fishermen, journeymen, factory workers and, above all, peasant agriculturalists).

Although generally correct, this scheme was subject to local variations. The few officials residing in the rural districts, in fact, usually had access to farms and carried out farming activities just like the peasants, even if there was no social intercourse between them. Furthermore, it is impossible to describe Norwegian society as if districts were all identical. In the south-eastern part of the country and in Trøndelag, for example, there was a class of idle land-owning proprietors who were dependant on the physical work of hired labourers, but the so-called *husmenn* (those who had been given access to small parts of the owner's land for their subsistence in exchange for long days of work) also worked on the main farms. Although, as folklorist Eilert Sundt reports, there had been a time in which the wealthy farmer worked together with his servants, and all had eaten around the same table, the proprietors eventually interrupted social intercourse with their labourers and tried to imitate the lifestyle of the social layer above them.[18] Traces of the old habit of socialisation across classes, however, survived on the western coast and in the mountain valleys, where even poor *husmenn* were invited to funerals and weddings of their wealthy neighbours, and there was no 'leisure class'. Most importantly, as Sundt argues, these and other behavioural patterns often emerged from the propagation of 'high' models of behaviour through the social hierarchy. In a desire to emulate the local elites, residents in the community normally adopted their patterns and transferred it to their descendants.[19] In the space of some generations, the community developed a homogenous behavioural structure, often in more than one sphere (e.g. dialects, music, wood carving).

Aspects of Norwegian Knowledge in Veblen's Works

Case 1: The Thrane movement

Although scholars have generally acknowledged the influence of utopian socialism on Veblen, its origins and precise nature have yet to be explored.[20] Rick Tilman traces it back to Edward Bellamy's *Looking Backwards*, but I suggest the Norwegian socialist leader, Marcus Thrane, whom Veblen seems to have met in his youth, had an even stronger effect on him.[21] Thrane, who founded a short-lived Norwegian socialist movement around 1850, coordinated his activity as a social agitator with that of editor of a newspaper – *Arbeiderforeningens Blad* – which at its culminating point had about 20,000 subscribers. Although the newspaper's main focus was on Norwegian reforms, these had a clear utopian character; articles by Proudhon, Weitling and Capet were translated and reprinted in the newspaper, and Thrane frequently refers to these writers and other socialists in his editorials. Thrane also urges the downtrodden – particularly in the urban districts – to organise themselves, and about 20,000 persons, possibly 30,000, enrolled in his unions. Initially the unions kept a low political profile, but gradually they moved in a more revolutionary direction. Thrane (together with other leaders of his movement) were arrested and sentenced to long jail terms. Some years after his release, Thrane sailed to America. In Chicago, Thrane edited a socialist/anarchist newspaper, and as an agent of a railway company he used his privilege of free travel to tour the Midwest giving lectures on socialism. When one subscriber to his newspaper asked if there was aristocracy in America, he answered in the affirmative and added: 'The worst of it'. As well as social problems, he attacked biblical inconsistencies and complained against the 'false prophets' crowding the American scene, even in the Lutheran community.[22]

For several years, while Veblen was sojourning in Minnesota, Thrane lived in Eau Claire, which could be reached by horse-and-buggy on a two-day trip from the Veblen farm.[23] We may at least surmise that Veblen had heard of Thrane, although it is highly probable that he visited him. After all, the Thrane movement was the biggest political issue in Norway around the middle of the century, and Veblen never lost sight of Norwegian politics. Even after it had been crushed in Norway, Thrane's movement continued to make converts in Norway. As a poor student, Henrik Ibsen shared his lodging with the movement's second in command, taught voluntary evening courses for the movement and wrote articles in its newspaper; he was almost arrested when the police raided the editorial premises of the newspaper. We have already noticed the similarities between Ibsen's and Veblen's ideas, and it is possible that many of their similarities were rooted in Thrane's utopianism. Like Ibsen, in fact, Veblen shares Thrane's contempt for exhibition and conspicuous consumption. Both share a philosophical conception which drew them to fight against nationalism, war and the power of finance, and to glorify liberty, dignity, justice, equality and work; both transform Locke's justification of private property as based on the work applied to it into an intellectual weapon to fight against the privileges of absentee owners. These similarities had visible manifestations in their respective lives and, curiously enough, in the dispositions they left regarding their burials. Thrane had left a message, ordering that his burial should be carried out without ceremonies or speeches, that only free thinkers should be allowed to attend, and that no monument should be raised in his honour. Similarly, Veblen requested that his funeral be carried out without rituals and that no monument should be raised in memory of him.

Case 2: Conspicuous leisure

On 6 April 1850, Marcus Thrane's newspaper *Arbeiderforeningens Blad* carried a caricature of a rich farmer resting on his sofa and obviously belonging to a 'leisure class'. In fact, the

Norwegian expression *sofabonde* (literally 'couch farmer') is a general term for people who do not like to work. The text below the caricature reads in translation:

> *We literally live in a topsy-turvy world. Not only do those who work hardest get least, but what is even more striking: those who do everything are abused and called tramps, wretches etc. He who sits immobile in his sofa and smokes tobacco and otherwise does nothing, lives so well that he gets sick.*

The target of the caricature is the land-owning farmer in the fertile districts of south-eastern Norway and Trøndelag, who did not work in the fields, but let their subordinates do all the work. I suggest that this social character was the prototype of Veblen's 'conspicuous classes'. Veblen skilfully extracted this character from the political-polemical context in which Thrane had placed him, and constructed a theory of evolutionary change around him. According to Veblen, the transformation of the social strategies adopted by the leisure class to signal its own prestige varied over time and the real causes of institutional transformation are hidden. Emblematically, pure leisure as a way of advertising wealth declined when small and transparent societies were replaced by anonymous cities, which required more effective ways of communicating rank and wealth, above all what Veblen calls 'conspicuous consumption'.[21] If Veblen had looked for Norwegian counterparts to the conspicuous consumption of American industrial cities, the districts of Hedmark, Toten, Hadeland and Biri would have offered accurate examples of conspicuous leisure. Thorstein's father and other relatives might have had direct knowledge about this phenomenon.

Case 3: Quaker influences

Quakerism reached Norway after 1814, when the converted Norwegian sailors who had been interned as a result of the Napoleonic blockade were released from the British jails. Beginning from the mid-1820s, Quakers escaped Norwegian persecution by sailing to America, and continued emigrating until 1845, when the process of religious liberalisation was started. In 1840, however, as a result of persecution, Quakers coalesced in a movement based in Høre, which survived the persecution and prospered until 1860. The Høre Quaker movement was led by the blacksmith Tømmøs Tumbløigarn, who seems to have been a highly respected person, and was known by the Veblen family. In a letter which Thorstein wrote to his brother Andrew in 1899, he refers to Tømmøs as having made the blade of the knife which his grandfather habitually had carried and, in an explanatory note, calls him 'Kvekørn' which is a Valdres equivalent to the English 'the Quaker'.[25]

  The little we know about the Quakers in Høre comes from a short article written by Ødegaard in 1911.[26] Fiercely egalitarian, they refused to honour persons of rank by lifting their caps, refused doing military service and did not submit themselves to the rituals and dogmas of the Lutheran church. Each person of the congregation had the right to express his or her opinion on religious matters. Notwithstanding their religious heterodoxy, Quakers were respected in the community on account of their helpfulness, and appreciated for seldom touching alcohol or smoking tobacco. The general Quaker ideology, which we may assume was shared by the Høre congregation too, held a high regard for the individual, preaching that all persons should be treated with the same degree of respect, irrespective of age, sex or ethnicity. Strictly correlated to this principle was a strong belief in the importance of education, also for women.[27]

The Veblens' connection with the Quaker community of Høre could explain their decision to leave Norway for America. True enough, when they left the country in 1847, Quakers were no longer legally persecuted, but we know that the Veblens took their decision to emigrate several years earlier, and under any circumstances an open declaration of Quaker affiliation could have compromised the position of Veblen's father as a tenant farmer on a property which was owned by the Lutheran pastorate, even after the ban against Quakers had been lifted.

It is only inferentially that we can assign a Quaker identity to Thorstein Veblen's parents. Their behaviour in America was, however, more characteristic of Quakers than of Norwegians in general. We know that the Quakers respected and helped the Indians,[28] while Norwegians shared a general contempt for ethnic minorities. While most Norwegian peasants considered education of their children, particularly the girls, as a waste, the Veblen children – both boys and girls – were given a good education. Contrary to most Norwegian-Americans, Thorstein's father hardly drank alcohol, nor did he smoke tobacco. It is also indicative that he never had any honorary employment in the Lutheran synod, and that the Lutheran pastor confessed that he felt that he never had his full support.[29] The crucial question is how consistent Thorstein Veblen's radical beliefs were with Quaker ideas. His contempt for religious dogmas and his assumption that the practice of brotherly love would prevail over the pursuit of business-like interests are certainly in accordance with Quaker thoughts.[30] So would also be his humanitarian approach and his dislike of war and killings. However, we must not take for granted that Veblen was a Quaker. Veblen must rather have received Quaker principles from his familial environment, and filtered them through his academic knowledge.

Conclusions

In this chapter, I have tried to draw attention to Veblen as a Norwegian. Although he lived nearly his whole life in America, his Norwegian heritage was part of him. Undoubtedly he was a marginal man and wore this status in order to disengage himself from both American and Norwegian values. Therefore I find it curious that some researchers, with reference to a hypothetical set of Norwegian values, have made a model Norwegian out of him. Veblen's sociological and economical thinking were the fruits of his exceptional ability to mould and articulate already existing ideas into new concepts. He is no more a typical Norwegian than his brother John Edward, who was a businessman with no sympathy for his brother's radical economic thoughts.

Veblen had a thorough knowledge of Norwegian culture. His knowledge of the Thrane movement might have contributed to his assumption that the solution to the economic contradictions and injustice was a socialist or syndicalist state, which also was at the heart of the Thrane reforms. The foundational knowledge of Quakerism, communicated to him by his parents, might have constituted an ingredient that was included in his scheme of evolution; his knowledge of the 'sofa farmers' on Hedemarken may have inspired his writings on conspicuous consumption. Emulation, however, might have shaped Veblen's ideas not only as an object of sociological study. Both on his father's and mother's side Veblen had a number of strong personalities who intellectually rose above their fellow parishioners. The most remarkable was probably Øystein Thorsteinsson (of the Bunde branch), who wrote letters to the Danish Governor in Christiania on behalf of his fellow peasants complaining about the behaviour of Danish solicitors in Valdres, and even more remarkably, won his support.[31] Drawing upon Bourdieu's concept of different types of capital, one may say that Øystein created a fund of capital of knowledge, which his descendents and neighbours tried to emulate. Both the Bunde and Veblen kin had strong affinities to the farm cluster of Øygard,[32] as Thorstein's father revealed in dictating to his son Andrew that the people coming from Ødegård were considered more knowledgeable than the rest.[33] Thorstein might have modelled himself on these expectations.

Notes and References

1　In an exchange of toasts between the president and King Harald V, the president said among other things: 'I think it is worth noting a few of them [Americans of Norwegian descent], for their descendants include many luminaries from our past and present: national leaders from Congressman Sabo's home State, like Walter Mondale and Hubert Humphrey; great jurists like the late Chief Justice Earl Warren; great thinkers like Thorstein Veblen; giants of entertainment like Jimmy Cagney; sports heroes like Knute Rockne; and, of course, Secretary Albright's predecessor, Warren Christopher' (The White House, Office of the Press Secretary, 1 November 1999).

2　Arvid Brodersen, *Sosiologi som Opplevelse* (Oslo: Universitetsforlaget, 1994); Wesley C. Mitchell in Irving Louis Horowitz, *Veblen's Century: A Collective Portrait* (New Brunswick: Transaction Publishers, 2002).

3　O. K. Ødegaard, *Gamalt fraa Valdres* (Fagernes: Valdres Historielag, 1977).

4　Rick Tilman, *The Intellectual Legacy of Thorstein Veblen. Unresolved Issues* (Westport: Greenwood, 1996); Stephen Edgell, *Veblen in Perspective: His Life and Thought* (Armonk: Sharpe, 2001), 64.

5　Andrew Veblen, *The Veblen Family: Immigrant Pioneers from Valdris*. The collection of Andrew Veblen's papers at the Minnesota Historical Society, St. Paul, MN, n.d., 68–9.

6　L. Hustvedt, *Rasmus Bjørn Anderson: Pioneer Scholar* (Northfield: Norwegian American Historical Association, 1966).

7　Joseph Dorfman, *Thorstein Veblen and His America* (New York: Viking, 1934), 43.

8　Letter from Thorstein B. Veblen to R. Anderson 1899. Wisconsin State Historical Society. Rasmus Anderson File.

9　Letter from Charles E. Stangeland (Board of Administration, ND) to Thorstein B. Veblen, 31 October 1919. Historical Society Archives, Madison, WI.

10　J. M. Schwartz, 'Tracking down the Nordic Spirit in Thorstein Veblen's Sociology', *Acta Sociologica* 33 (1990): 115–24.

11　Veblen, in his introduction to *The Laxdæla Saga*, translated by Thorstein Veblen (New York: Huebsch, 1925), ix.

12　Dorfman, *Thorstein Veblen*, 575–80.

13　Douglas Dowd, quoted in Horowitz, *Veblen's Century*, 18.

14　This community had existed for centuries at the margin of Danish/Norwegian civilisation. Although Denmark and Norway nominally had been converted to Protestantism in 1534, Catholic features had survived in the local church and were still present around 1800. The church in question was Thomaskirken (Church of St Thomas) at Filefjell, Valdres. The church was built during the Middle Ages, torn down in the early nineteenth century, but has been rebuilt in modern times. The Lutheran clergy disliked the social and religious life that took place when people from several valleys congregated here annually on 7 July in order to get rid of their physical sufferings. This was considered a Catholic reminiscence. A local poem says that many horses were burst, many virgins violated and many lusty lads thrashed (*'Der var mang ein hest sprengt, o mang ei møy krenkt, o mang ein sprek kar dengt'*).

15 Theodor W. Adorno, 'Veblen's attack on culture', *Studies in Philosophy and Social Science* 9.3 (1941): 394–5; Edgell, *Veblen in Perspective*, 120–21.

16 This said, the majority of emigrants between 1825 and 1840 were Quakers or Quaker sympathisers.

17 T. Pryser, *Norsk historie 1800–1870. Fra standssamfunn mot klassesamfunn* (Oslo: Det Norske Samlaget, 1985).

18 E. Sundt, *Om sædelighetstilstanden i Norge. (Om sædelighets-tilstanden i Norge* (1–263); *Fortsatte bidrag angaaende sædelighetstilstanden i Norge* (264–410); *Om sædelighetstilstanden i Norge, tredje beretning* (411–516)), ed. by H. O. Christophersen, N. Christie and K. Petersen (Oslo: Gyldendal, 1976).

19 Sundt, *Om sædelighetstilstanden i Norge.*

20 John Diggins, *The Bard of Savagery: Thorstein Veblen and Modern Social Theory* (Brighton: Harvester Press, 1978); Tilman, *Intellectual Legacy*; Edgell, *Veblen in Perspective.*

21 Tilman, *Intellectual Legacy*, 29.

22 In his so-called 'Wisconsin Bible' he mockingly criticised the 'false prophet' Tubalcain, whom he identified with Pastor Muus, who once had examined Thorstein Veblen in Lutheran confessions on the church floor.

23 In the 1880s, Thrane lived with his son in Eau Claire, Western Wisconsin, where he died in 1891.

24 Thorstein Veblen, *The Theory of Leisure Class* (New York: Mentor, 1953), 74

25 Dorfman, *Thorstein Veblen*, 191.

26 Ødegaard, *Gamalt fraa Valdres.*

27 G. H. Gorman, *Kvekerne, en innføring* (Oslo: Dreyer Perspektivbøker, 1972).

28 Tilman, *Intellectual Legacy*, 10.

29 A. Veblen, *Veblen Family*, 41.

30 Thorstein Veblen, 'Christian Morals and the Competitive System', *International Journal of Ethics* January (1910): 168–85.

31 G. Beitrusten, *Gardar og slekter i Vestre Slidre* (Valdres: Valdres Bygdelags Forlag, 1979).

32 Ødegård, *Gamalt fraa Valdres.* Thorstein Veblen's paternal grandfather, Andris, was born and grew up at Øygard, but his older brother Haldor inherited the farm and Andris had to move. Thorstein's mother, Kari, was a descendant of Øystein Thorsteinson Helle (1705–1765), who was born at Øygard but moved to Helle as an adult.

33 Andrew Veblen, *Notes recording statements by Thomas Anderson Veblen at Iowa City, Iowa, summer of 1895.* Written down from dictation by his son Andrew A. Veblen 1895. The collection of Andrew Veblen's papers at the Minnesota Historical Society, St. Paul, MN.

Chapter 6

THE PHYSICAL WORLD OF THORSTEIN VEBLEN: WASHINGTON ISLAND AND OTHER INTIMATE SPACES

Russell H. Bartley and Sylvia Erickson Bartley

Veblenists from Mars

It would seem that one's life experience refracts his or her perceptions and thoughts and that the physical spaces we inhabit influence our sense of who we are and what ultimately matters. Yet in the case of Norwegian-American political economist Thorstein Veblen this existential aspect of his seminal contributions to social science has for the most part been misconstrued or discounted altogether. In its most familiar version, Veblen has been portrayed as the marginal man from Mars whose cultural alienation as the product of the American immigrant frontier moved him to become an alienated critic of the prevailing socio-economic order. Joseph Dorfman bears primary responsibility for this misreading of Veblen's spatial groundings but others have contributed to the distortions as well.[1] Happily, considerable effort has been made in recent years to address this shortcoming in our understanding of Veblen's life and work. Stephen Edgell provides an excellent corrective in his concisely written 2001 volume, *Veblen in Perspective*, while Elizabeth Watkins Jorgensen and Henry Irving Jorgensen likewise have contributed useful new material for a rethinking of past assumptions about Veblen the man. We, too, have added our own grains of revisionist sand.[2]

The most common flaw of historical interpretation is the unwitting projection of contemporary perspectives and assumptions onto remote times and realities. This holds for biography as well, which is but one aspect of historical inquiry. In the case of Thorstein Veblen, virtually all of his earlier interpreters have committed this methodological sin despite the fact that Veblen's time is not so very remote. Significantly, the one exception is John Kenneth Galbraith, who has drawn on his own experience as a Scotch-Canadian reared among clansmen farmers on the north shore of Lake Erie to access the rural Minnesota milieu of Veblen's youth. Like town-based Yankees of the nineteenth-century Upper Midwest, English residents of Ontario towns and especially Toronto 'dominated the economic, political, religious, and social life of Upper Canada to their own unquestioned advantage'. Invariably, they saw themselves as socially superior to the non-English farming populace of the countryside. The Galbraiths, for their part, together with the neighbouring Scotch clans generally, considered themselves superior 'to the storekeepers, implement dealers, poolroom operators, grain dealers, and other entrepreneurs of the adjacent towns […] [whose] work, if such it could be called, did not soil the hands'.

Galbraith was raised to view claims to social prestige based on the vacuous criteria of English-Canadians as nonsense. Just as the Veblens regarded with contempt the social posturing of Minnesota's Anglo-Saxon elite, the Galbraiths likewise disdained the pretence of Canada's Anglophile establishment. More than one Upper-Midwestern reader of Galbraith's memoirs remarked to him that the social attitudes he described from his Ontario childhood were identical to those of their own Scandinavian and German communities. That Galbraith should have grasped the nuance of Veblen's origins which so persistently eluded other scholars ought not to come as a surprise. They shared a common experience.[3]

Joseph Dorfman, David Riesman, Robert Heilbroner and John Diggins, to cite four of the more familiar names among academic commentators on the life and work of Veblen, have little or no life experience in common with him. They typify the great majority of scholars who have felt compelled to appraise Veblen's legacy. 'Veblen,' remarks Diggins, 'was surely one of the strangest creatures ever to walk in the groves of academe.'[4] He was indeed 'a very strange man', Heilbroner concurs, 'a peasant in looks [whose] strange appearance hid a yet stranger personality'.[5] Riesman made him still stranger with a fanciful portrayal based on Freudian analysis accomplished without the benefit of patient or couch.[6] To a greater or lesser degree, all three rest their depictions of Veblen on Dorfman's erroneous notions about the nineteenth-century immigrant frontier and country life generally.

There is here a distinct urban bias that has prevented all but a very few Veblenists from fully accessing the world of their subject. Galbraith was the first to explode the prevalent myth of the Veblens as impoverished farmers and of presumed childhood deprivations as the source of Thorstein's later critique of the prevailing socio-economic order. 'There can be no farming country anywhere in the world with a more generous aspect of opulence', he writes, in describing the Veblens' Nerstrand farm. 'The soil is black and deep, the barns are huge, the silos numerous as also the special bins for sealing surplus corn, and the houses big, square, comfortable, if without architectural pretense'.[7] The legend of Thorstein's deprived upbringing, Galbraith notes, is wholly false. In Minnesota, his family became 'considerably more affluent than almost any farm proprietors in Norway. We would certainly estimate that they were far more affluent than the Canadian Galbraiths'.[8]

The overriding urban bias of Veblen scholars has distorted not only their version of his Norwegian-American farming origins, but virtually every other aspect of his life as well. For Veblen, Heilbroner tells us, the world was 'uncomfortable and forbidding' and he moved through it 'as if he had descended from another world'.[9] Yet nothing could be further from the truth. As we have noted elsewhere, it would be difficult to find another academic – especially, perhaps, an American academic – who today experiences the world as completely and easily as did Thorstein Veblen in his own day.[10] Over the course of his life he lived in, visited or passed through the full range of landscapes, geographies and human settlement from remote hinterland to occupied countryside, towns, cities and great metropolises. He traversed the North American continent repeatedly and on four occasions sailed to Europe. He was as comfortable in Copenhagen, London or Manhattan as he was on his parents' Nerstrand farm or at a primitive campsite among the ghosts of the ancient Anasazi.

While Veblen's formative years were spent in rural Wisconsin and Minnesota, it is important to recall that he lived more than a third of his life in major metropolitan areas, plus another 15 years in small and medium-size towns. And in none of these urban settings do we encounter a scintilla of evidence to suggest that he found his surroundings 'uncomfortable and forbidding'. On the contrary, he appears to have moved with complete ease and an abiding interest in every aspect of his immediate environment. Indeed, his full engagement with the world around him sets him apart from later generations who in the main tend not to be very observant of their surroundings and for whom distance is an obstacle to be surmounted as quickly as possible. Whereas many today have only a virtual sense of reality filtered through proliferating electronic media and the circadian-altering displacement of jet aircraft, Veblen retained a visceral sense of the world as he moved through it, always at a measured pace; always in contact with the ground and water beneath him.

To Veblenists' prevailing urban bias must be added a cultural parochialism all too common among the cloistered savants of the academy. Only a handful have been able to appreciate the nature and importance of Veblen's Norwegian heritage in the evolution of his ideas, while most – certainly in the United States – have considered that heritage quaint or exotic and above all an impediment to social as well as intellectual success. It was the primary source of his 'alienation', they mistakenly averred, and the burden that frustrated his academic career. Appropriately, perhaps, it has fallen to scholars from that same Norwegian heritage to provide the critical insights that now allow us to correct this habitual misreading of Veblen.

The first was John R. Christianson, an historian at Luther College in Decorah, Iowa, who dismisses the simplistic Norskie immigrant/Yankee entrepreneur opposition propounded by Dorfman and others as the origin of Veblen's marginalised place in American academic culture. Veblen's unique bent of mind, observes Christianson, developed 'in a variety of Norwegian-American rural, urban, and academic communities, as well as in the tension between these communities'. The cultural choices open to Veblen as he was growing up

were not choices between the horizontally distinct social values of Norwegian peasants on the one hand and educated Yankees on the other, but rather between the learned values and cultural and intellectual preoccupations of parallel Anglo-American and Norwegian-American academic communities.[11]

Christianson further notes that Veblen exhibited the characteristic traits of the 'folk savant', a recognisable sociological type present in the Norwegian-American farming communities of the Upper Midwest. The folk savant, he explains, 'never fully abandoned the values of his or her native community but always measured [them] against the values of a variety of elites'.

This learned misfit – Veblen's wandering Jew – amounts to 'a spokesman for ethnic values, reaching out to a new, educated audience'. Veblen's great genius, Christianson concludes, was that he managed 'to bring his community-based Norwegian-American system of social values to the attention of the English-speaking world'. Moreover, it is precisely because those values were not exclusively Norwegian-American values that his writings have 'found a wide national and international audience and remain powerful to this day'.[12]

More recently, the late University of Oslo scholar Knut Odner has offered additional insight into the Norwegian component of Veblen's thought. Just as Christianson calls attention to the socio-cultural diversity of the Norwegian-American communities of the Upper Midwest, so, too, Odner emphasises the complexity of nineteenth-century Norwegian society. What, exactly, might the specifically Norwegian content of Veblen's thought have been? It is quite impossible, Odner suggests, to identify a coherent body of old-country values and beliefs that transferred intact to America and were subsequently inculcated into Thorstein Veblen. If anything, Veblen's parents differed from most other Norwegians in their values and beliefs, perhaps influenced by Quakerism but also by other local factors at play in the Valdres area whence they came.[13] This, in turn, likely goes far to explain the uncommon success of the Veblens in America noted by Galbraith, not least the formal education of all the Veblen offspring.

There can be no doubt that Veblen was steeped in his Norwegian and more broadly Scandinavian heritage nor that his Norwegian roots formed an integral part of his personal identity. His grasp of the language, including the Valdres dialect of his parents' home region, was thorough, as was his knowledge of Scandinavian history, culture and politics. But he was a good deal more as well – and certainly not Riesman's nostalgic Norwegian, who confects a cultural suit of armour for protection against the slings and arrows of predacious Yankees.[14] A letter he penned to his older brother Andrew upon visiting their parents' ancestral valley in the summer of 1899 captures well the place Norway and things Norwegian occupied in his mind: 'The people here view me with alarm because I talk Valdres but look like an Englishman – which is held to be fundamentally wrong'.[15]

It would be illuminating to compare the two brothers' respective attitudes toward their Norwegian roots, for Andrew and Thorstein were always close and held each other in highest esteem, yet did not seem to internalise their ethno-cultural identity in precisely the same way. Both were fluent in Norwegian as well as the Valdres dialect and both knew well the history, customs and folklore of their parents' homeland. Whereas Andrew, however, served as the Veblen family historian and became the premier keeper of Valdres lore in America,[16] Thorstein seemed disinclined to concern himself with the particulars of their Norwegian ancestry, preferring instead to use his family heritage as a ready window on the human experience more broadly. Something of his attitude in this regard is apparent in his letter from Valdres:

> I came here over Bergen and Lærdal. So far there is nothing to tell in the way of adventures. I have seen some relatives and some of the places connected with the ancient tribe, but there is not a great deal to say for either […] I shall spend a couple of weeks in Christiania and in Sweden and then go to Copenhagen. What I want there is mostly Northern antiquities and ethnographic material.[17]

Among the ethnographic material he acquired in Copenhagen that summer were two recent editions of Icelandic sagas: the *Njáls Saga* and the *Ljósvetninga Saga*.[18] In striking contrast to the chivalric romances of mediaeval Europe, the thirteenth-century prose sagas of Iceland constitute a rich historic record of the settlement and earliest development of that outlying North Atlantic territory, offering unique insight into the functioning of a predatory social order in the remoter times of barbarism. For this reason Veblen found the sagas of especial interest and studied them closely throughout his adult life, eventually publishing his own translation of the *Laxdæla Saga*. The *Laxdæla* in particular, he noted, was above all 'an ethnological document of a high order […] [that] reflects the homely conditions of workday life in its time, together with the range of commonplace sentiments and convictions that animated this workday life'. It was, in sum, an invaluable record

> of late-Pagan and early-Christian manners, customs, convictions and ideals among the Germanic peoples at large, but more particularly touching the Scandinavian and the English-speaking peoples at the point of their introduction into their feudal and ecclesiastical status in early-Christian times.[19]

The anthropological insights to be gained from saga literature, in turn, were central to the entire corpus of Veblen's work, which explains the time and effort he expended to master the Icelandic language.[20] The Icelanders, after all, were not 'his people', their ancient links to Norway's western fjord country notwithstanding. Had Veblen been inclined to indulge himself in such personal nostalgia, he would have focused on Høre and the folkways of the surrounding Valdres region, as did his brother Andrew, not on the predatory culture of tenth-century Icelandic clans. While historically Icelandic derives from Old Norse, it was not a language that Veblen knew by virtue of his native fluency in modern Norwegian. He had to learn it in both its modern and literary variants, which required prolonged study. Unable to travel to Iceland for that purpose, he pursued the convenient alternative of sojourning periodically among the Icelandic immigrants of Washington Island, Wisconsin. It was an association that spanned three decades of his life and therefore constituted one of the key intimate spaces in his mental universe.

Washington Island

Washington Island is an irregularly shaped expanse of rolling woodlands and farms lying six miles off the tip of Wisconsin's Door Peninsula between Green Bay and Lake Michigan. The local Potawatomi Indians were pushed aside in the 1830s and 40s by New Englanders, Irish and other whites anxious to exploit the island's timber and surrounding fresh-water fishery. Its population dwindled during the American Civil War but recovered again in the 1870s with an influx of Icelanders, Danes and other Scandinavian immigrants.

Exactly when Thorstein Veblen first journeyed to Washington Island is uncertain, but oral testimony and documentary evidence confirm that it was while he was on the faculty at the University of Chicago. The first place he stayed on the island was at the Detroit Harbor home of John Gislason, one of the first Icelandic settlers who arrived in

1870.[21] In 1963, Gislason's son Lawrence recalled that when he was a young lad of nine or ten Veblen had appeared at their door to inquire if he might board with them for the summer and that he remembered the occasion distinctly because Veblen had insisted that the Gislasons speak only Icelandic in his presence. Lawrence Gislason was born in 1886, which would place Veblen's initial visit in the mid-1890s.[22]

In subsequent summers Veblen boarded at different establishments in both Washington and Detroit Harbors, situated on the island's north and south shores respectively. In the first years he appears to have travelled to the island alone, reflecting perhaps the strains of his marriage to Ellen Rolfe or simply his determination to immerse himself in the study of Icelandic, from which a companion untutored in that language would have been a distraction. We know few details of these early visits beyond his immediate purpose of immersing himself in the island's Icelandic-speaking milieu. We know as well that there were years when he did not summer on the island because he was travelling abroad (1896, 1899, 1904, 1914) or was otherwise occupied, as in 1911, 1912 and 1913. It is possible that he made brief visits to Washington Island in these years as well, but we cannot say for certain.

Once Veblen's divorce from Ellen was final and he had remarried, he was moved to acquire property on the island. In 1915 he and his new wife, Ann Fessenden (*née* Bradley), or 'Babe' as family members affectionately called her, purchased a 15-acre parcel from Kari and Sigurline Bjarnarson, Icelanders Veblen had come to know on the island's north-west shore. The property was situated on a wooded stretch of land separating Green Bay and a small body of water called Little Lake. For a vacation camp it was one of the most desirable sites on the island. The Bjarnarsons sold the property to the Veblens for the sum of three hundred dollars.[23] According to Veblen's stepdaughter Becky, this parcel had been burned over twenty years earlier and at the time they acquired it was now covered with 'young birch, balsam fir and cedar'.[24]

The following summer the Veblens pitched their tent on the Little Lake property and Thorstein set about building a permanent shelter. He constructed a two-room cottage with a sleeping porch and, a short distance away by the edge of Little Lake, a small study cabin for himself. His two stepdaughters, Becky and Ann, assisted the accomplished carpenter as best they could. 'We girls thought we helped a lot with handing out nails!' – reminisced Becky, more than three quarters of a century later – 'Ann and I were mostly lugging nice polished limestone [...] for the fireplace'.[25]

The study cabin was a one-room board-and-batten structure measuring roughly ten feet by twelve feet (~3 m x 4 m). It was constructed of milled lumber, had doors at either end, small six-pane windows set in its south, west and north walls and a large twelve-pane window on the east end by Veblen's work corner. Inside, Veblen fashioned an attached writing surface next to this larger window, put in several shelves above and next to it, installed a small laundry stove for heat, and affixed wooden packing crates to the opposite wall to accommodate his books. On warm days, he could sit at his built-in writing table with both doors open and listen to the sounds of the surrounding woods while contemplating the view across the water to the cedar-lined far shore of Little Lake.[26]

The result was rustic but functional, a clear reflection of Veblen's practical aesthetics and minimalist sense of material requirements displayed throughout his life. It recalls, for example, a flat he had maintained years earlier near the University of Chicago campus, described by a former graduate student as having only the barest furnishings possible: 'a table lamp, a few plain chairs, a set of plain boxes placed on top of one another containing books crowded into the shelf-like open side'.[27] It also brings to mind a previous cabin he had built in the coastal hills west of the Stanford University campus, which was strikingly similar to the Washington Island study cabin in basic concept and construction, albeit somewhat larger and differing slightly in floor plan.[28]

However Spartan Veblen's Washington Island retreat may appear to others, it fully provided for his essential needs, above all a place to work. And the workplace he built for himself leaves little doubt that much of his time on the island was in fact devoted to his work. This is reflected in the books that occupied the shelves and wooden packing crates in the Little Lake study cabin – several hundred volumes comprising Veblen's working library – as well as an extensive collection of clippings, papers and research materials left behind when, in 1926, he left the island for what, unbeknown to him, was to be the last time. That the packing crates were affixed to the cabin wall, the very same crates in which he had previously transported his books from place to place, suggests a sense of permanence not observed in him before.[29]

Veblen moved the bulk of his books to Washington Island when he left the University of Missouri in 1918,[30] although in subsequent summers he continued to arrive on the island with trunks of books. 'He'd bring them every year,' recalled Ted Bjarnarson from his early childhood. 'Regular steamer trunks they were. And they were heavy! Ninety-nine percent books!'[31]

From Chicago one typically reached Washington Island by steamship, although it was also possible to travel north by a combination of rail and stage to Gill's Rock at the tip of the Door Peninsula, thence by ferry to Detroit Harbor. The fact that Veblen first lodged with the Gislasons at Detroit Harbor suggests that he made his initial journey to the island via this overland route. In subsequent years, he preferred the more direct lake route served by the famed Goodrich boats – large, well-appointed passenger vessels serving the principal ports and resort destinations of Lake Michigan and Green Bay.[32] Because of their deeper draft, they docked at Washington Harbor on the island's north shore rather than the shallower Detroit Harbor served by the Washington Island ferry.

The Bjarnarsons would meet Veblen at the Washington Harbor boat dock and cart his trunks and other luggage by horse and wagon along an old logging road to the Little Lake camp. 'I remember him coming with [the books] in the spring,' Ted Bjarnarson recalled, 'but I don't remember what he did with them in the fall. [...] I know those bookshelves, those orange crates he had nailed to the wall, they always stayed pretty full. We used to check the place every so often'. Those trunks, added Ted's older brother Fritz, 'lined the whole walls. [...] They used them for seats. They were all full.' Veblen had constructed the trunks himself, according to his stepdaughter Becky, and left them filled with books and manuscripts when he departed the island 'to go into cold storage', as he had put it, in California.[33]

While Veblen was first drawn to Washington Island as a convenient place to hone his knowledge of Icelandic, over the years it came to occupy a central place in his personal universe. The acquaintances he initially cultivated with local Icelanders for the utilitarian purpose of language evolved into lasting friendships, for example with the Bjarnarsons, from whom he purchased his Little Lake property, and with the Gislasons, who would occasionally come from Detroit Harbor to visit with him at his Little Lake camp.[34]

Once Veblen and his new spouse had purchased the Little Lake property and constructed their permanent camp, it became an extended family destination as well as his own personal retreat. And as we have noted elsewhere, it is perhaps the one place where Veblen the man most fully reveals himself.[35] Contrary to what many have assumed, we observe here a family-oriented man ready to share space with kith and kin; one sensitive to the needs of others and, in general, giving of himself for the enjoyment and edification of those around him. We see, too, a person intimately aware of his own connection to the natural world and the cosmos beyond, yet dismissive of ancient as well as modern teleologies. In the most unpresuming way, Veblen sought to guide others, especially children, toward a fuller understanding of the world and themselves. With both his transient summer coterie and his Little Lake neighbours he exhibited a fundamental human solidarity that informed his merciless skewering of the vested interests who, in his day as in ours, shackle the species and frustrate our collective well-being.

He would organise camp activities with constant humour and purpose: birthday celebrations, berrying expeditions, nature walks. He constructed a raft for the children with a wry protuberance at one end vaguely suggestive of an ancient Viking vessel and christened it *The Mock Turtle*. At meals he would tell funny stories and recite verses from Yeats, Swinburne and Kipling. At age 89, his stepdaughter Becky still recalled 'The King of the Cannibal Islands, who dined on cucumbers cold and raw', and 'King Solomon and King David [who] led merry, merry lives/with many, many concubines and many, many wives'. She recalled as well Kipling's long poem about 'The Sons of Martha' and could recite Yeats's 'The Land of the Heart's Desire'.[36]

On one occasion Veblen quietly observed his mother-in-law, Harriet Ayer Towle Bradley, as she sat at the edge of Green Bay enjoying the sunset, an evening ritual that gave her particular pleasure. Making mental note of her proportions, he proceeded to fashion a waterside bench for her that she might thereafter watch the sunsets in greater comfort.[37] On another occasion, he awakened everyone in the night to observe an exceptional display of the aurora borealis. 'Lights of pastel to rainbow colors were flashing from all sides of the horizon', recalled Becky. They reached to the zenith, 'encircling the whole sky'. Never again would she witness so spectacular a display.[38] Yet another time Veblen awakened Babe and the girls in the night to watch the mist spiralling into 'a dozen ghost-like people', who in the pale moonlight passed eerily over the surface of Little Lake. Becky believed that he 'assembled his thoughts at night' to be written down the next day. 'He wrote neatly without cross-outs or anything [thrown in] the waste basket, as if it was clear in his head!'[39]

Veblen took special interest in the offspring of his immediate and extended families, seeking at every opportunity to stimulate their curiosity and mental development. His grandniece Colette Sims Van Fleet recalled, for example, how on nature walks he would 'always walk with his hands behind his back and a hatchet in his hand' and how he insisted that the children not raise their voices in the woods. 'He never made a big deal about it', she recounted, 'but we did learn what a lot of things were. He really knew his stuff [and] we were interested in what he had to tell us'.[40]

Veblen often combined activities or drew creatively on the oral tradition of his own upbringing to help teach children larger lessons about the world around them. A short distance up the shore from his Little Lake camp stood a large conifer that he named the 'Chief Spruce' and made the focal point of family birthday celebrations. After an expedition for favours and decorations to the Koyens' general store near the south end of Washington Harbor, the tree would be decorated and 'Toyse', as Veblen was familiarly called, would preside over the party beneath its stately boughs. Embellishing for effect a favourite lesson about the importance of snakes in the balance of nature, he would relate with a straight face how one day he happened upon a convention of water snakes assembled beneath the 'Chief Spruce', all listening raptly to one of their fellow serpents. The point of his tale was that snakes are useful and should not be killed. His two stepdaughters would reinforce this lesson by ostentatiously handling live snakes in the presence of whoever might be visiting.[11]

In striking contrast to Veblen's poor classroom performance at Chicago, Stanford, Missouri and the New School for Social Research, he revealed a subtle pedagogical sense where children and young people were concerned. Islanders and relatives alike marvelled at the lessons they learned from him. Oliver Bjarnarson once stated that Veblen 'was the smartest man he'd ever met'. He and his brothers queried their erudite neighbour at every opportunity about the most diverse subjects. 'No matter what you asked him', Oliver insisted, 'he knew more than any book'. Orville Cornell and the Bjarnarson boys often visited Veblen at the Little Lake camp, where, seated on a bench outside his cabin, he would talk and read to them about plants and the natural world. 'He noticed every new flower, every new growing thing', confirmed Becky. 'He was very observant about nature'.[12] Veblen explained to his young interlocutors how balsam sap could be used to heal blisters and wounds and on their frequent treks in the woods he would identify mushrooms, flowers and whatever else they happened to encounter along the way.[13]

Veblen's method with the younger generations was typically indirect and low-key, yet honed to whet their curiosity. In conversation, he would purposely drop new words to encourage youthful listeners to expand their vocabularies. His grandniece Colette remembered it as an ongoing word game in which Thorstein's older brother Andrew also participated. 'My grandfather and Uncle Thorstein used to sit around and introduce new words', she told us, 'and wait to see how [we] would pick them up and misuse them, or not misuse them; how quickly [we'd] catch on. We got quite a vocabulary that way'.[14]

Veblen would also leave books he thought appropriate where the young people at his Little Lake camp would find them. 'He was good at bringing things that he thought we might enjoy', noted Becky. 'Or perhaps *should* enjoy…' In a variation on this tutorial approach, Becky recalled how, in Columbia, Missouri, she and her sister Ann had both been enthralled by the illustrations in Peter Christen Asbjørnsen's 'neat little volume of Norwegian fairy tales', and Veblen had offered it to whichever of them learned to read it first. Their mother had already mastered Norwegian well enough to read Ibsen in the original but neither of the girls got past the wonderful illustrations, so the handsome book remained in Veblen's personal library.[15]

It was Veblen's method, according to his grandniece, to introduce unobtrusively some new element and then sit back to observe the results. It was a method that he applied as well to the university classroom, where, despite mixed reviews of his teaching, it remained pedagogically sound, quickly separating creative minds from the conventional. Veblen's cardinal transgression as an educator would appear to have been his refusal to play the role of 'teacher as authority', in Riesman's formulation;[46] that is, his rejection of the prevailing scholasticism of the day in defence of critical minds and free-standing intellect. A teacher, Veblen believed, 'is, properly, a student, not a schoolmaster'. One teaches 'by precept and example', not as a 'vehicle of indoctrination'.[47]

While personally frugal, Veblen was generous with his limited resources. In Becky's memory, he could not refuse a friend, relative or neighbour in need, even if it meant that he and his family had to go without. He continued to support his two stepdaughters after their mother died in 1920. He loaned money to his brothers Ed and Orson, financed his niece Hilda Sims through teacher certification at UC Berkeley, and in his final years fretted over his stepdaughters' ability to manage their affairs once he was no longer there to look after them. He even loaned money to the Bjarnarsons, who for their part looked after his Little Lake property when he was absent and lent him whatever assistance he required when he was there.[48]

Veblen's relationship with the Bjarnarsons grew into an especially warm and lasting friendship – the kind of association that so perplexed some of his fellow academics, who could not understand his tendency to prefer farmers and working people over scholars and intellectuals.[49] The Bjarnarsons delivered milk and mail to the Little Lake camp, in addition to which Veblen would purchase butter, eggs, vegetables and an occasional chicken from them. Often accompanied by his stepdaughters and his grandniece and grandnephew, Colette and Allan Sims, he would regularly call on the Bjarnarsons. While the youngsters entertained themselves with Katzenjammer Kids comic books, he would visit with Kari and Sigurline, Bjarnarson's wife. During these visits Veblen would share his stogie-like cigarettes with Kari, occasioning much envy among the Bjarnarson boys, who desired nothing more than to be able to smoke that exotic tobacco. Veblen, recalled Oliver Bjarnarson years later, 'treated my father like royalty!'[50]

Among the several hundred Veblen-related books we recovered from Washington Island in the early 1990s were a number that Veblen had either gifted or loaned to the Bjarnarsons, books that were later inherited by the Bjarnarsons' granddaughter Bernadette Rainsford, who in turn donated them to the Carleton College Archives.[51] Those inscribed to Kari and Sigurline reveal much about the quality of his relationship with them. Like many Icelanders of their day, the Bjarnarsons were highly literate in their own language, while Sigurline appears to have been so in English as well.[52] Books were a natural medium for the expression of friendship and Veblen frequently shared meaningful volumes with the Bjarnarsons.

Some of those books offer insight into Veblen's personality. His gift of Vogt's *Illustrated Bible History*,[53] for example, reflects a marked sensitivity and ability to accept others on their own terms. While he himself had long since abandoned the rituals of formal religion and was no longer a churchgoer ('bunk houses' was his term for churches),[54] he acknowledged the Bjarnarson's traditional religiosity and readily shared with them a book that spoke to that tradition. Swedish writer Selma Lagerlöf's *Jerusalem* and *The Holy City* provide two additional examples.[55]

Among the books Veblen shared with his Washington Island neighbours were several versions of the ancient sagas, including three in the original Icelandic that he had acquired during his 1899 visit to Copenhagen: the *Ljósvetninga Saga*, the *Njáls Saga* and the *Færeyínga Saga*, this last an edited volume that included Faroeish and Danish translations.[56] Veblen had also loaned the Bjarnarsons *The Saga of Grettir the Strong. A Story of the Eleventh Century*, translated from the Icelandic by George Ainslie Hight, volume one of *Sturlunga Saga, including the Islendinga Saga of Lawman Sturla Thordsson and other works*, and a copy of his own translation of *The Laxdæla Saga*. That Veblen shared these editions of the sagas with the Bjarnarsons attests to his longstanding interest in medieval Icelandic literature and further confirms the presence of native Icelanders as the primary attraction that brought him to Washington Island in the first place. His stepdaughter Becky recalled him working on *The Laxdæla Saga* while summering on the island and that when they were living in Columbia, Missouri, he had a shelf of Icelandic sagas in the original as well as in translation.[57] So, too, Kari Bjarnarson possessed his own leather-bound collection of sagas, including the *Laxdæla*, that he had brought from Iceland.[58] There can be little doubt that the sagas constituted a regular topic of conversation between the two men and that Veblen probed his Little Lake neighbour for all the insight he could offer into the sagas' ethno-historical content.

Veblen was most interested in the continuities of human behaviour through time (habit) and the Icelandic sagas, especially the *Laxdæla*, offered him a useful point of departure. He observes in the introduction to his translation:

> That occupation which gave its name and character to the Viking Age was an enterprise in piracy and slave trade, which grew steadily more businesslike and more implacable as time went on. It was an enterprise in getting something for nothing by force and fraud at the cost of the party of the second part; much the same, in principle, as the national politics pursued by the statesmen of the present time.[59]

Based on a close reading of the sagas' historical subtext, he likewise dismisses the celebrated legend of Iceland's primal parliamentary governance as a tradition of 'boss rule' cloaked in the trappings of representative commonwealth (regional *Þings* and the national *Alþing*) aided and abetted by medieval Christian clerics. The *Laxdæla*, he notes, recounts only the initial, 'more genial inchoate phase' of this new order, but is important because it describes the basic civil and ecclesiastical elements that led to its collapse in the mid-thirteenth century. Other documents closer to the events, he adds, were available for an appreciation of the 'tangle of corrosive infelicities' that brought about an end to Iceland's self-governance, notably the *Saga of Gudmund the Good* and the *Islendinga Saga*, together with the additional accounts included in Vigfusson's *Sturlunga Saga*. As for the Norwegians, the *Heimskringla*, together with certain detached sagas of the later kings of Norway, would show 'how the fortunes of that people, from the advent of Christianity onward, swiftly tapered off into a twilight-zone of squalor, malice and servility, with benefit of Clergy'.[60]

Washington Island was Veblen's access to mediaeval Iceland, as it appears also to have been the physical space in which some of his seminal ideas were refined or even, perhaps first formulated. But, as suggested above, it became something more for him as well, beyond this convenient bridge to the remote past – one of but three geographical places to which he revealed some deeper personal attachment. Most significantly, it was a gathering place for the extended family 'tribe', over which he presided whether in person or from afar. 'The place is quite the right thing for children and old folks,' he wrote his sister Emily in 1927. Then in final retirement in California and only two years away from his demise, he urged Emily to go to the Little Lake camp together with her daughter, Rakel, son, Edgar, Edgar's family and in-laws, and the younger generation, 'as many as may be', and to stay for 'as long as may be'.

   Anyone who went to the island, he explained:

> should go, preferably, by Green Bay, take stage or car to Sturgeon Bay and on to Elison's Bay or Gill's Rock, ferry to Detroit Harbor and car to Kari Bjarnarson's (pronounced 'Cowry') who has the keys and will do any carting or other work. This is the right route unless one can get a boat (Goodrich) from Escanaba or Sturgeon Bay.

He hastily wrote Emily a follow-up note saying he had forgotten to tell her 'that there is a cap on the chimney in camp which has to be taken off before lighting a fire in the kitchen' and cautioning her that 'one should not go on the roof without rubber soles to prevent slipping'. Also, he added, 'there is a better pair of oars for the skiff in the woodshed than those in the skiff'.[61] Veblen enjoyed his Little Lake camp most fully during the three or four summers he was able to spend on the island with his new wife and two stepdaughters. Once he had built the cabins and otherwise developed the camp, he happily shared the space with an ever expanding circle of extended family and close friends, including colleagues who would come to work with him on pending academic projects. A good sense of the spirit of the place and the special pleasure he derived from enticing those citified colleagues to visit his remote island retreat can be had from a letter he wrote to Isador Lubin in the summer of 1917. Lubin, then Veblen's assistant at the University of Missouri and a stalwart among the small coterie of former graduate students and loyal friends, was to join Missouri colleagues Max Handman and Leon Ardzrooni at the Little Lake camp.

   'Dear Lubin,' Veblen wrote, 'We are now beginning to look for you with every boat that blows. Unless you come on soon you won't get the work done that you are scheduled for.' Lubin should keep in mind, Veblen advised, 'that this is comparatively cool country, requiring woolens and warm bedding. It is also rough country which will tolerate nothing elegant.' It would be necessary, he added, to sleep under shelter and allowed that he could offer the use 'either of a tent or of a partly enclosed roof, in any case sufficient to keep out the weather'. As for getting to the island, Veblen recommended that Lubin 'take the Goodrich boat "Carolina" ', which left Chicago at 1 p.m. on Tuesdays and arrived at Washington Island at 5 p.m. the following day. Mrs Veblen added her invitation 'to come on and join this company of rustlers, accordingly, on such terms of Liberty, Equality and Fraternity as any person of your affiliation should appreciate'. Veblen enclosed a Goodrich timetable and urged Lubin to 'make haste'.[62]

Babe had herself written Lubin two weeks earlier saying they would be glad to see him and that if he let them know ahead of time what day he would be arriving, they would 'try to send a runner down to the dock' to meet him, although that was not a simple matter 'on account of the irregularity of the boats'. She anticipated they would 'have some good times' that summer and were expecting Max Handman and his wife the following week and Leon Ardzrooni before long. She emphasised the need for warm clothing and bedding and that there was 'no demand for any good clothing in the strict leisure-class sense of the word'. Lubin would have to do his own washing as well. 'In spite of all the hardships,' Babe concluded, 'this is the best life I know of and this is certainly a pretty place'. She was sure he would enjoy being there as they would enjoy having him.[63]

Eighteen months later Babe suffered an emotional breakdown in New York City and was confined first to Manhattan's Bellevue Hospital, then transferred to McLean Hospital in Belmont, Massachusetts, where she died of a massive lung infection in early October 1920. Numerous factors contributed to her distress, including the emotional trauma of having miscarried a child by Veblen in her seventh month of pregnancy. It was an especially cruel denouement of their peripatetic relationship, one that Veblen appeared to accept with characteristic stoicism but which privately he could only have suffered intensely. Thereafter, the Little Lake camp became his own intimate link to this woman who had meant as much to him as anyone else in his life, and he would return there each summer until ill health ended those annual sojourns.[64]

Veblen fully intended to return to Washington Island when he closed up camp in the fall of 1926. He had 'fallen in love' with that plot of land 'where he could see the sunrise over [Little Lake] and the sunset over Green Bay', as Sigurline Bjarnarson later expressed it.[65] Moreover, he had left his library behind together with work-related papers and sundry personal items.[66] At one point during his California retirement Leon Ardzrooni persuaded him that his book *The Theory of Business Enterprise* should be revised to include a discussion of the Federal Reserve System and suggested that the two of them go to Washington Island to accomplish that task. But Veblen's debilitated health prevented him from making the journey.[67]

In the spring of 1928 he and his stepdaughter discussed driving to Wisconsin in his Erskine automobile to spend the summer at their Little Lake camp. He had what Becky described as 'a nostalgia' for the place and in fact seems to have contemplated the possibility of ending his days there. His longstanding confidante and former love interest Sadie Hardy Gregory reported that he spoke of 'waiting for the clock to strike', which, he said, it would do wherever he was, implying that it might as well be on Washington Island.[68] His health, nonetheless, obliged him to postpone the trip another year.

In January 1929, Veblen wrote to the Bjarnarsons asking them to retrieve a map that he had left in his Little Lake study cabin and which he now needed. Upon receipt of his letter they went immediately to look for the map but could not find it. 'We found a pasteboard tube, most likely the one you described in your letter, laying on the shelf,' Sigurline informed him, 'but it was empty so most likely you have put it some other place. We also looked in the boxes on the floor. It could be in the boxes or trunks that are locked'.[69]

In March of that year Becky informed the Bjarnarsons that she and Veblen planned to come for the summer. By July, however, they had not yet arrived and Sigurline wrote Veblen saying that she and Kari had been expecting them already for two weeks. Had they given up the idea of coming? 'The other night we drove over to your place', she informed him, 'The road has been improved some, but it's still rough in places. Your place seemed lonely without anybody there'.[70]

Once again Veblen's precarious health, plus an unresolved real-estate matter, had kept him in California. Then, on the first Saturday of August 1929, he died of heart failure and Becky conveyed the sad news to the Bjarnarsons. It was too bad, Sigurline wrote her, that they had been unable to make even a brief visit to the island that summer, for Little Lake had 'never been prettier', its water standing much higher than usual. The fall weather, too, had been lovely and, already into the third week of October, the leaves were still on the trees but 'now turning beautiful red and yellow'.[71] Among these local Scandinavians, speculated island writer Anne Whitney, Veblen had found the 'spiritual affinity' and 'peace of mind' he needed for his study and writing.[72]

Sandhill Road, La Honda Ridge and Other Private Spaces

When Veblen went into his final California retirement in 1926, it was not to the alien exile suggested by his sardonic 'cold storage' remark, rather to a poignantly familiar setting that intersected with the most intimate moments of his then 69 years. His primary destination was a two-lot parcel with a rustic two-story cottage and two outbuildings by Sandhill Road along the western edge of the Stanford University campus, just over the San Mateo County line on the outskirts of Menlo Park. The property had been acquired and the cottage constructed in 1907–08 by his then estranged first wife, Ellen Rolfe Veblen, while he was on the Stanford faculty and residing at the university's adjacent Cedro Cottage property. It had been, according to the legend, a case of the spurned spouse seeking to keep an eye on her wayward husband.[73]

There remains considerable confusion about the timing and purpose of Ellen's Menlo Park real-estate venture. In a recent, well-researched article about Veblen's Stanford years authors Roxanne Nilan and Karen Bartholomew establish that Ellen's title to the Sandhill Road property was not recorded in the San Mateo County Recorder's Office until 27 January 1912, a full two years after Veblen had moved to Columbia, Missouri.[74] Robert Duffus, in turn, recalled that Ellen had lived 'for several years in a rented bungalow in the meadow near Cedro' before deciding to build 'a shack of her own'. A unique feature of this 'shack' was a movable section of roof 'which could be lifted by means of pulleys to allow the direct sunlight to come in during the daytime or the glimmer of moon and stars at night'.[75]

Jorgensen and Jorgensen, for their part, imply that this unusual feature was to serve as an observatory from which to view Veblen's activities on the adjacent Cedro Cottage grounds. They quote Ellen's friend Alice Millis to the effect that her presence next to Cedro was at best in 'questionable taste' and had been 'much remarked on'. Citing Ellen herself, they state that she built her two-story cottage in the spring of 1908 and that it was to be a rental property, a seeming contradiction of their cottage-as-watchtower scenario.[76]

Nilan and Bartholomew speculate that for her own reasons Ellen may have worked out some arrangement with the developer who owned the Sandhill Road property, Edward Fitzpatrick, whereby she could delay actual purchase while enjoying the right to build. There is room for additional speculation that by then Ellen could foresee the inevitability of her divorce and may have wanted to protect her property against potential settlement claims by her husband. It would seem a striking coincidence, if coincidence it be, that title to this property was not recorded until two weeks after her divorce had been granted.[77]

The Veblens' marital difficulties, now well documented, had their origin in Ellen's compromised physiology and were accordingly more complex than their contemporaries ever knew, such that through all their bitter disillusionment Ellen and Thorstein remained close.[78] When Ellen moved to the Halcyon theosophist colony in southern California, she decided to sell her Menlo Park property and offered it to her ex-husband. 'I have hung on to my house next [to] Cedro with the idea you might like it sometime', she wrote him in June 1923. 'Can't do it much longer'.[79] Veblen was on Washington Island at the time and first considered the possibility of acquiring Ellen's Sandhill Road place while summering at his Little Lake camp.[80]

Veblen's decision was immediate. On 21 August, he sent Ellen a cheque for $500 as an initial payment, thinking that she might 'have present use for it', and promised to pay the remaining $1,500 upon receipt of the deed 'or any other arrangement' that proved satisfactory to her. He was sending the cheque directly to her rather than to the real-estate agent she had mentioned, he explained, 'because if you sell direct you will have no agent's fee to deduct'. He had seen the place three years earlier, he allowed, but only 'from the road'. Within two weeks he received the deed from Ellen and on 10 September sent her a cheque for $750 rather than the entire balance, explaining that he was not certain there were sufficient funds in his New York account to cover the full amount. He would send her the remainder before the end of the month and in the meantime would not send in the deed to be recorded until what he still owed her had been duly paid.[81]

Something of the continuing emotional bond between the two former spouses can be sensed in this transaction and, above all, in their correspondence around it. In first broaching the possibility of Veblen's buying the Menlo Park property Ellen began by writing him about her circumstances in Halcyon. She had been living in a pleasant but rustic place on two acres of land next to a twenty-acre 'eucalyptus hill' but was now of a mind to sell it and to move into a second 'little place nearer other people'. Before doing so, however, it had occurred to her to invite him to come visit. She had not given it much thought, she said. It just struck her as 'so natural'. From her new theosophical perspective, it seemed a place 'for the undoing of Karma', where such a visit would be 'understood and approved without binding ties'. After all, they had 'a little to make up to each other' and should do so as much as possible while still able. Knowing that Veblen could never enter her world at Halcyon, she appears to have offered her Menlo Park property as an alternate medium for mending their mutual wounds.[82]

Veblen, for his part, surely understood what was in play with Ellen's offer and readily agreed to the purchase as a tangible gesture of reconciliation. 'I shall be very glad', he wrote from Washington Island, 'to have you look in on the place when you are near, and to suggest anything to be done and how to do it. And if there is anything on the place which you would like to use or keep, I should like you to feel quite free about it. It is not likely that I will see the place for a year', he added, 'and I am likely to ask Mrs. Storm [Grace Camp] to take care of the taxes and the deed for me as she has done in another connection before'.[83]

This opaque mention of a previous real-estate matter referred to a second intimate parcel near the summit of the Santa Cruz Mountains west of Stanford which likewise exerted an emotional draw on Veblen. It was an irregular half acre of steeply timbered land on the upper far slope of La Honda Ridge that he had purchased two decades earlier and where he had built two successive cabin retreats, the second of which was still on site, albeit in disrepair and need of renovation. He had fashioned the first cabin out of lumber salvaged from a chicken coop that had been wrecked on the grounds of his Cedro Cottage residence by the 1906 San Francisco earthquake. A large old-growth redwood stump served as its primary support at the uppermost edge of the parcel's tree cover, affording Veblen an unobstructed vista across the adjoining grassy opening and receding hills all the way to the ocean.

Robert Duffus, who as a Stanford undergraduate shared the Cedro Cottage quarters with Veblen, once visited the cabin. Veblen, he wrote,

> had a shack in the hills, among the redwoods, on the road to Pescadero and the coast […] It was erected on stumps on an elevation of the main ridge, and it commanded a view of the Pacific Ocean. Inside, it was plain but, to my outdoor eyes, pleasant and comfortable. He kept cooking utensils there, and some food. The dirt road that ran near by was not much traveled.[84]

How Veblen first happened upon this remote mountain parcel and what, precisely, moved him to purchase it eludes us. Interestingly, he acquired the ridge property and put up his little cabin within a year of joining the Stanford faculty. He had already built the shack by the time Duffus took up residence at Cedro Cottage in the fall of 1907. Many years later Duffus would idly wonder what attraction this rustic retreat might have held for Veblen. He did not think Veblen went there 'to commune with nature', which in Duffus's view he could have done well enough right there at Cedro had he not elected to surround himself 'with a menagerie of hens, cats, cows, horses and students'. Nor did he believe that Veblen 'went up to the hills to worship God, for his universe contained no God'. Neither would the attraction have been 'to see the chipmunks or deer, though there were some there, or to study birds'. It had been rumoured that Veblen used the place for discreet trysts with female acquaintances, but Duffus had no direct knowledge of such affairs and was unwilling to speculate beyond observing that 'it would have been a beautiful spot for two persons […] who loved each other and wished to be alone'. However it may have been, Duffus concludes, the shack was there 'and the fogs came over from the sea and covered it deep and wet, and rolled away from it again, and let its occupants or occupant view the glory of nature, if not the glory of God'.[85]

From our present remove it is impossible to know what Veblen's private motives may have been. As rural as the Cedro Cottage setting seemed to Duffus, it was hardly the same as the isolated mountain landscapes just a few miles away and could well have failed to satisfy some deeper desire on Veblen's part to experience nature beyond the bounds of human intervention. Duffus himself acknowledges the distinctly 'untamed quality' of La Honda Ridge, where, as he expressed it, 'things were never quite matter-of-fact' and there was yet some element 'that hadn't surrendered to the presence of man'. Even years later, having rambled all over that mountain and discovered its concealed places, Duffus was ready to believe 'any well-constructed mythology' about it, 'would have wanted to believe', because 'there was actually something there that needed explaining'.[86]

This elusive quality of the place itself could have moved Veblen to acquire the mountain parcel and, absent other objective factors in his life, might reasonably be considered his primary motive. We cannot ignore, however, his painful marital tribulations nor the developing relationship with his former Chicago acquaintance, Babe Bradley, who in the fall of 1907 matriculated at UC Berkeley for graduate study in economics and, on at least one occasion described by Duffus, visited Veblen at Cedro Cottage.[87] Presumably, they visited on other occasions that year, perhaps in Berkeley or maybe elsewhere around the San Francisco Bay Area. Whether they ever shared time together on La Honda Ridge is not known.

At the end of that academic year, Babe returned to her young daughters, Becky and Ann, who had remained in Chicago in the care of their Bradley grandparents. When the Cedro Cottage lease came up for renewal prior to the start of classes in the fall of 1908, Veblen decided to change his residence and moved to Alvarado Row on the opposite (south-east) side of the campus, where he rented a room for the remainder of his time at Stanford.[88] He wished, we surmise, to place a comfortable distance between himself and his then estranged wife, Ellen, who had moved onto the adjoining property and was in the process of building the house that was to be his some two decades later. Before abandoning Cedro, he enlisted the assistance of Duffus, Duffus's brother William and a third Stanford student who shared the premises to help him dismantle the shack on La Honda Ridge and return the lumber to the cottage grounds whence he had requisitioned it two years before.[89]

Veblen kept his ridge 'woodlot', as he once referred to it, and two years later would resurrect his shack on the precise spot where the first one had stood, this time in direct association with Babe Bradley and her two girls, who may actually have helped him build it.[90] This followed upon a dramatic incident at a remote cabin in Idaho where Veblen had gone in late December 1909 to visit Babe and the girls and almost succumbed to double pneumonia contracted while riding on horseback through a snowstorm from the Grangeville railroad depot. A local doctor had opined that Veblen would not survive but Babe, through determined ministrations that left his chest tender from mustard plasters and his back peeling from repeated passes with a stove-heated sadiron, managed to pull him through. It took Veblen many weeks to regain sufficient strength to make the return trip to California, where he faced unemployment and an uncertain future, his irregular marital situation having finally moved Stanford president David Starr Jordan to demand his resignation from the university.[91]

The Idaho cabin was on property belonging to Babe's Bevans in-laws, who had acquired it as a rustic retreat for restorative sojourns in the mountains of the West. Because of its remoteness they had named the place 'Nowhere'. Babe had gone there with Becky and Ann to spend a year living the pioneer life and to test her survival skills as a single woman (she and the girls' father had gone their separate ways and would ultimately divorce). She and Veblen had remained in communication following her year at Berkeley and his fateful visit to Nowhere was a natural progression in their gradually evolving relationship. His near-fatal bout with pneumonia from which Babe saved him appears to have qualitatively deepened and in effect sealed that relationship, as Veblen himself once confided in an unguarded moment. If Veblen were ever to remarry, a Missouri acquaintance told Joseph Dorfman many years later, there was little doubt that he intended to wed 'Mrs. Bevans', for 'she had saved his life once […] and he always remembered that'.[92]

As his difficulties at Stanford unfolded in predictable fashion, Veblen corresponded with his old Chicago colleague and close friend Herbert Davenport, now chair of the Department of Economics at the University of Missouri who, for more than a year, had sought unsuccessfully to bring him to Missouri. When Veblen informed Davenport that Jordan had asked for his resignation and that, in light of the reasons, he doubted he would again be able to obtain an academic appointment, Davenport invited him to come stay in his home in Columbia, then redoubled his efforts to open a position for him at the university. Veblen thanked Davenport for his kindness, but declined to accept his invitation into the Davenport household without a proper academic appointment.[93]

When Veblen left Nowhere in the spring of 1910 to return to California he could only assume that he would be unemployed for the next year. Accordingly, he and Babe appear to have decided that she and the girls should follow him to California and find a convenient but inconspicuous place to live while he sorted out his practical affairs. Although he and Ellen were by then legally separated, Ellen had not yet agreed to a divorce and he did not wish to muddy the waters unnecessarily. He would find a cottage for Babe and the girls in Pescadero along the Pescadero–La Honda Road a dozen or more winding mountain miles from his parcel on La Honda Ridge, where they arrived later that summer. At the time they settled on these plans they did not know that University of Missouri president A. Ross Hill would recommend to the university's trustees ('Board of Curators') that Veblen be appointed Lecturer in Economics for the second semester of the 1910–11 academic year, which Hill did on 6 April of that year.[94]

We do not know exactly when Veblen received notification of his Missouri appointment, only that the plans he and Babe had made were already in motion by the time he learned of it. Even if it was prior to Babe and the girls' arrival in Pescadero they had the remainder of summer and the entire autumn before them, as he would not leave for Missouri until the latter part of December. And if the offer reached him sometime after their arrival, it would shorten by half the time they had anticipated but still leave them what remained of summer and fall together. So the ridge shack was rebuilt, presumably with lumber unencumbered by the proprietary strictures of the Cedro period, and now became part of their shared experience – an extension, perhaps, of their intense time together earlier that year at the cabin in Nowhere.

Veblen's appointment at the University of Missouri was renewed on a regular basis after that initial spring semester of 1911 and Columbia would thereafter anchor his life financially and geographically for the next seven years.[95] Each of the following three

summers he and Babe spent camping at remote sites in the west, first with the girls at the
Murphy cattle ranch outside Ashland, Oregon, then at the Murphys' Buck Prairie high-
country range in the western Cascades; the second summer by themselves in Mancos and
Mesa Verde, Colorado; and the third, again accompanied by Becky and Ann, outside
Fort Garland, Colorado, on the western flank of the Sangre de Cristo Mountains.[96]
Once Veblen had left the Bay Area Ellen finally agreed to a divorce, which was granted
in January 1912. Thorstein and Babe took special precautions during the interlocutory
period, however, not to compromise his academic appointment at Missouri and even
after the divorce had become final they continued to be judicious in their association until
they at last married in June 1914.

While probably of no transcendence, two details from this period nonetheless recall
Veblen's Scandinavian heritage and suggest that it always informed his awareness of
himself as a conscious actor in the world. The first was his interest in the archaeological
sites of the ancient Anasazi ruins at Mesa Verde, probably aroused by the Swedish scholar
Gustaf Nordenskiöld, who in 1891 undertook the initial dig, mapping and description of
the place, as well as by the subsequent work of Smithsonian archaeologist Jesse Fewkes.[97]
Nordenskiöld, notes Mesa Verde National Park historian Duane Smith, made 'the first
conscientious attempt to excavate and record Mesa Verde archaeology systematically' and
his published study provided 'the first extensive examination and photographic record
of [the area's] prehistory'.[98] Perhaps of additional interest to Veblen was the fact that
Nordenskiöld had contracted tuberculosis and travelled to south-western Colorado to
regain his health in the region's restorative climate. Once there, he determined to combine
his recuperation with continued scientific endeavour, an attitude and circumstance that
would have resonated with Veblen, whose own respiratory system had been seriously
compromised and who might well have been inspired to emulate Nordenskiöld.

In any case, he and Babe did visit Mesa Verde in the summer of 1912 and, like
Nordenskiöld, Veblen devoted himself to scientific work there in the restorative clime
of the Colorado Plateau. That the disciplined Swedish archaeologist who preceded
him to Mesa Verde may have inspired him to go there himself is perhaps suggested by
Veblen's ready interest in the work and perspective of Scandinavian archaeologists and
ethnographers generally. A clear reflection of that interest is Kristian Bahnson's elegant
turn-of-the-century ethnographic treatise containing detailed descriptions of North
American indigenous cultures, a copy of which survives from Veblen's Washington Island
library.[99]

The second element of this period that bespeaks Veblen's Scandinavian sense of self
was the choice of Lindsborg, Kansas, for Babe and the girls' residence during the final
year before they became a 'proper', legally sanctioned family. Lindsborg was once the
cultural and religious centre of the region's extensive Swedish settlement dating from
the late 1860s and has preserved notable elements of its Scandinavian heritage down to
the present day. Veblen helped Babe and the girls get settled in a rented cottage there
following their summer in the Fort Garland area, then returned to Missouri for the start
of the new academic year. Babe enrolled her daughters in a local school and secured
a job for herself. Veblen would visit them periodically over the next nine months until
they all returned to Chicago, where Babe and Thorstein were married, then set out for

Norway. That Veblen and Babe should have opted precisely for Lindsborg as the final 'way station' en route to the normalisation of their personal relationship once again points to the subjective influence of Veblen's cultural identity. It was not an obvious choice, as other locations a prudent distance from Columbia, Missouri, offered equal or greater practical advantage. Lindsborg's unique Swedish heritage, therefore, would appear to have been the deciding factor.

It would be almost ten years from the time Veblen left the Bay Area until he again visited his La Honda Ridge property. In his absence, he relied upon Palo Alto acquaintance Grace Camp, later Mrs Hans Otto Storm, to look after tax and other property-related matters for him both on the ridge and in Menlo Park. The ridge parcel proved especially vexatious from the outset due to its diminutive size, irregular configuration and anomalous position between much larger properties whose owners more than once sought, in connivance with the San Mateo County surveyor and tax collector, to swindle him out of it. The first such incident occurred in 1910 and others followed over the years.[100] As late as spring 1929, he informed his sister Emily that he had run 'into a muddle about the title to a small piece of woodland up in the hills'. He had counted on going to Washington Island that summer but now would be unable to make the trip. Although the matter was then well on its way to being resolved, he told her, in light of past experience he thought it prudent to remain on hand 'to see the end of it'.[101]

The most remarked upon, and misapprehended, incident concerning the La Honda Ridge property occurred in the summer of 1920. Veblen had returned from the East Coast for the purpose of rehabilitating the ridge cabin, where he intended to bring Babe to regain her physical and emotional health. He evidently had reason to expect that she would soon be discharged from McLean Hospital and considered this the ideal place for her to recuperate. According to Dorfman, when Veblen arrived at the cabin he found for sale signs on the structure, assumed the neighbouring rancher had seized his property and flew into a blind rage, smashing the cabin's windows with a hatchet so as to make it uninhabitable. Afterward he allegedly made a sardonic remark about 'absentee ownership', then 'had a sign put on the property stating that it was the private property of Thorstein Veblen' and, upon his return to New York, commenced writing *Absentee Ownership and Business Enterprise*.[102]

This incident has always been recounted in a manner suggestive of emotional instability on Veblen's part, or at the very least, of a diminished ability to deal appropriately with the world around him. Even Jorgensen and Jorgensen, who allude to the ridge property's deeper significance for him, repeat Dorfman's description of that crazed moment and, like Dorfman, could not resist depicting Veblen as the ironic victim of his own 'absentee ownership'.[103] Yet everything we now know about Veblen's relationship with Babe Bradley points to her as the emotional link to that wooded parcel on La Honda Ridge with its curious little cabin and unobstructed vista out over the coastal hills to the ocean beyond. It was there that he seemed to imagine she could get well; there where they could restore the fullness of their intimacy, all too briefly shared in the four years prior to her breakdown. What he had in mind for his own future we cannot know, inasmuch as bringing Babe back to California would seem to imply having to leave the East Coast in order to attend to her needs. In any event, he seemed determined to do for her what she had done for him a decade before in that other cabin in Nowhere, Idaho. And it was in all likelihood the momentary dread that a neighbour's predacious chicanery would prevent him from doing so that precipitated his uncharacteristic outburst of raw emotion that strange afternoon up on the ridge.

Babe died unexpectedly the following October. Demanding that she be released from her captivity, she had gone on a hunger strike, was force fed and, probably as a consequence of the procedure, developed a massive pulmonary infection which ultimately caused her death.[104] We can only suppose that Veblen experienced her passing as a severe blow, although he kept his emotions to himself and with them the privacy of the relationship he and Babe had shared.[105] Those emotions, in turn, would appear to have been inextricably tied to both the woodlot on La Honda Ridge and his Little Lake property on Washington Island, the two places on earth where he most wished to be at the end of his life.

Heritage, Place and Self

Four years after Babe's death, Veblen described himself to an admiring correspondent by the name of Pritchard as 'an average person with few and slight ties of family or country, being born of Norwegian parents in America and educated at various American schools, and having never been hard at work or very busy'.[106] The wry self-deprecation is signal Veblenian understatement best understood in the light of his views about higher learning, idle curiosity, utilitarian purpose and the sabotage of the commonweal by businessmen. It is also characteristic of his Scandinavian heritage, which refocuses our attention on what he implies about his cultural identity and sense of place in the world.

'Born of Norwegian parents in America' and 'educated' in American schools, with minimal 'ties of family or country' – a facile response to a stranger's impertinent inquiry that tells nothing but in fact reveals much. Veblen here disclaims national allegiances beyond the inescapable formalities of citizenship, which accords fully with his well-known views on patriotism and the predacious nature of nation-states. His disavowal of extensive family ties, in turn, alluded to the relatively few living relations with whom he had personal bonds as well as to his basic disinterest in ancestral lines. ('I have seen some [Norwegian] relatives and some of the places connected with the ancient tribe, but there is not much to say for either [...]'[107]) What Veblen did not convey to Mr Prichard, however, and what scholars interested in Veblen have often misinterpreted, was the centrality in his personal universe of family, friends, and his Norwegian heritage.

The issue of Veblen's cultural persona is as elusive as it is central to how he experienced the world and to how he thought. Knut Odner was correct in dismissing the notion that Veblen's critical view of the prevailing profit-driven economic order stemmed from a peculiarly Norwegian system of values, no such homogeneous set of beliefs and assumptions ever having existed within the geo-historic confines of Norway, much less having been transmitted to America. He also notes correctly that Veblen's ideas about human society and economic arrangements derived from a multiplicity of sources and experiences across cultures and that in this sense he had much in common with the emancipated ('wandering') Jew whose intellectual pre-eminence he greatly admired.[108]

But Odner is equally ready to acknowledge the breadth and depth of Veblen's familiarity with Norwegian language and culture and that his Norwegian heritage 'was part of him'. Thorstein Veblen, he writes, 'had a thorough knowledge of Norwegian culture and […] he integrated this knowledge [into] his writings'.[109]

Odner suggests that Veblen consciously selected the elements of Norwegian culture that he added to his knowledge bank, just as he picked and chose the data he would retain from other cultural traditions. But this seems to beg the question of Veblen's primary store of Norwegian inputs received as a child and youth, above all language. Every language comprises a psychological, historical and cultural universe in which the fluent speaker experiences, thinks and acts in culturally particular ways. And one's first language, if not abandoned in favour of another, will tend to shade a speaker's window on the world even when she or he later accesses additional linguistic universes. Without dwelling on possible interferences, crossovers and perceptual mutations, suffice it to say that our first childhood language, if mastered and maintained, will endow us with life-long cultural filters that prevail over whatever other tongues and associated filters we may acquire in the course of our lives.

In Veblen's case, his primary cultural filters were unmistakably 'Norwegian', as verified by ample anecdotal testimony. Isador Lubin, for example, once remarked: 'Despite everything [Veblen] said and wrote about patriotism and the self-aggrandizement of "the vested interests" in the name of patriotism, when it came to Norway he was as great a chauvinist as anybody I ever knew. When he talked about the country his face lit up. I used to chide him about his attitude toward Norway', Lubin said. 'I went there for the first time in 1929, and I wrote him a letter from Oslo in which I said that having been there I now agreed with his feelings about Norway and forgave him for being chauvinistic about the country'. Veblen died the very week Lubin wrote that letter and so never saw it.[110]

This primal Norwegian sense of self permeates Veblen's life and work in evident as well as imperceptible ways. While not synonymous with what Lubin characterised as 'chauvinism', it nonetheless suffused his private spaces and animated his closest personal relationships, notably with his brother Andrew, sister Emily, and Washington Island neighbours Kari and Sigurline Bjarnarson; also with his companion and second spouse Babe Bradley, who herself endeavoured to learn Norwegian and accompanied him to Norway on their honeymoon. That the newlyweds should have chosen Valdres as their destination on so personal an occasion itself testifies eloquently to the depth of Veblen's Norwegian identity.

Philosophically, Veblen rejected all teleological belief systems and seemed to derive sustaining comfort simply from the knowledge that he was part of an infinitely larger and complex natural order with no knowable ultimate purpose, yet governed by its own imperatives and internal logic. Indeed, he appears to have looked upon humankind as a rather dubious life form with poor prospects for long-term survival, an attitude that offended some of his hidebound critics but which explains his ability and inclination to spend prolonged periods of time in rustic circumstances communing with nature and his own private thoughts.[111] At his La Honda Ridge woodlot where he passed much of the last year of his life, an observant neighbour who occasionally accompanied him has written that 'not a leaf nor a weed nor an insect was disturbed', the woodrats 'were free to share the larder', and more than once a prowling skunk 'would brush against Dr. Veblen's leg' as he stood or sat 'so very quietly for long periods'. Yet Veblen 'was never sentimental concerning "nature", nor even articulate', so far as the neighbour could recall. He simply held the view 'that the human was not so comparatively important among living things'.[112]

Individuals from many cultures have held this view of our place in the larger scheme of things, including the authors of this essay, so while it is perfectly compatible with Veblen's Norwegian heritage, no particular cultural significance can be attached to it. Indeed, none of Veblen's siblings exhibited this non-anthropocentric outlook on life, even though they shared a common upbringing and had been fully exposed to the natural world as youngsters. All we can say, then, about Veblen's diminished view of humankind is that it emerged from his own intellectual processes and reflected his particular personality. It probably imprinted as well the cultural filters through which he refined his Scandinavian identity, although we doubt that so subtle a psychological process could be discovered and persuasively described. What we can say confidently is that Veblen's detached view of himself in the world, together with the memory of past relationships and certain biographical links to his Norwegian heritage, are the interwoven threads that connected him to these discrete places where he desired to spend his final years.

Washington Island was where each of these psychological factors were fully played out and the one place Veblen most wished to be in the final decade of his life. He summered there virtually every year from 1915 to 1926 and, as indicated above, would have continued to do so in his last three years had ill health and other pressing matters not prevented it. He was at his Little Lake camp just three weeks before Babe died, unaware of her impending distress and himself just then recovering from 'something in the way of a collapse of the whole nutritive system' that had followed upon his frustrated attempt to rehabilitate the cabin on La Honda Ridge for Babe's anticipated convalescence. At the time, he was negotiating an offer to teach at the University of Oslo but did not expect the Norwegians to meet his terms.[113] During subsequent island sojourns following Babe's death he devoted himself to honing his translation of the *Laxdæla Saga* and preparing it for publication.

Veblen had ceased lecturing at the New School for Social Research and left New York City in 1926 on the advice of his personal physician, Dr Benjamin Gross, who had warned him that his debilitated system would not tolerate another East Coast winter.[114] Winters, of course, were considerably more severe in the Upper Midwest and Washington Island, for all its personal attraction, was never a viable year-round retirement option. Veblen's San Francisco Peninsula properties were the obvious alternative. 'Veblenstadir', as Hans Otto Storm humorously referred to the Sandhill Road compound,[115] was at the time occupied by renters who proved difficult to dislodge, as a consequence of which Veblen and his stepdaughter Becky, who accompanied him to California, had to make alternate living arrangements until the tenants were finally persuaded to vacate the premises.

The 'Veblenstadir' reference here has multiple layers of significance, both for its Veblenesque irony as well as for what it reveals about Veblen's own cultural vantage. The root of this playful name is the Icelandic word *stadur*, denoting a main regional church to which subordinate churches paid tithes. Following the introduction of Christianity into Iceland in the eleventh century, the *staður* (plural *staðir*) became a primary source of revenue for secular chieftains who retained control over the land on which the churches were built.[116] The wry comparison of Veblen to a mediaeval Icelandic *goði* in relation to his difficult Menlo Park renters, and of his Sandhill Road property to the tithe-extorting *staður*, is too exquisite for words.

Veblen had gifted a copy of his *Laxdæla* translation to Storm and Storm had read it by the time he wrote Veblen about the state of affairs at 'Veblenstadir' (the correct singular would have been 'Veblenstadur'), but he would not have come up with such a witticism himself since he knew no Icelandic, and the historic period in which events unfold in the *Laxdæla* antedates the institutionalisation of the *staður–goði* relationship. It could only have been Veblen who saw the ironic parallel between mediaeval Icelandic *goðar* and his own circumstances as a challenged absentee landlord. It was Veblen, surely, who formulated the sardonic Icelandic designation for his presently embargoed property, which provides yet another glimpse of his underlying Nordic identity.

Hans Otto Storm, for his part, was pleased to have received the *Laxdæla*. Himself an aspiring and gifted writer, he found this initial exposure to Icelandic literature a new experience that opened up for him 'a considerable vista'. It left him perplexed, however. 'Short of learning the Icelandic,' he remarked to Veblen, 'I shall never know whether your own terse and sardonic style has been written into the translation, or borrowed originally from the Icelanders!' Storm's readiness to consider this last possibility in effect attests to the depth and vitality of Veblen's Scandinavian heritage.[117]

In the spring of 1928, with Veblen and Becky at last settled in at the Sandhill Road cottage, William Camp and Hans Storm rehabilitated the La Honda Ridge cabin under Veblen's close direction. The aging *goði* of *Veblenstaður* now lacked the stamina to do any of the heavy work himself but knew precisely how he wanted the job done. Repairs began with the shack's floor, joists and foundation supports, proceeding upward to the walls and roof and included replacement of the windows that had succumbed to Veblen's frenzied hatchet eight years before. Once renovation was complete the cabin again afforded rustic but cosy shelter at the crest of the Santa Cruz Mountains, a pair of large second-growth redwoods flanking its doorway, redwood forest to one side of the structure, 'a sheer view over tier after tier of hills to the sea' on the other. It had always been Veblen's intention, Storm thought, to return to this cabin on La Honda Ridge.[118]

By all accounts Veblen spent the better part of his final year up on the ridge. Unable to go to Washington Island, he might well have died there and likely would have preferred it that way, although it hardly mattered since, as he put it, 'the clock would strike equally anywhere'. Yet so long as he was alive, the mountain shack is where he wished to be. Food, water and other supplies had to be brought from town, then lugged up the slope through the trees to the cabin, a regular chore with which Veblen could no longer offer much assistance. It was difficult enough to climb the slope himself. Becky saw to these tasks with assistance from their Palo Alto friends.[119]

She also kept Hans and Grace Storm apprised of their activities, the Storms having relocated temporarily to the East Coast in connection with Hans's employment as an electrical engineer for the Mackay Radio and Telegraph Company. 'The accounts of your cabin and wood pile, even with animalculae, sound as rumours of paradise', Hans wrote her from Sayville, New York, in late September 1928.[120] 'They tell me you are spending most of your time on the ridge now', he wrote Veblen that December. 'The more we see of Long Island, the more inviting seems your cabin in the redwoods. We have not forgotten the night we spent there under the trees in the summer',[121] 'Becky writes of your being marooned up in the redwoods for days at a time', he wrote the following February. 'The situation excites my envy. Sayville is too devilish far from any redwoods'.[122]

Alone on the ridge with his thoughts for days and nights on end, we must suppose that in his mind Veblen revisited the intimate spaces of his past, both distant and close at hand. We suspect as well that he returned to those moments and places through the inner prism of his Norwegian heritage. As his neighbour Mrs Fisher recalled:

Living alone so much of the time up on the "Ridge", he was somewhat occupied with memories. He told me that he heard members of his family, long since dead, speak to him in Norwegian as clearly as I was speaking to him then. I was sitting alone with him on the mountain overlooking the ocean where his shack was built', she explained. 'I believe that he never told anyone else of his conversations with people not present. But he certainly told me in no equivocal terms.[123]

Notes and References

1 Joseph Dorfman, *Thorstein Veblen and His America* (New York: Viking, 1934). See also David Riesman, *Thorstein Veblen. A Critical Interpretation* (New York: Scribner's, 1953); Robert Heilbroner, 'The Savage Society of Thorstein Veblen', in *The Worldly Philosophers. The Lives, Times and Ideas of the Great Economic Thinkers* (New York: Simon and Schuster, 1980), 210–44; and John P. Diggins, *The Bard of Savagery. Thorstein Veblen and Modern Social Theory* (New York: The Seabury Press, 1978).

2 See especially Edgell's first chapter, 'The Times, Life, and Works of Thorstein Veblen', *Veblen in Perspective. His Life and Thought* (Armonk: M. E. Sharpe, 2001); Elizabeth Watkins Jorgensen and Henry Irvin Jorgensen, *Thorstein Veblen. Victorian Firebrand* (Armonk: M. E. Sharpe, 1999). Of our own work, see, for example, Russell H. Bartley and Sylvia Erickson Bartley, 'In Search of Thorstein Veblen: Further Inquiries into His Life and Work', *International Journal of Politics, Culture and Society* 11.1 (Fall 1997): 129–73; Russell H. Bartley and Sylvia Bartley 'In the Company of T. B. Veblen: A Narrative of Biographical Recovery', *International Journal of Politics, Culture and Society* 12.2 (Winter 1999): 273–331; Russell H. Bartley and Sylvia Bartley, 'Stigmatizing Thorstein Veblen: A Study in the Confection of Academic Reputations', *International Journal of Politics, Culture and Society* 14.2 (Winter 2000): 363–400.

3 John Kenneth Galbraith, 'A New Theory of Thorstein Veblen', *American Heritage* 24.3 (April 1973): 33–40, esp. 39. See also John Kenneth Galbraith, *A Life in Our Times. Memoirs* (Boston, MA: Houghton Mifflin, 1981), 1–4, 30–31.

4 Diggins, *Bard of Savagery*, 33.

5 Heilbroner, *Worldly Philosophers*, 215–16.

6 Riesman, *Thorstein Veblen*; see also Bartley and Bartley, 'Stigmatizing Thorstein Veblen', 384–8.

7 Galbraith, 'A New Theory of Thorstein Veblen', 34.

8 John Kenneth Galbraith to Paul Veblen, Cambridge, MA, 1 June 1972. Copy in authors' possession.

9 Heilbroner, *Worldly Philosophers*, 216.

10 Bartley and Bartley, 'In the Company of T. B. Veblen', 276.

11 J. R. Christianson, 'Thorstein Veblen: Ethnic Roots and Social Criticism of a 'Folk Savant'', *Norwegian-American Studies* 34 (1995): 3–22, esp. 3, 11.

12 Ibid., 16.

13 Knut Odner, 'New Perspectives on Thorstein Veblen, the Norwegian', in this volume.

14 See Riesman, *Thorstein Veblen*, 4ff.

15 Thorstein Veblen to Andrew Veblen, Valdres, Norway, 16 August 1899. Andrew Veblen Papers, Box 1, Minnesota Historical Society (St. Paul).

16 See, for example, the obituary account of Andrew Veblen's life in the quarterly *Samband* (Minneapolis) 8.3 (September 1932): 74–6. Andrew Veblen Papers, Box 1, Minnesota Historical Society (St. Paul, MN).

17 Thorstein to Andrew, Valdres, 16 August 1899. Andrew Veblen Papers, Box 1, Minnesota Historical Society (St. Paul, MN).

18 *Njáls Saga* (Reykjavik: Kostnaðarmaður: Sigurður Kristjánsson, 1894); *Ljósvetninga Saga* (Reykjavik: Kostnaðarmaður: Sigurður Kristjánsson, 1896). In May 1994 we recovered both volumes from Bernadette Rainsford, a descendant of Veblen's Washington Island Icelandic neighbours, Kari and Sigurline Bjarnarson, to whom he had apparently loaned the books during what turned out to be his final visit in the summer of 1926. In each his name was pencilled on the back of the title page. The books have since been incorporated into the surviving portion of Veblen's Washington Island library now housed at the Veblen Collection, Carleton College Archives (Northfield, MN).

19 Veblen, introduction to *The Laxdæla Saga* (New York: Huebsch, 1925), v.

20 Dorfman, *Veblen and His America*, 492; Riesman, *Thorstein Veblen*, 206.

21 For the history of Icelandic immigration to Washington Island, see Conan Bryant Eaton, *Washington Island, 1836–1876. A Part of the History of Washington Township* (Sturgeon Bay: Privately published, 1980), 49–74. See also idem, 'The Icelanders in Wisconsin', *Wisconsin Magazine of History* 56.1 (1972): 2–20.

22 Esther V. Gunnerson, 'Washington Island's Thorstein Veblen' (unpublished research paper, Oshkosh State College, 1963), 2–3. Copy in authors' possession. Gunnerson conducted valuable research for this paper, including a number of oral interviews with persons who had known Veblen on Washington Island. Ironically, the Gislason children had to struggle that summer to comply with Veblen's wishes inasmuch as they were not accustomed to speaking Icelandic at home.

23 State of Wisconsin, Door County, Register of Deeds (Sturgeon Bay), vol. 27 of Deeds, No. 180814, 77. A copy of this deed dated 6 November 1915, bearing the signatures of Kari and Sigurline Bjarnarson and witnessed by Arni Gudmundsen and Edward H. Cornell is preserved in the Veblen Collection, Carleton College Archives (Northfield, MN).

24 Becky Meyers to John Diggins, San Francisco, 18 January 1982. Copy from Diggins's Veblen file.

25 Authors' tape-recorded interview with Becky Veblen Meyers, Sandpoint, Idaho, 27 August 1993; Becky Veblen Meyers, handwritten notes for memoirs, August 1990. Copy of the Bartley interview and Meyers' original handwritten memoirs are preserved in the Veblen Collection, Carleton College Archives (Northfield, MN). The 'limestone' was actually dolomite, which comprises the bedrock of Washington Island and on the surface has been broken into rounded and polished cobbles by overriding glacial ice in the late Pleistocene. They are abundant in the Little Lake area and Veblen made use of them to fashion unmortared piers for both the cottage and his study cabin.

26 Amy Koyen Eichelberger, telephone conversation, 17 April 1990. Eichelberger's description of the interior of Veblen's cabin was based on her personal recollection of the property at the time it was acquired by her father and mother. We have confirmed and elaborated aspects of her description based on our own inspection of the property. At the time (29 April 1990), the

cabin stood in its original location and was in essentially sound condition. The Eichelbergers subsequently moved the study cabin up against the main cottage and attached it for use as an additional room.

27 Cited in Dorfman, *Veblen and His America*, 276.

28 See photographs in Joseph Dorfman Papers, Box 65, Rare Book and Manuscript Library, Columbia University (New York, NY); also two snapshots in the Carleton College Archives, Veblen Collection (Northfield, MN).

29 A local realtor who grew up on Washington Island related to us how, as a boy, he once entered Veblen's study cabin via a window and rummaged through its contents. This would have been a dozen years or more after Veblen's death but before his stepdaughter Becky had sold the property. Our informant recalled how he had been especially struck by a trunk filled to the top with clippings and pages torn from newspapers. There were also boxes of papers in the cabin, as well as books and even some sheet music. Authors' interview with Eldred Ellefson, Washington Island, 10 October 1993; follow-up telephone conversation with Ellefson, 7 December 1993. Eugene Gislason recalled seeing the boxes of papers when, as a boy, he and his father visited Veblen at the Little Lake property. Esther Gunnerson, handwritten notes from interviews with former acquaintances of Veblen conducted in August 1963. Copy in Carleton College Archives, Veblen Collection (Northfield, MN).

30 Meyers, Memoirs, 7.

31 Interview with Ted and Fritz Bjarnarson conducted by Carleton College Archivist Eric Hillemann, Washington Island, 6 August 1993. Original tape cassette in the Veblen Collection, Carleton College Archives (Northfield, MN); dub in authors' possession.

32 For a detailed history of Lake Michigan steamships, see George W. Hilton, *Lake Michigan Passenger Steamers* (Stanford: Stanford University Press, 2002). On the history of the Goodrich boats, see James L. Elliott, *Red Stacks over the Horizon. The Story of the Goodrich Steamboat Line* (Grand Rapids: William B. Eerdmans Publishing Company, 1967).

33 Hillemann/Bjarnarson interview; Meyers to Diggins, 5. Diggins, Veblen file.

34 Gunnerson, interview notes.

35 Russell H. Bartley and Sylvia E. Yoneda, 'Thorstein Veblen on Washington Island: Traces of a Life', *International Journal of Politics, Culture and Society* 7.4 (1994): 589–613.

36 Interview with Colette Sims Van Fleet, Eureka, CA, 23 July 1993. Transcript in Veblen Collection, Carleton College Archives (Northfield, MN); snapshots of 'The Mock Turtle' preserved here as well; Meyers, Memoirs, 2–3.

37 Meyers interview.

38 Meyers, Memoirs, 1–2.

39 Meyers to Diggins, 3. Becky may here be describing a more mature and self-confident Veblen, for it would seem that he did not always write with such ease. To a former graduate student and close friend, for example, he described the great difficulties he was having in drafting *The Theory of the Leisure Class*, at one point having achieved 'nothing beyond contributing some half-dozen sheets of handwriting to the waste basket'. See Bartley and Bartley 'In Search of Thorstein Veblen', 152–5.

40 Van Fleet interview.

41 Ibid.; Gunnerson, 'Thorstein Veblen', 5. The trip to the Koyens' general store began with Veblen's rowboat. 'We'd go in the rowboat across the lake and then climb the hill to the Bjarnarson farm and from there we'd walk out to the Koyens' store', related Becky. 'We made this long trip through the woods', elaborated Veblen's grandniece Colette. 'It was the old-fashioned general store that had a barrel of stale chocolate [...] [the kind] with white centers and coated, always a little crisp because they were so old! We'd buy candles and flashlight batteries and staples' (Meyers interview; Van Fleet interview).

42 Gunnerson, interview notes; Meyers interview.

43 Van Fleet interview.

44 Van Fleet interview.

45 Meyers interview; Peter Christen Asbjørnsen, *Norske Folke-og Huldre-Eventyr i Udvalg* (Kristiania and Copenhagen: Gyldendalske Boghandel, Nordisk Forlag, 1909). This volume was among the books recovered from Veblen's Washington Island study cabin and is now preserved in the Veblen Collection, Carleton College Archives (Northfield, MN).

46 Riesman, *Thorstein Veblen*, 24. Cognizant as he was of the university's socialising function and of the fetters it imposed on students and faculty alike, Veblen chose to address only those students and colleagues agile enough intellectually to transcend the rote of prevailing ideology.

47 Thorstein Veblen, *The Higher Learning in America. A Memorandum on the Conduct of Universities by Business Men.* (New York: B. W. Huebsch, 1918), 18, 19–20. 'The student who comes up to the university for the pursuit of knowledge', Veblen held, 'is expected to know what he wants and to want it, without compulsion. If he falls short in these respects, if he has not the requisite interest and initiative, it is his own misfortune, not the fault of his teacher. What he has a legitimate claim to is an opportunity for such personal contact and guidance as will give him familiarity with the ways and means of the higher learning – any information imparted to him being incidental to his main work of habituation. He gets a chance to make himself a scholar, and what he will do with his opportunities in this way lies in his own discretion' (ibid., 20).

48 Bartley and Yoneda, 'Thorstein Veblen on Washington Island', 597; Jorgensen and Jorgensen, *Thorstein Veblen. Victorian Firebrand*, 262, 25n.

49 For more on this see our article 'Thorstein Veblen on Washington Island', 598.

50 Veblen to Emily Veblen Olsen, Palo Alto, CA, 26 June [1927]. Veblen Collection, Carleton College Archives (Northfield, MN); Meyers, Memoirs, 2; Van Fleet interview; Gunnerson, 'Thorstein Veblen', 7.

51 For a description of books Veblen loaned or gifted to the Bjarnarsons see: Russell H. and Sylvia Erickson Bartley, 'Veblen-associated Books Donated to Carleton College by the Descendants of Kari & Sigurline Bjarnarson of Washington Island, Wisconsin'. (Fort Bragg: Noyo Hill House, 1994). Copy in Veblen Collection, Carleton College Archives (Northfield, MN).

52 Ted Bjarnarson confirmed that his mother achieved greater fluency in English than did his father and that Sigurline, in fact, read a great deal in English. Telephone conversation with R. H. Bartley, 1 June 1994.

53 Volrath Vogt, *Illustrated Bible History and Brief Outline of Church History*, trans. by N. C. Brun (Minneapolis: Augsburg Publishing House, 1919). 'To Sigurline Bjarnarson from Thorstein Veblen' penned on flyleaf. Ted Bjarnarson confirmed that his parents held traditional religious convictions and were active churchgoers, while according to his mother Veblen was not religiously inclined.

54 Motier Fisher to Joseph Dorfman, n.p., 26 February 193??. Photocopy provided to authors by Veblen's step-granddaughter, Esther Meyers Baran, of San Francisco, from a collection of photocopied papers she had assembled from the Joseph Dorfman Papers at Columbia University. Veblen's sardonic word play here revolves around the double entendre of 'bunk' in its slang meaning of nonsense or balderdash, and 'bunkhouse', signifying a rustic dormitory for ranch hands, loggers, and other outdoor workers.

55 Selma Lagerlöf, *Jerusalem* (Garden City: Doubleday, Page, 1917); Lagerlöf, *The Holy City. Jerusalem II* (Garden City: Doubleday, Page, 1918).

56 *Færeyinga Saga eller Færøboernes Historie i den Islandske Grundtext med Færoisk og Dansk Oversættelse*, ed. by Carl Christian Rafn (København: Trykt Hos Directeur Jens Hostrup Schultz, Kongelig og Universitets-Bogtrykker, 1832).

57 Meyers, Memoirs, 7, 78.

58 Hillemann interview.

59 *The Laxdæla Saga*, ix.

60 *The Laxdæla Saga*, xi–xii.

61 Thorstein Veblen to Emily Veblen Olsen, Palo Alto, CA, 7 July 1927; Veblen to Olsen, Palo Alto, 8 July 1927. Copy in Veblen Collection, Carleton College Archives (Northfield, MN).

62 Thorstein Veblen to Isador Lubin, Detroit Harbor, 12 July 1917. Typed copy. Photocopy in Baran, Dorfman Papers (San Francisco).

63 Ann B. Veblen to Isador Lubin, Detroit Harbor, 29 June 1917. Typed copy. Baran, Dorfman Papers (San Francisco).

64 Commonwealth of Massachusetts, Standard Certificate of Death, Ann B. Veblen, Belmont, MA, 7 October 1920; McLean Hospital, Autopsy No. 11525: Veblen, Ann B. Copies of both documents in authors' possession.

65 Thorstein Veblen, *Essays, Reviews and Reports. Previously Uncollected Writings*, ed. by Joseph Dorfman (Clifton: Augustus M. Kelley, 1973), 189, 222n.

66 See our *Washington Island Library of Thorstein B. Veblen. A Description and Partial Listing* (Milwaukee: self-produced, 1990). Copies in Washington Island Archives (Washington Island, WI) and Veblen Collection, Carleton College Archives (Northfield, MN).

67 Dorfman, *Thorstein Veblen and His America*, 500.

68 Sadie Gregory to Clair Mitchell, Berkeley, 26 April 1928, 1–2. Joseph Dorfman Papers, Box 61, folder 'G'.

69 Sigurline Bjarnarson to Thorstein Veblen, Washington Island, 20 January 1929. Veblen Collection, Carleton College Archives (Northfield, MN).

70 Sigurline Bjarnarson to Becky Veblen, Washington Island, 26 April 1929; Sigurline Bjarnarson to Thorstein Veblen, Washington Island, 7 July 1929. Veblen Collection, Carleton College Archives (Northfield, MN).

71 Sigurline Bjarnarson to Becky Veblen, Washington Island, 22 October 1929. Veblen Collection, Carleton College Archives (Northfield, MN).

72 Anne T. Whitney, *Let's Talk about Washington Island, 1850–1950* (Chicago: Techni-Graphics/ Graphic Dimensions, 1973), 101.

73 Ellen R. Veblen to Thorstein B. Veblen, Halcyon, CA, 13 August 1923; Estate of Thorstein B. Veblen, Order and Decree of Settlement of Account and Final Distribution, No. 4886 (8 October 1931), 3–4. Superior Court of the State of California, County of San Mateo. Veblen Collection, Carleton College Archives (Northfield, MN). For a representative version of the Sandhill Road legend see Jorgensen and Jorgensen, *Victorian Firebrand*, 112–13.

74 Roxanne Nilan and Karen Bartholomew, 'No More "The Naughty Professor". Thorstein Veblen at Stanford', *Sandstone & Tile* (Stanford Historical Society) 31.2 (2007): 13–33, esp. 32, 8n.

75 R. L. Duffus, *The Innocents at Cedro. A Memoir of Thorstein Veblen and Some Others*, with the Advice and Consent of William M. Duffus (New York: Macmillan, 1944), 145.

76 Jorgensen and Jorgensen, *Victorian Firebrand*, 112–13, 242, 37n.

77 Nilan and Bartholomew, 'No More "The Naughty Professor"', 32, 38n.

78 For a detailed account of their marital tribulations, see our article: 'In Search of Thorstein Veblen'.

79 Ellen R. Veblen to Thorstein B. Veblen, Halcyon, CA, 18 June 1923. Veblen Collection, Carleton College Archives (Northfield, MN).

80 Ellen R. Veblen to Thorstein B. Veblen, Halcyon, CA, 13 August 1923. Veblen Collection, Carleton College Archives (Northfield, MN).

81 Thorstein B. Veblen to Ellen R. Veblen, Detroit Harbor, Washington Island, 21 August 1923; Thorstein to Ellen, Detroit Harbor, 10 September 1923. Copies in Veblen's hand. Veblen Collection, Carleton College Archives (Northfield, MN).

82 Ellen R. Veblen to Thorstein B. Veblen, Halcyon, CA, 18 June 1923. Veblen Collection, Carleton College Archives (Northfield, MN).

83 Thorstein B. Veblen to Ellen R. Veblen, Detroit Harbor, 10 September 1923. Veblen Collection, Carleton College Archives (Northfield, MN).

84 Duffus, *Innocents at Cedro*, 9.

85 Ibid., 93–4.
86 Ibid., 131–2.
87 Ibid., 131–2.
88 Nilan and Bartholomew, 'No More "The Naughty Professor"', 21.
89 Ibid., 129–33.
90 Becky Veblen Meyers, interview by Paul Veblen, Sand Point, ID, 10 June 1992. Transcription copy in Veblen Collection, Carleton College Archives (Northfield, MN). The 'woodlot' reference occurs in a letter from T. B. Veblen to Miss Grace Camp, Columbia, MI, 28 March 1918, Veblen Collection, Carleton College Archives (Northfield, MN). At age 92, Becky spoke of having helped Veblen build the ridge shack but we cannot be certain that she was not confusing La Honda Ridge with Washington Island, where as a teenager she did, in fact, participate in the construction of those later cabins. She was a nine-year-old when Veblen reconstructed the ridge shack and an adult when she would have formed her most lasting memories of the place. First childhood impressions, of course, also can be long-lasting, so we are here left with an irresolvable question.
91 For an account of Veblen's personal situation at and forced resignation from Stanford University, see: Jorgensen and Jorgensen, *Victorian Firebrand*, 121–9; also Bartley and Bartley, 'In Search of Thorstein Veblen', 159–61.
92 Maude Radford Warren to Joseph Dorfman, n.d., Joseph Dorfman Papers, Box 64. Warren, a good friend and occasional house guest of the Herbert Davenports, in whose home Veblen lived for a time, could only have learned of the Idaho episode directly from Veblen or perhaps one of the Davenports inasmuch as Veblen was not given to discussing his personal life and not even his closer acquaintants knew the details of that incident. 'Bevans' was Babe Bradley's first married name, which she continued to use until she wed Veblen in 1914.
93 Thorstein Veblen to Davenport, Stanford University, 6 September, 21 October and 9 November 1909. Joseph Dorfman Papers, Box 2 (N–Z of catalogued correspondence).
94 A. Ross Hill to the Honorable Board of Curators, University of Missouri (Columbia, MO), 6 April 1910. University of Missouri Archives, Box 11, fol. 4.
95 For a discussion of this period in Veblen's life see Bartley and Bartley, 'In the Company of T. B. Veblen', 291–309.
96 We have recounted in some detail their two Colorado sojourns (ibid., 309–22), and have compiled our raw research on their time together in Oregon in an unpublished compendium of notes, photocopied documents and photographs that also contains source material for the previous episode in Nowhere, Idaho. We have titled this collection of primary sources 'Tracking Thorstein Veblen in Idaho & Oregon: 1909–1911. A Working Compilation of Sources and Field Notes' (June, 1997). Copy in the Veblen Collection, Carleton College Archives (Northfield, MN).
97 Gustaf Nordenskiöld, *The Cliff Dwellers of the Mesa Verde* (Stockholm: P. A. Norstedt, 1893); Jesse Walter Fewkes, *Antiquities of the Mesa Verde National Park. Spruce-Tree House*. Smithsonian Institution, Bureau of American Ethnology, Bulletin 41 (Washington: Government Printing Office, 1909).
98 Duane A. Smith, *Mesa Verde National Park. Shadows of the Centuries* (Lawrence: University of Kansas Press, 1988), 27–32.
99 Kristian Bahnson, *Etnografien. Fremstillet i dens Hovedtræk* (København: Det Nordiske Forlag, 1900). Veblen Collection, Carleton College Archives (Northfield, MN).
100 See Thorstein Veblen to Miss Grace Camp, Columbia, MI, 25 March 1918. Veblen Collection, Carleton College Archives (Northfield, MN).
101 Thorstein Veblen to Mrs. Sigurd Olsen, Palo Alto, CA, 12 June 1929. Veblen Collection, Carleton College Archives (Northfield, MN).
102 Dorfman, *Thorstein Veblen and His America*, 455–6. There is, of course, no operative relationship whatsoever between Veblen's personal properties and the speculative investment capital to which he referred with his original, albeit not entirely appropriate, 'absentee ownership'

designation. The only conceivable connection here might be a vague parallel that Veblen saw in the heat of his own conundrums over title challenges and problematic renters between the inefficiencies of managing personal, non-investment, real estate from afar and the sabotage of industrial production by profit-seeking investors.

103 Jorgensen and Jorgensen, *Victorian Firebrand*, 163.

104 Ann B. Veblen, medical records, McLean Hospital (Belmont, MA). Copies in possession of patient's granddaughter, Esther M. Baran (San Francisco), who kindly allowed the authors to examine and selectively photocopy them.

105 The day after his wife's demise Veblen informed his brother Andrew of her passing in a brief letter that Dorfman described as 'laconic', groundlessly insinuating emotional detachment. 'Dear Andrew,' Veblen wrote. 'Ann died yesterday in the hospital at Waverley [Belmont], where she has been for something over a year past, from the effects of an abscess in the lung, complicated with symptoms of pneumonia. I have been here, with her sister's folks, the past week, going back and forth between Waverley and here. Next week I am to return to New York, where work begins at the New School on the fifteenth.' In an unusual departure from his customary habit of signing letters to Andrew: 'Your brother Thorstein Veblen', on this occasion he closed with a curiously formal 'Sincerely Thorstein Veblen' – perhaps a lapse in his rush to notify in-laws and mutual acquaintances with whom he normally was more formal. Whatever the case, this particular letter offers no insight at all into Veblen's emotional state following the death of his spouse and Dorfman was wrong to suggest otherwise. Thorstein Veblen to Andrew Veblen, Worcester, MA, 8 October 1920. Andrew Veblen Papers, Box 1, Minnesota Historical Society (St. Paul), Box 1; Thorstein Veblen, *Essays, Reviews and Reports. Previously Uncollected Writings*, ed. by Joseph Dorfman (Clifton: Augustus M. Kelley, 1973), 221, 188n.

106 Thorstein Veblen to [?] Pritchard, Minneapolis, MN, 28 October 1924. Previously unknown letter displayed in June 2007 as part of a Veblen exhibit at the Vang Public Library in Valdres, Norway, mounted on the occasion of the 150th anniversary of Veblen's birth. The letter was acquired in the 1990s from a Boston book dealer by Norwegian scholar Erik Reinert and now forms part of Reinert's private collection of Vebleniana.

107 Supra, 7.

108 Thorstein Veblen, 'The Intellectual Pre-eminence of Jews in Modern Europe', *Political Science Quarterly* 34 (1919): 33–42.

109 Odner, 'New perspectives on Thorstein Veblen, the Norwegian', in this volume.

110 Isador Lubin, 'Recollections of Veblen'. In *Thorstein Veblen. The Carleton College Veblen Seminar Essays*, ed. by Carlton C. Qualey (New York: Columbia University Press, 1968), 135.

111 Riesman's dismissive comparison of Mark Twain's and Veblen's shared preference for the company of animals over that of humans comes immediately to mind. See Riesman, *Thorstein Veblen*, 200.

112 Motier Fisher to Joseph Dorfman, n.p., 26 February 19??, 3–4. Copy in Baran, Dorfman Papers (San Francisco).

113 Thorstein Veblen to Miss Grace Camp, Detroit Harbor, WI, 20 September 1920. Veblen Collection, Carleton College Archives (Northfield, MN).

114 Becky Meyers to John Diggins, n.p., 18 March 1982, 2. Diggins, Veblen file; also Veblen Collection, Carleton College Archives (Northfield, MN).

115 Hans Otto Storm to Thorstein Veblen, Palo Alto, CA, 6 January 1926. Veblen Collection, Carleton College Archives (Northfield, MN).

116 Torfi H. Tulinius, 'Capital, field, illusio. Can Bourdieu's sociology help us understand the development of literature in medieval Iceland?' (2004): 3–4; online: http://w210.ub.uni-tuebingen.de/dbt/volltexe/2004/1080/pdf/27_tor~1.pdf (accessed 24 August 2007). Tulinius, a literary scholar at the University of Iceland (Reykjavik), has independently taken Veblen's view that the medieval Icelandic sagas represent social documents as well as literary works and has carried their historical analysis well beyond the suggestive observations offered

by Veblen in the introduction to his translation of *The Laxdæla Saga*. See also by the same author: 'Saga as a myth: the family sagas and social reality in thirteenth-century Iceland' n.d.; online: www.arts.usyd.edu.au/ departs/medieval/saga/pdf/526-tulinius.pdf (accessed 24 August 2007).

117 Hans Otto Storm to Thorstein Veblen, Palo Alto, CA, 6 January 1926.

118 Hans Otto Storm, Notes on Thorstein Veblen to Joseph Dorfman, Palo Alto, CA, November 1932. Copy in Storm (Hans O.) Papers, BANC MSS C-H 73, Bancroft Library, University of California (Berkeley).

119 Meyers to Diggins, 18 March 1982, 2. Diggins, Veblen file.

120 Hans Otto Storm to Meyers, Sayville, NY, 25 September 1928. Storm Papers.

121 Hans Otto Storm to Thorstein Veblen, Sayville, NY, 24 December 1928. Storm Papers.

122 Hans Otto Storm to Thorstein Veblen, Sayville, NY, 9 February 1929. Storm Papers.

123 Fisher to Dorfman, n.p., 26 February 193??, 1–2. Copy in Baran, Dorfman Papers (San Francisco).

Part Two

AMERICAN EDUCATION

Chapter 7

ITHACA TRANSFER: VEBLEN AND THE HISTORICAL PROFESSION

Francesca Lidia Viano[1]

Thorstein Bunde Veblen has passed into the annals of history as an academic *enfant terrible*: a womanising economist, atheist and iconoclast who mercilessly dissected the vices of the American leisure class, denounced the speculative vocations of their captains of industry and dismissed the entire corpus of contemporary economics and jurisprudence as empty theologies. Born to a Norwegian immigrant family on a Wisconsin farm in 1857, he grew up in a settlement inhabited by Irish and German settlers, from whom he learned both English and German early on. His foreign origins and segregated childhood, along with the autarkic principles and Lutheran morals of his parents, have often been invoked to explain Veblen's harsh denunciation of the American system. Indeed, he has been described as an 'unacclimated alien', an intellectual 'wanderer', and even an 'interned immigrant'; a marauder on the border between the old world and the new who, like Peder Victorious in Rølvåg's epic saga about Norwegian-American immigration, nonetheless identified himself fully with neither of them.[2]

Even if Veblen grew up on the outskirts of American culture, his career followed a path which was quite mainstream among his fellow intellectuals. In 1881, one year after graduating from Carleton College, where he had studied philosophy and political economy, Veblen enrolled for a PhD at Johns Hopkins University, then at the cutting edge in the teaching of history and political economy. Veblen, however, majored in Philosophy, taught at the time by the Hegelian G. S. Morris and the *sui generis* pragmatist Charles Sanders Peirce, and only took Herbert Baxter Adams's course in 'Sources of early European history'.[3] Apparently forced to leave for lack of funding, Veblen made his way to Yale, where he continued his philosophical studies under the supervision of the Kantian Noah Porter, alongside those of economics, then taught by William Graham Sumner, one of Herbert Spencer's American acolytes. After graduating from Yale in 1884, Veblen's career came to a standstill; in spite of fiery letters of recommendation, like those of his Carleton College professor John Bates Clark and his Yale mentors Sumner and Porter, Veblen had not been able to procure any academic position, and languished for seven years, first in his parents' house and then in that of his father-in-law.[4]

Veblen's difficulty in finding a permanent university position has often been taken as a confirmation of his marginality, resulting from his Lutheranism and 'Scandihoofian' heritage. However, as Mary O. Furner has documented, the 1880s were an extremely uncertain period in American academia, and particularly so for historians and economists. Very much like Veblen, the economist Simon Patten returned jobless to his father's Illinois farm, the philosopher and mathematician Peirce only got an untenured position at Johns Hopkins, and the economist James Laurence Laughlin left a temporary position at Harvard to work as an insurance agent.[5] Veblen entered Cornell University, perched on the gorges of Ithaca, New York, in 1891 to launch his professional career *ex novo*, passing, one might say, through a less showy entrance. For Cornell was by far the most rural of the great American institutions of higher learning: benefiting from the sale of public lands granted the State of New York by the Morrill Land Grant Act (1862) to those educational institutions aimed at diffusing agricultural and technical knowledge, Cornell was founded as a co-educational university admitting people of every or no religious denomination and allowing poor students to finance their studies by working on campus.[6]

According to Veblen's principal biographer, Joseph Dorfman, Veblen enrolled at Cornell in the beginning of the winter term, 1891, to work for an 'advanced degree' and only registered for two courses, 'one in American history and one in American constitutional history and law' with Moses Coit Tyler.[7] Eventually, the story goes, Veblen found 'better opportunities in economics', where professor James Laurence Laughlin, recently hired as head of the department, procured him a fellowship. Two years later, after moving to the newly founded University of Chicago, Laughlin would appoint Veblen associate professor in the Department of Economics.[8] It was at Chicago, where he taught until 1906, that Veblen composed the manifesto of a new current in economics, which he coined 'evolutionary economics', asking for the application of anthropology to the field of economics, and published his most famous book, *The Theory of the Leisure Class*, which immediately became a best-seller.[9]

Veblen's sojourn at Cornell has always been considered a brief and insignificant parenthesis in his intellectual development, a 'phase of transition' as Lev E. Dobriansky called it, between the philosophical studies of his youth and his intellectual maturation at Chicago.[10] At that university Veblen indeed came into contact with biologists Jacques Loeb and George Romanes, probably met British zoologist C. Lloyd Morgan, then visiting professor at Chicago University, and made friends with anthropologist William I. Thomas, the expert in comparative animism.[11] But Chicago also disclosed to Veblen the realm of pragmatism which, though introduced to him already in Peirce's classes at Johns Hopkins, now presented itself far more clearly through the influence of John Dewey, who began teaching at that university in 1896.[12] On this basis, economists in the early 1930s started presenting Veblen as a 'post-Darwinian' intellectual who used 'Darwinian methodological injunctions' to 'undermine the presuppositions of mainstream economics'.[13] Historians, on the contrary, saw in Veblen a kind of agitator who tried to give academic credibility to socialist and populist causes. Henry Steele Commager held that Veblen was a product of frontier reformism and argued that his criticisms of captains of industry 'might have been made by any Kansas Populist comparing the constructive work of building the transcontinentals with the destructive work of exploiting them',[14] and Daniel Aaron simply anchored Veblen to the 'political agitators' who, like Henry

George, Edward Bellamy, Henry Demarest Lloyd, and William D. Howells, had founded the progressive movement.[15] Morton G. White rightly placed him among the 'rebel' intellectuals who helped unhinge the old romantic and idealistic approach but, instead of assimilating his point of view to those of the rebel historians, like James Harvey Robinson and Charles A. Beard, he went back to the old myth of Veblen 'the pragmatist' and put his name beside that of John Dewey.[16]

In the long run, even though progressivism and populism continued to be counted among Veblen's influences, the image of Veblen as neo-Darwinian scientist outlasted the one sketched by post-war historians, particularly after the failure of communism made it urgent to replace his theory of economic and social development with a new kind of evolutionism, free from Marxist mnemonics. This essay will shed light on a further, important influence on the development of Veblen's thought, which hitherto has been neglected: history. It is absent from the list of Veblen's 'intellectual antecedents' elaborated by Stephen Edgell and Rick Tilman in one of the articles responsible for the recent Veblen Renaissance,[17] and Veblen scholars have habitually emphasised his distance from the world of historiography ever since his death in 1929. He was 'less the historian than the biologist of human institutions', Paul T. Homan remarked, while Wesley C. Mitchell emphasised that 'he was trained not in history but in natural science and philosophy'.[18] Historians themselves, although they did not endorse this narrative, indirectly contributed to its success by nurturing the myth of Veblen's alienation from historiography.

Even if it was part of Veblen's curricula since he took Herbert Baxter Adams's course at Johns Hopkins,[19] history crystallised as one of Veblen's principal interests only in the winter of 1891, when he enrolled at Cornell.[20] His historical studies there would prove fundamental for his intellectual development for a number of reasons: first, they gave him a vocabulary of institutions, covering every kind of historical expression, from law to constitutions to politics to psychology; second, they trained him to understand the development of institutions in a Darwinian way without resorting to the teleology of contemporary sociologists and legal historians, rather drawing his attention towards the frequent discrepancies between factual conditions and their ideological re-elaborations, or between economic conditions and political structures. Third, by insisting on the continuing 'survival' of ancient institutions and practices, Cornell historians would help him grasp the inertia of social as compared to biological development. Finally, Veblen familiarised himself with this historical-Darwinian method in an educational context dominated by certain priorities, above all by the necessity of applying the study of constitutional history, politics and economics to *practical* questions in order to prepare students for careers in politics and civil service.

The first section of this essay seeks to reconstruct Veblen's stay at Cornell, including the hitherto unknown archival evidence for his course of studies, in order to demonstrate its centrality to Veblen's career. The second and third section position Veblen's encounter with the history of political institutions at Cornell in the context of the transformations through which American social science gained a professional status. The fourth and fifth sections analyse the influence of Cornell historiography on Veblen's most celebrated theories. The Appendix, finally, reproduces Veblen's Cornell dossier.

Crossing the Cornell Frontier

An anecdote circulating at Cornell already in the 1890s, first popularised by Homan in 1927 and then taken up by Dorfman, describes Veblen entering the office of James Laurence Laughlin, then chair of the Department of Economics, in an unspecified moment of the winter semester of the academic year 1890–91, only to leave his study with the promise of a 'teaching fellowship' which he supposedly enjoyed until he left for Chicago.[21] Dorfman's special talent consisted in embellishing this anecdote so cleverly that it became an integral and picturesque part of Vebleniana for generations to come.[22] Not only did he add an air of authenticity to it by attributing it directly to Laughlin, but he gave it a romantic twist by portraying Veblen as a prototypical frontiersman:

> Laughlin often told the story of his first meeting with Veblen. He [Laughlin] was sitting in his study in Ithaca when an anaemic-looking person, wearing a coonskin cap and corduroy trousers, entered and in the mildest possible tone announced: 'I am Thorstein Veblen'.[23]

Veblen's pioneer-like appearance, reminiscent of Davy Crocket, alongside his ostensibly Lutheran profession of faith and his informal manners – revealed by his abrupt decision to visit Laughlin – were well suited to Cornell's unceremonious climate and its politics of supporting poor, religiously heterodox and rural students. Even if he was born in Ohio to a well-off, Scotch-Irish Presbyterian family, Laughlin himself was 'in the broadest sense of the term a self-made man', who once famously claimed that only 'a poor boy' could know what it meant to 'achieve something'.[24] When Veblen met him at Cornell, Laughlin had recently arrived from Philadelphia, where he had been working in the insurance business, after his hopes of being hired at Harvard had been frustrated by his mentor's decision to give tenure to his other *protégé*, the more mainstream historian and economist Frank William Taussig.[25] Given Laughlin's self-made education and difficulties in finding a permanent job in academia, it is not surprising that, after hearing of Veblen's sad academic history, 'of his enforced idleness and his decision to go on with his studies', Laughlin went straight to the president to secure him a source of funding.[26]

As narrated by his biographers, Veblen's Cornell admission was an important step towards his realignment with American culture. At Cornell, Veblen apparently freed himself from the uncomfortable role of a European immigrant in a foreign country to play that of a pioneer and 'rural intellectual' along the internal frontier, thus identifying himself with one of the central characters of American national mythology. This cultural sublimation is made even more credible by the fact that Cornell was constructed according to the Western model established by universities like Michigan, where Cornell's first president, Andrew Dickson White, and most of Veblen's professors at some point had taught.[27] Like all historiographical myths, however, the one of Veblen's arrival at Cornell remains problematic for at least two reasons. First of all, his modestly rural upbringing notwithstanding, Veblen's prospective professor at Cornell, Laughlin, was anyway a product of Harvard: described by his pupils as 'perfectly dressed and groomed', his manners and speech 'were always as perfect as he could make them, which was very perfect indeed'.[28] His contrast with Veblen could not have been clearer, and Laughlin himself confessed – in an oral account that largely has been ignored by scholars – to have found 'somewhat incredible … that a man could be so lacking in polish and yet have the ability which he recognized in Veblen'. It was 'because Veblen was different in his background, in his point of view, and even in his personal characteristics' – Laughlin would admit – that he 'liked him', not because of his conformity to the academic environment at Cornell.[29] Veblen 'was a luxury' for Laughlin, a kind of exotic plant in the academic greenhouse he was trying to construct at Cornell and later would realise at the University of Chicago.[30]

Most importantly, the narrative of Veblen's stay at Cornell propagated by Homan and later resumed as canonical by the secondary literature rests on faulty foundations. Contrary to what is commonly argued, Veblen's turn to economics was not triggered haphazardly, by his disappointment with historical disciplines. Veblen was attracted to Cornell by the perspective of studying 'History and Political Science', as he wrote in a letter to the administrative office of 25 November 1890,[31] but his 'graduate student report card' shows he was enrolled for an 'advanced course of study leading to the degree of Ph.D. in Economics, American History and English Constitutional History' on 9 January of the following year.[32] His 'committee' was comprised of 'James Laurence Laughlin, Moses Coit Tyler, and Herbert Tuttle', and his programme of study was structured as follows:

Major Subject: Economics; courses 20, 21 and 22 of 'History and Political Science'
First Minor: courses 10 and 12 of Do[ctorate?]
Second Minor: English Constitution; course 14.[33]

Since economics was still part of the political science programme at Cornell, and was taught at the School of History and Political Science, Veblen's final decision to match Laughlin's courses with those in history was not surprising. The three courses in economics indicated by Veblen (20, 21 and 22), all offered by Laughlin, consisted of a seminar on 'Special Topics' such as 'Bimetallism, Shipping, Railway Transportation' (20), one on the 'History of Tariff Legislation of the US' (21) and a 'Special Seminar' on a topic to be decided (22). The courses Veblen proposed to take as his First Minor were 'American History from the end of the War for Independence to the end of the War for the Union' (10) and 'American Constitutional History' (12), both held by Professor Tyler. Finally, Veblen's proposed 'Second Minor' was Professor Tuttle's course on the 'English Constitution' (14).[34]

Veblen maintained this programme of studies until the summer of 1891 when, before returning to Ithaca in the fall, he declared his intention to study 'European as well as American socialism' at Cornell in the coming year. No specific courses bearing this name were scheduled for the autumn and winter semesters of 1891, but on 19 November 1891 Veblen applied to replace his two minors in American History and English Constitutional History with 'The Science of Finance' and 'Socialism', both almost certainly held by Laughlin.[35] Even if he taught economics, Laughlin was an historian by formation, like Tuttle and Tyler, and all of them shared a profound interest in German historical jurisprudence. Under their supervision, Veblen would write an article – 'Some Neglected Points in the Theory of Socialism' – in which he articulated the core of his future economic theory by claiming that patterns of consumption derived from status competition rather than actual material needs.[36]

Objectivity and Reform

Until the 1880s, economics had generally been taught under the heading of philosophy or moral philosophy in America because, following the examples of Adam Smith and John Stuart Mill, economists saw their task as that of combing history in search of recipes for realising the highest philosophical goals, whether the common good or public happiness.[37] Philosophical curricula such as those pursued by Veblen during his education, from Carleton to Yale, were emblematic of this approach. Since the late 1860s, however, select American universities had become the stage of a major shift, eventually leading to the emancipation of social science from moral philosophy; a shift that Thomas Haskell has reconstructed elegantly by resurrecting Kuhnian models of explanation.[38]

In the wake of the Civil War, when transcendentalism gradually was superseded by a more constructive spirit of institutional reform, social science crystallised around an amateur association called the American Social Science Association (ASSA). Conceived by one of the leading characters of the abolitionist movement, Franklin B. Sanborn, the association shared all the ambiguities of its founder. Still alien to the pursuit of objective knowledge, and following rather the typically Victorian ambition of establishing intellectual 'authority',[39] this association gathered scientists, university reformers, ministers, lawyers and physicians who still confused social analysis with social reform; not in the sense that they politicised social questions, as Charles Wright Mills had once suggested, but in the sense that they tried to depoliticise social questions to make them the exclusive domain of social scientists, whose *professional* expertise was meant to guide political action, not become one with it.[40] Even if they lacked the later preoccupation of professionals with the problem of objectivity, these social scientists made a first effort to anchor their fields to factual analysis rather than to philosophical arguments. But historians and economists within the association eventually grew discontented with this system and, since they came to think that objective research was incompatible with reformist engagement, embarked on the further process of creating autonomous associations devoid of reformist goals: the American Historical Association was founded in 1884 at a Saratoga meeting of the ASSA, thanks to the initiative of its members, while the American Economic Association was born under similar circumstances one year later.

In freeing the AHA and the AEA of 'reformist ballast', the secession accelerated a shift of paradigm that, once defined by Morton White as a 'revolt against formalism', more recently has been described as a reconfiguration of old explanatory patterns to address the problems of 'uncertainty' and 'interdependence' posed by the growing complexity of modern societies and the new discoveries in biology and physics, particularly Darwinism.[41] Even after overcoming the old reformist ambitions, however, and for reasons of historical inertia, historians maintained the sociologists' and reformers' old faith in the state as an agent capable of redistributing wealth and intervening in the course of the social and economic life of communities, as well as a strong bias against free trade per se. Indeed, although Herbert Spencer had been inspirational in the founding of the American Social Science Association because of his ambition to ground the explanation of society on a scientific basis, neither the body of the ASSA nor the majority of historians agreed with his determinism and his hatred of the state.[12] They were closer to an old school 'free trader' like Adam Smith who, as Donald Winch demonstrates, had approached economics from the perspective of a science of legislation to highlight the interdependence of economic, social and political variables.[13]

When Veblen entered Johns Hopkins in 1881, the historians and economists of this university were in the processes of separating from the ASSA,[14] and Veblen's professor of history there, Herbert Baxter Adams, was one of the principal architects of the American Historical Association.[15] In his classes, Veblen had his first taste of professional historiography, i.e. of a kind of teaching which focused on the construction of a professional language, without engaging with its practical repercussions.[16] Cornell, on the contrary, where he ended up 10 years later, was still the headquarters of the old reformist movement. Former president White had been one of the earliest members of the American Social Science Association and among the few historians who continued trusting it even after professional historians had generally grown disenchanted with it.[17] This is the reason why he envisioned a university in which the study of history was combined with that of 'Jurisprudence, Political and Social Science' and specially designed to prepare students to fight against 'the present abuses in Politics and Religion'.[18] Already in 1871, after noting how 'the most glaring ignorance, not merely of the first principles, but of the simple, ordinary practice regarding great social interests' dominated 'our legislatures, county, state', White recommended 'the study of social problems arising among us, of the various solutions that have been proposed and tried, and of the result of these attempted solutions'. Among the topics he mentioned were 'the prevention and remedy of vice and crime [...] questions as to the management of pauperism, insanity, and inebriety; questions as to the means of infusing more comfort and more incentive to right thinking into the masses in the cities'.[19] To realise this goal, Cornell gave the first professorship of 'social science' to Frank Sanborn, the founder of the ASSA, in 1884, and, even if White resigned one year later, his policy and Sanborn's teachings deeply marked the subsequent development of Cornell's curricula. In 1891, the courses in 'History and Political Science' still promised to meet White's hopes by offering 'such training as will be valuable to students intending to go into the profession of the law, into journalism, into the civil service, or into active political life'.[20]

Veblen's social theory emerged from the unique climate created by White at Cornell, where reformism was combined with historical research and analysis. As will become clear later, Veblen's originality derived from his exploitation of an old historiographical pattern, still submitted to social analysis and practically indistinguishable from it. But what was historiography like at the time of Veblen's studies at Cornell?

Veblen and British Historiography

The pressure to emancipate historiography from social analysis was originally fuelled by the arrival in America of a new kind of academic culture. As the French historian and politician Édouard de Laboulaye once acknowledged, it was in Germany that legal history first developed as an academic discipline under the influence of Friedrich Karl von Savigny in the early nineteenth century.[51] This historical methodology was later extended from the study of law to that of language and folklore by the jurist Jacob Grimm, in what Grimm himself called the 'history of institutions'.[52] Since institutions were believed to be the fruit of a living subject – the 'spirit' of a people in Humboldt's words – their development could be assimilated to the process of continuous growth characterising the development of natural organisms.[53] The task of the historian therefore consisted in identifying the ancient nucleus of contemporary institutions or, in other words, in charting the 'survival' of primitive institutions in modern society.[54] German and British institutional historians agreed on tracing the origin of Anglo-Saxon civilisation back to the Teutonic 'mark-community' or 'township' of mediaeval times, where bands of kinsmen gathered to resolve common affairs and shared an 'undivided proprietorship over a definite tract of land'.[55] From this premise, they followed the organic development of the ur-community from early German settlements to the Anglo-Saxon occupation of England by tracing the evolution of its basic institutions – 'possession of land', 'rank', 'public law', 'family relations' and 'social conditions' – as they emerged from the study of local documents, oral or written traditions, and folktales.[56] Some British political historians, like Sir Henry Maine, Edward Augustus Freeman and Goldwin Smith, and a few of their American followers (notably William Francis Allen) even brought America into the scheme by presenting the early British settlements in New England as the latest development of German and Anglo-Saxon communitarian institutions.[57]

When Veblen enrolled as a graduate student at Johns Hopkins University, in 1881, this Anglo-German historical approach had already taken root in the university and had found its major spokesman in Adams, who believed in a continuous and uninterrupted development from the common land tenures of the German Middle Ages to the town-meetings of New England.[58] Since 1878, he had taken the habit of bringing students to the sites of ancient plantations so that they could study the 'survivals' of their original system of 'co-proprietorship' or 'proprietorship in common', as Maine once defined it.[59] Veblen took Adams's course and participated in his discussion seminar held at the Historical and Political Science Association, in which 'half a dozen advanced students' coming 'from various parts of the Union' met together twice a week 'in a small lecture-room of the Peabody Institute' to compare and confront the institutions of their different states.[60] No traces are left of Veblen's contribution to the discussions, except that one of his colleagues at the seminar, the later renowned social historian John Franklin Jameson, would report having learned from him that Norwegian communities in the Midwest were historical 'fossils', preserving the 'old dialectic forms' of their mother country from the modernising contaminations 'of the Danish newspapers from Copenhagen and Christiania [now Oslo]'.[61]

It is also probable that, while studying under Adams's supervision, Veblen met the British historian James Bryce, who had been invited by Adams in the autumn of 1881 to give lectures at Johns Hopkins on the history of political institutions, and whose books soon would be adopted as required reading in the history courses of some American universities.[62] At Yale, on the other hand, where Veblen arrived in 1882, scientific history had influenced the teaching of economics ever since Sumner read the English historian Henry Thomas Buckle's *History of Civilization* and discussed 'with other students at Oxford the possibility of a science of society based upon a study of history'.[63]

The history of institutions that Veblen practiced first at Johns Hopkins and then at Yale has left no visible mark in his writings, although it is almost certain that it sparked his future interest in land rents and problems of agricultural property, which were crucial in the discussion of village communities.[64] As a matter of fact, the only piece of published work Veblen produced at the end of this cycle of study was a long analysis of Kant's theory of judgment, in which he singled out the question of agency and re-interpreted Kant's reflective judgment as a means of research, while hinting at a dichotomy between intellectual theorisation and empirical observation.[65] It was at Cornell, the first American university to host British institutional historians in the new role of 'visiting professors' – most famously Goldwin Smith and Edward Augustus Freeman – that Veblen put the study of philosophy on hold and began studying economics from the perspective offered by the history of institutions, and particularly the history of political and legal ones.[66]

Given White's actualising agenda, it is not surprising that all of Veblen's professors combined the historical profession with journalism, demonstrated a clear trust in the state and its capacity to correct the corruption of American life by means of reform. Known among colleagues for his 'remarkable quick wit' and his 'love of nature', Veblen's professor of English Constitution History, Herbert Tuttle, was a passionate observer of politics and a strong supporter of the cause of civic reform.[67] Although he had trained as an historian under the supervision of Vermont professor James B. Angell, he began his career as a journalist, first in Paris, where he worked as a correspondent for the *New York Tribune*, and later as a correspondent of the London *Daily News* and of various American newspapers in Berlin.[68] It was in Berlin that Tuttle first became acquainted with Cornell president White, who not only invited him to teach in the newly founded university, but also encouraged him to write a history of Prussia, for which Tuttle began collecting materials in 1875 with extensive research in the Prussian Military Archives.[69] Tuttle set himself the goal of contrasting the cult of heroism and individualism instilled in historiography by Thomas Carlyle by emphasising the workings of governments and states; in the case of Prussia, this brought him to leave Frederick the Great's deeds in the relative shadows to concentrate on 'the life of Prussia as a State, the development of polity, the growth of institutions, the progress of society'.[70] Tuttle's historiographical agenda would resonate in Veblen's famous essays on 'The Evolution of the Scientific Point of View', where he complained about the fact that 'historians of human culture' had commonly dealt with facts that had occurred 'on the higher levels of intellectual enterprise', while 'the lower range of generalisations, which ha[d] to do with work-day experience, ha[d] in great part been passed over with scant ceremony'.[71]

Scepticism towards the cult of historical heroes was in the air when Veblen attended Cornell. His Cornell professor of 'American History' and 'American Constitutional History', Moses C. Tyler, wholeheartedly shared Tuttle's critique of past historians' veneration for heroes, although he retained Carlyle's belief in the supremacy of morals as the major engine of historical development. Before entering Yale University thanks to an uncle's generous donation, he had been a schoolteacher in a hamlet north of Detroit, a bookseller in Chicago, a student at Michigan, and a journalist for the *The Nation* and the *Christian Union*.[72] Under the guidance of Dr Dio Lewis, the director of an institute in which he recovered from a nervous breakdown by practising something called 'musical gymnastic[s]', Tyler began developing literary interests which led him to England and familiarised him with the writings of Matthew Arnold, Thomas Carlyle and Walter Pater, all of whom shared the romantic idea that historical processes could be reduced to the development of morals or, to put it more simply, that history could be taken as a 'moral standard'.[73] Tyler was fascinated by this current of thought, to the point of envisaging a history of the American Revolution based on the study of morality as it emerged from literary sources, an enterprise that was still occupying him when Veblen attended his courses.[74] Even more interestingly, and under the influence of William E. H. Lecky's studies on public opinion, Tyler extended the frontiers of 'literature' to incorporate any sort of manifestations of 'public opinion', like 'spiritual moods', 'motives', 'passions', even 'sportive caprices' and 'whims'.[75] Described by Veblen's biographer Dorfman as an idealistic bigot and a rampant patriot,[76] Tyler subverted historiographical priorities by subordinating the traditional subjects of political history – 'the proceedings of legislative bodies, the doings of cabinet ministers and of colonial politicians, the movement of armies' – to 'the ideas and the emotions which lay back of them or in front of them, which caused them or were caused by them'.[77] This attention to psychological phenomena would pave the way for the American Studies movement that, under the leadership of Perry Miller and Howard Mumford Jones, focused primarily on the study of mentalities, a method of which Veblen would give an embryonic expression in his essay on socialism written while he was at Cornell.[78]

Having received his BA in mediaeval history, Veblen's professor of economics James Lawrence Laughlin too was by vocation a historian. After writing his PhD thesis on mediaeval Anglo-Saxon Legal Procedure under the supervision of Henry Adams, at Harvard, he gave a series of courses which presumably combined comparative history and political economy to investigate the 'economic effects of land tenures in England, Ireland, and France'.[79] Before coming to Cornell, however, he worked first as secretary and later as president of the Boston Insurance Company, which was headed by the anti-imperialist activist Edward Atkinson.[80] Although allergic to European socialism, to the point of refusing membership in the American Economic Association because it was too socialistically inclined, Laughlin was drastic in his rejection both of the classical quantity theory and of the new marginalist approach coming from Austria. In tune with White's practical agenda, he would always remain critical of theoretical and abstract economics, and instead conceived of the subject as rooted in historiography and bearing upon politics and reform.[81] In 1884, the same year in which Tuttle wrote in the *Atlantic Monthly* to compare the structures of parties in Europe, England, and America, Laughlin wrote in the same journal on the corruption of the republican party generated by the massive use of the so-called 'Spoils system', and a year later to lament the absence of legislative responsibility in Congress.[82]

Although detailed accounts of Tyler's and Laughlin's courses at the time of Veblen's stay in Ithaca are missing, one can make educated guesses as to their content from the brief descriptions appearing in the *Cornell Register* and from their contemporary writings on topics they treated in class. In sketching the outline of the Cornell history programme, White had made clear that the 'history of England' had a place of honour in it, since England should be considered 'a typical example of a great modern state'.[83] In his course on the 'History of the English Constitution', Tuttle conformed to White's programme by reconstructing the gradual development of the English state from the first Anglo-Saxon settlements to the rise of parliamentary government. Judging from his lecture notes, the course was deeply indebted to the evolutionary scheme first elaborated by German and British institutional historians; very much like them, Tuttle believed that freedom was born in the tribal assemblies of mediaeval Germany, and traced its development through the German occupation of England and its later invasion by 'Romanised' Scandinavians – the Normans. More specifically, he followed the lead of institutional historiography in claiming that, even if the Normans had 'modified Anglo-Saxon institutions by superimposing upon them institutions of another branch of Germans, as modified by closer contact with the laws of Rome', the old Saxon liberties survived and gave a peculiar and more 'democratic' character to feudal England. Tuttle listed three main 'points of difference between Anglo-Norman and continental feudalism':

(1) Greater strength of Central Govt, owing to circumstances of conquest, to [...] personal possessions [...] to character of king [...] to relations between races
(2) Greater compactness or unity of barons or people [...] against King
(3) Survival of old Saxon institutions or their influence

Tuttle's treatment of Anglo-Norman feudalism was a prerequisite for his discussion of English democracy. In his lectures on English constitutional history, as in his previous ones on the 'History of Political and Municipal Institutions', he maintained that the English government was 'more democratic than that of the United States', and traced English democracy back to the singularity of Anglo-Norman feudalism, which combined the old Saxon idea of liberty with a stronger notion of central power and the egalitarianism of early German assemblies.[84] Like William Stubbs, whose *Constitutional History of England* figured in his reading list, Tuttle seemed to interpret the parliamentary system, as it evolved in modern times from the Anglo-Saxon resistance to the king, as the only medium capable of reconciling the nation-state with self-government. His discussion of how taxes shifted from being a mere war fund destined for the king to a 'national fund', in the lectures dedicated to 'REVENUES OF KING', 'CROWN AND MILITARY', and 'PARLIAMENTARY GOVERNMENT', might well have been instrumental in arguing so.[85]

Such an idea of government, able to combine democracy with a strong central authority invested with economic powers, was difficult to reconcile with the image of Britain drawn by authors like Herbert Spencer. In the wake of the Industrial Revolution, Spencer had envisioned a society in which old feudal conventions would have been replaced by purely industrial and commercial relations. Although sceptical of any form of abstract reasoning, Maine had followed his lead in defining modernity as the passage from the 'co-proprietorship' of the first Teutonic communities ('systems of status') to private property and contractual intercourse ('systems of contract'), and he condemned every form of state intervention as tyrannical and socialist.[86] Both of them, finally, had drawn on Darwin to demonstrate that the passage from communitarian to individualistic institutions was conditioned by rules of biological necessity. More subtly, Tuttle distinguished the institution in itself from its 'spirit': already in 1872, while explaining the character of the 'French Democracy' to the readers of the *Atlantic Monthly*, Tuttle maintained that 'there may be democratic peoples without strictly democratic institutions; and there may be popular institutions with a very weak democratic spirit'.[87] He then went a long way in presenting the Americans as more democratic in spirit than the English, but less so in their institutions, because 'the government of England feels more directly than that of the United States the force of public opinion'.[88]

In 1883, Tuttle applied the distinction between institutions and spirit to the analysis of socialism with the specific aim of questioning Spencer's visions of progress. Tuttle's intervention was a typical example of the way in which the social scientists of the old generation used to mix social analysis and historical inquiry and, above all, of the faith they put in the state. Like other social scientists, Tuttle believed in Darwinism, which President White had once described as 'the result of a study of the history of nature carried on in a scientific spirit', but he (no less than White) thought that Spencer and Maine overturned its very essence by projecting its past mechanisms teleologically into the future.[89] First of all, Tuttle clarifies, even when it was possible to identify an 'organic relation' or 'at least' an 'historical affinity' between ancient and modern institutions, that this did not necessarily mean the latter represented a perfection of the former. Secondly, some institutions appearing 'in different countries and different ages' were nonetheless 'without a clearly ascertainable order of progress'.[90] As an example of this, Tuttle discussed 'that tendency or aspiration variously termed agrarian, socialistic, or communistic', which was neither the fruit of a blind and violent populace as argued by Spencer, nor a movement which invariably sought to reinstate a system of status as Maine believed. Socialism, Tuttle argued, was determined by a 'pervading and peremptory instinct of human nature' present 'in all races and ages', in despotic and in liberal states alike, i.e. 'the instinctive demand that those who are less fortunate shall receive the greatest service', a demand prompted by 'the inevitable inequality of fortunes, or by a base jealousy of superior moral and intellectual worth'.[91] All political communities, no matter how liberal, had to consider this 'instinctive demand', and the contents of their policies were always found between 'the two extreme attitudes held towards this demand, – that of absolute compliance, and that of absolute refusal'. The Prussian state, the political economy of which derived from the often protectionist programme of the Socialists of the Chair,

> neglects many charges, or, in other words, leaves to private effort much that a rigid application of the prevailing political philosophy would require it to undertake; while England conducts by governmental action a variety of interests which the Utilitarians reserve to the individual citizen.[92]

Finally, the United States, also traditionally considered a haven of utilitarian and liberal doctrines, 'witnessed at an early day the apparent triumph of certain great schemes of policy, such as protection and public improvements, which are clearly socialistic' and which it had achieved 'chiefly by the aid of considerations of practical, economical, and temporary nature'.[93]

Veblen expressed his desire to study socialism after having taken Tuttle's lectures, and his first article on the subject, written while he was still studying at Cornell, was centred on the example of the English-speaking peoples.[94] As we will see soon, Tuttle's distinctions between economic institutions and their ideological substratum, his questioning of teleological applications of Darwinism to institutional development, along with Tyler's insistence on mentalities, fitted perfectly with the system of mental development Veblen started developing in his first academic article, in which he started out from Kant's philosophy to discuss the different ways of knowing external reality: one more adapt to intellectual reasoning, the other to empirical perception.[95] Philosophical Kantianism and historiography conjured to push Veblen towards the study of socialism, seen as the fruit of a divergence between real economic conditions and the 'popular sentiment' of social dissatisfaction.[96]

Socialism was then regarded as an 'economic' phenomenon, and Veblen might have found the clues for studying the economic implication of American and English socialism in Laughlin's course. Very much like the legal historian Maine, Laughlin had once maintained that, in the earliest phases of German history, 'land belonged as property in partnership with the community', and the ownership of things and people was seen as an extension of the *persona* and not as a 'real right' or *dominium*.[97] Laughlin followed Maine's lead also in claiming that competition was the only guarantee of efficient production and that progress consisted in the gradual emancipation from ancient forms of co-ownership. But his historical and institutional training allowed Laughlin to observe economic phenomena from a different angle. Faithful to Adam Smith's original approach to economics, Laughlin not only considered his theory of the 'division of labour' the cardinal principle of economic analysis; he thought that economics should be grounded in the practical observation of reality, from the statistical record of prices to the actual observation of accounting practices, and aimed at influencing or even directing governmental action. Already at Cornell, and then more decisively at Chicago, Laughlin had devoted special courses to 'Economic Problems' and 'Practical Economic Questions', in which he had explained how production depended on the 'state of art' of a certain community and the level of education provided by its schools and universities.[98] As to consumption, Laughlin had highlighted the influence of fashions on production and investment. Already in his 1884 *History of Bimetallism* – and possibly in his Cornell lectures devoted to the same topic – Laughlin had anchored the vicissitudes in the price of silver and gold through the centuries to the institutions and the traditions of peoples dealing with these precious metals. He had explained, for example, how, after being displaced by gold in the Western world, silver was siphoned into Asia as a cheap source of 'ornaments':

Although the people of India are very poor, and are miserably housed, yet they place their little all in the form of ornaments, when the peasantry of England would have added to their stock of utensils or of furniture. The natives never invest their money in the way in which civilized nations look upon an investment.[99]

Since then, and certainly at the time of his Cornell lectures, Laughlin began taking psychological influences, too, into account to explain consumption in Western societies. In an article he would publish in 1894, one year after moving to Chicago with Veblen, and in his 1906 German lectures, Laughlin would demonstrate how, though unable to ignite crises of overproduction, 'changes in fashions', particularly in the field of women's dress, could redirect the employment of capital between different options of investment and even stop industrial plants entirely.[100] Eventually, Laughlin would trace the origins of American Socialism back to the working classes' difficulty in acquiring luxurious, not essential goods.[101] In 'too many places' – he would then complain in a quite Veblenian vein – 'success is judged wholly by pecuniary results, so that the moral sense as to methods of acquisition has become blunted'.[102]

Since Laughlin's conception of consumption as prompted by psychological and institutional motives was already well developed at the time of his Cornell lectures, he clearly preceded the Chicago anthropologists in conveying to Veblen the importance of 'ornamentation' as a psychological force affecting the economic life of a nation. Besides, his seminars on 'Railroad Transportation' and 'History of Tariffs in America' certainly reinforced Tuttle's argument on the constitutional and legislative overlapping between individual and state property. Any discussion of railroads and trusts, in fact, necessarily involved a definition of the form and extent of state intervention through tariffs, 'the power to regulate rates' and the exercise of 'eminent domain' which – to use the almost contemporary definition of R. Newton Crane – was 'the power of public corporations to acquire lands for public uses under rights similar to those afforded by the Lands Clauses Acts' of England, 'intended to prescribe a general form for expropriation acts' by 'compulsory power of purchase'.[103] The economic discussion of railroads, therefore, along with Tuttle's historical analysis of the various forms of economic interference at disposal of the English Parliament, would reinforce Veblen's diffidence towards the inevitability of 'free trade'.

As demonstrated by the topics of their lessons and articles, Cornell historians shared a common interest not only in history, but in the present state of politics. Even if their method derived from the same roots as those practiced by Johns Hopkins historians, they combined it with a stronger public engagement in favour of reform, a more pronounced interest in sociological and political problems and a starker awareness of the discrepancy between facts and their ideological representations. These elements urged them to question Maine's and Spencer's optimistic faith in invisible hands and their resulting distrust of state interventions. More specifically, what linked Cornell historians to the old reformers of the American Social Science Association was their shared belief that reforms were made urgent by the increasing level of institutional integration of modern societies brought about by industrial development and urbanisation.[104] If Spencer thought that modern integration always would resolve itself in fruitful coordination among individuals, Tuttle, Tyler and Laughlin thought that integration also could be a source of corruption and that it therefore should be regulated. This led them to consider urban life responsible for the moral degradation of politicians and for the transformation of parties into machines manipulating votes and public opinion. The opposition between the corruption of urban and the purity of rustic life was therefore the red thread linking Tuttle's lectures, where he explained how mediaeval cities 'had become richer, more powerful, but also more turbulent and more ambitious', with his, Tyler's and Laughlin's public outcries against the corruption of party men and of party systems on the pages of the *Atlantic Monthly* and the *Nation*.[105] The latter's editor, E. L. Godkin (a member of the ASSA alongside White, Tyler and Tuttle), had already denounced the fact that 'all classes [entertain] such hope of material enjoyment as has never pervaded human society before', fuelling in everyone the 'secret belief that luxury is within his reach' and utterly discrediting the 'practice of industry and frugality', 'the display of punctuality' and 'integrity'.[106]

Veblen and the History of Ideas

In November 1891, Veblen published 'Some Neglected Points in the Theory of Socialism' in the *Annals of the American Academy of Political and Social Science*. According to Dorfman, the article pleased Laughlin so much that he secured Veblen financial support for the following year. Since Veblen's name appears among the recipients of the 'Fellowships in Political Economy and Finance' for the year 1891–92, one has to infer that he wrote the article between May 1891, when Laughlin advertised the fellowships (the first in economics) and the summer, while he was still attending Tuttle's, Tyler's and Laughlin's classes, or immediately after that.

Veblen's article was a commentary on the theory of progress and modernity elaborated by Maine and picked up, almost without amendments, by Spencer. Revealing, already at the onset, the typical ambiguity of the old social scientists towards Spencer, Veblen reassured the reader that it was not his purpose 'to controvert the position taken by Mr Spencer as regards the present feasibility of any socialist scheme', and respectfully presented his paper as 'mainly a suggestion, offered in the spirit of the disciple, with respect to a point not adequately covered by Mr Spencer's discussion'.[107] Like Maine, Spencer argued that any form of state interference in the economic life of a nation would reintroduce the most despotic elements of the ancient regimes of 'status', voiding the hard-won victories of modernity.[108] While Veblen agreed with Spencer and Maine on the fact that 'the development of industry, during its gradual escape from the military system of status, has been, in the direction of a system of free contract', he did not think that the system of free contract necessarily resulted in an absolute advantage for the community, nor that its only alternative was a return to the system 'of status'. The major flaw in Maine's system, Veblen thought, was its incapacity to take account of psychological factors, the importance of which Tyler had made abundantly clear in his courses. Since 'the result of the last few decades of our industrial development has been to increase greatly the creature comforts within the reach of the average human being', Veblen argued, the 'cause of discontent must be sought elsewhere than in any increased difficulty in obtaining the means of subsistence or of comfort'.[109]

Like Tuttle, Veblen interpreted the institutional framework of contemporary societies as the result of a shifting of the Darwinian 'struggle of subsistence' from the material to the psychological world, that is, as a 'struggle to keep up appearances', or 'jealousy' as Tuttle had defined it, or a taste for 'ornamentation' to use Laughlin's terminology.[110] Veblen noted that socialism was not generated by a *real* decline in working class living standards, but rather by its *subjective* deterioration: Americans felt themselves poorer 'in their own eyes, as measured in terms of comparative economic importance', since 'the modern industrial organization of society' had encouraged them to spend money on superfluous commodities at the expense of useful goods.[111] The escalation in luxurious consumption was caused by the increased accessibility to all kinds of 'means of sustenance and comfort' and, 'most importantly', by an increased 'freedom of movement of the individual' which, 'widening the environment to which the individual is exposed – increasing the number of persons before whose eyes each one carries on his life, and *pari passu*, decreasing the chances which such persons have of awarding their esteem on any other basis than that of immediate appearances', had 'increased the relative efficiency of the economic means of winning respect through a show of expenditure for personal comforts'.[112]

Others before Veblen had counted such emulation among the forces conditioning the economic lives of individuals: in the wake of Bernard de Mandeville's *Fable of the Bees*, Adam Smith and David Hume had recognised the important role played by envy and invidious comparisons of consumption in urban contexts.[113] Veblen himself admitted that 'the misdirection of effort through the cravings of human vanity is of course not anything new, nor is 'economic emulation' a modern fact'.[114] Like Laughlin before him, Veblen therefore understood the suitability of Smith's interdisciplinary approach to the social and economic conditions brought about by urban immigration and the increased integration between countryside and cities. Under the cover of objectivity, however, made even more credible by the recourse to the notion of Darwinian 'struggle for existence', Veblen gave scientific dignity to a moralistic argument, which presented conspicuous consumption as a form of psychological disturbance caused by the divorce of the individual from his neighbourhood or, in other words, by his moral corruption.[115] In his *The Theory of the Leisure Class*, Veblen dramatised the contrast between rural and urban context and, almost paraphrasing the reformist arguments harnessed by ASSA reformers, as well as by his Cornell professors, delineated a sharp distinction between the patterns of consumption in the two:

> Consumption becomes a larger element in the standard of living of the city than in the country. Among the country population its place is to some extent taken by savings and home comforts known through the medium of neighbourhood gossip sufficiently to serve the like general purpose of pecuniary repute [...][116]

From this major premise, Veblen subsequently drew the conclusion that non-communitarian, urban contexts led people to invest their surplus wealth (or even to cannibalise necessities) in emulating their social superiors, thus lowering their long-term material welfare and withdrawing large sums of wealth from productive investment.[117] Veblen did not push himself to the point of elaborating a project of reform, as his Cornell professors would have done, and, in abstaining from doing so, he revealed already what the Cornell historian Hull would later call 'a stronger bent towards social diagnosis than social therapeutics'.[118] And, in fact, notwithstanding Veblen's effort at clothing his criticism of conspicuous consumption in the aseptic language of utilities and subjective values,[119] the *Theory of the Leisure Class* was a curious compromise between the analytical effort to objectively describe a social problem that needed to be cured (the effects of urban social intercourse on patterns of consumption) and a moralist judgment of it. The combination of factual analysis, reformist *intents*, and moral conservatism were all typical of the pre-professional stage of social research as conducted by the first generations of ASSA thinkers, but clearly evident at Cornell as well. What made it hard for Veblen to transform the reformist *intent* of his Cornell professors and historian colleagues into concrete plans for reform was the fact, of which Hull was entirely oblivious, that Veblen approached history and politics from a philosophical background that, by giving an ontological dimension to the discrepancy between facts and their theoretical elaboration, made it very difficult for him to embark on any reformist projects at all.[120]

More in tune with the taste of Cornell historians for the incongruities and fractures of institutional development than with their reformism, Veblen agreed with them on the inertia of institutional evolution. As Henry James noted in the same year that Veblen's article on socialism appeared, in the wake of Darwin's *Descent of Man*, the construction of habits (institutions) was the distinctive element of man and what made societies possible: institutions were the 'fly-wheel' of society', its 'most precious conservatory agent'.[121] Any history of societies, written by both historians and biologists, had to be conservative. This is why Veblen presented the *Theory* as 'discussing the survival of archaic traits of human nature under the modern culture', rather than analysing their gradual disappearance or transformation.

Veblen's History of Politics and Economics

Veblen's criticisms of Spencer and Maine became the basis of a further argument that, while less influential in *The Theory of the Leisure Class*, would leave its mark on his *The Theory of Business Enterprise*, his *Imperial Germany and the Industrial Revolution* and his *An Inquiry into the Nature of Peace*.[122] Except for the first of these books, which Veblen composed while still teaching at Chicago, the second and the third books date back to a later period, during which he was more directly involved with public affairs. In *Imperial Germany*, Veblen analysed the peculiarity of Germany, which combined a recently developed industrial system with an autocratic form of government, against the background of WWI. Furthermore, by relying once more on the comparative method he learned from the British historiographical tradition, Veblen compared German institutions with those of the other dynastic states as well as those of the 'constitutional democracies'. Written four years later, at the end of the war, the *Inquiry into the Nature of Peace* complemented the previous book with a proposed scheme of diplomatic policy through which to bring peace to the world, assure its durability and neutralise the militaristic and 'feudal' institutions fuelling Germanic bellicosity.[123]

The seeds of Veblen's comparative studies in economics and politics were clearly planted in the second part of the Cornell essay on socialism. After having attacked Spencer's and Maine's systems for their incapacity to explain psychological reactions and moral standards, Veblen went on to criticise their blindness to the differences between political and economic institutions. If Veblen recognised that Maine was right in explaining the industrial revolution as a gradual development toward the 'institution of property', he expressed doubt that industrial progress would follow the path envisaged by Maine and

Spencer. Like Tuttle, Veblen argued that the categories of status and contract failed to exhaust all the industrial and political typologies observable in Europe and America. In fact, even if 'the industrial system, in the case of all communities with whose history we are acquainted, has always in the past been organised according to a scheme of status or of contract, the latest development of the industrial organisation among civilized nations … has not been entirely a continuation of the approach to a régime of free contract'.[124] In America, for example, one of the world's most industrially advanced countries, Veblen saw numerous municipalities that, while responsible for 'elementary education, street-lighting, water-supply, etc.' for the simple sake of 'industrial expediency', did not impede the system of free trade, nor the liberties of the citizens. In arguing this, Veblen once again showed a strong commitment to the ASSA's opposition to doctrinal economic liberalism. At Cornell, White had audaciously played with the idea that a cooperative solution might be the operational compromise between socialism and laissez-faire: he 'would have the student examine the reasons why the communistic solution of the labour question has failed, and why the co-operative solution has succeeded'.[125]

The same mixture of control and liberty towards which Veblen thought the economic system was headed had its equivalent in the political sphere, particularly 'in the development of those communities whose institutions we are accustomed to contemplate with the most complacency, e.g., the case of the English-speaking peoples'.[126] English 'Constitutional democracy', as he called it, echoing Tuttle's theses, 'does not fall under the head of either contract or status', since it requires subjection 'not to the person of the public functionary', as with the status system described by Maine, but 'to the powers vested in him'. Similarly, 'the right of eminent domain and the power to tax, as interpreted under modern constitutional forms' – and almost certainly made clear to Veblen by Laughlin's discussion of railways and tariffs – guaranteed public functionaries ample room for economic intervention, without interfering with civil liberties. It was in this subtle distinction that Veblen found 'a large part of the meaning of the boasted free institutions of the English-speaking people'.[127]

In essence, if Veblen's first blow to evolutionary determinism highlighted the autonomy of psychological motives with regards to material needs and necessities, of economic factors with regards to their perception and intellectual theorisation, his *coup de grâce* consisted in differentiating the dynamics of economic from that of political evolution: no matter how liberal the governmental system was in political questions (like the English or the American), it could always allow for economic intervention; no matter how developed and at the vanguard the economic system was (as in Germany), it could always allow for autocracy. Veblen revisited and widened these topics in his *The Theory of Business Enterprise*, *Imperial Germany* and *An Inquiry into the Nature of Peace*. In constitutional governments like that of eighteenth-century England, Veblen explained by drawing on Lecky's and Tyler's methods once more, public opinion was the emanation of 'small commerce and petty entrepreneurship, which asked for absence of mandatory restrictions' and a 'system of natural liberty'.[128] In Germany, Italy and Japan, on the contrary, laws retained the mark of their autocratic pasts because 'the transition to a constitutional government' had 'not been completed'.[129] Contrary to Spencer, who had forecasted the final triumph of the liberal scheme and seen it as instrumental to industrial progress, Veblen demonstrated how constitutional governments could turn into autocracies through the medium of 'parliamentary voting on the budget',[130] and how autocratic states could foster industrial progress and technological advance through the examples of Germany and Japan.

Conclusion

What made Veblen's encounter with Cornell historians unique and seminal for his subsequent works was the fact that the university in some ways had resisted the professionalisation of the social sciences, nurturing a combination of social inquiry, moralising attitudes and institutional historiography. In this partially segregated community of historians, all sharing a distaste for Carlyle's heroism and the common goal of grounding historical inquiry in the analysis of mental and social institutions, Veblen planted the seeds of his future *Theory of the Leisure Class* and his later political works. The former book was born out of a general reflection on the friction between factual history, which Veblen interpreted as consisting in a series of material improvements, and the history of human ideas, more and more dominated by a sense of dissatisfaction with those improvements. *Imperial Germany* and *An Inquiry into the Nature of Peace*, on the other hand, were the result of a parallel work of dismemberment of the post-Darwinian and Spencerian models of social evolution, conducted his time from the point of view of the history of economic institutions and that of political structures. Taken together, all of Veblen's criticisms of evolutionary sociology reflected the insistence placed by some of Veblen's Cornell professors on the non-linearity of historical development in polemics with Maine's and Spencer's 'teleological' accounts of human history. It was the Cornell historians who formulated the inertial and path-dependent interpretation of evolution to which Veblen clung all his life, in which survivals tended to outnumber innovations and politics evolved independently from economics. The ASSA's and Cornell's vocation for public commitment would reveal itself even stronger in Veblen's later works, *Imperial Germany* and *An Inquiry into the Nature of Peace*, after Veblen had overcome his earlier philosophic scepticism.

The eminent Oxonian Matthew Arnold, who did not share Freeman's and Bryce's curiosity about the New World, once observed that 'the university of Mr. Ezra Cornell, a really noble monument of his munificence', seemed 'to rest on a misconception of what culture truly is, and to be calculated to produce miners, or engineers, or architects, not sweetness and light'.[131] Although Veblen's predilection for engineers and industry shows that Arnold's stereotyped criticism of Cornell might have contained some grains of truth, Veblen gained something much more important from his days at Cornell: the empirical confirmation of his philosophical intuition about the curious discrepancy between ideology and reality, ideals and concrete institutions.

Appendix

Document A

Stacyville, Homer, Nov. 25-,1890

Registration, Cornell University

Ithaca, New York

Dear Sir:--- Will you kindly inform me if there is anything to hinder the admission of a new student to a regular graduate work from the beginning of the winter term. If not, are the fees for the remainder of the year the same for such student as for a student registered at the beginning of the year? The work I have in view is in History and Political Science. I have had some graduate work before.

Very truly yours

T. B. Veblen

Document B

CORNELL UNIVERSITY.
GRADUATE WORK AND ADVANCED DEGREES.

Ithaca, N. Y., Jan. 9 1891

DEAR SIR :—*The application of M*r. J. B. Veblen, A. B. 1880 *of* Carleton College. Ph. D. Yale 1884, *for an advanced course of study leading to the degree of* Ph. D. *in* Economics, Am. Hist. Eng. Con st. Hist.

was referred to the following Committee, which will have the special direction of h.. *studies : Professors* Laughlin. Tyler and Tuttle.

To Professor

Chairman.

The student will present this card to the Chairman of his committee, who will report for record the course assigned. All graduate students are required to file a statement of their work in the Registrar's Office at the beginning of every University year, also to register at the opening of every term.

105 N. Tioga St. This card is to be retained by the student.

Document C

Application of Graduate Student.

Full name and residence (home): *Thorstein B. Veblen, Northaus Minn.*

Place and date of graduation: *Carleton Coll. 1880; Yale 1884*

Degree: *B.A., Ph.D.*

Details of previous course of study: *At Carleton Coll; the regular classical course.*
At Yale; Philosophy as a primary and Economics and Social Science as a secondary course.

Degree applied for: *Ph. D.*

Outline of proposed course of study:

Major subject: *Economics; courses 20, 21 and 22 of "History and Political Science."*

First minor: *courses 10 and 12 of Do.*

Second minor: *English Constitution; course 14.*

Graduate students whose course of study has already been approved, will state what subjects or parts of their work have been completed to date.

Special Committee: *Laughlin, Tyler + Tuttle.*

Memorandum of action of Committee on Graduate Work and Advanced Degrees:

Document D

GRADUATE STUDENT

[To be filled out by the student.]

Name: *Thorstein B. Veblen*

Residence in Ithaca: *105 N. Tioga,*

Date of Application: *Jan. 8, 1891.*

Where graduated: *Carleton Coll.*

Degree applied for: *Ph. D.*

Committee:

Document E. Verso

[TO BE FILLED OUT BY STUDENT.]

Name   *T. B. Veblen*

Date   *19 Nov. 1891.*

Referred to Professors
Laughlin. Tyler and
Tuttle for their
recommendation
Mr. T. Hewett.

20 Nov. 1891.
approved   J. Laurence Laughlin.
M. C. Tyler.
{Tuttle absent, but
gave assent, with some
reservation}
Reported
Granted S

Document E. Recto

COMMUNICATION TO THE FACULTY.

DIRECTIONS.—Petitions must be deposited in the box in the door of the Faculty room not later than 12 o'clock on the day when the Faculty meeting is held. They should in all cases where a change of registration is involved, include *the number of the course and the number of hours,* and in order to receive prompt consideration should be endorsed *with the opinion of the heads of departments* in which lies the work to be taken *or dropped.* The action taken will be posted on the Faculty bulletin board, and entered upon the record cards. All petitions should be expressed as clearly as possible, and should contain a statement of the reasons for the request. *Attention is called to sections 6, 7, 8, and 9 of the Rules for the Guidance of Students.*

TO THE FACULTY OF CORNELL UNIVERSITY,

GENTLEMEN:—*I,* Thorstein B Veblen [NAME] { Course Graduate { Year ....

respectfully ask permission to change the two minors for which I am registered.

I have, since January last, been registered for a major in Political Economy and minors in American History and English Constitutional History. I now wish to replace these two minors with Socialism and The Science of Finance.

It is my present expectation to continue in the University until June 1893.

The reason for my petition is partly the altered opportunities now offered by the University, partly a change of opinion on my own part as to what I had best do.

Respectfully, T. B. Veblen (See other side.)

Document F

Apr. 27, 1905

President David Starr Jordan
    Stanford University, Cal.

Dear Mr. Jordan :

As you probably know, Thorstein Veblen was one
time a graduate student in Cornell University, but that was the year
before I first taught here, and my personal acquaintance with him
is not extensive.   I met him then and two or three times since in
Ithaca, have seen him repeatedly at meetings of the Economic Association, and have had from time to time a little correspondence with
him.   I also have read two of his books.

Veblen is a man of undeniable ability and much originality of
mind.   He writes in a brilliant but somewhat paradoxical manner
and has, it seems to me, rather a strong bent towards social diagnosis than social therapeutics.   To what extent the temperament
which seems to pervade his books characterizes his everyday intercourse, I scarcely feel able to say.   Such relations as have existed between us have been always very pleasant,-I even have ventured
to think at times that Veblen had rather a liking for me, and remember having heard that commented upon and with some slight accent of
wonder by one of our acquaintances.   I can not now recollect who
the acquaintance was and would prefer not to conjecture why he was
surprised at the circumstances.   Veblen apparently does not get
along particularly well with Laughlin, but for my part I know nobody
who does.   It is the common gossip of the craft that Veblen does
much of the work of the Chicago Department of Economics and does not
receive there the recognition which he deserves because he is either
too modest or too proud to push himself.   At the same time, nobody

Document F. Continued

in any of the other colleges has tried to get Veblen away from Chicago, so far as I know, although every one seems to think that it would be easy to move him.   I can not say why this is so.

This is all very negative as you see, and ought not to count against Veblen in a degree in which it may seem to be lacking in appreciation, for my acquaintance with the man is unfortunately not sufficient to warrant a confident opinion.   In spite of an occasional bepuzzlement by his devotion to paradox, I have a high opinion of him intellectually and really know nothing that would warrant any different opinion of him socially or academically.

While we are glad that Farrand is to be here next year, we never anticipated any such good luck as keeping him permanently would involve.   As for Marx, you know what our feelings and desires hopeand we know yours, and it will all depend, I suppose, upon Marx's if he proves able to know his own.

Very truly yours

Notes and References

1 I would like to acknowledge the kind assistance of Cornell University's Carl A. Kroch Library, and particularly the Division of Rare and Manuscript Collections, the staff of which has gone well beyond the call of duty. I am particularly grateful to Evan Fay Earle and Laura Miriam Linke. Glenn Altschuler, Richard Bensel, Robert Fredona, Jeremy Jennings, Michael Kammen, Isaac Kramnick, Peter Mandler, Sophus A. Reinert, Carlo Augusto Viano and Richard Whatmore provided significant comments and criticisms, and I am deeply grateful for their help. This is an elaborated version of the paper given at the Veblen conference, circulated in manuscript form in spring 2008, and published in *The History of European Ideas* 35 (2009): 38–61.

2 The Norwegian writer Rølvåg wrote four famous volumes (*I De Dage, Riket Grundlaegges, Peder Seier* and *Den Signede Dag*) narrating the fictional history of Per Hansa, a fisherman who left Norway to settle in Dakota, of his family and descendants. The American translations, the two first volumes published as *Giants in the Earth* (New York: Harper & Brothers, 1927), followed by *Peder Victorious* (New York: Harper & Brothers, 1929), and *Their Father's God* (New York: Harper & Brothers, 1931), appeared around the time of Veblen's death, but to some extent they give an idea of what his early childhood in America might have been like. The myth of Veblen's marginality, established by his first biographer, Joseph Dorfman, in the early 1930s, was fuelled by the psychological historiography of the 1850s, but survived until the 1970s, when it was challenged by a new, revisionist current in Vebleniana. As the most representative of the traditionalist approach see Joseph Dorfman, *Thorstein Veblen and His America* (Clifton, NJ: Kelley, 1973); Richard V. Teggart (ed.), *Thorstein Veblen: A Chapter in American Economic Thought* (Berkeley: University of California Press, 1932); Wesley C. Mitchell, 'Thorstein Veblen', in *What Veblen Taught. Selected Writings of Thorstein Veblen*, ed. by Wesley C. Mitchell (New York: Viking, 1947), vii–xlix; Lewis Feuer, 'Thorstein Veblen: The Metaphysics of the Interned Immigrant', *American Quarterly* 5 (1953): 99–112; George M. Fredrickson, 'Thorstein Veblen: The Last Viking', *American Quarterly* 11 (1959): 403–15; David Riesman, *Thorstein Veblen: A Critical Interpretation* (New York: Transaction Publishers, 1995). Veblen's marginality has fascinated literati too, like John Dos Passos, *The Big Money* (London: Harcourt, Brace, 1936), and Jorge Louis Borges, 'El escritor argentino y la tradición', in Borges, *Selected Non-Fictions*, ed. by Eliot Weinberger (New York: Viking, 1999), 420–27, esp. 426; Jorge Louis Borges, 'Prologue to *A Personal Library*', in id. *Selected Non-Fictions*, 511–22, esp. 512, 518. The revisionist reaction, which dates from the 1970s, was (and still is) led by Rick Tilman, Russell H. Bartley and Sylvia Erickson Bartley, and Stephen Edgell.

3 The earliest and until now most detailed account of Veblen's sojourn at Hopkins dates from Dorfman's biography (Dorfman, *Thorstein Veblen*, 38–55). In this volume, Charles Camic has elegantly placed this phase of Veblen's life in the context of his education, adding some new insights to the former accounts and, above all, shedding new light on its 'positional' importance in the sequence of Veblen's formative experiences. It is true that, as far as I know, the original Hopkins documents, with the number of courses taken by Veblen and their division into Major and Minors, are still missing. See Charles Camic, in this volume.

4 Rick Tilman, *The Intellectual Legacy of Thorstein Veblen. Unresolved Issues* (Westport: Greenwood Press, 1996), 26; Dorfman, *Thorstein Veblen*, 56–67.

5 Mary O. Furner, *Advocacy & Objectivity. A Crisis in the Professionalization of American Social Science, 1865–1905* (Lexington: University Press of Kentucky, 1975), 57.

6 Morris Bishop, *A History of Cornell* (Ithaca, NY: Cornell University Press, 1962), 58–64; Carl L. Becker, *Cornell University: Founders and the Founding* (Ithaca, NY: Cornell University Press, 1967), 93. The non-religious commitment clause was on the one hand fruit of Cornell's first president Andrew Dickson White's so-called radicalism, as shown by Glenn C. Altschuler in his *Andrew D. White, Educator, Historian, Diplomat* (Ithaca, NY: Cornell University Press, 1979), 19–21, and on the other of Ezra Cornell's Quakerism. In this sense, Veblen's fortune at Cornell must be seen in light of Knut Odner's study on the Veblen family's possible Quakerism, *Thorstein Veblen: Forstyrreren av den Intellektuelle Fred* (Oslo: Abstrakt Forlag, 2005), 23–46.

7 Dorfman, *Thorstein Veblen*, 79.

8 Ibid., 87–8.

9 Thorstein Veblen, 'Why is Economics Not an Evolutionary Science?', *Quarterly Journal of Economics* 12 (1898): 373–97; Thorstein Veblen, *The Theory of the Leisure Class. An Economic Study in the Evolution of Institutions* (New York: Macmillan, 1899).

10 Lev E. Dobriansky, *Veblenism. A New Critique* (Washington: Public Affairs Press, 1957), 13.

11 Dorfman, *Thorstein Veblen*, 125–7, 139; Geoffrey M. Hodgson, 'On the Evolution of Thorstein Veblen's Evolutionary Economics', *Cambridge Journal of Economics* 22 (1998): 415–31, esp. 417, 420; Geoffrey M. Hodgson, *How Economics Forgot History* (London: Routledge, 2001), 141–2.

12 Dorfman, *Thorstein Veblen*, 120, 125.

13 Geoffrey M. Hodgson, *The Evolution of Institutional Economics* (London: Routledge, 2004), 157.

14 Henry Steele Commager, *The American Mind. An Interpretation of American Thought and Character since the 1880s* (New Haven: Yale University Press, 1965), 237–8.

15 Daniel Aaron, *Men of Good Hope. A Story of American Progressivism* (New York: Oxford University Press, 1951), 208–42.

16 Morton G. White, *Social Thought in America: The Revolt Against Formalism* (New York: Viking, 1952), 21–7.

17 Stephen Edgell and Rick Tilman, 'The Intellectual Antecedents of Thorstein Veblen: A Reappraisal', *Journal of Economic Issues* 23 (1989): 1003–26.

18 Paul T. Homan, 'Thorstein Veblen', in *American Masters of Social Science: An Approach to the Study of the Social Science*, ed. by Howard Washington Odum (Port Washington: Kennikat, 1965), esp. 263; Wesley C. Mitchell, *Types of Economic Theory. From Mercantilism to Institutionalism*, ed. by Joseph Dorfman (New York: Kelley, 1969), 2:615.

19 Harris E. Starr, 'William Graham Sumner: Sociologist', *Journal of Social Forces* 3 (1925): 622–6, esp. 623. Revised accounts of Veblen's stay at Johns Hopkins are offered by Francesca Lidia Viano, 'Passaggio a Cornell: Veblen e gli esordi della storiografia Americana', *Annali della Fondazione Einaudi* 39 (2005): 91–123; Francesca Lidia Viano, 'From Staple Rent to Conspicuous Rent: Veblen's Case for a New Theory of Distribution, *International Review of Sociology – Revue Internationale de Sociologie* 14 (2004): 471–85; 'Camic's chapter in this volume, where Veblen's stay at Yale is also revisited.

20 I have discussed the documents related to Veblen's stay at Cornell, previously unknown, partially in 'From Staple Rent to Conspicuous Rent', where I shed light on the influence of Cornell economist James Laurence Laughlin on Veblen's ideas on overproduction, finance and prices, and more in detail in 'Passaggio a Cornell', where I reconstruct Veblen's stay at Cornell on the background of the administrative struggles for the emancipation of the teaching of economics from that of politics and history.

21 Homan, 'Thorstein Veblen', 235–6.

22 According to Dorfman, Laughlin was only able to procure a 'special grant' for Veblen; Dorfman, *Thorstein Veblen*, 80.

23 Dorfman, *Thorstein Veblen*, 79–80.

24 E. S. Mead quoted in James Bornemann, in *James Laurence Laughlin. Chapters in the Career of an Economist*, ed. by Leon C. Marshall (Washington: American Council on Public Affairs, 1940), 7; Laughlin quoted in Edward Chalfant, *Improvement of the World: A Biography of Henry Adams: His Last Life, 1891–1918* (North Haven: Archon Books, 2001), 627n.

25 Furner, *Advocacy & Objectivity*, 57.

26 Dorfman, *Thorstein Veblen*, 80.

27 After graduating from Harvard, Andrew Dickson White responded to the appeal of President Wayland of Brown University to join the educational movement in the West and began teaching at the University of Michigan, where President Tappan already had introduced the German system of seminars, library facilities, teaching in all fields of knowledge (Altschuler, *Andrew D. White*, 36–7).

28 Bornemann, *James Laurence Laughlin*, 7.
29 From an interview with Adolph C. Miller quoted in Bornemann, *James Laurence Laughlin*, 27. Miller, associate professor of economics at Cornell, would follow Laughlin to Chicago along with Veblen and the philosopher William Caldwell in 1893. See also William C. Mitchell, 'James Laurence Laughlin', *Journal of Political Economy* 49 (1941): 876–81, esp. 877, Bornemann, *James Laurence Laughlin*, 26. Bornemann's contention is further proved by a letter Charles Hull wrote to David Starr Jordan (Charles Hull Papers, #14–17–249. Division of Rare and Manuscript Collections, Cornell University Library), see the Appendix, letter F.
30 Bornemann, *James Laurence Laughlin*, 27.
31 Cornell University Graduate School Records #12–5–636. Division of Rare and Manuscript Collections, Cornell University Library. For the complete text, see the Appendix, Document A.
32 Cornell University Graduate School Records # 12–5-636. Division of Rare and Manuscript Collections, Cornell University Library, see the Appendix. Document B contains a reproduction of Veblen's ID card, where his local address also is provided. Document C contains Veblen's 'Application of Graduate Student'. Document D contains his 'Graduate Student' statement.
33 See the Appendix for Documents B, C and D.
34 *The Cornell University Register, 1890–91* (Ithaca, NY: Cornell University Press, 1891), 103–4.
35 Veblen's letter and application for the change of his curriculum (recto and verso) is contained in Document E of the Appendix (Cornell University Graduate School Records #12–5–636. Division of Rare and Manuscript Collections, Cornell University Library). Veblen had announced his decision to study socialism to the *Carleton Voice* before leaving for Ithaca in the summer of 1891. The journal reported that Veblen and his wife, Ellen Rolfe, said they were to follow 'their interest in socialism, studying both American and European socialist thought'. See *Carleton Voice* 29 (1891), quoted in Elisabeth Watkins Jorgensen and Henry Irvin Jorgensen, *Thorstein Veblen. Victorian Firebrand* (Armonk: M. E. Sharpe, 1999), 31. No such course as 'Science of Finance' was listed in *The Cornell University Register* for 1891–92, but it is probable that Veblen took Adolph C. Miller's course no. 33 in 'Taxation. Public Finance. Banking' (*Cornell University Register*, 103). Miller, associate professor of economics at Cornell, would follow Laughlin to Chicago together with Veblen in 1893. See William C. Mitchell, 'James Laurence Laughlin', *Journal of Political Economy* 49 (1941): 876–81, esp. 877. The course in 'Socialism' is again missing from the 1891–92 list of 'Courses of Instruction'. In a previous article, I have discussed the possibility that Veblen took Jeremiah Whipple Jenks's course in 'Political and Social Institutions'. See Francesca Lidia Viano, 'Un Elitismo Democratico: La classe politica in Thorstein Veblen (1891–1917)', in *Classe dominante, classe politica ed élites negli scrittori politici dell'Ottocento e del Novecento*, ed. by Sergio Amato (Florence: Centro Editoriale Toscano, 2008). I now think it more plausible, however, that Veblen studied socialism with Laughlin. Being listed for the year 1892–93 under the section 'Economics' and taught by economist Edward Alsworth Ross, the course in 'Socialism' might have been taught already in 1892 by professor Laughlin in one of his special seminars. The possibility that Veblen decided to study socialism in view of Ross's arrival at Cornell in September 1892, news of which might well have been in the air the year before, cannot be excluded.
36 Thorstein Veblen, 'Some Neglected Points in the Theory of Socialism', *Annals of American Academy of Political and Social Science* 2 (1891): 57–74; republished in *The Collected Works of Thorstein Veblen*, ed. by Peter Cain (London: Routledge, 1994), 7:387–408. Veblen also wrote two notes before entering Chicago, possibly when he was still at Cornell and certainly under Laughlin's influence: Thorstein Veblen, 'Boehm-Bawerk's Definition of Capital, and the Source of Wages', *Quarterly Journal of Economics* 6 (1892): 247–50, republished in his *Collected Works*, x, 132–6; Thorstein Veblen, 'The Overproduction Fallacy', *Quarterly Journal of Economics* 6 (1892): 484–92, republished in his *Collected Works*, x, 104–13. I have already analysed these two works in the wider context of the American controversy debate over capital and rational expectations (Viano, 'From Staple Rent to Conspicuous Rent').

37 Mary O. Furner, *Advocacy & Objectivity*, 35. Edward S. Mason and Thomas S. Lamont, 'The Harvard Department of Economics from the Beginning to World War II', *Quarterly Journal of Economics* 97 (1982): 383–433, esp. 384. As Donald Winch has demonstrated, Smith's economics was originally meant as a branch of the science of government. See *Adam Smith's Politics: An Essay in Historiographic Revision* (Cambridge: Cambridge University Press, 1978).

38 Thomas L. Haskell, *The Emergence of Professional Social Science. The American Social Science Association and the Nineteenth-Century Crisis of Authority* (Urbana: University of Illinois Press, 1977); Thomas L. Haskell, *Objectivity Is Not Neutrality* (Baltimore: Johns Hopkins University Press, 2000).

39 As John Higham and Thomas L. Haskell have pointed out, the archetype of public intellectual which informed Sanborn's cultural and reformist projects dated back to the Victorian conception of 'authority'. Matthew Arnold once famously described the 'great men of culture' as 'those who have had a passion for diffusing, for making prevail, for carrying from one end of society to the other, the best knowledge, the best ideas of their time; who have labored to divest knowledge of all that was harsh, uncouth, difficult, abstract, professional, exclusive; to humanize it, to make it efficient outside the clique of the cultivated and the learned, yet still remaining the best knowledge and thought of the time, and a true source, therefore, of sweetness and light' (quoted by Stefan Collini, *Matthew Arnold: A Critical Portrait* (Oxford: Oxford University Press, 1988), 86. See John Higham, Leonard Krieger and Felix Gibert, *History: The Development of Historical Studies in the United States* (Englewood Cliffs: Prentice-Hall, 1965), 9–10; John Higham, *From Boundlessness to Consolidation: The Transformation of American Culture 1848–1960* (Ann Arbor: University of Michigan Press, 1969). For a detailed account of how the principle of authority found application in the real history of the ASSA and its derivative institutions see Haskell, *Emergence*, 64–5, 97 following.

40 Charles Wright Mills, *The Sociological Imagination* (London: Pelican Books, 1970), 96. Haskell has introduced this distinction in his *Emergence of Professional Social Science*, 121.

41 Morton White, *Social Thought in America: The Revolt against Formalism* (New York: Viking, 1949); Haskell, *Emergence*, 24–47.

42 Haskell, *Emergence*, 139–43; Andrew D. White, *On Studies in General History and the History of Civilization* (New York: Putnam, 1885). The state-oriented heritage will be particularly evident in the platform of the American Economic Association. See the statute in Richard T. Ely's famous article on the *American Economic Association Quarterly: 'The American Economic Association 1885–1909'* 3.11 (1910): 47–111. Cornell's President White himself would endorse the platform by saying 'I agree with you entirely that the *laissez-faire* theory is entirely inadequate to the needs of modern states. I agree, too, entirely with the idea that we must look not so much to speculation, as to an impartial study of actual conditions of economic life […]' (quoted in Ely, 'The American Economic Association', 63).

43 Winch, *Adam Smith's Politics*, 172. On Smith and the question of the 'interdependence' see also Haskell, *Emergence*, 29–33.

44 Curiously enough, the mathematician and ASSA member Benjamin Peirce (father of Veblen's professor of logic at Johns Hopkins) had a prominent role in drafting the proposal. The role that Johns Hopkins President Gilman played in the event is discussed in Haskell, *Emergence*, 144–5, 160.

45 Haskell, *Emergence*, 169, 171.

46 The only exception was probably his professor of 'History of Political Economy' at Johns Hopkins, Richard T. Ely. Although he promoted the foundation of the American Economic Association in 1885, Ely was, as Haskell has stressed, not a typical representative of the professionalising spirit in economics (Haskell, *Emergence*, 185); as documented by his platform, which was modelled on that of the German *Verein für Sozialpolitik*, Ely asked for a stronger public commitment of economists in favour of state action, and not for their estrangement from it. His courses at Johns Hopkins, however, did not impress Veblen, who, according to Dorfman, 'doubted that 'Ely' had read the works he was discussing' (Dorfman, *Thorstein Veblen*, 40). Even

if one does not take Dorfman's statement at face value, confirmation of Veblen's distaste for Ely can be found in an article Veblen wrote to criticise the German '*Katheder Sozialismus*', of which Ely was one of the staunchest advocates in America. See Veblen, 'The Army of the Commonweal', *Journal of Political Economy* 2 (1894): 456–61, esp. 460. Veblen's critical attitude towards Ely is recognised by Haskell (*Emergence*, 163) and must problematise Camic's ongoing re-evaluation of Veblen's dependence on Ely ('Schooling for Heterodoxy').

47 Haskell, *Emergence*, 175, 190, 192.

48 Quoted from a letter asking for support from Gerritt Smith, 1 September 1862, in Haskell, *Emergence*, 193.

49 Quoted in Frank L. Tolman, 'The Study of Sociology in Institutions of Learning in the United States. A Report of an Investigation Undertaken by the Graduate Sociological League of the University of Chicago', *American Journal of Sociology* 7 (1902): 797–838, esp. 801. See also Albion Small, 'Fifty Years of Sociology in the United States (1865–1915)', *American Journal of Sociology* 21 (1916): 721–864, esp. 733.

50 'School of Social and Political Science', *Cornell University Register, 1891–92* (Ithaca, NY: Cornell University Press, 1892), 64. More importantly, Cornell history professors such as Herbert Tuttle and Moses Tyler maintained their membership in the ASSA, although they were also members of the Historical and the Economic Associations. For the list of the founders of the AHA, see Richard T. Ely, 'The American Historical Association', *Science* 4 (1884): 312–13; Richard T. Ely, 'The American Economic Association'; Richard T. Ely, 'The Meeting of the Economic and Historical Associations', *Science* 9 (1887): 527–8.

51 Édouard de Laboulaye, *Essai sur la vie et les doctrines de Frédéric Charles de Savigny* (Paris: A. Durand, 1842), 21–2.

52 Stefan Collini, Donald Winch, John Burrow, *The Noble Science of Politics* (Cambridge: Cambridge University Press, 1983, 1987), 211. Ulrich Wyss, *Die wilde Philologie* (Munich: Beck, 1979), 60–61.

53 Wilhelm von Humboldt, *Schriften zur Sprachphilosophie* (Stuttgart: Wissenschaftliche Buchgesellschaft, 1979), 414. The Grimm brothers began working on the collection of folklore and fable under the inspiration of Savigny, their professor at Marbourg. In 1808, Jacob became court librarian to the king of Westphalia and then in Kassel, where Wilhelm too was employed. They both were elected professors at Göttingen in 1830. In the nationalist atmosphere of Romanticism, the study of laws – particularly historical jurisprudence – was naturally conducive to the study of fables and folklore, a transition which is possible to detect also in Veblen, who seconded an interest in history and archaeology with one in sagas and folklore.

54 Giuliano Marini, *Jacob Grimm* (Napoli: Guida, 1972), 29, 53, 143–4.

55 John W. Burrow, *A Liberal Descent: Victorian Historians and the English Past* (Cambridge: Cambridge University Press, 1981), 162; Collini, Winch and Burrow, *That Noble Science*, 221. On the British assimilation of German historiography, Collini, Winch and Burrow highlighted the role played by English mediators such as John Mitchell Kemble, whose *The Saxons in England* (London, 1848) was faithful to the teachings of his German professors, and the legal historian Sir Henry Maine. In his famous *Ancient Law* (London: John Murray, 1861), and more decisively in his later *Village Communities* (London: John Murray, 1871), Maine combined the co-proprietorship thesis with the study of Roman law into a scheme of gradual evolution from common property and status to individual property. Maine was particularly sensitive to the work of German scholars of the early European village community, George von Maurer and Erwin Nasse, who were Grimm's students. See John W. Burrow, 'The Village Community' and 'The Uses of History in Late Nineteenth-Century England', *Historical Perspectives. Studies in English Thought and Society in Honour of J. H. Plumb*, ed. by Neil McKendrick (London: Europa, 1974), 255–84; Burrow, *A Liberal Descent*, 262, 265; Collini, Winch and Burrow, *That Noble Science*, 199, 211, 215–18. Collini, Winch and Burrow also made the fundamental distinction between those historians subscribing to the original co-proprietorship thesis (i.e. John Mitchell Kemble, Sir Henry

Maine) and those renouncing it, like Edward Augustus Freeman and Goldwin Smith (Burrow, *Liberal Descent*, 172; Collini, Winch and Burrow, *That Noble Science*, 219–20).

56 John Mitchell Keble, *The Saxons in England. A History of the English Commonwealth till the Period of the Norman Conquest* (London: Quaritch, 1876), 2:viii, 35.

57 Sir Henry Maine, *Village Communities*, 201; Edward Augustus Freeman, 'An Introduction of American Institutional History', in *Johns Hopkins Studies in Historical and Political Science* 1 (1883): 13–39; Goldwin Smith, *The Foundation of the American Colonies. A Lecture Delivered before the University of Oxford* (Oxford: Oxford University Press, 1861); Goldwin Smith, 'England and America', *Atlantic Monthly* 14 (1864): 749–69, esp. 750. Smith's specific interest in the 'familiarity' between English and North Americans is further documented by Andrew Dickson White. See the *Diaries of Andrew D. White*, ed. by Robert Morris Ogden (Ithaca, NY: Cornell University Press, 1959), 154; William Francis Allen, 'A Survival of Land Community in New England', *Nation* 10 (January 1878). The penetration of the 'Teutonic School' into American academia has been described in a cursory manner by Edward N. Saveth, *American Historians and European Immigrants 1875–1925* (New York: Columbia University Press, 1948). The array of liberal ideas which took shape around a common interpretation of the Teutonic origins of English institutions has been defined 'Democratic Teutonism' by Peter Mandler in his '"Race" and "Nation" in Mid-Victorian Thought', in *History, Religion and Culture*, ed. by Stefan Collini, Richard Whatmore and Brian Young (Cambridge: Cambridge University Press, 2000), 224–44, esp. 239. As Duncan Bell has pointed out, the historiographical pattern utilised by the liberals believing in Teutonism also took 'Greek and Roman ingredients' into account and, specifically in the case of Goldwin Smith, did not accept the model of the Aryan-Indian ancestry, which was crucial in Maine. See Bell, *The Idea of Greater Britain. Empire and the Future of World Order, 1860–1900* (Princeton: Princeton University Press, 2007), 191.

58 Herbert Baxter Adams (1850–1901) graduated from Amherst in 1872 and two years later embarked on a three-year doctorate in 'Philosophie, Geschichte und Politikstudium' in Heidelberg with Johann Bluntschli. After his return to the United States, Adams taught at Smith College, in Baltimore, from 1878 to 1880, before entering Johns Hopkins University. See Raymond J. Cunningham, 'Is History Past Politics? Herbert Baxter Adams as Precursor of the 'New History', *History Teacher* 9 (1976): 245; John Higham, 'Herbert Baxter Adams and the Study of Local History', *American Historical Review* 89 (1984): 1225–39. Adams's contribution to the history of institutions is condensed in a series of essays he published in the *Johns Hopkins Studies in Historical and Political Science:* see Herbert Baxter Adams, 'The Germanic Origin of New England Towns', *Johns Hopkins University Studies* 1.2 (1883): 5–38; Herbert Baxter Adams, 'New Methods of Historical Study', *Johns Hopkins University Studies* 2.1–2 (1884): 25–137. The nature and role of scientific history have been fully explained in Higham's *History* and analysed in the wider perspective of American historiographical development by Michael Kraus, *The Writing of American History* (Norman: University of Oklahoma Press, 1953), and Michael Kraus and David D. Joyce, *The Writing of American History. Revised Edition* (Norman: University of Oklahoma Press, 1985), 136–51. Deborah L. Haines has enriched the discussion by focusing on the didactic side of scientific history (Deborah L. Haines, 'Scientific History as a Teaching Method: The Formative Years', *Journal of American History* 63 (1977): 892–912).

59 Henry Maine, *Ancient Law: Its Connection with the Early History of Society and Its Relation to Modern Times* (London: Murray, 1908), 232.

60 Herbert Baxter Adams, 'Special Methods of Historical Studies', 2.1–2 (1884): 5–23; H. B. Adams, 'New Methods', 101–3, both republished in the same volume with the title *Methods of Historical Study* (Baltimore: John Murray for Johns Hopkins University, 1884).

61 John Franklin Jameson to James Bryce, 31 October 1917. Curiously enough, Jameson does not mention Veblen as the author of the *Theory of the Leisure Class* nor reveal his name. He called him 'a young Minnesota Norwegian who was one of my companions'. Bryce on the other

hand might have met Veblen during the time of his visit at Johns Hopkins (letter reproduced in Dorfman, *Thorstein Veblen*, 545).

62 Historian James Bryce was the famous winner of the Arnold Historical Essay Prize in Oxford for his *Holy Roman Empire* (1863), in which he drew heavily on both German idealism and legal history to demonstrate the continuity of Teutonic practices of government and ideals of empire from Roman times down to modern Germany. According to Albert Shaw, one of Adams's students at Johns Hopkins, Bryce visited Adams's seminar at Johns Hopkins in October 1881 to deliver a course on 'English Problems' and to refute the analysis of American institutions provided by Alexis de Tocqueville. For a discussion of this otherwise neglected chapter of Bryce's life see Albert Shaw, 'James Bryce As We Knew Him in America', *American Review of Reviews* 65 (1922): 277–84. Jeremiah Whipple Jenks, the professor who replaced Tuttle as professor of the History of Political and Social Institutions beginning from the Fall Semester of 1891, and later took over the courses in 'Political Science' and 'Economic Legislation', required students to read Bryce's *American Commonwealth* (New York: Macmillan, 1888), along with William Stubbs's *The Constitutional History of England, in Its Origin and Development*, vol. 3 (Oxford: Clarendon Press, 1874–78), Edward Augustus Freeman's *The History of the Norman Conquest of England: Its Causes and Its Results*, vol. 6 (Oxford: Clarendon Press, 1867–1879), and James Fitzjames Stephen's *A General View of the Criminal Law of England* (London, Cambridge: Macmillan, 1863), among others (see the notes from Jenks' classes taken by Herbert D. A. Donovan, in the Donovan papers, # 41–5–115, box 2. Division of Rare and Manuscript Collections, Cornell University Library). Freeman travelled to the United States from October 1881 until April 1882, and paid visit to both Johns Hopkins University and Cornell. See W. R. W. Stephens, *The Life and Letters of Edward A. Freeman*, vol. 2 (London: Macmillan, 1895), 178; B. Norton, *Freeman's Life. Highlights, Chronology, Letters and Works* (Farnborough: Norton, 1993), 39.

63 H. E. Starr, 'William Graham Sumner', 623.

64 While at Hopkins, in fact, Veblen gave a paper on the topic of rent and 'taxation of land' and applied for a scholarship to study the 'Relation of Rent to the Advance of Population'. Even if, Dorfman argued, Veblen commented upon the 'land boom in the West', the surviving resume of his essay showed that he treated the question of rent from a purely philosophical angle, arguing that its eventual confiscation, famously proposed by Henry George to enact a redistribution of wealth, would increase 'the compactness of population, making possible a saving of labor' rather than a redistribution of it (Dorfman, *Thorstein Veblen*, 40–41).

65 Veblen began his philosophical career by questioning traditional explanations of causality in his 1884 article on Kant's *Critique of Judgment*. See Veblen, 'Kant's Critique of Judgement', *Journal of Speculative Philosophy* 18.3 (1884): 260–74. On the probabilistic implications of this article, which already demonstrated Veblen's sensibility to pragmatism and the new theories of causation, see Francesca Lidia Viano, 'Guesswork and Knowledge in Evolutionary Economics: Veblen Revisited', in *Cognitive Developments in Economics*, ed. by S. Rizzello (London, 2003), 338–70; Sophus A. Reinert and Francesca Lidia Viano in this volume.

66 The Morrill Act granted public lands to the states endowing *only* those colleges 'which would emphasize agriculture and the mechanic arts'. By harnessing the principle that *any kind of* education was essential for the construction of the future political classes – a principle he learned in Germany – Andrew Dickson White widened the interpretation of the Morrill Act as to comprehend 'other scientific and classical studies' besides agriculture and engineering (Altschuler, *Andrew D. White*, 58–9), 73; Bishop, *History of Cornell*, 58). Since the beginning, he attracted famous scholars from Europe and other parts of the United States by offering them non-resident professorships. The Regius Professor of Modern History at Oxford, Goldwin Smith, accepted the professorship in 1868, and, notwithstanding his status of non-resident professor, spent the first two years of his tenure at Cornell. After settling in Toronto in 1869, Smith would frequently come back to lecture at Cornell. Edward Augustus Freeman too was hired as non-resident professor from Oxford and gave a series of lectures at Cornell in 1881

(on the same tour that brought him to Johns Hopkins). See Bishop, *History of Cornell*, 104–5; Altschuler, *Andrew D. White*, 85.

67 Herbert Baxter Adams, 'The Historical Work of Prof. Herbert Tuttle', *Annual Report of the American Historical Association for the Year 1894* (Washington: Government Printing Office, 1895): 29–37, esp. 30. Tuttle (1846–1894) was born at Bennington, Vermont and, after graduating from university there, devoted himself to journalism until 1880.

68 H. B. Adams, 'Historical Work', 31.

69 *New York Tribune*, 28 June, 1894. White was then in Germany as American ambassador. See Altschuler, *White*, 119–31 and Wolfgang Drechsler, *Andrew D. White in Germany. The Representative of the United States in Berlin, 1879–1881 and 1897–1902* (Stuttgart: Academic Publishing House, 1989). Before entering Cornell, however, Tuttle taught at Michigan. On Tuttle's hiring at Cornell see also *The Diaries of Andrew Dickson White*, 213, 227.

70 Herbert Tuttle, *History of Prussia*, 4 vols (London, 1884–1896), 1:i, vii. Tuttle had become Associate Professor of History and Theory of Politics and of International Law in 1883; Professor of the History of Political and Municipal Institutions and of International Law in 1887; and of Modern European History and English Constitutional History in 1891. Beginning September 1891, Tuttle's courses in the history of political institutions were passed on to Jeremiah Whipple Jenks, who would combine them with the history of social institutions.

71 Veblen, 'The Evolution of the Scientific Point of View', in *The Place of Science in Modern Civilization and Other Essays* (New York: Huebsch, 1819), 32–55, esp. 43.

72 Michael G. Kammen, *Selvages and Biases: The Fabric of History in American Culture* (Ithaca, NY, 1989), 223, 225. Tyler began editing the *Christian Union* in 1873. As a former member of the American Social Science Association, along with White and Tuttle, he represented Cornell at the constitution of the American Historical Association and was also member of the American Economic Association (Haskell, *Emergence*, 170–72).

73 Kammen, *Salvages and Biases*, 239.

74 Tyler would publish *The Literary History of the American Revolution, 1763–1783* in two volumes in 1897 (New York: G. P. Putnam's Sons).

75 Tyler, 'Introduction', in id. *Literary History*, 1:v. Since the early Sixties, British thinkers such as James Bryce and Edward Lecky had brought the German and moralist tradition a step further in the direction of the history of public opinion and ideas. Emblematic, in this sense, are James Bryce's *History of the Holy Roman Empire* (Oxford: Oxford University Press, 1864), and Lecky's *History of the Rise and Influence of the Spirit of Rationalism in Europe* (London: Longman, 1865).

76 Dorfman, *Thorstein Veblen*, 79.

77 Tyler, Introduction to the *Literary History*, i, vi.

78 Veblen, 'Some Neglected Points'. Not to say that Tyler was also the founder of the American Studies Movement. Before Tyler started his courses in American history at Cornell, instruction on the subject had been provided by William C. Russell, who was professor of modern languages, by visiting professor Hermann von Holst in May 1879 and, also, by Cornell professor John Fiske in 1881 (Kammen, *Savages*, 231).

79 H. B. Adams, *New Methods*, in *Methods of Historical Studies*, 89.

80 Born in Ohio in 1850, James Laurence Laughlin 'worked his way through Harvard', where he took his degree *summa cum laude* in history and supported himself during the university years by teaching in Boston. Laughlin's dissertation was published alongside those of other Adams's students in a 1876 book of collected essays: Laughlin, 'The Anglo-Saxon Legal Procedure', in *Essays in Anglo-Saxon Law* (Boston, MA: Little, Brown, and Company, 1876). In 1878, he was appointed instructor of political economy at Harvard by Dunbar, under whose influence Laughlin began developing a strong interest in monetary questions which would lead him to the composition of his famous *History of Bimetallism in the United States* (New York: D. Appleton & Co., 1886). A 'nervous breakdown' seemingly forced Laughlin to resign from Harvard in 1888, to travel to the West Indies, and later to find employment in Philadelphia. By that time, he was

simultaneously teaching as non-resident professor at Cornell, where he was often invited to give talks, such as the one on 'The Relation of Christianity to Economics', in 1889–90 (*Cornell Register* 1889–90). He was elected to the professorship of political economy and finance at Cornell, with a salary of $3,000 per year, in 20 May 1890, and began teaching permanently in September of that year. See the *Proceedings of the Board of Trustees of the University of Cornell* (Ithaca, NY: Cornell University Press, 1890), 345, 347–8.

81 It 'was my hope' – Laughlin wrote at the beginning of his *History of Bimetallism* – 'that the effect of an historical inquiry in suppressing some of the theoretical vagaries of the day might be realized by showing what our actual experience with bimetallism has been, in contrast with the assertions of some writers as to what it may be. *The practical lessons from facts in such a subject are more instructive than the suppositions of theory*' (*History of Bimetallism*, v; emphasis added). Laughlin was a conservative who believed in Smith's and Mill's theories at a time in which Austrian marginalism was becoming fashionable. Combined with his practical biases, his conservatism made Laughlin a kind of heterodox at the time (Dorfman, *Veblen*, 79). Laughlin began correcting what he thought to be the current failures of mainstream economics in his own textbook, which was an abridged and annotated version of John Stuart Mill's *Principles of Political Economy*, bringing the latter's ideas to bear on practical problems in the American economy. This textbook was to be followed by a second one, made up of a selection of Laughlin's articles also dealing with contemporary problems, and by a third aimed at introductory courses. See John Stuart Mill, *Principles of Political Economy*, ed. by James Laurence Laughlin (New York: D. Appleton & Co., 1884); James Laurence Laughlin, *Study of Political Economy. Hints to Students and Teachers* (New York, 1885); James Laurence Laughlin, *The Elements of Political Economy, with Some Applications to Questions of the Day* (New York: D. Appleton, 1887). On Laughlin and his teachings of Political Economy see Bornemann, *J. Laurence Laughlin*, 3, 15, 18; William C. Mitchell, 'J. Laurence Laughlin', 875–6.

82 James Laurence Laughlin, 'The New Party', *Atlantic Monthly* 53 (1884): 837–40; Herbert Tuttle, 'The Despotism of Party', *Atlantic Monthly* 54 (1884): 374–84; James Laurence Laughlin, 'Our Political Delusion', *Atlantic Monthly* 55 (1885): 826–35.

83 Andrew Dickson White, 'Historical Instruction in the Course of History and Political Science at Cornell University', in *Methods of Teaching History*, ed. by Granville Stanley Hall (Boston, MA: Heath, 1885), 73–6, esp. 74.

84 In the Fall Term examination of 20 December 1890 for the course 'History of Institutions', Tuttle asked his students to answer the following question: 'How can the English Government be called more democratic than that of the United States?'. In his notes for the course in 'English History' he dwelled on the 'popular and democratic character' of the English Constitution. Tuttle Papers, #14–17–163. Division of Rare and Manuscript Collections, Cornell University Library. Finally, Tuttle clearly states his ideas on the superior character of English democracy in his 'French Democracy', *Atlantic Monthly* 29 (1872), 560–65.

85 *Charles Tuttle Papers*, Lecture Notes for the Course in English Constitutional History, Tuttle Papers, #14–17–163. Division of Rare and Manuscript Collections, Cornell University Library. Final examination (25 March 1891). Question IV: 'REVENUES OF THE KING: As Feudal Lord, and when surrendered? From crown domains, and when surrendered? As affected by the Reformation; control over as defined in Magna Carta, petition of Right, and Tonnage and Poundage Act'. Question V. 'CROWN AND MILITARY: Feudal System of service; question of standing army as affected by parliamentary control of purse, by insular position of England, by Bill of Rights, and by the annual mutiny bill; advantage of all this to English liberty'. Question VI. 'PARLIAMENTARY GOVERNMENT: Rise of; relation of Cabinet to Privy Council, to King, to Parliament; the Premier'.

86 Maine, *Ancient Law*, 312–15; Henry Sumner Maine, *Popular Government. Four Essays* (London: Murray, 1909), 188–9; Herbert Spencer, 'From Freedom to Bondage', in *A Plea for Liberty. An Argument against Socialism and Socialistic Legislation* (London: Murray, 1891), 6–7.

87 Tuttle, 'French Democracy', 562.

88 Ibid., 562. Both Tuttle's notes and his questionnaires for the finals demonstrate that he included the distinction between spirit and institutions among the topics of his course. He even asked his students to problematise the statement 'the English government be called more democratic than that of the United States' and to place it in the context of the evolutionary scheme he had formulated as an alternative to the teleological visions of Maine and Spencer (Tuttle Papers, 'History of Institutions', Fall Term 1890, Examination 20 December).

89 Andrew Dickson White, 'On Studies in General History and the History of Civilization', *Papers of the American Historical Association* 1 (1885): 19. The same concept can be found in C. K. Adams, 'Recent Historical Work in the Colleges and Universities of Europe and America', *Annual Report of the American Historical Association for the Year 1889* (Washington, 1890), 19–42, esp. 19; James Schouler, 'The Spirit of Historical Research', *Annual Report of the American Historical Association for the Year 1889* (Washington, 1890), 43–51; Albert Bushnell Hart, 'Imagination in History', *American Historical Review* 15 (1910): 227–51, esp. 233–34.

90 Herbert Tuttle, 'Academic Socialism', *Atlantic Monthly* 52 (1883): 200–10, esp. 202.

91 Ibid., 202.

92 Ibid., 203.

93 Ibid., 203.

94 The fact that a kind of affectionate relationship developed between them while Veblen took Tuttle's courses, or at least one of reciprocal esteem, is further suggested by the latter's resistance to Veblen's decision to substitute his courses in history with Laughlin's seminar on socialism. See the Appendix, Document E verso ('Tuttle absent. He gave assent, but with some reservations').

95 See Sophus A. Reinert and Francesca Lidia Viano in this volume.

96 Veblen, 'Some Neglected Points', 390.

97 James Laurence Laughlin, 'The Anglo-Saxon Legal Procedure', in *Essays in Anglo-Saxon Law*, 183–305, esp. 197–218.

98 *Cornell Register 1890–91*, 104; Bornemann, *Laughlin*, 3. See Laughlin, 'Economics and Socialism', *Chautauquan* 30.3 (1899): 252: 'In the start, it must be clearly understood that those who deny the collective power of the state to exert any influence in bettering the conditions of distribution are certainly in the wrong. The social power of a community, by its ideals and education, can make great changes in the moral standard of living of labourers; it can make great changes in the skill and efficiency of labour, by establishing industrial schools whereby labourers can add to production and thereby obtain greater wages, even under the present régime'.

99 Laughlin, *History of Bimetallism*, 123.

100 Laughlin, 'Economic Effects of Changes of Fashion', 9.

101 In 1906, Laughlin was invited to lecture before the *Vereinigung für Staatswirtschaftliche Fortbildung* in Berlin. He lectured in German, and his lectures were subsequently translated into English. See, more particularly, James Laurence Laughlin, 'Die Arbeiterfrage in den Vereinigten Staaten', in id. *Aus dem Amerikanischen Wirtschaftsleben* (Leipzig: Teubner, 1906), 44–59, esp. 46; translated into English as James Laurence Laughlin, 'The Labor in the United States', *Industrial America. Berlin Lectures of 1906* (London: Hodder & Stoughton, 1907), 67–99, esp. 70–71.

102 Laughlin, 'Labor', 70–71.

103 James Laurence Laughlin, 'Das Eisenbahnproblem in den Vereinigten Staaten', in *Aus dem Amerikanischen Wirtschaftsleben*, 90–113, esp. 104; translated into English as James Laurence, 'The Railway Problem', in *Industrial America*, 140–83, esp. 164; R. Newton Crane, 'United States of America: State Legislation', *Journal of the Society of Comparative Legislation*, New Series 6 (1905), 315–18, esp. 318; Arthur Lenhoff, 'Development of the Concept of Eminent Domain', *Columbia Law Review* 42 (1942): 596–638, esp. 604.

104 Haskell, *Emergence*, 24–47.

105 *Tuttle Papers*, lecture notes for the course in 'English History'.

106 *Tuttle Papers*, lecture notes for the course in 'English History' (Tuttle, 'The Despotism of Party'; Laughlin, 'The New Party'; Laughlin, 'Our Political Delusion'). Tyler identified the 'ideal community' with the New England towns, where – he thought – intercourse was exclusively intellectual and sustained by a longstanding tradition of self-government and mutual help: 'In its inception New England was not an agricultural community, nor a manufacturing community, nor a trading community: it was a thinking community; an arena and mart for ideas; its characteristic organ being not the hand, nor the heart, nor the pocket, but the brain'. 'The outward arrangements which they had constructed for themselves […] were the authentic expression of their characters, and fitted them as the garment does the man who wears it: closely related communities; local self-government […] every man a soldier; every man a scholar; constant friction of mind with mind; not labor but idleness seemed disgrace', Tyler, *A History of American Literature*, 1:85, 95. See also Nina Baym, 'Early Histories of American Literature: A Chapter in the Institution of New England, *American Literary History* 1 (1989): 459–88, esp. 466. E. L. Godkin, 'Commercial Immorality and Political Corruption', *North American Review* 107 (1868): 248–66, esp. 249. The same concern for urban corruption had been displayed by Herbert Baxter Adams and his pupils and was passed on to eminent British guests of the historical seminar such as historian James Bryce. See for example, Albert Shaw, *Municipal Government in Great Britain* (New York: The Century Co., 1895), 1–19.

107 Veblen, 'Some Neglected Points', 387.

108 Spencer, 'From Freedom to Bondage', 7–8, 14.

109 Ibid., 404.

110 Ibid., 399; Tuttle, *Academic Socialism*, 202.

111 Veblen, 'Some Neglected Points', 395–96.

112 Ibid., 396.

113 Bernard de Mandeville, *The Fable of the Bees; or Private Vices, Publick Benefits*, vol. 1, ed. by F. B. Kaye (Indianapolis: Liberty Fund, 1988), 452. On Veblen's use of Mandeville, see Edward Hundert, *The Enlightenment's Fable: Bernard Mandeville and the Discovery of Society* (Cambridge: Cambridge University Press, 1994), 247, cf. Joseph J. Spengler, 'Veblen and Mandeville Contrasted', *Weltwirtschaftliches Archiv* 82 (1956): 35–67.

114 Veblen, 'Some Neglected Points', 395.

115 As G. D. H. Cole has illustrated, moralising tendencies had always been an important component of socialism, particularly the utopian version of which traced moral deficiencies back to the corrupting influences of the environment and set out to cure them by acting upon institutions. See G. D. H. Cole, 'What is Socialism?' in *Political Studies* 1 (1953): 21–33; and in *Socialism. Critical Concepts in Political Science*, ed. by Jeremy Jennings (London: Routledge, 2003), 24–44; See also Jeremy Jennings, 'Socialism: an Introduction', in id. *Socialism. Critical Concepts in Political Science*, 1–20, esp. 7–8.

116 Veblen, *Leisure Class*, 85–7, 88.

117 Ibid., 112. See also ibid., 205: 'The requirements of decency in this matter are very considerable and very imperative; so that even among classes whose pecuniary position is sufficiently strong to admit a consumption of goods considerably in excess of the subsistence minimum, the disposable surplus left over after the more imperative physical needs are satisfied is not infrequently diverted to the purpose of a conspicuous decency, rather than to added physical comfort and fullness of life. The institution of a leisure class hinders cultural development immediately (1) by the inertia proper to the class itself, (2) through its prescriptive example of conspicuous waste and of conservatism and (3) indirectly through that system of unequal distribution of wealth and sustenance on which the institution itself rests'.

118 Letter of Hull to President Jordan, 27 April 1905, Charles Hull Papers, #14–17–249. Division of Rare and Manuscript Collections, Cornell University Library. See Appendix, Document F. The letter was first discovered and kindly shown me by Sophus A. Reinert.

119 On Veblen's re-elaboration of the utilitarian and hedonistic bequest to economics, see Sophus A. Reinert and Francesca Lidia Viano in this volume.

120 Ibid.

121 Henry James, *Psychology* (New York: Holst, 1892), 143.

122 Thorstein Veblen, *The Theory of Business Enterprise* (New York: Charles Scribner's Sons, 1904); Thorstein Veblen, *Imperial Germany and the Industrial Revolution* (New York: Macmillan, 1915); Thorstein Veblen, *An Inquiry into the Nature of Peace and the Terms of its Perpetuation* (New York: Macmillan, 1917).

123 For a more detailed description of Veblen's treatment of international politics and his project for a perpetual peace see the essays by Sidney Plotkin, Stephen Edgell and James K. Galbraith in this volume.

124 Veblen, 'Some Neglected Points', 402.

125 Quoted in Tolman, 'The Study of Sociology', 803.

126 Veblen, 'Some Neglected Points', 402.

127 Ibid., 404.

128 Veblen, *Business Enterprise*, 270.

129 Ibid., 284.

130 Ibid., 285.

131 Matthew Arnold, *Culture and Anarchy and Other Writings*, ed. by Stefan Collini (Cambridge: Cambridge University Press, 1993), 200.

Chapter 8

SCHOOLING FOR HETERODOXY: ON THE FOUNDATIONS OF THORSTEIN VEBLEN'S INSTITUTIONAL ECONOMICS

Charles Camic

Attentive observer that he was of discoveries occurring at the frontiers of the biological sciences a century ago, Thorstein Veblen, were he transported to our own time, would almost certainly be fascinated by the research of contemporary biological scientists, perhaps especially by the work of those in the thriving field of comparative genomics. Findings by genomics researchers that, for example, human DNA and the DNA of chimpanzees differ by less than 1.2 per cent would have captivated Veblen, who – we may confidently assume – would have followed with great interest scientists' current efforts to plumb this comparatively small zone of interspecies genetic difference and to specify the particular bundle of genes that differentiates humans from chimps (and others species), as well as to identify precisely when and how these distinguishing genes emerged in the course of human evolution. At the least, Veblen would have understood the reasoning of present-day evolutionary anthropologists, paleo-neurologists and other genomic scientists when they hold that finding the *human genetic differentia* furnishes one of the keys to our origins as humans.

For nearly 80 years, historians and social scientists have sought Thorstein Veblen's own origins – the intellectual origins of the distinctive body of ideas to which he gave voice and which would subsequently bear the label of (American) institutional economics. With few exceptions, however, the quest by scholars for the origins of Veblen's thought has followed a strategy fundamentally at odds with the logic that underpins comparative genomics and many other fields of inquiry in the biological and the human sciences.[1] Consider, by way of illustration, Stephen Edgell and Rick Tilman's major 1989 article on Veblen's 'intellectual antecedents'. Synthesising the extensive scholarship on Veblen available to them, Edgell and Tilman identify 'the following dozen sources of influence' on Veblen's thought:

'1. German philosophy and economics, including German idealism, especially Immanuel Kant and the historical school of economics, particularly Gustav Schmoller.
2. British empiricism, notably David Hume.
3. American pragmatism, especially C. S. Peirce and John Dewey.

4. European socialism, most notably Karl Marx, Marxists and Marxism.
5. Anglo-American evolutionary thought, particularly Charles Darwin, Herbert Spencer and […] W.G. Sumner.
6. American socialist thought, including […] Edward Bellamy and anarcho-syndicalism [of the I.W.W].
7. British socialism, especially John Hobson.
8. French utopian socialism, particularly Charles Fourier and Henri St. Simon.
9. Scottish political economy, notably John Rae.
10. Norwegian Lutheranism.
11. Psychology, notably Jacques Loeb and William James.
12. Anthropology, including Franz Boas and Edward Tylor.'[2]

If we set aside Norwegian Lutheranism, John Rae and perhaps Jacques Loeb, the remaining 10 'intellectual antecedents' that constitute the core of this list have a striking characteristic. Not only are they sources with which scholars have shown that Veblen was familiar, they are sources with which virtually every American intellectual who was Veblen's contemporary was also familiar. Indeed, the enumeration almost amounts to the academic 'Top 10 Hits List' for the period that runs from roughly 1880 to 1910. For, as one can verify by perusing biographies of nearly all of Veblen's contemporaries, Kant, Hume, Marx, the German Historical School, the pragmatists, the new psychology, the new anthropology, Spencer and Darwin – this was the literature of the age, the staples known to practically everyone engaged with and participating in the intellectual life of the period. The point may be hard for social scientists of our own era fully to appreciate, for we do *not* all read the same things; with hundreds of articles relevant to our interests published each week, scores of pertinent new books appearing each month, each of us must pick and choose. But this is a phenomenon of the past half century. Unlike ourselves, academics of Veblen's period – while they no doubt attended selectively to the various specialised literatures that were already emerging as separate academic disciplines took shape – simultaneously remained conversant with the dominant streams of contemporary thought: that is to say, with precisely those intellectual developments that appear in the Edgell-Tilman summary of the 'main sources' of Veblen's characteristic ideas.[3]

Notice here the substantial contrast between the approach of Veblen scholars and the approach of the researchers in comparative genomics. Where the latter seek humankind's distinctive origins by analysing wherein human DNA and chimp DNA *differ*, Veblen scholars have sought the sources of Veblen's thought using a procedure that is the equivalent of dwelling on the large area of *similarity* between the human and the chimpanzee genomes. In other words, Veblen scholars have focused on intellectual antecedents *common* to Veblen and large numbers of his contemporaries, rather than on the *Veblen differentia*. The same objection applies to scholars whose accounts lay emphasis on the *social context*, in addition to the intellectual background, of Veblen's work, as Diggins does when he links Veblen's ideas to the 'new, menacing economic forces' and diverse 'protest movements' of the late nineteenth century, for these forces and movements were factors in a social environment that Veblen shared with legions of his contemporaries – not 'genetic' factors that differentiate him from others.[4]

We have here a circumstance that may partly explain why the notion that Veblen was a being from outer space – the man-from-Mars – persisted for so long (and still sometimes reappears) in the literature on Veblen, with the various elaborations, onward from Joseph Dorfman's biography, which the Bartleys have carefully traced.[5] In Diggins's version of this idea, 'Veblen was surely one of the strangest creatures ever to walk in the groves of academe'[6] – and a claim of this sort makes it very easy to account for how Veblen's distinctive ideas emerged from so many of the same intellectual and social influences that also impinged on his contemporaries. The reason is simply that Veblen was too eccentric – too strange, aloof, marginal, alienated, detached – to filter these common influences in the same way that other academics of his time did. In other words, to continue the above analogy, Veblen was a genetic mutant or had the equivalent of a genetic defect, so that when 99 of a 100 contemporaries saw green, he reacted to the same stimuli by seeing red. The appeal of this argument is obvious; but in light of the historical research that scholars have done during the past 15 years to dismantle the Veblen-as-Martian thesis, there seems little to gain for present purposes by pursuing this argument further.[7] As this chapter hopes to suggest, the origins of Veblenian institutional economics may, in any case, partly admit of a more straightforward account.

Before proceeding, however, a caveat is in order regarding the Edgell-Tilman list. This listing is cited as the point of departure here because it provides an able summary of the literature on the intellectual sources of Veblen's thought; but this is not to say that the enumeration represents Edgell's or Tilman's own position. Their own approach is cautious, and they express scepticism about the adequacy of much of the evidence that previous scholars provided to support arguments about Veblen's intellectual antecedents. Sensibly urging higher standards for establishing the sources that actually influenced Veblen, Edgell and Tilman favour narrowing down the possible antecedents and concentrating on 'the two pervasive intellectual influences on Veblen's social thought':[8] evolutionism, particularly the positive influence of Darwin and the negative influence of Spencer; and socialism, especially the positive impact of Bellamy and the negative impact of Marx – highly plausible candidates all of them, but at the same time probably among the most widely known and widely discussed sources from Edgell's and Tilman's longer list. An American academic located in any area of the human sciences at Veblen's time who was *not* familiar with at least certain of the ideas of Spencer, Darwin and Marx and/or with the best-selling Bellamy, would have been the true creature from Mars.

That this is so does not mean – and the qualification merits emphasis – that we should discount the importance of these sources for Veblen. The DNA that humans and other species have in common is no less fundamental to our genetic make-up than the DNA that is unique to humankind, even as the shared DNA fails to afford an explanation of the human differentia. And so it is with Veblen: to the extent that our interest in Veblen's intellectual development is an interest in the origins of *the distinctive thinker who was Veblen*, it behoves us to consider the possibility of complementing accounts focused on intellectual sources that Veblen shared with his contemporaries by giving greater attention to what was not shared. Among other things, this may eventually help us to understand why Veblen's engagement with thinkers like Darwin, Spencer and Marx took the precise form it did – although this latter challenge is a task beyond the scope of the present paper.

To be sure, some valuable moves in the direction just indicated have been made in the literature on Veblen. Edgell and Tilman's analysis of John Rae and Tilman and Charles Rasmussens's analysis of Jacques Loeb in relation to the development of Veblen's ideas; Geoffrey M. Hodgson's examination of the connection between C. Lloyd Morgan's work and that of Veblen; and the growing scholarship on Veblen's Norwegian Lutheran background, his family, and the rural immigrant communities of America's upper Midwest – here is research that does shed light on Veblenian sources that were far less commonplace to intellectuals of Veblen's time, and the same applies to a handful of other studies cited below.[9] But which of these lines of investigation is most fruitful?

The answer to that question depends on a very careful specification of the particular features of Veblen's thought with which one is concerned. An obvious point but a point often muted in writings about the sources of Veblen's thought is that Veblen's 'thought' was multi-layered and multi-dimensional: an ensemble of abstract ontological and epistemological assumptions; of economic, historical, anthropological, sociological and psychological arguments; of assertions about scientific method and about aesthetics; of technical concepts; of critiques of pre-existing bodies of academic work; of commentary on different aspects of his own society; of very many highly specific statements and observations. Seen from this point of view, accounts of Veblen's origins that lay emphasis on Morgan or Loeb, rather than on Rae or Norwegian Lutheranism, are not necessarily at odds with one another, insofar as they are addressed to different aspects of Veblen's complex body of work.

The analysis in this chapter is concerned with three interrelated aspects of Veblen's thinking:

1. His critique of orthodox (classical and marginalist) economics for its ahistorical preconceptions – i.e. its individualistic, rationalistic assumptions about human beings and static view of social conditions.
2. His programme to reconstruct economics as a modern evolutionary science, focused on the genesis and growth of economic institutions, including those necessary for understanding practices of economic consumption – e.g. property ownership and the leisure class.
3. His effort to put this reconstruction on solid empirical foundations by the use (*inter alia*) of contemporary research in anthropology (or ethnology) and psychology.

These are neither the most abstract features of Veblen's thought, nor the most technical or specific. Instead, they fall between these extremes, although by no means does this diminish their significance. To the contrary: to the extent that consensus exists among Veblen scholars at the present time, surely these three ideas constitute central defining features of Veblen's institutional economics.[10] What is more, these ideas broadly accord with Veblen's own characterisation of his project at the point at which he began writing *The Theory of the Leisure Class* and was embarking on the celebrated critical and constructive articles that he published in the late 1890s. In December, 1895, Veblen wrote to Sarah Hardy: '*The Leisure Class* is on the boards again [...] . As the writing proceeds, or rather in the attempt to proceed, I find myself embarrassed by an excessive invention of unheard-of-economics doctrines'. A month later, in what is probably the most revealing letter he ever wrote, Veblen elaborated to Hardy on the substance of these doctrines:

> I have a theory which I wish to propound [...]. My theory touches the immediate future development of economic science, and it is not so new or novel as I make it out to be. It is [...] that the work of the [coming] generation of economists [...] is to consist substantially in a rehabilitation of the science of modern lines. Economics is to be brought into line with modern evolutionary science, which it has not been hitherto. The point of departure for this rehabilitation, or rather the basis of it, will be the modern anthropological and psychological sciences [...] Starting from [the] study of usages, aptitudes, propensities and habits of thought, [...] the science, taken generally, is to shape itself into the science of the evolution of economic institutions.[11]

Taking this set of ideas as the focus, this chapter seeks to pursue the question of the Veblen differentia and – rather than concentrating on those intellectual sources on the 'Top 10 Hits List' of the period, the sources that were known to Veblen and to all those contemporary academics who were *not* Veblen – to consider certain antecedents that may have gone to set him apart.

As a chapter-length treatment of this topic, however, the background scope of this inquiry must be circumscribed. Accordingly, the analysis will take for granted two essential preliminary matters that a full-length study would need to cover in detail. The first of these is the *documentation* of the presence and role in Veblen's writings of the three ideas just listed. Because such documentation is widely available in the scholarship on Veblen,[12] the present work omits the textual examination of these aspects of Veblen's work. Related to this exclusion is a second and perhaps more fundamental omission: *historically-informed conceptual specification*. The expressions just quoted to characterise Veblen's views – e.g. 'modern evolutionary science', 'the modern anthropological and psychological [...] study of usages [...] and habits', 'the evolution of economic institutions' – are not transparent terms with stable referents, but mutable and highly complex ideas. Hodgson has shown, for instance, that in the 2–3-year period after Veblen wrote to Sarah Hardy, he greatly refined his own conception of 'the evolution of economic institutions', and this chapter does not dispute this finding.[13] Stepping back from Veblen himself to his context, moreover, all of these expressions have rich and variegated histories; thus, in the second half of the nineteenth century, as Peter J. Bowler documents, not only were there many 'kinds of evolutionism', but even the very same evolutionary 'theory was often understood in different ways by the scientists who supported it'.[14] Given this situation, the following exploration of the Veblen differentia furnishes no more than a prolegomenon to a full-scale analysis that would carefully unpack the historical meanings of each of the freighted ideas under discussion here.

Bearing these limitations in view, it seems apposite to turn our attention to Veblen's formal schooling – that is to say, to the education that he received at the college-level and in the three graduate-level programs in which he enrolled. A thinker's formal schooling is, to be sure, just about the most obvious avenue to pursue in quest of the origins of his ideas. Yet, with a handful of recent exceptions that are acknowledged below, this obvious avenue has been completely neglected by Veblen scholars, as Bartley and Bartley recently observed.[15]

This neglect is another instance of the pernicious effect of Joseph Dorfman's biography. This is so because Dorfman gives every appearance of covering Veblen's education as fully as it merits coverage – so what more is there to do? His account marches through the institutions where Veblen studied, identifies most of his teachers and seems to summarise what they taught, reaching the conclusion that Veblen gained next to nothing from his time in college and graduate school except a determination to rid himself of stale platitudes.[16] In light of this very significant conclusion, later Veblen scholars have generally either bypassed Veblen's education altogether or dispensed with it in four or five sentences that name a handful of his teachers and then stop, saying almost nothing about the content of their ideas except to wave the problematic expression 'social Darwinist' to characterise William Graham Sumner, who taught Veblen at Yale.[17] Here, however, is another instance where trust in Dorfman is unwarranted, for his account of Veblen's education (like his account of so much else in Veblen's life) is riddled with errors of omission and commission. On the omission side, not only does Dorfman simply ignore the teachings of some of the major figures involved in Veblen's education, but he conceals the ideas of those he does analyse in a swamp of undigested quotations drawn seemingly at random from their works. On the commission side, he perpetrates the argument that, wherever Veblen studied, what he principally met with was suffocating religious orthodoxy: an argument Dorfman mounts with the almost-comical tactic of inserting the title 'Reverend' before the name of anyone that Veblen encountered who had ever been a preacher – as if a clerical background meant, of necessity, hopeless intellectual backwardness.[18]

Nevertheless, as other aspects of Dorfman's biography have come under scrutiny, a few scholars have begun to re-open the investigation into Veblen's education. Bartley and Bartley and Eric Hillemann have done path-breaking research into Veblen's time at Carleton College, and Donald Stabile has written briefly on Veblen in relation to his Carleton teacher, J. B. Clark.[19] In addition, a few papers have appeared on Veblen and C. S. Peirce, who taught Veblen at John Hopkins; while Francesca Lidia Viano has turned her attention to Veblen's time at Cornell, particularly to the influence of J. L. Laughlin.[20] So far, however, these contributions have been somewhat ad hoc, rather than addressed to Veblen's formal education as a whole.

Considering that education as a whole, Veblen's schooling occurred in four segments, which we may think of as sustained intellectual encounters[21] with:

1. The Carleton College faculty, particularly John Bates Clark (1877–80).[22]
2. The faculty of Johns Hopkins University, particularly Herbert Baxter Adams and Richard T. Ely in the Department of History and Political Economy; also G. S. Morris and C. S. Peirce in the Department of Philosophy (fall term of 1881–82).
3. The philosophy and social science faculty at Yale University, Noah Porter, George Trumbull Ladd and William Graham Sumner (winter/spring term of 1882 to winter/ spring term of 1884).
4. The social science faculty at Cornell University, especially James L. Laughlin; also Moses Coit Tyler (winter/spring term 1891 to winter/spring term 1892).

This listing has almost as many names as the Edgell-Tilman summary listing, but is arguably better suited to shed light on the Veblen differentia. This is especially so if one focuses on the teachings of these men during the specific years when Veblen encountered each of them, as the following analysis does by drawing on what they published near to the time of Veblen's contact with them and, where possible, also on lecture notes, from near this same time, of the courses that Veblen actually took with them. During the years in question, Porter and Laughlin were already widely known – though scarcely so widely read at those of the front-ranks like Darwin, Spencer and Marx – but the rest of these figures were not. Some achieved renown later in their careers, while others (most notably, Adams) never commanded more than a limited audience. But not only was Veblen the *only one* among his contemporaries versed in the ideas of all of these men as their ideas stood during the years at issue; he was also the *only one* to meet these ideas in this particular chronological sequence.

This point about sequence bears emphasis. According to educational psychologists, sequence is a decisive factor with regard to schooling for the reason that education is a thoroughly 'path-dependent' process.[23] Consider two otherwise similar individuals, Alfred and Boris, and two dissimilar sets of ideas, Alpha and Beta. At Time 1, present Alfred with Alpha, and Boris with Beta; at Time 2, present Alpha to both Alfred and Boris, and their intellectual reactions will differ; just as their responses will differ again, at Time 3, if Boris now reencounters Beta but Alfred meets Beta only for the first time – for ideas encountered early on and later reinforced tend to gain strength,[24] whereas late-arriving, discordant ideas may receive less notice or exert less permanent impact.[25] Re-order the listed four segments of Veblen's schooling, or delete any one of them, and his would have been a different education.[26]

These observations set the stage for a brief consideration of these four episodes in this order, and this is the task of the following four sections. I say 'brief consideration' because I have been pursuing this line of research for several years and can here present only a selection of relevant illustrations and representative bits of supporting evidence on behalf of my larger argument as to how Veblen's formal education set him on the path to the features of his institutional economics emphasised above – i.e. his critique of orthodox economics, his programme to rebuild economics as a modern evolutionary science and his appeal to research in ethnology and psychology. To be sure, none of Veblen's teachers was Thorstein Veblen or nearly Thorstein Veblen, and (to return to Hodgson's point about the significance to Veblen's intellectual development of the 1896–98 period), it was not until after the completion of his formal education that Veblen worked out and refined his position in these areas and so gave life to his own intellectual project. Recognising this point, the tentative suggestion of the sections below is that this particular combination of teachers and the sequence in which such a combination occurred were among the factors that brought Veblen, step by step, to the point from which his great project began.[27] Perhaps it was this that Veblen was telling Hardy when his letter to her said: 'My theory […] is not so new or novel as I make it out to be'.

Carleton College

According to Dorfman's biography, Carleton College of the late 1870s was a remote intellectual backwater in the grip of a faculty of devout clerics, who stressed traditional subjects (religion, moral philosophy) and virtually ignored the modern natural sciences; the only genuine scholar in its ranks, J. B. Clark, so pale a presence that a 'lecture on suavity' was all that Veblen remembered of Clark from this time.[28] The research of Bartley and Bartley and of Hillemann has established that Dorfman was mistaken about the college as a whole: that although Carleton was an avowedly Christian institution, its faculty was predominately non-clerical, consisting of specialised teachers, several with advanced degrees in their fields, who offered a curriculum that required students to take 'courses in chemistry, geometry, trigonometry, calculus, surveying, botany, physiology, astronomy, geology, mechanics, and natural philosophy'.[29]

Because these men and women did not publish, the closest indicators of their teachings are the books that they assigned during Veblen's time at Carleton: texts such as Joseph LeConte's *Elements of Geology*, James Dana's *Manual of Geology* and James H. Orton's *Comparative Zoology*.[30] Significantly, not only were the authors of these texts among America's leading scientific researchers in their fields at the time; but what they all brought to their student readers were (stronger or weaker) versions of contemporary evolutionary doctrines. According to historians of science, LeConte was 'America's "apostle of evolution"';[31] Dana, a path-setter in 'his adoption of Darwin's theory' in the 1870s;[32] Orton's text, a positive and lucid exposition of 'Darwin's "Natural Selection" [as well as] Herbert Spencer's "Survival of the Fittest"'.[33] What was more, all of these writers perceived the implications of evolutionism for the study of humankind. Whether or not Veblen-the-student noticed these anticipations of his own future interests, for example, LeConte's text concluded with a lengthy discussion of the 'antiquity of man', the division of 'the history of civilization into epochs or ages' (stone, bronze, iron), and the economic activities of 'primeval man in Europe'.[34] At any rate, the content of the Carleton science curriculum supports the recollection of Andrew Veblen, who attended the college three years earlier than his brother Thorstein, that '[e]volution was often spoken about at Carleton [...] and discussed; and no one appeared to question its validity'.[35]

For Thorstein Veblen himself, moreover, reading texts by scientists like LeConte, Orton and Dana coincided with the study of political economy under John Bates Clark, who joined the college faculty during Veblen's freshman year and played a major role in his coursework during his combined junior/senior year. Nearly 30 years later, Veblen would publish a sharp attack on 'Professor Clark's Economics'; but his target when he did so was specifically Clark's influential work from the turn-of-the-century period – work written after the intellectual reorientation that Clark underwent from the late 1880s onward.[36] Back in the late 1870s, however, when he was Veblen's teacher at Carleton, Clark – fresh from his encounter abroad with members of the German Historical School – took a position that interwove his own version of marginal utility theory with ideas of a very different complexion. This is evident in *Philosophy of Wealth*, which did not appear until 1885 but presented arguments that Clark had been publishing in instalments during the preceding years.

Clark's explicit objective's during this time was to contribute to 'the needed reconstruction of economic theory'.[37] In Clark's view 'the traditional system [of political economy] was obviously defective in its premises, [which] were assumptions rather than facts',[38] and he singled three of these assumptions out for particular criticism. The first was economists' view of human nature: 'The motives attributed to men [by leading economists] have been erroneous; […] the assumed man is too mechanical and too selfish to correspond with the reality'.[39] Second, economists misconceived the relationship of man to other men: 'The great fact that society is an organic unit has been […] forgotten, and attention has been fixed on individuals and their separate and intricate actions in valuing and exchanging commodities […] The subject can never be grasped and understood until the organic whole is made the primary object of attention'.[40]

Third, economists viewed the economic conditions that existed at the founding of their field as if these were constant and unchanging – this error being their most fundamental, as well as the source of their other misconceptions. 'The reasoning of Ricardo is based on the existence of unrestricted competition'[41] such as prevailed 'at the time when economic science was in the process of formulating' an historical 'era […] of uneconomical methods of work, of divided and localized production', etc.[42] The epoch of 'free individual competition is not permanent', however; just as it arose, so too, observes Clark, was it in the process of 'rapidly passing out of existence', meaning that 'the principle which is at the basis of Ricardian economics is ceasing to have any general application to the system under which we live'.[43]

But Clark was not content simply to identify the errors of political economy. He was interested as well in why economists had gone astray and in what might rectify the problems in their work. On the why question, Clark charges that economists had 'troubled themselves very little with anthropological investigation', with the result that 'economic science has never been based on adequate anthropological study'.[44] And, from this assessment, his proposal for corrective action directly followed, as Clark insisted that 'the science […] needs to be built on a permanent foundation of anthropological fact'; that 'anthropological studies […] would give a new character to Political Economy', transforming it into a science that 'treats of man […] as he has become by ages of social development'.[45]

Apparently, Clark intended this proposal to set an agenda for future work since his work at the time actually drew very little on anthropological facts or studies of social development. Sometimes, he distinguished among 'tropical savages', 'nomads', 'agriculturists' and 'civilized man';[46] other times, he spoke of 'primitive tribes', 'intermediate types' and 'high civilization' – his most general claim being that, for 'social organisms' as for 'lower animals', 'organic development' was marked by growing social differentiation and cephalisation.[47] Principally what Clark sought to accent was the long-term historical transformation of human psychological motives, culminating in civilised man's wider and more elevated palate of wants,[48] although he also stressed the role of a neglected 'want that is universal and insatiable, […] the desire for personal esteem'.[49] Of this he continued:

[Here] is a main spring of the energetic action on which the accumulation of wealth depends […] It is a chief incentive to the prodigal expenditures of the very wealthy; and at the same time, it impels to the accumulation which make large expenditures possible […] This motive creates a highly expansive market for whatever acts as a badge of social caste. Yet it is this identical want the working of which produces the most frequent and sudden fluctuations of value. It demands conformity to a changing style in clothing, furnishing, decorations, dwelling, equipage and infinitude of semi-aesthetic form utilities.[50]

According to Clark, however, the era of high civilisation was still very much in flux in the aftermath of the passing of the competitive conditions that Ricardian economics assumed. In their stead, he saw at the time the spread of more 'openly predatory' trade practices, accelerating 'accumulations of vast fortunes' spent on vanity-driven consumption, the entrenchment of 'non-competing groups' embodied in massive 'combinations of capital and labor', and 'the chaotic condition of industrial society open[ing] wider than it was ever open before the door for new forms of organization'.[51] Among these forms, Clark considered alternatives as varied as arbitration, profit-sharing and socialism, offering the 'prospect that the fittest [of these historical options] will, in the end, survive'.[52]

Clark's ideas in this period were thematically rich, and this brief summary not only truncates many of his arguments, but also omits other aspects of his thinking, including its marginalist strands.[53] When Veblen took Carleton's course in political economy with Clark, the student may well have been hazy about his teacher's overall position, and we do not know which of Clark's specific teachings – or, for that matter, which of the teachings of Veblen's other instructors at Carleton – registered or failed to register at the time. Even so, what is clear is that Veblen's first full-dose exposure to economics was in the presence of a thinker deeply critical of political economy and determined to reconstruct it. And, no less important, this experience was only the first in a sequence; for, whatever their initial impact on Veblen, certain elements in Clark's teachings would soon receive significant reinforcement.

Johns Hopkins University

Veblen's semester of study at Johns Hopkins occurred at the moment when the university was the 'flagship of postgraduate studies' in the United States and the Mecca for those seeking advanced training in the natural sciences.[54] Leading researchers in the evolutionary sciences filled the faculty and set the standard for scholars in the nascent fields of the social sciences and the humanities to follow.[55] With his brother Andrew then pursing coursework at Hopkins in physics and mathematics, Thorstein Veblen was directly connected to the scientific life of the institution, although he concentrated his own work in two other departments of the university, philosophy and history/political economy. In the former, he took three courses with G. S. Morris, a Hegelian who specialised in Kant, and one with C. S. Peirce, the pragmatist logician, and the teachings of these men echo in the philosophical reaches of Veblen's own subsequent work, particularly when he writes on scientific method and on epistemological and ontological issues. In different ways, Morris and Peirce also broadly championed certain kinds of evolutionary thinking.[56] However, it is his work in Hopkins's combined department of history and political economy that merits primary attention.

In this department, Veblen took two courses, one with Richard T. Ely and the other with Herbert Baxter Adams, both men products of the German Historical School and, indeed, close associates of John Bates Clark. Of the two, Ely identified more exclusively with economics, and the 20-lecture course that Veblen took with him, 'History of Political Economy', formed the basis of a monograph that Ely published immediately afterwards.[57]

The keynote of Ely's position at the time was that political economy existed in a thoroughly 'unsettled' condition that beckoned for 'the younger men in America [to] abandon [...] the dry bones of orthodox political economy' and to build thoughtfully on the foundations of the 'German school'.[58] Too long mired in 'scholastic wrangling concerning nomenclature and verbal quibbling concerning definitions',[59] the English approach erred in multiple ways. First, it reduced all human conduct to the workings of 'universal self-interest', whereas the Germans correctly emphasised that 'the most diverse motives come into play, and the desire of wealth is only one of these; others are generosity, love of mankind, a desire to see those about one happy, pride, sentiment, etc.'.[60] Second, the English school was too individualistic and atomistic; in contrast, the Germans understood that 'it is impossible to separate the individual from his surroundings in state and society', that a 'people does not consist simply of a sum of individuals', and that 'the economic life of a [...] people is to-day a most delicate organism'.[61] Third, the English assumed the constant workings of immutable 'natural laws', while the Germans sought to do

> for the social body what physiology does for our animal bodies. Account is taken of time and place; historical surrounds and historical development are examined. Political economy is regarded as only one branch of social science, dealing with social phenomena from one special standpoint, the economic. It is not regarded as something fixed and unalterable, but as a growth and development, changing with society.[62]

For Ely, the proper choice between these two alternatives was self-evident, and he particularly credited the German approach with furnishing insight into the distinctive features of '*economic life in modern times*', including 'the growing power of corporations', the rule of the 'captains of industry', 'the tendency of wealth to accumulate in a few hands', the possible polarisation of society into 'two great hostile camps' – 'one class devoted to luxury and self-indulgence, the other given up to envy and bitterness' – and the development of the labour movement and of socialism.[63]

Although Ely's involvement in Veblen's education is commonly overlooked, Ely stands even today as a prominent figure both in the history of economics and in American intellectual history more generally.[64] In this respect, he differs from Herbert Baxter Adams, whose name remains unknown except to scholars who study the professionalisation of history as a discipline in the late nineteenth century.[65] During Veblen's time at Johns Hopkins, however, Adams was the more prominent intellectual figure, towering at the intersection of history *and* political economy in the final years before their academic separation. An academic entrepreneur, as well as a scholar and teacher, Adams organised a monthly forum – which he called, rather pretentiously, the 'Historical and Political Science Association' – where faculty members and graduate students presented papers, and he launched a monograph series ('Johns Hopkins University Studies in Historical and Political Science') to distribute this work.

While at Hopkins, Veblen participated in the Historical and Political Science Association, and although he left the university just before the monograph series went to press, Adams's programme for these projects was already well established. The goal of Adams's programme was expressly to encourage historical research on 'institutions' – the titles of the first two series volumes were 'Local Institutions' and 'Institutions and Economics'.[66] 'At the present moment', avers Adams, 'there await the student pioneer vast tracts of American Institutional and Economic History almost as unbroken as were once the forests of America'.[67] Further, Adams urged students to view every institution as an organism of historical growth, developing from minute germs by processes akin to those found in nature, elaborating this doctrine with the claim that America 'and all its institutions, though they adopt the best which the Old World can teach, [...] constitute a New World still by natural selection, and by independent organization in harmony with a new environment'.[68]

How seriously Adams took this thesis was evident in his own historical writings. As he explained at the opening meeting of the Historical and Political Science Association during Veblen's semester at Hopkins:

> The object of [my] entire research was to investigate the *economic beginnings* of Massachusetts and the results show that *English enterprise, English capital, and English local institutions constitute the material basis of New England.* [Not only is it] impossible to ignore the significance of English capital in thus founding Massachusetts, [...] [but] free socage tenure, the Kentish custom of Gavelkind, the old Saxon village community, [and] other local institutions, [...] all contribute to a better understanding of Puritan [...] local democracy [...] Here lie historic germs of the leading institutions which formed the town-life of New England [...] Even the Yankee disposition to truck and trade, hunt and fish, was inherited from a nation of traders and adventures, and by them from their Germanic forefathers.[69]

Whether or not Veblen spotted Adams's deft recasting of a feature of human nature that Adam Smith had taken as universal – 'the disposition to truck, barter, and exchange'[70] – into an historically-specific motivational set produced by institutional factors, Adams's focus on the development of economic institutions was unmistakable. And, in exactly this same vein he continued at the Association's next monthly meeting, where his companion paper on the evolution of 'the Saxon Institution of the Hundred' was immediately followed by a short paper that Veblen himself gave on 'J.S. Mill's Theory of the Taxation of Land'.[71]

But Veblen's association with Adams went much further than this public forum. During the semester in question, Adams offered for the first time a graduate course that would soon emerge as the centrepiece of historical training at Hopkins – his 'seminary' on 'the sources of early European history' – and Veblen was one of the handful of students in the course.[72] A monument to Adams's conviction that history was not about dates but about those larger forces that 'have entered into the life of the race' – viz. 'agriculture, industries, art, science, literature, religion, social culture' – the seminar combined lectures with hands-on exposure to the materials for original research.[73] These included everything from contemporary newspapers and a vast collection of pamphlets on 'institutions' – subdivided into 'family; marriage; contracts; slavery; serfdom; nobility; land tenure' etc. – to artefacts from an 'anthropological museum' that Adams had assembled, complete with a 'collection of lacustrine relics from Neuchatel, – axes, spear-heads, knives, spindle-whorls, ornaments representing the stone and bronze ages of Switzerland'.[74] These last items accorded with Adams's belief that 'ethnology' is 'one of the greatest topics in universal history', as well as with his particular interest in 'the Social Condition of Primitive Man, his Moral and Religious Condition, his Knowledge of the Useful Arts'.[75] Not surprisingly, Adams's lectures for the course followed suit, concentrating on the Dark Ages, on 'the tide of Teutonic invasions [that] led to the inundation of the Roman empire' and peopled Europe with a Bronze Age race 'possessed of a knowledge of agriculture' and associated 'institutions, modes of life dress, habits of making forays and the love of war'.[76] Veblen's classmate, the future eminent historian J. Franklin Jameson, cared little for these sundry odds and ends, although one suspects that Veblen himself, in the aftermath of his time with Clark, may already have found Adams's teachings, as well of those of Ely, more congenial intellectual fare.

Yale University

Although Veblen intended to continue his studies at Hopkins, his hope to do so ended when he failed to win one of the university's fellowship awards, at which point he reverted to an earlier plan to attend Yale University, where opportunities for support seemed greater and where his two fields of interest, philosophy and political economy, were more securely established. For, if Hopkins revolved around the natural sciences, Yale remained firmly anchored in philosophy and the liberal arts. Even so, among the traditional institutions of the east coast, Yale of the early 1880s stood out not only for the presence of several internationally renowned scientists on the college faculty, but also for its prominent affiliate, the Sheffield Scientific School, which was then a hotbed of scientific research.[77] This combination gave Yale a 'reputation for work at the forefront of American science'[78] and provided the context in which a commitment to science – understood as original scholarship based on disciplined methods of empirical observation – gripped members of the Yale faculty in fields ranging from geology and American history to philology and art history.[79]

A prime mover in this process was Noah Porter, professor of moral philosophy and metaphysics and Yale president from 1871–86, with whom Veblen took several philosophy courses and thereafter pursued research on Kant for his 1884 article 'Kant's *Critique of Judgment*' and his dissertation in the same year on the 'Ethical Grounds of a Doctrine of Retribution'. At the time, Porter, too, was engaged in the study of Kant's ethics, amid the Kant revival then underway in the US, and his ideas both on Kant and, more generally, on ontology, epistemology and scientific methodology directly informed Veblen's thinking on these subjects.

Porter was a complex figure, often misperceived in later decades through the lens of quarrel that occurred, just prior to Veblen's arrival at Yale, when Porter sought to disallow

William Graham Sumner's use of Spencer's *Principles of Sociology* in an undergraduate course. What was mainly at stake, however, in this particular episode, as John D. Heyl and Barbara S. Heyl have shown, was local campus in-fighting, not ideas, for 'Porter had nothing against evolution per se, nor against an intellectual encounter with Spencer', whose works Porter himself assigned in graduate courses and publicly commended (along with the work of Darwin).[80] Indeed, Porter followed the researches of evolutionary natural scientists closely and with intense interest; and, while strongly opposing any attempt to justify a 'negative theology' from scientific findings, he nonetheless accepted that 'evolution as a theory, fact or law, must stand or fall by its appropriate evidence' and that, in particular, Darwinian 'theory is perfectly legitimate as an hypothesis, and is supported by the unquestioned [...] presence and operative forces of the two tendencies or laws to which Darwin attached supreme importance', the laws of struggle for existence and survival of the fittest.[81]

Similarly, Porter championed closer ties between the natural sciences and the human sciences, averring that

> the student of mind and of man, who has been schooled by a close and stern wrestling with the forces and laws of matter, cannot but [avoid the] romancing by which the science of man and the logic of science have been dishonored in the past.[82]

From this perspective, he urged the development of 'anthropology' ('the study of man as a complex whole, as varied in temperament, race, sex, and age'), of 'history, philology, literature, art, politics, ethics and theology' (which together treated 'those principles and institutions, those manners and laws, that civilization and culture which give security [...] to present life') and of his own area of specialty, the field of psychology.[83] What was more, with regard to the latter, he himself took the lead: his massive work, *The Human Intellect* (1868) was the first American text to hold that 'Psychology [is] a science [based on] exact observation, precise definition, fixed terminology, [...] and rational explanation'[84] and to take seriously the research that the European pioneers of the New Psychology were then pursuing, with 'Porter actually view[ing] Fechnerian psychophysics favorably as confirming that the "mind" was a legitimate object of scientific study'.[85]

Given how fundamental these ideas were to all of Porter's thinking, the possibility that Veblen was unfamiliar with them after his many long walks with Porter (and the reading he almost surely did of Porter's works) is remote; but even in that unlikely scenario, very similar ideas buffeted him through another Yale source. This is George Trumbull Ladd, whose position as professor of philosophy and psychology at Yale began shortly after Veblen's arrival. The background of Veblen's relationship with Ladd is unclear. Like Porter, Ladd was a Kant specialist, and Veblen's interest in Kant perhaps drew him to Ladd. Then, too, Ladd was at the time engaged with bringing into English the works of Hermann Lotze; and, according to Dorfman,[86] 'Veblen translated for Ladd a volume of [Lotze's] lectures', possibly his 1884 *Outlines of Metaphysic*. In any case, Andrew Veblen long recalled that his brother 'spoke of Ladd in such a way that it impressed me as of some importance that he worked under him' while at Yale.[87]

In this period, Ladd was involved in two major projects. The first, *The Doctrine of Sacred Scripture*, earned him wide public condemnation as a 'heretic' for his insistence on 'the importance of ascertaining the *historical origins* of the Bible without assuming its inspirational or mythical creation, as [Ladd] time and again [forced] the question, what are the *historical facts*'.[88] His second, larger project was his all-out crusade on behalf of the science of psychology, particularly his determined effort to import European physiological psychology and lay the groundwork for empirical research in the field. Prior to moving to Yale, Ladd had already begun what he characterised as 'the detailed study of the relations between the nervous system and mental phenomena', and he immediately resumed this research at Yale, first inside a medical school laboratory and then by founding his own experimental lab.[89] Simultaneously, and throughout the entire time that Veblen knew him at Yale, Ladd worked on his monumental *Elements of Physiological Psychology*, a work with the distinction of predating by three years William James's *Principles of Psychology* as the first American book on physiological psychology *and* of crystallising the case for 'the relevance of science to the study of mental life',[90] as Ladd carefully examined mind 'in its relations to the human physical organism' and expounded 'the laws of the mind', chief among them the widely operative 'law of Habit'.[91] Still further, Ladd (who professed great admiration for Darwin) insisted that the 'distinctive feature of *modern* science', the '*modern* impulse', is an overriding concern with 'evolution', 'growth', and 'development' – the 'historical and genetic way of studying everything' – and, in this spirit, he sought to elucidate (ontogenetically) the 'evolution of mind' itself, 'the stages and laws of the development of mind'.[92] On the basis of this work, historian Merle Curti has ranked Ladd, along with James and Dewey, as the period's leading American proponents of an 'evolutionary conception of the human mind'.[93]

The counterpart to this conception, an evolutionary perspective on the social world, was the special province of the third of Veblen's teachers at Yale, William Graham Sumner. During this period in Sumner's mercurial career, he was less an academic scholar than a controversialist, speaking out in opposition to protectionism, paper currency, state aid, strikes and socialism in newspapers, high-brow magazines and public lectures to educated audiences.[94] Apart from a collection of his popular writings,[95] his principal work from these years was a short undergraduate workbook, *Problems of Political Economy*, which he wrote as a current-topics supplement to standard Anglo-American texts on the principles of political economy. Insofar as Veblen knew Sumner's workbook (as presumably he did), it may well have illustrated for him Ely's complaint about classical economists' preoccupation with nomenclature and definitional quibbling, although what may also have stood out was Sumner's rather unusual emphasis on 'the need of investigating consumption as a department of political economy', as well as his repeated references therein to 'waste', 'extravagant expenditure', 'luxurious consumption' and the 'idle rich'.[96]

At an earlier point in this research, I wondered how Veblen, whose education in economics had previously been in the hands of critics of classical economics (Clark, Ely, Adams), responded when he encountered Sumner's pro-classical position, but this would now seem to be the wrong question. For, while Sumner was certainly a partisan of the English school and while Veblen was doubtless aware of this fact, Sumner's ideas did far more to compromise than to shore up the orthodox tradition. This was so because Sumner was then relocating himself into the field of sociology, which he conceived as the 'science of life in society' as a whole; and this move led him to regard political economy as a mere 'branch of sociology' – the branch concerned specifically with the dynamics of wealth in 'industrial civilization'.[97] Sumner elaborated this cardinal point as follows:

> To compare the economy of the hunting stage, the patriarchal stage, the Asiatic States, the classical States, the feudal period, &c., is an enterprise by itself, […] and one which sociology is constantly enabling us to accomplish better […] Political Economy […] is the science of things within the conditions and experience of men who have to live in the highest civilized nations. Those conditions are changing so rapidly, and new phenomena of growth are presented so constantly, that the science is all the time overwhelmed to keep up with the new demands on it.[98]

In line with this position, Sumner maintained that 'the Ricardian "economic man" could not be further from the men of today than any type of man in the feudal period'[99] – and with Sumner on its side, one wonders if the English school was then suffering more from its enemies or its friends? It is true that when Sumner came to state the basic 'natural laws' by which societies operate and evolve overtime, his formulations were little more than Spencer-esque variants on some of the time-honoured tenets of English political economy, as in his central claim that humankind's

> struggle for existence is aimed against nature; it is from her niggardly hand that we have to wrest the satisfactions for our needs, but our fellow-men are our competitors for the meagre supply; competition, therefore, is a law of nature'.[100]

Unlike political economists, however, Sumner appealed to such laws for the express purpose of advancing 'the scientific study of the structure and functions of the social body' by illuminating the processes by which 'human society takes its various forms and social institutions grow and change'.[101]

What makes Sumner's stance here especially important is that this was the side of Sumner with which Veblen was most directly familiar. One of Veblen's primary points of contact with Sumner occurred, for example, when he took Sumner's year-long graduate course, 'Lectures on Political Economy'. The conventional title may conjure up the image of a course dealing with the concepts and principles of Smith, Ricardo and Mill; yet notes from Sumner's lectures reveal none of this, but something much closer in content to Veblen's course at Hopkins with Herbert Baxter Adams.[102] For Sumner's course was entirely historical in focus and rich in evidence from 'anthropo-geography' and 'ethnography', as he addressed the economies of 'hunting', 'pastoral' and 'tribal' groups, dealt at length with ancient societies, and worked his way slowly through the agricultural communities of the Middle Ages, the growth of commerce during the Renaissance and the rise of modern industry, giving particular emphasis throughout to the transformation of economic 'institutions' such as property ownership, land tenure, contract, technology and social class divisions. Further, as befit this focus, the sources Sumner recommended to his students were not the classics of political economy but contemporary works on evolution and economic history: Darwin, Spencer, Maine on *Village Communities* and the *Early History of Institutions*, Pollock on *Land Laws*, Laveleye on *Primitive Property*, Connell on economic conditions in India, and on and on. Little wonder then that Veblen wrote to a friend that he was 'very well pleased' with Sumner's classes.[103]

Veblen's reaction to other aspects of Sumner's thought is more difficult to gauge because Sumner was then turning out literally dozens of commercial articles and reviews each year, and how familiar Veblen was with any particular argument that Sumner put forth is unknown. A common thread in Sumner's oeuvre at that time was that society's natural laws confer 'rewards to the fittest' – to persons and classes exhibiting 'industry, energy, skill, frugality, prudence, temperance, and other industrial virtues' – as surely as they penalise the indolent and improvident;[104] and Veblen no doubt felt the cold draft of this smug doctrine, which, years afterwards, his own evolutionary theory would turn upside down. But, while at Yale, Veblen was likely aware as well of other constant themes in Sumner's thinking, including: his contention that 'all civilized governments [tend] toward plutocracy', or to control, manipulation, and corruption by the 'force of wealth';[105] his wariness of the auxiliary institutions of 'the governing classes', namely, 'the church, the academy the army, [and] the palace', 'the oligarchy of priests and soldiers';[106] and his running diatribe against 'waste and extravagance', 'the thirst for luxurious enjoyments [that] has taken possession of us all', the spreading belief that 'leisure, not labor is dignified', and the prospect that modern 'advance[s] in the arts and in wealth [...] sufficient to banish poverty and misery' would be aborted by the pursuit of 'luxury'[107] – an analysis of contemporary society that distinctly echoed themes from Clark and Ely.

Cornell University

Between the time that Veblen completed his PhD at Yale and his enrolment in the graduate programme at Cornell University, there occurred a 6-and-a-half-year hiatus. As Erik H. Erikson long ago observed, the lives of many creative thinkers are punctuated by a 'moratorium' period, a voluntary or involuntary time away from career demands and responsibilities;[108] and this notion of a moratorium may perhaps serve to characterise the shadowy interval, from mid-1884 to late 1890, when Veblen was away from the academic world and living back with family members in Minnesota and Iowa.[109] In any case, these were years when Veblen was unsuccessful in his intermittent efforts to obtain a college teaching position in a field related to philosophy (the discipline of his doctorate), and so eventually decided to seek an additional PhD in economics – hitherto his secondary area of interest – probably encouraged by the sudden rise in demand for teachers of political economy in American colleges. With this aim in view, he set off to Cornell University, which had recently established a School of History and Political Science, complete with a department of economics, as well as funds for graduate student fellowships.[110]

At the time, Cornell more closely resembled Johns Hopkins than Yale, as it was among America's new universities and, accordingly, dominated by the natural sciences, with departments of natural history, physics, chemistry, geology, zoology, entomology and botany[111] – the last the department in which Veblen's wife enrolled. As a student in the School of History and Political Science, Veblen himself spent his first two terms at Cornell taking courses on 'American Constitutional History' and 'American History from [...] Independence to the End of the War for the Union' with historian Moses Coit Tyler. And, while nothing is known about the content of these particular two courses, Tyler held very definite views regarding the teaching of history, as he explained:

[I] organize the work of American History[112] so as to cover [...] the whole field from the prehistoric times of this continent down to the present [...] From this point of view, I decide upon the selection of historical topics for special study, [as in] the following: The native races, especially the Mound-builders and the North American Indians; the alleged Pre-Columbian discoveries; the origin and enforcement of England's claims to North America as against competing European nations; the motives and methods of English colony-planting in America[;] [...] the development of ideas and institutions in the American colonies, with particular reference to religion, education, industry, and civil freedom; [...] the causes and progress of the movement for colonial independence; [...] the origin and growth of political parties under the constitution; the history of slavery as a factor in American politics, culminating in the civil war.[113]

'Prehistoric times', 'native races', 'the origins and growth of economic and social institutions': here was history once again in the key of Herbert Baxter Adams and William Graham Sumner; and Tyler was explicit in contrasting this type of approach to the traditional historiographic focus on 'statesmen and generals', 'party leaders', 'ministerial agents' and the like, instead urging a 'new scientific method' attentive to social-psychological forces, i.e. to 'public opinion' and its 'moods, its motives, its passions, even [its] caprices and its whims'.[114] An emphasis of this kind accorded well with several other features of Cornell's School of History and Political Science during Veblen's time there. This is so because not only was it the school's goal to offer courses on 'municipal institutions', 'political institutions' and 'the history of industrial, charitable, and penal institutions',[115] but because economist Jeremiah Jenks then occupied a special chair for the study of 'political and social institutions', while economist Adolph Miller pursued research on the history of American financial institutions. Still further, historian Herbert Tuttle, with whom Veblen was in direct contact, was then completing a multi-volume history of eighteenth-century Prussia: a project Tuttle undertook in order to break from the historian's conventional emphasis on 'the character of kings' and on 'wars, treaties, dynastic intrigues [and] territorial conquests', and to concentrate, instead, on the 'origins' and 'development of polity' and the 'growth of [social] institutions' by tracing modern Prussian arrangements back to 'the[ir] earliest times' – i.e. to the 'primitive and medieval' epochs – and examining 'the early institutions of Brandenburg' as well as the 'process' of their subsequent transformation.[116] Despite the presence of this contingent of scholars interested in institutions, however, Veblen chose to study primarily with another local figure, the head of Cornell's economics department, J. Laurence Laughlin.

Veblen's choice may seem a peculiar one. By the early 1890s, Laughlin had 'gained a reputation for being one of [America's] greatest defenders (if not the champion) of the classical tradition in economics',[117] while Veblen's thinking was set on a different course. The clearest evidence regarding the latter is an article that Veblen published a few months after arriving at Cornell, 'Some Neglected Points in the Theory of Socialism'. Here, one finds Veblen already concerned with 'the evolution of institutions', specifically with the 'economic ground' of 'modern society' – as contrasted with 'more primitive forms of social organization' – and the prospects for 'the modern industrial system, […] based on the institution of private property' and on attendant social inequalities, as the 'system of competition' increasingly recedes.[118] To examine this issue, Veblen's analysis immediately introduces a psychological factor, an 'element of human nature', namely, 'human vanity' or man's regard for 'the esteem of his fellowmen' – a force that, in modern society, mutates into a desire to 'display' 'economic success' by wasteful spending on 'articles of apparel' and the 'show of luxury',[119] thus transforming the age-old economic 'struggle for existence […] into a struggle to keep up appearances'.[120] Among persons of modest means, according to Veblen, this situation gives rise to 'popular discontent' – to a widespread 'feeling of injured justice' – that favours the development of socialism: an economic system whose possibilities can only be correctly assessed when account is taken of the political institutions that would accompany socialism, i.e. 'modern constitutional government – the system of modern free institutions – […] of the English-speaking people'.[121] I call attention to these passages because they nicely capture Veblen-in-progress, chronologically somewhat more than halfway between Carleton College and his seminal turn-of-the-century publications. Here in 1891 he promiscuously intermingles the ideas, the topics and even the language of Clark, Ely, Adams, Ladd, Sumner and Tyler – and others, no doubt, as well – and simultaneously foreshadows themes that later appear in *The Theory of the Leisure Class* and his critical articles from the same period.

But why would Veblen then study with the ultra-orthodox Laughlin? Recall Veblen's reason for attending Cornell: he was seeking to re-tool himself professionally, to make himself a suitable candidate for faculty positions in political economy. At the advanced age of 33, he was not returning to the lowly status of a student again for more of what his previous schooling had already given him – critiques of political economy or proto-institutionalist alternatives – but in order to acquire what he was conspicuously lacking: advanced training in orthodox economics. And, for this purpose, Laughlin was ideal, for not only was he a pre-eminent figure in the academy with the ability to place his students as teachers of political economy, but he also was the high intellectual authority on the classical doctrine. Indeed, the standard American edition of John Stuart Mill's *Principles of Political Economy* had been 'abridged and supplemented' by Laughlin – who gave particular emphasis to Mill's concepts of 'unproductive consumption' and 'unproductive classes'[122] – and Laughlin was likewise the author of two leading texts, *The Study of Political Economy* and *The Elements of Political Economy*, the latter a vast (and uncritical) survey of the traditional provinces: production, exchange, distribution, wealth, value, capital and wages, supply and demand and all the rest. In these areas, Veblen did not prove himself to be an unwilling pupil. To the contrary, his studies with Laughlin resulted, exactly at this time, in his writing four highly technical articles, two of them taxonomic, dealing with definitional issues regarding capital, wages, value and overproduction, and two of them applications of supply-and-demand principles to the analysis of fluctuations in wheat prices.[123]

Yet, Veblen's dalliance with economic orthodoxy proved to be short-lived – possibly because Laughlin's traditional teachings were 'too little, too late' to uproot Veblen's nascent but already-voiced interest in the evolution of institutions; possibly because these teachings paled when Veblen's *subsequent* experiences revived and reinforced lessons from Carleton, Hopkins and Yale; more probably, because of a combination of such factors. That said, we do well also to appreciate that Laughlin himself gave significant aid to the enemy, unwittingly compromising the orthodox position in the very process of staunchly defending it. This was so in three ways.

First, Laughlin was an inveterate historiciser, unable to represent economic conditions as timeless and unchanging. Prior to becoming a professional economist, Laughlin had obtained a doctorate in history, trained in the field in Germany, and written specifically on 'German political institutions' prior to the era of 'private property in land'[124] – and, ever afterward, he took historical change to be a matter of course. When in the mid-1880s, at the height of the American debate over the English versus the German approaches to economics, Laughlin dismisses the German critique of orthodoxy, this was because he presumed that recognition of historical variety was inherent to the English approach itself – that the 'old English school […] economist does not pretend that his assumptions are descriptions of economic conditions existing at a given time'.[125] Accordingly, in expositing the principles of political economy, Laughlin takes care to limit these mainly to 'the wonderful industrial system around us', albeit with the further proviso that changes in industrial organisation were increasingly invalidating assumptions about 'free competition'.[126] Still further, Laughlin sought to focus students of economics chiefly on 'the leading questions of the day' (e.g. socialism, tariffs, taxation, the national debt),[127] and in fact wrote extensively on such questions himself – his best-known book being his *History of Bimetallism in the United States*, a study he touted as resting on 'the historical method' and the careful investigation of contemporary historical facts.[128]

Second, particularly at the time of his association with Veblen, Laughlin was gravitating even more emphatically in historicising directions. For example, in these years, he rewrote *The Elements of Political Economy* to begin with a lengthy chapter framing his presentation of economic principles in terms of highly distinctive features of 'the industrial system', as contrasted with life in 'rural communities' and Adam Smith's 'archaic description' of the division of labour;[129] and he grew more insistent that the 'result of applying this body of principles […] to the conditions of any particular country, at any given time, *will depend upon just what the facts are in each case*'.[130] More generally, seeking at this point a rapprochement between the contending parties of the 1880s, Laughlin found common cause for the old and new schools alike in the 'vast […] opportunities for economic study and investigation' opened up by the historically-specific 'conditions of our industrial life', including 'the modern growth of large production and the control of enormous capitals under single management', the development of new 'methods of production', the dissolution of 'agricultural communities', and the emergence of powerful labour organisations.[131] Here, rather than in the further pursuit of definitions and principles, Laughlin saw a 'free field' for the coming 'young leaders' of American economics.[132]

Third, there was the factor of Laughlin's own academic style. Often autocratic to the extreme in his writings, Laughlin apparently wore a different persona to his students and colleagues, exhibiting a 'readiness to welcome many points of view' and tolerance for those 'of very different persuasions from his own'.[133] Laughlin held that a teacher's aim is the cultivation 'of independent power and methods of work, rather than specific beliefs'; and although he trained dozens of renowned economists, he 'did not establish a "school" in the sense of implanting his views in the mind of his pupils', very few of whom 'accept[ed] his characteristic doctrines in a form that would satisfy him'.[134] Instead, through hours spent meeting with his students individually, Laughlin forced them to work out their grounds for dissenting from his views and so to 'think independently'.[135] Little wonder then that Laughlin counted Veblen among his best students, took Veblen with him when he relocated to the University of Chicago in 1892 and stood loyally by him during the 15 years that Veblen remained at Chicago.

Since Veblen's move to Chicago brings to an end this short account of the four main episodes of his formal schooling, we might at this point very briefly take educational stock by returning to the three aspects of his institutionalism that were identified at the outset. First, as regards the critique of orthodox economics for its ahistorical preconceptions, here a leitmotiv of Veblen's schooling, sounded in succession by Clark, Ely, Adams and Sumner, often in identical terms. Second, the idea of making economics the study of the genesis and development, the origins and growth, of institutions: this is an idea initially voiced by Clark and Ely, then brought to life in the lectures of Adams and Sumner, and later supported by Tyler and even Laughlin – all situated within colleges and universities that highly valorised work in the modern evolutionary natural sciences. And, third, the appeal to the findings of anthropology and psychology: this is a practice championed by Porter and Ladd as exponents of the new psychology, and by Clark, Adams, Sumner and Tyler as partisans of the use of evidence from anthropology and ethnology. The full sum of all these parts, to hand for Veblen by 1892, was – to be very sure – still considerably less that the Veblenian whole that took form between 1896 and 1900.[136] Even so, I would tentatively submit that these teachings were among the *makings* of the corpus of work that Veblen brought forth in those years – key elements of the *Veblen differentia*.

But two final points bear mention. First, the process of education, quite obviously, does not end at the conclusion of formal schooling. When Veblen moved to Chicago, he remained Laughlin's graduate student for only one more academic year, thereafter becoming a member of the University of Chicago faculty and slowing rising though the ranks in later years. Having ceased to be a student, however, Veblen continued to learn, both from all that he read and observed,[137] *and* from his new colleagues – most notably, W. I. Thomas, Frederick Starr, Carlos Closson, John Dewey and Jacques Loeb – whose ideas enriched, refined, extended and, in some instances, reconfigured and redirected the teachings with which Veblen had previously become familiar.[138] Without this additional learning, Veblen's early educational experiences would likely never have come to fruition, let alone to the particular kind of fruition that occurred in his work after 1895.

Second, in examining Veblen's teachers, the focus of this chapter has been on the specific substance of their ideas in relationship to the specific substance of Veblen's ideas. But among the things that give Veblen's work its force is the *intellectual ambition* that enfolds his specific ideas – for, as Veblen made clear in his letter to Hardy and repeated in many subsequent writings, his goal was nothing less than the reconstruction of economics in its entirety, the 'rehabilitation' of the field for the future, for the coming 'generation of economists'. Like individual ideas themselves, however, ambition is to some degree learned, and in this regard another characteristic of Veblen's teachers' merits attention. Insofar as the names of the teachers treated in the preceding account trigger mental images for us, they are probably of frail, elderly Victorian professors, with white beards and walking sticks – hardly invigorating company, it would seem, for a young man like Veblen.

Yet this is not how most of these men would have appeared to Veblen at the time. True, the two biblical-sounding figures – Noah (Porter) and Moses (Tyler) – were 71 and 56, respectively, and very much senior in years to Veblen at the time he met them. But the other six were more like a band of older brothers, wising up the new kid and daring him to take part in a high new adventure. The oldest members of the remaining pack, at the time Veblen encountered them, were Sumner at 42, Laughlin at 41 and Ladd at 40, men of great intellectual vigour right at the prime of their careers. The others were younger still, and full of irreverent early-career energy: Clark only 32 (10 years older than Veblen, just like his brother Andrew), Adams 31 (only 7 years older), Ely 27 (barely 3 years older). And every one of these men was a self-anointed visionary, each convinced not only that his field – whether history, psychology, sociology or economics itself – urgently needed a new scientific direction but that he knew exactly what that direction was and could lead the next generation forward to the Promised Land. Of the many lessons that Thorstein Veblen learned from his teachers, here was another that would ramify in his programme for institutional economics.

Notes and References

1   The common name for this logic, which research in genomics so well exemplifies, is the 'method of difference', classically formulated by John Stuart Mill. See John Stuart Mill, *A System of Logic* (London: Parker, 1843), 2:541–3.

2   Stephen Edgell and Rick Tilman, 'The Intellectual Antecedents of Thorstein Veblen: A Reappraisal', *Journal of Economic Issues* 23.4 (1989): 1003–26, esp. 1003–4.

3   This is not to overstate the point. To say that nearly all academics of Veblen's time were familiar with the dominant intellectual developments of the age is not to say that Veblen's contemporaries all read the same writings by thinkers such as Spencer, Darwin and Marx, or that they all read these thinkers in the same manner and with the same effect.

4   John Patrick Diggins, *Thorstein Veblen: Theorist of the Leisure Class* (Princeton: Princeton University Press, 1999), 3.

5   Joseph Dorfman, *Thorstein Veblen and His America* (Clifton: Augustus M. Kelley, 1972); Russell H. Bartley and Sylvia Erickson Bartley, 'Stigmatizing Thorstein Veblen: A Study in the Confection of Academic Reputations', *International Journal of Politics, Culture and Society* 14.2 (2002): 363–400; Stephen Edgell, *Veblen in Perspective: His Life and Thought* (Armonk: M. E. Sharpe, 2001).

6   Diggins, *Thorstein Veblen*, 32.

7   Russell H. Bartley and Sylvia Erickson Bartley, 'In Search of Thorstein Veblen: Further Inquiries into His Life and Work', *International Journal of Politics, Culture and Society* 11.1 (1997): 129–73; Edgell, *Veblen in Perspective*; Jorgensen and Jorgensen, *Thorstein Veblen*; Rick Tilman, *The Intellectual Legacy of Thorstein Veblen: Unresolved Issues* (Westport: Greenwood Press, 1996).

8   Stephen Edgell and Rick Tilman, 'The Intellectual Antecedents', 1004.

9 Stephen Edgell and Rick Tilman, 'John Rae and Thorstein Veblen: A Neglected Intellectual Relationship', *History of Political Economy* 23.4 (1991): 167–80; Tilman, *The Intellectual Legacy*; C. Rasmussen and Rick Tilman, *Jacques Loeb: His Science and Social Activism and Their Philosophical Foundations* (Philadelphia: American Philosophical Society, 1999); Geoffrey M. Hodgson, *How Economics Forgot History: The Problem of Historical Specificity in Social Science* (London: Routledge, 2001); Geoffrey M. Hodgson, *The Evolution of Institutional Economics: Agency, Structure and Darwinism in American Institutionalism* (London: Routledge, 2004); Jonathan A. Larson, 'Speculations on the Origins of Veblen's Aesthetic Criticisms: As Revealed by the Restoration of the Veblen Family Farmstead', presented at the 1st International Thorstein Veblen Association Conference (1994); Edgell, *Veblen in Perspective*.

10 See especially Hodgson, *Evolution of Institutional Economics* and the vast literature cited therein

11 These letters are dated 15 December 1895 and 23 January 1896. They are reproduced in full in the Appendix of Elisabeth Jorgensen and Henry Irvin Jorgensen, *Thorstein Veblen: Victorian Firebrand* (Armonk: M. E. Sharpe, 1999), 190–96.

12 Geoffrey M. Hodgson, *Evolution of Institutional Economics*; Charles Camic, 'Thorstein Veblen', in *International Encyclopedia of Economic Sociology*, ed. by Jens Beckert (London: Routledge, 2005).

13 Hodgson, *Evolution of Institutional Economics*, 134–42.

14 P. J. Bowler, *The Eclipse of Darwinism* (Baltimore: Johns Hopkins University Press, 1992), x, 7; see also P. J. Bowler, *The Non-Darwinian Revolution: Reinterpreting a Historical Myth* (Baltimore: Johns Hopkins University Press, 1988).

15 Russell H. Bartley and Sylvia Erickson Bartley, 'The Formal Education of Thorstein Veblen: His Carleton Years, 1874–1880', paper presented at the 4th International Thorstein Veblen Association Conference (2002), 1.

16 A minor exception here is Dorfman's brief paragraph on C. S. Peirce (*Thorstein Veblen*, 41), whose stature among Dorfman's own contemporaries may have led him to a more circumspect treatment.

17 For recent examples, see Diggins, *Thorstein Veblen*; Edgell, *Veblen in Perspective*; Jorgensen and Jorgensen, *Thorstein Veblen*; Tilman, *The Intellectual Legacy*.

18 Dorfman thus introduces Veblen's teachers as 'Reverend Noah Porter', 'Reverend George Trumbull Ladd' and 'Reverend Moses Coit Tyler'; see Dorfman, *Thorstein Veblen*, 41, 53, 79). Likewise, while neglecting the content of the books in question, Dorfman is careful to report that the economic text that Veblen used at Carleton was by 'Bishop Francis Wayland as revised by the Reverend A. L. Chapin', while the logic text was the work of 'Reverend Lyman Atwater' (ibid., 22, 26). Bartley and Bartley properly call attention to how 'Dorfman proceeds from an unexamined anti-clerical basis rooted in the fallacious opposition of science and religion, which blinds him to the subtleties of intellectual inquiry in nineteenth-century America' ('The Formal Education of Thorstein Veblen', 2).

19 D. Stabile, 'The Intellectual Antecedents of Thorstein Veblen: A Case for John Bates Clark', *Journal of Economic Issues* 31.3 (1997): 817–25.

20 Bartley and Bartley, 'The Formal Education', (2002); E. Hillemann, 'Thorstein Veblen and Carleton College, and Vice Versa', paper presented at the 5th International Thorstein Veblen Association Conference (2004); Alan Dyer, 'Veblen on Scientific Creativity: The Influence of Charles S. Peirce', *Journal of Economic Issues* 20.1 (1986): 21–41; Robert Griffin, 'What Veblen Owed to Peirce – The Social Theory of Logic', *Journal of Economic Issues* 32.3 (1998): 733–57; Francesca Lidia Viano, 'Guesswork and Knowledge in Evolutionary Economics: Veblen Revisited', in *Cognitive Developments in Economics*, ed. by Salvatore Rizzello (London: Routledge, 2003), 338–70; Francesca Lidia Viano, *Thorstein Veblen: Tra utopia e disincanto* (Aosta: Stylos, 2002); Francesca Lidia Viano, 'From Staple Rent to Conspicuous Rent: Veblen's Case for a New Theory of Distribution', *International Review of Sociology* 14.3 (2004): 471–85; Francesca Lidia Viano, 'Between New England and the Western Frontier: Veblen's Encounter with Institutional History at Cornell', paper presented at 'Thorstein Bunde Veblen (1857–1929): Transatlantic

Social Scientist', conference, Beitostølen, Norway, 6–9 June 2007; Francesca Lidia Viano, 'Veblen and the Historical Profession', *History of European Ideas* 35 (2009): 38–61.

21 I say 'sustained' because to study first-hand with a figure is arguably a qualitatively different learning experience than to read a thinker's disembodied writings or to meet him/her on isolated occasions; see Randall Collins, *The Sociology of Philosophies* (Cambridge, MA: Harvard University Press, 1998). Veblen's encounters with his teachers would have extended for several hours each week over periods ranging from three months (in the case of Johns Hopkins) to several years (in the case of the other institutions). Further, as the size of the settings for these contacts involved very few other students, these encounters would have been face-to-face and relatively intimate, rather than impersonal or anonymous. At Carleton, Veblen was one of three in his graduating class (Hillemann, 'Thorstein Veblen', 13), while at Hopkins – then America's largest graduate programme – a typical course found Veblen in the classroom with five other students and the professor; see *Johns Hopkins University Circular* (1881), 155–6.

22 Veblen's association with Carleton actually began three years earlier. From 1874 to 1877, he was a student in Carleton's sub-collegiate, or Preparatory Department, pursuing its classical course of study (Hillemann, 'Thorstein Veblen', 3–8).

23 I use this concept following Paul Pierson, 'Increasing Returns, Path Dependence, and the Study of Politics', *American Political Science Review* 94 (2000): 251–672. One might as well invoke Veblen's own notion of 'cumulative causation' here.

24 This observation about reinforcement is important to prevent misunderstandings in the course of the following analysis. When I state that J. B. Clark, for example, presented Veblen with idea X, I am not making a claim about Clark's influence per se, nor asserting the idea X necessarily even registered on Veblen at that point. However, as Ely, Adams and Sumner over time reiterated idea X, it was an idea with which we may assume that Veblen was closely familiar and well grounded. (The contrast case would be an idea that received no subsequent reinforcement in the course of Veblen's education. Ideas of this type do not figure into my account.) My argument, in other words, is not about the impact of any one teacher per se, but about the impact of an entire process.

25 This is, of course, a generalisation which admits of various exceptions.

26 The same would apply had Veblen commenced his education with different *prior* experiences. The process I describe started when Veblen stood at the ripe age of 20 and had already encountered many ideas about many topics. Until scholars are able to learn more about Veblen's family, his schooling prior to 1877 (cf. 7n above) and other sources of his early intellectual development, however, the 20-year-old Thorstein Veblen remains largely an unknown. Nevertheless, based on what scholars have reported about the Veblen family, its ethnic and religious background, the Norwegian communities of the Midwest, and Veblen's sibling position in his family, I would offer – for future research – the hypothesis that Veblen at 20 was already disinclined to look favourably upon religions and political institutions or to include church and state among his main intellectual interests. Insofar as this is true, Veblen may have begun his college education already somewhat inoculated against the religious and political enthusiasms of his teachers, even as he remained open to their teachings in other areas.

27 Most emphatically, the following account does not seek to deny the role of other intellectual and social factors in this process.

28 Dorfman, *Thorstein Veblen*, 18, 31.

29 Bartley and Bartley, 'The Formal Education', 3; Hilleman, 'Thorstein Veblen'.

30 Bartley and Bartley ('The Formal Education') brought Carleton's use of these texts to light. The following remarks on their content are based on my own research. There were a few women at Carleton, teaching mainly in fields like modern foreign languages and the fine arts. This arrangement, however, was not unique to Carleton. It was found at other small liberal arts colleges of the time, where faculty (men and women) were more akin to high-school teachers than to 'professors'.

31 Lester D. Stephens, 'Joseph LeConte's Evolutional Idealism: A Lamarckian View of Cultural History', *Journal of the History of Ideas* 39.3 (1978): 465–80, esp. 469.

32 William F. Stanford Jr, 'Dana and Darwinism', *Journal of the History of Ideas* 26 (1965): 531–46, esp. 543–4

33 Robert Ryal Miller, 'James Orton: A Yankee Naturalist in South America, 1867–1877', *Proceedings of the American Philosophical Society* 126.1 (1982): 11–25, esp. 18.

34 Joseph LeConte, *Elements of Geology* (New York: Appleton, 1878), 560–65.

35 Andrew Veblen to Joseph Dorfman, 12 July 1930 (Andrew A. Veblen Papers, Minnesota State Historical Society).

36 Thorstein Veblen, 'Professor Clark's Economics', in Thorstein Veblen, *The Place of Science in Modern Civilization* (New Brunswick: Transaction Books, 2003), 180–230. See John F. Henry, *John Bates Clark: The Making of a Neoclassical Economist* (London: Macmillan, 1995).

37 John Bates Clark, *The Philosophy of Wealth: Economic Principles Newly Formulated* (New York: Augustus M. Kelley, 1967), iv.

38 Ibid., iii.

39 John Bates Clark, 'Unrecognized Forces in Political Economy', *The New Englander* 36 (1877): 710–24, esp. 710–12.

40 John Bates Clark, 'The Philosophy of Value', *The New Englander* 40 (1881): 457–69, esp. 457.

41 John Bates Clark, 'Business Ethics, Past and Present', *The New Englander* 39 (1879): 157–68, esp. 158.

42 Clark, *The Philosophy of Wealth*, 120–22.

43 Ibid., 150, 147.

44 Clark, 'Unrecognized Forces', 710–11.

45 Clark, 'Unrecognized Forces', 711, 713. Stabile's analysis of the relationship between Clark and Veblen (in his 'The Intellectual Antecedents') also takes note of these passages, but insufficiently attends to Clark's critique of political economy.

46 Clark, 'Unrecognized Forces', 714.

47 Clark, *Philosophy of Wealth*, 38–39.

48 Clark, 'Unrecognized Forces', 714–24.

49 Clark, *Philosophy of Wealth*, 46.

50 Ibid., 46, 96.

51 John Bates Clark, 'Non-Competitive Economics', *The New Englander* 41 (1882): 837–46, esp. 841; Clark, *Philosophy of Wealth*, 173–73, iv–v, 189–90.

52 Clark, *Philosophy of Wealth*, 189.

53 Lest I leave the impression, however, of inflating those elements in Clark that anticipate Veblen, I would call attention to Paul Homan's emphasis on the very same elements in Clark's early work. Comparing the ideas of the early Clark with those of Veblen in later years, Homan wrote: 'There is the same insistence that economic theory must be built upon a correct view of human nature, the same attack upon economic laws which represent no more than competitive normality, the same appeal to the evolutionary viewpoint'. See Paul T. Homan, 'John Bates Clark: Earlier and Later Phases of his Work', *Quarterly Journal of Economics* 42.1 (1927): 39–69, esp. 45. That Dorfman would have had Homan's analysis available to him and still have neglected Clark's importance is telling.

54 William J. Barber, 'Political Economy in the Flagship of Postgraduate Studies: The Johns Hopkins University', in William J. Barber, *Breaking the Academic Mould: Economists and American Higher Learning in the Nineteenth Century*, ed. by W. J. Barber (Middletown: Wesleyan University Press, 1988), 203.

55 Jane Maienschein, *Transforming Traditions in American Biology, 1880–1915* (Baltimore: Johns Hopkins University Press, 1991).

56 With regard to Peirce and Veblen, see Dyer, 'Veblen on Scientific Creativity'; Griffin, 'What Veblen Owed to Peirce'; Viano, 'Guesswork and Knowledge'. Scholars have yet to examine

the Veblen-Morris connection, but Morris's ideas are usefully analysed in biographies of John Dewey, who Morris also taught at Hopkins. See, for example, Robert B. Westbrook, *John Dewey and American Democracy* (Ithaca, NY: Cornell University Press, 1991).

57 *Johns Hopkins University Circular* (1881, 162) presents the outline of Ely's course for the semester when Veblen attended (Fall, 1881); this outline parallels the content of Ely (1884). The same issue of the *Circular* is the source of the other information cited above about the university's curriculum and the coursework of Thorstein and Andrew Veblen.

58 Richard T. Ely, 'The Past and the Present of Political Economy', *Johns Hopkins University Studies in Historical and Political Science*, Series 2, 3 (1884): 143–202, esp. 156, 202.

59 Ibid., 195.

60 Ibid., 148, 171.

61 Ibid., 173, 188, 189.

62 Ibid., 177, 183.

63 Ibid., 174, 187; Richard T. Ely, *The Labor Movement in America* (New York: Crowell, 1886), 6; Richard T. Ely, *French and German Socialism in Modern Times* (New York: Harper, 1883), 28; emphasis added.

64 Note, for example, his role in James T. Kloppenberg, *Uncertain Victory: Social Democracy and Progressivism in European and American Thought, 1870–1920* (New York: Oxford University Press, 1986).

65 See, for example, Peter Novick, *That Noble Dream: The 'Objectivity Question' and the American Historical Profession* (Cambridge: Cambridge University Press, 1988).

66 Cf. Hodgson's title more than a century later, *Economics and Institutions: A Manifesto for a Modern Institutional Economics* (Cambridge: Polity Press, 1988).

67 Herbert Baxter Adams, 'Cooperation in University Work', *Johns Hopkins University Studies in Historical and Political Science*, Series 1, 2 (1882): 39–57, esp. 51.

68 Adams, 'Cooperation', 49, 48, 44.

69 *Johns Hopkins University Circular* 12 (December 1881): 164; emphasis added. The last sentence reveals Adams's embrace of what Novick has called the 'Teutonic-germ theory', which then 'dominated American historical thought', and had Adams as its 'most zealous promoter' (Novick, *That Noble Dream*, 87–8). Novick continues: 'Briefly summarized, the theory held that English and American democratic and liberal institutions had grown out of an institutional germ which developed in the forests of Germany in the remote past, and was transported to Britain by the Teutonic tribes in the fifth and sixth centuries […] This seed was responsible for the development of English institutions. When, in the seventeenth century, the descendants of the Teutons carried the seed to America, it grew with renewed vigor in the forests of New England' (ibid., 87). See also Garry Wills, *Henry Adams and the Making of America* (Boston, MA: Houghton Mifflin, 2005), 92–5. Traces of this theory arguably linger in Veblen's views on the historical role of dolicho-blonds.

70 Adam Smith, *The Wealth of Nations*, Part 1 (New York: Collier, 1902), 59–60.

71 *Johns Hopkins University Circular* 13 (February 1882): 176. For published versions of the two papers, see Herbert Baxter Adams, 'Saxon Tithingmen in America', *Johns Hopkins University Studies in Historical and Political Science*, Series 1, 4 (1883); Herbert Baxter Adams, 'Village Communities of Cape Anne and Salem', *Johns Hopkins University Studies in Historical and Political Science*, Series 1, 9/10 (1883): 3–81.

72 On the history of this course, see Adams (1884). On Veblen's enrolment in it, see *Johns Hopkins University Circular* (1881): 156–7.

73 Herbert Baxter Adams, 'New Methods of Study in History', *Johns Hopkins University Studies in Historical and Political Science*, Series 2, 1–2 (1884): 25–137, esp. 27, 102–3.

74 H. B. Adams, 'New Methods of Study in History', 115, 125.

75 Ibid., 28, 45.

76 Herbert Baxter Adams Papers, 'Sources of Early European History', Class Lecture Notes, series 2, box 27, folder 17 (Special Collections, Milton Eisenhower Library, Johns Hopkins University).

77 Stephen G. Alter, *William Dwight Whitney and the Science of Language* (Baltimore: Johns Hopkins University Press, 2005).

78 William J. Barber, 'The Fortunes of Political Economy in an Environment of Academic Conservatism: Yale University', in id. *Breaking the Academic Mould*, 141.

79 Louise L. Stevenson, *Scholarly Means to Evangelical Ends: The New Haven Scholars and the Transformation of Higher Learning in America, 1830–1890* (Baltimore: Johns Hopkins University Press Stevenson, 1986).

80 John D. Heyl and Barbara S. Heyl, 'The Sumner-Porter Controversy at Yale', *Sociological Inquiry* 46 (1976): 41–50, esp. 43, 3n.

81 Noah Porter, *Evolution* (New York: Bridgman, 1886), 3–6. Porter's Spencerised rendition of Darwin notably omits consideration of the principle of natural selection.

82 Noah Porter, *The Sciences of Nature versus the Science of Man. A Plea for the Science of Man* (New York: Dodd & Mead, 1871), 87–8.

83 Noah Porter, *The Elements of Intellectual Science: A Manual for Schools and Colleges* (New York: Scribner, Armstrong, 1874), 3; Porter, *Sciences of Nature*, 89–90.

84 Noah Porter, *The Human Intellect: With an Introduction upon Psychology and the Soul* (New York: Charles Scribner & Company, 1868), 1.

85 Graham Richards, 'Noah Porter's Problem and the Origin of American Psychology', *Journal of the History of the Behavioral Sciences* 40.4 (2004): 353–74, esp. 358.

86 Dorfman, *Thorstein Veblen*, 53–4.

87 Andrew Veblen to Dorfman, 18 March 1930 (Andrew A. Veblen Papers, Minnesota State Historical Society).

88 Eugene S. Mills, *George Trumbull Ladd: Pioneer American Psychologist* (Cleveland: Case Western Reserve University Press Mills, 1969), 86–7), emphasis added; also Ronald L. Numbers, 'George Frederick Wright: From Christian Darwinist to Fundamentalist', *Isis* 79 (1988): 624–45, esp. 631.

89 Ladd, Letter to the Editor, *Science* 2 (November 1895), 626–7, esp. 627.

90 Mills, *George Trumbull Ladd*, 103.

91 Ladd, *Elements of Physiological Psychology; A Treatise of the Activities and Nature of the Mind from the Physical and Experimental Point of View* (New York: C. Scribner's Sons, 1887), 4, 300ff.

92 Ibid., 614–16; emphasis added.

93 Merle Curti, *The Growth of American Thought* (New York: Harper & Row, 1964), 542; see also Thomas Dixon, 'The Psychology of the Emotions in Britain and America in the Nineteenth Century', *Osiris* 16 (2001): 288–320.

94 The principal study of Sumner's career during this period is Donald C. Bellomy, 'The Molding of an Iconoclast: William Graham Sumner, 1840–1885', PhD dissertation, Harvard University (1980). Bellomy describes Sumner as America's great 'iconoclast'. It is perhaps significant that, having studied with Ladd the 'heretic' and Sumner the 'iconoclast', Veblen would later wear these same appellations in the annals of American intellectual history.

95 William Sumner, *What Social Classes Owe To Each Other* (New York: Harper & Brothers, 1920).

96 William Sumner, *Problems in Political Economy* (New York: Holy, 1885), 4, 50, 3, 52.

97 Ibid., 3, 89.

98 As quoted in Bellomy, 'The Molding of an Iconoclast', 441–2.

99 As quoted in ibid., 442.

100 William Sumner, 'Socialism', in *On Liberty, Society, and Politics: The Essential Essays of William Graham Sumner*, ed. by Robert C. Bannister (Indianapolis: Liberty Fund, 1992), 164.

101 Ibid., 173; William Sumner, 'Sociology', in id. *On Liberty, Society, and Politics*, 183.

102 While neither Sumner's own notes nor Veblen's survive, a full set of notes taken on the course a few years after Veblen attended exists as 'Lectures on Political Economy, 1886–87', J. C. Schwab Notes, William Graham Sumner Papers, group 219, series 2, box 67, Manuscripts and Archives, Yale University Library. I base the statements in this paragraph on these notes.

103 Thorstein Veblen to J. Franklin Jameson, New Haven, Conn., 2 April 1882, in Dorfman, *Thorstein Veblen*, 542. Veblen also took and enjoyed Sumner's course on the History of the United States, which was even further removed from a traditional course in political economy. See J. C. Schwab Notes, 'Lectures on the History of the U.S. [of] America, 1824–1876', William Graham Sumner Papers, group 219, series 2, box 67, Manuscripts and Archives, Yale University Library.

104 Sumner, 'Socialism', 164–5.

105 Sumner, *Social Classes*, 103–4; William Sumner, 'Democracy and Plutocracy', in id. *On Liberty, Society, and Politics*, 143–4.

106 Sumner, *Social Classes*, 30–32.

107 Sumner, ibid., 145, 181–2; Sumner, 'Sociology', 198; William Sumner, 'The Philosophy of Strikes', in id. *On Liberty, Society and Politics*, 129.

108 Erik H. Erikson, *Young Man Luther* (New York: Norton, 1958).

109 Bartley and Bartley have augmented Dorfman's brief account of this period. See their 'In the Company of T. B. Veblen: A Narrative of Biographical Recovery', *International Journal of Politics, Culture and Society* 13 (1999): 273–331.

110 Since this chapter was completed, Francesca Lidia Viano's major study of Veblen's time at Cornell (in this volume) substantially enriches the scholarship on the subject.

111 Waterman Thomas Hewett, *The History of Cornell University in the Twenty-five Years of Its Existence, 1868–1893* (Syracuse: University Publications Society, 1894).

112 Tyler's particular stress on *American* history reflects his appointment specifically as 'Professor of American History'. Tyler took this mandate seriously, as his position at Cornell was 'the first professorship of United States history created at any American university'. See Michael Kammen, 'Moses Coit Tyler: The First Professor of American History in the United States', *History Teacher* 17 (1983): 61–87, esp. 61.

113 Cited in Adams, 'New Methods of Study', 32.

114 Moses Coit Tyler, *The Literary History of the American Revolution, 1763–1783* 1 (New York: Frederick Ungar, 1897), 1:v–vii; see also Kammen, 'Moses Coit Tyler'.

115 Morris Bishop, *A History of Cornell* (Ithaca, NY: Cornell University Press, 1962), 274.

116 Herbert Tuttle, *History of Prussia*, 2 vols (Boston, MA: Houghton, Mifflin and Company, 1892), see in particular, *To the Accession of Frederic the Great, 1134–1740*, 'Preface' [n.p.], 1:1–3, 24; and *Under Frederic the Great, 1740–1745*, 2:vii. While these comments on the content of Tuttle's work are based on my own research, I wish to thank Francesca Lidia Viano (2007) and Russell and Sylvia Bartley (personal communication) for calling attention to Veblen's association with Tuttle.

117 Clair Edward Morris Jr, 'J. Lawrence Laughlin: An Economist and His Profession', PhD dissertation, University of Wisconsin-Madison (1972), 16.

118 Thorstein Veblen, 'Some Neglected Points in the Theory of Socialism', in Thorstein Veblen, *The Place of Science in Modern Civilization* (New Brunswick: Transaction Books, 2003), 404, 387, 392, 395, 391, 402.

119 Ibid., 392–5.

120 Ibid., 399.

121 Ibid., 390, 406, 404.

122 John Stuart Mill, *Principles of Political Economy*, abridged and supplemented by J. Laurence Laughlin (New York: Appleton Mill/Laughlin, 1888), 62–4.

123 Thorstein Veblen, 'Boehm-Bawerk's Definition of Capital, and the Source of Wages', *Quarterly Journal of Economics* 6.2 (1892): 247–52; Thorstein Veblen, 'The Overproduction Fallacy', *Quarterly Journal of Economics* 6.4 (1892): 484–92; Thorstein Veblen, 'The Price of Wheat since 1867', *Journal of Political Economy* 1.1 (1892): 68–103, 156–61. Thorstein Veblen, 'The Food Supply and the Price of Wheat', *Journal of Political Economy* 1.3 (1893): 365–79.

124 James Laurence Laughlin, *Essays on Anglo-Saxon Law* (Boston, MA: Little, Brown and Company, 1876), 183, 227.

125 Laughlin, 'Sketch of the History of Political Economy', 34.

126 James Laurence Laughlin, *The Elements of Political Economy* (New York: Appleton, 1887), 5, 131.

127 Ibid., viii.

128 James Laurence Laughlin, *The History of Bimetallism in the United States* (New York: Appleton, 1886), 3.

129 James Laurence Laughlin, *The Elements of Political Economy* (New York: Appleton, 1902), 9, 15.

130 James Laurence Laughlin, 'The Study of Political Economy in the United States', *Journal of Political Economy* 1.1 (1892): 1–19, esp. 6; emphasis added.

131 Ibid., 14–16.

132 Ibid., 19, 7.

133 John U. Nef, 'James Laurence Laughlin (1850–1933)', *Journal of Political Economy* 42.6 (1934): 1–5, esp. 5.

134 Wesley C. Mitchell, 'J. Laurence Laughlin', *Journal of Political Economy* 49, 6 (1941): 875–81, esp. 879–80.

135 Ibid., 880.

136 Geoffrey M. Hodgson, 'On the Evolution of Thorstein Veblen's Evolutionary Economics', *Cambridge Journal of Economics* 22.3 (1998): 415–31.

137 And likely witnessed as well, as in the case of the early 1896 visit and public lecture of C. Lloyd Morgan at the University of Chicago. See Hodgson, *Evolution of Institutional Economics*, 134–42.

138 This point is developed at length in Camic (forthcoming).

Part Three

VEBLEN'S POLITICS

Chapter 9

THORSTEIN VEBLEN AND THE POLITICS OF PREDATORY POWER

Sidney Plotkin

Among Thorstein Veblen's most influential essays, one asks why economics is not an evolutionary science.[1] Orthodox economics took market-based institutions to be natural, the expression of eternally rational principles of exchange. Their inherent logic of competition brought universal beneficence. Veblen's standpoint could not be more different. His economics is a study of the ceaseless evolution of institutions and industry, and beneficial outcomes are not assured. The material production of things useful to mankind, what Veblen called 'industry', was acutely vulnerable to contamination by practices and habits of exploit, 'the coercive utilization of man by man'.[2] Reflecting qualitatively different patterns and norms of human action, industry and exploit are not easily separated in evolving social life. In complex human institutions, habits of production and of power remain inextricably connected. An economic theory that fails to grapple with the evolution of exploit masks the darker, ugly half of human experience. Veblen's work is a constant reminder that the right hand must be called to account for the activities of the left.[3] A pretence to science is no excuse.

In the Veblen canon there is no equally well-drawn critique of political science; but Veblen's theoretical perspective justifies an interrogation along comparable lines. It is reasonable to ask why political science is not an evolutionary science.

A Veblenian answer might note that much of conventional Western political science rests on normative assumptions about human behaviour drawn, as in the case of orthodox economics, from the various individualistic strains of modern liberalism. Political science as we know it in the United States constituted itself with presuppositions concerning what a supposedly normal, liberal democratic order looks like when individual citizens motivate themselves to concert and execute their political goals within a system of legally regulated institutions. Understandings of political modernisation run on similar lines. The latter is governed by a sequence of historical moves veering toward some semblance of the forms and procedures of Western liberal democracies, themselves the product of a calculation of individual interests like those governing the market. In a different way, Marxist theories of the capitalist state take class relations as their starting point, but they resemble liberal political science in their embrace of teleology, in this case teleology of historical materialism, class struggle and the determined route to emancipation of the working class.

Liberal and Marxist political theorists, more or less convinced of the certainty of their starting points, arrive at conclusions about the state that tend to support and reflect the claims of their presuppositions. Prevailing modes of analysis steer toward self-closure. It is the same tendency that Veblen criticised in orthodox economics. The logic of that critique is no less apt for much of political science. Veblen took occasional methodological slaps at political science and jurisprudence, accusing them of being essentially ceremonial disciplines. But with the partial exception of his idea of the monarchical origins of the modern state system, Veblen never made the evolution of political institutions central to his work. On this score John Diggins is quite correct.[4]

Even within Veblen's own frame of reference, however, this omission is actually a bit odd, for the evolution of social and economic power is a central theme of Veblen's work. As a critic of predatory power wherever it emerged, we might reasonably expect a theorist like Veblen to undertake serious study of the state and politics. Yet Veblen's most important theoretical works, all published between 1898 and 1914, including *The Theory of the Leisure Class*, *The Theory of Business Enterprise* and *Instinct of Workmanship*, offer only passing observations about politics. These subjects remain at best secondary preoccupations, subordinate to emphases on culture, technology and the dynamics of evolutionary change. Simply stated, neither *The Theory of the Leisure Class* nor *The Instinct of Workmanship* devotes as much as a single chapter to the subject matter of politics.[5]

However, chapter titles do not tell the whole story. Closer looks suggest a more nuanced picture of Veblen's relevance to political analysis. It is the purpose of this essay to provide a more exacting view of Veblen's idea of the political. I begin with his concentration on coercive human relationships, and follow with suggestions about parallels and divergences between Veblen's perspective and classic realism. I argue that Veblen's more radical version of realism is rooted in an anthropological understanding of the cultural evolution of power, an understanding that implicates his working notion of 'the political'. With this claim in mind, I turn to Veblen's view of the state, comparing certain plainly instrumental notions of the state in his work with a contrasting view of its potential for autonomy, an analysis based on his discussion of pre-World War I military spending. The chapter concludes with reflections on the theoretical implications of the armaments case for Veblen's understanding of institutional and individual action.

Searching for the Political

Few scholars would debate the point that there is little overt political science in Veblen's writings. On the other hand, he never gave politics a pass in his critique of institutions. To the contrary, governments and political behaviour in general meet many unkind receptions in Veblen's books and essays. This is not merely because Veblen found politics distasteful; it is because Veblen understood political life to be of a piece with other conflict-based, non-productive, predatory institutions – competitive sports, warfare, organised crime and the system of business enterprise – whose common feature is a singular pattern of habits, practices and patterns of behaviour, a distinctively aggressive, conflict-centred scheme of thought and action, a design for 'the coercive utilization of man by man'. Veblen conceived of exploit and conflict as elements in a common configuration of human habit, each bound to the same root: an evolutionary tendency, originating in late savage cultures, toward the making of invidious comparisons among individuals and groups on the basis of imputed capacities for the skilled use of power.[6] 'Coercive utilization of man by man' may be the most graphic demonstration of native prowess, but its exhibition through the more passive intellectual forms of fraud and cunning loom larger as predatory culture assumes increasingly pecuniary, businesslike form. Amid institutions of exploit, tests of power are inevitable; conflict is to be expected, and with it, politics. These are precisely hallmarks of what classic political realism has regularly identified as distinctively political phenomena.

'All political structures use force', observes Max Weber.[7] In the face of this coercive reality, '[a]ll politics is a struggle for power'.[8] This omnipresence of force and power helps to explain why, in the words of a distinguished American political scientist, '[a]t the root of all politics is the universal language of conflict'.[9] Friedrich Nietzsche's 'will to power', an idea of fundamental significance for Weber and for Hans Morgenthau, creates an unbreakable human circle of power and resistance, politics and conflict.[10] Realism normalises connections between power, conflict, politics and human nature. In treating these phenomena as essential features of the species, realism defines their grip on human institutions as an eternal human problem. It is just this normalisation of conflict that distinguishes the genus of 'exploit' in Veblen. Realism makes power inexpugnably a feature of human existence: Veblen treats it as a particular, culturally shaped motivation or habit, the most conspicuous interest of barbaric cultures, the point of view that guides and shapes 'the predatory phase of culture [...] when the fight has become the accredited spiritual attitude for the members of the group'.[11] I explore the content of Veblen's idea of this early evolution later in this essay. Here I want to stress the historicity of the argument. Only with the emergence of exploitative institutions, argues Veblen, does conflict begin truly to furnish a working framework for perceiving the course, imperatives and needed skills of a belligerent life. With the evolution of predatory habits, life comes to be understood and experienced as series of competitive struggles with other human beings, its primary challenges and limitations governed by forces of conflict and power. Once relations and inequities of power become the decisive, qualitative, invidious difference among people, equally within and among different communities, the normative, desired, emulated personality becomes the narcissistic, aggressive personality.[12] Only in the face of such a life, one ordered by presumptions of battle and fight, does 'the occurrence of a habitual bellicose frame of mind – a prevalent habit of judging facts and events from the standpoint of the fight' fully take hold.[13] And in the context of this evolution of exploitation, the various *political* institutions of exploit begin to share the common feature of favouring and rewarding 'coercive utilization of man by man'.

Thus, it comes about that it is in the political domain that members of the human species deny their generic commonality. Here they divide; they fight; they struggle; they dominate; they resist; and they ultimately yield to the powerful. Increasingly habituated to struggle within their own species, as well as with other species, humans begin to question, to doubt, indeed to suppress their consciousness of an impersonal, undivided, generic well being of their community. Yet, Veblen insists, a lingering sensibility of generically human interests and needs stubbornly persists in the human spirit. Suppressed perhaps, but not suffocated, the instincts of workmanship and parental bent continue to function as its most powerful instinctive sources.[14] But if in the age of savagery industry and community were habits blended into the practicalities of everyday life, with the coming of barbarism they retreat to a seemingly unattainable moral realm; they become utopian, their practical significance muted by facts of power and exploit; the here and now dominated by partisan solidarities, the ideological camouflage of cynical and exploitative interests.[15]

It is in these respects that the political – a preoccupation with power, struggle and conquest – appears for Veblen in any form of human activity whose central features are those of an emulative contest for mastery: war, sports, judicial combat, the sharp elbows of business competition and, of course, the struggle for power in and among states. The political in Veblen, as it grows out of phenomena of exploit and conflict, is a sphere of separateness, alienation and competition; its inherent tendencies favouring war, not peace, the forging of enmity, not the solidarity of the species. If the state as we know it is one, but by no means the only, predatory institution to emerge in human culture, an adequate study of the political should encompass any analysis of bellicose and power-motivated habits wherever they emerge and evolve. An evolutionary study of the political will thus be, as indeed it tends to be in Veblen, a historical study of changes in the forms, direction and purposes of 'the coercive utilization of man by man'.

Coercive Utilisation

To identify politics with competitive, predatory and coercive features of human behaviour is, of course, hardly shocking or original. The view of humans as naturally aggressive and lusting after power is virtually emblematic of Western culture. 'It is held' as a commonplace of the going scheme of things, Veblen writes in *The Vested Interests and the Common Man*, that 'men are inclined to fight, not to work – that the end of action in the normal case is damage and not repair'.[16] Human beings are purposive beings; they do not act randomly or without intelligent reason, and it is not that they are naturally sadistic. Evolution and function running together, the appeal of aggressiveness must therefore be serviceable to certain human ends. People seek power over others for rational reasons, although perhaps not exclusively for rational ones.

The coercive use of others has had significant economic implications, of course, as Karl Marx insisted. But it has been just as deeply engaged in cultural processes. Honour, status and prestige are in many different cultures regularly enlisted to infuse coercive success with spiritual and moral dignity. As Veblen stresses, it is the very dignity to be got from exhibitions of power, a dignity closely associated with rank and class that is the chief motive of power seeking.[17] In this sense, the inner political substance of claims to status and class is the claim to power. Dignity derives from reputations for unusual competence in the uses of power, just as the 'concept of dignity, worth or honor, as applied either to persons or to conduct, is of first-rate consequence in the development of classes and class distinctions'.[18]

The fusion of honour, dignity, class and power virtually defines the social structures of predatory civilisation. Triumphant generals, victorious athletes, clever lawyers, daring business executives and masterful politicians enjoy enhanced status not available to ordinary workers. The trophies of their power are many and various, none perhaps more expressive of these governing habits of mind than the symbol of 'trophy wife'. 'The coercive utilization of man by man' may have well begun, after all, with the coercive utilisation of woman by man.[19] But whatever its specific evolutionary start, in whatever variant combinations of intimidation and guile, the bringing of power to bear carries with it a thorough social organisation of spiritual gratifications, an elaborate institutional process of rituals and regalia, the overall thrust of which is an unmistakable celebration of abilities to compel others toward action and purpose not of their own choosing.

Such observations, as we have noted, characterise the realist tradition in political thought. As Morgenthau explains in a classic essay, Jean Jacques Rousseau made a profound error when he said that man is born free yet finds himself everywhere in chains. Not only is man born in chains and condemned to live in them; the deeper tragedy is that he seeks to escape those chains not to become free, but precisely to establish mastery over others. The inevitability of politics lies in the nature of human aspirations to dominate and control other human beings. These motivations affirm both the inescapability of power and the eternal conflict over its possession and use. 'Man's aspiration for power', he insists, is 'not an accident of history [...] a temporary deviation from a normal state of freedom; it is an all-permeating fact which is of the very essence of human existence'.[20]

This presupposition is, of course, pervasive in Western political thought, from Plato's Thrasymachus, through the works of St Augustine, Machiavelli, Spinoza, Hobbes, the American Framers and Nietzsche.[21] Veblen's analysis of the power implications of exploit also follows this trail, but only as it evolved through epochs of barbaric feudalism and quasi-peaceable capitalism. Precisely in this qualified but still revealing sense does Veblen's account dovetail with realism. Veblen, like the realists, posits power and its associated prestige to be decisive motivations of belligerent action. However, and this distinction is crucial to our qualified analogy, Veblen radically differed with realism on the fundamental issue of the origins of power. All views of power, exploit and conflict that make these things 'the very essence of human existence' are excluded by his evolutionary analysis of institutions. Veblen refused to take power lust, or humanity's supposedly combative, aggressive nature, for granted. He objected to any theory of a natural drive toward power, to any theory that refers to connections between human nature and power as essential qualities of a fixed, eternal human nature. Above all, he wanted to understand, from within an anthropological and hermeneutic perspective, how and why humans learned to court reputations for power, how and why they were attracted by its special lure in the course of their evolution as a species. This is not a question of Morgenthau's reference to an historical accident, but an inquiry into the social evolution of the human enchantment with power. Veblen tried, in other words, to explain 'why man, unlike the rest of the animal kingdom, was not content to confine himself to what life objectively requires'.[22] In short, Veblen sought to account for how power obtained its mystique, why it is that human beings make a fetish of power.

He engages this analysis comparatively, drawing contrasts with forms of action and value that, from his evolutionary viewpoint, must have preceded the development of exploit into a full-blown cultural practice and norm.

Right from the beginning, his basic evolutionary distinction between industry and exploit put the nature of power into doubt – that is, Veblen made it a relative rather than an absolute or essential human concept. In his writings, he consciously situates power within a theory of exploit that describes its gradual separation from industry, as a distinctively personalised, egoistic phenomenon that increasingly estranges itself from impersonal work. In a sense, the most profound difference between Veblen and most realists is that his evolutionary perspective considers all human phenomena not from a personal or individual viewpoint, but from the standpoint of the species and its life process considered generically. Phenomena of power grow, however unwittingly at first, from out of this indispensable process. In contrast, the great German realist thinker Friedrich Meinecke reflected the realist tendency to offer a qualitatively different judgment of the appropriate derivation of power. An understanding of the distinctively human quest for power, he observed, cannot begin in 'the mere satisfaction of bare physical needs'. This domain of industry, of 'mere technique […] belongs to the realm of physical nature'. As Meinecke adds, 'That which is merely useful and necessary can never lead beyond the static technique of animals and animal communities'.[23] This industrial or 'scientific' man', as Morgenthau described him in 1946, can tell us nothing about 'political man'.

Veblen's perspective was fundamentally different. He posits an ongoing set of successive comparisons between two tightly related, but increasingly distinctive phenomena. There is, first of all, the life process and the generic needs and capacities of the species – all those organic activities of labour and technique that most immediately function to reproduce human life – realms that Meinecke and Morgenthau specifically identify with nature and science. Then there is the evolutionary fact of humanity in its gradually differentiated cultural evolution as a collection of disparate groups – the realists' domain of politics – each community with its own particularised version of the life process, human needs and institutional capacities, each increasingly organised through relations of power, but always relying upon industry for life.

For Veblen, then, power relations did not represent an analytically discrete, much less a nobler human realm than the economic. Rather, he saw them as an outgrowth of human experience and interpretation, shaped initially by pressures, techniques and habits learned in the course of humanity's material or 'animal' life. Veblen was dealing with what he conceived as a subtle and mutually reinforcing web of human developments, a network of closely knit industrial activity and hermeneutic experience that refuted the familiar separation of disciplines and fields of knowledge. In other words, Veblen refused to treat power as a natural phenomenon, but he was committed to a naturalistic explanation of its evolution.[24] Power lust is not inscribed in humanity's DNA, we might say today; but its influence as a factor in the growth of human institutions, and its identification with something called human nature, can be explained within an evolutionary frame of reference, as a logical if not a determined product of changing pressures and opportunities. An understanding of this distinction is imperative both for an appreciation of his evolutionary naturalistic perspective and its implications for the specific kind of radical realism that it led Veblen to embrace.

Veblen refused to accept orthodox realism's insistence that there is some kind of unfathomable mystery to human interests in power. His method – indeed his normative standpoint on the illuminating possibility of reason – urged him against such claims as Meinecke's that humanity's 'higher and lower abilities, the element of mind and the element of physical nature, can be in Man at one and the same time both causally connected and yet essentially separate', a fact that expresses 'the dark mystery of life'.[25] If the vital elements of the mind become attracted and habituated to power, this attraction does not lie in 'the dark mystery of life'. Veblen made no concession to an opaque, enigmatic barrier to what reason can fathom. For him, there is a rational explanation for the attraction to power. It can be found in hermeneutic processes characteristic of the human mind. The mind projects itself – or rather applies features of knowing that it experiences within itself – to explain its relation to the mysteries it encounters outside. We can find the sources of humanity's enchantment with power, Veblen suggests, by understanding how such imputation unfolds and how it influences a reshaping of habits and institutions. To follow this evolution, it is imperative to say a little more about Veblen's theory of the instincts and their contribution to human survival.

Psychological factors, what Veblen calls instincts, enter into the complexity of life only through the mediation of human institutions and environmental forces, but their orientation tends to be generic, or species based. Reflecting his strong Darwinian influence, Veblen believed that most of these psychic factors evolved by way of natural selection to favour survival of the species.[26] Although the duration and cumulative effects of human experience give increasingly greater weight to culture, habit and environment in the evolving human make-up, the basic instinctual factors in human psychology have enduring significance. The prime instinctive factors include instincts of workmanship, which encourages proclivities toward useful, effective work; a parental bent that stimulates concerns for the future well-being of children, community and species; and an 'idle curiosity', that searches for conceptual, theoretical understanding of the world and its phenomena. The latter brings with it a unique sort of gratification that comes from acquiring knowledge as a value in itself. Within a Veblenian psychological framework, the matrix of these generic, psychic factors helps us to understand and evaluate human behaviour. That is, Veblen's psychology is both descriptive and normative. Insofar as the instincts support human endurance and change within the life process – the empirical aspect – they hold an objective or generic species value for his theory. Veblen valued not only the life of the individual human being; above all, he ascribes value to the flourishing of human life in its most collective, generically human, species aspect.[27]

The fundamental or primary instincts enable the species to live, for it is only through species activity that individuals can have any biological chance. This is why, as the psychic trait that stimulates useful work, the 'instinct of workmanship' has such definite and firm moral implications. The instinct of workmanship encourages more than biologically necessary work. It also guides a generic, impersonal standpoint for considerations of economic judgment. More, in general, the instinct of workmanship not only helps humans to develop more efficient production techniques and skills, these developments are crucial to satisfaction of essential human needs. In this sense, the instinct of workmanship is not only an expression of an industrious self; as a matter of implicit 'economic conscience', it motivates us to evaluate and compare the products of labour in terms of serviceability to social needs. The instinctive intelligence governing labour is oriented not to coercive utilisation of the other, but to an alliance of mutual aid and generalised benefit. Inspired by the instinct of workmanship, economic conscience makes 'the test' for all matters touching use and expenditure of resources the measure of 'whether it serves directly to enhance human life on the whole – whether it furthers the life process taken impersonally', apart from any specific personal or group advantage to any particular member of a politically divided species.[28]

This orientation of economic conscience is definitively industrial, mundane, matter of fact, material and profoundly social, without being, in the slightest realist sense, political, a phenomenon of power. At a fundamental level, Veblen suggests, humans can live without politics and exploitative power; without economic conscience, the species would perish.

These inclinations, for Veblen, were not metaphysical speculations. They were hypotheses anchored to an empirical conception of evolution and human behaviour. Put squarely, for Veblen, most of the human species, for most of the time it has occupied the planet, has busied itself with the immediate material experience of working to support its chances of survival. Most humans, in whatever civilisation, spend the preponderance of their time and energy 'at work to turn things to human use'.[29] They live, act, produce, think and feel in small worlds of work, clan and village; even the experience of community for most people tends to be felt through more or less intimate circles and small milieu. The cumulative consequence of intimate association with work and community extends beyond the pleasures of family and parental bent, however. Without necessarily intending it in any conscious way, ordinary working people, by their everyday activity, serve to enhance the life process generally. The drama of power politics, the intensity of political conflict, the will to exploit, are aspects of experience, that if not quite alien to daily life are for most human beings secondary, marginal and exceptional. Murray Edelman's observation that '[p]olitics is for most of us a passing parade of abstract symbols' reflects the Veblenian point that ordinary life, enmeshed in industrial concerns, unfolds close to home, in an 'immediate world in which people make and do things that have directly observable consequences', not at a distance, the way power politics does. Where, as Edelman notes, the absentee drama and spectacle of political, military and athletic exploit 'exhausts men's energies in passionate attachments to abstract and remote symbols', life for most members of the species draws on the instincts of workmanship and parental bent to get by in the village, neighbourhood or city, with ample gratifications stemming from 'planned manipulation of the environment'.[30]

In light of the disproportionately small amount of time and effort devoted to predation by a disproportionately small percentage of the human species, an evolutionary framework, for Veblen, must reject a priori judgments about the political nature of man. 'Coercive utilization' of the other is an impressive feature of the human story, to be sure. And habits of exploit have had a vast influence on the development of human productive energies and partisan human loyalties. But it is precisely the development, the *evolution* of institutions and habits, which must be explained. Power may dominate industry, but as the vast majority of the species spends its time at work of one kind or another, rather than in struggles over power, claims for the naturalness of power lose their force. However important aggression is to the human experience – and Veblen thought it is very important indeed – aggression is not to be identified with something pervasively and generically human, *until humans begin slowly to re-make themselves as creatures of the habits and institutions of power.*

Duly acknowledging acute differences between the presuppositions of realists and Veblen, we still cannot help but be struck by certain commonalities. Veblen's study of human institutions, especially in the post-savage epochs of barbarism and quasi-peaceable industry, portrays a comparable human interest in power, its workings, celebration and its human cost. There is in Veblen's writing, as with the realists', a pervasive sensitivity to the unavoidable institutional and human facts of power, and to the psychic, political and economic toll exacted by chronic dissatisfaction in its use. There is an air of the tragic in both views. Those who possess whatever passes for a given society's instruments and rewards of power seem chronically anxious, uncertain, unsure, disquieted, ever intent on certifying their strength and prowess with further extensions of its use. Frustration drives power even as power yields more frustration. Insecurity abounds. Even for the most celebrated among the powerful, sufficiency of power and honour seems elusive. As a human motive, power is inhabited, haunted really, by a ceaseless, restless pressure to guarantee its claims, to vouchsafe its status, to affirm its possession and to justify its necessity. This very insecurity of power is no small part of what Morgenthau called 'the all-permeating fact' of power, an energising force of supreme importance in the dynamic of politics.

Animism and Power

In the opening pages of *The Theory of the Leisure Class*, Veblen offers a view of power that parallels realist thought. He declares his purpose for the study to establish the 'derivation of the institution' of a leisure class, a class whose singular trait is the capacity not only to avoid industrial work, but to be honoured for doing so. However, much the leisure class may have changed forms in the millennia since its first appearance; Veblen's evolutionary method presumes that traces of its likely origin are discoverable in modern societies. 'All that has gone before was not lost', Veblen liked to say; 'many things were carried over'.[31] Thus, 'before we can even begin to talk about overcoming' relations of power and alienation, 'we need to discover the beginnings of such phenomena in early archaic society', and '[i]t was this task', as John Diggins notes, that 'constituted the anthropological imperative' of Veblen's theory.[32]

Gently pruning away accumulated layers of cultural evidence, searching carefully back in time, Veblen discerned an epoch of the 'lower barbarism', where 'we no longer find the leisure class in fully developed form'.[33] At this cultural moment, when distinctions between leisure and other classes are murky and opaque at best, when social relations that we take for granted seemed at first vague and shifty, it becomes possible, aided by the available anthropological evidence, to hypothesise – and that is all that Veblen does – the factors that influenced the original development of social classes.

The root of this tendency, he supposes, lays in efforts to explain 'the dark mystery of life', to comprehend a mysterious and enchanted world. In this respect, exploit owes not a little of its earliest history to a certain premature and confused development of humanity's reaching effort to know. Instincts of workmanship and idle curiosity, Veblen suggests, energised human beings to better comprehend and use their world. It was, he thinks, quite likely that they drew from within themselves to perceive their environment. In short, they fashioned categories of understanding that reflected their subjective experience of themselves. They took what they experienced of themselves psychologically to explain phenomena outside themselves. Primitive humans imputed certain generalised features to phenomena, separating them into two more or less distinct categories, one apparently rather more like themselves than the other. On the one hand, some aspects of the environment seemed to be made of inert, brute, material stuff, qualities that lacked vibrancy or inner spirit, a lively sense of purpose or will. These elements of the external world did not seem alive and human-like. Absent a will of its own, such brute stuff is more or less complacent in a way that humans are not; it yields to intelligent human purpose and skill, to the instinct of workmanship.[34]

Action aimed at inert material was more or less one-sided and instrumental, the activity of human brain, mind and hand, of body, of controlled force and intellect; all these occupied in uneventful, quiet industry. The community employed itself putting such inert things to industrial and economic use. Perhaps it was a want of humanlike spirit in such things that accounted for their compliance with human purpose. In any event, human abilities to work effectively with these relatively benign materials favoured harmonious and productive relationships with the environment. Human industry, cooperation, nature and peace went together. On the other hand, the economic dimension of savage life was probably as unexciting and dull as it was productive and functional.

Other features of the environment proved less tractable or compliant. They did not submit readily to human purpose; they resisted; they opposed human action. These resistant forces were a considerably more complicated problem for action. First of all, there is the issue of how such obstruction might be explained? With the answer to this problem, we encounter propositions that become fundamental to Veblenian political thought.

'Man's life is activity, and as he acts, so he thinks and feels'.[35] If human life is activity, its keynote is the sense of purpose that drives action. It follows that humans tend to think and feel in teleological, goal-oriented terms. Activity, wherever humans found it in the outer world, must have seemed to possess an equally inspired, human-like wilfulness. So, as early humans met frustration, they tended to construe its source 'in the only terms that are ready to hand – the terms immediately given in his consciousness of his own actions'.[36] When humans met resistance to their ends, the inner experience of their own activity – 'the only terms that are ready to hand' – suggested a sense that they were dealing with phenomena more or less like themselves. Formally speaking, Veblen hypothesises that primitive people interpreted refractory phenomena in mimetic ways, as mirrors of their own wilfulness.[37] The world of resistant things, in other words, seemed to be inhabited by spiritual forces like those that humans felt inside themselves, including the very purposes and energies that drove human action. As such things act, so *they* must think and feel. Unlike the inert stuff, animate phenomena seemed to reflect a defiant inner capacity to oppose human purpose.

In a sense, Veblen observes, primitive peoples explained the mysteries of resistance to themselves by an imputation that suggested how animate phenomena are actually less alien, but potentially more dangerous to man than inert things. A defiant animate presence in the neighbourhood created occasions for tests of will, for the first stirrings of a primal power struggle. In direct contrast with Meinecke's view – that 'the striving for power is an aboriginal human impulse, which blindly snatches at everything around until it comes up against some external barriers' – Veblen holds that 'aboriginal' humans probably had no interest in conquest at all until the very presence of 'external barriers' stimulated that interest. Power does not meet its limit in barriers or in some sense of a reality principle, according to Veblen; to the contrary, barriers stimulate desires to express power, to smash through barriers and limits.

This difference in perspective has momentous consequences. It profoundly informs Veblen's anarchism. It inspires his doubt that power holders will recognise or respect prudential limits to their reach, or that such limits can be built into reliable systems of checks and balances. If power's very origin, in other words, lies in self-delusion, such delusion is embedded in the evolutionary cast of power. This is why, for Veblen, human power remains ever vulnerable to self-destructive over-reach. The motivation of power, after all, is not untamed desire; people 'blindly snatching at everything around'. It is a specific gratification that comes with breaching barriers and overcoming resistance. To expect that power holders will temper their dispositions with wisdom or prudence, or that they will defer to external checks, is, for Veblen, excessively optimistic, even utopian. Checks and limits are precisely what power abhors. In this respect, Veblen, the anarchist sympathiser, is more realist than the realists.

At the same time, we can see how ancient animistic and anthropomorphic tendencies of mind support Veblen's emerging understanding of human alienation itself. As humans mistake their relation with aspects of nature, so they begin to misapprehend their relation to society.[38] Experience of conflict led human intelligence gradually to set for itself the question of how to discipline the energy and will of obtrusive forces, turning them to human account. The agent's animating purpose became a matter of 'exploit […] the conversion to his own ends of energies previously directed to some other end by another agent'.[39] Contrary to Adorno, who claims 'what Veblen dislikes about capitalism is its waste rather than its exploitation',[40] the critique of exploit not only literally precedes the critique of waste in Veblen's analysis; exploit is the very social pre-condition of waste. Far from being secondary, the critique of exploit is fundamental to Veblen's whole theoretical assault on predation, capitalism and politics.

Exploit is the process by which one agent aims to capture, control and displace for his own purposes another's ability to direct her own energies to her own ends.[41] It is a violation of another's organic spontaneity, a triumph of one will over another's capacity for self-generated purpose, an act of predation against another's intentionality, a process of turning another's independent life force to the cause of one's own. It is a radical violation of that very purposefulness that Veblen identifies with the human trait most necessary to survival. Tragically, it is both an affirmation of the other's powers of spontaneity and independence and a denial of those very powers. Also it is a supremely political act, for it aims to realise Morgenthau's sense of mastery, although, for Veblen, humans' earliest experience of such power was inspired by mystified relationships with animate nature.[42] It is this exploitative engagement with the animate world that

Veblen identified with clever applications of strategic thought and power, with fraud and force.

As a classic instance of cumulative causation, the crucial evolutionary point is that the experience of exploit built on itself. Gradually it laid the foundation for an unmistakably different human experience of the world than was to be found in industrial activity. Here is the anthropological root of both the separation between industry and exploit and the beginnings of industry's submission to power. Industry dealt with compliant materials, objects with no notable capacity wilfully to resist human purpose. Industry lacked drama and intensity; it involved little emotional tension or strain. It was a domain without the experience of personal pressure, without the kind of excitement created in the sharp encounter of clashing wills. Industry was matter of fact, dispassionate; it lacked the acute nervous stimulation created by the presence of occult forces and wilful challenge.[13] Exploit possessed all of these aspects of acute interest and intensity. It sparked the human fascination with power.

Exploit placed experience in a theatrical, tension-ridden, political context. Because it put humans face to face with something like themselves, Veblen suggests that acts of exploit seemed to touch human beings in an especially stimulating way, to enliven them in a more directly, intimately human way. Perhaps, then, it was not really alienation, a feeling of strangeness – or difference – that favoured the evolution of power and politics. Instead it may well have been a kind of implicit, imputed recognition, a certain sympathetic comprehension of the spirit of obtrusive things that led the way to the political. Exploit may set us against the other, but it can do so only because we are able to imagine the other as like us. Because we can put ourselves in its place, sympathise with that other, we can imagine its purposefulness, anticipate its strategies and act to defeat them. The target of exploit is an adversary, an enemy, who shares in the most distinctive features of the human. The enemy is an 'other' whose identity with the predatory self is the very condition of exploitation. It is this dialectic of exploitative sympathy that, for Veblen, best explains why humans evolved from conquerors of nature to become masters of their own species.

The great Veblenian irony of exploit is that it grew out of a peculiar sense of familiarity, not out of perceptions of foreignness. Indeed, it was the very recognition and identification with the 'other' as quasi-human that turned humans into actors capable of violating others, at least others who are perceived as worthy competitors. It was the stimulating presence and obstinate recalcitrance of animate phenomena that inspired human proficiency to aim at improved techniques of 'coercive utilization'.

Better tools made exploit more efficient, but it was not technological change that defined the beginnings of barbarism. 'The substantial difference between the peaceable and the predatory phase of culture', Veblen argues, 'is a spiritual difference, not a mechanical one'.[44] Primitive forms of sympathy and projection spawned a new spirit of combative estrangement and alienation: here is the inaugural history of domination.[45] Paradoxically, then, human alienation really began in mimesis, in a striving to bridge gaps of recalcitrant difference. This peculiar dialectic explains how Veblen saw humans enter into dynamic, conflict-ridden relationships, the political domain of intrigue, strategy, deception and gamesmanship.[46]

As humans act, so do they think and feel. In activity of predation and exploit, they act, think and feel as if they are dealing with phenomena most like themselves; they think, act and feel as members of a singular but divided community of others, a kind of proto-political community. In short, Veblen suggests, as they began slowly to inhabit relations and activities of exploit, and as such habits began slowly to inhabit them, humans began their long historical acquaintance with their political, predatory selves.

As hinted above, Veblen distinguishes between what we might call the material or objective conditions for the full-blown development of predatory culture, and a change in the human spirit that led to humanity's enduring interest in the personal qualities associated with power. Institutionally, the onset of predatory culture required sufficient economic and technical means to produce a surplus of wealth, 'a margin worth fighting for'. Technology, tools and especially weapons had to have developed to a point 'as to make man a formidable animal'.[47] But material change alone did not transform the culture of peaceable industrial savagery. 'The substantial difference' in the emergence of a new human order was 'a spiritual difference', a difference in the way that humans calibrated value among themselves, in the personal qualities, talents and skills they came to admire and to emulate. Gradually, skills displayed in the defeat of oppositional phenomena were seen as more admirable, more worthy and honourable than those employed in the relatively spiritless domain of industry. Slowly, the community associated honorific acts with 'assertion of the strong hand'.[48] Now 'the predatory phase of culture is attained'. In Veblen's words,

> [u]nder this common-sense barbarian appreciation of worth or honor, the taking of life – the killing of formidable competitors, whether brute or human – is honorable in the highest degree. And this high office of slaughter, as an expression of the slayer's prepotence, casts a glamour of worth over every act of slaughter and over all the tools and accessories of the act. Arms are honorable, and the use of them, even in seeking the life of the meanest creatures of the fields, becomes a honorific employment.[49]

The combative human personality that realism presumed to be natural has now evolved to become a 'human nature' that is most fit for the fight. At this point, 'the predatory attitude' becomes 'the habitual and accredited spiritual attitude for the members of the group'. Fighting becomes 'the dominant note in the current theory of life' and 'common-sense appreciation of men and things' comes 'to be an appreciation with a view to combat'.[50] Here we can see how the most uniquely personal and spiritual of the human claims to power, Max Weber's concept of charisma, can take on a whole new light.

As Weber explains, the most telling aspect of charismatic leadership is the followers' imputation of 'supernatural, superhuman, or at least exceptional powers or qualities' to the charismatic leader. 'It is recognition on the part of those subject to authority which is decisive for the validity of charisma'. As Weber warns, charisma must not to be understood sociologically as indissolubly part of the leader's being or person. Imputation, action and results are crucial to the political relation of charismatic authority, and these exist in the eyes of its beholders. 'If proof and success elude the leader […] if he appears deserted by his god or his magical or heroic powers, above all, if his leadership fails to benefit his followers, it is likely that his charismatic authority will disappear'.[51] What Weber calls charisma appears in Veblen as an ideology of 'the strong hand' in its most perfected, most personalised and spiritualised form. In effect, the latter gives a socio-political account of how predatory culture leads to the social, political and psychological conditions that underpin possibilities for charisma. In this connection, the main point is precisely the recognition of the followers, or, in Veblen's terms, the identification and emulation of the underlying population with the virtues of power, that enables the legitimacy of charismatic appeals.

The evolution of exploit, with its various versions of predatory legitimation, including the charismatic, has increasingly absorbed human relations in institutions and networks of power, emulation, prestige and waste. Thus, it is Veblen's focus on the predatory or *political* aspects of economic life that explains his critique of business enterprise as the master predatory institution of the twentieth century. Absentee ownership, after all, is the currently legitimate means by which a predatory social minority uses power, in the form of abstract claims to ownership, to convert to their own ends the energies and purposes of an economic majority of workers and consumers. The sociology and economics of this business-led exploit dominated Veblen's early works and lent them a decidedly economic cast. But politics – the pursuit of mastery and dignity for their own sake – was very much inside the economic, defining its purposes, directing it strategies, contaminating industry and giving ulterior meaning to its pecuniary standards of triumphal success.[52]

Instrumentalism and Predation

In the age of quasi-peaceable capitalist industry, coercion assumed predominantly pecuniary and fraudulent forms – economic force through the price system – and fraud via salesmanship and the credit system. With one important qualification, therefore, Veblen tended to treat politics, especially in his earliest writings, mainly as a manifestation of economic predation, and the state as an instrument of business imperatives.[53] There are, however, illuminating exceptions to this tendency. Early examples can be found in *The Theory of Business Enterprise*, the first book in which Veblen honours the subject of politics with a distinct chapter all its own, 'Business Principles in Law and Politics'. Its placement, eighth among ten chapters, clearly suggests its subordinate relationship to Veblen's main concerns with industry and 'the machine process' (Chapter 2) and exploit and 'business enterprise' (Chapter 3). Indeed, this first extended statement on politics and the state would hardly lead one to conclude that Veblen believed in the independent impact of political forces. Veblen shows no faith here in the possibility that US government would move aggressively to regulate business in the public interest, that democratic politics should be taken seriously as a force for popular control, or that the state enjoyed any significant degree of political independence at all. 'A constitutional government is a business government', after all; its dominant political parties constitute little more than different rings of business interests.[54]

From such materials it is natural to conclude that Veblen's thinking on politics exemplifies 'the recurrent thesis that the state is an instrument of class rule', a view that can be linked to 'economic reductionism', through the assumption that the economic base determines both the balance of social and political power and the institutional forms of the state.[55] Like Marx in his most reductionist moments, Veblen seemed to see democratic politics as little more than a swindle, a complex of 'methods whereby the bourgeoisie utilized [...] democratic forms for the purpose of stabilizing its socioeconomic rule'.[56]

The resulting indifference of orthodox political scientists to Veblen is, in this sense, understandable. Since Veblen offers little more than crude, unsophisticated images of state-business relationships, some Veblen critics decry him as venting the spleen of a petty shopkeeper. On the other hand, such important radical theorists as Paul Sweezy understood that Veblen's state theory was rather subtler than that, especially in the way that it assigned 'a decisive role in the development of capitalism to the reciprocating interaction of business principles and national politics'.[57] Close inspection of Veblen's work supports Sweezy's point: Veblen's thinking about the state was less than consistently instrumental; indeed, it was not strictly an instrumental view at all; nor could it be, given the ambiguity and variability of the cumulative forces at work in institutional evolution.

The key point is that it is insufficient to deduce a superficial political theory from Veblen's observations about the workings of government-business relations as they unfolded under one set of institutional conditions. Veblen made a comparable point about the critics of Marx, many of whom extract aspects of the work from its theoretical framework, subjecting them to criticism outside the logic of the very system that gives them meaning. Critics should attend to relationships between main concepts and the theory to which they are anchored. To criticise a given concept apart from its relationship to a larger theoretical framework is not only intellectually unfair; it bespeaks ignorance of the theory itself. 'Except as a whole and except in the light of its postulates and aims', such a theory as Marx's or Veblen's 'is not only not tenable, but it is not even intelligible. A discussion of a given isolated feature of the system', such as Veblen's treatment of political institutions apart from his evolutionary framework, 'is as futile as a discussion of solids in terms of two dimensions'.[58]

Seen in this light, it is true that Veblen's more nuanced view of economic and political relations tended in the early writings to be reserved to methodological critiques of others, or to be immersed in frequently murky statements of his own method, leaving the serious political implications of his ideas unstated. Provoked by the coming of World War I, as well by a sense of foreboding about its aftermath, Veblen spent the last two decades of his life carefully, explicitly, even bitterly, extending his framework of cultural and institutional analysis to problems of war and peace, the nation-state and democratic politics.[59] But even this point should not be exaggerated.

Veblen's interest in the cultural, economic and political implications of war appears very early in his work, indeed it flows directly out of his first focus on exploit in *The Theory of the Leisure Class*. The principle governing much of what he says later about the peculiar dynamic of war and politics is clearly discussed as early as *The Theory of Business Enterprise*, which appeared a decade before the outbreak of global hostilities. In other words, even as he devoted closer attention to the state, Veblen neither abandoned nor significantly changed his existing approach to studies of predatory culture. To the contrary, his increasingly specific preoccupations with the state, war, politics and democracy closely reflected pre-suppositions, methods and frameworks, the basic structure of which underpinned the early theoretical works and which he continued to employ throughout the later more concrete studies. There is no methodological or theoretical leap as Veblen moves across the disciplinary boundaries of sociology and economics to the subject matter of political science.

The fact that Veblen made politics more central to his work after 1912 signals a new thematic emphasis. But this political turn represented only a more overt application of his familiar methods and theories to political matters. Politics remains for Veblen a subject best treated within a wide cultural frame and within the terms of a distinct theoretical framework that he holds to throughout his career. Even in his most polemical writings, the working principles of what is always an inter-disciplinary analysis are constantly evident. It is not as if late in life Veblen abandoned some presumed disciplinary allegiance to sociology or economics – he had none. As far as he was concerned, the prevailing disciplinary categories were arbitrary designations anyway, representing little more than administrative divisions of intellect for the purposes of university management and scholarly advancement, matters for which he had little patience and even less interest. Similarly, the later polemical writings in *The Dial* and other journals only reproduced in more colourful and unmistakable language, language called into being by the post-war political crisis, a series of conclusions that derived directly from arguments advanced more soberly in other places.

Many examples can be cited to substantiate the view taken here; the present study as a whole is an extended argument for it. But one especially revealing illustration of the point is worth examining here in a little detail. It is Veblen's discussion of the international arms race that preceded World War I. A review of this argument has the benefit of providing a clear empirical example from which we can develop insight into Veblen's methods and presuppositions. An extra benefit of the case is that it also shows how Veblen applied his theory of cumulative causation to a select instance of institutional change, and how, depending on the dynamic of cumulative causation, he could assign a differential or variable weight to the political factor in social change.[60]

The War Case

I begin with a straightforward exegesis of the example and then move in the next section to some reflections on what it reveals about Veblen's understanding of the social scientific implications of cultural evolution, especially for conceptions of human action, critiques of rationality and the state.

The subject of military spending is the last issue taken up in 'Business Principles in Law and Politics', appearing after a survey of various incarnations of commercial factors in public policy and law. As he launches the discussion, Veblen offers a curious suggestion: spending on weapons has a dual character. It typifies the general 'manner' of business influence in politics, but it is also 'an extreme expression of business politics'.[61] What Veblen means by 'extreme' is not made clear until the end of the discussion, although we can say already that it concerns the potentially negative impact of war spending on business dominance of the state. In other words, typical or otherwise unexceptional features of the political influence of business can threaten to generate consequences at the extreme margin of its position in society, potentially shifting the asymmetrical relationship of economic and political power in the state's favour. Neither business leaders nor state officials are especially aware of this potential result. Such blindness to the consequences of cumulative causation is at the heart of Veblen's scepticism of business rationality.[62]

On the face of things, military spending and business interests have a clear instrumental rationality. Rising levels of arms spending by the state are, in part, a deliberate result of business activity. The nature of business enterprise stimulates capitalists to seize on every possible competitive advantage. Insofar as modern business is international, encompassing a world market, large corporations will seek all kinds of 'legislative, diplomatic, and military' assistance from their home governments.[63] Increased state military power helps to open wider markets for corporations, between arms makers themselves and the various nation-states, and then in the broader world market for goods. Such power is especially useful in expanding capitalism to the furthest reaches of the global hinterland, advancing 'the pecuniary culture' in lands occupied by non-capitalist peoples, where profit margins, based on a 'traffic [...] adequately backed by force', can be especially 'handsome'. Business influence on the state thus leads to a coercive capitalist imperialism, as non-capitalist, 'pecuniarily unregenerate' populations, refusing to enter the market system freely and of their own will, are compelled to do so at gunpoint. Exploit follows. More, rival business and dynastic states are themselves ready to pounce on such opportunities with their own armies. Military power is thus made necessary both by the resistance of the colonised and by the competition of rival empires.[64]

As the scope of economic conflict becomes global, the nature of that widening commercial conflict cannot escape the impact of the historically political character of international relations. As war is the *ultima ratio* of global relations between states, business finds itself faced with a political terrain that is useful to, but not by any means identical with, the purely economic rationality of capital. On the one hand, within the capitalist context, militarism follows from the nature of expanding world trade. Its conscious, rational purpose is to establish 'the peace and security necessary to an orderly development of business'.[65] This commercialised peace cannot be pursued, however, without managing deep-seated conflicts unloosed by colonialism. These conflicts are overtly political in character, as they are organised within a framework of competitive, belligerent relationships among existing or erstwhile nation-states, each attempting to seize opportunities to put its rivals at a disadvantage. It is this shift from the commercial to the political domain that is most important to Veblen, because the shift of the institutional context introduces precisely those forces that produce the extreme case, i.e. its significance for 'the present and immediate future of business enterprise'.[66]

To back his claim, Veblen looked to the specific conditions of arms races in Europe over the previous half-century, an era that takes in a series of contained wars, numerous imperial ventures and, most important, the military build-up in the first years of the twentieth century. The key facet of this 'warlike emulation' is that competitive military expenditure tended to assume 'a cumulative character'.[67] In other words, over time, populations will come to accept levels of military spending as normal and acceptable 'which would at the outset' of the competition 'have seemed absurdly impossible'.[68]

The driving force of such expansion is the impact of the competitive predatory relationship itself. In the political competition for military power, as in the emulative expenditure of private consumers, the 'absolute magnitude' of spending is secondary, while 'it is comparative size that counts'.[69]

The more nations spend to enhance their military power the greater '*the political need*' to spend still more.[70] Accordingly, ever-larger shares of national output go to military ends. Furthermore, as magnitudes of warlike expenditure increase, so does sensitivity to the threatening character of global political relations: national resentments grow proportionately sharp. In other words, once military competition assumes the character of an emulative race for political standing, the social nature and dynamic of the situation changes. As economic interest gives way to national pride as the chief factor in military spending, the disciplinary or limiting effects of economic rationality lose much of their force. Military budgets inflate beyond the limits of economic reason. The motivating question is no longer how much the nation must spend on arms to increase the global opportunity of business, but rather how much the nation's resources and economy will tolerate in the interest of enhanced military and political standing. The economic domain becomes a means used by statesmen to further their increasingly autonomous political aspirations for prestige and power. As this political relation is fundamentally intangible, much more governed by perceived reputation and slights than fixed magnitudes of objective power, the participating states are prone to continue their military efforts 'with no stopping point in sight', or at least none other than war itself, or their 'emulative' and economic 'exhaustion'.[71]

But then Veblen raises a crucial question, the answer for which calls into doubt any claim that he was an economic or technological determinist: why wouldn't the various national capitalist classes, who have substantial influence within their states, and whose own economic fortunes are endangered by the fiscal irrationality of cumulative war expenditures, call 'a halt when the critical point is reached'.[72] In essence, why doesn't a presumably dominant economic power curb the claims of political-military power?

There are, in fact, from a Veblenian perspective, several reasons to believe that a businesslike curtailment of arms spending might well fail. From the corporate side, a key limitation on collective business rationality is the intensely individualistic, competitive nature of capitalism. As long as super-profits are available through the military contracting system, large individual corporations will continue to seize available opportunities. For the corporate mind, after all, 'it is always profits [...] not livelihood' that matters.[73] But crucial features of capitalism well beyond the immediate interests of stakeholders also shape the outcome. Already by 1905, the system of business enterprise was of 'so pronounced an international or cosmopolitan character', that the various international corporations and their investments were heavily and pervasively involved in different states and global markets. As commercial entanglements abounded, business rationality itself could be subverted by the obfuscating consequences of its own global extension. Individual capitalists and their firms were no longer necessarily aware of the complexities or implications of all their connections. Firms might well lend economic aid and comfort to potentially hostile powers, increasing their competitor's capacity to spend, 'without fully appreciating the fact', thus enhancing the overall chances for war and/or an economic system breakdown.[74]

More than economic factors are at work too. The political situation also changes in ways that curtail collective business rationality while enhancing the power interests of the state. Rising military expenditures, national animosities and emulative competition encourage partially suppressed dynastic habits of mind. Statist and military bureaucratic interests take on a momentum all their own. In addition, 'A warlike animus' awakens a host of anti-democratic changes, including arbitrary rule by the executives in charge and unquestioning loyalty and obedience on the part of citizens. The latter begin to act compliantly, more like subjects of a dynastic state than sceptical and insubordinate agents of their own democratic destiny. Moreover, as expansion of military institutions and the allied civilian administration of warfare gain more prominence, the two fuse increasingly together to spur the internal power drives of state-based interests in their own 'employment and display'. Overall, the threat of war and the growth of military and statist institutions combine to induce anti-democratic cultural effects on society as a whole, effects that have equally subversive effects on business rationality.

In the end, whether originally inspired by economic interests, as in capitalist states, or the imperial ambitions of dynastic ones, once competitive war spending takes root, it is political aspirations and motives that tend to overtake the aspiring powers, including capitalist ones. The more such processes unfold, the more it comes to pass that the state 'makes use of business interests as a means rather than an end'.[75] Under such conditions, therefore, an unfolding military policy tends, without the aid of any conscious change in capitalist or state priorities, to shift the ground of state policy 'from business advantage' to *raison d'etat*. And once this development assumes its self-propelling, cumulatively reinforcing momentum, economic rationality risks falling by the wayside. Consequently,

[b]arring accidents and untoward cultural agencies from *outside* of politics, business, or religion, there is nothing in the logic of the modern situation that should stop the cumulative war expenditures short of industrial collapse and consequent national bankruptcy, such as terminated the carnival of war and politics that ran its course on the Continent in the sixteenth and seventeenth centuries.[76]

The advent of the First World War surely exemplifies Veblen's thesis, particularly for the cases of Germany and Russia.

Theoretical Implications: Institutions

This discussion of capitalism and militarism typifies how Veblen applied his theoretical framework to explain a dynamic complex of institutional relationships, one in which a self-propelling logic of cumulative causation seems to outwit even the shrewdest, most calculating interests. Here, the pattern of cumulative causation, partly rooted in constricted, but enduring patterns of statism, can threaten to sabotage the interests and plans of highly motivated economic agents, actors keenly aware of their predatory interests, who nevertheless find themselves gradually facing subordination to an institution hitherto seen as instrument and ally. Instrumental rationality suffers a cruel fate at the hands of a cumulative process of institutional interaction that is increasingly dominated by power motives. The gradually developing logic of these relationships and forces increasingly situates the state at the centre of vital cultural and political changes, changes that tend to dissolve the claims of the rationality of capital on behalf of an alternate political rationality. Caliban becomes master; predator become prey.

Such an analysis presupposes, first of all, the idea that relationships between economic and political power are potentially fluid, moving and changeable; they are not fixed by a definite or logically construed functional relationship between the state and economy. The many instrumental services that states may provide to business, as important as they are, remain contingent on a set of conditions the permanence of which cannot be taken for granted, nor is their logic written into the scheme of things. Nor are these controlling conditions limited to factors of popular compliance with capital. Pressures to alter connections between state and capital can arise in the dynamic relationship between these predatory institutions, as economic forces themselves influence and enhance hierarchical power claims in the state.[77]

Consider how this standpoint differs from familiar pluralistic and radical arguments. As we saw earlier, a main problem with conventional, non-evolutionary political theories, in their various liberal or Marxist forms, is a tendency to assume *a priori* that a pre-given logic or structure of institutional relations is governed by an imputed purpose, or *telos*, of the system, one that defines and limits the functions, character and direction of institutions. Marxists identify this logic with the imperatives of capital accumulation and legitimation; pluralists and neo-pluralists stress how the separation and disconnection of institutions, as much within the state as between state and society, preserves a market-like steering of the system. Marxist critiques have difficulty conceiving of states that produce outcomes inconsistent with capitalist interests, while pluralists have equal difficulty anticipating cohesion within a state whose executive is presumably incapable of autonomous predatory action. Such preconceptions go far to explain Veblen's impatience with orthodox political science, as well as his debate with Marxism.

Each of these views suffers from a common teleological flaw; the shared presumption is that social forms obey an immanent, normal logic, favouring a specific end or *telos*. The idea of this outcome infuses the theory, affecting the total comprehension of a system's features, limits and direction. Absent this underlying conception of logic and purpose, the theory would make little sense. Such teleological conceptions may be more or less overtly apologetic as with pluralism, or critical as in Marxism. But in either case, the resulting theories are normative in ways that can obstruct understanding of important problems.[78] Such obstruction results from the fact that the 'notion of a legitimate trend in the course of events is an extra-evolutionary preconception and lies outside the scope of an inquiry into the causal sequence in any process'.[79] This 'legitimate trend' derives from the fact that both Marxism and pluralism share a social-centric view of the state as an expression, or tool, of social forces, whether class or group based.[80]

Veblen hardly wants to oppose the analytical potential in studies of connections between social and political structures. But in his view these connections are not to be taken as given or static; they are best understood as products of institutional action and reaction, ever subject to ceaseless forces of cumulative change. More, the state, as a reasonably distinctive institution in its own right, embraces political actors with their own peculiar habits, patterns of thought and action, their own interests and purposes, interests associated with the most violent form of predatory exploit: war. There is a considerable overlap between Veblen's appraisal of the power potential of the state and the 'organizational realism' of such contemporary theorists as Skocpol, Skowronek and Tilly. Organisational realists, who bear a distinctly Weberian influence, conceive of states as organisations that strive to 'extend coercive control and political authority over particular territories and the people residing within them'.[81]

Veblen agreed that coercive expansionism has deep institutional roots in the history of the state. But this analogy must not be pressed too far. Veblen was disinclined to attribute autonomy to the state except under very specific historical conditions, and for the most part his analysis of the state in contemporary business settings does bear more likeness to instrumental than organisational realist theory. The notable convergence with organisational realism comes in the way Veblen's evolutionary theory of the state keeps open the question of how state–economy interactions may develop, including possibilities that states, as in the case of Imperial Germany, take the lead in economic development. Notice, however, that in the present example, the state takes the lead not by dint of a conscious policy aimed at controlling development of capital – a pattern more akin to that analysed in *Imperial Germany* – but threatens to do so only in the throes of a process of blind cumulative change, the impetus of which began elsewhere. This pattern is, in fact, very typical of how social change happens in Veblen's perspective.

As the military case suggests, Veblen's evolutionary model understands cultural change to be cumulative, opaque, undirected by any pre-given purpose or norm, either logical or historical. History is a continuous process, but not a very transparent one. Seemingly decadent and archaic habits can intrude in what seem like contexts utterly foreign to their nature. No particular logic of development determines the outcome. Analysts must be open to the contingent and cumulative movements of forces, what Veblen liked to call opaque cause and effect, a slew of interactions that may at any moment be less than visible to the naked eye. For this reason, Veblenian assessments of institutional trends can be no more than provisional and tentative, especially where so many of the weighted factors in change unfold unconsciously, as in the gradual politicisation of imperialism.[82]

Veblen's evolutionary perspective stresses the need to remember that any starting point for analysis of social institutions can only be an arbitrary analytical cut into dense constellations of institutional patterns. The 'base of action' in an evolutionary framework, 'the point of departure – at any step in the process is the entire organic complex of habits of thought that have been shaped by the past process'.[83] There is no social contract to define and constrain the political relations of pluralism; no specific moment of historical division between mental and physical labour that prefigures and governs all subsequent class relations, as in Marx. Similarly, there is no inherent terminus for social systems: markets do not necessarily reach equilibrium, nor does history lead inexorably to socialism or to anything else. By the same token, there is no guarantee of the state's pre-eminence as the master of the means of violence in a given territory. These are matters for investigation, not deduction. Institutions will appear in any number of curious interrelationships and connections, depending on specific patterns of evolution, the particular complex of environmental forces that have impinged upon them, including the wide array of possible human adaptations to such circumstances as people may face, equipped as they are with the institutions, habits and resources available to them.

A consequence of this framework is the strongest possible caveat against assuming that economic, political and cultural factors can be neatly isolated for study, an observation that has the greatest importance for seeing how something called 'the political', or power, figures in Veblen's theory.[84] He knew how useful it is analytically to set up categories of economic or political institutions; but such utility ceases at the point where analysts forget that no category can be more than a 'convenient caption, comprising those institutions in which the economic (or political) interest most immediately and consistently finds expression, and which most immediately and with the least limitation are of an economic (or political) bearing'.[85]

If, for example, we conceive of the political interest as 'the coercive utilization of man by man', it would make sense to associate the political with the state, because it is in the state, especially during the modern era, where struggles for power are most overtly coercive in their bearing, where the interest in coercive power finds its most obvious expression. But such an association does not any more preclude recognition of power motives and struggles in other institutions than it precludes recognition of economic or cultural motives inside the state.[86] Nor should such a 'convenient caption' pre-empt recognition of power either as a factor in pre-statist institutions, or in non-state institutions, where its workings may be less immediate and direct, and where, for various reasons, its appearance may be disguised by a surface of more explicit and socially approved motives.

Implications for Action

Veblen's treatment of human action at the individual level forms a direct counterpart to the cumulative causation that affects institutions. Institutional complexity and subtlety has its analogue in the comparable density of individual behaviour. No less than in his critique of the teleological bias of non-evolutionary theories, Veblen attacked a related error in what he called the hedonistic theory of causation. Such models were the norm of social science in Veblen's day; to a considerable degree they remain so today, as important to Weberian sociology as to Marxian and rational choice versions of political science.

Veblen understood 'hedonistic' models to specify conditions of rationality as the paradigmatic context of causation in human behaviour. 'Human conduct' is conceived 'as a rational response to the exigencies of the situation in which mankind is placed'.[87] This is a model familiar to any one who has studied neoclassical economics, but it applies to Marx as well, at least to the extent that he linked his otherwise objective materialistic account of history to a theory of class struggle that depended on a subjective, pain-induced conception of political revolt.[88] Whether the driving rationality of behaviour is seen as economic, social or political, the weakness of such analyses, for Veblen, is that they specify the causative pressure of internal and external forces on individuals, who are expected to rationally respond to such forces in the immediacy of the moment, and who are themselves left unchanged and 'intact' by the experience of action. State managers, who are subjected to the immediate political pressure of corporations for military spending, for example, might therefore be expected to remain unchanged by the cumulative logic of armament, state competition, national rivalry and increasing global risk. In this way, the human agent conceived by hedonistic accounts is 'an isolated human datum, in stable equilibrium except for the buffets of the impinging forces that displace him in one direction or another'.[89]

Against 'hedonistic' theories of agency, with their stress on isolated human choices in response to external or internal pressures, Veblen argues for an 'action' theory, one whose foundations lie in an evolutionary conception of the relation between behaviour, institutions and heredity. Here human activity is not a direct, reflexive response to preceding pressures – be they material, emotional or moral. 'Activity' is 'itself the substantial fact of the process, and the desires under whose guidance the action takes place are circumstances'.[90] In turn, these circumstances reflect the influence of existing as well as past institutions, habits of mind, cultural biases and tendencies, as well as hereditary factors, a whole cluster of social, material and biological factors, coming together in what Veblen calls 'circumstances of temperament'.[91]

Notice Veblen's emphasis: it is not temperament as such that influences action, but an accumulation of 'circumstances' that influence such temperament. This shaping includes what individuals perceive or do not perceive, count or do not count, as factors worthy of their motivation. These 'circumstances of temperament' embrace much of what we call culture, the economy, political ideas, as well as organic factors of heredity and genetic disposition; all the elements that accumulate to shape an existing frame of mind of the agent, and that are

> the outcome of the antecedents and his life up to the point at which he stands. They are the products of his hereditary traits and past experience, cumulatively wrought out under a given body of traditions, conventionalities, and material circumstances; and they afford the next step in the process.[92]

As Erkki Kilpinen points out in an important essay that compares Veblen's and Weber's theories of action, neither internal nor external determinants, neither physical forces nor internal psychological motivations, '*precede* the ensuing more concrete action'.[93] The inner or outer impulsions co-exist with, or 'emerge in the midst of an already ongoing process of action, one without any definable starting point, final end, or resting place'.[94] In arms racing, economic pressures applied to secure profits for individual firms centre in a state that has its own cumulative legacy, patterns and habits of aggressive interest and action. These traditions fuel an institutional capacity to initiate power motivations of its own, including turning the very corporate powers that target the state into its instruments. Both sets of actors, state officials and business lobbyists, are changed by consequences flowing from their interaction. Not only do institutions shape expectations, demands and responses, but also the cumulative effect of institutional processes can change the actors who drive such institutions. In this way, a predatory instrumental rationality can turn back on itself, but now as an openly political logic of power rather than as an economic logic of profit.

This insight underscores the significance of Veblen's observation that '[m]an's life is activity; and as he acts, so he thinks and feels'. Thinking and feeling are not mere responses to motivations and impulses; thinking and feeling are part of action, can be modified by action, and are inseparable from the agent as an actor who lives and moves within a wider field of shaping influences. 'This was the revolutionary conclusion', writes Kilpinen, that Veblen took from Darwinian science, and that influenced such like-minded thinkers as John Dewey, George Herbert Mead and the psychologist Jacques Loeb, a close associate of Veblen's at the University of Chicago.[95] Alternatively, as Geoffrey M. Hodgson puts it,

> Veblen used this idea of an unbroken historical chain of cause and effect to undermine the presuppositions of mainstream economics [...] Essentially, because the human agent was a subject of an evolutionary process, she could not be taken as fixed or given. Neither could the opposite error be committed: of subsuming agency under the heading of mysterious social forces.[96]

Clearly, Veblen's model precludes a systematic, consistent instrumentalism, favouring instead a consistent evolutionism. From Veblen's standpoint, we can see how one problem with instrumental theories of politics is that they presuppose a sequence of cultural borrowing that oversimplifies the density and opacity of cultural change, in a way that too sharply distinguishes capitalist from other forms of state. Liberals believe that with the model of the social contract in mind, free 'individuals' effectively establish a voluntary basis of political authority. In effect, they harness the pre-existing, arbitrary political powers of older state forms to a new system of impersonal legal responsibility. Liberals introduced constitutional arrangements, based on rule of law, to terminate the subjective arbitrariness of absolutism; not completely perhaps, but by and large and for the most part. In a parallel universe of theory, Marxists argue that the capitalist class appropriated the powers of the absolutist state even as they expropriated, albeit under a wide range of variant circumstances, the peasantry from their occupation of the soil. The bourgeoisie carefully devised new pro-property institutions and rules to sanctify and assure the accumulation of capital and legitimation of social relations. The economic and political powers of capital constricted any remaining autocratic tendencies within the state system, or they harnessed such tendencies to the needs of capital, i.e. the implicit Marxian idea of a dictatorship of the bourgeoisie. Like the liberals, Marxists are prepared to qualify their arguments. The complexity and incompleteness of history, with all its variation and distinction, ensure that any particular capitalist state will bear specific features uniquely the product of its past. But the main drift is clear: by and large, the modern state has become a capitalist state. Liberals and Marxists alike tend to argue as if the modern state inherited just those qualities of stateness essential to their expectations, leaving the rest to the dustbin of history. This is the central historical presupposition of claims about political modernisation.

Veblen's studies of the state/business relationship find much truth in these theories. Political individualism and class power are certainly features of capitalist politics about which he has much to say. But as against both Marxist and liberal concepts of the state, each of which tends to emphasise a highly selective process of borrowing and exclusion as a precondition of political modernisation, Veblen's genetic, evolutionary method approaches the state in ways that are considerably more sceptical of the modernisation thesis. For 'all that had gone before was not lost [...] Many things were carried over'.[97]

Notes and References

1   Thorstein Veblen, 'Why is Economics Not an Evolutionary Science?', in *Veblen on Marx, Race, Science and Economics* (New York: Capricorn Books, 1969), 56–81.

2   Thorstein Veblen, *The Theory of the Leisure Class*, ed. by Robert Lekachman (New York: Penguin Books, 1979), 10.

3   Veblen, *Absentee Ownership, Business Enterprise in Recent Times: The Case of America*, ed. by Marion Levy Jr (New Brunswick: Transaction, 1997). Veblen suggests that it may well have been in the 'moral penumbra' of the slave trade that the founders of the American enterprise 'learned how not to let its right hand know what its left hand is doing; and there is always something to be done that is best done with the left hand' (171).

4   John Diggins, *Thorstein Veblen, Theorist of the Leisure Class* (Princeton: Princeton University Press, 2000), published originally as *The Bard of Savagery* (New York: The Seabury Press, 1978).

5   On the other hand, several of Veblen's early essays and reviews do in fact offer suggestive and important observations about politics, especially radical and socialist movements. See for example, Thorstein Veblen, 'Some Neglected Points in the Theory of Socialism', in id. *Veblen on…*, 387–408; 'The Army of the Commonweal', in Thorstein Veblen, *Essays in our Changing Order*, ed. by L. Ardzrooni (New York: Augustus Kelley, 1964), 97–103; Thorstein Veblen, 'The Socialist Economics of Karl Marx and His Followers, Parts I, II', in *Veblen on…*, 409–56. See also Louis Pastouris, *Thorstein Veblen and the American Way of Life* (Montreal: Black Rose Books, 2004), 41–8.

6   Though it is a phenomenon central to his thought, Veblen does not regularly use the now familiar term 'power', i.e. as a noun, to name the character or implications of exploit and predation. Still, a careful review of his work suggests that Veblen identifies at least four reasonably distinct forms of political power as a cohesive and controlling factor in social order. Most frequently, Veblen's references to the phenomenon of power emphasise the *personal* and *irresponsible* qualities popularly imputed to predominant individuals, groups or classes. For example, in one of his two formulations of the emergence of class society, Veblen invokes power as an adjective to indicate the strength of a social class and its capacity for irresponsible use of coercive means, a capacity forged on the *personal* authority of its chieftains. In this account, to be found in his *The Instinct of Workmanship*, ed. by Murray G. Murphey (New Brunswick: Transaction Publishers, 1990), 168, the early priestly stratum becomes 'a *powerful* despotism and nobility resting on a servile people […] in which the final arbiter is always *irresponsible* force' and 'the all-pervading social relation is *personal subservience* and *personal authority*'; emphasis added. Or to cite an other illustration, from his *Imperial Germany and the Industrial Revolution*, ed. by Joseph Dorfman (New York: Viking, 1954), 67, Veblen describes the habit of mind essential to the structure of feudal power in strikingly similar terms: 'the habit of mind which makes it a practicable form of political organization', he notes, 'is the […] habit of personal subservience to a personal master. In such a polity subordination, *personal allegiance*, is the prime virtue, the chief condition precedent to its carrying on; while insubordination is the fatal vice, incompatible with such a coercive system'. In one of his earliest essays, Veblen contrasts as a principle of social organisation such 'personal' and 'irresponsible' authority with two other types, voluntary, market-based self-coordination via 'contract' and the 'system of modern constitutional government' as 'a system of subjection to the *will of the social organism*, as expressed in *an impersonal law* […] Here, subjection is not to the person of the public functionary, but to the powers vested in him' ('Some Neglected Points', 404; emphasis added). Invoking a comparably democratic notion, Veblen will later observe, 'it is the frame of mind of the common man that makes the foundation of society in the modern world' ('The Socialist Economics of Karl Marx', 16). However, Veblen's scepticism about the authenticity or reality of the people's power in 'ostensible democracy' hinges heavily on his appraisal of people's enduring sentimental attachment 'to admire and defer to *persons* of achievement and distinction', a 'predilection for deference' so strong that it will 'find merit even in a personage who, for all that is known of him, has no personal attributes, good, bad,

or indifferent', such as 'the Mikado in the times of the Shogunate', or in 'only less perfect instances of the same [...] the kings and prelates of Christendom', or the absentee owners of contemporary America. See Thorstein Veblen, *Absentee Ownership, Business Enterprise in Recent Times: The Case of America*, ed. by Marion Levy, Jr (New Brunswick: Transaction, 1997), 115–17. In contrast with each of these first three types, Veblen also identifies a fourth mixed type, one that unites 'the individualistic or democratic conception', and which he calls 'the anarchistic conception' of 'live and let live, subject only to 'the margin of tolerance rooted in the moral common sense of the neighbors' (*Imperial Germany*, 328–9). Clearly, then, while Veblen does not habitually use the term power, he is in fact quite attentive to the phenomenon and especially to differences and similarities in its forms and contents as a factor of cohesion in social structure. See also on this point, 12n below. My gratitude to Francesca Lidia Viano for calling attention to the infrequency of Veblen's usage of the term 'power'.

7   Max Weber, 'Politics as a Vocation', in Max Weber, *From Max Weber, Essays in Sociology*, trans., ed. by H. H. Gerth and C. Wright Mills (New York: Oxford University Press, 1948), 159.

8   Hans J. Morgenthau, *Scientific Man vs. Power Politics* (Chicago: University of Chicago Press, 1967), 25.

9   E. E. Schattschneider, *The Semisovereign People, A Realist's View of Democracy in America* (New York: Holt, Rinehart and Winston, 1960), 2.

10 For Nietzsche's influence on Weber and Morgenthau, see John Diggins, *Max Weber, Politics and the Spirit of Tragedy* (New York: Basic Books, 1996), 129–31; Cristoph Frei, *Hans Morgenthau, An Intellectual Biography* (Baton Rouge: Louisiana State University Press, 2001), 98–108. As Weber himself stated, 'One can gauge the intellectual honesty of today's scholar [...] by examining his attitude toward Nietzsche and Marx. Anyone who fails to acknowledge that he could not have accomplished a significant part of his own work without the contribution of these two men is deceiving himself and others. We now dwell in a world that has been intellectually shaped to a large extent by Marx and Nietzsche' (cited in Frei, *Hans Morgenthau*, 108). Veblen certainly acknowledged Marx's contribution to contemporary thought, but nowhere in his work, to the best of my knowledge, does he show any familiarity with Nietzsche. There are Nietzschean aspects to Veblen's cold assessments of the realities of power, as well as in the latter's insistence on relativity of values. But Nietzsche would doubtlessly find Veblen's affection for the principle of live and let live evidence of just that weakness of Christian spirit against which he protested. In any case, a careful study comparing Nietzsche and Veblen remains to be written.

11 Veblen, *Leisure Class*, 19.

12 Stjepan Mestrovic, *Thorstein Veblen on Culture and Society* (London: Sage, 2003).

13 Veblen, *Leisure Class*, 19.

14 Veblen, *Leisure Class*, 97–101; *Instinct*, 25–7.

15 Indeed, it is just because the values most essential to survival lose primacy to habits of power, difference and invidious discrimination, Veblen reads history as recording 'more frequent and more spectacular instances of the triumph of imbecile institutions over life and culture than of peoples who have by force of instinctive insight saved themselves alive out of a desperately precarious institutional situation'; Veblen, *Instinct*, 25.

16 Thorstein Veblen, *The Vested Interests and the Common Man* (New York: Augustus Kelley, 1964), 83, 82.

17 Of course, it might just as well be said that denial of dignity – humiliation – is within a Veblenian framework an equally compelling motive for struggle and power. Many recent discussions of Muslim support for Islamist resistance to the West, for example, stress how much Hezbollah's popularity in the Arab world is traceable to its revival of a sense of dignity for a people so habituated to defeat. See e.g. 'And Now Islamism Trumps Arabism', *The New York Times*, 20 August 2006, sec. 4: 1.

18 Veblen, *Leisure Class*, 15.

19 Ibid., Ch. 2. As one historian of warfare notes, until recently, women have generally been 'excluded from [...] organized combat (sieges and wars with genocidal overtones being special exceptions). In this regard it would appear that, rather than serving as the equivalent of the hunt (an activity in which female predators frequently participate), warfare preserved the intraspecific role of the female as prize and object of combat. If nothing else, this helps to account for the aura of sexuality which has hung about war and weapons throughout history, serving as both a thematic equipoise to its ruthlessness and an indication of the complexity of the subject and the motives behind it'; in Robert O'Connell, *Of Arms And Men, A History of War, Aggression, and Weapon* (New York: Oxford, 1989), 37. For valuable discussions of Veblen's ideas about women and their place in cultural development, see Clare V. Eby, 'Veblen's Anti-Anti-Feminism', *Canadian Review of American Studies*, Special Issue 2 (1992): 215–38; Jeffrey Waddoups and Rick Tilman, 'Thorstein Veblen and the Feminism of Institutional Economists', *International Review of Sociology* 3 (1992): 182–204.

20 Morgenthau, *Scientific Man vs. Power Politics*, 3–4.

21 As Veblen put it, 'Until recently there has been something of a consensus among those who have written on early culture, to the effect that man, as he first emerged upon the properly human plane, was of a contentious disposition, inclined to isolate his own interest and purposes from those of his fellows, and with a penchant for feuds and brawls'; see Thorstein Veblen, 'The Instinct of Workmanship and the Irksomeness of Labor', in id. *Essays in our Changing Order*, 82.

22 Diggins argues that Veblen failed to provide such an explanation; in fact, his account of the evolution of power constitutes precisely that answer; see Diggins, *Bard of Savagery*, 76–7.

23 Friedrich Meinecke, *Machiavellianism. The Doctrine of Raison d'Etat and its Place in Modern History*, tr. Douglas Scott, intr. Werner Stark (New Brunswick: Transaction, 1957), 4, 7, 11.

24 Rick Tilman, *Thorstein Veblen and the Enrichment of Evolutionary Naturalism* (Columbia: University of Missouri Press, 2007).

25 Meinecke, *Machiavellianism*, 11.

26 The question of Veblen's understanding of Darwin, as well as his changing understanding of contemporary developments in biology and psychology, falls outside the scope of this paper. For a variety of detailed discussions of the Darwinian influence on Veblen see Rick Tilman, *The Intellectual Legacy of Thorstein Veblen: Unresolved Issues* (Westport: Greenwood Press, 1996), Ch. 2–3; Geoffrey M. Hodgson, 'On the Evolution of Thorstein Veblen's Evolutionary Economics', *Cambridge Journal of Economics* 22.4 (1998): 415–31; Geoffrey M. Hodgson, 'Darwin, Veblen and the Problem of Causality in Economics', *History and Philosophy of the Life Sciences* 23.3–4 (2001): 385–423; Richard Wiltgen, 'The Darwinian Evolutionary Perspectives of Engels and Veblen', *International Journal of Social Economics* 17.4 (1990): 4–11; William M. Dugger and Howard J. Sherman, *Reclaiming Evolution* (London: Routledge, 2000); Murray G. Murphey, 'Introduction to the Transaction Edition' in Thorstein Veblen, *The Instinct of Workmanship and the State of the Industrial Arts* (New Brunswick: Transaction Publishers, 1990), vii–xlv; Cynthia Eagle Russett, *Darwin in America, The Intellectual Response, 1865–1912* (San Francisco: W. H. Freeman, 1976), Ch. 6; Abram L. Harris, 'Economic Evolution: Dialectical and Darwinian', *Journal of Political Economy* 42.1 (1934): 34–79; Idus Murphree, 'Darwinism in Thorstein Veblen's Economics', *Social Research* 26 (1959): 311–24. Also see Peter J. Bowler, *Evolution: the History of an Idea*, 3rd edn (Berkeley: University of California Press, 2003); Paul Crook, *Darwinism, War and History* (Cambridge: Cambridge University Press, 1994).

27 Veblen carefully distinguishes between the immanent value of human life as an organic feature of the species in the throes of its constant evolution, and a teleological belief in the ultimate vindication of the life process, the belief 'that the goal of the life history of the race in a large way controls the course of that life history'. Species survival is by no means assured, after all. In his critique of Marx, for example, Veblen claims that the problem with the theory of the geometric growth of the labour reserve army is that Marx failed to understand that workers might not be willing to increase their progeny beyond the means of their own survival.

This error Veblen attributes to Marx's teleological commitment to 'the growing volume of human life' as a necessary, indeed as 'the main fact' of humanity's economic life history. See Veblen, 'Socialist Economics of Karl Marx and His Followers', I, II, 429–30.

28 Veblen, *Leisure Class*, 98–9.

29 Veblen, 'Instinct of Workmanship', 83–4.

30 Murray J. Edelman, *The Symbolic Uses of Politics* (Urbana: University of Illinois Press, 1964), 5, 9.

31 Veblen, *Absentee Ownership*, 20.

32 Diggins, *Bard of Savagery*, xiv. Diggins's suggestion of Veblen's anthropological interest in the origins of power may also help, I think, to explain why Veblen tended to steer away from use of the term power. As suggested in 6n, Veblen's critique of power centred on its enduringly pre-modern 'personal', or magical qualities. Insofar as its modern usage tends to carry legalistic or formally political connotations, Veblen may have wanted to preserve his accent on the archaic by stressing the personal quality of predatory authority. More, it should be added that the modern social scientific interest in the systematic study of power is a rather post-Weberian – and thus also a post-Veblenian pre-occupation – deriving in no small measure not only from Weber's work itself, but from the various and contrasting influences it had on such disparate American students of power as Talcott Parsons, C. Wright Mills and Robert Dahl.

33 Veblen, *Leisure Class*, 1–3.

34 Ibid., 11–12.

35 Veblen, 'Instinct of Workmanship', 85.

36 Veblen, *Leisure Class*, 12.

37 One need only attend the gaming tables of Las Vegas or Atlantic City to see that this habit of mind is alive and well, i.e. consider the belief in 'lady luck'; see Veblen, *Leisure Class*, Ch. 11.

38 Diggins, *The Bard of Savagery*, 75. In 'Why Is Economics Not an Evolutionary Science?', Veblen describes the process as a projection of human personality onto 'inanimate nature', in which those 'processes' are construed as 'agencies whose habits of life are to be learned, and who are to be outwitted, circumvented and turned to account, much as the beasts are'; see Veblen, 'Why is Economics Not an Evolutionary Science?', 63. Veblen does not argue that animism inherently gave rise to exploit, however. In some cases, women farmers, for example, established benign relationships with 'the wordless others' among plants and animals, and thus laid the basis for matrilineal societies based on peaceable industry, suggesting why 'the ancient assumption of a primitive state of nature after the school of Hobbes cannot be accepted'; see Veblen, *Instinct of Workmanship*, 100, and passim. In this respect, Veblen's account resembles some trends in contemporary eco-feminism. See Catriona Sandilands, *The Good-Natured Feminist: Ecofeminism and the Quest for Democracy* (Minneapolis: University of Minneapolis Press, 1999).

39 Veblen, *Leisure Class*, 12–13.

40 Theodore W. Adorno, 'Veblen's Attack on Culture' in *Prisms*, ed. by Theodore J. Adorno and Samuel M. Weber (Cambridge, MA: MIT Press, 1941), 404.

41 The use of gendered pronouns is, of course, quite deliberate here. It reflects Veblen's theory that the beginnings of male exploitation of women constituted the crucial change from exploitation directed at animate phenomena in the environment to the social relations of human beings themselves. See Veblen, *Leisure Class*, Ch. 2.

42 Curiously, Veblen's critique of the animistic sources of power consciousness parallels Morgenthau's criticism of 'scientism', the view that 'problems of social life are in essence similar to the problems of physical nature' and equally subject to technical control; see Hans Morgenthau, 'The Escape from Power', in Hans Morgenthau, *The Decline of Democratic Politics* (Chicago: University of Chicago Press, 1962), 312. As primitive people misapplied their knowledge of nature in ways that underpinned evolving distinctions between industry and exploit, so modern peoples mistakenly impute scientific knowledge of nature to rationalise relations of domination. To understand this parallel is to begin to appreciate why Veblen's 'soviet of the engineers' is, perhaps, best understood as a satire rather than a realistic political project.

43 Not surprisingly, Veblen argued that human technical or industrial proficiency, the most effective applications of 'the instinct of workmanship', needs 'circumstances of moderate exigence', while 'seasons of great stress' and pressure tend to encourage 'a crudity of technique'; *The Instinct of Workmanship*, 33–4. In direct contrast with this assertion of a relationship between quiet industry and inventiveness, Joseph Schumpeter conspicuously distinguished and valorised the entrepreneurial or business function in precisely the terms Veblen used to criticise the elitist psychology of exploit. 'To act with confidence beyond the range of the familiar beacons and to overcome resistance requires aptitudes that are present in only a small fraction of the population [...] This (entrepreneurial) function does not essentially consist in either inventing anything or otherwise creating the conditions which the enterprise exploits. It consists in getting things done'; Joseph A. Schumpeter, *Capitalism, Socialism and Democracy* (New York: Harper Torchbooks Schumpeter, 1962), 132. Schumpeter's entrepreneur, in short, is Veblen's exploiter, master of others' activity and purposes, the political organiser of their industrial activity.

44 Veblen, *Leisure Class*, 20.

45 The question of how human beings come to distinguish between friend and foe, the definitive political phenomenon for such realists as the authoritarian Carl Schmitt and the liberal E. E. Schattschneider is thus a theme crucial to Veblen's political thought as well. Suffice it to say here, a Veblenian account of this issue is inseparable from conservation of predatory traits built into the evolving distinction between exploit and industry. At work are ancient habits of demonisation, tendencies to put a mimetic sense of likeness to work as the conceptual underpinning of difference understood as hostility.

46 Reading Veblen from a Marxist perspective, Paul Baran insists that Veblen's preoccupation with exploit failed sufficiently to specify how particular social and economic forms of exploitation characterised different forms of society. Setting aside the obvious rejoinder that Veblen did distinguish between feudal and capitalist modes of exploit, among others, including biblical empires of conquest, what Baran calls Veblen's 'morbid engrossment in the sameness of iniquity' suggests how Veblen's interests in power lay more with its continuities and mystification than with the specific social mechanics of economic exploitation; see Paul Baran, 'The Theory of the Leisure Class', *Monthly Review* 9 (1957): 83–91, esp. 85, and the discussion in Rick Tilman, *Thorstein Veblen and His Critics, 1891–1963* (Princeton: Princeton University Press, 1992), 214–17.

47 Veblen, *Leisure Class*, 20.

48 Ibid., 17.

49 Ibid., 8.

50 Ibid., 19.

51 Max Weber, *Economy and Society, An Outline of Interpretive Sociology*, 2 vols, ed. by Guenther Roth and Claus Wittich (Berkeley: University of California Press, 1978), 1:242. Veblen is, if anything, rather less insistent than Weber on performance or empirical success to secure legitimate authority. See 6n above.

52 This interpretation emphasises what Veblen liked to call the 'inosculation', the cultural blending and mixing of different, often conflicting habits, such as industry and exploit. See e.g. Veblen, *Instinct of Workmanship*, li. Here Veblen notes his stress on the fundamental role of the technological factor in human development, 'but not in such a sense as to preclude or overlook the degree to which [...] other conventions of any given civilization in their turn react on the state of the industrial arts'. In contrast to the view taken here, Mestrovic argues, incorrectly, I think, that Veblen understood the human agent to split industrial and barbaric habits into 'separate, logic-tight compartments'; Mestrovic, *Thorstein Veblen*, 8–9.

53 The important qualification comes at the end of Veblen's discussion of the state's pro-business character in Ch. 8 of *The Theory of Business Enterprise*, to be discussed below. Concluding his analysis of casual connections between business interests, the arms industry, imperialism and war, Veblen notes that, under some conditions, the drive toward war can indeed assume a dynamic

and force of its own, driven by military and political motives independent of economic rationality, a logic that can lead to the bankruptcy or utter exhaustion of a state and ruination of its business conditions. Indeed, on the very last page of the book, Veblen speculates that the continued rule of business enterprise is put at risk as much by the rising strength of 'aggressive politics' as by the potentially emancipatory implications of 'the machine process'. In either case, business institutions appear to be endangered because they are 'incompatible with the ascendancy' of technical and/or political forces; see Veblen, *Instinct of Workmanship*, 292–301, 400, passim.

54 Thorstein Veblen, *The Theory of Business Enterprise*, ed. by Douglas Dowd (New Brunswick: Transaction Books, 1978), 285, 293–4. Just a few years later, in his first foray at analysis of America's country towns, an eleven page 'supplementary note' that appears at the end of his study of *Imperial Germany and the Industrial Revolution*, Veblen offered an equally dour assessment of American local government, a view that would not change at all when the same material appeared in revised form in Absentee Ownership. In both books Veblen described municipal government in the strictly instrumental terms that he earlier used to describe business dominance of the national government. Each level of the state was merely 'a public or overt extension of that private or covert organization of interests that watches over the joint pecuniary benefit of [...] business'. See Veblen, *Absentee Ownership*, 142–65; Veblen, *Imperial Germany*, 333.

55 Bob Jessop, *The Capitalist State, Marxist Theories and Methods* (New York: New York University Press, 1982), 12; Ralph Miliband, *The State in Capitalist Society, An Analysis of the Western System of Power* (New York: Harper Colophon, 1969).

56 Hal Draper, *Karl Marx's Theory of Revolution: State and Bureaucracy* (New York: Monthly Review Press, 1977), 1:306.

57 Paul Sweezy, 'Veblen on American Capitalism', in *Thorstein Veblen, A Critical Appraisal*, ed. by Douglas Dowd (Ithaca, NY: Cornell University Press, 1958), 195. For a thoughtful reflection on the relationship between Veblen's ideas and Sweezy's, see Phillip Anthony O'Hara and Howard Jay Sherman, 'Veblen and Sweezy on Monopoly Capital, Crises, Conflict, and the State', *Journal of Economic Issues* 38.4 (2004): 969–87.

58 Veblen, 'Some Neglected Points', 410.

59 Michael Spindler, *Veblen and Modern America* (London: Pluto Press, 2002); Sweezy, 'Veblen on American Capitalism'. Veblen was hardly alone in this respect. The war was a major factor influencing the works and outlooks of many important sociologists across Europe and the US, and in this way had a major influence on 'the history of sociology' itself. See Hans Joas, *War and Modernity* (Cambridge: Polity Press, 2003), 57.

60 The point, it should be emphasised, is not to question claims that Veblen frequently insisted upon business dominance of the state, especially where appropriate conditions were in force, nor is it to make the case that Veblen predicted that the warfare state would necessarily dominate business enterprise. Rather, the importance of the case is that it reveals how Veblen's concept of the state contains its own institutional legacy, including a potential, in some circumstances, to assert strong claims for political predominance over business. That said, this discussion does point with striking force and clarity to the galvanising power of militarism in the prelude to World War I. No serious reader of *Theory of Business Enterprise* could have been surprised by the advent of war. More, it also anticipates C. Wright Mills' more famous 'power elite' thesis, with its stress on 'the political directorate' and 'warlords' in the higher circles of US power. And, perhaps most presciently, the theory anticipates the logic of economic collapse of the Soviet Union following its futile effort to emulate US military spending. On the other hand, the analysis does undermine interpretations of Veblen as a deterministic theorist for whom 'nothing [...] can be done in a society dominated by the spirit of business enterprise that is not congruous with that spirit', in John Gambs, *Beyond Supply and Demand* (New York: Columbia University Press, 1946), 55–6.

61 Veblen, *The Theory of the Business Enterprise*, 292; Douglas Dowd, *Thorstein Veblen*, intr. Michael Kearney (New Brunswick: Transaction, 2000), 51–3.

62 Sometimes Veblen suggests that political contamination of industrial know-how reflects a more general 'cycle of industrial growth, commercial enterprise, princely ambitions, dynastic wars, religious fanaticism and industrial collapse'. His point is not that history moves in cycles, but that industrial, commercial and political motivations tend to evolve in tandem, with potentially ruinous consequences for all concerned. A notable exception is the case of England, whose relative isolation from the continental wars of Europe between the sixteenth and eighteenth centuries helped it to avoid 'political exhaustion' in favour of the economic dynamism that propelled 'the industrial revolution'. See Veblen, *Instinct of Workmanship* (1990), 247–51; Veblen, *Absentee Ownership*, 269.

63 Veblen, *Business Enterprise*, 293, 295.

64 Ibid., 295.

65 Ibid., 296.

66 Interestingly, certain aspects of Veblen's analysis here anticipate two classic treatments of American politics. One is David Truman's argument that when business enters the field of the state it must do so on the state's political terms; David Truman, *The Governmental Process, Political Interests and Public Opinion* (New York: Knopf, 1962), 258–9. This shift, he argues, creates a 'discount rate' on the translation of economic into political power, one necessitated by popular pressures on elected officials to represent wider than business interests. In a similar vein, E. E. Schattschneider insists that changes in scope and locus of conflict inevitably affect the character and outcome of the conflict; see his *Semisovereign People*. Both theories were advanced with the intention of suggesting why, in democratic pluralistic political systems, state power cannot easily be reduced to economic power. Veblen's model suggests the truth of the observation that changes in institutional domain matter. However, for reasons to be developed below, Veblen does not believe that centring the locus of institutional conflict within the political sphere is necessarily, or is even especially likely, to favour democratic outcomes. For one thing, Veblen is sceptical about the forces of democratic counterbalance to corporate power. For another, institutional habits within the state are likely to favour quasi-monarchical, dynastic and centralising outcomes, results corrosive for democracy and capitalism alike.

67 The question of what implications might result from the political logic of military spending where one superpower, i.e., the US, enjoys a vast asymmetric military advantage against all other states, constitutes a radically different situation from one in which a handful of more or less equal states compete to build up their arms. Veblen's discussion centres on the latter case.

68 Veblen, *Business Enterprise*, 297–8.

69 Ibid., 298.

70 Ibid., 298.

71 Ibid., 299. In his positive assessment of Veblen's thoughts on international relations, radical historian William Appleton Williams well captures his understanding of the complex 'interrelationship between foreign and domestic policies, and the parallel interaction between foreign policies' that shaped contemporary world politics and the forces making for war. But curiously, Williams pays no attention to the evolutionary analysis of the state and the state system, the *political* institutions whose history figures so prominently in a Veblenian theory of war. See William Appleton Williams, 'The Nature of Peace', *Monthly Review* 9.3–4 (1957): 112–17.

72 Veblen, *Business Enterprise*, 299.

73 Ibid., 301.

74 Here, if anything, Veblen probably understates the conscious willingness of capitalists to invest in the economic opportunities of rival states, all the while aggravating the causes of war as well as economic collapse. Citing the example of Alfred Krupp, who displayed and sold his military wares to all comers, one historian notes, 'The arms trade and the technological progress which fuelled it remained, and would remain, very much an international phenomenon'; Robert O'Connell, *Of Arms And Men, A History of War, Aggression, and Weapons* (New York: Oxford,

1989), 205. See also, for example, reports on US business involvement with the Third Reich, such as Kevin Phillips, *American Dynasty; Aristocracy, Fortune, and the Politics of Deceit in the House of Bush* (New York: Viking Phillips, 2004); Edwin Black, *IBM and the Holocaust: The Strategic Alliance Between Nazi Germany and America's Most Powerful Corporation* (New York: Three River's Press; Crown Black, 2001).

75 Veblen, *Business Enterprise*, 300.

76 Ibid., 301; emphasis added.

77 Not for nothing have conservative economic theorists warned socialists against taking war planning as a model for planning of entire economies. See Friedrich Hayek, *The Road to Serfdom*, ed. by John Chamberlin (Chicago: University of Chicago Press, 1945). Veblen was no enemy of socialism, but he had comparable trepidations about its potential to encourage statism. See Veblen, 'Army of the Commonweal', 100.

78 The great benefit of the teleological in theory is the rigor and direction that it imparts to analysis. Testable propositions may be easily discovered. The defects of this virtue however are two-fold. One is that empirical relations in the system may defy the imputed purpose, creating logical paradoxes of the sort we see in the military spending example, the kind of accumulating puzzles that Kuhn suggests lead to scientific revolutions. The other is foundational; it goes to the heart of Veblen's understanding of an evolutionary as opposed to a teleological approach to social science. See Thomas S. Kuhn, *The Structure of Scientific Revolutions* (Chicago: University of Chicago Press, 1970).

79 Veblen, 'Some Neglected Points', 76.

80 There are important exceptions to instrumentalism in each school of thought. Among the classic mid-twentieth-century pluralists, some such as Schattschneider (see *Semisovereign People*), Robert Dahl, Richard E. Neustadt, Raymond A. Bauer, I. de Sola Pool and Lewis A. Dexter have attributed significantly more independence to political actors than other interest group oriented thinkers such as Arthur F. Bentley, Earl Latham and David Truman. Among Marxist scholars, advocates of structural approaches, such as Nicos Poulantzas and the later work of Ralph Miliband also tend to assign relative autonomy to the state. See Robert Dahl, *Who Governs? Democracy and Power in an American City* (New Haven: Yale University Press, 1961); Richard. E. Neustadt, *Presidential Power, The Politics of Leadership* (New York: New American Library, 1964); Raymond A. Bauer, I. de Sola Pool and Lewis A. Dexter, *American Business and Public Policy; the Politics of Foreign Trade* (Chicago: Aldine, Atherton, 1972); Arthur F. Bentley, *The Process of Government; a Study of Social Pressures* (Bloomington: Principia Press, 1949); Earl Latham, *The Group Basis of Politics, a Study in Basing-Point Legislation* (Ithaca, NY: Cornell University Press, 1952); David Truman, *The Governmental Process, Political Interests and Public Opinion* (New York: Knopf, 1962); Nicos Poulantzas, *Political Power and Social Classes*, trans. Timothy O'Hagan (London: Verso, 1978); Nicos Poulantzas, *State, Power, Socialism*, trans. Patrick Camiller (London: Verso, 1980); Ralph Miliband, *Marxism and Politics* (New York: Oxford University Press, 1977). See also Clyde W. Barrow, *Critical Theories of the State, Marxist, Neo-Marxist, Post-Marxist* (Madison: University of Wisconsin Press, 1993).

81 Although Weber had a clear eye for the militarily and expansive thrust of state power, he cautions against presupposing that 'all political structures use force [...] against other political organizations'. Indeed, his famous definition of the state as that institution claiming 'the *monopoly of the legitimate use of physical force* within a given territory', suggests a primary stress on the internal dynamics of state power. Max Weber, 'Structures of Power', in id. *From Max Weber*, 159; Weber, 'Politics as a Vocation', in id. *From Max Weber*, 78, emphasis original. Organisational realists likewise argue that the competitive nature of international relations may encourage state elites to follow strategies that enhance the political power of the state, even against the resistance of domestic social forces. See Charles Tilly, *Coercion, Capital, and European States, AD 990–1992* (Cambridge: Blackwell, 1992); Barrow, *Critical Theories*, 129.

82 Veblen, 'Socialist Economics of Karl Marx and His Followers, I, II', 416.

83 Veblen, 'Some Neglected Points', 76–7.

84 Charles F. Gattone, *The Social Scientist As Public Intellectual* (Lanham: Rowman & Littlefield, 2006), 36. Gattone made the point well when he observes, 'Veblen did not treat business and government as separate entities but framed them as components of an integrated institutional order'.

85 Veblen, 'Why is Economics Not an Evolutionary Science?', 77; parenthesis added.

86 Among the most critical factors of power in business-run societies is legal support for systematic application of 'pecuniary pressure', a pressure that can be inflicted on any individual, group, or institution, at any time. In fact, for capitalist societies, economic coercion may well have a greater great effect than public law in regulating and channelling the ends and energies of most members of society most of the time; see Veblen, *Business Enterprise*, 274.

87 Thorstein Veblen, 'The Limitations of Marginal Utility', in *Veblen on Marx, Race, Science and Economics*, ed. by Sidney Plotkin and Rick Tilman (New York: Capricorn Books, 1969), 234.

88 The pain of exploit would, at some definitive point, cause the revolutionary spirit to break out, a spirit structurally embedded in the dialectics of history. Veblen argued, however, that Marx understated how much prevailing institutions and habits affect what workers might construe to be illegitimate pain. Obviously, as Veblen certainly knew, Marx understood ideological power. The problem is, as Veblen saw it, that Marx conflated the materialistic dimension of capitalist development, a process of blind, opaque cumulative causation, with a different, largely subjective, conception of causation, that he derived from natural rights, utilitarian and subjective conceptions of political behaviour. Instead, the development of political class consciousness, for Veblen, emerges largely apart from material factors. When it comes to political consciousness, for most people, their 'sequence of reflection, and the consequent choice of sides to the quarrel, run entirely alongside the material facts concerned'. See Veblen, 'Socialist Economics of Karl Marx and His Followers, I, II', 417. In other words, what counts in Marx as the identification of political class interests, the question of which kinds of groups align against one another in political combat, is not in fact pre-determined economically or materialistically, but rather emerges 'on the spiritual plane of human desire and passion'; ibid., 415. The difference subsisting in Marx between materialistic and hedonistic lines of explanations goes far to explain not only why 'the revolution' has not happened in the West, but also perhaps why organised labour seems to be growing less organised all the time.

89 Veblen, 'Why is Economics Not an Evolutionary Science?', 73.

90 Ibid., 74.

91 Ibid., 74.

92 Ibid., 74.

93 Erkki Kilpinen, 'How to Fight the 'Methodenstreit'? Veblen and Weber on Economics', paper presented at the Meetings of the International Thorstein Veblen Association, Carleton College (Northfield, MN, 2004), 18; emphasis added.

94 Ibid., 18.

95 Ibid., 18.

96 Geoffrey M. Hodgson, 'Darwin, Veblen and the Problem of Causality in Economics', 403; Anne Mayhew, 'Human Agency, Cumulative Causation, and the State: Remarks upon Receiving the Veblen-Commons Award', *Journal of Economic Issues* 35.2 (2001): 239–50.

97 Veblen, *Absentee Ownership*, 20.

Chapter 10

VEBLEN, WAR AND PEACE

Stephen Edgell

In 1957, on the 100th anniversary of Veblen's birth, the Department of Economics at Cornell University, where Veblen had studied in 1891–92, sponsored a series of lectures to commemorate this event. The main purpose of these commemorative lectures, which were published subsequently in a book, was to celebrate Veblen's seminal contribution and stimulate an interest in it.[1] However, not a single lecture focused on Veblen's writings on war and peace, although this topic was mentioned in passing on a couple of occasions.[2] This was in part possibly because the analysis of war is not a central issue in either mainstream economics[3] or indeed heterodox economics,[4] and partly perhaps because international conflicts were at a relatively low point in the late 1950s by the standards of the twentieth century. Yet the twentieth century was one of almost perpetual war with an estimated 180 million people killed, the vast majority civilians rather than combatants, a higher total than for any other century in the history of humankind.[5]

At the beginning of the twenty-first century, the prospect of perpetual peace looks no nearer being achieved than it did at the beginning of the last century (notwithstanding the creation in 1919 of the first international organisation in modern history, the League of Nations, and its replacement in 1945 by the United Nations).[6] At a time of increased actual and potential international conflict, the 150th anniversary of Veblen's birth is, therefore, an apposite time to reconsider Veblen's relatively neglected contribution to the social scientific understanding of war and peace. Thus the purpose of this chapter is to address some of the key aims of this conference: firstly, to increase awareness of Veblen's original and profound social thought by reviewing his analysis of war and peace; and secondly, to consider briefly its relevance to international conflict at the beginning of the twenty-first century with reference to the Middle East and the current war in Iraq.

Veblen's Evolutionary Theoretical Framework

In my first foray into the world of Veblen scholarship, I argued that Veblen's 'theory of evolutionary change is the central and unifying aspect of his contribution to social science'.[7] Over twenty-five years later, I reiterated this view by noting that 'the core of Veblen's contribution, which may be called sociologial economics to indicate Veblen's lack of respect for disciplinary boundaries, concerns his theory of evolutionary change'.[8] The claim that Veblen was, above all, an evolutionary theorist, and that this is pivotal to an understanding of his account of social change in general, and his specific analyses of issues such as conspicuous consumption, industrial capitalism, war and peace, has been endorsed by many commentators.[9] Thus, the logical starting place for a reconsideration of Veblen's account of international relations is his evolutionary theoretical framework.

In the following outline of Veblen's evolutionary theory of social change, the twin issues of war and peace will be highlighted to a greater degree than is usually the case. Veblen's evolutionary theoretical framework comprised four broad stages of social evolution; the peaceable era, the barbarian era, the handicraft era and the machine age or industrial capitalism. At each stage, the key dynamic involved the slow historical interaction of technology, instincts, habits and institutions and the main thrust of Veblen's theory of evolution was that some economic environments are more favourable than others to the expression of thoughts and actions that ultimately derive from the basic propensities of workmanship and predation, and that these fundamental orientations typically work at 'cross-purposes'.[10] Workmanship is conceived by Veblen to be a productive orientation concerned with a 'sense of the merit of serviceability or efficiency and the demerit of futility, waste, or incapacity' and as such is absolutely fundamental to the survival of the group.[11]

Conversely, predation is conceived as an acquisitive orientation concerned with obtaining goods and services by 'seizure or compulsion' and correspondingly is essential to the advancement of self-interest.[12] In short, the former is characterised by peaceful cooperation among equals, the latter by aggressive competition among unequals; or in Veblen's own words, workmanship expresses itself via 'industry' and is invariably the product of the collective technical knowledge of the community, whereas predation expresses itself via 'exploit' and is invariably a matter of individual aggrandisement.[13] Workmanship and predation were not the only 'instincts' discussed by Veblen, but they sum up the tendency for them to fall into one of two basic cultural categories, namely group-regarding or self-regarding attitudes and behaviour.[14]

The first stage of the evolution of human societies, often referred to as the Stone Age, since this material was used for tools, was the most protracted. In this earliest type of society workmanship prevailed as the major factor which shaped the culture. This is because the low level of technology put a premium on sharing knowledge and caring about production by all members of the group if it is to survive, let alone succeed economically. Thus:

> Predation cannot become the habitual, conventional resource of any group or any class until the industrial methods have been developed to such a degree of efficiency as to leave a margin worth fighting for, above the subsistence of those engaged in getting a living.[15]

The first stage of the evolution of human societies is, therefore, a relatively peaceable and egalitarian one, with minimal recourse to fighting since there was nothing worth fighting over.[16] It is not that there was no conflict, since there would have been some sexual competition; but more a case that it was not the norm during the protracted first stage of cultural evolution.

Under this 'savage plan of free workmanship', there is no state as such, merely a 'peaceable, non-coercive social organization', a form of anarchistic 'local self-Government' characterised by among other things 'insubordination'.[17] For Veblen, archaeological evidence, limited though it is, provides support for the peaceable origins of the earliest human societies insofar as there is more evidence of tools than of weapons. In a relatively weapon-free culture, the gods tend to be female not male and the rituals and symbols expressive of life not death. Thus, the state, such as it is in the earliest small-scale, self-sufficient, agrarian, relatively peaceable human communities, is organised loosely in a participatory democratic manner with minimal hierarchy:

> This civil system might be described as anarchy qualified by the common sense of a deliberative assembly that exercises no coercive control; or it might, if one's bias leads that way, be called a democratic government, the executive power of which is in abeyance.[18]

Veblen acknowledges that the use of the concept state when it is essentially anarchistic, is a 'misnomer'.[19]

With the development of technical knowledge and the use of tools, an economic surplus is produced; 'it becomes worth while to own the material means of industry', which provokes aggression and promotes the institution of ownership.[20] In due course, this change in material conditions leads gradually to the 'growth of predatory aptitudes, habits, and traditions' as predators rather than producers begin to dominate the society and its culture.[21] Self-interest advanced via exploitative predation replaces common interest advanced via productive workmanship. This second stage of evolution witnesses the emergence and eventual predominance of Veblen's famous leisure class, that parasitic ruling class who 'lives by the industrial community rather than in it'.[22] In other words, a class that lives off the surplus created by others. For example, in the case of the pagan, prehistoric kingdoms of Norway, Veblen refers to the 'war-lords installed for purposes of war and predation'.[23] At this barbarian stage, Veblen claims that there is a clear gender as well as class pattern of predation: 'War is honourable, and warlike prowess is eminently honorific in the eyes of the generality of men; and this admiration of warlike prowess is itself the best voucher of a predatory temperament in the admirer of war'.[24] He adds that the typical ruling class occupation of government is also predatory in terms of origin and content and that the only class that matches the leisure class for predatory attitudes and behaviour is that of working-class delinquents. Hence for Veblen, the ruling class are the original and bigger criminals, yet thanks to the prescriptive bias of the societies they dominate, they are not conventionally perceived in this way; in fact, the obverse is the case.

Veblen contrasts the first evolutionary stage and the second by noting that the former's 'most impressive traits' concern workmanship and therefore industrial efficiency, not politics, religion or art, whereas the second stage concerns predation in the form of 'dynastic power, statecraft, priestcraft, or artistic achievement'.[25] Thus, during the emergence of the barbarian era, obtaining goods and services either by priestly 'fraud' or royal 'force', or a combination of the two types of seizure, the state takes the form of a dynastic enterprise in which the culture is 'tempered by a large infusion of predatory concepts, of status, prerogative, differential respect of persons and classes, and a corresponding differential respect of occupations'.[26] In such a culture, 'warlike exploits and ideals become habitual in the community' and the 'sentiment of common interest [...] comes at the best to converge on the glory of the flag instead of the fulness of life of the community', or more specifically, 'in subservience to the common war-chief and his dynastic successors'.[27] Thus, the dynastic state is autocratic rather than democratic. It is concerned internally with issues such as political succession, managing those competing for power, and the provision of financial support for those in power; externally, 'the object end was dynastic prestige and security, military success, and the like', since the dynastic state is focused on maintaining domination at home and extending domination abroad.[28] Furthermore, Veblen argues that when a dynastic state is established via conquest, or when it is involved in perpetual conflict, and imbued with a religious fervour, the predatory and coercive character of society is likely to be excessive, as for example, suggests Veblen, the dynastic states during the barbarian era in what is now referred to as the Middle East.[29]

The hegemonic character of the values and institutions of a predatory parasitic plutocracy has profound implications for workmanship: 'The discipline of life in such a culture, therefore, is consistently unfavourable to any technological gain; the instinct of workmanship is dominated constantly by prevalent habits of thought that are worse than useless for any technological purpose'.[30] For instance, arguably the most significant negative consequence for workmanship is the tendency for productive labour to become a mark of disrepute, thereby discouraging it and encouraging exploit. However, the predatory culture of the barbarian era is not entirely bad news for workmanship since during the later years of this stage, when ownership has developed more fully as an institution, it 'conduces to diligence in work, if no more expeditious means of acquiring wealth can be devised'.[31] Thus, the outcome may be largely unfavourable for industry during the early phase of the barbarian era, but more favourable during the later phase.

The transition to the third evolutionary stage, the quasi-peaceable handicraft era, is like all such changes, a complex and drawn out one, according to Veblen. The defining feature of this stage, as its name implies, 'is a formal observance of peace and order', yet 'this stage still has too much coercion and class antagonism to be called peaceable in the full sense of the word'.[32] On a more positive note, Veblen claims that during this era 'workmanship again came into a dominant position among the factors that made up the discipline of daily life'.[33] After a slow start, Veblen argues that Britain was able to take the technological and hence economic lead during this stage due to its physical isolation, natural resources, cultural borrowing from its continental neighbours and above all, especially in the later phase of this era, minimal involvement in any 'international war, nor, except for the civil war of the Commonwealth period, in destructive war of any kind'.[34] As a consequence, the outcome in Britain was the Industrial Revolution, rather than 'the exhaustion of politics' and 'collapse' of the economic system as in mainland Europe.[35]

Yet more positively, and pertinently given the focus of this analysis, the freedom enjoyed by workmanship during the handicraft era, personified by the 'skilled masterless workman' who escaped from the 'bonds of that organization in which arbitrary power of the landed interests held dominion', gave rise to modern democratic principles and institutions.[36] Specifically those individual civil rights and legal equalities that developed into what we now refer to as liberal democracy are traceable, according to Veblen, to the pivotal role of the class of 'ungraded free men' referred to above, during the handicraft era. In other words, for Veblen, the emergent, and at that time limited, system of Natural Rights and Natural Liberty, are a 'by-product of workmanship under the handicraft system'.[37] Veblen noted that civil rights that developed during the quasi-peaceable handicraft era were more like those that prevailed in the peaceable savage era than the predatory barbarian era, due to the cultural significance and impact of workmanship which tended to undermine notions of differential class or individual privilege.

The emergence of the fourth and final stage, that of industrial capitalism, initially in Britain and later in other parts of western Europe and north America, involved the transformation in production methods but not in the methods of business which are still predicated on private ownership. During the handicraft era, the small scale of industry was well suited to the institution of ownership which ensured that the worker who owned the tools received the benefit in the form of a reasonable livelihood, namely the English doctrine of the '"natural" right of property'.[38] But with the growth in the size and complexity of industrial capitalism, especially in America, the main focus of Veblen's life work, '[t]he pecuniary side of the enterprise came to require more unremitting attention, as the chances for gain or loss through business relations simply, aside from mere industrial efficiency, grew in umber and magnitude'.[39] This caused profit on investment for private benefit to supplant industrial serviceability for the common good as the primary object of production, in effect reversing the priorities of the handicraft era insofar as predation in the form of pecuniary concerns now takes precedence over workmanship with its focus on useful production. Moreover, the 'technological knowledge, that so enables the material equipment to serve the purposes of production and of private gain, is a free gift of the community at large to the owners of industrial plant'.[40] To achieve the goal of maximum profit rather than maximum production, capitalists attempt to consolidate their competitive advantage by engaging in a variety of strategies which disrupt production and disadvantage rivals. Such was, and still is, the inevitability and ubiquity of what Veblen called 'capitalistic sabotage' by virtue of its indispensability to business success, that it attracted hardly any attention, public or academic, in marked contrast to such methods when undertaken by employees.[41] Thus, the key problem for Veblen was that the theory of the heroic entrepreneur creating goods and services where none existed before, belongs to the eighteenth-century era of handicraft production but has survived, enhanced even, into the machine age where it no longer applies. This point is simultaneously the source of Veblen's critique of mainstream economics and the springboard for his critique of contemporary industrial capitalism.

The domination of industry (workmanship) by business (predation) has significant ramifications beyond the derangement and consequent retardation of production; it impacts on both national and especially international politics in ways that are detrimental to the common good in general and the underlying population in particular. As the process of business domination over industry and the wider culture took effect, Veblen argued that: 'Representative government means, chiefly, representation of business interests'.[12] The main institutional supports for constitutional governments under the sway of business interests are patriotism and property. These predatory habits of thought and action predate the machine era, and although the material conditions have changed, these habits and institutions have not. It was not just a matter of the '(ostensibly) democratic' state protecting business interests domestically, but promoting them abroad in the mistaken view that what is good for business is good for everyone.[13] According to Veblen's analysis, the businessman is not qualified to run industry, let alone the government and determine its domestic and foreign policies. Hence, for Veblen, the clearest expression of the tendency for business to dominate society is the close connection between the financial interests of business and military policies. Business has always been competitive, but it is now international, consequently, 'the business men of one nation are pitted against those of another and swing the forces of the state, legislative, diplomatic and military, against one another in the strategic game of pecuniary advantage'.[14] It is partly a matter of providing military support for the maintenance and extension of business interests abroad, but it is also the case, according to Veblen, that 'when warlike emulation between states of somewhat comparable force has once got under way it assumes a cumulative character'.[15] In addition, large military expenditure is particularly lucrative for the companies involved as those in business tend to drive a harder bargain than government officials. Unsurprisingly, Veblen argued that state military expenditure benefits business at the expense of the common good and common people, since from this standpoint it is entirely wasteful. Moreover:

> Habituation to a warlike, predatory scheme of life is the strongest disciplinary factor that can be brought to counteract the vulgarization of modern life wrought by peaceful industry and the machine process, and to rehabilitate the decaying sense of status and differential status.[16]

Thus, warfare is not only profitable for some, but also helps to promote social integration, thereby minimising social unrest.

Veblen was unsure about the eventual outcome of the historical struggle between workmanship and predation. Notwithstanding his frequent protestations to the contrary, there is a clear moral dimension to his writings, and his preferred alternative was for workmanship to prevail in the form of an industrial republic and perpetual peace, rather than predatory capitalism and perpetual war.

Veblen's Analysis of War and Peace

It is significant to note that Veblen discusses war and peace in all his book-length studies, including his introduction to the *Laxdœla Saga* and many of his articles and reviews, and the two books that focus specifically on these twin issues are among those which were published during the First World War, namely *Imperial Germany and the Industrial Revolution* in 1915 and *An Inquiry into The Nature of Peace and the Terms of its Perpetuation* in 1917. Thus, Veblen was concerned with international relations throughout his career and he was especially animated by the international conflict that engulfed Europe between 1914 and 1918.

In *Imperial Germany*, Veblen compares and contrasts the links between the economic and political development of Germany and Britain, and to a lesser extent Japan and America, with a view to accounting for the industrial advancement and excessive predation of the unified German nation-state. Veblen's thesis is that Germany borrowed the latest technological knowledge from the English, 'without the cultural consequences which its gradual development and continued use has entailed among the people whose experience initiated it and determined the course of its development'.[47] In terms of Veblen's evolutionary theory, Germany adopted the new technology of the machine age into a society still organised politically in a way associated with the barbarian era, i.e. a dynastic state. According to Veblen, this was a potentially explosive combination that could lead to war since it involved the ability to use advanced military technology by a nation-state characterised by predatory notions of prowess, militant nationalism and territorial aggression. In an article published in the same year as *Imperial Germany*, Veblen argues that there were marked similarities between Germany and Japan. He sums up neatly his theory that the mixture of non-democratic archaic political institutions and modern industrial institutions is a recipe for war rather than peace: 'It is this unique combination of a high-wrought spirit of feudalistic fealty and chivalric honour with that material efficiency given by the modern technology that the strength of Japan lies'.[48] Thus, Veblen's account of the success of German industrial capitalism at the beginning of the twentieth century and its military ambitions is rooted in his theory of evolutionary change, emphasising its uneven development due to the cultural lag of political institutions and the cultural borrowing of technology. Veblen's distinction between dynastic states and their subjects on the one hand and democratic states and their citizens on the other, corresponds to his fundamental conceptual categories predation and workmanship in that the former is a highly coercive type of political organisation characterised by 'subordination', whereas the latter places a high value on 'insubordination'. More specifically, 'the dynastic State being necessarily of a competitive or rapacious character and free to use any expedient that comes to hand', including a 'system of bureaucratic surveillance and unremitting interference in the private lives of subjects', i.e. the suppression of dissent, censorship and repressive police powers as it prepares for and engages in expansionist conflict.[49] Memorably, Veblen concludes that '[a] dynastic State can not be set afloat in the milk of human kindness'.[50] Veblen emphasises that although the dynastic German nation-state is 'appreciably more arbitrary and bureaucratic' than the British, the difference between the two 'is only a matter of degree'.[51] Hence, Veblen notes that Germany is merely 'a distinctive form of the current compromise between the irresponsible autocracy of the medieval State and the autonomy of popular self-government'.[52] The validity of this point was underlined by the banning of *Imperial Germany* by US Mail on the grounds that it was 'damaging to America'.[53]

In short, state censorship in times of war is not unique to dynastic states. While Veblen was completing this book, war erupted in Europe and he considered Germany to be the main source of this disturbance of peace, but he also felt that the other European nations were equally culpable although everyone professed that their aim was peace not war.

He contends that Germany was likely to lose the war, since the other European nations had also been increasing their arsenals and their combined fighting capacity outweighed that of Germany. Veblen further discusses the material consequences of war, such as the loss of life, property, the cost of financing war in terms of loans and taxes,[54] and the immaterial consequences, notably the 'state of the industrial arts considered as a system of habits of thought'.[55] He opines that as long as the conflict was not too prolonged the damage to the latter would not be great. However, just like the modern predatory business enterprise, the predatory state both depends on the industrial system (workmanship) yet is disabled by its cultural effects. Veblen had argued this point in his analysis of the future of the business enterprise:

> The growth of business enterprise rests on the machine technology as its material foundation. The machine industry is indispensable to it; it cannot get along without the machine process. But the discipline of the machine process cuts away the spiritual, institutional foundations of business enterprise; the machine industry is incompatible with its continued growth; it cannot, in the long run, get along with the machine process.[56]

In *Imperial Germany* Veblen repeats this important evolutionary point using almost identical phrasing with reference to the future of the state:

> Nothing short of the fullest usufruct of this technology will serve the material needs of the modern warlike State; yet the discipline incident to a sufficiently unreserved addiction to this mechanistic technology will unavoidably disintegrate the institutional foundations of such a system.[57]

Consequently all states 'may be said to be unable to get along without the machine industry, and also, in the long run, unable to get along with it'.[58] Veblen considers this cultural eventuality to be of the utmost importance for all advanced industrial capitalist societies whether they were dynastic or democratic nation-states.

Veblen's other war book, *The Nature of Peace*, begins where *Imperial Germany* ends. Instead of analysing the conditions that lead inexorably to war, Veblen focuses on the conditions that favour the establishment of peace on a permanent basis. Veblen's objective in writing his book in the midst of an international conflict between nations of unprecedented scale was to analyse what can be done to achieve the Kantian ideal of perpetual peace rather than consider this aspiration in moral terms.

Veblen's point of departure is that in modern societies, 'any breach of the peace takes place only on the initiative and at the discretion of the government or State', who have a monopoly on the legitimate use of violence, and that 'in furtherance of such warlike enterprise to cherish and eventually to mobilise popular sentiment in support of any warlike move'.[59] In all modern states, whether dynastically offensive or democratically defensive, this is 'indispensable to the procuring and maintenance of a suitable equipment with which eventually to break the peace, as well as to ensure a diligent prosecution when once it has been undertaken'.[60]

Following Kant's idea of a 'truce' agreed by warring states,[61] Veblen notes that when a state establishes peace, it is effectively an 'armistice' since such a peace can be broken at any time, even by the most peaceably inclined states.[62] All governments, suggests Veblen, operate 'under the precept, "Speak softly and carry a big stick"', and comments wryly that 'the "big stick" is an obstacle to soft speech'.[63] This reflects Veblen's earlier claim that the modern state, whether dynastic or democratic, can be traced back to the barbarian era and is, therefore, in essence 'of a predatory origin and of an irresponsible character'.[64] By the same token, Veblen reiterates that his distinction between dynastic and democratic states is a matter of variation not one of opposites as all modern states encourage and require its subjects/citizens to show allegiance to the state which operates legitimately in its authority over them. Consequently, in all modern states it is one's patriotic duty to support the state, especially in times of war, to do otherwise is not just a matter of bad form but ultimately a treasonable offence, which for Veblen reveals that coercion is at the core of all states.

Patriotism is the key concept in *The Nature of Peace* and a whole chapter is devoted to its character and consequences, although, as noted above, it had been mentioned in his earlier studies, in addition to *Imperial Germany*, where he argues that territorial expansion at the 'cost of other communities, particularly communities at a distance, and more especially such as are felt to be aliens', typically gains the approval of the patriotic populace.[65] Veblen is suggesting that it is not difficult to mobilise popular support for war against 'culturally distinct communities' on the other side of the world.[66]

For Veblen, patriotism was a 'sense of partisan solidarity in respect of prestige' and the 'patriotic spirit is a spirit of emulation'.[67] Hence, patriotism 'belongs under the general caption of sportsmanship, rather than workmanship' and 'finds its fullest expression in no other outlet than warlike enterprise; it highest and final appeal is for death, damage, discomfort and destruction of the party of the second part'.[68] Moreover, patriotism is often aided and abetted in a moral sense by appeals to aims above and beyond that of national prestige, notably liberation from dictatorship, to spread democracy, or religious ideals. To illustrate the last point Veblen notes that,

> among the followers of Islam, devote and resolute, the patriotic statesman (that is to say the politician who designs to make use of the popular patriotic fervour) will in the last resort appeal to the claims and injunctions of the faith.[69]

The predatory nature of patriotism belies its origins in the peaceable era when a sense of group solidarity was essential to survival. Following the improvement in the industrial arts and consequent growth of a surplus in the barbarian era, the

> development of the rights of property, and of such prescriptive claims of privilege and prerogative, it has come about that other community interests have fallen away, until collective prestige remains as virtually the sole community interest which can hold the sentiment of the group in a bond of solidarity.[70]

In a modern society in which the material interests are divided between a superordinate ownership class and a subordinate class who works, the idea of a shared interest is a myth: 'The substantial interest of these [dominant] classes in the common welfare is of the same kind as the interest which a parasite has in the well-being of his host'.[71] Yet those in charge, notably the civil and military authorities, take advantage of the patriotic sentiments of the underlying population to further their predatory political policies. For their part, the common people have the doubtful honour of sharing vicariously the 'prestige value' or 'psychic income' of the state's increased power, albeit at the cost of paying the bill.[72] The business class engaged in foreign trade also make use of the patriotic sentiments of the underlying population to advance policies that discriminate in their favour and against those of their international competitors, such as the 'patent imbecility' of the protective tariff which inhibits the growth of technical knowledge.[73] Such strategies are only in the private interest of the minority business class; the majority do not share the profits and may suffer from the international conflict that is provoked. Furthermore, according to Veblen, when it comes to supporting a war, there is little to choose 'between the sluggish and shamefaced abettor of a sordid national crime, and a raving patriot who glories in serving as a cat's-paw to a syndicate of unscrupulous politicians bent on domination for dominion's sake'.[74] Thus, for both democratic citizens and dynastic subjects, patriotism, along with emulative consumption, contributes to social cohesion in a divided society.

Veblen was not unaware of the irony that the increased capacity to propagandise and propagate predation on an international scale was enhanced greatly by technological advances applied to the instruments of war. Yet he also argues that the culture of the modern technological system is cosmopolitan and that consequently 'the patriotic spirit fits like dust in the eyes and sand in the bearings'.[75] By retarding industrial progress, the material interests of the majority are again thwarted by the dominant minority interests of the predatory state and its ruling class. Veblen concludes that '[p]atriotism is useful for breaking the peace not for keeping it'.[76] Moreover the persistence of patriotism in modern societies is increasingly malignant due to the internationalisation of the technological system.[77] Veblen's proposed solution to international predation was the same as the one that he suggested for the problem of the dysfunctional rule of predatory institutions within any one industrially advanced nation-state, namely the rehabilitation of workmanship.[78]

Veblen is not interested in a temporary peace, but a lasting peace; a Kantian perpetual peace: 'what is necessary to assure a reasonable expectation of continued peace is the neutralization of so much of those relations as the patriotic self-conceit and credulity of these peoples will permit'; that is, the business enterprise and the idea of national prestige, both of which are embodied in and emboldened by, the modern state.[79] In terms of the above discussion of Veblen's evolutionary theory and the tendency for habits of thought to change more slowly than the material conditions, it is clear that in the long run, the prospects for economic and political predation on an international scale are damaging, thanks to the corrosive effect of workmanship. However, in the meantime, to ensure perpetual peace, those archaic expressions of predation, the price system and patriotism, need to be abolished forthwith. Retaining the price system is conducive to international economic competition, which is more than likely to lead to conflict. Similarly, the persistence of patriotism is conducive to international political competition which is also likely to lead to conflict. Patriotism is the older habit that has persisted into the modern world and Veblen comments that '[i]t is easily acquired and hard to put away', even in democratic states where it survives in a diluted form, but its extinction is essential because it is 'an enduring obstacle to a conclusive peace'.[80] In the case of the price system, Veblen expects it to 'gain in volume and inclusiveness' and concludes that its retention 'is incompatible with an unwarlike state of peace and security'.[81] How these radical changes were to be achieved is not discussed in depth by Veblen in *The Nature of Peace*, although he was aware that the adoption of either or both was highly unlikely given the contemporary power and historical authenticity of these obsolete predatory institutions, including the coercive business state under the controlling influence of the owners of capital. In the context of an attempt to create a League of Nations to prevent the outbreak of war in the future, Veblen warns that if his remedies for the culturally obsolete forms of predation were not implemented, the prospect of war in the future would be improved significantly. This is the source of Veblen's famous prediction that Germany and Japan were likely to disturb peace as soon as the opportunity arises since the 'prospective comity of nations Imperial Germany (and Imperial Japan) fit like a drunken savage with a machine gun'.[82]

In addition to a theoretical analysis of war and peace with special reference to World War I, *The Nature of Peace* contains Veblen's views (dated January 1917 in parenthesis in the text) on the debate about how a projected league of pacific nations could best secure a lasting peace at the end of the international hostilities. Political engagement of this practical kind marked a new departure for Veblen, although the first item in his list of six points is entirely in keeping with his theoretical conclusions: 'The definitive elimination of the Imperial establishment, together with the monarchical establishments of the several states of the Empire and the privileged classes'.[83] In addition to the Kantian priority of democratisations, the other items in Veblen's list are mainly concerned with practical details, covering such issues as war equipment and war debt. Later in the same year, Veblen submitted two memoranda to the US government containing his suggestions regarding the implementation of a programme for peace after the war, with special reference to the role of America, which echoed his previously stated views on democracy and the vested interests of business.[84] Veblen's keenness to contribute in a constructive way to the debate about peace at this juncture is also indicated by his willingness to pay a publisher to get *The Nature of Peace* published.[85] Further evidence of the strength of Veblen's political concerns regarding WWI and peace on a permanent rather than temporary basis is provided by his controversial employment by the state in the Food Administration in 1918, which could be interpreted as working for the enemy (i.e. the coercive business state), and his subsequent switch to political journalism as a prominent member the editorial staff of *The Dial*.[86] These moves by Veblen into the realm of policy making resulted in a raft of publications, including one book, *The Vested Interests and the Common Man*, plus several articles and editorials, many of which appear in the book *Essays in Our Changing Order*. In these works, Veblen reiterates his thesis regarding the need to advance the primacy of workmanship at the expense of predatory institutions, especially the nation which 'is an organization for the collective offence and defence, in peace and war, – essentially based on hate and fear of other nations'.[87] They also focus on some of the concrete issues noted in *The Nature of the Peace* that needed to be taken to enhance the prospect of perpetual peace, such as the abolition of national frontiers because they inhibited the workmanship internationally and encouraged animosity between nations and are critical of the aim to make the world safe for the vested interests and 'commercialised democracy'.[88] Thus, contrary to the view that Veblen 'failed to carry through from theory to policy',[89] his policy-making activities as a government advisor and political journalist suggest otherwise and reveal a consistency between his theoretical analysis of war and peace and his practical recommendations.

The salience of war and peace is still apparent in Veblen's last book, *Absentee Ownership and Business Enterprise in Recent Times: The Case of America*. This is most noticeable in the first two chapters and the last in which Veblen updates his argument that '[t]he Great War arose out of a conflict of absentee interests and the Peace was negotiated with a view to stabilize them'.[90] States continue to threaten and use force if necessary as indicated by the aforementioned 'big stick' principle, and this invariably 'resolves itself in to an expenditure of life and substance on the part of the underlying population of all contending parties'.[91] Veblen also reaffirms his view that 'external politics is a blend of war and business and combines the peculiar traits of both'.[92] These familiar themes concerning the persistence of 'imbecile' predatory institutions, such as patriotism and the price system, which are more conducive to war than the free, global development of workmanship, are covered once again.[93] However, he achieves this with the added emphasis that the democratic nations are the offspring of the dynastic states of an earlier era since their

> national establishments, and the spirit of national integrity on which they trade, are still essentially warlike and predatory. That is to say, predation is still the essence of the thing. The ways and means of the traffic are still force and fraud at home and abroad.[94]

Moreover, when confronted by a perceived threat to the vested interests of business and, therefore, the (mistaken) interests of the whole society, there will be a demand for repressive measures to ensure the safety of the public. With the state operating in the special interests of business, it is, as usual, at the cost of the advance of workmanship and the masses. Veblen is pessimistic that in the near future the dominance of 'imbecile' institutions will be removed, but in the long run their supremacy is at risk due to the indispensability of workmanship and its peaceful habits of thought.

Conclusions and Contemporary Relevance

World War I was arguably a turning point in Veblen's life; in addition to analysing the twin issues of war and peace within his evolutionary theoretical perspective, he became involved professionally in the process of policy formation for the first time and later a political journalist. It was also a turning point for Veblen personally since he married his second wife on 17 June 1914 and was on his honeymoon in Norway when the war in Europe was ignited by the assassination of Archduke Franz Ferdinand on 28 June. According to his second wife's daughter Becky, it was a 'perfect marriage'.[95] Needless to say, the political context of this union was less than perfect, but it perhaps galvanised Veblen's long-standing theoretical interest in the issues it raised to such an extent that he focused on them in more detail than before and became engaged in political policy making. Thus, Veblen spent the final years of his life preoccupied with the conditions that were conducive to peace and workmanship and with those that favoured predation and the prospect of war. Veblen clearly felt strongly about war and peace, as his less cautious post-1914 style indicates.[96] This review of Veblen's writings on war and peace has shown that his analysis of these issues is entirely consistent with his earlier works, namely his evolutionary theory of change with its emphasis on the consequences of cultural lag. Specifically, the thrust of his theoretical analysis of war and peace is that the survival of obsolete predatory institutions into the modern machine era, notably the price system, patriotism and the coercive state that operates primarily to further its own interests and those of business, will be undermined in the long run by the cultural impact of workmanship. In the meantime predatory institutions not only retard workmanship but ensure the persistence of conflict within and between nations.

Veblen's proposed solution to the problem of international predation was also consistent with his earlier writings which had centred on the evolution of workmanship and predation in different historical periods and the need to abolish institutions associated with the latter proclivity so that the former could thrive to the benefit of all. Veblen argues that if the price system, patriotism and the nation-state are preserved, peace will be temporary and not lasting since these predatory habits and institutions favour competition and conflict, not cooperation and comity. Moreover, his practical suggestions regarding the establishment of an enduring peace are broadly in line with his theoretical analysis and, hence, include recommendations such as the abolition of protective tariffs and national frontiers to reduce international enmity and encourage the free flow of technical knowledge.[97]

The one apparent inconsistency revealed by this review of Veblen's analysis of war and peace concerns the relationship between his critical theory of the predatory business state, however democratic, and his brief stint as an employee of a state infused with a heightened sense of patriotism and dominated by aggressive political and business interests. A full account of this short period of Veblen's life that considers his role as a government policy maker, his political policies and his analysis of war and peace is beyond the scope of this paper. This possible contradiction has been addressed most recently by Christopher Capozzola who was less concerned to resolve it than argue that Veblen does not 'fit easily into a single category of pro-war or anti-war'.[98] I am not so sure. Veblen's pacifist inclinations are too clear in all his writings to dismiss his wartime state employment as non-problematic on the grounds that the pro-/anti-war dichotomy is a false one and, hence, unhelpful when interpreting Veblen's complex writings. Veblen's theoretical and policy writings all point in the same direction, that of an anti-war public intellectual. The recently unearthed clue by Knut Odner that Veblen's family of origin were Quakers is of possible relevance here given their well-documented pacifist tradition and role in peace movements.[99] Thus, the apparent inconsistency between Veblen's words and actions on war needs to be revisited in greater depth than has hitherto been the case.

At the beginning of the twenty-first century, one does not need to go to the Middle East to appreciate the destructive horrors of war facilitated by the latest military technology, it can be seen every day via a multitude of twenty-four-hour television news channels beamed around the world. Were Veblen alive today, he would not be surprised to find clear parallels between the contemporary tinderbox situation in the Middle East and the one he analysed in Europe nearly a hundred years ago. That is to say, an explosive mixture of expansionist and highly militarised dynastic and democratic states, all competing for political power and economic resources, notably the increasingly scarce and, hence, strategic energy resource: oil. Moreover, these states vary in their religious affiliations and the extent to which their religious institutions are integrated or separated from state and business institutions. In addition, there are several Western states and business corporations that have taken an active interest in the political and economic circumstances and rivalries in the Middle East throughout the past century and continue to do so. This applies especially to the UK and the USA and their armaments and oil companies, such as British Petroleum which was founded in 1909 as the Anglo-Persian Oil Company. The nation-states in the Middle East are mostly dynastic and combine archaic political institutions with the latest military technology. In keeping with Veblen's evolutionary understanding of predation, they tend to resort frequently to military force to further their imperial ambitions and/or defend their national integrity. Thus, the whole region has a long and ongoing history of conflict that is entirely predictable in the light of Veblen's theoretical analysis of war and peace.

In the case of the most recent outbreak of war in the Middle East, the decision by the US government and its main ally, the UK, to invade Iraq in 2003 confirms Veblen's critical view that democracies have never shed their predatory tendencies, their justifications for this pre-emptive war notwithstanding. The influence of the neoconservative agenda, which predates this war and emphasises the right of nations to start wars in the interests of spreading democracy,[100] is within the logic of Veblen's analysis and has contributed to the rise in bellicosity. Veblen's misgivings about patriotism have been affirmed by the passing of the Patriot Act of 2001 in response to the terrorist attacks of 9/11 (updated and re-authorised in 2005), which enhanced the power of the state to pry into the lives of US citizens, including data about the books they buy or borrow. The US government is not quite at the book-burning stage, 'just yet', as Veblen would say, but these powers by a supposedly democratic state would not have surprised him although they would have remained a cause for concern.[101] The phrase 'war on terror', preferred by the US government to less aggressive alternatives such as 'policy on terrorism', is instructive in a Veblenian sense in that it signifies the use of force.

Finally, the conflagration currently consuming Iraq is entirely predictable on the basis of Veblen's evolutionary theory of war and peace which at its core warned of the lethal mix of pre-modern political institutions and modern military technology. Perhaps, if Bush had read Veblen, he would have been less surprised by the violence that 'Operation Iraqi Liberation' (OIL) has unleashed. Above all, Veblen teaches us not to underestimate the power of the vested interests and that when the captains of industry, war and superstition are in charge of quasi-feudal societies and have access to the latest military technology, there is more chance of perpetual war than perpetual peace.

Notes and References

1 Douglas Dowd (ed.), *Thorstein Veblen: A Critical Appraisal* (Westport: Greenwood, 1958).

2 On the occasion of the centennial year of Carleton College, Veblen's alma mater, a seminar programme was organised in 1966 and published subsequently as a book: Carlton Qualey (ed.), *Thorstein Veblen* (New York: Columbia University Press, 1968). The issue of war and peace is also overlooked in the essays.

3 Jim Horner and John Martinez, 'Thorstein Veblen and Henry George on war, conflict and the military', *Journal of Economic Issues* 31.3 (1997): 633–9.

4 The classic American heterodox economics textbook by Allan Gruchy similarly fails to discuss war and peace. See Allan Gruchy, *Modern Economic Thought: The American Contribution* (New York: Prentice-Hall, 1947). Jim Horner and John Martinez 'Thorstein Veblen and Henry George on war, conflict and the military', *Journal of Economic Issues* 31.3 (1997): 633–9. Notable exceptions to this generalisation include more politically minded economists such as John K. Galbraith who updates Veblen's theory of the 'arms race' with reference to the Cold War and, of course, all those who have written about imperialism. See John K. Galbraith, *The New Industrial State* (New York: Mentor, 1972).

5 Matthew White, *Wars, Massacres and Atrocities of the Twentieth Century* (November 1999). Online: http://users.erols.com/mwhite28/war-1900 (accessed 7 December 2009).

6 Francis Hinsley, *Power and the Pursuit of Peace: Theory and Practice in the History of Relations between States* (Cambridge: Cambridge University Press, 1980), 149.

7 Stephen Edgell, 'Thorstein Veblen's Theory of Evolutionary Change', *American Journal of Economics and Sociology* 34.3 (1975): 267–80, in particular 278.

8 Stephen Edgell, *Veblen in Perspective: His Life and Thought* (New York: Sharpe, 2001), 162.

9 Although Veblen's evolutionary approach enjoyed a 'remarkable revival in the 1980s', as Geoffrey M. Hodgson put it, his legacy in this regard has been considered 'unfulfilled'. See Geoffrey M. Hodgson, 'Thorstein Veblen and Post-Darwinian Economics', *Cambridge Journal of Economics* 16.3 (1992): 285–301, in particular 286; Anne Mayhew, 'On the Difficulty of Evolutionary Analysis', *Cambridge Journal of Economics* 22.4 (1998): 449–61, in particular 449.

10 Thorstein Veblen, *The Instinct of Workmanship and the State of the Industrial Arts* (New York: Kelley, 1964), 11.

11 Thorstein Veblen, *The Theory of the Leisure Class: An Economic Study of Institutions* (London: Unwin, 1970), 29.

12 Ibid., 30.

13 Ibid., 28.

14 Edgell, *Veblen in Perspective*, 80.

15 Veblen, *Leisure Class*, 32.

16 Accounts of the first contact between the Portuguese and hunting and gathering groups in what is now Brazil confirm Veblen's peaceful and egalitarian depiction of such communities. See Charles Ley, *Portuguese Voyages 1498–1663* (London: Dent, 1947). Perhaps this is why Veblen's Washington Island library contained so many books on the European voyages of discovery, such as those by James Cook (Thorstein Veblen Collections, Carleton College Archive).

17 Veblen, *Instinct*, 153; Thorstein Veblen, *Imperial Germany and the Industrial Revolution* (Ann Arbor: University of Michigan Press, 1966), 326–7.

18 Veblen, *Imperial Germany*, 46.

19 Ibid., 166.

20 Veblen, *Instinct*, 150–51.

21 Veblen, *Leisure Class*, 32.

22 Ibid., 164.

23 Veblen, *Imperial Germany*, 315.

24 Veblen, *Leisure Class*, 165.

25 Veblen, *Imperial Germany*, 43.
26 Veblen, *Instinct*, 159–60.
27 Ibid., 157, 161.
28 Thorstein Veblen, *The Theory of the Business Enterprise* (New York: Kelley, 1975), 284.
29 Veblen, *Instinct*, 166–7.
30 Ibid., 169.
31 Ibid., 173.
32 Veblen, *Business Enterprise*, 58.
33 Veblen, *Instinct*, 234.
34 Ibid., 251.
35 Ibid.. 251.
36 Ibid., 276.
37 Ibid., 341.
38 Veblen, *Business Enterprise*, 79.
39 Ibid., 24.
40 Thorstein Veblen, *The Nature of Peace and the Terms of its Perpetuation* (New York: Kelley, 1964), 321.
41 Ibid., 324.
42 Veblen, *Business Enterprise*, 286.
43 Veblen, *Nature of Peace*, 9.
44 Veblen, *Business Enterprise*, 293.
45 Ibid., 297.
46 Ibid., 393.
47 Ibid., 86.
48 Thorstein Veblen, *Essays in Our Changing Order*, ed. by Leon Ardzrooni (New York: Kelley, 1964), 251.
49 Veblen, *Imperial Germany*, 79–80.
50 Ibid., 216.
51 Ibid., 224.
52 Ibid., 230.
53 William Hard quoted in Joseph Dorfman, *Thorstein Veblen and His America* (New York: Viking, 1934), 382.
54 The UK finally repaid the last of 50 instalments of its WWII debts to the US and Canada in 2006 that were negotiated by John Maynard Keynes in 1945; online: www.news.bbc/co.uk/2/hi/uk-news/magazine/4757181stm (accessed 7 December 2009).
55 Veblen, *Imperial Germany*, 272.
56 Veblen, *Business Enterprise*, 375.
57 Veblen, *Imperial Germany*, 270–71.
58 Ibid., 270–71.
59 Veblen, *Nature of Peace*, 4.
60 Ibid., 4.
61 Immanuel Kant, *Perpetual Peace: A Philosophical Essay* (London: Swan Sonnenschein, 1903), 107.
62 Veblen, *Instinct*, 7.
63 Ibid., 7. See also Thorstein Veblen, *Absentee Ownership and Business Enterprise in Recent Times: The Case of America* (New York: Kelley, 1964), 23. Veblen is referring to Roosevelt who first used this phrase in a letter written in 1900. A carbon copy of the letter in the US Library of Congress and the original was put up for sale at $200,000 earlier this year (*Guardian*, 5 April 2007).
64 Veblen, *Nature of Peace*, 9.
65 Veblen, *Imperial Germany*, 48.

66 Ibid., 138.

67 Veblen, *Nature of Peace*, 33.

68 Ibid., 33.

69 Ibid., 35.

70 Ibid., 53–4.

71 Ibid., 57.

72 Ibid., 71.

73 Ibid., 68.

74 Ibid., 106.

75 Ibid., 40.

76 Ibid., 78.

77 Veblen's friend Isador Lubin from their time at the University of Missouri and who worked with him at the Food Administration in Washington has alleged that 'when it came to Norway he was as great a chauvinist as anybody'. See Isador Lubin, 'Recollections of Veblen', in Qualey, *Thorstein Veblen*, 131–47, in particular 135. However, this is denied by Veblen's brother Andrew who wrote in one of his letters to Dorfman, dated 23 June 1930, that 'he was not particularly "strong for all things Norwegian"'. He had no use for chauvinists' (Joseph Dorfman Papers, Columbia University).

78 Edgell, *Veblen*, 137–59.

79 Veblen, *Nature of Peace*, 205.

80 Ibid., 283.

81 Ibid., 336, 366.

82 Ibid., 238.

83 Ibid., 271.

84 Veblen, *Essays*, 355–82.

85 Dorfman, *Thorstein Veblen*, 356.

86 Lubin, 'Recollections', 131–47.

87 Thorstein Veblen, *The Vested Interest and the Common Man* (New York: Capricorn, 1969), 147.

88 Veblen, *Essays*, 457, 383–90; Veblen, *Instinct*, 264; Veblen, *Vested Interest*, 141–2.

89 Richard Brinkman and June Brinkman, 'Cultural Lag: In the Tradition of Veblenian Economics', *Journal of Economic Issues* 40.4 (2006): 1009–28.

90 Veblen, *Absentee Ownership*, 3.

91 Ibid., 23.

92 Ibid., 29.

93 Ibid., 38.

94 Veblen, *Absentee Ownership*, 439.

95 Elizabeth Jorgensen and Henry Jorgensen, *Thorstein Veblen: Victorian Firebrand* (New York: Sharpe, 1999), 145.

96 It is difficult to write about war without feeling, and my impression is that Veblen is no exception since his tendency to deny, via numerous caveats, that he uses words such as waste in a technical sense only, is far less noticeable in his analyses of this issue. Notwithstanding this point, Veblen arguably underestimated the long-term impact of war on the families of combatants.

97 It is interesting to note the parallels between Veblen's analysis of post-war peace policy and a recent contribution to this topic, such as Martin Alexander and John Keiger, 'Limiting Arms, Enforcing Limits: International Inspections and the Challenges of Compellance in Germany post-1919; Iraq post-1991 Introduction', *Journal of Strategic Studies* 29.2 (2006): 345–94.

98 Christopher Capozzola, 'Thorstein Veblen and the Politics of War, 1914–1920', *International Journal of Politics, Culture and Society* 13.2 (1999): 255–71, in particular 256.

99 Knut Odner, 'New Perspectives on Veblen the Norwegian', paper originally presented at the 150th Anniversary Conference, Beitostølen, Norway, June 2007, and now part of this edited

book; April Carter, *Peace Movements: International Protest and World Politics since 1945* (Harlow: Longman, 1992).

100 Alex Danchev and John MacMillan (eds), *The Iraq War and Democratic Politics* (London: Routledge, 2005).

101 Thorstein Veblen, *The Engineers and the Price System* (New York: Harcourt, 1963), 114.

Chapter 11

VEBLEN'S 'HIGHER LEARNING': THE SCIENTIST AS SISYPHUS IN THE IRON CAGE OF A UNIVERSITY

Eyüp Özveren

And so I learned things, gentlemen. Ah, one learns when one has to; one learns when one needs a way out; one learns at all costs. One stands over oneself with a whip; one flays oneself at the slightest opposition. My ape nature fled out of me, head over heels and away, so that my first teacher was almost himself turned into ape by it, had soon to give up teaching and was taken away to a mental hospital. Fortunately he was soon let out again.

But I used up many teachers, indeed, several teachers at once. As I became more confident of my abilities, as the public took an interest in my progress and my future began to look bright, I engaged teachers for myself, established them in five communicating rooms and took lessons from them all at once by dint of leaping from one room to the other.

That progress of mine! How the rays of knowledge penetrated from all sides into my awakening brain! I do not deny it: I found it exhilarating. But I must also confess: I did not overestimate it, not even then, much less now. With an effort which up till now has never been repeated I managed to reach the cultural level of an average European. In itself that might be nothing to speak of, but it is something in so far as it has helped me out of my cage and opened a special way out for me, the way of humanity. There is an excellent idiom: to fight one's way through the thick of things; that is what I have done, I have fought through the thick of things. There was nothing else for me to do, provided always that freedom was not to be my choice.

Franz Kafka[1]

As with most literary texts that have become classics, Franz Kafka's 'A Report to an Academy' lends itself easily to several interpretations. For the sake of our discussion of the institutions of higher learning, however, it offers us a most convenient point of departure. The main character of this short story is an ape caught in the jungle of West Africa. Once placed in a cage, it is faced with a choice between freedom and imitating his new masters. The route to freedom is by escape. On the other side, once the choice is made in favour of imitating his new masters, the ape has first to observe them closely and study the way they behave so as to be able to mimic them to the point of perfection when it could actually become one of them. The ape chooses the second route. This way the ape avoids being exhibited in a zoo and instead finds his way to a variety show where his talents can be displayed. However, it must constantly improve and renew its talents in order to keep the spectators' attention, and to this effect the ape hires some private instructors and sets up a school of his own with a certain division of labour and specialisation among the teachers. Eventually, the ape is summoned to the summit of the institutions of higher learning, i.e. the academy, in order to report his own version of this uncommon progress. In this universal parody of the individual's condition in the learning process, learning is equated with imitating, or more explicitly aping, and the route to education by way of division of labour and specialisation is specified as *not* the route to freedom. It is instead described as a movement through successive cages starting with the one on the boat, followed by the cage, the stage of the variety show, onwards by way of the private school in his apartment to the highest floor of the ivory tower, the academy. There is thus a progression of cages from the most to the least obvious that corresponds with the climb up the ladder of education. The last in the line, the prestigious academy on the tip of the educational pyramid, also happens to be the one where the distinction between the performer/student and the spectators/literati is finally abolished for good, making everyone equally a prisoner of the situation, which they can no longer discern thanks to their indoctrination throughout their painfully long process of previous education.

The above epigraph from Kafka – which nevertheless does not distinguish between higher and lower learning[2] – serves as a useful pointer for a contemporary discussion of higher learning that I pursue below. The recent debate over the privatisation, reshuffling and supranational (within the European Union) as well as global standardization of higher education has attracted increasing attention for practical if not outright academic reasons.[3] The global spread of neo-liberalism, as well as the theoretical elaboration of the concepts of human capital and innovation systems, over the past few decades constitutes the two pillars of the widening debate over educational policy. It is now high time to look back at the precedents of this debate over the nature of higher learning.

Thorstein Veblen's *The Higher Learning in America* and Max Weber's seminal speech-turned-essay, 'Science as a Vocation', cast a critical light with important theoretical bearings on the turn-of-the-century structural shift and the dynamics of higher education.[4] It has already been correctly pointed out that Veblen wrote at a time when the worldwide influence of the German scheme of higher learning had already marked the orientation of better American universities.[5] He was as critical of the parochialism of the church-influenced good old American campus college committed exclusively to undergraduate instruction as he was of the intrusive challenge of the power of capital over academic institutions.[6] In a similar vein, Weber was well aware of the transatlantic influence of the American way of business-minded university administration over the German mode of higher learning when he voiced his opinions. 'In very important respects', Weber begins his account in 'Science as a Vocation', 'German university life is being Americanized'.[7] Therefore, the process described by Veblen was not restricted to the USA but was of wider relevance. What Weber had in mind was the increasing rationalisation of academic life, which trapped individual academics in something akin to an 'iron cage', an effective, rules-based system emerging from the encounter of hierarchical capitalist enterprise, on the one hand, and bureaucratic means of organisation on the other. More importantly, both Veblen and Weber were, on opposite sides of the Atlantic, equipped with a bird's eye view of the global processes at work. This chapter essentially synthesises the complementary views of Veblen and Weber by linking them with certain ideas of Joseph A. Schumpeter and Karl Polanyi, not to mention Albert Camus.[8] This broader synthesis will hopefully provide us with an institutional economic perspective on higher education that can ultimately help us to better understand the debates occupying the contemporary academic scene, as well as our own professional prospects.

The Order of Sciences

While developing his own critique of classical political economy, Karl Polanyi felt obliged to evaluate the general knowledge context of the Industrial Revolution, the origins of which overlap with Adam Smith's time. Polanyi had an important point to make:

> *Social not technical invention* was the intellectual mainspring of the Industrial Revolution. The *decisive contribution of the natural sciences* to engineering *was not made until a full century later*, when the Industrial Revolution was long over. To the practical bridge or canal builder, the designer of machines or engines, knowledge of the general laws of nature was utterly useless before the new applied sciences of mechanics and chemistry were developed [...] The *triumphs of natural science had been theoretical* in the true sense, and *could not compare in practical importance with those of the social sciences* of the day. It was to these latter that *the prestige of science as against routine and tradition* was due, and, *unbelievable though it may seem to our generation*, the standing of natural science greatly gained by its connection with the human sciences. The discovery of economics was an astounding revelation which hastened greatly the transformation of society and the establishment of a market system, while the *decisive machines had been the inventions of uneducated artisans* some of whom could hardly read or write. It was thus both just and appropriate that *not the natural but the social sciences* should rank as the intellectual parents of the mechanical revolution which subjected the powers of nature to man.[9]

According to Polanyi, there was a time when the social sciences were considered as more structurally influential on daily life, insofar as they were more able to resist routine and tradition. During that very same epoch, mechanical inventions of critical importance for the technologies of the Industrial Revolution had been stimulated not by the theoretical natural sciences hosted by the universities but by the routine and tradition of the arts and crafts that continued to prevail among the uneducated laymen.[10] Finally, Polanyi assesses those days as being essentially quite different from his and our times, and dates the origins of this paradigmatic shift to the end of the nineteenth century when the natural sciences, by way of their engineering effect, came to set the tune for scientific knowledge in general. This was the new state of things characteristic of modernity, to the rigorous investigation of which Veblen addressed himself.

According to Veblen, science '[gave] its tone to modern culture', and a 'cult of science' was already well in place by the turn of the century.[11] The advance of science and its attainment of an authoritative position in the modern civilisation was largely 'the result of the spread of machine process' characteristic of industry and its inevitable effect on the matter-of-fact scheme of knowledge:

> Since the machine technology has made great advances, during the nineteenth century, and has become a cultural force of wide-reaching consequence, the formulations of science have made another move in the direction of impersonal matter-of-fact. The machine process has displaced the workman as the archetype in whose image causation is conceived by the scientific investigators. The dramatic interpretation of natural phenomena has thereby become less anthropomorphic; it no longer constructs the life-history of a cause working to produce a given effect – after the manner of a skilled workman producing a piece of wrought goods – but it constructs the life-history of a process in which the distinction between cause and effect need scarcely be observed in an itemized and specific way, but in which the run of causation unfolds itself in an unbroken sequence of cumulative change.[12]

With this statement, Veblen indicates what he thought the relationship between technology and knowledge to be, and in so doing he incorporates Polanyi's definition of the industrial era into his own perspective as one bearing the imprint of artisanal craftsmanship. The increasingly matter-of-fact-oriented nature of knowledge derived its momentum from the impact of industry on daily life and necessitated a modern science that would go beyond a simple cause-and-effect sequence and take as its subject-matter the process of cumulative causation typical of the new era. This requirement echoes strongly Veblen's turn-of-the-century path-breaking critique of economics not yet being an evolutionary science because of the persistence in it of an 'archaic habit of thought'.[13] Whether or not science in general and economics in particular could measure up to this task is beside the point here. In tune with this overall transformation, a reversal of the order of prestige among the social and natural sciences had taken place:

> The so-called 'sciences' associated with these pragmatic disciplines, such as jurisprudence, political science, and the like, is a taxonomy of credenda. Of this character was the greater part of the 'science' cultivated by the schoolmen, and the *large remnants* of the same kind of authentic convictions are, still found among the tenets of the scientists, *particularly in the social sciences*, and no small solicitude is still given to their cultivation.[14]

Anxious to be recognised as full sciences, social sciences nevertheless remained parasitic upon the prestige of natural science. In fact, social sciences lagged behind the natural sciences by about a century, serving as a bastion of old scholastic habits.[15] However, the greatest loser of this re-ordering process would soon be the humanities, which Veblen linked with conspicuous and wasteful consumption as early as 1899:

> During the recent past some tangible changes have taken place in the scope of college and university teaching. These changes have in the main consisted in a *partial displacement of the humanities* – those branches of learning which are conceived to make for the traditional 'culture', character, tastes, and ideals – by those more matter-of-fact branches which make for civic and industrial efficiency. To put the same thing in other words, those *branches of knowledge which make for efficiency (ultimately productive efficiency) have gradually gained ground against those branches which make for a heightened consumption* or a lowered industrial efficiency and for a type of character suited to the regime of status.[16]

In this context, Veblen is most critical of the humanities' tradition which inspired an aversion to what was merely useful knowledge and consumed 'the learner's time and effort in acquiring knowledge which is of no use'.[17] He regrets that their decline in status was slowed down by the institutions of the leisure class.

The shift in the social perception of the order of sciences had further important consequences. The social scientists in general and economists in particular mimicked natural scientists and engineers, and this had important bearings on their schooling and orientation:

> Meantime, *detailed monographic and itemized inquiry, description, analysis, and appraisal of particular processes going forward in industry and business, are engaging the best attention of the economists*; instead of that meticulous reconstruction and canvassing of schematic theories that once was of great moment and that then brought comfort and assurance to its adepts and their disciples. *There is little prospect that the current generation of economists will work out a compendious system of economic theory at large.*[18]

Furthermore, within the domain of higher learning, the relative weights of the two compartments, namely scholarship and science, shifted considerably in favour of the latter at the expense of the former:

> Scholarship – that is to say an intimate and systematic familiarity with past cultural achievements – still holds its place in the scheme of learning, in spite of the unadvised efforts of the short-sighted to blend it with the work of science, for it affords play for the ancient genial propensities that ruled men's quest of knowledge before the coming of science or of the outspoken pragmatic barbarism. Its place may not be so large in proportion to the entire field of learning as it was before the scientific era got full under way.[19]

Despite their changing weights, scholarship and science were alike insofar as neither had an ulterior end other than the pursuit of knowledge for the sake of knowledge. This structural and motivational affinity between science and scholarship made them the two major elements of the modern scheme of higher learning.[20]

Veblen's 'Report' between the Lines

Veblen chose to describe the above major shift and transformation in a most disinterested scientific manner befitting his customary style. Even though science was seen as the crowning achievement of modern civilisation, the ideals of mankind were far from being caught by it: 'The ideal man, and the ideal of human life, even in the apprehension of those who most rejoice in the advances of science, is neither the *finikin skeptic* in the laboratory nor the *animated slide-rule*'.[21] Veblen was neither of the two, nor did he aspire to become either. The dark side of the above transformation was nevertheless reflected in his own words as if he were making an autobiographical statement about where the strongly passionate and rebellious Veblen himself stood within the scientific enterprise:

> The ancient human predilection for discovering a dramatic play of passion and intrigue in the phenomena of nature still asserts itself. In the most advanced communities, and *even among the adepts of modern science, there comes up persistently the revulsion of the native savage against the inhumanly dispassionate sweep of the scientific quest*, as well as against the inhumanly ruthless fabric of technological processes that have come out of this search for matter-of-fact knowledge. Very often the savage need of a spiritual interpretation (dramatization) of phenomena breaks through the crust of acquired materialistic habits of thought, to find such refuge as may be had in articles of faith seized on and held by sheer force of instinctive conviction. *Science and its creations are more or less uncanny, more or less alien, to that fashion of craving for knowledge that by ancient inheritance animates mankind.*[22]

A decade after these words were written, Veblen was realistic enough to see that, as a non-conforming scholar within the academic establishment, the most he could hope for was the tolerance of his peers:

> It is not an easy or a graceful matter for a businesslike executive to get rid of any *decorative or indecorous scientist, whose only fault is an unduly pertinacious pursuit of the work for which alone the university claims to exist*, whose failure consists in living up to the professions of the executive instead of professing to live up to them. Academic tradition gives a broad, *though perhaps uncertain*, sanction to the scientific spirit that moves this *obscure element* in the academic body. And then, their more happily gifted, more worldly-wise colleagues have also a degree of respect for such *a single-minded pursuit of knowledge*, even while they may view these naïve children of impulse *with something of an amused compassion*; for the general body of the academic staff is still made up largely of men who have started out with scholarly ideals, even though these ideals may have somewhat fallen away from them under the rub of expediency.[23]

Another decade was enough to lead the elder Veblen, in much the same spirit, to conclude his overview of the regrettable state of economics in a highly personal way by connecting it to the institutions of higher learning in the mid-1920s:

> So also the schools are turning their powers to the same purpose, in so far as they cultivate economic science. Increasingly *the faculties of economic science are taken up with instruction in business administration*, business finance, national trade, and salesmanship, with particular and growing emphasis on the last-named, the art of salesmanship and the expedients of sales-publicity. Such is the current state of academic economics, and such appears to be its promise as conditioned by the circumstances that promise to surround it in the near future. *Of course, there still stand over certain perfunctory antiquities out of the Victorian age, in the way of standard articles of economic theory, and these are given a perfunctory hearing in the schools; but that has little else than a historical interest. It is a matter of survival, not of proliferation.*[24]

It was as if he now saw himself as also one of the disillusioned academics who did not get the hearing they deserved and, in fact, as belonging to a species on the verge of extinction that strove hard to persist. In spite of it all, Veblen was no pessimist at heart because he insisted, to the very end of his career, on making himself heard by continuing to write with his 'condemning, biting, sardonic, and insightful' style.[25]

Higher Learning as the Iron Cage from Without

Veblen's academic disillusionment manifest in the above statements had deep roots in his personal experiences as an academic. Veblen made good use of his own unwritten autobiography in order to develop a thoroughly scientific analysis of higher education. As he matured, a subtle change in his approach to higher learning took place. Veblen's earliest substantial piece of writing on this theme is found in the final chapter of *The Theory of the Leisure Class*. In this piece, he treats higher learning as an adjunct to his theory of conspicuous consumption and waste. As such, his original emphasis is on the consumption side. When approached this way, he is highly critical of the wasteful nature of higher learning as far as resources were concerned:

> It is true, since conspicuous consumption has gained more and more on conspicuous leisure as a means of repute, the acquisition of the dead languages is no longer so imperative a requirement as it once was, and its talismanic value as a voucher of scholarship has suffered a concomitant impairment. But while this is true, it is also true that classics have scarcely lost in absolute value as a voucher of scholastic respectability, since for this purpose *it is only necessary that the scholar should be able to put in evidence some learning which is conventionally recognized as evidence of wasted time*; and the classics lend themselves with great facility to this use. Indeed, *there can be little doubt that it is their utility as evidence of wasted time and effort, and hence of the pecuniary strength necessary in order to afford this waste, that has secured the classics their position of prerogative in the scheme of higher learning*, and has led to their being esteemed the most honorific of all learning.[26]

In the place of this ritualistic education, he wanted to see a concern with usefulness from the viewpoint of material advance. In his later work, he would approach higher learning with an emphasis on its relevance for production and profitability. This time, he would delineate a narrow short-sighted and pecuniary-minded concern with utility as distinct from usefulness, and defend the essentially disinterested nature of the scientific enterprise, arguing that it would prove itself serviceable to the community at large in the long term. Afterwards, in addition to his articles already quoted above, he wrote *The Higher Learning in America*, which still remains unsurpassed in its own genre and provides a solid foundation, as well as a referential point of departure for any further treatment of higher education, institutional economic or otherwise.[27] Even so, there remains a connecting thread between his earliest work and this crowning achievement, insofar as the discussion of the architecture and material equipment of the institutions of higher learning from the viewpoint of the principle of conspicuous consumption and waste persists, despite being reduced in overall theoretical significance.[28] Nevertheless, Veblen himself admitted that this important book started off from his first-hand observations at the University of Chicago.[29] Be that as it may, his argument attains a level of sophistication, consistency and generality that undoes whatever element of subjectivism that plausibly may have been there in the first place.[30]

For Veblen, because scientific knowledge constitutes the apex of modern civilisation, humans approach the modern schooling system in general, and the university in particular, as the prime vehicles for further advancing it by way of scientific and scholarly inquiry and of the instruction of students.[31] Veblen defines the university as follows:

> [T]he university is a corporation of learning, *disinterested and dispassionate*. To its keeping is entrusted the community's joint interest in esoteric knowledge. *It is given over to the single-minded pursuit of science and scholarship*, without afterthought and without a view to interests subsidiary or extraneous to the higher learning. It is, indeed, *the one great institution of modern times that works to no ulterior end* and is controlled by no consideration of expediency beyond its own work.[32]

Yet this is more the definition of what a university *ought to be* rather than what it actually *is*, and, in any case, the fact that it will soon be further from what it ought to be becomes quite obvious from Veblen's discussion. According to Veblen, the university moves further from this ideal because of the imposition upon it of vested interests by way of the governing boards and the presidency. It is through this channel that the power of business penetrates into the university and shapes it after the image of a business enterprise. The most effective tools in the hands of the business interests are the governing board's control of the budget and its last say over hiring and firing of all staff members, academic or otherwise.[33] However, this business outlook is not necessarily restricted to the employment and spending policies of the university administration:

> Men dilate on the high necessity of a businesslike organization and control of the university, its equipment, personnel and routine. What is had in mind in this insistence on an efficient system is that these corporations of learning shall set their affairs in order after the pattern of a well-conducted business concern. In this view, the university is conceived as a business house dealing in merchantable knowledge,

placed under the governing hand of a captain of erudition, whose office it is to turn the means in hand to account in the largest feasible output.[34]

Therefore, with the gain motive characteristic of its outlook, business considers the university as essentially a business enterprise and seeks to re-orient the university's inner resources away from disinterested science and scholarship towards utilitarian ends.[35] On the one side, there are the academic needs of higher learning, and on the other side, the demands of business interests formulated in terms of business principles and pecuniary gain.[36] These two ends are essentially irreconcilable. As Veblen puts it, 'If the higher learning is incompatible with business shrewdness, business enterprise is, by the same token, incompatible with the spirit of higher learning'.[37] As such, the university becomes torn between two conflicting ends, tilting gradually towards the latter, but in the meantime betraying its own self-image as it does so. According to Veblen, as long as 'the community's workday material interests continue to be organized on a basis of business enterprise', this 'foolish arrangement' is bound to remain with us as the inevitable effect of the former on the structures of higher learning:[38]

> Plato's classic scheme of folly, which would have the philosophers take over the management of affairs, has been turned on its head; the men of affairs have taken over the direction of the pursuit of knowledge. To any one who will take a dispassionate look at this modern arrangement it looks foolish, of course, – ingeniously foolish, but, also, of course, there is no help for it and no prospect of its abatement in the calculable future.[39]

The reinforcement of the business yoke over the university has several dire consequences that distort the primary characteristics and objectives of a university. First of all, the penetration from outside the pecuniary mode of business conduct affects the choice and quality of the academic personnel:

> The two lines of interest – business and science – do not pull together; a competent scientist or scholar well endowed with business sense is as rare as a devout scientist – almost as rare as a white blackbird. Yet the inclusion of men of scientific gifts and attainments among its faculty is indispensable to the university, if it is to avoid instant and palpable stultification.
>
> So that the most that can practically be accomplished by a businesslike selection and surveillance of the academic personnel will be a compromise; whereby a goodly number of the faculty will be selected on grounds of businesslike fitness, more or less pronounced, while a working minority must continue to be made up of men without much business proficiency and without pronounced loyalty to commercial principles.[40]

The result of this compromise is inevitably a net reduction in the academic quality of the faculty. But this is not the sole negative effect of the commercialisation of universities. Far more importantly, commercialisation causes a structural distortion of the university.

In fact, it creates a kind of incurable obesity. In Veblen's view, a university without undergraduate departments and professional schools is quite conceivable whereas one without 'non-utilitarian higher learning' is not. In other words, in principle, the *sine qua non* of a university is the graduate school.[41] In practice, however, because the business logic gives primacy to marketable education and output, the undergraduate programs, as well as vocational training, have expanded considerably in size and have thereby gained precedence at the expense of the graduate programs. The distortion comes not only in the relative importance and shares of these constituent units of the university but also with the more subtle process of homogenisation that pervades all divisions of the university and imposes a most unfitting straightjacket on the graduate school:

> The businesslike order and system introduced into the universities, therefore, are designed primarily to meet the needs and exploit the possibilities of the undergraduate school; but, by force of habit, by a desire of uniformity, by a desire to control and exhibit the personnel and their work, by heedless imitation, or what not, it invariably happens to the same scheme of order and system is extended to cover the graduate work also.[42]

Although far from complete, Veblen sees this process nevertheless as unfolding according to its own logic and anticipates a bleak outcome:

> The advanced work falls under the same stress of competition in magnitude and visible success; and the same scheme of enforced statistical credits will gradually insinuate itself into the work for the advanced degrees; so that these as well as the lower degrees will come to be conferred on the piece-work plan.[43]

Thus the university, at odds with its ideal definition, betrays its founding principles and becomes practically a generalised undergraduate college because its inner rhythm is increasingly dictated by the latter:

> [I]t comes about that the college in great measure sets the pace for the whole, and that the undergraduate scheme of credits, detailed accountancy, and mechanical segmentation of the work, is carried over into the university work proper.[44]

This amounts to no less than remodelling the graduate division, i.e. higher learning proper, after the undergraduate division that 'puts a premium on mediocrity and perfunctory work' and caters degrees to students who esteem 'an honourable discharge' higher than their 'love of knowledge'.[45] This is the sad story of how a 'republic of learning' degenerates in the hands of the 'unlettered' business community.[46]

Veblen has retrospectively been criticised for overemphasising the influence of business on institutions of higher learning, and especially for making a universal trend out of a specific tendency among the private American universities of his time.[47] In retrospect, we can say that the penetration of business into the university was not restricted to the appointment of presidents and governing board members but was a matter of mentality that still spreads in fits and starts. Moreover, while Veblen told the specific story of the intrusion of business as an outside force into the university, what was important for him was to recognise how this process diverts the university from the pursuit of long-term goals to a myopic concern with short-term usefulness. This is a more general diagnosis and applies equally well when the external 'yoke' comes not from business interests but from governments, or local communities that provide public funds in return for extracting short-term services or benefit from these institutions of higher learning that fall prey to their utilitarian ends. In any case, the contemporary university is placed within a field of force, the two poles of which are the market and the state, with the state yielding to the primacy of market, if not actively engineering it in favour of the principles that Veblen had emphasised.[48]

Put differently, this is the description of the process of devaluation of the university as the ultimate institution of higher learning. According to Veblen, 'the business regime' imposed upon the university from without corrupts it and subjects it to an irreversible process of devaluation.[49] Given this downward trend, Veblen observes a tendency to counter it by attempting to upgrade higher learning by designing new institutions. In the institution of the fellowship, Veblen identifies one such institution that 'acquired a use not originally intended',[50] thereby ultimately losing its meaning and value:

> At its inception the purpose of these fellowships was to encourage the best talent among the students to pursue disinterested advanced study farther and with the greater singleness of purpose and it is quite plain that at that stage of its growth the system was conceived to have no bearing on intercollegiate competition or the statistics of registration.[51]

As the undergraduate school lost its value and corrupted the graduate school by its influence, Veblen sees attempts at creating still 'higher' institutions of learning such as the 'extra-academic foundations for research' (of which the Carnegie Institution was one example) as proofs of the failure of the university system:[52]

> So it is that, with a sanguine hope born of academic defeat, there have latterly been founded certain large establishments, of the nature of retreats or shelters for the prosecution of scientific and scholarly inquiry in some sort of academic quarantine, detached from all academic affiliation and renouncing all share in the work of instruction [...] This move looks like a desperate surrender of the university ideal. The reason for it appears to be the proven inability of the schools, under competitive management, to take care of the pursuit of knowledge.[53]

Veblen thought this was only a second-best solution that could in no way compensate for the losses that resulted from the devaluation of the university. In these highly artificial quarantine environments where instruction did not take place, a major limitation was sooner or later bound to make itself felt and distort the direction of the scientific body of knowledge:

> Only in the most exceptional, not to say erratic, cases will good, consistent, sane and alert scientific work be carried forward through a course of years by any

scientist without students, without loss or blunting of the intellectual initiative that makes the creative scientist. The work that can be done well in the absence of that stimulus and safeguarding that comes of the give and take between teacher and student is commonly such as can without deterioration be reduced to a mechanically systematized task-work, – that is to say, such as can, without loss or gain, be carried on under the auspices of a businesslike academic government.[54]

In spite of the warning note, organised research was gradually divorced from the teaching faculty and students and shifted deliberately to off-campus buildings as the exclusive privilege of a separate 'research faculty'.[55] Be that as it may, this double movement consisting of a constant devaluation of degrees[56] and a counter-tendency of upgrading higher learning through the creation of upper-echelon institutions has been going on for about a century since Veblen wrote these lines. Whereas the graduate school was considered a novelty to compensate for the insufficiency of college education at the turn of the previous century as a result of which the US doctorate degree became increasingly a universal standard, we now have numerous *post*graduate programs under the tutelage of overarching research foundations. In the meantime, R&D activities have increasingly been dissociated from the institutions of higher learning in favour of industry and government agencies.[57] Time has proven Veblen right as far as his identification of this primary evolutionary trajectory of the institutions of higher learning is concerned.

Higher Learning as the Iron Cage from Within

Veblen has been much misunderstood and unfairly criticised for a variety of reasons, only one of which is overemphasising the role in higher learning of research motivated by the quest for science for the sake of science at the expense of instruction.[58] As we readily see from the last quotation, Veblen insisted that a certain level of instruction was a condition of existence not only for the institution of higher learning at large but also for the continuation of academic research per se. In Veblen's mind, faculty–student relationships ought ideally to follow the example of a master–apprentice relationship. The emphasis Veblen puts on the stimulating yet safeguarding effects of the give and take between faculty and students indicates the necessity of a 'disciplining' force within the academic establishment. Although Veblen did not spell it out, what is at work here is also an inter-generational process which we might as well call an inter-generational competition. This competition is by no means unbound, but rather contained within certain institutional parameters that entail a cooperative dimension insofar as the exclusive virtues of the two rivalling generations complement as well as compete with one another. Whereas the elder generation possesses a mastery of the established professional habits of thought together with wisdom that comes with age and experience, the younger generation, as yet unburdened with the conventions of the discipline, brings a freshness and flexibility of outlook conducive to risk-taking and novelty.[59] Therefore, in the above quotation from Veblen we can identify a window of opportunity for incorporating a positive effect of competition into his analytical scheme. This is important because Veblen appears hostile to competition, at least when it is either among the multiple institutions of higher learning or within the numerous departments and programs of a single university. Veblen notes that inter-university competition is modelled after the inter-enterprise competitive system under the impact of the business principle of pecuniary gain:

> It is one of the unwritten, and commonly unspoken, commonplaces lying at the root of modern academic policy that the various universities are *competitors for the traffic in merchantable instruction*, in much the same fashion as rival establishments in the retail trade compete for custom.[60]

Furthermore, competition is contagious and pervasive as it inevitably spreads also within the very same university in question:

> So the chief of bureau, with the aid and concurrence of his loyal staff, will aim to offer as extensive and varied a range of instruction as the field assigned his department will admit. Out of this *competitive aggrandizement of departments* there may even arise a diplomatic contention between heads of departments, as to the precise frontiers between their respective domains; each being ambitious to magnify his office and acquire merit by including much of the field and many of the students under his dominion.[61]

Veblen assesses competition as the greatest obstacle in the way of the American system of higher learning: 'This competitive parcelment, duplication and surreptitious thrift, due to a businesslike rivalry between the several schools, is perhaps the gravest drawback to the American university situation'.[62] Resentful of both inter-university and intra-university competition, Veblen accuses competition of essentially being wasteful of resources the full potential of which could be realised if only cooperation and coordination could replace it:

> As is well known, there prevails today an extensive and wasteful competitive duplication of plant, organization and personnel among American universities, as regards both publications and courses of instruction. Particularly is this true in respect of that advanced work of the universities that has to do with the higher learning. At the same time, these universities are now pinched for funds, due to the current inflation of prices. So that any proposal of this nature, which might be taken advantage of as an occasion for the pooling of common issues among the universities, might hopefully be expected to be welcomed as a measure of present relief from some part of the pecuniary strain under which they are now working.[63]

In light of our interpretation concerning inter-generational competition, we can infer that Veblen may have been more receptive to competition in certain domains than in others, rather than rejecting it in principle. As a matter of fact, the German university that served as a model for Veblen as well as most of his contemporaries had also been characterised by a very specific type of institutionalised competition. The central 'institution of the *Privatdozent*' facing the 'incorruptible jury of fee-paying German students' secured that selection through competition would ensure a dynamic process of improvement for the universities:[64]

> The introduction of universal enrollment fees on the French model, however, and the abolition of individual lecture fees paid in accordance with the law of supply and demand threatened to bring about not only the decline of the German university but also the decay of the sciences, *whose progress was guaranteed by, among other things, the institution of the Privatdozent.* For the *Privatdozent* was debarred from teaching in any branch of study to which the professor for the time being himself laid claim – rivalry was prevented if only because it would lead to a ruinous competition for lecture fees. *Thus, because they were obliged to compete with one another but forbidden to compete with the professors, the Privatdozenten were compelled to develop new ways of asking questions, new specialties, indeed even new disciplines, and their need to survive economically became a gurantee* [*sic*] *of scientific innovation.*[65]

Hence an original mix of competition with regulation had, at the back of Veblen's mind, been the key to the success of German institutions of higher learning.

Creating room for some kind of competition in Veblen's analytical framework is important because we need to specify a kind of mechanism that helps explain the tendency for change from within universities. This is because universities are institutions of higher learning and like every other institution they possess a certain rigidity and resistance to change. Unless we specify an internal prime cause for such change, we would be left to assume that the institutions of higher learning could only change from without due to those external factors that impact upon them through penetration. The business yoke imposed upon the higher learning was one such major external factor. It was also the most recent one. As evident from Schumpeter's following description, universities tended to resist rather than catalyse change in much the same fashion at an earlier turning-point in history:

> It is highly significant that modern mathematico-experimental science developed, in the fifteenth, sixteenth and seventeenth centuries, not only along with the social process usually referred to as the Rise of Capitalism, but also *outside the fortress of scholastic thought and in the face of its contemptuous hostility.* In the fifteenth century mathematics was mainly concerned with questions of commercial arithmetic and the problems of the architect. The utilitarian mechanical device, invented by men of the craftsman type, stood at the source of modern physics [...] The *artist who at the same time was an engineer and an entrepreneur* – the type immortalized by such men as Vinci, Alberti, Cellini; even Dürer busied himself with plans for fortifications – illustrates best of all what I mean. *By cursing it all, scholastic professors in the Italian universities showed more sense than we give them credit for. The trouble was not with individual unorthodox propositions. Any decent schoolman could be trusted to twist his texts so as to fit the Copernican system. But those professors quite rightly sensed the spirit behind such exploits* – the spirit of rationalist individualism, the spirit generated by rising capitalism.[66]

As this description attests to, the university as an institution has been quite change-resistant, and in that particular instance, had to be revolutionised from without. Veblen was also well aware of this fact. In his earliest work on higher learning, in the context of his theory of the leisure class, he claimed:

> On this head, it is well known that the accredited seminaries of learning have, until a recent date, held a conservative position. *They have taken an attitude of deprecation towards all innovations. As a general rule a new point of view or a new formulation of knowledge have been countenanced and taken up within the schools only after these new things have made their way outside of the schools.* As exceptions from this rule are chiefly to be mentioned innovations of an inconspicuous kind and departures which do not bear in any tangible way upon the conventional point of view or upon the conventional scheme of life; as, for instance, details of fact in the mathematico-physical sciences, and new readings and interpretations of the classics, especially such as have a philological or literary bearing only. Except within the domain of the 'humanities', in the narrow sense, and except so far as the traditional point of view of the humanities has been left intact by the innovators, it has generally held true that *the accredited learned class and the seminaries of the higher learning have looked askance at all innovation.* New views, new departures in scientific theory, especially new departures which touch the theory of human relations at any point, *have found a place in the scheme of the university tardily and by a reluctant tolerance,* rather than by a cordial welcome; and the men who have occupied themselves with such efforts to widen the scope of human knowledge *have not commonly been well received by their learned contemporaries.* The higher schools have not commonly given their countenances to a serious advance in the methods or the content of knowledge *until the innovations have outlived their youth and much of their usefulness* – after they have become commonplaces of the intellectual furniture of a new generation which has grown up under, and has had its habits of thought shaped by, the new, extra-scholastic body of knowledge and the new standpoint.[67]

In spite of the change-resistant nature of a university as an institution and the business yoke which distorted it under the weight of vested interests, Veblen nevertheless identified a certain inner dynamics that accounted – at least in part – for its functioning. The very existence of such dynamics makes higher learning – illuminated as it is by the 'dry light of science' from within[68] – all the more an 'iron cage', which Weber associates in a resonant manner with the 'disenchantment of the world' and the 'polar night of icy darkness'.[69] Whereas Veblen thinks that the 'instinct of workmanship' by way of habit formation contributed to the formation and growth of the corpus of knowledge in general after the image of the material conditions of daily life, the 'instinct of idle curiosity' was for him active within the particular domain of higher learning that constitutes the tip of the pyramid of scientific knowledge:

> In so far as it may fairly be accounted esoteric knowledge, or a 'higher learning', all this enterprise is actuated by an idle curiosity, a disinterested proclivity to gain a knowledge of things and to reduce this knowledge to a comprehensible system.

The objective end is a theoretical organization, a logical articulation of things known, the lines of which must not be deflected by any consideration of expediency or convenience, but must run true to the canons of reality accepted at the time.[70]

In Veblen's view, 'the university is after all a seat of learning, devoted to the *cult of idle curiosity*, – otherwise called the scientific spirit'.[71] In short, what makes a university is the central role idle curiosity occupies in it. Moreover, not only does idle curiosity make a university, it also makes it move. Idle curiosity is the 'animus' of higher learning.[72] It animates the quest for knowledge for the sake of knowledge; it is the principal *modus operandi* of higher learning. Veblen takes great pains to avoid a misunderstanding that could originate from the use of 'idle' as an adjective in this phrase. One could plausibly be misled to think that a curiosity of the idle type could work occasionally, i.e. only from time to time, and thereby display a *discrete* pattern. This, for Veblen, is far from being the meaning intended. The 'idleness' in question implies a search for knowledge independently of 'any ulterior use of the knowledge so gained';[73] neither is idle curiosity 'idle' in any other sense than that it is extra-economic, not without derogation to be classed as a gainful pursuit.[74] In short, it is 'idle' as far as the practical gainful employment of its subject-matter is concerned. Otherwise it is a *continuous* activity that has to do with the human quest for knowledge for the sake of knowledge, as a result of which one periodically hits upon new ways of thought and doing things.

In retrospect, we can identify the role attributed to 'instincts' as the one theoretical element in Veblen's scheme of analysis that could not pass the test of time in the medium term. The concept had its fall from grace into a state of century-long social scientific 'taboo' as early as with the replacement by behaviourism of the 'instinct-habit psychology', only to experience a gradual revival more recently.[75] To this day, instincts have remained the Achilles' heel in Veblen's theoretical scheme. However, we can circumvent some of the difficulties associated with them by saying that Veblen's specification of the consequences of 'idle curiosity' as a pattern of behaviour remains convincing, irrespective of whether it results from nature or nurture.[76] We can then take the next step to elaborate how this process works.

The Scientist as Sisyphus?

In 1918, the same year as Veblen's *The Higher Learning in America* came out, Weber delivered a speech entitled 'Science as a Vocation' at Munich University, published the following year. In it, Weber reflects upon his lifelong experience as an academic, distilling from it a certain vision of science and higher learning in much the same way as Veblen. Like Veblen, Weber also emphasises the behavioural characteristic of the scientist as essentially disinterested in the practical consequences of his undertaking. For Weber, too, the scientist 'engages in "science for science's sake" and not merely because others, by exploiting science, bring about commercial and technical success and can better feed, dress, illuminate, and govern'.[77] In a way reminiscent of Veblen, Weber compares the status of the academic who held fast to his personal library to the artisan of the past who had been trapped in the whirlpool of capitalism and rationalisation only to be dispossessed of his tools of trade and his independence.[78] Science cultivated further rationalisation of all enterprises, academic or otherwise, and the university was caught in the process of an ever-expanding specialisation. Once '[s]cientific work is chained to the course of progress',[79] a certain dynamics of the scientific activity becomes manifest:

> In science, each of us knows that what he has accomplished will be antiquated in ten, twenty, fifty years. That is the fate to which science is subjected; it is the very meaning of scientific work, to which it is devoted in a quite specific sense, as compared with other spheres of culture for which in general the same holds. *Every scientific 'fulfillment' raises new 'questions'; it asks to be 'surpassed' and outdated. Whoever wishes to serve science has to resign himself to this fact.* Scientific works certainly can last as 'gratifications' because of their artistic quality, or they may remain as a means of training. *Yet they will be surpassed scientifically – let that be repeated – for it is our common fate and, more, our common goal.* We cannot work without hoping that others will advance further than we have. In principle, this progress goes on ad infinitum. And with this we come to inquire the meaning of science. *For after all, it is not self-evident that something subordinate to such a law is sensible and meaningful in itself. Why does one engage in doing something that in reality never comes, and never can come, to an end?*[80]

With this statement Weber provides us with the best elaboration to this day of the process-view of scientific activity from within that surpasses anything Veblen accomplished. Yet Weber falls short of giving an equally convincing and straightforward answer to the paradox he raises at the end of the paragraph. This relates to the fact that this is the truth, but not the whole truth.

To understand better what is missing from this picture, it may be worthwhile to take a detour and to relate this process-view of scientific activity with another similar process-view of a more fundamental economic mechanism, i.e. the entrepreneurial process as the motor-force of capitalism aimed towards perpetual 'creative destruction' working in fits and starts from within the domain of economic life.[81] According to Schumpeter, the quest for novelty by way of innovation is the *modus operandi* of the entrepreneur and is rewarded with an entrepreneurial profit. Schumpeter views the entrepreneur as a leader in a special sense, insofar as he opens up new ground with his innovation, by blazing the trail and creating a model for his followers,[82] only to be imitated by them who will gradually undermine his essentially monopolistic 'entrepreneurial' profits and reduce him to the ultimate status of one among the many:

> [The entrepreneur] also leads in the sense that he draws other producers in his branch after him. But as they are his competitors, who first reduce and then annihilate his profit, this is, as it were, leadership against one's own will.[83]

Bound to become one among the many at the end, the entrepreneur is nevertheless far from being the *homo economicus* incarnate. Unlike his rivals who merely imitate him, he is motivated, first of all, by 'the dream and the will to found a private kingdom, usually, though not necessarily, also a dynasty'. In addition, he possesses the 'the will to conquer: the impulse to fight, to prove oneself superior to others, to succeed for the sake, not of the fruits of success, but of success itself'. Last but not least, 'there is the joy of creating, getting things done, or simply of exercising one's energy and ingenuity'.[84] It goes without saying that Schumpeter's characterisation of the entrepreneur has much in common with Veblen's and Weber's scientist. In much the same way, Weber's description of the process of scientific activity is similar to Schumpeter's definition of the entrepreneurial competition. And, while discussing the psyche of the businessman, Schumpeter himself draws a parallel between the domains of science and business. This parallelism should come as no surprise to us, as 'entrepreneurship' is a concept that has to do with creativity in general, irrespective of the domain concerned: [85]

> It is not only objectively more difficult to do something new than what is familiar and tested by experience, but the individual feels reluctance to it and would do so even if the objective difficulties did not exist. *This is so in all fields. The history of science is one great confirmation of the fact that we find it exceedingly difficult to adopt a new scientific point of view or method.* Thought turns again and again into the *accustomed track* even if it has become unsuitable and the more suitable *innovation in itself presents no particular difficulties.* The very nature of *fixed habits of thinking, their energy-saving function,* is founded upon the fact that they have become subconscious, that they yield results automatically and are proof against criticism and even against contradiction by individual facts. But precisely because of this they become *drag-chains when they have outlived their usefulness. So it is also in the economic world.* In the breast of one who wishes to do something new, the *forces of habit rise up and bear witness against the embryonic project. A new and another kind of effort of will is therefore necessary* in order to wrest, amidst the work and care of the daily round, scope and time for conceiving and working out the new combination and to bring oneself to look upon it as a real possibility and not merely as a day-dream. This *mental freedom* presupposes a great surplus force over the everyday demand and is *something peculiar and by nature rare.*[86]

Notwithstanding the similarity of the dynamic descriptions of scientific and entrepreneurial activities, there remains an important difference, since 'positive' entrepreneurial profits are conspicuously absent in the former. In light of this fact, we are faced with an entrepreneurial competition *minus* the entrepreneurial profits. This may now seem to us as an oxymoron because we have arrived at this point by way of Schumpeter. For Schumpeter, who started off from Léon Walras only to arrive at his own theory of economic development as a dynamic process, this looked more like a riddle to be solved. Because Walras had concentrated his analysis on what Schumpeter calls the 'circular flow of economic life', which repeated itself from one year to the next, and more specifically on the snapshot of the state of general equilibrium under the assumption of perfect competition, he was forced to depict an entrepreneur who made neither profits nor loss, or in Schumpeter's own words, an entrepreneur who 'simply does not exist'.[87] It was paradoxical that the entrepreneur was a *sine qua non* to bring the economy to a state of general equilibrium in the model; yet because no out-of-equilibrium trading was allowed in the Walrasian auction markets he remained unrewarded for his specific contribution in the very same model. This economic agent who helps move the economy to equilibrium just for nothing has been appropriately termed as the 'Sisyphus entrepreneur'.[88] With the paradox of the 'Sisyphus entrepreneur' it creates, the above incomplete description of the economy by Walras actually approximates, better than that of Schumpeter,[89] Weber's specification of the scientific dynamics that gives rise to the equally paradoxical question of why anyone would participate in such a process.

In discussing monopoly, Schumpeter noted that competition in the wider sense of the term (covering not only price competition but also product and technological competition) as an 'ever-present threat' due to the potential entry of competitors into the business in question, disciplined the monopoly and forced it to behave as if it were actually in a competitive situation in the long term.[90] In other words, the monopolist competed against the potential rival. With this statement, Schumpeter took one further step in the right direction for squaring off the agency behaviour involved in the scientific enterprise. However, he stopped short of fully realising it. The scientist in Weber's or Veblen's scheme of higher learning does not only compete with his potential rival who might enter the scene at any moment, but more importantly with himself. Whether this is for the sake of social recognition or approbation, *pace* Polanyi, or for self-fulfilment, *pace* Veblen, is beside the point. Like Sisyphus, the scientist competes with himself in a fruitless labour even though he knows in advance that his endeavours will be in vain. By admitting the possibility of an inter-generational competition in addition to his insistence on the importance of an idly curious inner drive, Veblen came very close to hitting upon this deeper meaning of a self-centred competition as the *modus operandi* of the scientific enterprise. Even if he did not quite articulate this concept in his theory of higher learning, he certainly, in real life as an academic, struggled against all odds to outperform himself under increasingly less favourable institutional circumstances.

I began this essay with an epigraph from Kafka, which I used in order to trace all types of learning back to the principle of opting out of freedom for the sake of a progression through a series of cages that became increasingly invisible yet all the more confining. I might as well end here with a quotation from Albert Camus, hinting at how we can rediscover from within the most invisible cage the one freedom we are left with; that is, the right to resist. This lesson Camus illustrated by recourse to the mythological figure of Sisyphus would be all the more obvious to us if only we knew how to interpret the meaning of Veblen's own lifelong struggle against all odds within the academic establishment:

But Sisyphus teaches the higher fidelity that negates the gods and raises the rocks. *He too concludes that all is well.* This universe henceforth without a master seems to him neither sterile nor futile. Each atom of that stone, each mineral flake of that night-filled mountain, in itself forms a world. The struggle itself toward the heights is enough to fill a man's heart. One must imagine Sisyphus happy.[91]

Notes and References

1 Franz Kafka, 'A Report to an Academy', in Franz Kafka, *Wedding Preparations in the Country and Other Stories*, trans. by Willa and Edwin Muir (Harmondsworth: Penguin Books, 1978), 154–5.
2 Kafka made the distinction between higher and lower learning elsewhere. In another story named 'The Great Wall of China', posthumously published but written the very same year in

which he wrote 'A Report to the Academy', Kafka had this further elaboration to make: 'Now one of the most obscure of our institutions is that of the empire itself: In Peking, naturally, at the imperial court, there is some clarity to be found on this subject, though even that is more illusive than real. Also the teachers of political law and history in the schools of higher learning claim to be exactly informed on these matters and to be capable of passing on their knowledge to their students. The farther one descends among the lower schools the more, naturally enough, does one find teachers' and pupils' doubts of their own knowledge vanishing and superficial culture mounting sky-high around a few precepts that have been drilled into people's minds for centuries, precepts which, though they have lost nothing of their eternal truth, remain eternally invisible in this fog of confusion'. See Franz Kafka, 'The Great Wall of China', in Franz Kafka, *The Complete Stories*, trans. by Tania and James Stern (New York: Schocken Books, 1972), 242.

3   On the one hand, the American system of higher education, which has served as a model since the Second World War for an increasing number of countries, has itself been showing signs of deterioration. See Richard H. Hersh and John Merrow (eds), *Declining by Degrees: Higher Education at Risk* (New York: Palgrave Macmillan, 2005). On the other hand, the attempts to create a rival European system of higher education by 2010 via the Bologna Process have intensified such worries about the quality and competitiveness of the American system. As for the theoretical side of the question, see Pierre Bourdieu, *Homo Academicus* (Stanford: Stanford University, 1988); Immanuel Wallerstein et al., *Open the Social Sciences, Report of the Gulbenkian Commission on the Restructuring of the Social Sciences* (Stanford: Stanford University Press, 1996); Tony Becher and Paul R. Trowler, *Academic Tribes and Territories: Intellectual Enquiry and the Culture of Disciplines* (Buckingham: The Society for Research into Higher Education & Open University Press, 2001); Jürgen Enders (ed.), *Academic Staff in Europe: Changing Contexts and Conditions* (Westport: Greenwood, 2001).

4   In the beginning it was, not surprisingly, once again, Adam Smith who wrote critically about the leading universities of his time in his *Wealth of Nations: The Production and Distribution of Knowledge in the United States* (1776). His theoretical insights have unfortunately been overlooked, perhaps because of the sarcasm in which they were clothed.

5   Wolf Lepenies, 'The Direction of the Disciplines: The Future of the Universities', *Comparative Criticism* 11 (1989): 51.

6   Veblen was a vociferous critic of the once dominant religious yoke over higher education. This was because the autonomy of the university was won within the context of the struggle for the separation of the church and the state. See Alvin W. Gouldner, *The Dialectic of Ideology and Technology* (New York: The Seabury Press, 1976), 188; Paul Woodring, *The Higher Learning in America: A Reassessment* (New York: McGraw-Hill, 1968), 12.

7   Max Weber, 'Science as a Vocation', in *From Max Weber: Essays in Sociology*, ed. by H. H. Gerth and C. Wright Mills (London: Routledge, 1991), 131.

8   To some extent Veblen stood as a loner in the American scene because of the scope of his vision and the range of his thematic interests. Recent attempts to situate Veblen's thought and intellectual formation within the broader European milieu of his times demonstrate that Veblen had indeed at least one foot in Europe as far as his standing as a transdisciplinary social philosopher is concerned. See Stjepan G. Mestrovic, *The Barbarian Temperament: Toward a Postmodern Critical Theory* (Routledge: New York, 1993); Rick Tilman, 'Thorstein Veblen and Western Thought *Fin de Siècle*: A Recent Interpretation', *Journal of Economic Issues* 36.1 (2002): 107–29.

9   Karl Polanyi, *The Great Transformation: The Political and Economic Origins of Our Time* (Boston: Beacon Press, 1944), 119; emphases added.

10 The same view has been confirmed much later by a prominent authority on the 'two cultures' of academia: 'The academics had nothing to do with the industrial revolution, as Corrie, the old Master of Jesus, said about trains running into Cambridge on Sunday, "It is equally displeasing to God and to myself". So far as there was any thinking in nineteenth-century industry, it was

left to cranks and clever workmen'. See C. P. Snow, *The Two Cultures* (Cambridge: Cambridge University Press, 1993), 23–4. The modest role of science in the 'development' stage of basic inventions has also been acknowledged by another authority, Mokyr, who nevertheless rightly puts great emphasis on the importance of what he calls 'Industrial Enlightenment' that coincided with a major reduction in 'access costs' to knowledge and the historic narrowing of the gap between promoters of scientific knowledge and those engaged in applying it to production. See Joel Mokyr, *The Gifts of Athena: Historical Origins of the Knowledge Economy* (Princeton: Princeton University Press, 2002), 48, 65.

11 Thorstein Veblen, 'The Place of Science in Modern Civilization', *American Journal of Sociology* 11.5 (1906): 585–609, esp. 608.

12 Veblen, 'Place of Science', 597.

13 Thorstein Veblen, 'Why is Economics not an Evolutionary Science?', *Cambridge Journal of Economics* 22.4 (1998): 403–14, esp. 406.

14 Veblen, 'Place of Science', 601; emphases added.

15 Thorstein Veblen, *The Higher Learning in America: A Memorandum on the Conduct of Universities by Business Men* (New York: Augustus M. Kelley, 1918), 189.

16 Thorstein Veblen, *The Theory of the Leisure Class: An Economic Study of Institutions* (New York: Mentor, 1953), 251–2; emphases added.

17 Ibid., 254.

18 Thorstein Veblen, 'Economic Theory in the Calculable Future', *American Economic Review* 15.1 (1925): 48–55, esp. 51; emphasis added.

19 Veblen, 'Place of Science', 607.

20 For the sake of brevity, we will collapse the two concepts and adopt the usage of 'science' as the equivalent of German '*Wissenschaft*' indicating 'any systematic body of enquiry' (Snow, *The Two Cultures*, l–li) and refer to any academic as a 'scientist', while being fully aware that especially people like Veblen and Weber were in fact scholars when the narrower meaning of 'science' is deployed. Moreover, Weber's distinction between the 'cultivated man' and the 'specialist' overlaps with Veblen's. See Max Weber, *Economy and Society* (Berkeley: University of California Press, 1978), 1001–2.

21 Veblen, 'The Place of Science', 609; emphases added.

22 Ibid., 605–6; emphases added.

23 Veblen, *Higher Learning*, 173; emphases added.

24 Veblen, 'Economic Theory', 55; emphases added.

25 E. K. Hunt, *History of Economic Thought: A Critical Perspective* (Belmont: Wadsworth, 1979), 327.

26 Veblen, *Leisure Class*, 255–6; emphases added.

27 This genealogical connection is so strong as to reflect itself even in the titles of some of the subsequent works. See, for example, Robert Maynard Hutchins, *Higher Learning in America* (New Haven: Yale University Press, 1936); Woodring, *The Higher Learning*. A recent study that has attracted much attention, while not adopting the title of Veblen's work outright, nevertheless starts off with an epigraph from this trendsetting book and engages in a dialogue with Veblen in order to introduce the theme of commercialization of American higher education. See Derek Bok, *Universities in the Marketplace: The Commercialization of Higher Education* (Princeton: Princeton University Press, 2003), 1, 4. In contrast, the central importance of Veblen's work in this field remains largely unrecognised in Europe.

28 Veblen, *Higher Learning*, 135–47.

29 Ibid., v–vi.

30 Even so, the book had hit its target well as it aroused much hostility, including that of Nicholas Murray Butler, the one time president of Columbia University 'who instigated the vilification of Veblen for writing *The Higher Learning in America*'; Rick Tilman, *Thorstein Veblen and His Critics, 1891–1963* (Princeton: Princeton University Press, 1992), 102.

31 Veblen, *Higher Learning*, 15–6.

32 Ibid., 59; emphases added.

33 Ibid., 80–81.

34 Ibid., 85.

35 Ibid., 31.

36 Ibid., 48.

37 Ibid., 75.

38 Ibid., 78.

39 Ibid., 77–8.

40 Ibid., 149–50.

41 Ibid., 41.

42 Ibid., 100.

43 Ibid., 127.

44 Ibid., 108.

45 Ibid., 104–5.

46 Ibid., 84, 144.

47 Woodring, *Higher Learning*, 146.

48 Enders, *Academic Staff*, 4–6; Becher and Trowler, *Academic Tribes*, 166.

49 Veblen, *Higher Learning*, 119.

50 Ibid., 131.

51 Ibid., 130.

52 Ibid., 55.

53 Ibid., 272.

54 Ibid., 273.

55 Fritz Machlup, *The Production and Distribution of Knowledge in the United States* (Princeton: Princeton University Press, 1962), 83.

56 When contemporary critics (Enders, *Academic Staff*, 1–2) speak of the 'decline, erosion, and deprofessionalization' of the academic profession as well as a pervasive 'feeling of impoverishment', they provide us with further evidence of this devaluation dynamics.

57 Machlup, *The Production and Distribution of Knowledge*, 145.

58 Woodring, *Higher Learning*, x–xi.

59 The idea of an inter-generational rift occupied Veblen's mind so much that it became manifest once again in his discussion of the then present state of economics and economists in his 1925 article: 'Therefore any distinctive or peculiar traits to be looked for in the science, in the way of scope and method, in the range of its inquiry and the drift and bias of its guiding interest, its logic and its data, will be due to arise out of those characteristic habits of thought that are induced in the incoming generation of economists in the course of that habituation to which they will have been exposed during the period of their growth and adolescence and during those marginal years of waning flexibility that make up the initial phase of adult life' (Veblen, 'Economic Theory', 48).

60 Veblen, *Higher Learning*, 89; emphasis added.

61 Ibid., 113; emphasis added.

62 Ibid., 232.

63 Ibid., 54–5. In much the same way as Veblen envisaged, the current Bologna process is designed to steer the European institutions of higher learning through the rough seas of international competition by way of cooperation *and* (not *or* as Veblen emphasises!) competition at the European level.

64 Lepenies, 'The Direction of the Disciplines', 53.

65 Ibid., 53–4; emphases added.

66 Joseph A. Schumpeter, *Capitalism, Socialism and Democracy* (New York: Harper, 1942), 124; emphases added.

67 Veblen, *Leisure Class*, 245–6.

68 Veblen, *Higher Learning*, 7.

69 Max Weber, 'Science as a Vocation', in *From Max Weber: Essays in Sociology*, ed. by H. H. Gerth and C. Wright Mills (London: Routledge, 1991), 155; Max Weber, 'Politics as a Vocation', in *From Max Weber: Essays in Sociology*, ed. by H. H. Gerth and C. Wright Mills (London: Routledge, 1991), 128.

70 Veblen, *Higher Learning*, 8.

71 Ibid., 176; emphasis added.

72 Ibid., 75.

73 Ibid., 5.

74 Ibid., 117.

75 Geoffrey M. Hodgson, *The Evolution of Institutional Economics: Agency, Structure and Darwinism in American Institutionalism* (London: Routledge, 2004), 39, 162–7, 265–72, 347, 401–3.

76 The possibility of learned habits brings us very close to the fashionable concept of 'habitus' used by Bourdieu to characterise the *homo academicus* (Bourdieu, *Homo Academicus*).

77 Weber, 'Science as a Vocation', 138.

78 Weber carried the analogy further by recourse to the alternative process of rationalisation by way of bureaucratisation: 'In the field of scientific research and instruction, the bureaucratization of the inevitable research institutes of the universities is also a function of the increasing demand for material means of operation. Liebig's laboratory at Giessen University was the first example of big enterprise in this field. Through the concentration of such means in the hands of the privileged head of the institute the mass of researchers and instructors are separated from their "means of production", in the same way as the workers are separated from theirs by the capitalist enterprises' (Weber, *Economy and Society*, 983).

79 Weber, 'Science as Vocation', 137.

80 Ibid., 138; emphases added.

81 Schumpeter, *Capitalism*, 82–4.

82 Schumpeter, *The Theory of Economic Development* (New Brunswick: Transaction Publishers, 1983), 133.

83 Ibid., 89.

84 Ibid., 93.

85 Alvin Gouldner also refers to the 'early ideologues' of the critical era prior to the expansion of the universities as 'intellectual entrepreneurs' (*Dialectic*, 181); Daniel Hjorth, 'In the Tribe of Sisyphus: Rethinking Management Education from an 'Entrepreneurial' Perspective', *Journal of Management Education* 27.6 (2003): 637–53, esp. 646–8.

86 Schumpeter, *Economic Development*, 86; emphases added.

87 Ibid., 76.

88 Ernesto Screpanti and Stefano Zamagni, *An Outline of the History of Economic Thought* (Oxford: Clarendon Press, 1993), 167. Sisyphus is a mythological character whom Homer describes as the most prudent and sage of all mortals, and was yet condemned by the gods to an endless punishment of carrying a rock uphill, only to find that, once reaching the summit, the rock would roll back, thus obliging Sisyphus to start all over again. According to Albert Camus, who reinterpreted the legend and found in Sisyphus who was condemned to labour without fruit the ultimate example of an absurd hero, gods must have thought with some reason that there was no worse punishment than being engaged in useless labour that came with no foreseeable end; Albert Camus, 'The Myth of Sisyphus', *The Myth of Sisyphus and Other Essays*, trans. Justin O'Brien (New York: Vintage Books, 1990), 163.

89 To be fair to Schumpeter, we should remind ourselves that he actually noted that 'profit is a symptom of imperfection' and that 'there is a monopoly element in profit in a capitalist economy' (Schumpeter, *Economic Development*, 31, 152). By implication, in the state of perfection at the back of his mind, there would be no monopoly element and zero profit, and we would be back to a model that converges with Weber's description. Of course, for Schumpeter the imperfect state is the normal course of things whereas the state of perfection is an asymptote.

90 Schumpeter, *Capitalism*, 85.

91 Camus, 'The Myth of Sisyphus', 91; emphases added.

Part Four

VEBLEN'S ECONOMICS

Chapter 12

THORSTEIN VEBLEN: THE FATHER OF EVOLUTIONARY AND INSTITUTIONAL ECONOMICS

Geoffrey M. Hodgson

Being 'institutional' and 'evolutionary' is currently fashionable for economists.[1] Since the early 1990s, almost every economist has learned to stress the importance of institutions and several Nobel Prizes have been awarded to institutionalists, including Ronald Coase, Douglass North, Elinor Ostrom and Oliver Williamson. Evolutionary themes pervade game theory and other approaches in mainstream economics. We are all institutional and evolutionary economists now.

Of course, these widely shared terms obscure a variety of different basic assumptions and approaches. There is also no unanimity on what 'institutions' are and what 'evolution' means. Given the broad coverage of these terms, it is also possible to point to a wide variety of progenitors. Adam Smith, Karl Marx, Carl Menger, Alfred Marshall, Joseph Schumpeter, Friedrich Hayek and others were all, in a meaningful sense, evolutionary economists; they all developed an understanding of the dynamic processes of structural change. They all, furthermore, paid much attention to the effects of social institutions on economic performance. Accordingly, evolutionary and institutional economics as found today have a rich variety of ancestors, in part accounting for the diversity of contemporary approaches.[2]

I argue, however, that the additional name of Thorstein Veblen is not only highly significant but rather special in this context. In a narrower and more well-defined understanding of 'evolutionary and institutional economics' that I shall discuss below, Veblen emerges in a sense as its father. Although others are also extremely important in its genesis, Veblen to some degree stands above them.

My arguments concern core ideas in Veblen's thinking and their relevance today. Of course, there is a historical case for Veblen as well. The term 'institutional economics' first emerged in a public forum at the December 1918 meeting of the American Economic Association.[3] Among the leading active promoters of institutionalism in the immediate post-1918 period were Walton Hamilton, John Maurice Clark and Wesley Clair Mitchell. At that time, Veblen was in poor health, but he was widely acknowledged as the principal inspiration for this new school of thought. In that sense, he was the father of institutional economics, in its first explicit incarnation. However, I wish to place even more stress on Veblen's inspirational paternity as a theorist for modern rather than original institutional economics.

Much inspired by Veblen's contribution, the original American institutional economics reached the high point of its influence in the 1920s and 1930s. While it remained highly influential in policy circles until the 1950s, its core theoretical presuppositions were questioned and attacked much earlier. Among these was its evolutionary approach. The critic Paul Homan once remarked that 'in introducing the evolutionary approach, Veblen claimed too much for it'.[1] He accuses Veblen of 'an exaggerated insistence on the evolutionary viewpoint'. After Veblen's death, at a Round Table held at the American Economic Association annual meeting, Homan argued that 'Veblen's attempt to make of economics an evolutionary science has been little developed by other economists' and the 'differentiating characteristics of an institutional economics are hard to find'.[5] Homan failed to see why 'the language of the evolutionary process is having or is likely to have any substantial effect upon either the knowledge or the analysis relevant to the solution of our economic problems'.[6] Homan noted forcefully that the meaning of 'institutionalism', and how it differed from any other kind of economics, was entirely unclear.[7]

These points hit home because, as I have argued elsewhere, later institutionalists largely abandoned Veblen's evolutionary and Darwinian research programme and its links with instinct-habit psychology.[8] Although later generations of American institutionalists in this tradition remained fond of the word 'evolutionary', they abandoned Veblen's particular evolutionary approach.

Veblen himself carries part of the blame. He was a brilliant but unsystematic thinker. His prose is lucid, witty and finely crafted. But he was interested more in penetrating observation, biting irony and the spectacular turn of phase than systematic theory. He left behind no comprehensive and systematic text to describe his approach, like Marx's *Capital*, Walras's *Elements* or Marshall's *Principles*. Pursued by scandal and marred by illness and personal tragedy, he never reached a senior academic position and his career was unfulfilled.[9]

Veblen's 'institutionalism' is widely acknowledged; but Veblen the 'evolutionary economist' is often neglected. This is strange because Veblen did not embrace the term 'institutional economics', yet he called repeatedly for economics to become an 'evolutionary science' and for it to be transformed along 'Darwinian' or 'post-Darwinian' lines.[10]

Despite this, even writers in the original institutionalist tradition thought Veblen's emphasis on Darwinian natural selection was misplaced. In 1924, John R. Commons argued mistakenly that 'artificial selection' was an alternative, whereas Darwin saw the latter as a special case of the former.[11] The influential Clarence Ayres treated Darwinism as an outmoded embarrassment.[12] Veblen's student Wesley Clair Mitchell departed from his mentor by rejecting both Darwinism and instinct-habit psychology.[13]

Within the much later revival of modern varieties of evolutionary economics in the 1980s and 1990s, Veblen is often neglected. In their seminal volume that did much to establish modern evolutionary approaches, Richard Nelson and Sidney Winter give him no mention (although they do later rectify this deficiency).[14] This widespread negligence persisted into the 1990s. For example, in an essay entitled 'What is evolutionary economics?' involving a substantial attempt to trace its history, Richard Langlois and Michael Everett see Menger, Marshall, Schumpeter, Hayek and others as major progenitors of the modern doctrine.[15] Yet Thorstein Veblen, who is the first to import core Darwinian ideas into economics, is entirely ignored.

Given this widespread neglect, my claim that Veblen is the father of the most viable and important strain of 'evolutionary economics' today may seem even more remarkable and absurd. Nevertheless, I propose it here.

This chapter pursues this idea in three distinct ways. In the following section, I address the psychological and ontological core of Veblen's thinking on institutions. The third section discusses Veblen's militantly Darwinian version of evolutionary economics. The final section concludes the paper by examining the relevance of Veblen's institutional and evolutionary ideas today.

The Foundations of Veblen's Institutionalism

Many contemporary 'new institutional economists' see institutions as the outcomes of rational choices by interacting individuals.[16] The problem with this approach is that the preferences or purposes of these individuals are left unexplained. By contrast, Veblen draws from Darwin and others the imperative that the causal origin of all evolved phenomena had to be explained. With the psychologist William James he also takes up the fundamental idea expressed by Darwin that reason emerges on a substrate of instincts and habits.[17] As Darwin himself wrote in 1856: 'Men are called "creatures of reason", more appropriately they would be *"creatures of habit"*'. Habit is the central concept in Veblen's institutional analysis.[18]

In Veblen's writings, the term 'habit' suggests a propensity or disposition, not behaviour as such. For example, Veblen wrote in 1898 of 'a coherent structure of propensities and habits which seeks realization and expression in an unfolding activity'.[19] Here habit is tied in with other propensities and 'seeks realization', suggesting that habit itself is a disposition, rather than a mode of behaviour. Even more clearly, Veblen also remarked in 1898 that 'man mentally digests the content of habits under whose guidance he acts, and appreciates the trend of these habits and propensities'.[20] Here habits are not actions, but the dispositions that guide them.

Accordingly, Veblen adopts a pragmatist theory of action in which activity and habit formation precede rational deliberation. For the pragmatist, activity itself does not require reason or deliberation; we only have to consider the habitual or instinctive behaviour of non-human animals to establish this truth. According to the Darwinian principle of continuity, but contrary to much of twentieth-century social science, the uniqueness of humanity does not lie in any relegation of instinct or habit, but in the critical supplementary deployment of conscious rational deliberation when a novel situation or problem demands it. Reasons and intentions emerge in a continuous process of interaction with the world, while we are always driven by habits and other dispositions. As Veblen writes in 1908: 'habits of thought are an outcome of habits of life'.[21] Veblen later explains:

> History teaches that men, taken collectively, learn by habituation rather than precept and reflection; particularly as touches those underlying principles of truth and validity on which the effectual scheme of law and custom finally rests.[22]

Reason is intimately connected with doing, because activity is the stimulus for habits of thought, and because reason and intelligence guide action through difficulties.

Deliberation and reason are deployed to make choices when habits conflict, or are insufficient to deal with the complex situation. In turn, these particular patterns of reason and deliberation themselves begin to become habituated, so that when we face a similar situation again, we may have learned to deal with it more effectively. Reason does not and cannot overturn habit; it must make use of it to form new habits. Knowledge is an adaptation to a problem situation; it stems from and assists activity.

For Veblen, as the philosopher Stanley Daugert explains, our concepts evolve in interaction with the world: 'Ideas or concepts, that is, habits of thought, are thus not merely the passive products of our environment but are active, dynamic, and creative instruments searching for conduct adaptable to changing circumstances'.[23]

Instinct is prior to habit, habit is prior to belief and belief is prior to reason. That is the order in which they have evolved in our human ancestry over millions of years. That too is the order in which they appear in the ontogenetic development of each human individual. The capacity for belief and reason develops on a foundation of acquired instinctive and habitual dispositions. That too is the order in which they are arranged in a hierarchy of functional dependence, where the current operation of reason depends upon belief, belief depends upon habit and habit upon instinct. Lower elements in the hierarchy do not entirely determine the higher functions, but they impel them into their being, where they are formed in their respective natural and social context. The lower elements are necessary but not sufficient for the higher.[24]

For Veblen, shared habits are the formative material of institutions. In 1909, Veblen describes institutions as 'settled habits of thought common to the generality of men. [...] [I]nstitutions are an outgrowth of habit'.[25] In *The Theory of the Leisure Class*, Veblen explains:

> institutions are, in substance, prevalent habits of thought with respect to particular relations and particular functions of the individual and of the community [...] The situation of today shapes the institutions of tomorrow through a selective, coercive process, by acting upon men's habitual view of things, and so altering or fortifying a point of view or a mental attitude handed down from the past. [...] The evolution of society is substantially a process of mental adaptation on the part of individuals under the stress of circumstances which will no longer tolerate habits of thought formed under and conforming to a different set of circumstances in the past.[26]

Because habits are the constitutive material of institutions, the building or changing of an institution involves the formation or adjustment of shared habits of thought. As Veblen writes elsewhere in the same volume: 'Social evolution is a process of selective adaptation of temperament and habits of thought under the stress of the circumstances of associated life. The adaptation of habits of thought is the growth of institutions [...] a process of selection'.[27]

Part of Veblen's achievement in this area was to connect the analysis of institutional structures and their change with human psychology. This meant much more than the establishment of interdisciplinary connections. By focusing on particular psychological mechanisms rather than the abstract axioms of rationality, it became possible to consider the conditions under which institutions could affect individual dispositions or preferences.

People do not develop new preferences, wants or purposes because mysterious 'social forces' control them. The framing, shifting and constraining capacities of social institutions give rise to new perceptions and dispositions within individuals. The key mechanism is habit formation. Upon new habits of thought and behaviour, new preferences and intentions emerge.[28]

Accordingly, Veblen reduces explanations of social or economic phenomena to neither individuals nor institutions alone.[29] In these senses, he is neither a methodological individualist nor a methodological collectivist. Explanations *always* involve both individuals *and* social structures.[30] In these broad terms, his stance is similar to several other modern social theorists. However, several of these approaches take individuals and their beliefs as given, or propose not mechanism to explain reconstitutive causal effects from structures to individuals. Veblen's analysis fills this gap and goes further to examine the psychological mechanisms that are involved.[31]

Veblen's Darwinian Evolutionary Economics

There is no Darwinian copyright on the word 'evolution'. It is perfectly legitimate to use the word in different ways, reflecting its varied origins and uses. It carries necessarily no more precise a meaning than 'change'.

Veblen's contribution was to bring Darwinian ideas into the economic arena. This meant much more than the importation of biological analogies. Along with a number of thinkers at that time – including David Ritchie, William James, Charles Sanders Peirce and John Dewey – Veblen upheld that Darwinism was more than a biological theory: it was a new philosophical system, offering a framework of explanation for *all* complex systems involving entities that compete for resources. Consequently, it was possible to generalise the core Darwinian principles of variation, inheritance and selection, and apply them to social phenomena. In the century and a half since Darwin's ideas first appeared, no adequate alternative explanatory framework has been devised to explain such phenomena.[32]

This Darwinian aspect of Veblen's thinking has been somewhat neglected, even by devotees of his ideas. Yet it is abundantly clear in his writing. The idea that Darwinian ideas can be generalised to cover socio-economic as well as biological evolution does not mean that socio-economic phenomena are explained entirely in biological terms. Generalising Darwinism does not mean biological reductionism. As Veblen wrote in 1909:

> if men universally acted not on the conventional grounds and values afforded by the fabric of institutions, but solely and directly on the grounds and values afforded by the unconventionalized propensities and aptitudes of hereditary human nature, then there would be no institutions and no culture.[33]

Despite his extensive knowledge of biology, Veblen was too careful to commit himself in the then ongoing debate over Lamarckism. Darwin himself believed in the inheritance of acquired characters. Whether this happens in reality is an empirical question. Even if it were true, the Darwinian principles of variation, inheritance and selection would be required to complete the explanation.[34] Veblen remained neutral on whether or not acquired characters could be inherited.[35] But he was not neutral between the theories of Darwin and Lamarck. Veblen writes: 'Darwin set to work to explain species in terms of the process out of which they have arisen, rather than out of the prime cause to which the distinction between them may be due'.[36] What Darwin had tried to do, albeit without complete success, was to provide a processual explanation of the origin of species where the causal mechanisms involved were fully specified. Veblen continues in a highly perceptive footnote: 'This is the substance of Darwin's advance over Lamarck, for instance'.[37] On this basis of more adequate causal explanations of process, Veblen rightly judges Darwin to be superior to Lamarck.

Like Darwin, Veblen emphasises the importance of processual, causal explanation, over explanations that assume a fixed outcome or end point. Although he does not use the word, he had an appreciation of Darwinian evolution as an 'algorithmic' process. Veblen uses phrases such as 'cumulative causation', 'theory of a process, of an unfolding sequence' and 'impersonal sequence of cause and effect' to connote the same idea.[38] This focus on algorithmic processes is revolutionary and modern; it directs attention to ongoing processes rather than static equilibrium alone.[39]

Consequently, rather than taking individual reasons or preferences as themselves sufficient to understand motivations, Veblen points to the need for causal explanations of reasons or preferences themselves. In this respect, he contrasts with Lionel Robbins and others who take preferences as given.[40] Contrary to many who misunderstand Veblen on this point, he did not underestimate the importance of human intentionality – but felt it had to be explained rather than assumed. Here again, he contrasts with many social theorists that take beliefs or reasons as given data. For Veblen, adequate explanations involved the evolution of social institutions and their interplay with biological and psychological characteristics. He thus acknowledges processes of dual inheritance or co-evolution (again to use modern terms) where there was evolution and transmission at both the instinctive and the cultural levels.[41]

Veblen understood that the process of Darwinian evolution had three important features. First, there must be sustained variation among the members of a species or population. Variations may be random or purposive in origin, but without them, as Darwin insisted, natural selection cannot operate. This is the concept of variation. Second, there must be some mechanism of heredity or continuity, through which offspring have to resemble their parents more than they resemble other members of their species. In other words, there has to be some mechanism through which individual characteristics are passed on through the generations. Third, natural selection itself operates either because better-adapted organisms leave increased numbers of offspring, or because the variations or gene combinations that are preserved are those that bestow an advantage in the struggle to survive. This is the concept of the struggle for existence. Consider these three features in turn, as they appear in Veblen's work.

For Veblen, a Darwinian science must address 'the conditions of variational growth'.[42] Veblen saw a 'Darwinistic account' in economics as addressing 'the origin, growth, persistence, and variation of institutions'.[43] Veblen also refers to 'a selection between the predatory and the peaceable variants'.[44] This indicates that for Veblen, and in conformity with Darwin, variation exists *prior* to (as well as after) evolutionary selection.

Veblen does not provide a full account of the sources of variation of social institutions. In general, Veblen saw cultural variation as cumulative. 'The growth of culture is a cumulative sequence of habituation', but 'each new move creates a new situation which induces a further new variation in the habitual manner of response' and 'each new situation is a variation of what has gone before and embodies as causal factors all that has been effected by what went before'.[45]

For Veblen, the 'instinctive propensity' of 'idle curiosity' is also a major source of variety and invention. 'This instinctive curiosity' may 'accelerate the gain in technological insight', as well as 'persistently disturbing the habitual body of knowledge'.[46]

In 1901, the Dutch biologist Hugo De Vries published *Die Mutationstheorie* in German. Veblen adopts the metaphor of mutation, applying it to social and economic institutions. He writes of 'business capital and its mutations', 'effects of these institutions and of the mutations they undergo' and 'growth and mutations of the institutional fabric'.[47] Veblen also writes of 'the mutation of habits' and proposes that 'the state of the industrial arts has been undergoing a change of type, such as followers of Mendel would call a "mutation"'.[48]

We now turn to the second Darwinian concept, the question of inheritance. It is clear from several passages in *The Theory of the Leisure Class* – including some quoted above – that the institution was regarded as the unit of relative stability and continuity through time, ensuring that much of the pattern and variety is passed on from one period to the next. This relative stability and durability of habits and institutions made them key objects of evolutionary selection in the socio-economic sphere. But Veblen did not examine the processes or institutional replication or inheritance in detail.

Turning to the concept of selection, Veblen famously promotes the idea that in social evolution there was a 'natural selection of institutions':

> The life of man in society, just like the life of other species, is a struggle for existence, and therefore it is a process of selective adaptation. The evolution of social structure has been a process of natural selection of institutions. The progress which has been and is being made in human institutions and in human character may be set down, broadly, to a natural selection of the fittest habits of thought and to a process of enforced adaptation of individuals to an environment which has progressively changed with the growth of community and with the changing institutions under which men have lived. [...] So that the changing institutions in their turn make for a further selection of individuals endowed with the fittest temperament, and a further adaptation of individual temperament and habits to the changing environment through the formation of new institutions.[49]

It was no accident that Darwin's phrases 'natural selection' and 'struggle for existence' appear here. Veblen writes also in the same work of 'the law of natural selection, as applied to human institutions'.[50] Elsewhere Veblen poignantly but infrequently applies the specific phrase 'natural selection' to habits of thought or to social institutions.[51] The decisive implication was that Darwinism could be applied to human society without necessarily reducing explanations of social phenomena entirely to individual psychology or biology.

Although Veblen uses the phrase 'natural selection' only a few times, the concept of selection is common and persistent in his works. Words such as 'select', 'selection' and 'selective', used in the Darwinian sense of a process of sifting and preservation of fortuitous adaptations, are used with conspicuous frequency. I have counted well over a hundred appearances. A large number of these appearances concern the selection of institutions, customs or habits of thought. Confining ourselves to *The Theory of the Leisure Class* alone, the following are a small sampling:

> In whatever way usages and customs and methods of expenditure arise, they are all subject to the selective action of this norm of reputability; and the degree in which they conform to its requirements is a test of their fitness to survive in the competition with other similar usages and canons.[52]
>
> There is a cumulative growth of customs and habits of thought; a selective adaptation of conventions and methods of life.[53]
>
> Social evolution is a process of selective adaptation of temperament and habits of thought under the stress of the circumstances of associated life.
>
> The adaptation of habits of thought is the growth of institutions. […] a process of selection […] a selective process […][54]
>
> Wherever the pecuniary culture prevails, the selective process by which men's habits of thought are shaped, and by which the survival of rival lines of descent is decided, proceeds proximately on the basis of fitness for acquisition.[55]

This and much other textual evidence on his use of the concept of selection, along with his understanding of the importance of variation and inheritance in the Darwinian theory, decisively favours an interpretation of Veblen's work as an application of Darwinian principles to the analysis of social evolution.

It must again be emphasised that Veblen's Darwinian economics did not involve the assertion that economic evolution can or must be reduced substantially to biological terms. Furthermore, Veblen's use of Darwinian terminology was *not confined to metaphor*. Veblen makes it abundantly clear that he believed that socio-economic systems *actually evolved* in a manner consistent with the Darwinian concepts of variation, inheritance and selection. Veblen did not believe that the domain of Darwinian theory was confined to nature. His use of Darwinian theory is much more than mere word play. The difference between natural and social evolution was in the units of selection and in the details of the evolutionary processes, not in the exclusion of variation, inheritance or selection from the social sphere. Variation, inheritance and selection are present and real in both the social and the natural context.

The relatively infrequent appearance of the phrase 'natural selection' does not undermine the claim that Veblen was an evolutionary economist in a Darwinian genre. As mentioned above, he uses the concept of selection frequently. But it remains to consider why Veblen did not often choose to attach the adjective 'natural' to the abundant instances of 'selection' or 'selection process' in his work. We may guess why. First, and most obviously, Veblen was concerned with the evolution of society, and not of the non-human, natural world. As his attention was directed at society rather than nature, the term 'natural' was dropped. Second, the 'natural selection' of institutions could be misinterpreted by the reader in terms of 'nature' doing the selecting, or that the selection was taking place according to 'natural' rather than economic or other social criteria. Third, economists and others who advocate a 'natural' order, or 'natural rights', are the persistent objects of Veblen's devastating criticism. Resistance to the likely interpretations of the word 'natural' as 'normal' or 'predestined' can lead to the rejection of the term, especially when the word 'selection' on its own will do. Hence there are several possible reasons why Veblen more frequently uses the word 'selection' rather than 'natural selection'. As a result, the marginalisation of the word 'natural' in his writing should not be taken to imply that Veblen lost any of his Darwinian inspiration.

While Veblen generally saw institutions as units of selection in a process of economic evolution, he did not make the context, criteria or mechanisms of selection entirely clear. Prompted by the notion that the social 'environment' itself evolves, Veblen moved towards, but does not complete, a causal analysis of that evolutionary process.[56] Insofar as an evolutionary analysis exists, we have to impute it from passages such as the one quoted above, where Veblen writes that the 'selective adaptation can never catch up with the progressively changing situation in which the community finds itself at any given time'.[57] This suggests a process of imperfect institutional adjustment and cultural lag. But it does not sufficiently explain the evolution of the 'progressively changing situation' in which institutions are selected.

Nevertheless, Veblen was clearly attempting to move towards a theory of institutional evolution. In its time and context, this sketchy and preliminary analysis of institutional evolution in *The Theory of the Leisure Class* was a major achievement, standing significantly above its precursors. However, having started this research programme he failed to move it forward.[58] Cynthia Russett's verdict is apposite and accurate:

> If Veblen failed to develop an evolutionary methodology, he also failed to develop a comprehensive evolutionary theory to explain in detail how institutions evolve in the cultural environment and what sorts of interaction occur between economic activity and institutional structures. Veblen was something of an intellectual butterfly, and he often lacked the patience to elaborate his ideas into a coherent system. But he teemed with fragmentary insights, and these can be pieced together to suggest the outlines of a Veblenian scheme of cultural evolution – what might be called a 'pre-theory' of cultural change.[59]

Today, with benefit of hindsight and a richer knowledge of evolutionary processes, it is possible to build on Veblen's achievement and construct a Darwinian theory of economic evolution. Despite his failure to systematise, Veblen today stands out as the first economist to propose this project and to set out its key features.

Conclusion: Veblen's Relevance Today

Like many modern evolutionary thinkers,[60] Veblen saw Darwinian evolutionary processes as open-ended and suboptimal. Unlike advocates of laissez faire, he did not use Darwinian principles to justify market competition. He was critical of apologetic tendencies in social science which regard existing institutions as necessarily efficient or optimal. He described particularly regressive or disserviceable institutions as 'archaic', 'ceremonial' or even 'imbecile'. Furthermore, he used Darwinian ideas to rebut of Marx's teleological suggestions that history was leading inevitably to a communist future.

Along with the assumption of fixed preference functions, Veblen also criticised the widespread assumption in economic theory of a fixed set of technological possibilities. Technological change can challenge established institutions and vested interests. In *The Theory of Business Enterprise* and elsewhere, Veblen distinguished between industry (making goods) and business (making money). This dichotomy parallels the earlier suggestion in *The Theory of the Leisure Class* that there is a distinction between serviceable consumption to satisfy human need and conspicuous consumption for status and display.[61]

However, Veblen's modern relevance extends beyond these relatively familiar topics. With his key concept of habit, Veblen built a bridge between psychology and the analysis of social institutions. He explained that habits are the constitutive material of institutions and that institutional change necessitates the adaptation of habits in the social group. This insight not only forms a keystone of a viable social ontology but also distances Veblen from the extremes of both methodological individualism and methodological collectivism. In sum, Veblen has made an important contribution not only to our understanding of institutions but also to fundamental social theory.

Veblen followed Darwin and others in stressing the importance of processual, causal explanation. Rare among thinkers of his epoch, he grasped the essence of Darwinian ideas and saw them as applicable to social as well as biological evolution. Many modern evolutionary economists are sceptical of this claim, but others have seen the relevance of Darwinism for the social sciences and, in spirit if not the letter, have returned to this Veblenian theme.

In the last two decades of the twentieth century, evolutionary and institutional ideas again became prominent in economics. Pragmatism has once more become fashionable in philosophy and the concept of habit has returned to psychology. Many of Veblen's ideas, including those on institutional evolution and the role of knowledge in economic growth, now seem strikingly modern. The conditions exist for a much deeper appreciation of his contribution to economics and social science. We can still learn a great deal from his writings and build on them for the future.[62]

Notes and References

1 This chapter makes use of some material from Geoffrey M. Hodgson, *The Evolution of Institutional Economics: Agency, Structure and Darwinism in American Institutionalism* (London: Routledge, 2004).

2 For discussions of different types of 'evolutionary economics' see Geoffrey M. Hodgson, *Economics and Evolution: Bringing Life Back into Economics* (Cambridge, MA and Ann Arbor: Polity Press and University of Michigan Press, 1993); Geoffrey M. Hodgson, *Evolution and*

Institutions: On Evolutionary Economics and the Evolution of Economics (Cheltenham: Edward Elgar, 1999). For discussions of different types of institutionalism see Eirik Furubotn and Rudolf Richter, *Institutions in Economic Theory: The Contribution of the New Institutional Economics* (Ann Arbor: University of Michigan Press, 1997) and Malcolm H. Rutherford, *Institutions in Economics: The Old and the New Institutionalism* (Cambridge: Cambridge University Press, 1994).

3   Walton H. Hamilton, 'The Institutional Approach to Economic Theory', *American Economic Review* 9 (Supplement), no. 1 (1919): 309–18.

4   Paul T. Homan, 'Thorstein Veblen', in *American Masters of Social Science*, ed. by Howard W. Odum (New York: Holt, 1927), 231–70, esp. 258–9.

5   Paul T. Homan, 'An Appraisal of Institutional Economics', *American Economic Review* 22.1 (1932): 10–17, see esp. 10.

6   Ibid., 15.

7   Ibid., 16.

8   Hodgson, *Evolution of Institutional Economics.*

9   Elizabeth W. Jorgensen and Henry I. Jorgensen, *Thorstein Veblen: Victorian Firebrand* (Armonk: M. E. Sharpe, 1999).

10 Thorstein Veblen, *The Place of Science in Modern Civilization and Other Essays* (New York: Huebsch, 1919), 37, 58, 72, 77, 79, 176, 191–2, 265, 328, 369, 370, 413–17, 436, 441.

11 John R. Commons, *Legal Foundations of Capitalism* (New York: Macmillan, 1924), 376.

12 Clarence E. Ayres, *Huxley* (New York: Norton, 1932), 95.

13 Wesley C. Mitchell (ed.), *What Veblen Taught* (New York: Viking, 1936), xlix.

14 Richard R. Nelson and Sidney G. Winter, *An Evolutionary Theory of Economic Change* (Cambridge, MA: Harvard University Press, 1982).

15 Richard N. Langlois and Michael J. Everett, 'What is Evolutionary Economics?' in *Evolutionary and Neo-Schumpeterian Approaches to Economics*, ed. by Lars Magnusson (Boston: Kluwer, 1994), 11–47.

16 Andrew R. Schotter, *The Economic Theory of Social Institutions* (Cambridge: Cambridge University Press, 1981); Furubotn and Richter, *Institutions in Economic Theory.*

17 William James, *The Principles of Psychology*, 2 vols (New York and London: Holt and Macmillan, 1890).

18 Charles R. Darwin, *Metaphysics, Materialism, and the Evolution of Mind: Early Writings of Charles Darwin* (Chicago: University of Chicago Press, 1974), 84, 115.

19 Veblen, *Place of Science*, 74.

20 Thorstein Veblen, *Essays On Our Changing Order*, ed. by Leon Ardzrooni (New York: Viking Press, 1934), 80.

21 Veblen, *Place of Science*, 38.

22 Thorstein Veblen, *The Vested Interests and the Common Man* (New York: Huebsch, 1919), 15.

23 Stanley Matthew Daugert, *The Philosophy of Thorstein Veblen* (New York: Columbia University Press, 1950), 36.

24 Howard Margolis, *Patterns, Thinking and Cognition: A Theory of Judgment* (Chicago: University of Chicago Press, 1987); James Bernard Murphy, 'The Kinds of Order in Society', in *Natural Images in Economic Thought: 'Markets Read in Tooth and Claw'*, ed. by Philip Mirowski (New York: Cambridge University Press, 1994), 536–82; Geoffrey M. Hodgson, 'Instinct and Habit before Reason: Comparing the Views of John Dewey, Friedrich Hayek and Thorstein Veblen', in *Advances in Austrian Economics*, 9 (2006): 109–432.

25 Veblen, *Place of Science*, 239.

26 Thorstein Veblen, *The Theory of the Leisure Class: An Economic Study in the Evolution of Institutions* (New York: Macmillan 1899), 190–92.

27 Veblen, *Leisure Class*, 213.

28 Geoffrey M. Hodgson, *Economics in the Shadows of Darwin and Marx: Essays on Institutional and Evolutionary Themes* (Cheltenham: Edward Elgar, 2006); Geoffrey M. Hodgson and Thorbjørn

Knudsen, 'The Complex Evolution of a Simple Traffic Convention: The Functions and Implications of Habit', *Journal of Economic Behavior and Organization* 54.1 (2004): 19–47.

29 Veblen, *Place of Science*, 241–3.

30 Geoffrey M. Hodgson, 'Institutions and Individuals: Interaction and Evolution', *Organization Studies* 28.1 (2007): 95–116; Geoffrey M. Hodgson, 'Meanings of Methodological Individualism', *Journal of Economic Methodology* 14.2 (2007): 211–26.

31 Hodgson, *Evolution of Institutional Economics*.

32 Geoffrey M. Hodgson and Thorbjørn Knudsen, 'Why We Need a Generalized Darwinism: and Why a Generalized Darwinism is Not Enough', *Journal of Economic Behavior and Organization* 61.1 (2006): 1–192; Geoffrey M. Hodgson and Thorbjørn Knudsen, *Darwin's Conjecture: The Search for General Principles of Social and Economic Evolution* (Chicago: University of Chicago Press, 2010).

33 Veblen, *Essays on Our Changing Order*, 143.

34 David L. Hull, 'The Naked Meme', in *Learning, Development and Culture: Essays in Evolutionary Epistemology*, ed. by Henry C. Plotkin (New York: Wiley, 1982), 273–327; Richard Dawkins, 'Universal Darwinism', in *Evolution from Molecules to Man*, ed. by D. S. Bendall (Cambridge: Cambridge University Press, 1983), 403–25; Paul T. Hodgson and Thorbjørn Knudsen, 'Why We Need a Generalized Darwinism: and Why a Generalized Darwinism is Not Enough', *Journal of Economic Behavior and Organization* 61.1 (2006): 1–192.

35 Veblen, *Leisure Class*, 190, 192.

36 Thorstein Veblen, *Business Enterprise* (New York: Charles Scribners, 1904), 369.

37 Ibid., 369n.

38 Veblen, *Place of Science*, 61, 58, 61, 64, 68, 326, 436.

39 Daniel C. Dennett, *Darwin's Dangerous Idea: Evolution and the Meanings of Life* (London: Allen Lane and Simon and Schuster, 1995); Brian W. Arthur, 'Out-of-Equilibrium Economics and Agent-Based Modeling', in *Handbook of Computational Economics, Vol. 2: Agent-Based Computational Economics*, ed. by Kenneth L. Judd and Leigh Tesfatsion, 2 vols (Amsterdam: North-Holland, 2006).

40 Lionel Robbins, *An Essay on the Nature and Significance of Economic Science* (London: Macmillan, 1932).

41 Robert Boyd and Peter J. Richerson, *Culture and the Evolutionary Process* (Chicago: University of Chicago Press, 1985).

42 Veblen, *Place of Science*, 176–7.

43 Ibid., 265.

44 Ibid., 217.

45 Ibid., 241–2.

46 Thorstein Veblen, *The Instinct of Workmanship, and the State of the Industrial Arts* (New York: Macmillan, 1914), 87.

47 Veblen, *Business Enterprise*, 149; Veblen, *Place of Science*, 243.

48 Thorstein Veblen, *The Vested Interests and the Common Man* (New York: Huebsch, 1919), 5, 40.

49 Veblen, *Leisure Class*, 188.

50 Ibid., 207.

51 Veblen, *Place of Science*, 5, 149. 171, 416; Veblen, *Essays on Our Changing Order*, 79.

52 Ibid., 166.

53 Ibid., 208.

54 Ibid., 213–4.

55 Ibid., 241.

56 Ibid., 188–98.

57 Ibid., 191.

58 Malcolm H. Rutherford, 'Veblen's Evolutionary Programme: A Promise Unfulfilled', *Cambridge Journal of Economics* 22.4 (1998): 463–77.

59 Cynthia Eagle Russett, *Darwin in America: The Intellectual Response 1865–1912* (San Francisco: W. H. Freeman, 1976), 153.

60 John A. Dupré (ed.), *The Latest on the Best: Essays on Evolution and Optimality* (Cambridge, MA: MIT Press, 1987).

61 Subsequently, institutionalists such as Clarence E. Ayres elevated the different conflicts between technology and institutions into a universal principle, and dubbed it the 'Veblenian dichotomy'. This is misleading, because Veblen never saw such a conflict as universal, and he saw institutions as the indispensable fabric of economic life (Hodgson, *Evolution of Institutional Economics*).

62 Geoffrey M. Hodgson, 'The Revival of Veblenian Institutional Economics', *Journal of Economic Issues* 41.2 (2007): 325–40.

Chapter 13

VEBLEN'S WORDS WEIGHED

Paul Burkander

Thorstein Veblen made significant contributions to economics. As the father of institutionalism, he was an important critic of capitalism and what he termed neoclassical economics. Interestingly, for an economist, Veblen's style of writing has gained as much attention as his ideas. His writing has been described as biting, ironic and satirical.[1] Some of his phrases, like 'conspicuous consumption', have so penetrated our culture that they are familiar even to those who never heard the name Veblen.

Yet some of his phrases are so abstruse that even the economists whom he addressed failed to understand them. For instance, in his essay 'Why is Economics Not an Evolutionary Science', he asks,

> if we are getting restless under the taxonomy of a monocotyledonous wage doctrine and a cryptogamic theory of interest, with involute, loculicidal, tomentous and moniliform variants, what is the cytoplasm, centrosome, or karyokinetic process to which we may turn, and in which we may find surcease from the metaphysics of normality and the controlling principles?[2]

This sentence is not easy to understand, although one economist, James Galbraith, describes it as his favourite sentence in all of economics.[3] Yet in that same article, Galbraith declines to help those who don't understand it. It is therefore the purpose of this essay to decipher this cryptic sentence. In order to do so, I first examine the essay in which it appears. In turning to my analysis of the sentence in question, I recall the advice of John K. Galbraith, James's father, who wrote that to understand Veblen 'the words must be weighed'.[4]

Veblen begins 'Why is Economics Not an Evolutionary Science' with the following quotation by M. G. Lapouge: 'Anthropology is destined to revolutionise the political and social sciences as radically as bacteriology has revolutionised the science of medicine'.[5] Veblen suggests that, at least with regard to economics, Lapouge is not alone in pointing to the need for revolution. Indeed, Veblen says that professionals from many branches of science, including political and social sciences, felt that economics was seriously behind the times and in need of rehabilitation. He cites Alfred Marshall's humility, contrasted with the arrogance of previous classical economists, as evidence of the uncertain state of economics. He even criticised the historical school for not keeping its original pace.

He then outlines his main complaint against economics: that while the other modern sciences were evolutionary sciences, economics was still based on 'natural rights, utilitarianism, and administrative expediency'.[6] Veblen next turns to examine the precise ways in which economics fell short of being an evolutionary science. He offers several suggestions which he then refutes. First, he suggests that it may be because the other sciences are based in reality, but he counters this suggestion by citing the extreme insistence on data by the historical school. Next, he suggests that an evolutionary science is one which has a close-knit body of theory that explains an unfolding sequence. Again, though, he finds that economics met the criteria and cites the work of John Stuart Mill and of James Elliot Cairnes.

Veblen then admits that fact collection and theories of processes existed in the other sciences before they were considered evolutionary. Thus, these are not the correct criteria by which to judge a science as evolutionary or not. But he puts forth the appropriate distinction: that the pre-evolutionary sciences, as well as economics, had different 'terms which were accepted as the definitive terms of knowledge'.[7] Clearly this is a distinction that needs to be expounded upon. Veblen does so, saying that the evolutionary scientist asks questions about 'why' things happen and answers them in terms of causation and quantitative sequence.

Veblen points out that the pre-evolutionary scientist, on the other hand, relied on concepts of natural law for answers. Thus, a sequence of events tends toward some 'spiritually legitimate end'.[8] Any sequence contrary to this accepted end point is a 'disturbing factor' which takes us away from a normal state.[9] Upon the foundation of an agreed-upon end a logical structure is built, which constitutes the scheme of knowledge. He considers this to be a spiritual framework, the roots of which could be traced from animism through metaphysics. Veblen then asks how this preconception of a normal state has fared against modern-science and the new preconception of non-spiritual sequence. Veblen says that answering this question could help us determine whether the preconception of a normal state would persist indefinitely.

He then traces the preconception of a normal state from primitive conditions through the post-evolutionary sciences, where it is still generally present, if in a weakened form. Veblen says that the process of disavowing the normal state has been gradual, that it has touched the different sciences unequally and that economics in particular still showed too many signs of this preconception. Moreover, in economics, the character of the normal state was dependent on the 'common sense of the time'.[10] The purveyors of economic thought, in relying on a normal state, were irreparably biased by their own sense of the ideal economic life.

He admits that writers of his time used the language of a normal state only metaphorically. An example of this metaphorical use is the idea of a 'natural' wage and 'normal' value. Veblen's response is significant: 'it is this facile recourse to inscrutable figures of speech as the ultimate terms of theory that has saved the economists from being dragooned into the ranks of modern science'.[11] The use of such metaphors allowed economists to avoid questions of sequential causation and to avoid examining the institutions of money, wages and land ownership outside of their contribution to a predetermined end. As a result, economists were left with a cost of production theory of value recalling the times when nature abhorred a vacuum, i.e. when something was deemed not possible because it was assumed to be contrary to nature's preference.

Veblen described the outcome of this process as, at best, 'a body of logically consistent propositions concerning the normal relations of things',[12] i.e. what he termed a system of economic taxonomy. It was precisely such a system under which other scientists grew restless, and this led them to ask why and to form theories of causal sequences. He cites talk about 'cytoplasm, centrosome, and karyokinetic process' as evidence that these scientists were looking to the processes of life itself, and attempting to develop causal explanations to explain it.[13] They had moved beyond a system of mere classification to the study of process.

On the other hand, Veblen states that economics had reached the pinnacle of taxonomy. He recalls the work of Cairnes 'taxonomy for taxonomy's sake',[14] and credits him with bringing economics nearest to the ideal dismal science. However, he chastises economics for losing its charm by abandoning the application of common sense to questions of what ought to be. In so doing, according to Veblen, economics lost the support of the common person and became a pursuit interesting only to those either born into it or educated enough to understand it. He argues that economists were getting restless under this discipline and asks, 'what does all this signify?'[15]

The next sentence is the one we began with and is one which, I presume, continues to perplex readers. It is to this sentence that I now turn my attention. The first part of the sentence has been anticipated already: Veblen has already described the reaction of scientists and of economists to taxonomy as restless. He has also described what he means by taxonomy, i.e. a body of logically consistent propositions, as contrasted with a study of causation. Taxonomy is a system of classification; it comes from the Greek words for order (τάξις) and distribution (νομία). In biology, it was the exercise of classifying living things into kingdom, phylum, class, etc. Biological taxonomy is related to taxidermy, both linguistically and practically. They share the same root: taxidermy comes from the Greek words order (τάξις) and skin (δέρμα). Taxonomy in practice often meant grouping a collection of taxidermied animals and distinguishing between groups based on subtle differences. In all this, taxonomy is not the examination of the process of life. The object of study in taxonomy might as well be dead – it is only their appearance and character that matters, not how they live.

Veblen continues in the language of biological, or specifically botanical, taxonomy. He describes the wage doctrine as monocotyledonous. The root is again Greek, μόνο, for one, and κοτυληδών, which means hollow. Monocotyledonous refers to plants that only have a single seed lobe; these plants aren't particularly fruitful. Thus, Veblen has described the wage doctrine, not as something that has given birth to many fruitful ideas, but rather as something with limited capabilities to produce at all. He describes the theory of interest as being cryptogamic, a word derived from the Greek κρυπτός, which means hidden, and γάμος, which means wedlock. Cryptogamic plants are those that are destitute of stamens, pistils and true seeds. These plants do not flower. Examples include ferns, mosses and fungi. A cryptogamic theory of interest is perhaps worse than a monocotyledonous wage doctrine: it isn't fruitful in any way.

Veblen next describes the variants of this taxonomy as 'involute, loculicidal, tomentous and moniliform'.[16] Involute comes from the Latin involūtus, which means to roll up or in.

Loculicidal also comes from Latin, *loculus*, meaning locus or place, and *cid*, meaning to cut. It describes bud of a plant that, while blooming, splits longitudinally – it opens like a clam shell stood on its end. Examples include irises and some lilies. Tomentous is derived from the Latin word *tōmentōs*, which refers to pillow stuffing. It describes plants that are short and densely matted. Moniliform comes from the Latin words *monīle*, meaning necklace, and *forma*, meaning, of course, form or shape. Moniliform refers to something that is necklace-like, often something that has globular protuberances, suggesting a beaded necklace.

This is not a very exciting image that Veblen has drawn for us. Indeed, it is intentionally boring – in the garden of sciences economics is a plant that is rolled up in itself; its flowering is simple and uninteresting; it is short and densely matted; it consists of globular protuberances. Such a plant would be dismal indeed in any garden. The variants of the taxonomy of economics are not consistent with complex life processes.

In the next part of the sentence, he asks, 'what is the cytoplasm, centrosome, or karyokinetic process to which we may turn'.[17] Veblen has already made reference to these terms. Earlier in the article, he cites talk of such things in other sciences as indicative of a shifting focus towards the processes of life. A cytoplasm is the general protoplasm of the cell. The protoplasm, as described by Huxley, is 'the physical basis of life'.[18] It forms the essential substance of cells. The centrosomes are minute bodies believed to influence cellular division. Karyokinetic is the science of the nucleus, its development and history.

The use of these three words well indicates that biology had come to consider the processes of life. The cytoplasm, centrosome and karyokinetic processes are the driving forces of life at the simplest level, the cell. The study of the processes of the cell is far removed from the categorisation of animals according to genus and species. Veblen asks if there are analogous processes to which economics can turn. Where are the processes of life in economics?

In turning to them, he argues we could 'find surcease from the metaphysics of normality and the controlling principles'.[19] Again, these are phrases that Veblen has already defined earlier in the article. The metaphysics of normality refers to the preconception that there is a normal state to which all things tend by natural law. It is the secularised idea of the 'spiritually legitimate end'.[20] The controlling principles are the underlying forces, assumed to exist, which forever guide us toward that end.

To rephrase the sentence, Veblen asks: if we are getting tired with a system of logically consistent propositions and classifications; with a wage doctrine of limited productivity and a theory of interest that is not at all fruitful; with variations that are like small, rolled up, densely matted flowers whose blooming is simple and uninteresting, then what is the driving life force, the key elements, the study of the process of life to which we may turn and in which we may end the preconception of a normal state and the forces that guide us there?

He follows up this question by stating that the material in which we can study the life process exists before our eyes; it is the human material. Veblen suggests that, rather than thinking of changes in capital as driving the production process, we must focus on changes in human understanding. The resources of the world will forever maintain their properties; it is human understanding that changes to better understand these properties. That is, we must scrutinise the economic actions of man.

Veblen criticises earlier attempts to study the economic actions of man for thinking in hedonistic terms that man is an immutable expression of wants. He suggests that instead man is consistently habitual, and that economic action is expressed in ever-unfolding activity. Past experience thus has a cumulative effect on present decisions. As this is true for the individual, so too would it be true for the community. He suggests that economic action is properly conceived as teleological, i.e. man is always seeking something. Understanding what that something is will require scrutinising human activity. We should not, however, assume some legitimate end or preconceived path – these preconceptions remain indicative of pre-evolutionary thought.

Since economic interest follows individuals everywhere, and it follows mankind through cultural development, all institutions were therefore economic in a sense. Thus, evolutionary economics becomes defined as 'a theory of a process of cultural growth as determined by the economic interest, a theory of a cumulative sequence of economic institutions stated in terms of the process itself'.[21] Veblen goes on to examine the degree to which this has been achieved and finds it sorely lacking.

Having analysed this particularly abstruse sentence, I find that it in fact presents a beautifully descriptive metaphor. Veblen borrows language from biology, which is appropriate considering that Veblen's article recommends that economists learn from biology. Unfortunately, this sentence is an example of style clouding meaning.

This prompts two questions. Have economists responded to this message? And is it still applicable today? In my opinion, we rely less these days on the language of normality. It's still there, though. We still focus on equilibrium conditions. I also suspect that we impose our concept of the ideal economic life onto our analysis, whether or not it's accurate. For instance, we assume that firms are profit-maximisers, when in fact they may be only profit-seekers, and that workers will forego work if the opportunity cost of leisure is low. I suppose we have yet to find the surcease Veblen sought.

Notes and References

1 Stephen Edgell, *Veblen in Perspective: His Life and Thought* (Armonk: M. E. Sharpe, 2001).
2 Thorstein Veblen, 'Why is Economics Not an Evolutionary Science', *Quarterly Journal of Economics* 12.4 (1898): 373–97.
3 James Galbraith, 'Smith vs. Darwin', *Mother Jones* (December 2005). Online: http://www. motherjones.com/commentary/columns/2005/12/smith_darwin.html (accessed March 2007).
4 John K. Galbraith, 'Foreword', in Thorstein Veblen, *The Theory of the Leisure Class* (Boston: Houghton Mifflin, 1973), v–xxv.
5 Veblen, 'Evolutionary Science?', 373.
6 Ibid., 374.
7 Ibid., 377.
8 Ibid., 378.
9 Ibid., 378.
10 Ibid., 382.
11 Ibid., 383.
12 Ibid., 384.
13 Ibid., 384.
14 Ibid., 385.

15 Ibid., 386.
16 Ibid., 386.
17 Ibid., 387.
18 Thomas Huxley, *Methods and Results; Essays* (New York: D. Appleton and Company, 1925), 130.
19 Veblen, 'Evolutionary Science?', 387.
20 Ibid., 378.
21 Ibid., 393.

Chapter 14

THE GREAT CRASH OF 2007 VIEWED THROUGH THE PERSPECTIVE OF VEBLEN'S *THEORY OF BUSINESS ENTERPRISE*, KEYNES'S MONETARY THEORY OF PRODUCTION AND MINSKY'S FINANCIAL INSTABILITY HYPOTHESIS

L. Randall Wray

It has long been recognised that Thorstein Veblen and John Maynard Keynes share a common approach to the nature of 'business enterprise' or 'monetary production' in the modern capitalist economy. While the influence of Keynes on Hyman Minsky's 'investment theory of the cycle and financial theory of investment'[1] is obvious and well known, this chapter demonstrates that Veblen's approach is in some ways closer to Minsky's. Further, Veblen's approach is in many important respects more informative, and still relevant for developing an understanding of modern business practice. On the one hand, this is not surprising as Keynes had let many of the monetary details 'fall into the background'.[2] However, it is surprising that most followers of Keynes have not mined Veblen's 1904 *The Theory of Business Enterprise* for arguments that nicely complement and extend Keynes's better known approach. This chapter concludes with an assessment of these theories in light of the global financial collapse.

Veblen and the Distinction between the Money Economy and the Credit Economy

Probably following his teacher Richard Ely, Veblen distinguishes the 'natural economy' from the 'money economy' and the 'credit economy'.[3] The first refers to an economy in which distribution is 'in kind' without reliance on markets. The money economy refers to a system in which there is 'ubiquitous resort to the market as a vent for products and a source of supply of goods. The characteristic feature of this money economy is the goods market.'[4] This is the sort of economy addressed by classical political economy, in which 'the welfare of the community at large is accepted as the central and tone-giving interest, about which a comprehensive, harmonious order of nature circles and gravitates'.[5] The end of production is consumption; the means is 'monetary' in the sense that money is used in markets. While the conventional theory can be criticised for misunderstanding the nature of production even in the money economy, Veblen argues that regardless of the 'merits of such a point of view', they 'need not detain the inquiry' because '[m] odern business management does not take that point of view'.[6] By the 1870s, the money economy had been displaced by the credit economy.[7]

Veblen's main purpose in *The Theory of Business Enterprise* was to examine the operations of the credit economy. His distinction between industrial and pecuniary pursuits and his argument that 'the motive of business is pecuniary gain' are too well known to require explication.[8] What is more interesting is his argument that in the credit economy, it is not the goods market that dominates, for '[t]he capital market has taken the first place [...] The capital market is the modern economic feature which makes and identifies the higher "credit economy" as such.'[9] By 'capital' he means the 'capitalized presumptive earning capacity', 'comprised of usufruct of whatever credit extension the given business concern's industrial equipment and good-will will support'.[10] This is different from 'effective industrial capital', the aggregate of the capitalised material items engaged in industrial output, as 'business capital' adds goodwill plus the credit that can be obtained using industrial capital and other non-industrial property as collateral. The key to his analysis is the divergence between the value of industrial capital and the value of business capital, because this is the basis for credit extension that ultimately generates liquidation crises, as well as trust formations.

The 'putative earning-capacity' is subject to fluctuation (and, as we will see, manipulation) because it

is the outcome of many surmises with respect to prospective earnings and the like; and these surmises will vary from one man to the next, since they proceed on an imperfect, largely conjectural, knowledge of present earning-capacity and on the still more imperfectly known future course of the goods market and of corporate policy.[11]

When presumptive earning capacity rises, this is capitalised in credit and equity markets, with the '[f]unds obtained on credit [...] applied to extend the business; there is thus 'in the nature of things a cumulative character' because 'the money value of the collateral is at the same time the capitalized value of the property, computed on the basis of its presumptive earning-capacity'.[12] In this manner, credit fuels capitalised values, which fuels more credit and further increases the discrepancy between industrial and business capital values.

Management's interest is to maximise this differential, to increase capitalised value.[13] This then encourages the concentration of ownership through two processes. First, credit expansion will normally proceed to 'abnormal' levels as putative earnings are 'over-capitalised'. The inflation of the value of the business capital as collateral will rise faster than prospective earnings that ultimately depend on final sales, the majority of which is constituted by sales to consumers (see below).[14] Eventually the over-capitalisation will be recognised, credit will not be renewed, loans will be called-in and assets will be sold. Because in a period of 'buoyancy' 'not only is the capitalization of the industrial property inflated on the basis of expectation, but in the making of contracts the margin of security is less closely looked after', hence there will be a general reliance on an extensive network of 'contracts for future performance'.[15] A general liquidation crisis can follow – all it requires is the realisation by one large creditor that the earning capacity of some debtor is not as great as the capitalisation requires. When credit is cut off, the debtor is forced to default on contracts, and to call-in others, with forced sales of assets following. This snowballs into a general liquidation that allows creditors to accumulate and concentrate industrial capital; however, the nominal value of the business capital must shrink to effect concentration of ownership along these lines.

Second, credit is used in reorganisation through corporate takeover, as industrial capital plus 'goodwill' created through concentration of ownership serves as collateral for loans.[16] Further, there is something of a 'widow's curse' to goodwill, as 'it is of a spiritual nature, such that, by virtue of the ubiquity proper to spiritual bodies, the whole of it may undividedly [sic] be present in every part of the various structures which it has created' – it is never diminished but rather can augment the capitalised value 'of the next corporation into which it enters'.[17] The business capital is packaged and sold at a price based on the discrepancy between the putative and actual earning capacity. Increasing this discrepancy is the prime motivation driving the 'business interest' of the managers – 'not serviceability of the output, nor even vendibility of the output', but rather 'vendibility of corporate capital'.[18] They are 'able to induce a discrepancy [...] by expedients well known and approved for the purpose. Partial information, as well as misinformation, sagaciously given out at a critical juncture, will go far [...] [i]f they are shrewd business men, as they commonly are.'[19] Note that like liquidation, trusts achieve concentration; however, they do it without diminishing capitalised values.

Trust formation, in turn, is impelled by rising efficiency of industrial capital, which destroys the actual earning capacity of business capital. Technological advances ensure that newer industrial capital will reduce the pecuniary capacity of older industrial capital that is burdened with the credit that was advanced based on the discrepancy between capitalised presumptive earning-capacity and industrial capital – a discrepancy that now cannot be maintained. However, recapitalisation based on lower prospective earnings is not possible due to credit obligations – interest must be paid. The only solution is to prevent rising industrial efficiency from lowering price, but so long as competition exists this is not possible. As prices fall, production becomes unprofitable and chronic depression sets in. Veblen argues that while this is frequently described as a situation of 'over-production' or of 'under-consumption', it is really due to a 'malady of the affections' – earnings will not cover contracted commitments with a net profit that 'bears a reasonable relation to the current rate of interest'.[20] While a burst of temporary 'wasteful' spending (on wars, colonies and the 'employment of the courtly, diplomatic and ecclesiastical personnel', for example) can maintain sales and prices, waste cannot long keep up with rising industrial efficiency.[21] The solution is 'a business coalition on such a scale as to regulate the output and eliminate competitive sales and competitive investment [...] to neutralize the cheapening of goods and services effected by current industrial progress'.[22] Thankfully, '[t]he higher development of the machine process makes competitive business impracticable, but it carries a remedy for its own evils in that it makes coalition practicable' through collateralised credit expansion that can finance trust formation.[23]

Similarities with Keynes

Those familiar with John Maynard Keynes's *General Theory of Employment, Interest and Money* will recognise many similarities in the previous discussion. These include:

1. Both make a distinction between historical epochs based on the role played by money. In his preparation of the *General Theory*, Keynes spoke of the 'monetary theory of production', that would deal with an economy in which money plays a part of its own and affects motives and decisions and is, in short, one of the operative factors in the situation, so that the course of events cannot be predicted, either in the long period or in the short, without a knowledge of the behavior of money between the first state and the last. And it is this which we ought to mean when we speak of a monetary economy.[24] He distinguishes this from a 'real-exchange economy' that might use money, but 'does not allow it to enter into motives or decisions'.[25] Like Veblen, Keynes insists that in the modern economy, 'the firm is dealing throughout in terms of money. It has no object in the world except to end up with more money than it started with.'[26] Keynes's 'monetary economy' is thus similar to Veblen's 'credit economy' stage.[27]

2. Both emphasise the spending decisions of business, rather than consumer sovereignty. Investment is the critical variable in Keynes's approach and, as in Veblen's theory of business enterprise, it is forward looking, a function of expected future profits. In both approaches, expected profits are weighed against 'the' current interest rate. Because the future is uncertain, investment fluctuates with changes to confidence or 'affections'. In both approaches, new capital competes with old investments. While Veblen focuses on the improved efficiency of the new industrial capital, Keynes emphasises the importance of different interest rates: if interest rates have fallen, the newer investment goods are satisfied with a lower profit rate – a point Veblen also recognised.[28]

3. Finally, both recognised a tendency toward insufficient aggregate demand. Where Veblen attributed this to a tendency for the nominal value of the capitalised firm to rise faster than prospective earnings that depend largely on final sales for consumption, Keynes argued that a 'demand gap' opens because the marginal propensity to consume is less than unity. By distinguishing between two kinds of spending, one (mostly, consumption) a function of income and the other (mostly, investment) autonomous, Keynes created the possibility that aggregate demand (D curve) would not rise as fast as aggregate supply (Z curve). The 'special properties' of money are then invoked in Keynes's argument that investment will not normally be at the level required to generate the point of effective demand at full employment.[29] Still, both blame the unemployment of productive resources on the profit-seeking behaviour of entrepreneurs. Further, both find a temporary expedient in 'wasteful spending' to prop up demand. In spite of the tendency of 'Keynesians' to present Keynes's theory

as 'fine-tuning', Keynes was as sceptical as Veblen concerning the use of wasteful spending to resolve problems of effective demand.[30]

Differences from Keynes

Let us turn to an assessment of the areas in which Veblen's analysis provides more insight into the operation of the modern capitalist economy.

1. Because Keynes was most concerned with demonstrating the determination of the point of effective demand, he primarily focused on the demand side (or multiplier) effects of investment and ignored the supply side (or, capacity) effects. This led, of course, to the extensions by Roy Harrod and Evsey Domar, which then spurred growth theory – unfortunately, mostly down a neoclassical synthesis path – and the Cambridge/capital theory debates. Work by Harold Vatter and John Walker shows how accounting for the capacity effects of investment leads to an explanation for the chronic stagnation that grips modern capitalism: capital-saving technological advance causes the capacity effects of investment to continually outstrip multiplier effects on demand, generating an excess capacity that depresses investment and growth.[31] This is closely related to the argument made by Veblen in *The Theory of Business Enterprise* that technological advance affects *all* production, increasing capacity faster than potential pecuniary earnings, thus 'chronic depression, more or less pronounced, is normal to business under the fully developed regime of the machine industry'.[32] Again, Veblen is pessimistic that increasing 'unproductive consumption', including that by a deficit-spending government, will allow demand to keep pace with growth of industrial efficiency.[33]

2. Veblen's discussion of the role played by credit in financing growth of capitalised values not only provides insight into the important distinction between industrial capital and business capital (less important in Keynes and in those extensions made by Vatter and Walker), but it is also critical to his description of the business cycle and the crisis phase that leads to liquidation. While Keynes provides a chapter titled 'Notes on the Trade Cycle', *General Theory* does not really provide a theory of the cycle. By contrast, Veblen ties his theory of the business enterprise to the theory of the cycle and links this to his theory of growing concentration of ownership. Keynes does address the distinction between ownership and control of the production process, arguing that the modern corporation's owners know little about operations, forcing management to focus on the short term out of fear of possible adverse impacts on stock prices.[34] However, unlike Veblen, Keynes is not wholly critical of the increasing corporatisation of the economy. Indeed, his call for increased 'socialization of investment' (explicitly in Chapter 24 of *General Theory* and less directly in his earlier essay on 'The End of *Laissez-Faire*') could be interpreted as a call for greater concentration of decision-making that would allow concerns with the long term and social interests to play a bigger role.

3. Chapter 12 of *General Theory* is famous for its discussion of 'whirlwinds of optimism and pessimism', speculation and uncertainty, and for its criticism of the operation

of the stock market, likened to a game of 'Old Maid, [or] of Musical Chairs', or in which 'each competitor has to pick, not those faces which he himself finds prettiest […] nor even those which average opinion genuinely thinks the prettiest […] [but rather] what average opinion expects the average opinion to be'.[35] While Veblen agrees that there is uncertainty and speculation involved in business enterprise, he emphasises pecuniary initiative in manipulating stock values to increase differential valuation between industrial and business capital. Keynes does address the distinction between ownership and control of the production process, arguing that the modern corporation's owners know little about operations. The ignorance of owners forces management to focus excessively on the firm's short term performance out of fear of possible adverse impacts on stock prices.[36] While the manipulation does carry risk, it is 'not so much to the manipulators as such, as to the corporations […] [and to] the business men who are not immediately concerned in this traffic'.[37] Veblen's preference for an explanation based on 'capitalisation' over 'speculation' would seem to apply much more readily to the dealings of the Milkens and Enrons of the world. While Keynes's description might have captured the experience of many who were duped by the NASDAQ 'buoyancy', those who actually *produced* the discrepancy between putative earnings on an imaginary scale versus actual earnings capacity in mostly negative territory did quite well.

None of this is meant to be a critique of Keynes's *General Theory*. Keynes's purpose there was narrower – to present an alternative to the neoclassical theory of the determination of the point of equilibrium. Further, Keynes wanted to provide an 'internal' critique, exploding neoclassical theory from within by adopting, where possible, some of the neoclassical assumptions. By contrast, Veblen was the eternal outsider, attacking 'on several fronts at once: nationalism, the business system, war, *de facto* political oligarchy, a corrupted educational system, and, most generally, irrationality'.[38] The purpose of this section has been to draw out some of the similarities between Keynes and Veblen and to point the way toward improving our understanding of what Keynes called the monetary production economy and what Veblen termed the credit economy.

Minsky and the Institutionalist Tradition

There are a number of traditions that have attempted to reject the self-adjusting vision of the system. Keynes, of course, had doubted that vision at least since his essay on the end of laissez-faire. Others within the institutionalist tradition, including Veblen and Minsky, share a similar framework of analysis that rejects the notion of an equilibrium-seeking system and sees money and finance as the major source of problems with capitalist systems – the pecuniary interests dominate. Minsky calls this a 'pre-analytic vision' of the operation of the financial markets and their role in directing the evolution of the economic system.[39] In contrast to the 'efficient markets' approach, this pre-analytic vision concerns decision-making in a system in which dynamics are not equilibrating, indeed in which rational behaviour by individuals leads to systemically irrational results. This goes beyond the acceptance of 'radical uncertainty', as in Shackle's approach or in the Austrian approach.

Instead, as Minsky put it, 'agents in the model have a model of the model' but they know their models are wrong. Their behaviour is based on a model they know to be incorrect and thus subject to revision; when their model changes, they change their behaviour.

In Minsky's financial instability hypothesis, uncertainty is the result of engaging in commitments to make future financial payments with financial receipts that are uncertain because they, too, will occur in the future. In turn, those future receipts will not be forthcoming unless, at that future time, there is a willingness to enter into additional financial commitments (since spending in the future will determine future receipts). Hence, what one does today depends on what one expects others to do today, as well as into the future. Since commitments made in the past may not be validated today, and those made today may not be validated tomorrow, the movement of the system through time need not be toward equilibrium. Minsky argues instead that behaviour will change based on outcomes, in such a manner that instability will be created. For example, a 'run of good times' (in which expectations are at least met) will encourage more risk taking, which increases financial leveraging that creates more risk. While many accounts of Minsky's work focus on the behaviour of non-financial firms (as in the investment decision of a manufacturing firm), Minsky argues that behaviour within financial institutions also evolves with innovations that stretch liquidity.

This provides an endogenous, rational explanation of the possible, volatile behaviour of asset prices, which is not self-equilibrating. Indeed, financial crises are usually the result of the impact of decisions taken within organised financial institutions – outside the market process – on the balance sheet stability of financial institutions. The 'run of good times' leads to changes of the rules of thumb guiding practice within financial institutions, leading decision makers to test the limits of acceptable practice. Minsky's theory explains the evolution of the balance sheet positions of financial institutions and the impact on financial markets through financial layering. In particular, financial institutions find it rational to increase leverage; and rising leverage plays a crucial role in the financial instability hypothesis.

Minsky argues that the endogenous process of profit-seeking innovation will be not only a source of instability, but also make it impossible to design financial reform proposals that produce financial stability. The search for such regulations only makes sense within a theory of self-adjusting equilibrium – where 'getting prices right' is all that is necessary. In an evolutionary theory of innovation and instability, the concept of stability and the regulations that would be required are completely different. It requires a completely different view of the operation of financial institutions.

In the next section, I quickly review the transformation of the financial system over the post-war period as fragility rose. In many ways, the trends up to the GFC of 2007 simply replicated the processes that Veblen had discussed before the 1929 crash.

The Transformation Away from Banking to Money Managers: Finance Capitalism Reprised?

Rudolf Hilferding identifies a new stage of capitalism characterised by complex financial relations and domination of industry by finance.[10] He argues that the most characteristic feature of finance capitalism is rising concentration which, on the one hand, eliminates 'free competition' through the formation of cartels and trusts and, on the other, brings bank and industrial capital into an ever more intertwined relationship.[41] Veblen, Keynes, Joseph A. Schumpeter and, later, Minsky also recognised the new stage of capitalism. For Keynes, it represented the domination of speculation over enterprise; for Schumpeter, it was the command over resources by innovators with access to finance; while Veblen distinguished between industrial and pecuniary pursuits.

By the 1870s, plant and equipment had become so expensive that external finance of investment became necessary. External finance, in turn, is a prior commitment of future gross profits. This creates the possibility of default and bankruptcy – the concerns of Minsky – while at the same time it opens the door for the separation of ownership from control. From this separation Keynes derives the 'whirlwinds of optimism and pessimism' addressed by Chapter 12 of his *General Theory* (attributed to the precariousness of valuing firms based on average opinion), while Veblen's analysis points to management's manipulation of the value of business capital to dupe owners. Schumpeter's view was obviously more benign, as his 'vision' of markets was much more orthodox, but he still recognised the central importance of finance in breaking out of a 'circular flow' where money merely facilitates production and circulation of a given size through the finance of innovation that allows the circular flow to grow. With the rise of finance capitalism, access to external finance of positions in assets was necessary. This fundamentally changed the nature of capitalism in a manner that made it much more unstable.

As discussed above, Veblen designated the early twentieth-century version of capitalism the 'credit economy', wherein it is not the goods market that dominates, for '[t]he capital market has taken the first place [...] The capital market is the modern economic feature which makes and identifies the higher "credit economy" as such.'[42] Keynes also distinguished between 'speculation' and 'enterprise' and discussed the transition from nineteenth-century capitalism where enterprise dominated toward the twentieth-century domination by Wall Street of business decision making. Recall Keynes's famous warning: 'the position is serious when enterprise becomes a bubble on a whirlpool of speculation. When the capital development of a country becomes a by-product of the activities of a casino, the job is likely to be ill-done.'[43] And, as discussed, Veblen insisted that from the view of Wall Street's traders, this was not high-risk activity.

As John K. Galbraith makes clear, stocks could be manipulated by insiders – Wall Street's financial institutions – through a variety of 'pump and dump' schemes.[44] Indeed, the 1929 crash resulted from excesses promoted by investment trust subsidiaries of Wall Street's banks. Since the famous firms like Goldman Sachs were partnerships, they did not issue stock; hence they put together investment trusts that would purport to hold valuable equities in other firms (often in other affiliates, which sometimes held no stocks other than those in Wall Street trusts) and then sell shares in these trusts to a gullible public. Effectively, trusts were an early form of mutual fund, with the 'mother' investment house investing a small amount of capital in their offspring, highly leveraged using other people's money. Goldman Sachs and others would then whip up a speculative fever in shares, reaping capital gains. However, trust investments amounted to little more than pyramid schemes (the worst kind of what Minsky called Ponzi finance) – there was very little in the way of real production or income associated with all this trading in paper. Indeed, as Galbraith shows, the 'real' economy was long past its peak – there were no 'fundamentals' to drive the Wall Street boom. Inevitably, it collapsed and a 'debt deflation' began as everyone tried to sell out of their positions in stocks, causing prices to collapse. Spending on the 'real economy' suffered and we were off to the Great Depression.

For some decades after World War II, 'finance capital' played an uncommonly small role. Memories of the Great Depression generated reluctance to borrow. Unions pressed for, and obtained, rising compensation – allowing rising living standards to be financed mostly out of income. In any case, the government guaranteed mortgages and student loans (both at relatively low interest rates) – so most of the household debt was safe, anyway. Jimmy Stewart's small thrifts and banks (burned during the Depression) adopted prudent lending practices. The Glass-Steagall Act separated investment banks from commercial banks, and various New Deal reforms protected market share for the heavily regulated portions of the financial sector. Military Keynesianism provided demand for the output of industry, often at guaranteed marked-up pricing. Low debt, high wages, high consumption and big government promoted stability.

The 1960s and 1970s saw the development of an array of financial institution liabilities circumventing New Deal constraints as finance responded to profit opportunities. After the disastrous Volcker experiment in monetarism (1979–82), the pace of innovation accelerated as many new financial practices were adopted to protect institutions from interest rate risk. These included securitisation of mortgages, derivatives to hedge interest rate (and exchange rate) risk and many types of 'off balance sheet' operations (helping to evade reserve and capital restraints). Favourable tax treatment of interest encouraged leveraged buy-outs to substitute debt for equity (with the take-over financed by debt that would be serviced by the target's future income flows). Another major transformation occurred in the 1990s with innovations that increased access to credit and changed attitudes of firms and households about prudent levels of debt. Now consumption led the way as the economy finally returned to 1960s-esque performance. Robust growth returned, now fuelled by private deficit spending, not by the growth of government spending and private income. All of this led to what Minsky called money manager capitalism.[45]

While many point to the demise of Glass-Steagall separation of banking by function as a key mistake leading to the crisis, the problem really was the demise of underwriting. In other words, the problem and solution are not really related to functional separation but rather to the erosion of underwriting standards that is inevitable over a run of good times when a trader mentality triumphs. If a bank believes it can offload toxic assets before values are questioned, its incentive to do proper underwriting is reduced. And if asset prices are generally rising on trend, the bank will be induced to share in the gains by taking positions in the assets. This is why the current call by some for a return to Glass-Steagall separation, or to force banks to 'put skin in the game' by holding some fraction of the toxic waste they produce are both wrong-headed.

Minsky argues that the convergence of the various types of banks within the umbrella bank holding company, and within shadow banks was fuelled by growth of money manager capitalism. It was also encouraged by the expansion of the government safety net, as Minsky remarks: 'a proliferation of government endorsements of private obligations'.[46] Indeed, it is impossible to tell the story of the current crisis without reference to the implicit guarantee given by the Treasury to the mortgage market through its GSEs (Fannie and Freddie), through the student loan market (Sallie), and even through the 'Greenspan Put' and the Bernanke 'Great Moderation', which gave the impression to markets that the government would never let markets fail. In the aftermath of the crisis, the government's guarantee of liabilities went far beyond FDIC-insured deposits to cover larger denomination deposits as well as money market funds and the Fed-extended lender of last resort facilities to virtually all financial institutions (with bailouts also going to automotive companies and so on). This really was a foregone conclusion once Glass-Steagall was gutted and investment banking, commercial banking and all manner of financial services were consolidated in a single financial 'big box' superstore with explicit government guarantees over a portion of the liabilities. It was always clear that if problems developed somewhere in a highly integrated system, the Treasury and Fed would be on the hook to rescue the shadow banks, too.

In the 1990s the big investment banks were still partnerships, so they found it impossible to directly benefit from a run-up of the stock market, similar to the situation in 1929. An investment bank could earn fees by arranging initial public offerings for start-ups and it could trade stocks for others or on its own account. This offered the opportunity to exploit inside information, or to manipulate the timing of trades, or to push the dogs onto clients. But in the euphoric irrational exuberance of the late 1990s that looked like chump change. How could an investment bank's management get a bigger share of the action?

In 1999, the largest partnerships went public to enjoy the advantages of stock issue in a boom. Top management was rewarded with stocks – leading to the same pump-and-dump incentives that drove the 1929 boom. To be sure, traders like Robert Rubin (who would become Treasury secretary) had already come to dominate firms like Goldman Sachs. Traders necessarily take a short view – you are only as good as your last trade. More importantly, traders take a zero-sum view of deals: there will be a winner and a loser, with the investment bank pocketing fees for bringing the two sides together. Better yet, the investment bank would take one of the two sides – the winning side, of course – and pocket the fees and collect the winnings. Why would anyone voluntarily become the client, knowing that the deal was ultimately zero-sum and that the investment bank would have the winning hand? No doubt there were some clients with an outsized view of their own competence or luck; but most customers were wrongly swayed by investment banks' good reputations. But from the perspective of hired management, the purpose of a good reputation is to exploit it for personal gain – what William Black calls control fraud.[47]

Before this transformation, trading profits were a small part of investment bank revenues – for example, before it went public, only 28% of Goldman Sachs's revenues came from trading and investing activities. That is now about 80% of its revenue. While many think of Goldman Sachs and JP Morgan (the remaining investment banks since the demise of Lehman, Bear and Merrill, which all folded or were absorbed) as banks, they are really more like huge hedge funds, albeit very special ones that now hold bank charters, granted during the crisis when investment banks were having trouble refinancing positions in assets – giving them access to the Fed's discount window and to FDIC insurance. That in turn lets them obtain funding at near-zero interest rates. Indeed, in

2009 Goldman spent only a little over $5 billion to borrow, versus $26 billion in interest expenses in 2008 – a $21 billion subsidy thanks to its access to cheap, government-insured deposits. The two remaining investment banks were also widely believed to be 'backstopped' by the government – under no circumstances would they be allowed to fail – keeping stock prices up. However, after the SEC began to investigate some of Goldman Sachs's practices, that belief was thrown into doubt, causing share prices to plummet.

In some ways, things were even worse than they had been in 1929 because the investment banks had gone public – issuing equities directly into the portfolios of households and indirectly to households through the portfolios of managed money. It was thus not a simple matter of having Goldman Sachs or Citibank jettison one of its unwanted trust offspring – problems with the stock or other liabilities of the behemoth financial institutions would rattle Wall Street and threaten the solvency of pension funds and other invested funds. This finally became clear to the authorities after the problems with Bear and Lehman. The layering and linkages among firms – made opaque by over the counter derivatives such as credit default swaps – made it impossible to let them fail one-by-one, as failure of one would bring down the whole house of cards. The problem we faced is that total financial liabilities in the US amounted to about five times GDP (versus 300% in 1929) – so that every dollar of income must service five dollars of debt. That is an average leverage ratio of five times income. That is one way to measure leverage, for as Minsky and Mayer argue, this is, historically, the important measure for bank profitability – which ultimately must be linked to repayment of principle and interest out of income flows.[48]

Another measure is the ratio of debt to assets. This became increasingly important during the real-estate boom, when mortgage brokers would find finance for 100% or more of the value of a mortgage, on the expectation that real-estate prices would rise. That is a trader's, not a banker's perspective because it relies on either sale of the asset or refinancing. While a traditional banker might feel safe with a capital leverage ratio of 12 or 20 – with careful underwriting to ensure that the borrower would be able to make payments – for a mortgage originator or securitiser who has no plans to hold the mortgage what matters is the ability to place the security. Many considerations then come into play, including prospective asset price appreciation, credit ratings, monoline and credit default swap 'insurance' and 'overcollateralization' (markets for the lower tranches of securities).

We need not go deeply into the details of these complex instruments. What is important is that income flows take a back seat in such arrangements, and acceptable capital leverage ratios are much higher. For money managers, capital leverage ratios are 30 and reach up to several hundred. But even these large numbers hide the reality that risk exposures can be very much higher because many commitments are not reported on balance sheets. There are unknown and essentially unquantifiable risks entailed in counter-parties – for example, in supposedly hedged credit default swaps in which one sells 'insurance' on suspected toxic waste and then offsets risks by buying 'insurance' that is only as good as the counter-party. Because balance sheets are linked in highly complex and uncertain ways, failure of one counter-party can spread failures throughout the system. And all of these financial instruments ultimately rest on the shoulders of some homeowner trying to service his or her mortgage out of income flows – on average with $5 of debts and only $1 of income to service them. As Minsky argues, 'National income and its distribution is the 'rock' upon which the capitalist financial structure rests.'[49] Unfortunately, that rock is holding up a huge financial structure, and the trend toward concentration of income and wealth at the top makes it ever more difficult to support the weight of the debt.

Moving away from income flows and to prospective asset price appreciation opened the door to Veblenian 'manipulation', just as it did in the late 1920s. A clever investment bank can always assign any price desired, pumping up fictitious 'goodwill' in the 1920s or using 'internal proprietary models' in the 2000s. Thus, we had a series of speculative bubbles (e.g. dot-com stocks, commodities, real estate) that allowed capital gains to dominate over income flows in price determination. The whole thing was fuelled by heavily leveraged lending. Collapse was a certainty, indeed desired by insiders who planned to get out first. And when it came, government intervened to save Wall Street. So unlike the 1929 crash, this time around there was no lesson learned, no cleaning of the financial house on Wall Street. Another bubble and bust awaits. But that is a story for another day.

Conclusions

In many important ways, the 2007 crash resulted from processes that replicated the problems analysed by Veblen and Keynes. While I think that Keynes's analysis provides the best theoretical framework from which to analyse the modern 'monetary production economy', Veblen's 'theory of business enterprise' provides a much more critical analysis of the actual processes. Minsky always argued that he stood on the shoulders of Keynes, borrowing the 'investment theory of the cycle' and adding 'the financial theory of investment'. But Minsky had been raised in the Chicago institutionalist tradition and it is obvious that institutional detail plays an important role in Minsky's approach. Indeed, Minsky was much less willing than Keynes to attempt to produce a 'general theory' – his theory was always specific, concerning the capitalism he observed. In that respect, he was much more like Veblen. His analysis of the transformation of US capitalism provides the insights we need to study the GFC. Unfortunately he died in 1996 so he cannot provide for us a study of 'the Great Crash' like the analysis that Galbraith provided for the 1929 crash. However, he does point the way.

Notes and References

1   Hyman Minsky, *Stabilizing an Unstable Economy* (New York: McGraw-Hill, 2008), 133.
2   John Maynard Keynes, 'Preface', *The General Theory of Employment, Interest, and Money* (New York and London: Harcourt Brace Jovanovich, 1964), 2.
3   In *Evolution of Industrial Society*, Richard Ely quotes German economist Bruno Hildebrand, founder of the German Historical School on this sequencing: truck economy (i.e. barter economy), money economy, credit economy. See Richard Ely, *Evolution of Industrial Society* (New York: Chautauqua Press, 1903).
4   Thorstein Veblen, *The Theory of Business Enterprise* (New York: Mentor Books, 1958), 75.
5   Ibid., 69.

6 Ibid., 16. Veblen argues that '[l]ooking at the process of economic life as a whole [...] [as if it were] a collective endeavor to purvey goods and services for the needs of collective humanity [...] need neither be defended nor refuted here, since it does not seriously touch the facts of modern business' (ibid., 196, 11n).

7 Of course, orthodoxy remains fixated on developing theory for the hypothesised economy dominated by the sovereign consumer and 'in which all things should work together for the welfare of mankind' (ibid., 69) – a theory that was not even appropriate to nineteenth-century capitalism.

8 Ibid., 16.

9 Ibid., 75.

10 Ibid., 65.

11 Ibid., 77.

12 Ibid., 55. Veblen goes on: 'competing business men bid up the material items of industrial equipment by the use of funds so obtained [...] the aggregate of values employed in a given undertaking increases [...] but since an advance of credit rests on the collateral as expressed in terms of value, an enhanced value of the property affords a basis for a further extension of credit' (ibid., 55). See also Patrick J. Raines and Charles G. Leathers, 'Veblenian stock markets and the efficient markets hypothesis', *Journal of Post-Keynesian Economics* 19.1 (Fall 1996): 137–51; Matthew C. Wilson, 'Budget Constraints and Business Enterprise: a Veblenian Analysis', *Journal of Economic Issues* 40.4 (December 2006): 1029–44, for discussions of use of collateral to support credit.

13 This is where the divergent interests of owners and managers become important, because 'the business interest of the managers demands, not serviceability of the output, nor even vendibility of the output, but an advantageous discrepancy in the price of the capital which they manage' (Veblen, *Business Enterprise*, 79).

14 Ibid., 56.

15 Ibid., 97.

16 This goodwill includes '[v]arious items, of very diverse character [...] the items included have this much in common that they are "immaterial wealth", "intangible assets"; which [...] are not serviceable to the community, but only to their owners' – precisely because it can be collateralised and thereby increase the divergence between the values of industrial and business capital (ibid., 70). Also, see Wilson, 'Budget Constraints' for discussion of market evaluation of goodwill.

17 Veblen, *Business Enterprise*, 85.

18 Ibid., 79.

19 Ibid., 77–8.

20 Ibid., 114; 105–6.

21 Ibid., 122–3.

22 Ibid., 115–16.

23 Ibid., 125.

24 John Maynard Keynes, *The General Theory and After, Part I Preparation, The Collected Writings of John Maynard Keynes*, ed. by D. E. Moggridge (London: Macmillan, 1973), 408–9.

25 Ibid., 408–9.

26 John Maynard Keynes, *The General Theory and After. A Supplement, The Collected Writings of John Maynard Keynes*, ed. by D. E. Moggridge (London: Macmillan and New York: Cambridge University Press for the Royal Economic Society, 1979), 89.

27 Interestingly, both Keynes and Veblen addressed the stability of the purchasing power of money. For Keynes, relatively stable value of money (especially in terms of the nominal wage) is essential to maintaining its liquidity (John Maynard Keynes, *The General Theory of Employment, Interest, and Money* (London: Harcourt Brace Jovanovich, 1964), 240–41, 270). For Veblen, the presumption of stability of nominal values is important for business practice (as opposed to

industrial pursuits): 'Capitalization as well as contracts are made in its terms, and the plans of the business men who control industry look to the money unit as the stable ground of all of their transactions', even though they know 'the value of money has varied incontinently throughout the course of history' (Veblen, *Business Enterprise*, 45).

28 '[A] low or declining rate of interest is effective in the way of depressing the business situation […] What gives effect to this drawback for the business enterprises which have such fixed interest charges to meet is the fact that the new investments […] come into competition with the old. These new or rejuvenated concerns are not committed to a scale of fixed charges carried over from a higher interest level' (ibid., 107). As Vining emphasises, in both Veblen and Keynes interest is eminently a pecuniary or monetary phenomenon; see Rutledge Vining, 'Suggestions of Keynes in the Writings of Veblen', *Journal of Political Economy* 47.5 (October 1939): 692–704.

29 L. Randall Wray, 'Keynes's Approach to Money: An Assessment after Seventy Years', *Atlantic Economic Journal* 34 (2006): 183–93.

30 For a discussion of similarities in Veblen and Keynes on this score, see Vining, 'Suggestions'. However, it is undoubtedly true that the policy recommendations in Chapter 24 of Keynes's *General Theory* are more optimistic than the prognosis of the 'natural decay of business enterprise' in Chapter 10 of Veblen's *Business Enterprise*.

31 See Harold G. Vatter and John F. Walker, *The Rise of Big Government in the United States* (Armonk: M. E. Sharpe, 1997).

32 Veblen, *Business Enterprise*, 112.

33 Ibid., 122–3.

34 As 'human nature desires quick results […] remoter gains are discounted by the average man at a very high rate' (Keynes, *General Theory*, 157).

35 'And there are some, I believe, who practice the fourth, fifth and higher degrees' (ibid., 156).

36 Veblen, *Business Enterprise*, 82.

37 Ibid., 82–3.

38 Douglas Dowd, *Thorstein Veblen* (New York: Washington Square Press, 1964), xii; see also Douglas Dowd, 'The Virtues of their Defects and the Defects of their Virtues: Reflections on John Kenneth Galbraith and Thorstein Veblen', in *Economics with a Public Purpose: Essays in Honour of John Kenneth Galbraith* (London: Routledge, 2001). Online: http://www.dougdowd.org/articlesAndCommentary/2000/TheVirtuesOfTheirDefects.php (accessed 26 July 2012).

39 Hyman Minsky, 'Schumpeter: Finance and Evolution', Hyman P. Minsky Archive, no. 314 (1988). Online: http://digitalcommons.bard.edu/hm_archive/314 (accessed 10 March 2012).

40 Rudolf Hilferding, *Finance Capital: A Study of the Latest Phase of Capitalist Development* (London: Routledge and Kegan Paul, 1981).

41 Hilferding 1981, 21–2.

42 Veblen, *Business Enterprise*, 75.

43 Keynes, *General Theory*, 159.

44 See John K. Galbraith, *The Great Crash 1929* (New York: Houghton Mifflin Harcourt, 2009).

45 Minsky defined it as follows: 'Capitalism in the United States is now in a new stage, money manager capitalism, in which the proximate owners of a vast proportion of financial instruments are mutual and pension funds. The total return on the portfolio is the only criteria used for judging the performance of the managers of these funds, which translates into an emphasis upon the bottom line in the management of business organizations'; see Hyman Minsky, 'Uncertainty and the Institutional Structure of Capitalist Economies', *Working Paper 155* (April 1996), Levy Working Papers.

46 Hyman Minsky, 'Reconstituting the Financial Structure: The United States' (prospective chapter, four parts) (13 May 1992), manuscript in Minsky Archives at Levy Institute, 39.

47 William K. Black, *The Best Way to Rob a Bank is to Own One: How Corporate Executives and Politicians Looted the S&L Industry* (Austin: University of Texas Press, 2005).

48 See Minsky, 'Reconstituting the Financial Structure'; Mayer, Martin, 'The Spectre of Banking', *One-Pager No. 3* (20 May 2010), Levy Economics Institute.

49 Minsky, 'Reconstituting the Financial Structure', part III, 2.

Chapter 15

PREDATION FROM VEBLEN UNTIL NOW: REMARKS TO THE VEBLEN SESQUICENTENNIAL CONFERENCE

James K. Galbraith

The language of the market serves a social function, which is to obscure and also to sanitise many economic encounters – especially encounters between the large business enterprise on one side and its customers, workers and suppliers on the other. On the blackboard, these encounters appear balanced: the supply curve matches that of demand; both are drawn in lines of equal width. The underlying thought is that by their weight of numbers, consumers, workers and suppliers just offset the mass of the organised firms. But of course no such balance exists in real life. There is every difference between an organised and a disorganised force, between an army and a mob. Thus, the lived experience of the relationship between the private individual and the business firm is, always and everywhere, one of a radical difference in power. The appropriate way to think about this is in terms that acknowledge the imbalance, and, although the fact is not very well known, for this purpose there already exists an economics of predator and prey.

In 1899, Thorstein Veblen published the first and still the leading tract on economic predation, a masterpiece called *The Theory of the Leisure Class*. The metaphor is evolutionary and Veblen's treatment is a high point in evolutionary political economy. Veblen writes that predation is a phase in the evolution of culture, 'attained only when the predatory attitude has become the habitual and accredited spiritual attitude […] when the fight has become the dominant note in the current theory of life'.[1]

Predation is not class struggle, and Veblen's approach is quite different from that of Karl Marx. Several decades before, Marx had written that the point and purpose of capitalism was accumulation – 'Accumulate! Accumulate! That is Moses and the Prophets!'[2] – while the contradiction of capitalism lay in its inability to bring wages above subsistence levels, in the 'immiseration of the proletariat'.[3] The increasing inequality between capitalists and workers would bring on revolutionary consciousness among workers, who would, Marx imagined, organise themselves under the leadership of the Communist Party. Veblen, looking at the world through a detached, anthropologist's eye, saw the forward projection of historical forces in this way as a fallacy of induction; he did not think it was very likely.

Writing two decades after Veblen, in the wake of the Great War, John Maynard Keynes would puzzle over the slow but steady improvement of living standards in the working class. This was something that classical political economy did not predict, and could not easily explain. Keynes concluded that it was the non-illusory result of an illusion: a 'double bluff'. The capitalists saved and invested, Keynes writes, thinking that the beneficiaries of their thrift would be their own children and grandchildren, when in fact the largest share of the benefits flowed instead to their own employees.[1] Meanwhile, the workers, conscious of their modest but unexpected gains, were largely content to continue to let the capitalists make the decisions respecting the allocation of resources, and, therefore, chose to cooperate with the system rather than to rebel against it. For Marx, revolutionary consciousness would lead to revolution, whereas for Keynes, romantic illusions were likely to prevent it.

Unlike Marx or Keynes, Veblen was quite free of any preoccupation with the tendency of society toward either salvation or upheaval. His interest was in the ongoing process of social life – in the character of 'the fight'. This was something that he saw as necessarily having long-term continuity in human society: as part of an evolutionary process, any pattern of social behaviour must have characteristics that permit it to persist over long periods of time.

Thus, the point of accumulation, as Veblen saw it, is not to advance class interest or the larger good; either of these objectives would have to be seen as relatively novel developments in human social life. Accumulation was part of an age-old pattern of behaviour, the point and purpose of which were to establish the ongoing dominance of one party over another. And this dominance is not that of capitalists over workers – that dominance was taken for granted on both sides; overthrowing it was a far-fetched possibility of interest largely to visionaries and romantics. The real fight – the ongoing battle in all societies, as Veblen saw it – was rather to establish rank and hierarchy *within and among the members of the leisure class.*

In the 'higher barbarian culture', Veblen writes, the 'industrial orders' comprise most of the women, servants, slaves and other chattel, plus the craftspeople and a smattering of engineers.[5] These people are underlings, and they alone perform what in modern societies is called work. Only for them, therefore, is it appropriate to think of wages and salaries as compensation for the drudgery of toil. Those who are higher up in the pecking order take a different view. And while (as Veblen writes) to an outsider the work of the hunter and that of the herder may seem functionally similar, this is not at all the 'barbarian's sense of the matter'.[6]

The non-industrial orders comprise the leisure class: warriors, government, athletes and priests. Captains of industry are an outgrowth of the warrior caste, which explains the organisation of much of business along military lines. Modern intellectuals form a minor offshoot of the priests. The leisure classes do not work. Rather, they hold offices. They perform rituals. They enact deeds of honour and valour. For them therefore income is not compensation for toil. It serves no functional purpose. It is, rather, a testament by the community to the prestige it accords them, to the esteem in which they are held. It is a way, in other words, of keeping score.

Predation is what the leisure class does. They prey on the industrial classes as a matter of course, and on each other as a matter of honour. Yet this does not mean that the industrial orders – the chattel – are driven to the brink of subsistence. On the contrary: the success of the predators depends, in part, on healthy prey. Wives and servants are fed and decorated to reflect the stature of their masters; engineers are kept comfortable with 'full lunch buckets' so as to keep the industrial machinery running smoothly. Since the lower orders generally understand this, they also realise that their own position could be worse than it is. For this reason, they are not intrinsically revolutionary nor inevitably destined to become so. But also contrary to Keynes, their understanding of their position is not based on illusion. It is, rather, part of the age-old order of things.

Instead, the ecology of predator–prey relationships is one of *mutual* interdependence. Predators rely on prey for their sustenance, but they also require and must motivate their assistance. The true function of the clan, tribe, family unit or company is not to enrich the owner/master at the expense of the underlings, but to enrich him at the expense of surrounding clans, tribes, families or companies. In this contest, the underlings naturally must enjoy some benefit: both to motivate their cooperation and to illustrate the success of the collective enterprise.

Meanwhile, the prey also relies on the predators – to enforce industrial discipline. This is a function they could, in principle, carry out for themselves – Veblen hoped, one day, for a 'soviet of technicians'.[7] But the mechanics of an effective soviet are not easily mastered, and when the experiment was eventually tried, it failed. (The communist societies that emerged in the mid-twentieth century proved to be rough on predators – 'class enemies' – but fatally lax on worker efficiency). Predator–prey societies can be efficient: harshly disciplined on the factory floor but otherwise comparatively free. This, of course, explains (in part) why the capitalist economies bested the Soviet Union over the course of the century after Veblen wrote.

Why go over this territory here and now? The reason is that Veblen's concept of predation neatly exposes what an analysis based on the notion of the market conceals – that there are always two strategies available to the predator. One is to mobilise resources and build organisation – comprised of the industrial orders – to compete against other enterprises. And the other is auto-predation: to prey directly on your own chattel. The first is difficult, while the second, in the short term, is comparatively easy. The first is a strategy for competitive self-enrichment, and the second is a strategy for eventual collective ruin. Yet the market mechanism cannot distinguish between them. Indeed it is prone, in the short run, to favour the second strategy over the first. This is the essential problem that predation poses for the market system.

It is not a new problem, nor a new way of framing a problem. It is merely a problem that a generation of economics has obliterated under a blizzard of forgetting. The whole history of the economics of the business firm in the first half of the twentieth century can be seen, in very large part, as a struggle to come to grips with this problem; while that of the second half was, very largely, an effort to rationalise a failure to do so. The first half of the twentieth century gave us the trust-busters, the progressive movement, institutional economics and the New Deal. The second half gave us neoclassical economics, competitive equilibrium theory, law and economics, and ultimately the economic practices of government from Reagan to Bush.

The solution arrived at during the first half of the twentieth century was a framework of law and regulation, a complex and pervasive set of limits and rules governing business practice. In the century since Veblen wrote, such limits and rules became practically universal: virtually no complex business activity escapes their effect. They also became the prime battleground of American politics, and they did so with a twist that Veblen, as a student of the sociology of economists, would have appreciated. For virtually all economists who specialise in the field now do so from a professional starting point that is profoundly hostile to public regulation of business practice. The 'perspective of economics' on this matter stands firmly with those who would – not in every particular, but as a general rule – rip up a century's worth of regulatory evolution and start again. The economists here stand with Friedrich von Hayek and Milton Friedman – and firmly against the sweep of history over 100 years. They are the romantics, the revolutionaries, standing against a pervasive practice and not quite understanding how it got that way.

Indeed the economics of the past generation has set up the regulator – and in particular the government regulator – as a bogey and a burden. He is at best a painful necessity and at worst a useless imposition. The doctrine and methods of cost–benefit analysis give this perspective an operational dimension: regulations should not be imposed, unless the 'benefits exceed the costs'. In the Reagan years, the cost–benefit approach found its champion in Murray Weidenbaum, Reagan's first chair of the Council of Economic Advisers, whose Center for the Study of American Business had attempted to aggregate the 'burden' of regulation: a convenient figure of $100 billion was duly uncovered and widely publicised. Later political battles against particular regulatory 'impositions' could then be fought, by the straightforward device of minimising benefits and exaggerating costs.

The cost–benefit approach thus frames the issue of regulation in a particular way. On one side, one finds business, the provider of goods and services to a general public that must pay the 'cost' of regulation. 'Business' here is taken, for purposes of simplicity that are by no means innocent, as a monolith: all business is supposed by the analysis to share the same technical characteristics and, therefore, to be influenced by regulation in the same way. On the other side, one finds 'advocacy groups' – environmentalists seeking uncarcinogenic water, consumer groups seeking non-lethal appliances or lower electric prices, unions seeking to reduce the loss of life and limb on the job. The economist's role is to act as arbiter between the conflicting interests. The presumption is always that while something may be gained, something is also always lost in the act of regulation. It is, after all, an interference with the market, and therefore a 'distortion' of the outcome that would otherwise occur.

In this view, in short, regulation arises from pressures emerging outside of economic life. It is an imposition, made possible by an (often mistaken) view of the weaknesses and failings of the market outcome.

Given such a view, one is hard-pressed to understand how regulatory regimes can arise in the first place. It is also difficult to understand why they tend to survive, at least in form, even the most hardened ideological challenges. Despite the mythic status they sometimes acquire in the eyes of business, advocacy groups are not by themselves particularly powerful. In an economy largely governed by business interests, heavier hitters are surely necessary.

And this is the solution to the conundrum. In the real world, economic regulation is not a uniform imposition on a monolith called 'business'. Rather, it is a device for governing business conduct and therefore for redistributing economic power, in part from one type of business to another. As such, it will enjoy the support of certain businesses and engender the opposition of others. In particular, it will tend to benefit newer, more flexible and technologically advanced business – those who can meet the regulatory standards at a lower cost, over older, more backward competitors. More generally, it is a device, for favouring businesses that compete within a framework of rules and restrictions over those who have greater difficulty prevailing in such competition. It is a device for favouring businesses that are not tempted by the path of auto-predation over those who are. The latter, therefore, form the backbone of opposition to a regulatory regime.

It is thus not the case that regulations, in most cases, 'distort' a marketplace that would otherwise come to a more efficient result. Left unregulated, markets generally do not come to efficient results. Rather, the point and purpose of regulation – and the necessity for its existence – is to channel the activities of predatory business leaders down socially efficient paths. That is why regulations arise, why they are accepted and why they survive. The genius of the American system of regulation was that for a long time – including the entire length of the Cold War – it worked reasonably well. The tragedy of the triumph of the market economists has been that, in weakening and often destroying the regulatory system, they have empowered auto-predatory business and, therefore, worked toward the general collapse of the system in which we all live and work.

At the most abstract level, there is a general reason why markets are not efficient, to which Joseph Stieglitz gave a technical name some years ago: *information is asymmetric.* Sellers always know more about their products than buyers do. Sellers always have an incentive to disguise the defects and understate the costs of their products; sharp practice, shady dealing, swindles and corruption all pay. Buyers know this. And so – as George Akerlof demonstrated in his classic article on lemons – buyers will blacklist markets wherever they lack confidence in the product. Specifically, they will demand discounted prices in order to cover their risks – discounts so deep that they preclude recovery of the full cost of production. Therefore, in the end, only those sellers who are actually offering inferior products can make money. This is Gresham's Law writ large: in information-asymmetric markets, bad products drive out good. Akerlof's example was the market for used cars, an industry of classically poor repute.

But although the analysis was brilliant, the example was poorly chosen in two respects. First, it misrepresented the actual market for used cars. And second, by focusing on that industry it gave the impression that the analysis dealt with a special case. In fact, used cars don't exhibit the properties Akerlof described, although many other products do. The reason is that regulation largely works for used cars, whereas it often fails in other product domains. Akerlof's argument is actually more general – and therefore more damning to the larger reputation of unregulated and competitive economic markets – than he let on.

In the real world, most used cars are not lemons. Why not? Because dealers, with the help of stiff laws against (for example) the resetting of odometer readings, have developed credible ways to overcome their own reputations. 'Pre-owned vehicles' have been around; typically, they have a service history; and one can know whether they have been maintained and if they have had structural defects or accidents. (There is also the option of having the car checked by an independent mechanic.) The information on any particular car is thus embodied in the car itself, and can be incorporated with some considerable reliability into the price. This solution does not depend on trust; one does not need to rely on the reputation of a particular dealer, or to have a favourable opinion of used-car salesmen in general. They either have credible documentation on the vehicles they sell, or they don't.

New cars on the other hand have no individual repair record. A new model also has no track record specific to make and model year. A new car one has only the reputation of the manufacturer to go on, and the guidance of *Consumer Reports*, which can at best assign probabilities for various kinds of trouble. For this reason, new cars only sell if they are accompanied by a very extensive warranty. The length of the warranty signals the confidence of the manufacturer in its product; this substitutes for the missing information. Without the warranty, the car could not, in general, be sold – let alone at a profit. The difference between the two markets for used and new vehicles – their stock-in-trade is, after all, functionally identical – lies precisely in the state of information. Every purchaser necessarily becomes a private expert on their own used car; for a new one, one demands a guarantee.

The market for used goods, although well-developed, is largely restricted to goods whose safety and reliability can be judged first-hand. It passes through the classified sections of the newspapers; as a general rule and with limited exceptions (such as books), one does not buy without personal inspection. There is no market in partly used pharmaceuticals (for instance) for this reason; while the market for illicit drugs carries well-known risks of contamination and dilution. Where one cannot inspect in advance, one inspects by reference to earlier work: this is the function of reputation. Contractors, housekeepers, independent hotels and restaurants, small shops, baby-sitters and the better class of drug dealers and prostitutes function on their references, longevity in one location and repeat customers. These are numerous cases but they do not represent the central productive activities of advanced capitalism.

Most merchandise – and especially merchandise incorporating advanced technologies – trades new. The market for new cars – which is the true potential 'market for lemons' – is, therefore, much more representative than the used-car market of the market for advanced commodities in general. Virtually all such marketplace transactions are *intrinsically* asymmetric. With motor vehicles, jet aircraft, electrical products and pharmaceuticals, you can't look inside the box – and your life is at stake in every transaction. *Every* such market is potentially a market for lemons. The more complex the product, which is to say the more we are talking about the output of the modern corporate economy, the more severe the asymmetry is.

Reputation provides a limited defence for the large seller. Along the Interstate Highway System, this is the function of the franchise: customers walking into McDonald's or Burger King are entering an independently owned small business, but they understand that the corporation guarantees the uniformity and salmonella content of the meal. (This, one trades against the trans fats.) But reputation can cut both ways; it does not take many cases of E. coli O157:H7 poisoning to pose a mortal threat to Taco Bell. The customer cannot tell, in these matters, the difference between an unavoidable accident and systematic negligence; moreover, substitutes are readily available and although they may be equally at risk, the customer doesn't know that either. Large corporations easily acquire, and only with difficulty shake off – reputations for cutting corners and indifference to product safety. Ralph Nader existed for a reason.

For the modern manufactured product – and for any food potentially riskier than, for instance, the potato – the rules of the industrial system have come to apply. This means that information about the product must be conveyed alongside the product itself. As in the case of the new car, the remedy for asymmetric information is additional information; the trick is to convey it in a credible way. To avoid the problem of the 'market for lemons', the necessary and sufficient condition is a *credible* guarantee of product authenticity and quality. The customer must have reason to believe that the product is what it claims to be, and that it will function as it is supposed to do. This is what a strong system of regulation provides.

In the real world, every decently functional modern market not only must meet this test, but *actually does so*. The mechanics of delivering a signal of quality are well developed. For clothing, there are brand names and country-of-origin labels, but also the little tag that tells of what the fabric is made. For electrical and electronic products and household appliances, there are safety ratings, measures of energy use and the ability to return something that doesn't work to the store. For software, there are product reviews, available on the Internet – imperfect but functional where the product doesn't matter too much. For cars and computers, as noted, there are warranties, backed by the authority of a corporation which the buyer can reasonably expect won't disappear before the product does. For air travel, there is the Federal Aviation Administration and lately the Transportation Safety Administration. For meat, fish and produce, there is the United States Department of Agriculture. For the prescription drug, there is that long insert; its function is not to be read but to reassure the buyer that the FDA is on the case. All of these are regulatory devices, intended to convey information alongside and in addition to the price signal. They do not exist because Ralph Nader is anti-capitalist or because, in some earlier time, a politics of anti-business activism somehow came to prevail in the United States. They exist because, in a world where the potential scale of abuse has become known, regulations are indispensable. Without them, the market would not survive.

This still leaves an open question: how much inspection is enough? At what point does the cost exceed the benefit? A moment's thought will make clear that the answer does not rest strictly on a measurement of the physical cost of inspection as against the benefit of health protection against, for instance, the E. coli hazard. The larger purpose of an inspections regime is the same as that of the new-car warranty: the purpose is to overcome the 'market for lemons'. It is not to generate a complete assurance that nothing bad will ever happen, but to generate sufficient assurance so that the markets function acceptably in the first place. This is a grey zone for which there is no absolute standard and no 'market test'. The political disputes in this area tend to be precisely over whether the regulatory regime should be strong enough in fact to overcome the problem of confidence, or whether it is sufficiently that it only appear so.

In the case of E. coli in vegetables, the consequences of failure to regulate effectively are plain to all. Without the regime, those who are lax with respect to feral pigs would not only win the competitive battle, but they would be seen to win it. Consumers would then correctly conclude that eating raw vegetables is unsafe – a conclusion that consumers in modern China or India actually live with, precisely because they lack institutions capable of persuading them otherwise. In the face of that conclusion, there would be no economic incentive to maintain the production of table-ready produce. Quite quickly, *all* producers would be driven to the low-cost, worst-practice techniques, feral pigs would roam freely in the fields, and fresh spinach would become something one only trusted if culled from one's own garden. One can live that way, of course – billions do – but the difference between a developed and an underdeveloped country is precisely that in the former one does not have to.

Inspection and regulation are thus not merely impositions on the industrial market system. They are not, as generally represented, a simple transfer of resources and welfare from producers to consumers and other interest groups. They are, instead, part of the essence of the extended production system. In exchange for a certain outlay of real resources, consumers gain something otherwise unachievable: confidence in the safety (or other desired properties) of the products they buy. In a large class of cases, the regulatory system makes production possible that would otherwise find no mass market at all, because otherwise customers could never effectively distinguish *ex ante* the functional and safe from the poisonous and explosive. The only problem is that a system which is seen to be credible and a system that actually is effective are two different things; while everyone agrees on the first goal, not everyone agrees on the second.

The costs of a regulatory system are of two kinds. Direct administrative costs are borne either through the tax system (by the general public) or in the price of the product (in which case, by the consuming public). In the latter case, we encounter another misleading analytical practice: it is common – but incorrect – to separate the 'cost' of the regulation from the product price. For the regulatory system is, like labour and capital, just another factor of production. Consumers *must* be willing to pay the price of an inspections regime sufficient to maintain confidence, otherwise raw spinach will not reach the table at all. There are thus three important questions:

a) Is the product itself important enough to justify the regulatory system required to get it to market?
b) Is the product of general enough value to society to justify paying the regulatory costs through the general tax system rather than through the price of the product? and
c) How much regulation is sufficient to maintain general public confidence in the product?

The second type of costs is costs of compliance: what it takes to get in line with an inspections regime. These costs are borne by producers, but they are not borne evenly by all producers. They fall more heavily on those producers who fail, or who would otherwise fail, the inspections regime. Those producers are obliged to bear the burden of bringing themselves into compliance. On the assumption that the regulatory regime is reasonable – that it seeks a goal that may be technically challenging but that can actually be achieved – e.g. the provision of uncontaminated produce over long distances – there must exist some producers who are capable of meeting the requisite standards at relatively low marginal cost. And the price of the final product must be set at a level at least sufficient to cover the cost of these producers, before any regulation is imposed.

Regulation per se, therefore, has *no effect* on the conduct of those producers who are already meeting the standards. Rather, regulation merely tells *other* producers that they must perform to the standards set by those deploying best-practice techniques. The entire burden of meeting the standards falls on the dirtier producers.

There is here a clear unity of purpose between the consuming public and the best-practice producers. One would like a class of product which the unregulated private market does not provide; the other can provide that product at a cost consumers are generally willing to pay. For this reason, regulatory product safety and similar quality regimes will tend to have a business constituency, among the more progressive firms in any affected industry.

But, equally clearly, there will also always be a group of producers whose interests are hurt by the regulation – and for whom there is relatively heavy burden of compliance. These will oppose the regime, and this is true, even though the survival and success of the industry in which they operate may depend entirely on that regime. The businesses affected care more about their relative position within the industry, than about the possibility that the industry could cease to exist altogether were regulation abandoned. This is the paradox of regulation. In any regulatory environment, there will always exist a temptation to enjoy the benefits of a secure and well-regulated market *without* having to conform to its standards. In a precise technical sense, we may call this group the auto-predators on the regulatory system.

We are now at a key point in the argument and it is worth restating the central propositions. First, apart from small-scale cases, modern consumer markets for manufactured goods and for foods are pervasively asymmetric. Products in such markets are inherently complex; price is never sufficient to establish quality. Rather, to function properly, an industrial market system requires that a flow of detailed and credible information be provided about the products on offer. The quality of this information must be guaranteed, which means that a credible authority must stand behind it. That authority can in principle be a corporation or a trade association – but only if the record of these organisations is such that it establishes their credibility with the buying public, which is commonly not the case. Therefore, the credible authority available for the task, as a matter of last resort (but of widespread last resort) in any advanced and developed economy, is and must be the government. As Margaret Thatcher used to say 'there is no alternative' to regulation, and often (not always), there is no alternative to compulsory regulation by the government. But, such regulation will always draw the opposition of those on whom the costs of compliance fall, who generally constitute some, but not all, of the producers.

We can go further. It is the presence, the existence, of a credible government authority – and therefore the willingness and ability of consumers to trust the regulatory system – that distinguishes a developed from an underdeveloped economy. The most advanced economies have the most advanced regulatory systems. There is a precise hierarchy in the development process, with the United States, Canada, Europe and Japan at its head, which is exactly correlated with regulatory power and practice. These are the governments allegedly most competent to handle the technical issues delivered up by the deployment of advanced technology in the production of goods and services. An incompetent government is one that cannot regulate effectively in the conditions under which it operates. The price of that incompetence is economic underdevelopment.

Predation – in the sense we now use the term – is the effort to subvert and undermine this regulatory system, for the sake of competitive advantage among and between businesses. It is an intrinsic temptation for those parts of the business community on whom the costs of the regulatory regime will fall. In no case is predation in this sense *the universal* instinct of the business classes as a whole; the political problem is that the future has no representation in the process. (Thus for any energy scheme, the claims of coal and oil outweigh those of successor industries, and always, of course, those of conservation.)

Predator enterprises will, therefore, typically be among the older and established firms – those with dated technology that is no longer on the cutting edge of cost reduction. Just as these are the weaker players in the marketplace, they are likely to be disproportionately represented in the political process. They may also have more labour-intensive modes of production, and perhaps as a result of that also an organised labour force whose interests are also likely to be threatened. Their predation against the regulatory system is, therefore, likely to take on a political cast and an ideological hue; this the economist abets in two ways: first, by pretending that all business interests are similar when they are not, and therefore that the opponents of regulation represent the 'interests of business'; and second, by assuming that the regulation is a cost or a burden on an economic system that would otherwise function through markets, when in fact the market could no more dispense with regulation than it could with capital or labour.

The ultimate goal of the predator is regulatory capture: to take charge of, and to dismantle, the regulatory structure itself. And the optimal strategy for predators in this sense is to achieve this goal from within, without alerting the larger public. The ideal situation, for this group, is one in which the broad public continues to think that they live under an effective system of regulatory protections, when in fact they do not.

This form of predatory conduct – partly visible, partly hidden – has now become the central problem of advanced regulatory systems. Dealing with it is, therefore, a central problem of a post-conservative economics. To go further, one may say that the administration of George W. Bush represented the pure political triumph of the anti-regulation predator class, in alliance with each other, to the near exclusion of all other economic interests. And they have worked toward their goal mutually, systematically and with remarkable success across a wide spectrum of advanced industry during their years in power.

In this respect, the Bush years represent an evolutionary step from the Reagan years. At that time, conservative theory held to a principle: markets usually worked, but sometimes failed. Regulations should be considered, but only in the case of market failure. And they should be implemented only when the benefits exceed the costs, with the burden of proof firmly on the advocates of regulation to show that the result would be superior to that provided by an unregulated market. Reagan did appoint famously anti-regulation chiefs at the Interior Department (James Watt) and the Environmental Protection Agency (Anne Gorsuch) – but in both cases, these appointments went beyond the official ideology of the administration.

The second Bush administration, in contrast, had no official ideology to which its own actions could be compared. It simply, and systematically, nominated the most aggressive anti-environment, anti-safety, anti-consumer-protection advocates it could find, to every regulatory position that it could not afford to leave unfilled. The result was a systematic empowerment, not of business in general, but of the reactionary wing within business. The political isolation into which the Bush administration eventually fell reflects the fact – the powerful reality – that much of business opposes open government by its own most reactionary wing. A functioning structure of regulation is the instrument, in other words, of that part of the business community that wishes, and chooses, to play by a common set of rules.

Once one sees this, the irrelevance of the common discourse on 'law and economics' becomes clear. That discourse assumes the efficiency of markets, and treats regulation as an imposition made necessary by a narrowly defined set of 'market failures' – externalities, public goods, incomplete markets and asymmetric information. But on examination, any one of those 'exceptions' can be seen to encompass nearly all actual economic relations, making effective regulation a universal, inescapable requirement for the functioning of markets. Yet even this fails to capture the full scope of the necessity. For once one recognises that the vast bulk of economic life must pass through large organisation for one reason or another, then it follows that regulation of a general and pervasive kind is required; not because of the particular characteristics of an activity but because all organisations are prone to predatory self-destruction. And this is something that only an effective system of economic regulation can systematically keep under control.

The political task facing a post-conservative polity in this area is, therefore, relatively simply stated. It is how to re-establish a tolerable, effective and politically successful regulatory regime, especially in the areas of finance and the environment, which can empower the firms of the future while keeping the pure predators under control. It is not an easy assignment – but it is one for which an overwhelming political consensus exists, provided only that the language of our discourse can be brought to bear on the problem correctly. No one wants business to fall entirely into the hands of crooks, and no one wants the planet to perish in a carbon haze. And that, of course, is exactly what is at stake.

Notes and References

1 Thorstein Veblen, *Theory of the Leisure Class, Introductory*, in *The Portable Veblen*, ed. by Max Lerner (New York: Viking, 1948), 70–71.

2 Karl Marx, *Capital*, vol. 1, Chapter 24, section 3.

3 Ibid.,

4 'The Economic Consequences of the Peace', in *The Collected Writings of John Maynard Keynes*, vol. 2 (London: Macmillan, 1971 [1919]), 11.

5 Veblen, *Leisure Class*, 57.

6 Ibid., 58.

7 Thorstein Veblen, 'The Technicians and Revolution', in id. *Portable Veblen*, 441.

Chapter 16

CAPITALISING EXPECTATIONS: VEBLEN ON CONSUMPTION, CRISES AND THE UTILITY OF WASTE

Sophus A. Reinert and Francesca Lidia Viano[1]

I see enormous conglomerates replace the individual capitalists. I see the stock markets fall prey to the same curse that now claims the casinos.

Friedrich Nietzsche

The doctrines which Adam Smith maintained with so much ability, never took so deep hold in this country as in England, and they have been more strongly opposed.

John Rae

Few authors are so perennially in the process of being rediscovered as Thorstein Veblen. Most recently, his authority has been summoned to combat the climate crisis, to uncover the meaning of life generally and what it means to be American particularly, and by those seeking to make sense of financial scandals such as those of Enron, Worldcom and Parmalat, not to mention the current global economic turmoil.[2] His theories regarding the moral and material costs of conspicuous consumption are today echoed for wider audiences in works such as Alain de Botton's *Status Anxiety* and Oliver James's *Affluenza*, and the phrase 'Gilded Age' again enjoys cultural and analytical currency.[3] This chapter contributes to this Veblen Renaissance, but neither by dwelling on the structural and cultural similarities between the crises of his time and ours, nor by using his writings to shed light on the technical origins of modern financial misdemeanours.[4] Rather, it demonstrates how Veblen perceived the important epistemological role played by 'expectations' and how, at a very early stage of modern corporate capitalism, he used them to explain not only systemic financial collapses but also patterns of individual consumption. This paper offers an inclusive study of Veblen's doctrines to shed light on the relationship he drew between the mechanisms of luxury expenditure and financial crises, and his resulting conclusions on the relation between consumption and production in complex economic systems.[5]

There is today a widespread consensus around the idea that, under the influence of the Darwinian evolutionary theories of contemporary American biologists, zoologists and psychologists, Veblen's theories matured in reaction to Bentham's 'hedonistic' utilitarian approach.[6] We will not challenge Veblen's dependence on Darwin, but will argue that his relation to the utilitarian tradition is far more complicated than is commonly assumed. The psychology of 'utilities', 'needs' and 'pleasures' had made its way into economics long before Bentham drew on it to draft his plans for legislative reform, and with very different results. French sensualists of the eighteenth century were perfectly aware of the importance played by subjective evaluations of utility in the economic process, but never shared Bentham's conviction that the maximisation of pleasures should go unrestrained by principles of morality, opportunity or even industrial efficiency, nor his confidence in the infallibility of 'the motive of *pecuniary* interest'.[7] Some utilities and some needs, according to these philosophers, were morally superior or simply 'more productive' than others, and anyway dependent on social institutions more than on abstract models of reasoning. As we will see shortly, it was this very distinction, which he freely reinterpreted in the light of more recent psychological theories, that set the stage for Veblen's theoretical explanation of the imbalances of modern economies generally and the inefficiencies of the industrial system more particularly.

Section I of this chapter proposes to reconsider the whole body of Veblen's economic doctrines as providing a new interpretation of the Aristotelian dichotomy between real and apparent wealth, one in tune with the late nineteenth-century economy of casino capitalism and compulsive consumption. Veblen, it will be argued, interpreted the relation between real and artificial wealth from the perspective of subjective utilities. His closest point of reference was John Stuart Mill, but Mill was in turn inspired by a long-standing tradition of hedonistic political economy, initiated by Étienne Bonnot de Condillac and continued by Jean-Baptiste Say, a tradition that Veblen had accessed not only through Mill's *Principles of Political Economy*, but also through the translation of Say's *Traité d'economie politique* or his later re-elaborations by various American economists.

Section II illustrates the theoretical implications of Condillac's and Say's hedonism for the treatment of luxury expenditure and the relations between industrial production and consumption. Section III then goes on to unpack the utilitarian jargon and contents of the *Theory of the Leisure Class*, and reconstructs its genesis in relation to Veblen's re-elaboration of the hedonistic elements of sensualist philosophy under the influence of Darwin's *Descent of Man* and nineteenth-century British theories of physiology and psychology. Neo-Darwinism and Pragmatism influenced Veblen only tangentially in his re-adaptation of old utilitarian tenets to a new economic landscape, since, as we argue in section IV, the cornerstone of Veblen's system was the notion that theoretical and empirical knowledge followed divergent paths and could not be assimilated under the concept of practical reason.[8] According to Veblen, indeed, intellectual reasoning was active only because it was based on a variety of 'expectations', 'discriminations' and comparisons, which distracted a subject from purely instrumental motives rather than driving it towards their accomplishment. Section V, finally, brings Veblen's epistemology to bear on the analysis of financial crises by focusing particularly on his debate with Irving Fisher over accounting techniques and methods of capitalisation. The economy was only one of several fields, including eugenics and racial hygiene, where Fisher and Veblen represented opposing approaches and traditions, and their juxtaposition remains illuminating on many points.[9] If Fisher was the champion of a hedonistic approach to economics which made pleasurable actions equivalent to useful ones, and preached the convergence of personal expectations and optimal market outcomes, Veblen applied his own notion of an 'attendant' or 'expectant' subject to show that value-based appreciations were based on 'expectations' that were completely unrelated to the *industrial* production of the 'community' and rather reflected its pecuniary assets and advertising goals.

To conclude, we argue that Veblen's theories of conspicuous consumption and financial crisis should not be seen as independent expressions of his anti-utilitarian take on economics, but rather as related, long-term results of Veblen's effort to re-elaborate the utilitarian tradition from the inside and bring it to demonstrate the chronic divergences between consumption and production in modern economies. Contrary to Fisher and other marginalist economists, who thought that utilitarian interpretations of wealth and capital made the old distinction between productive and unproductive activities obsolete, for Veblen the concept of 'utility' was an instrument with which to draw a line between consumption and investment, finance and production, and ultimately the real and the apparent economy. His insights on the matter echo harrowingly through this era that has so aptly been called 'Veblen's century'.[10]

The Real and the Apparent

It was an Aristotelian apothegm that commercial acquisition, based on the exchange or accumulation of 'fictitious entit[ies]' such as silver coins, and prompted by the desire for 'pecuniary profit', differed fundamentally from 'true wealth', which originated in 'nature'.[11] Incorporated into scholastic thought, the distinction between pecuniary acquisition and the production of real wealth became a mainstay of Western economic thinking, where it was codified polemically in reaction to the bullionist and metallist pretence to see a 'natural' reality in the value of silver and gold coins.[12] Veblen construed his interpretation of the relation between distribution and production by drawing on this 'anti-metallist' repertoire from the history of political economy. The Physiocrats, he recalled, built their economic system on the conviction that *real* wealth originated solely from the soil and – to use Veblen's own words – was 'directed to the shaping of the material means of life'.[13] This Physiocratic axiom became influential enough to survive even after the onset of the Industrial Revolution had given abundant proof of the economic potentialities of inventions and machines. Emblematically, and in spite of his appreciation of pin-factories, even Adam Smith remained convinced throughout his life that agricultural activities were the most productive, since they added 'a much greater value to the annual produce of the land and labor of the country, to the *real* wealth and revenue of its inhabitants', than industry and trade.[14] This, however, did not keep him from recognising the contribution rendered by human labour to production. On the contrary, Smith elevated man to 'the central figure in the process of production' and Veblen followed in his footsteps by making real wealth consist in the material result of human labour (both agricultural and industrial) and pecuniary wealth in the result of purely commercial exchanges, of catallactics: 'men at work', Veblen echoed Smith, are 'on the whole, occupied with production of goods; the business men, on the other hand, are occupied with the acquisition of them'.[15] What Veblen reproached Smith for was his having missed some of the most striking effects of the Industrial Revolution on business practice, which Smith continued to interpret as if nothing had changed from the era in which 'handicraft and agriculture' were the only 'obtrusive' features of the economy, 'with commerce as a scarcely secondary phenomenon'.[16] It was this assumption, Veblen argued, that made Smith's faith in the self-adjusting mechanisms of market economies possible and which instilled in his followers – who already were permeated by Benthamite optimism – the mistaken belief that real wealth and pecuniary wealth tended to coincide.[17] To adapt the core of Smith's theories to a more complicated economic environment and correct the Benthamite diversion, Veblen drew on a variety of sources, many of which he decided not to reveal with the provocative excuse (laid down in the *Theory of the Leisure Class* but valid also for his other works) that they were 'of the more familiar and accessible kind and should be readily traceable […] by fairly well-read persons'.[18] Our task is therefore that of investigating the library of Veblen's idealized average reader in order to make conjectures regarding the possible and plausible sources of his corrections to the Benthamite-Smithian tradition.

John P. Diggins long ago argued that the single most important source on which Veblen drew to forge his economic system as an alternative to those of Smith and Bentham was John Stuart Mill's *Principle of Political Economy*.[19] Veblen generically referred to Mill in his *Theory of the Leisure Class* to demonstrate that the increasing percentage of social income devoted to conspicuous consumption would prevent 'mechanical inventions' from lightening 'the day's toil of any human being', and repeatedly praised Mill in his historiographical essays for having shed light on the causes of the divergence between production and consumption.[20] The first of these causes was the impossibility of reducing the market value of a commodity to the cost of its production because of the unpredictability and incommensurability of the worker's economic motives and 'pleasures'; the second was the fact that ownership was not the fruit of labour applied to nature, as argued by Locke, but an institution entirely belonging 'within the theoretical realm of Distribution' and, therefore, completely dependent 'on the laws and customs of society', which were in turn determined by 'the opinions and feelings of the ruling portion of the community'.[21]

An essential lesson Veblen drew from Mill was that economics could reckon with imbalances and disequilibria only if based on sound psychological foundations. And these foundations, Veblen explained, were essentially two: a 'sophisticated hedonism', which assumed 'qualitative divergence among the different qualities of pleasures that afford the motives of conduct', and an improved 'theory of association', which hypothesised the existence of an organising mind able to compare 'impressions' and to engage in 'some degree of constructive work'.[22] While Veblen's first attribution to Mill is historiographically justified, the second is more controversial. Not only did Mill never use the concept of 'psychological association', but, as Alexander Bain and Herbert Spencer would later claim, he never completely emancipated himself from the eighteenth-century hedonistic tradition. And yet, even if somewhat imaginative and historiographically disputable, Veblen's reconstruction of Mill's theory of psychology is possibly one of the most illuminating means of reconstructing the intellectual genesis of his departure from Smith and the Physiocrats.

Veblen was right on one point: in showing that the economic motives driving men's economic choices ('choice of employments and of domicile', for example) differed 'from man to man to man and from class to class, not only in degree, but in kind', Mill had shown that pecuniary stimuli were no longer the fundamental motive driving human behaviour, as Bentham thought to have demonstrated.[23] This discovery, however, was not enough to dismantle the by then consolidated belief in the harmony of markets and economic interests, as Veblen must have realised in the light of his knowledge (direct or indirect) of pre-Millian hedonistic philosophy.

Veblen was certainly familiar with the 'subjectivist' trend initiated by Condillac with his *Le commerce et le gouvernement, considérés relativement l'un à l'autre* (1776) and introduced to American audiences through the mediation of Destutt de Tracy, Jean-Baptiste Say and Francis Wayland. According to Condillac and his followers, utility was never 'an absolute quality' inherent in a commodity or a service. It was rather the fruit of our 'esteem' or 'opinion':

> although things have a value because they have the qualities which make them suited to our needs, they will have no value for us, if we do not judge that they have in fact these qualities.[24]

The fact of taking 'judgments' and 'esteem' into account as crucial economic factors had made Condillac and his later followers particularly sensitive to the imbalances of economic systems. Condillac knew, for example, that an exaggerated perception of scarcity could induce a hoarder of grain to keep it for himself, thus subtracting it from the market in greater quantities than necessary.[25] It was 'in the opinion that one has of quantities, not in the quantities themselves', wrote Condillac, 'that abundance, overabundance, or scarcity lie'.[26] At the same time, Condillac was conscious of the crucial role played by subjective evaluations in directing the fluxes of consumption. Since nobody was 'wealthy in an absolute way but only relatively to his own class; and, within his own class, relatively to his country or to the century in which he lives', one should expect people to consume according not only to their primary needs (hunger, comfort) but also to the needs driven by social emulation.[27] Luxury itself, he argued, thus echoing a long line of French economic writers stretching back at least as far as Jean-François Melon, was a relative concept, depending on what people considered to be 'excess' or extravagance in a certain political or geographical context and in a certain period of time.[28]

Condillac did not ignore the fact that the subjectivisation of economics could bring his analysis to a blind spot, in which quantification was impossible and definitions of wealth loose enough to comprehend any kind of utilities, even the wildest eccentricities. But he eventually conceded that the relative measures of opinion, as expressed by market prices, tended to align with the utilities of the correspondent commodities according to their relative scarcity or abundance.[29] The belief in the harmony between measures of opinion and measures of quantity was made possible by the sensationalist belief in the substantial continuity between rational judgment and empirical life. Later on, Carl Menger and Ludwig Von Mises would argue that Condillac's premises could be held to be true if values were meant to refer to 'marginal' units.[30] Veblen, instead, received what was left of Condillac's subjective economy from sources, like Jean-Baptiste Say's *Traité d'economie politique* (1803), which treated the belief in the correspondence between subjective and objective values as a mere theoretical assumption, without inquiring into the causes of their discrepancy. Veblen's partly rigorous and partly ventriloquising analysis of Mill's thought revealed the strategy he himself had followed to bring to light the causes of the discrepancy between psychological and market values by exploring the deep roots of human needs and utilities from the point of view of an 'active' subject. But what did an 'active' subject exactly mean for Veblen?

Say and the 'Luxe Ostentation'

Famously lauded by Thomas Jefferson for being 'shorter, clearer and sounder' than Adam Smith's *Wealth of Nations*, Jean-Baptiste Say's 1803 *Traité d'economie politique* had made its way into the curricula of most American universities by the early nineteenth century.[31] It had inspired some of the most influential works of American political economy, among them Francis Wayland's *Elements of Political Economy*, which was part of Veblen's reading list at Carleton College, and was partially incorporated into J. S. Mill's *Principles of Political Economy*, which Veblen's professor of economics at Cornell, James Laurence Laughlin, abridged and edited for his students.[32] Not to mention the fact that John Rae's *New Principles of Political Economy* (1834), in turn deeply influenced by Say, was a favourite of Laughlin's professor at Harvard, Charles Dunbar, and of the latter's colleague Frank William Taussig.[33] Either directly or indirectly, therefore, Say had left a mark on his American audiences, particularly by assisting them in the adaptation of some of Smith's most important principles to an economic context in which industry mattered more than agriculture, titles of property were a pure matter of law and custom, and natural or acquired talent emerged as a source of productivity no less important than mechanic contrivances. To accomplish this task, Say had gradually abandoned not only the Physiocrats' claim that wealth originated solely from the soil, but also Smith's definition of value as 'the quantity of labor' invested in a good to eventually embrace the alternative view that the value of things and services ultimately depended on their utility. 'To create objects with a measure of utility whatsoever', explains Say, 'means to create wealth, since the utility of things is the first fundament of their value, and their value of wealth.'[34]

    Even if he built on the foundations laid down by Condillac and went even further than him towards reconciling the subjective theory of value with the objective position spearheaded by the Physiocrats and by Adam Smith, Say never thought that the utilities of goods and services (their *'natural values'*) could be quantified, nor did he deceive himself with the belief that exchange values (prices) could be taken as a substitute for 'natural values', since they only registered variations in price, which took 'place in favour of one class [of goods] or at the expense of another', and only 'affect[ed] particular fortunes'.[35] Like Aristotle, Say was all too aware that pecuniary gains and societal wealth, *exchange* values and *real* values, often diverged, but, like Smith, he assumed their long-term convergence under optimal conditions (perfect information, free markets, regular circulation). It was this *theoretical* assumption that impressed Say's audiences the most and made people (like John Maynard Keynes) think that he was the first theorist of full occupation and undisturbed growth. And yet, as has been correctly noted, Say devoted relatively little effort to demonstrate this long-term convergence, while indulging at length in the analysis of those factors potentially responsible for short term imbalances.[36]

As Condillac and Smith himself had realised, the most important of these disruptive factors was consumption. According to the Physiocrats, 'need' was a relatively simple concept; it 'solicits the artisan to gain his own subsistence, and solicits also all who can buy to procure his works'.[37] Their conclusion was therefore that consumption could keep the whole economic system running even in the absence of industrial or commercial investments: in other words, the more consumption the more production. Condillac had shaken the psychological foundations of this theory when he suggested that some needs were qualitatively 'better' than others. He distinguished between 'natural' needs, which were 'the continuation of our conformation' (hunger, thirst, sexual appetites and so forth), and 'fictitious 'needs, 'born from the habit of satisfying natural needs through *chosen* means'.[38] In the first stages of civilisation, he explained, the means at man's disposal were so narrow that it was hard to neatly delineate fictitious and natural needs. With the passing of time, however, and the widening of wealth and commodities, the gap between them would become ever larger to the point in which 'by continuously moving away from nature, fictitious needs will eventually change it completely, or corrupt it'. Since his focus was on advanced societies, Condillac had decided to call 'natural' all forms of needs satisfied by means which retained their utility over time or even increased them to the point of becoming indispensable for the society at large (i.e. raw materials, industrial contrivances) and '*fictitious*' those satisfied by means 'which have value only in the moment of their acquisition' and remained confined to 'a small number at the exclusion of the masses'.[39]

At the core of Condillac's evolutionary distinction between *natural* and *fictitious* needs lay the idea that disequilibria, inequalities and excesses arose from a disproportion of superfluous desires over concrete necessities (from hunger to industrial investment). Although formulated in terms of quantities of labour instead of utilities, Smith's distinction between 'productive' and 'unproductive' occupations presupposed the same dichotomy between concrete and superfluous wealth. While 'the labour of a manufacturer adds generally to the value of the materials which he works upon', Smith explained, the 'labour of a menial servant, on the contrary, adds to the value of nothing'.[40] All occupations, productive and unproductive alike, were 'maintained by the annual produce of the land and labour of the country' but, since the work of the unproductive ones 'perish[ed] in the very instant of their performance', Smith concluded that many forms of luxury consumption (both commodities and services) subtracted resources from the national stock of wealth.[41]

The novelty of Say's approach consisted in using Smith's dichotomy to perfect Cantillon's distinction between different needs or forms of consumption. Consumption, according to Say, always implied an act of destruction, a '*destruction of utility*' which in turn involved 'a *destruction of value*' and was accompanied by some form of compensation.[42]

The right way to assess the utility of consumption was to look not at the means of its satisfaction, as suggested by Condillac, but at the nature of its compensation. The use of fire, for example, could satisfy both an immediate need for heat and the industrial need to melt metals; in the first case, the destructed value was compensated by an enjoyment, neatly delineated in time and without further repercussions, in the second case, it was replaced by the additional value of a newly produced metal. Since only durable *compensation* was 'productive' or 'reproductive', while temporary *compensation* was 'unproductive', it was evident to Say that industrial growth could solely depend on the former. From this it followed that the old faith in the power of consumption as the engine of economic growth was entirely misplaced, for it was industrial investment which created values and purchasing power, whereas consumption per se did not necessarily create capacity for investment and often detracted resources from it.[43]

Even if adumbrated already by James Mill, the idea that consumption (as contrasted with investment) was a net detraction from the general wealth of a society was novel to the utilitarian tradition, and certainly there are few if any traces of it in Bentham's writings.[44] Had he developed his discussion to the point of noticing how consumption could chronically inhibit savings, Say would have increased his distance from Bentham even further. And he went very close to this conclusion when he proceeded to divide the group of *unproductive* consumptions into two subgroups, according this time not to their respective compensations (which were always temporary) but to the needs which they were meant to satisfy. In this case, as with the distinction between productive and unproductive forms of consumption/compensation, it was Smith who set the precedent. Starting from the general premise that behind any form of consumption there was the desire to 'be observed, to be attended to, to be taken notice of with sympathy', Smith had searched for a form of taxation that would limit the impact of this desire on the lower classes and on the economy at large.[45] Smith knew, in fact, that vanity was strong enough to push even 'the meanest labourer' to spend his wage upon 'conveniences' or even, on extraordinary occasions, on luxuries. He had accepted the first expense as legitimate, since he thought that a great part of goods not 'indispensably necessary for the support of life' were anyway necessary to both rich and poor to satisfy 'the established rules of decency' (like leather shoes and linen shirts), while condemning luxury expenditure, which he suggested to tax in order to force 'frugality' upon the lowers strata of population.[46]

Not unlike Smith, Say noted that the categories of 'necessity' and 'superfluity' blurred into one another, but he extended the former to include not only the consumption of those commodities that were prompted by '*real* needs', but also those satisfying a 'sensual' desire for what he called '*luxe de commodité*'.[47] What discriminated the '*luxe de commodité*' from other kinds of luxuries, according to Say, was best expressed by the Latin word *luxuria*, which the French language (differently from English) had divided into two words: *luxure*, a search for sensual pleasures, and *luxe*, a desire for '*ostentation*'.[48] Necessities were for Say all those commodities the desire for which was prompted by a concrete, material need for survival or even sensual pleasure (*luxure*), while luxuries were those goods which satisfied the desire to demonstrate status (*luxe*). The line of demarcation between necessary and superfluous consumption was in other words not determined by questions of decency, but depended on the nature and origins of the specific need driving any given act of consumption: needs originating in the consumer's concrete, even sensual desire were *real* and prompted healthy forms of consumption, while needs driven from the exogenously induced desire to 'strike the eyes' of the beholder were 'fictitious' and encouraged dangerous forms of consumption.[49]

It was Say, therefore, who taught nineteenth-century economists to condemn luxuries not so much for their sensual excesses but for the relative and exogenous nature of the needs prompting their consumption. Even if they were destructive of industrial values, sensual luxuries were at least compensated for by some more or less evanescent physical gratification, while the pleasure given by pure ostentation perished when the consumed object stopped 'to flatter the vanity of his possessor'; the object consumed for vanity, in other words, was 'destroyed ... even before it stopped to exist and without having satisfied any veritable need'.[50] Without ever completely fulfilling a desire, conspicuous consumption nurtured immaterial needs which distracted more and more resources from the satisfaction of 'real' needs (although superfluous) or from other forms of consumption (industrial investments) that would have contributed to the production (or 'reproduction', as Say called it) of national wealth.[51]

By focusing on the unhealthy concentration of consumption in only one sector of production (ostentatious luxuries), Say identified a social or psychological obstacle to productive investments and to the spread of consumption across different sectors, a source of potential and chronic disturbances in the economic system. In the end, however, he did not develop this insight into a theory of imbalances, and continued to believe, as James Mill did, that, as long as production was high, purchasing power would also be high and so demand would by necessity keep up with supply.[52] In the following section we will see how Veblen, armed with his idiosyncratic bifurcated theory of mental development, was able to show that natural and fictitious elements were constant and coexisting components of human needs and utilities, since individuals evaluated them on the base of both practical needs and 'expectations'.

Veblen's Bifurcated Utilitarianism

Even if Veblen's familiarity with the language of utility and values rarely has attracted scholarly attention, it plays a crucial role in both his *The Theory of the Leisure Class* and *The Theory of Business Enterprise*. We now turn to Veblen's approach to utility in the former work, which he described as a treatise on the '*value* of the leisure class as an economic factor in modern life'.[53] In his *The Theory of the Leisure Class*, Veblen advanced the unusual view that economics was a science predominantly about interpersonal comparisons; contrary to the point of view normally held in contemporary economics textbooks, according to which only commodities and services had utility or value in the eyes of their prospective consumers and producers, Veblen was convinced that people too had an economic value in the eyes of consumers and producers, and that the process of interpersonal evaluation, which he considered a process of 'rating and grading' people 'in respect of relative worth or value', preceded and influenced evaluation of goods.[54]

Use and waste, Veblen explained, had been the two main parameters according to which men had been establishing people's worth since the earliest stages of human civilisation, when (to take one notable example) 'women and other slaves' were 'highly valued, both as an evidence of wealth and as a means of accumulating wealth'.[55] With technological progress and economic development, however, the activities of demonstrating wealth and of accumulating it bifurcated: the former came to be accomplished by servants and women, while the latter fell upon an ever diminishing class of professional workers. In wake of venerable Benthamite teachings, marginalists such as John Bates Clark and Irving Fisher would have said that, as long as they produced pleasurable effects, all forms of service had a level of utility comparable to those rendered by professional workers. Veblen's stand on the question was controversial. Like Say, he never really emancipated himself from the Smithian belief in labour as the basis of production, and continued to discriminate between utilities on the base of the quantity and durability of work they comprised. He even followed Say in his effort to break the demand for luxuries down into a sensual component (that satisfying 'the psychical efficiency or comfort' of the consumers) and an ostentatious one. And yet, whereas Say thought that both components were destructive of value (with the first nonetheless offering more durable forms of pleasure in the act of destroying 'real' values), Veblen seems to have thought that even the most superfluous services such as those rendered by butlers and housekeepers involved a form of 'productive' work for the mere fact of satisfying some physical or psychological need.[56] He also admitted that '[e]ven in articles which appear at first glance to serve for pure ostentation only, it is always possible to detect the presence of some, at least ostensible, useful purpose'.[57] To be productive, in other words, work did not have to add 'to the value of the materials' employed, as Smith would have said, but simply to satisfy 'psychical' or 'physical' pleasures.

Veblen's correction of Smith brought him nearer to hedonistic currents than is commonly supposed. Whereas the hedonists, however, thought that *natural* needs were opposed to *fictitious* needs, Veblen believed that any assessment of utility included both components. He started to build this bifurcated model of utilitarianism very early in his career, in his first article on Kant's *Critique of Judgment*.[58] We will first investigate how Veblen developed his interpretation of judgments from Kant's *Critique*, then trace its consequences for his political economy.

Kant had, for a long time, been an indispensable point of reference for all those seeking to make a space for human volition in biological accounts of social evolution. Darwin himself had led the trend by tracing mental evolution back to the action of something similar to the Kantian imperative, a force that, in his view, could bend the individual to the dictates of his own his instincts, both inborn and acquired.[59] Herbert Spencer and Henry James followed suit by assuming that human evolution was a chain of adaptation of psychological structures to changing social environments and that reasoning consisted in purely 'internal' comparisons between external objects and inborn or acquired mental categories.[60] Veblen felt the influence of this literature, but he approached and domesticated it from a different angle. Contrary to the neo-Darwinians scientists (like George Romanes and C. Lloyd Morgan) and the Pragmatists, Veblen was scarcely motivated by the necessity to demonstrate the supremacy of spiritual factors over empirical experience. His main concern was with the way in which the old Laplacian positivist scheme of knowledge had chained scientific research to the analysis of cause and effect without encouraging a more adventurous animus, one able to deal with randomness and chaos through guesswork and 'forecast of the future'.[61]

In constructing his economic system, Veblen curiously enough seems to have drawn far more extensively on contemporary controversies in physics and psychology than normally assumed. Even more interestingly, he thought he had found the instrument by which to mediate between these two disciplines (physics and psychology), and to shift the fundaments of economics from a purely mechanical and deterministic approach to a probabilistic one, in Kant's *Critique of Judgment*.[62] Though originally intended 'for the purposes of morality', Veblen said, Kant's 'reflective judgment' could also be seen as a 'faculty of search' which allowed the subject to pass 'beyond the simple data of experience' and seek 'a universal which is not given in empirical cognition'. Instead of connecting pre-existing facts along causal chains, the reflective judgment had the potential to guide the research 'beyond the known' and let the subject grasp 'at that which cannot come within experience'.[63] And since, according to Kant, the reflective judgment thought 'things in a system *as though* they were made [...] with a view to the exigencies of our capacity of knowing', Veblen called it a 'principle of adaptation' of external reality to internal conditions.[64]

In so manipulating Kant's notion of reflective judgment Veblen seemingly echoed the likes of a Spencer or James, who had both invoked a 'principle of adaptation' as the engine of human evolution. But the similarity is deceiving. First of all, Veblen thought that the imputation of internal categories (categories of 'expedient conduct' or finality, as the Pragmatists would have defined them) to external reality was only one aspect of the process of acquiring knowledge. Since reflective judgment transcended experience, the knowing subject also needed a form of empirical and applied knowledge to satisfy his or her most practical needs.[65] This, Veblen argued, meant that 'natural' (instrumental) and 'fictitious' (intellectual or 'internal') considerations were not alternative ways of assessing utility, but complementary ones: shoes were chosen for being comfortable, but also for being expensive; serfs were hired for both their assistance in cleaning and for their symbolic and delegated job of showing off their employers' wealth. The different proportions of natural/pragmatic versus fictitious/idle motives entering into any given calculation of economic utilities were largely determined by the institutional structures of the community in which the calculus was made, which, as Darwin and the neo-Darwinians knew all too well, operated a form of secondary selection on human behaviour.

The second difference between Veblen's epistemology and that of Spencer and the Pragmatists lays in Veblen's pronounced emphasis on the role of anticipation as a vehicle of judgment. As Veblen said with regard to Mill's psychological theory, in which he (quite surreptitiously) found the seeds of his own approach, if one attributes to the subject the ability to perceive both similarities (and not only register associations) and qualitative distinctions between pleasures, one has to postulate some sort of expectation on the part of the subject:

> To perceive the similarity, he [the subject] must be guided by an interest in the outcome, and must 'attend'. The like applies to the introduction of qualitative distinctions into the hedonistic theory of conduct. Apperception in the one case and

discretion in the other cease to be the mere registration of a simple and personally uncoloured sequence of permutations enforced by the factors of the external world. There is implied a spiritual – that is to say, active – 'teleological' continuity of process on the part of the perceiver or of the discretionary agent, as the case may be.[66]

It was this element of expectation in human agents that, under certain circumstances, set interpersonal evaluations sometime above the mere evaluation of commodities.[67] Even if biologically programmed to pursue concrete accomplishments, Veblen explained, men had been driven by certain *social pressures* to direct their instinct of 'self-assertion' towards what he called 'pecuniary emulation', that is, a 'comparison with one's neighbours' in terms of wealth:[68] in order to guarantee 'his own peace of mind', an individual 'should possess as large a portion of goods as others with whom he is accustomed to class himself', but would find it 'extremely gratifying to possess something more than others'.[69] Veblen was categorical on the fact that these instincts of self-assertion varied in strength and intensity in the course of evolution. He recognised, for example, that they reached a peak in the modern era, when the chances of awarding personal esteem 'on any other basis than that of immediate appearance' had been drastically reduced.[70] Under these conditions, he thought, the optimal way of signalling status and wealth had become investing in apparel, particularly, in women's clothing, for – as Veblen argues in *The Theory of the Leisure Class* – women had, since time immemorial, been the indirect instruments of their masters' and (later) husbands' worldly success. In the modern era, therefore, the utility of goods resided more in their conspicuousness, which was instrumental in filling the information gap between strangers resulting from the anonymity of modern urban life, than in the concrete service they rendered to their owner:

> The means of communication and the mobility of the population now expose the individual to the observation of many persons who have no other means of *judging* of his reputability than the display of goods (and perhaps of breeding) which he is able to make while he is under their direct *observation*.[71]

Instead of denying the utility of superfluous goods, as scholars normally assume, Veblen showed that superfluities satisfied the 'internal' need for esteem and positive judgment, a need which was present in all economic agents and that increased under certain circumstances (urbanisation, anonymity and so on), without ever replacing the need for concrete expediency. If, for historical and institutional reasons, people were busy evaluating others 'in respect of relative worth or value', to the point of upgrading what was 'wasteful' and 'reputable' to a canon of beauty, and consumers felt constrained or were anyway influenced by what they perceived 'as the expectations of the community in the way of pecuniary decency', it was clear that the fictitious or 'immaterial' services offered by luxury commodities had a greater utility as 'informational goods' or 'advertizing media' (as Veblen called them) than for the material services they rendered.[72] People entrusted their commodities with the task of projecting their ideal images to anonymous audiences, and beholders relied on those commodities to adjust their expectations. 'As the community advances in wealth and culture', Veblen explain,

> the ability to pay is put in evidence by means which require a progressively nicer discrimination in the beholder. This nicer discrimination between advertising media is in fact a very large element of the higher pecuniary culture.[73]

This ever-changing advertising function not only required an alert beholder, but also shaped the very way in which manufacturers designed objects, anticipating the prospective consumer's desire to meet or intriguingly upset his or her beholders' expectations.

> [M]ost objects alleged to be beautiful, and doing duty as such, show considerable ingenuity of design and are *calculated* to puzzle the beholder—to bewilder him with irrelevant suggestions and hints of the improbable—at the same time that they give evidence of an expenditure of labor in excess of what would give them their fullest efficiency for their ostensible economic end.[74]

The importance Veblen accorded to the observation of present and future neighbouring expenditures becomes evident in his explanation of one of the main principles regulating conspicuous consumption, namely the 'requirement of novelty'.[75]

> As soon as a given item of luxurious apparel becomes accessible to a larger portion of the group or 'community', its consumption ceases to be attractive as a medium of exhibition, gradually becoming the mere baseline of further, ever more extreme displays of pecuniary power.[76]

As contemporary game theorists have recently demonstrated, the evaluation of our neighbour's abilities, to spend among other things, is a form of very subtle prediction. To quote Robert Half, 'there is something that is much more scarce, something rarer than ability. It is the ability to recognize ability'.[77] At the base of consumption, Veblen identified a complex interrelation of conjectures, 'imputations' and even 'deception', which complicated the traditional notion of utility by introducing an element of unpredictability in the evaluation process and making it less immediately dependent on empirical experience. As we will see in the next section, Veblen will attribute to similar imputations, deceptions and discriminations at the base of the productive system the disequilibria responsible for financial crises and disturbances.

Accounting for Standards of Thought

Ever since his doctoral studies at Cornell, Veblen had accepted Say's idea (echoed in Mill's *Principles of Economics*) that production created its own demand as a truism, and he had attributed apparent cases of maladjustment to 'matter[s] of price – of "values" in the commercial sense' or (as Say would have defined them) of 'exchange values'.[78] His research into conspicuous consumption, also inaugurated at Cornell, in effect convinced him that demand in itself could not foster production, and continued testing his and Say's scepticism throughout the 1890s. But Veblen soon extended his analysis of imbalances to the financial market. The major premises of this second area of study are contained in one of his Cornell articles, 'The Overproduction Fallacy', where he endorsed Say's and Mill's rejection of the 'general overproduction' theories to confute Uriel H. Crocker's conviction that crises could be generated by an excess of 'machinery for the production of the commodity' over 'the adequate demand for the product'.[79] The cry of 'general overproduction', Veblen clarified, had emerged in the past to explain the dynamics of 'depression' or 'liquidation' and, more particularly, the apparently inexplicable fact that 'machinery was run at a loss' by its owners or even stopped. Debating Crocker, who blamed the increasing efficiency of industrial machinery, Veblen here formulated the core of his future theory of business and financial cycles. He maintained that what is normally explained in terms of excessive efficiency is a situation in which 'the average profit obtainable on the capital invested falls short of the standard accepted as the proper, customary profit'.[80] Crises, in other words, could simply be explained as a shift in the standards by which the business community evaluated profits, rather than as the result of changes in the industrial assets of a nation.

It was a way of approaching financial crises that recalled the cultural and psychological treatment of consumption laid down by Veblen in *The Theory of the Leisure Class*: standards of thought were responsible not only for the increasing portion of income spent on luxuries, but also for fixing the rates of profits and investments. At the base of both phenomena there was a quite simple process of evaluation: evaluation of persons through commodities in the case of consumption, evaluation of firms through capital assets in the case of production. If understanding the psychological roots of consumption required the investigation of interpersonal comparisons, understanding financial crises meant exploring competitive comparisons between firms, the mechanisms of which, Veblen argued, emerged from the study of accounting practices.

Earlier economists, Veblen lamented, had constructed their theories by looking backward to a reality of 'household produced goods' and 'handicraftsmen' already partially superseded by Smith's time. From this outdated perspective, one could easily be convinced that 'business operations, the bargain and sale of goods' were 'subservient to their production and consumption'.[81] But things were no longer that way. The new corporate economy which Veblen had seen expanding around him made room for new services and jobs, purely commercial and with only the remotest connection to the productive process. The old 'business manager', who oversaw the 'mechanical processes' of a specific plant, had been replaced by the 'undertaker', whose function was that of superintending 'pecuniary affairs', 'coordinating and directing industrial processes' from far away. 'Speculators' were everywhere, exploiting the new market economy, in particular the 'real-estate men (land-agents) engaged in the purchase and sale of property for speculative gain or for a commission'.[82] Undertakers, speculators, real-estate men, 'promoters and boomers', with their followers of 'attorneys, brokers, bankers, and the like' who made their operations possible, were for Veblen actors in a new stage of the economic system, one in which commercial and financial operations had cannibalised the share of the economy historically occupied by labour and industry.[83]

Capital itself, Veblen argued, almost anticipating John Hicks, was a purely commercial entity: it was not a group of 'physically productive agencies', as the marginalists claimed in their longing for hedonistic certainties, but a 'fund' of values only partially corresponding to 'capitalized industrial material'. The best proof of this was that the 'total remaining assets after liabilities have been met' did not correspond to material capital, but only to a group of 'intangible' assets commonly labelled 'good-will'. And such 'good-will' had replaced the industrial plant as 'the nucleus of the capitalization'.[84] 'Good-will' was to production what luxury expenditures were to consumption: a pure matter of subjective opinions and expectations. It comprised every contract or title of property which was supposed to put its beneficiary (corporations were legally treated as individuals since the 1860s) into some kind of 'differential advantage' towards its competitors: 'customary business relations, reputation for upright dealing, franchises and privileges, trade-marks, brands, patent-rights, copyrights, exclusive use of special processes guarded by law or by secrecy, exclusive control of particular sources of material'.[85]

Indebted to the tradition of Say and Mill on this point, Veblen believed that titles of property were purely juridical documents with no justification in the labour originally applied to them by their owner: property was a matter of distribution, not of production.[86] Contrary to his predecessors, however, and in consonance with his previous considerations on conspicuous consumption, Veblen thought that, although intangible, titles of property were productive of some service or utility. In the same way in which the luxuries' utilities depended on their capacity to meet the expectations and opinions of their consumers' beholders, the utility of goodwill goods depended entirely on the expectations that they were able to raise in the business community at large. In order to incorporate these expectations into the current corpus of economic doctrines, Veblen invited his fellow economists to follow the common business habit and take 'account, under one name or another, of the various immaterial items of wealth classed as intangible assets', since 'any theory that aims to deal with the actualities of modern business will have to make its peace with the term by which these elements of capital are called'.[87]

In so doing, Veblen's path strangely converges with that of an anomalous marginalist, the Yale economist Irving G. Fisher. In his 1906 *Nature of Capital and Income*, Fisher engaged with the then available definitions of capital before confidently going on to provide his own, one which Veblen would honour with this epitaph: the 'most elaborate outcome of classificatory economics to this date'.[88] Fisher knew that the emergence of corporations had posed practical problems not only to theorists but to businessmen as well, and eagerly went out into the field to learn what they had to say. Instead of conceiving of capital as an aggregate of material assets of production, businessmen were to incorporate into capital all kinds of wealth, including commodities ready for immediate consumption such as an automobile, a lit cigar and financial assets of various kinds: not only stocks and bonds but also patents, copyrights and the ever-elusive goodwill.[89]

To implement the advice of contemporary businessmen, Fisher recognised, utilitarianism too had proved of some help. The German economist Wilhelm Roscher had paved the way by demonstrating that *any employment* of an article was essentially profitable and productive, even if it only produced the 'inwards goods' of enjoyment.[90] Following suit, Fisher maintained in 1896 and again in 1906 that the terms 'productive' and 'profitable' no longer served to delineate capital, for all wealth, all possessions were productive of some sort of good. 'Reading matter', 'animals', persons and 'jewellery', he argued, were integrated parts of capital alongside 'raw materials' (mineral, agricultural, manufactured), 'land improvements' and 'building improvements' for the simple reason that they were a source of *future* value to the people employed in the productive and consumptive process.[91]

The concept of time, as we have seen, had always played an important role in the utilitarian tradition: the Benthamites thought the estimates of future actions were important variables in the calculus of pleasure; the French utilitarians catalogued different forms of consumptions on the basis of the durability of their 'compensations'; while the marginalists dealt with current phenomena as conditioned by their future consequences. It was the Scottish-Canadian political economist John Rae, however, whose writings Fisher esteemed highly, who first familiarised him with the idea that wants and the corresponding 'instruments' of their satisfaction could be 'ordered' according to the worth of their product compared to their lifespan.[92] While Rae, however, in this matter closer to Say and the French tradition in general, introduced a chronological hierarchy in order to show the merits of 'technological' instruments, Fisher thought that any kind of good with a prospective capacity to satisfy wants could be considered a productive 'instrument', since wealth consisted not in concrete objects but in a flow of 'desirable' services or actions. This meant that bonds, stocks and even goodwill and money were 'instruments' of wealth, precisely like mechanical inventions, since they were rights to future services with a high degree of 'desirability', which necessarily implied some transactions in 'physical objects'.[93] '[T]o act in this physical world', he explained, it 'is necessarily to make use of physical objects – persons or things' and 'the physical objects used must always be wealth, for the right to use useless objects or unappropriated articles is not called property'.[94]

To establish the value of prospective wealth, however, was another matter, which Fisher could only settle by presupposing two conditions: first, that there existed an incorruptible correlation 'between social and individual income'; second, that consumers and producers alike were able to make prophetic guesses about their future income, so that 'the entire future history of the capital in question' could be assumed to be 'definitely known in advance':

> We assume that the expected income is foreknown with certainty, and that the rate of interest in foreknown, and also that it is constant during successive years […] [Given these assumptions] it is very simple to derive the capital value of the income to be yielded by any article of wealth or item of property; in other words, to derive the value of that wealth or property. That value is simply the present worth of the future income from a specified capital.[95]

Less trusting in the regularity and repetitions of economic history, which he had learned quite early to see through Darwinian eyes, Veblen had not only demonstrated that economic services did not always imply the exploitation of material resources and 'useful objects' and, vice versa, that rights and contracts had no connection whatsoever with real production, but had also shown in more general terms that the expectations of future outcomes was epistemologically remote from empirical perception. And this very discrepancy between empirical dimension and guesswork had a correspondent in the discrepancy between the production of goods and the production of wealth. 'Concretely', Veblen said, 'there is not always a consensus of imputations as to the expected value of a given flow of income' and, furthermore, such capitalizations 'proceed on an imperfect, largely conjectural, knowledge of present earning-capacity and on the still more imperfectly known future course of the goods market and of corporate policy'.[96] The income flowing from a contract, in fact, was not estimated on the base of the present worth of the 'physical' service flowing from it, but on the base of the present worth of the 'competitive' advantage with which it endowed the firm compared to its competitors. It was not the number and quality of the contracts making up the goodwill that brought utility to the firm, but the way in which they were advertised by traders, people who could invent sophisticated accounting techniques, make lucrative deals and obtain extensions of credit, by exclusively dealing with funds and phantasms, transferring them and creating corresponding credit obligations:[97]

> [The corporation] is a business concern only, and in the nature of the case its activities as a corporation are limited to business transactions of the nature of bargain and sale, and its aims are confined to results which can be brought into a balance sheet in terms of net gain.[98]

Like luxuries, goodwill contracts derived their utility from a capacity to fill some informational gap in competitive environments and to satisfy the needs for interpersonal comparisons among economic agents; they were 'advertizing media' with which both consumers and firms conveyed to their competitors the idea of their possessing some 'differential' or 'monopoly' advantage. Say and Veblen had already dissected, if in slightly different ways, the process through which immaterial needs for conspicuous consumption harmed society at large. Veblen alone explained the way in which a symmetrical phenomenon in the field of business management would produce analogous results and cause economic crises.

Like the consumers' speculation regarding the conspicuousness of certain objects, the evaluation of the utility or of the *future* utility of rights and contracts comprised in capital depended on purely immaterial projections elaborated on the basis of past information. And, differently from what Say suspected, these immaterial projections could have dramatic consequences for the real economy. In fact, the tendency to assimilate prospective income to present capital led corporations to expand beyond their own *real* limits, giving them the opportunity to extend their credit on the basis of immaterial, unsecured assets, particularly goodwill, and often in a cumulative fashion, something which Veblen had noted already in a 1900 review of Basil A. Bouroff's now forgotten *The Impending Crisis: Conditions Resulting from the Concentration of Wealth in the United States.*[99] Crises happened whenever a technological development or a speculative misstep revealed the discrepancy between past earning expectations and present earning capacity.

If, according to Veblen's French sources, the separation of labour and property did not have consequences serious enough to determine a divergence of production and demand, their theories had nonetheless led later economists to reach more dramatic conclusions. Daniel Raymond's early nineteenth-century works, for example, had introduced the idea that the mechanisms responsible for the accumulation of individual wealth were not the same as those responsible for the creation of national wealth to an American audience.[100] In line with Raymond, Veblen distinguished the processes of individual and national accumulation, but made it clearer that this distinction corresponded to the one between pecuniary interests on the one hand and industrial interests on the other. According to him, in fact, 'the material framework of modern civilization' was an incredibly complex network of interconnected economic activities: while 'the economic welfare of the community at large' was 'best served by a facile and uninterrupted interplay of the various processes which make up the industrial system at large', the 'pecuniary interests of the business men' depended on their 'disturbing' this technological 'concatenation' by way of those juridical privileges comprised in the goodwill.[101] Property was for Veblen an act of disturbance because it was used to create fictitious situations of monopoly or 'differential advantage' (by way of manipulative deals and credit extensions not supported by 'real' capital) which drew investments away from otherwise productive purposes, in the same way in which a constant application of available incomes to luxury expenditure withdrew funds from the productive capital of a nation.

Crises were only the most visible result of the constant discrepancy between distribution and production, pecuniary and productive values and, in the last analysis, expectations and empirical evidence: whenever the appearance of a new mechanical contrivance or the exhaustion of certain speculative moves annihilated the value of differential advantages and the corresponding expectations, the volatility of collaterals became patent and creditors pushed their 'aggregate claims ... beyond what the hypothecable material wealth of the debtors would satisfy'.[102] This brought capitalised values back to the level of the material values, thus revealing the discrepancy between expectations and reality:

> Hence, in a period of general liquidation, when the differential advantages of the various concerns greatly contract, the legitimate claims of creditors come greatly to exceed the paying capacity of debtors, and the collapse of the credit system follows. The failure of classical theory to give an intelligent account of credit and crises is in great part due to the habitual refusal of economists to recognize intangible assets, and Mr Fisher's argument is, in effect, an accentuation of this ancient infirmity of the classical theory.[103]

Like salutary shocks, crises were therefore those rare and cyclical experiences through which humanity realised the delusional nature of its pecuniary expectations, lost the utilities built on them and retained all others intact. Crises, in fact, left 'the community at large poorer in terms of market values, but not necessarily in terms of the material means of life', since the 'shrinkage incident to a crisis is chiefly a pecuniary, not a material, shrinkage'.[104] It was Veblen's faith in a cohabitation of fictional and necessary needs or utilities within individuals and societies at large that led him to think that crises only adjusted the former to the latter.

Conclusion

The corpus of Veblen's most celebrated theories can be seen as a system of symmetrical theses aimed at explaining the divergence between economic sectors normally conceived as convergent. To construct this system, Veblen availed himself not only of contemporary Darwinism, but also of French utilitarian sources, which he accessed either directly or through the mediation of Jean-Baptiste Say, J. S. Mill and John Rae. Even though the French utilitarians retained faith in the self-adjusting capabilities of the market, they identified significant areas of friction in the modern economy: on the one hand, the friction between 'fictitious' and 'real' needs and utilities; on the other, that between property rights and industry. Veblen developed his own bifurcated epistemology, drawing on Kant, Darwin and Spencer, to demonstrate that the frictions were much more serious than hitherto acknowledged and responsible for the chronic divergence between consumption and production, empirical perception and expectations.

In both *The Theory of the Leisure Class* and *The Theory of Business Enterprise*, Veblen showed that this gap between consumption and production was brought about by the consumers' and producers' pursuit of immaterial goods or utilities or 'advertizing media', which he traced back to the human reliance on expectations and interpersonal comparisons in the assessment of utility. In the case of consumption, those media were mostly (even if not only) luxuries, the main utility of which consisted in filling the informational gap so characteristic of urban, industrialised societies to the advantage of their consumers. The business equivalent of luxuries was the goodwill or the set of property rights capitalised by firms with nothing corresponding in their material assets. Luxuries and goodwill were both, although in different ways, immaterial goods, the utility of which was based on expectations, generally overblown, of future value: the value of individuals in the case of conspicuous consumption, the value of firms in the case of goodwill. By carefully propagating an illusion of success, projected through manipulative media such as clothing or goodwill, individuals and firms alike could capitalise on unrealistic expectations, at times to the detriment of everyone but themselves. Crises were salutary shocks that brought consumption and production back to their underlying values by momentarily annihilating the utility of advertising immaterial goods by briefly lifting the veil on the material and industrial fundaments of society.

Veblen's innovative take on utilitarianism was thus indebted to the French tradition for its conviction that the perception of utilities was socially and historically conditioned, but owed to the English utilitarian tradition the belief that immaterial or intangible goods were able to condition the economy at large. It was, however, not to the realignment of 'real' and 'market' values, as more influentially sustained by J. B. Clark and Irving Fisher, that this conditioning worked, but towards their tragic divergence.

Notes and References

1   An earlier version of this paper was presented at a conference on 'The Stock Market and New Technologies Conference', Cambridge Endowment for Research in Finance, Judge Business School, Cambridge University, 31 March–1 April 2006. The authors are grateful to the organisers and participants of that conference, in particular Lord John Eatwell and Carlota Perez, as well as Robert Fredona and Carlo Augusto Viano for their suggestions.

2   Ross E. Mitchell (ed.), *Thorstein Veblen's Contribution to Environmental Sociology: Essays in the Political Ecology of Wasteful Industrialism* (Lewiston: The Edwin Mellen Press, 2007); Rick Tilman, *Thorstein Veblen, John Dewey, C. Wright Mills, and the Generic Ends of Life* (Lanham: Rowman and Littlefield Publishers, 2004); Michael Spindler, *Veblen & Modern America: Revolutionary Iconoclast* (London: Pluto Press, 2002); Louis Patsouras, *Thorstein Veblen and the American Way of Life* (Montréal: Black Rose Books, 2004); James K. Galbraith, 'Enron May Spark Revolt of Professionals', *Newsday* 25 (2002); Eric R. Hake, 'Financial Illusion: Accounting for Profits in an Enron World', *Journal of Economic Issues* 39.3 (2005): 595–611. Finally, see http://www.veblen-institute.org.

3   Alain de Botton, *Status Anxiety* (New York: Penguin, 2004); Oliver James, *Affluenza* (London: Vermillion, 2007); Martin Wolf, 'A New Gilded Age', *Financial Times*, 25 April 2006; Paul Krugman, 'Gilded Once More', *The New York Times*, 27 April 2007.

4   Robert H. Frank, *Falling Behind: How Rising Inequality Harms the Middle Class* (Berkeley: University of California Press, 2007); Paul Krugman, 'Enron's Second Coming?', *The New York Times*, 1 October 2007; Eric R. Hake, 'Capital and the Modern Corporation', in *Thorstein Veblen and the Revival of Free Market Capitalism*, ed. by Janet T. Knoedler, Robert E. Prasch and Dell P. Champlin (Cheltenham: Edward Elgar, 2007), 31–68.

5   The relationship between Veblen's micro and macro analysis has of course been noted before, see for example Jeffrey Sklansky, *The Soul's Economy: Market Society and Selfhood in American Thought, 1820–1920* (Chapel Hill: University of North Carolina Press, 2002), 184.

6   John P. Diggins, *Thorstein Veblen: Theorist of the Leisure Class* (Princeton: Princeton University Press, 1978), 51; H. A. Innis, 'A Bibliography of Thorstein Veblen', *Social Science Quarterly* 60.3 (1979): 420–23; Stephen Edgell and Rick Tilman, 'The Intellectual Antecedents of Thorstein Veblen: A Reappraisal', *Journal of Economic Issues* 23.4 (1989): 1003–26, esp. 1016.

7   Jeremy Bentham, 'The Psychology of Economic Man', in W. Stark (ed.), *Jeremy Bentham's Economic Writings*, 3 vols (London: Allen, 1954), 3:421–50, esp. 434. For a recent effort to assimilate French and English strands of utilitarianism, see Evert Schoorl, 'Jean-Baptiste Say as a Benthamite Utilitarian', *History of Economic Ideas* 10.1 (2002): 33–47.

8   On the implications of Veblen's epistemology for his political economy, see the introduction to *Thorstein Veblen, Il posto della scienza*, ed. by Carlo Augusto Viano and Francesca Lidia Viano (Torino: Bollati Boringhieri, 2012).

9   Robert W. Dimand, 'Fisher and Veblen: Two Paths for American Economics', *Journal of the History of Economic Thought* 20.4 (1998): 449–65; Dimand, 'Echoes of Veblen's theory of business enterprise in the later development of macroeconomics: Fisher's debt-deflation theory of great depressions and the financial instability theories of Minsky and Tobin', *International Review of Sociology* 14.3 (2004): 461–70; Sophus A. Reinert, 'Iconoclastic Eugenics: Thorstein Veblen on Racial Diversity and Cultural Nomadism', *International Review of Sociology* 14.3 (2004): 51, 334.

10 Irving Louis Horowitz (ed.), *Veblen's Century: A Collective Portrait* (New Brunswick, NJ: Transaction Publishers, 2002).

11 Aristotle, *Politics*, I, 9. On this passage see Ricardo Crespo, '"The Economic" According to Aristotle: Ethical, Political and Epistemological Implications', *Foundations of Science* 13.3–4 (2008): 281–94.

12 Andrea Finkelstein, *Harmony and the Balance: An Intellectual History of Seventeenth-Century English Economic Thought* (Ann Arbor: The University of Michigan Press, 2000), 40.

13 Thorstein Veblen, 'The Preconceptions of Economic Science', *Quarterly Journal of Economics* 13.4 (1899): 396–426, esp. 408.

14 Adam Smith, *The Wealth of Nations*, 3 vols (New York: Collier, 1902), 2:50–51.

15 Veblen, 'The Preconceptions of Economic Science' (1899), 401. See also Thorstein Veblen, 'Industrial and Pecuniary Employments', in id. *The Place of Science in Modern Civilizations and Other Essays* (New York: Huebsch, 1919), 279–323, esp. 299.

16 Veblen, 'The Preconceptions of Economic Science' (1899), 407.

17 Ibid., 411–21.

18 T. Veblen, *The Theory of the Leisure Class: An Economic Study of Institutions* (New York: Macmillan 1912), vi.

19 Diggins, *Thorstein Veblen*, 51.

20 Veblen, *Leisure Class*, 111; cf. John Stuart Mill, *Principles of Political Economy* (New York: Appleton, 1888), 1:257.

21 Thorstein Veblen, 'The Preconceptions of Economic Science (1900), 244; Veblen, 'Industrial and Pecuniary Employments', 296; cf. Mill, *Principles*, 1:258, 278.

22 Veblen, 'The Preconceptions of Economic Science', *Quarterly Journal of Economics* 14.2 (1900): 240–69, esp. 243–44.

23 Veblen, 'The Preconceptions of Economic Science', 244.

24 Étienne Bonnot Condillac, *[Le] commerce et le government considérés relativement l'un à l'autre: ouvrage élémentaire* (Amsterdam and Paris: Jombert et Cellot, 1776), 19–20.

25 Ibid., 13.

26 Ibid., 4.

27 Ibid., 79.

28 Ibid., 298–99.

29 Condillac, *Le Commerce*, 11, 37.

30 Jörg Guido Hülsmann, *Mises: the Last Knight of Liberalism* (Auburn: Ludwig von Mises Institute, 2007), 113.

31 Jefferson quoted by Michael J. L. O'Connor, *Origins of Academic Economics in the United States*, ed. by Michael Hudson (New York: Garland Publishing, 1974), 23; Dorothy Ross, *The Origins of American Social Science*, 4th edn (Cambridge: Cambridge University Press, 1997), 4. Say's fourth edition of the *Traité* (1819) was translated into English by Charles Robert Prinsep and published first in London and then in Boston (Wells and Lilly) in 1821. The American edition was edited by Clement Cornell Biddle, who translated Say's introduction (omitted from the London edition) and added some notes to the English version. A second edition appeared in 1824, a third in 1827, a fourth in 1830, a fifth in 1832, a sixth in 1834; other reprints were published before 1880 (O'Connor, *Origins*, 124–5). The bifurcation of Western economics into a continental-American tradition inspired by Say and an English tradition inspired by Smith over the question of capital and profits was long ago traced by Lionel Robbins in his *Theory of Economic Development in the History of Economic Thought* (London: Macmillan, 1968), 104.

32 F. Wayland, *The Elements of Political Economy* (New York: Leavitt, Lord, 1837); Michael J. L. O'Connor, *Origins of Academic Economics*, 6, 23, 121; Joseph Dorfman, *Thorstein Veblen and His America* (Clifton: Kelley, 1972), 22. On Say's original intention to emigrate to the United States and his influence over other leading American economists, such as George Tucker and Thomas Cooper, see *Breaking the Academic Mould. Economists and American Higher Learning in the Nineteenth Century*, ed. by William J. Barber (Middleton: Wesleyan University Press, 1988), 26, 29, 30–31, 50, 60–61.

33 Francesca Lidia Viano, 'From Staple Rent to Conspicuous Rent: Veblen's Case for a New Theory of Distribution', *International Review of Sociology* 14.3 (2004): 471–85, esp. 477–8; Wesley C. Mitchell, *Types of Economic Theory. From Mercantilism to Institutionalism*, ed. by Joseph Dorfman, 2 vols (New York: Kelley, 1967), 1:563.

34 Say's utilitarian turn was completed in the second edition of his work. We are using here *Traité d'economie politique*, 2 vols (Paris: Crapelet, 1819), 1:4.

35 Say, *Traité* (Paris: Crapelet, 1803), 1: 5–6; 2: 94, 96, 103.

36 William J. Baumol, 'Say's (at Least) Eight Laws, or What Say and James Mill May Really Have Meant', *Economica, New Series* 44.174 (1977): 145–61, esp. 153.

37 François Quesnay quoted by Joseph Spengler, 'The Physiocrats and Say's Law of Markets. II', *Journal of Political Economy* 53.4 (1945): 317–47, esp. 318n.

38 Condillac, *Le commerce*, 7–8; emphasis added.

39 Ibid., 8–9, 47–50, 230, 236.

40 Smith, *Wealth of Nations*, 2:3.

41 Ibid., 4–5.

42 Say, *Traité* (1803), 2: 238–39; Say, *Traité* (1819), 2: 211–12.

43 Say, *Traité* (1803), 2: 339, 358–59; William J. Baumol, 'Say's [at least] Eight Laws', 147, 149.

44 For James Mill's formulation of something akin to Say's '*lois des débouchés*', see Baumol, 'Say's (at Least) Eight Laws', 148.

45 Adam Smith, *The Theory of Moral Sentiments* (Philadelphia: Anthony Finley, 1817), 78; Smith, *Wealth of Nations*, 3:289–90.

46 Smith, *Wealth of Nations*, 3:289–92.

47 Say, *Traité* (1803), 2: 350; Say, *Traité* (1819), 2: 211–12.

48 Say, *Traité* (1819), 2: 252–53.

49 Say, *Traité* (1819), 2: 252–53.

50 Ibid., 373.

51 Ibid., 373, 378–9.

52 Baumol, 'Say's (at Least) Eight Laws', 149.

53 Veblen, *Leisure Class*, 5; emphasis added.

54 Ibid., 34; Veblen, 'Some Neglected Points in the Theory of Socialism', in id. *Place of Science*, 387–408, esp. 394.

55 Veblen, *Leisure Class*, 53.

56 Ibid., 58.

57 Ibid., 100.

58 On Veblen's epistemological treatment of expectations and guesswork see Francesca Lidia Viano, 'Guesswork and Knowledge in Evolutionary Economics: Veblen Revisited', in *Cognitive Developments in Economics*, ed. by Salvatore Rizzello (London: Routledge, 2003), 338–70.

59 Charles Darwin, *Descent of Man, and Selection in Relation to Sex*, 2 vols (London: Murray, 1871), I: 92. For Darwin's reliance on Kantian morals, see Robert J. Richards, *Darwin and the Emergence of Evolutionary Theories of Mind and Behavior* (Chicago: University of Chicago Press, 1987), 211.

60 Richards, *Darwin*, 286; Henry James, *Principles of Psychology*, 2 vols (New York: Holt, 1891) 2:364; James, *Psychology* (New York: Holt, 1892), 3–4.

61 Thorstein Veblen, 'Why is Economics not an Evolutionary Science?', *Quarterly Journal of Economics* 12.4 (1898): 373–97, esp. 377; Thorstein Veblen, 'Kant's Critique of Judgment', *Journal of Speculative Philosophy* 18.3 (1884): 260–74, esp. 271, 274.

62 Francesca Lidia Viano, 'Veblen Revisited: Guesswork and Knowledge', 342.

63 Veblen, 'Kant's Critique of Judgment', 262, 264.

64 Ibid., 264, 265, 271.

65 Veblen, 'The Place of Science in Modern Civilization', in id. *Place of Science*, 1–31, esp. 9.

66 Veblen, 'The Preconceptions of Economic Science', *Quarterly Journal of Economics* 14.2 (1900): 240–69, esp.244.

67 Veblen, *Leisure Class*, 31–32.

68 Ibid., 17, 31, 243.

69 Ibid., 31.

70 Veblen, 'Some Neglected Points', 395.

71 Veblen, *Leisure Class*, 86; emphasis added.

72 Ibid., 34, 45, 113, 149, 187, 370, 396.

73 Ibid., 187.

74 Ibid., 152; emphasis added.

75 Thorstein Veblen, 'The Economic Theory of Woman's Dress', in id. *Essays in Our Changing Order*, ed. by Leon Ardzrooni (New York: Transaction, 1998), 65–77, esp. 72..

76 Veblen, *Leisure Class*, 31.

77 In Robert H. Frank, *Choosing the Right Pond: Human Behavior and the Quest for Status* (Oxford: Oxford University Press, 1985), 137.

78 Thorstein Veblen, 'Overproduction Fallacy', in id. *Essays in Our Changing Order*, 104–13, esp. 112. For a discussion of this article in the context of Veblen's studies at Cornell see Viano, 'From Staple Rent to Conspicuous Rent', 476; Viano, 'Ithaca Transfer', in this volume.

79 Uriel H. Crocker, 'The 'Over-Production' Fallacy', *Quarterly Journal of Economics* 63.3 (1892): 352–63; Thorstein Veblen, 'Overproduction Fallacy', 105.

80 Veblen, 'Overproduction Fallacy', 109.

81 Veblen, 'Industrial and Pecuniary Employments', 284, 286.

82 Ibid., 288–92.

83 Ibid., 293.

84 Thorstein Veblen, *The Theory of Business Enterprise* (New York: Scribner's Sons, 1904), 116–17, 127, 138. For analytical and historical assessments of the risk inherent in radical new financial innovations, see Carlota Perez, *Technological Revolutions and Financial Capital: The Dynamics of Bubbles and Golden Ages* (Cheltenham: Edward Elgar, 2002); Richard Bookstaber, *A Demon of Our Own Design: Markets, Hedge Funds, and the Perils of Financial Innovation* (Hoboken: John Wiley & Sons, 2007).

85 Veblen, *Business Enterprise*, 108, 116, 139.

86 Ibid., 29; Veblen, 'Industrial and Pecuniary Employments', 296.

87 Thorstein Veblen, 'Fisher's Capital and Income', in id. *Essays in Our Changing Order*, 148–74, esp. 154.

88 Ibid., 152.

89 Irving Fisher, 'Precedents for Defining Capital', *Quarterly Journal of Economics* 18.3 (1904): 386–408, esp. 400; Fisher, *The Nature of Capital and Income* (New York: Macmillan, 1923), 63–4.

90 Irving Fisher, 'What is Capital?', *Economic Journal* 6.24 (1896): 509–34, esp. 513.

91 Fisher, *The Nature of Capital*, 7.

92 John Rae, *The Sociological Theory of Capital: Being a Complete Reprint of the New Principles of Political Economy*, 1834, ed. by Charles Whitney Mixter (New York: Macmillan, 1905), 109, 114.

93 Fisher, *Nature of Capital*, 43–4; Fisher, 'Senses of "Capital"', *Economic Journal* 7.26 (1897): 199–213, esp. 202, 210.

94 Fisher, *Nature of Capital*, 211.

95 Ibid., 113, 202.

96 Veblen, 'Fisher's Capital and Income', 168; Veblen, *Business Enterprise*, 155–56.

97 Thorstein Veblen, *Absentee Ownership: Business Enterprise in Recent Times: the Case of America* (Piscataway: Transaction Publishers, 1923), 87.

98 Ibid., 83.

99 Thorstein Veblen, Review of Basil A. Bouroff, *The Impending Crisis: Conditions Resulting from the Concentration of Wealth in the United States*, in Thorstein Veblen, *Essays Reviews and Reports: Previously Uncollected Writings*, ed. by Joseph Dorfman (New York: Augustus M. Kelley, 1973), 491–3.

100 Daniel Raymond, *Thoughts on Political Economy: In Two Parts* (Baltimore: Lucas, 1820). Raymond revised this work heavily in its numerous subsequent editions: Daniel Raymond, *The Elements of Political Economy*, 2 vols (Baltimore: Lucas, 1823); Daniel Raymond, *The Elements of Political Economy: In Two Parts* (Baltimore: Lucas, 1836); Daniel Raymond, *The Elements of Constitutional Law and Political Economy* (Baltimore: Cushing, 1840).

101 Veblen, *Business Enterprise*, 1, 26–7, 28–36, 49, 57–8, 182.

102 Veblen, 'Overproduction Fallacy', 155.

103 Veblen, 'Fisher's Capital and Income', 155–56.

104 Veblen, *Business Enterprise*, 191.

Chapter 17

THORSTEIN VEBLEN: STILL MISUNDERSTOOD, BUT MORE IMPORTANT NOW THAN EVER

Robert H. Frank

More than a century has passed since the publication of Veblen's *The Theory of the Leisure Class*. And although the ideas he introduced in that book continue to be widely discussed today, they have never achieved the status that many feel they warrant. In this brief essay, I will attempt to explain why I think Veblen's ideas are so important and why they have not yet realised their full potential.

It is no accident that Veblen was moved to write about conspicuous consumption when he did. *The Theory of the Leisure Class* was published in 1899, near the end of the Gilded Age. In the United States, it was a time of almost unprecedented growth in inequality of income and wealth. People in every socio-economic group have always consumed in accordance with their income. When incomes are stagnant or rising at the same rate for all income groups, the consumption of the wealthy attracts little attention, because it doesn't stand out from the frame of reference that sets expectations. But because the incomes of top earners had been rising very rapidly during the 1890s, their consumption was particularly conspicuous, if only because no one had ever seen anything like it. Similar rapid growth of income and wealth among top earners today may help explain the current resurgence of interest in Veblen's ideas.

Veblen viewed conspicuous consumption as the outcome of a competitive signalling process. In his account, the wealthy consumed lavishly merely to demonstrate to others that they had the ability to do so. But as I attempt to explain, Veblen made a serious strategic error in having framed his explanation in these terms. Although, to be sure, there are specific individuals for whom Veblen's characterisation is apt; most of us dislike such people and make every effort to avoid them. That we are able to do so most of the time suggests that their number must be relatively small.

The upshot is that Veblen's characterisation of conspicuous consumption almost inevitably relegates the concept to fringe status. I will suggest an alternative way of characterising the phenomenon, one that reveals more clearly the breadth of its influence on spending decisions at every income level.

The Link between Context and Evaluation

I begin with two simple thought experiments. In each, you are to imagine that you confront a once for all choice between two worlds in which all conditions are identical except for a single difference. In the first experiment, what's different is house size:

World A. You and your family live in a neighbourhood with 400 sq. m houses, while others live in neighbourhoods with 600 sq. m houses;

World B. You and your family live in a neighbourhood with 300 sq. m houses, others in neighbourhoods with 250 sq. m houses.

If the conditions described would remain in place for ever, which world would you pick? In standard economic models, the utility from any good depends only on the absolute amount of it consumed. In these models, the uniquely correct choice is thus World A, since your house would be larger there.

When confronted with this thought experiment, however, most people end up choosing World B, where their house will be smaller in absolute terms but larger in relative terms. One could rationalise this choice within Veblen's framework by saying that they wanted to demonstrate their superiority over their neighbours. But as I will explain, there are other, more compelling, interpretations.

The second thought experiment involves two worlds that differ in workplace safety levels:

World C. Your job entails a 2 in 100,000 chance of death each year, while others' jobs entail a 1 in 100,000 chance of death;

World D. Your job entails a 4 in 100,000 chance of death each year, while others' jobs entail a 6 in 100,000 chance of death.

This time virtually all subjects choose World C, where their job safety is greater in absolute terms, but lower in relative terms, than in World D.

Following the late Fred Hirsch, I use the term *positional good* to describe goods which have a capacity to yield utility dependent to a relatively high degree on how they compare with other goods of the same type; and the term *non-positional good* to describe goods whose capacity to yield utility depends more heavily on the absolute amounts in which they are consumed.[1] In terms of the two thought experiments, housing is thus a positional good and workplace safety a non-positional good. It is not that context is irrelevant for non-positional goods. Indeed, someone who had a significantly more dangerous job than others would surely notice that fact and not like it. The important point is that such a person would not be willing to sacrifice much absolute safety to improve his relative position on the safety scale.

Positional Arms Races

As illustrated by the foregoing thought experiments, context shapes evaluation more heavily in some domains than in others. Although it matters for evaluations of both housing and safety, it matters more for housing. The fact that context is more important in some domains than others has important implications for whether private markets allocate resources efficiently.

Consider the tradeoff that workers face between safety and other forms of consumption. In competitive labour markets, riskier jobs pay more than safer ones because it costs money to make the workplace safer. In standard economic models, workers will sacrifice safety for higher wages up to the point that the resulting increment in utility from having a larger house (or more of some other consumption good) is just offset by the disutility of the higher risk. According to these models, self-interested choices in competitive markets give rise to socially optimal amounts of both housing and workplace safety.

But that result goes out the window if context matters more for housing than for safety. When a worker buys a bigger house with the extra money he earns by accepting additional risk on the job, he rationally expects two benefits: the extra utility from having an absolutely larger house and the extra utility from having a relatively larger one. Yet when all workers follow the same logic, no one ends up with a relatively larger house. As in the familiar stadium metaphor, all stand to get a better view, only to discover than no one sees better than if all had remained seated.

In short, when context matters more in some domains than others, a positional arms race ensues that is analogous to a military arms race. Too much ends up being spent on positional goods like housing, and too little on non-positional goods like safety. The logic of this claim is precisely the same as the logic that governs the analogous, and completely uncontroversial, claim regarding military arms races.

People in every nation want both a high material standard of living and protection from aggression from other nations. To protect against aggression, resources must be diverted from other forms of consumption into military armaments. Relative expenditures clearly matter more in the armaments domain than in the consumption domain. After all, a nation that spends less than its rivals on armaments puts its political independence at risk, whereas one that spends less than its rivals on consumption risks only a reduction in relative living standards. Military arms races result because most people believe that being less well armed than one's rivals is more costly than having fewer flat-panel television sets. By the same token, positional arms races result because consumption evaluations are more sensitive to context in some domains than in others.

Why Context is More Important in Some Domains than in Others

The argument just summarised could be adapted to map exactly onto Thorstein Veblen's argument about conspicuous consumption. Retaining his assumption that people's primary objective is to demonstrate their economic prowess, the practical question would be how to accomplish that goal most effectively. Clearly it would make no sense to spend heavily on items that others never saw. In Veblen's terms, people would divert money from inconspicuous consumption categories in order to finance additional consumption of items that are more easily observed by others. The result would be inefficient because the amount of economic power one's spending communicates to others depends almost entirely on the relative amounts spent on conspicuous consumption goods.

As a group, professional economists have been unwilling to embrace Veblen's narrative. In conversations with my colleagues over the course of many years, I have come to believe that their aversion to it has less to do with its internal logic than with their perception that embracing it would be to legitimise negative emotions such as envy and jealousy, which they feel merit no consideration in normative analysis. They reject Veblen's model for the same reason they would reject models that give policy weight to the preferences of sadists.

Society does indeed have a legitimate interest in discouraging envy. We should continue to teach our children not to be boastful or to envy the good fortune of others. But the influence of context stems less from negative emotions than from the fact that many important rewards depend on relative position.

Consider, for example, a middle-income family's decision about how much to spend on a house. The cost of sending a child to a school of average quality is closely linked to the price of the average house in the community. In the United States this is true in part because of the direct link between local school budgets and local property tax revenues. But in the light of evidence that any given student's achievement level rises with the average socio-economic status of his or her classmates, property values and school quality will be positively linked even in countries in which school budgets are largely independent of local property values. The upshot is that individual families can send their children to better schools if they are willing to stretch their budgets and spend a little more on housing.

We may safely assume that most middle-income families aspire to send their children to schools of at least average quality. Indeed, parents who felt completely at ease with the prospect of their children attending below-average schools would be judged harshly in most communities. Yet the notion of a good school is inherently context-dependent. No matter how much everyone spends on housing, only half of all children can attend top-half schools. The decision of how much to spend on housing thus confronts many middle-income families with a painful dilemma. They can either send their children to a school of average quality by purchasing a house that is larger and more expensive than they can comfortably afford; or they can buy a smaller house that is within their budget and send their children to a below-average school. To see why so many families might find the former option more compelling, we need not assume that they are strongly prone to envy or jealousy.

Similarly, we need not invoke envy to explain why people might perceive opportunities to get ahead by spending more than others on clothing. First impressions count for a lot during job interviews, but looking good is also a relative concept. It means looking better than others who are competing for the same job. If others are spending more, you must spend more as well, or else be prepared to live with reduced odds of landing the job you want.

A similar logic governs the decision of how much to spend on gifts. Suppose you have been invited to a professional associate's home for dinner and want to bring a bottle of wine for your host. What should you bring? John Brecher and Dorothy Gaiter, whose unpretentious, value-oriented wine column appears each Friday in *The Wall Street Journal*, devoted a recent column to precisely this question. 'Ask a respected wine merchant to suggest an unusual wine, one that your host is unlikely to have tried before', they sensibly recommended. 'And plan on spending about $30'.

Why should you spend so much, given that many wines available today for under $10 are far better than the wines drunk by kings of France in centuries past? In part because you have an interest not only in how the wine tastes, but also in how your gift will be interpreted. Giving a wine that has become inexpensive by today's standards might be read as a statement that you view your relationship with your host as unimportant. So unless you really don't care about the relationship, the extra $20 is probably worth spending. Here again, we need not invoke envy to explain why the spending of others might induce people to spend more than they can comfortably afford on gifts.

Context is the very wellspring of the every day quality judgments which drive consumer demand. That this point is not widely appreciated by economists first became clear to me during a dinner conversation that took place before a lecture I gave at the University of Chicago several years ago. Three of us were waiting outside a restaurant when the fourth member of our dinner party arrived at the wheel of a brand new Lexus sedan. Once we were seated at our table, the Lexus owner's first words to me were that he didn't know or care what kinds of cars his neighbours and colleagues drove. As it turned out, I had had numerous conversations with this gentleman over the years and found his statement completely credible.

I asked him why he had chosen the Lexus over the much cheaper, but equally reliable, Toyota sedan from the same manufacturer. He responded that it was the car's quality that had attracted him – things like the look and feel of its interior materials, the sound its doors made on closing and so on. He mentioned with special pride that the car's engine was so quiet and vibration-free that the owner's manual posted warnings in red letters against attempting to start the car while its engine was already running.

I then asked him what car he had been driving before trading up. I forget what he said, but for the sake of discussion will suppose that it was a five-year-old Saab. I asked him how he thought people would have reacted to his Saab if it had been possible to transport it back to the year 1935 in a time capsule. He answered without hesitation that anyone from that era would have been extremely impressed. They would have found the car's acceleration and handling spectacular; its interior materials would have amazed them; and its engine would have seemed unbelievably quiet and vibration-free. His own evaluations of his former car were of course strikingly different on each dimension.

We then discussed what a formal mathematical model of the demand for automobile quality might look like, quickly agreeing that any reasonable one would incorporate an explicit comparison of the car's features with the corresponding features of other cars in the same local environment. Cars whose features scored positively in such comparisons would be seen as having high quality, for which consumers would be willing to pay a premium.

Such a model would be essentially identical to one based on a desire not to own quality for its own sake, but rather to outdo, or avoid being outdone by, one's friends and neighbours. Yet the subjective impressions conveyed by these two descriptions could hardly be more different. To demand quality for its own sake is to be a discerning buyer. But to wish to outdo one's friends and neighbours is to be a boor, a social moron. To be sure, there are people whose aim is to flaunt their superiority over others. But such people are relatively rare.

I noticed that on the heels of this discussion, everyone at the table suddenly took much more interest in talking about the kinds of behaviour that are driven by contextual concerns. It was fine to talk about behaviours that result from context-dependent perceptions of quality, but not at all palatable to speak of behaviours that result from envy or a desire to outdo others.

In sum, if Veblen's core idea is really about context, which shapes perceptions of quality, which in turn drive demand, then it is not a peripheral concept. It applies to virtually every good, including basic goods like food. When a couple goes out to dinner for their anniversary, for example, the thought of feeling superior to their friends and neighbours probably never enters their minds. Their goal is just to share a memorable meal. But a memorable meal is a quintessentially relative concept. It is one that stands out from other meals.

Conclusion

Against all evidence, traditional economic models continue to assume that consumption decisions take place in social isolation. More clearly than any of his predecessors, Thorstein Veblen called attention to the absurdity of this presumption.[2] The plain fact is that evaluations of all types depend heavily on social context.

Veblen chose to focus on the battles among wealthy consumers in which the winner was whoever could consume the most conspicuously. That such battles occur in the real world there is no doubt. The footrests on the barstools aboard the late Aristotle Onassis's yacht, *The Christina*, were made of whale ivory and the vessel's faucets were of solid gold. At the flip of a switch its swimming pool could be covered by a retractable, mosaic-tiled dance floor. *The Christina* was just one salvo in Onassis's costly battle to outdo rival shipping magnate Stavros Niarchos, whose own yacht, the 375-foot *Atlantis*, was designed by an architect whose explicit instructions were to make it 50 feet longer than the Onassis vessel.

My claim is that Veblen made a strategic error to have focused so heavily on such battles. Rightly or wrongly, most economists do not believe that their own consumption decisions are driven by a desire to impress others or that they envy others who consume more than they do. And for this reason, they have been largely unreceptive to Veblen's message.

Yet context shapes evaluation even for people who are not eager to outdo their neighbours – indeed, even for those who would *prefer not* to outdo them. The same car that would have been experienced by most drivers as having brisk acceleration in 1950 would seem sluggish to most drivers today. Similarly, the 300 sq.m. house that would have seemed spacious to a corporate executive in 1980 would probably seem too small to most executives today. And an effective interview suit has always been one that compares favourably with those worn by other applicants for the same job.

Once we acknowledge that context shapes evaluation in these ways, the claims of standard economic models are altered profoundly. A new logic governs tax and regulatory policy. Consumption and savings decisions unfold in completely different ways.

Veblen's core idea remains poorly understood by modern economists, but it is more important now than ever.

Notes and References

1 Fred Hirsch, *Social Limits to Growth* (Cambridge, MA: Harvard University Press, 1976).
2 Thorstein Veblen, *The Theory of the Leisure Class* (New York: Modern Library, 1899).

NAME INDEX

SUBJECT INDEX

Numbers in boldface refer to figures in the text

Lightning Source UK Ltd.
Milton Keynes UK
UKOW040634160113

204942UK00002B/9/P